CHABOT COLLEGE - HAYWARD
2 555
D0378780

THE AMERICAN LEGION

AN OFFICIAL HISTORY

1919 – 1989

THOMAS A. RUMER

M. EVANS & COMPANY, INC.
NEW YORK

Library of Congress Cataloging-in-Publication Data

Rumer, Thomas A.
The American Legion: an official history, 1919-1989 / Thomas A. Rumer.
p. cm.
Includes index.
ISBN 0-87131-622-6: $24.95
1. American Legion—History. I. Title.
D570.A1R86 1990
369'.1861'0904—dc20

M. Evans and Company, Inc.
216 East 49th Street
New York, New York 10017

Manufactured in the United States of America

9 8 7 6 5 4 3 2 1

To The American Legion History Committee,
and particularly to its first chairman,
Ralph Godwin (MS),
this book is respectfully dedicted.

PREAMBLE TO THE CONSTITUTION

FOR GOD AND COUNTRY

WE ASSOCIATE OURSELVES TOGETHER FOR THE FOLLOWING PURPOSES

To uphold and defend the Constitution of the United States of America; to maintain law and order; to foster and perpetuate a one hundred percent Americanism; to preserve the memories and incidents of our associations in the Great Wars; to inculcate a sense of individual obligation to the community, state and nation; to combat the autocracy of both the classes and the masses; to make right the master of might; to promote peace and good will on earth; to safeguard and transmit to posterity the principles of justice, freedom and democracy; to consecrate and sanctify our comradeship by our devotion to mutual helpfulness.

ACKNOWLEDGMENTS

Past National Commanders Al Keller, Jr. (IL), Chairman, and members E. Roy Stone, Jr. (National Executive Committeeman, SC), and National Executive Committeeman U. S. "Udie" Grant (KS) have contributed essential services as members of The American Legion History Committee originally chaired by Ralph M. Godwin (MS, 1905–1986), along with national staff members: National Adjutant Robert W. Spanogle, National Judge Advocate Philip B. Onderdonk, and *The American Legion Magazine* Publisher Daniel S. Wheeler. Former Director of the American Legion Library, Museum, and Archives Thomas V. Hull located archival materials, helped select illustrations, and prepared the appendix of national officers. Current Librarian and Archivist Joseph Hovish and his staff have also aided the author in numerous ways.

In addition to these, many other national officers and staff persons of the American Legion past and present have contributed to this publication.

Critical readings of the manuscript were given by Dr. Robert D. Thornton; Wendell C. Phillippi, MG (Ret.); and Dr. George W. Geib.

CONTENTS

INTRODUCTION

The American Legion has established a motif in twentieth-century America unrivaled in recognition by any other organization. Since 1919 the familiar Legion emblem has signified service to veterans, community, and nation.

The emblem of which the organization is demonstrably proud and firmly protective has adorned countless patriotic events from National Convention parades to small-town 4th of July color guards; has identified thousands of local posts, the first community centers for numerous towns in the 1920s and later; and has appeared below the titles of hundreds of educational publications for public service over the years.

The Legion is no stranger to ideological jousts with other organizations and individuals, and it has recently gained notice most often for holding to the fire the clay feet of the new Department of Veterans Affairs, and for an undaunted campaign for a constitutional amendment prohibiting desecration of the American flag.

The world's largest veterans' organization has sought to maintain the original "basics" of its founding: veterans' rehabilitation, Americanism, child welfare, and national security. Each of these program areas has been expanded over the years to include relevant—the ordained term is *germane*—matters. But the organization has continued above all its mission as a consumers' advocate for veterans.

The Legion's presence on the American scene has been accepted as part of the social and cultural landscape here and in several foreign countries. Yet an organization with so many sides and surfaces tends to be known in parts, even by its members, according to what aspect of its existence most directly affects a group or an individual.

That is as it must be. But the Legion has been a presence in towns and cities across the land since the close of World War I. It has affected public policy in ways and to degrees that are sure to surprise the uninitiated. Therefore, a description of its birth, development, and many functions deserves to be treated in a narrative chronicle which, interwoven with the Legion point of view derived from the democratic process of its governance, can be viewed by members and nonmembers alike.

For certain, the seventy-year history of the organization and the amazingly complex nature of its operation invites such an effort. A look at its national convention mandates alone offers a review of American history from 1919 forward.

The process for producing mandates is one of the Legion's most distinguishing features. Possessed of the practice of resolving, the Legion has put many public laws on the books. The process can begin at the post level and continue through several levels of debate and voting until, transformed from resolution to mandate to legislation, a measure is introduced into Congress and then is handed to the President for signature. In developing the process and putting it to work, the Legion has made a difference in the way the federal and state governments have dealt with a wide range of matters.

The Legion, of course, has had its critics. A history of the organization may enlighten those believing:

- That Legionism is lockstep: The amount and quality of internal debate has been impressive; the membership is a political, religious, social, and cultural cross section of America.
- That it is strident and self-righteous in its patriotic fervor: Founded to serve others, the Legion firmly believes that its members have earned and continue to earn the right to express and expect an ardent brand of patriotism.
- That it unnecessarily and unceasingly demands veterans' benefits: Objectivity illuminates the truth about the nation's often lagging attention to essential veterans' rehabilitation, and about how we all stand to benefit by medical advances made in that field.

Countering the criticism of some, of course, is not the primary reason for compiling the history of the Legion. From its beginning the organization has relied on a vigorous brand of volunteerism. In the collective efforts of millions of Legionnaires over the years it has amassed a truly impressive record in whatever standards one chooses —hours, dollars, or achievements.

While yet in its infancy, the American Legion was spoken of not uncommonly as a "movement" and never as an organization of war veterans gathering merely to reminisce. Instead, there was in the programs proposed at the founding gatherings a readily apparent energy and determination to meet the needs of veterans and their dependents as well as an America beset, it was believed, by radicalism.

Inherent in the "movement," of course, was the citizen-soldier concept, particularly the postwar role. Those who attended the introductory caucuses in Paris and St. Louis in early 1919 determined that their concept of volunteerism should be expressed through public service. They imagined volunteerism on a national scale, then provided a system at their first National Convention in November 1919 that subsequently would constitute many times a first rank of help and aid for many needs.

Years later, the American tradition of the "citizen-soldier" would be enhanced by the establishment of the G.I. Bill of Rights, one of the most important socioeconomic innovations of the twentieth century and a progenitor of a succession of such measures.

An American phenomenon all the way, the G.I. Bill was typically pragmatic—it made good sense economically to facilitate the reentry into civilian life of several million persons after World War II. And appreciably involved in determining the focus of that practicality for those most needing the rehabilitative measures and the compassion of that far-reaching measure, was the American Legion in drafting the G.I. Bill, lobbying for it, and then in helping veterans understand and benefit from its many provisions.

Re-creating some semblance of order within the expanse of time and space in which have occurred seventy years of Legion activity and to package it all in a manageable, readable format requires the selection of a vantage from which to view the organization.

The vantage chosen is that from "National"—National Headquarters and the ranks of national volunteers and staff—in order to show the development and operation of the organization from 1919 to the present. In each chapter two or more themes of basic operational activity are developed in time frames artificially partitioned by events important to veterans. The text also includes capsule renditions of basic programs, events, and persons important to the story and deserving special notice.

Those who appear in these pages speak directly through oral history interviews, correspondence, speeches, or verbatim minutes of the myriad meetings, conventions, conferences, and other gatherings at which Legion policy is hammered out or reported. Most voice a prevailing point of view. Some express views proving the diversity of opinion within the organization. Others speak warnings based on long-standing Legion concerns, thereby pointing up a function of the organization as interpreter of events relating to the nation's security and to its citizens' general quality of life.

The larger context in which these Legionnaires speak is the story of national officers and staff members lobbying on Capitol Hill, planning and implementing strategy, searching the organizational heart, mind, and soul, and exercising the drive-ahead determination for principles regarded as Legion truisms.

For that is what national officers do. All those travel tickets only hint at the time-consuming advancements through the successive "chairs," during which time these Legionnaires strive to represent others back home as they consider, debate, and act on apace the ongoing concern and advocacy that is the essence of Legionism.

But the narration herein is at best a representation of the whole, an indication of what has happened and is happening, as well as an attempt to show why some key events have occurred as documented.

Objectivity has been welcomed and expected by the Legion, which has cooperated to the fullest extent in providing access to archival materials and introductions to those who sat patiently for oral history interviews.

PROLOGUE

AMERICA IN WORLD WAR I

America's first shot in the First World War was fired at 6:05.10 A.M. on October 23, 1917, from a French 75mm (3-inch) field piece in position 400 meters east of Bathlemont in the Luneville sector of the Western Front near Verdun, a sector which had seen little action since 1914.

The U.S. First Division, Regular Army, had been in place here for two days. The opposing line was about a mile distant across many strands of barbed wire. Corp. T. J. Varady of C Battery, 6th Field Artillery, loaded the gun, Gunner R. E. Braley sighted it, and Sgt. Alexander L. Arch fired a "target," hitting a bridge. The brass shell case was set aside to be sent to President Woodrow Wilson. The crew fired seventeen more shots, then went to breakfast.

American troops in Europe—this was truly the ultimate "European entanglement" warned against by U.S. presidents from Washington to Wilson (whose campaign slogan in 1916 was, "He kept us out of war"). Yet by the time Sergeant Arch and his crew fired their prebreakfast salvo, there were 62,000 American military personnel in France in a war that many American isolationists, noninterventionists, and neutralists insisted was strictly a European matter. In March 1917, German submarines had sunk three unarmed American merchant ships and the pleas from invaded nations had already had an effect in America. By the close of the war, the American Expeditionary Forces—the A.E.F.—would number over two million. (Another two million would serve in the military but remain in the U.S.)

Thus, accompanied by a repertoire of popular background music echoing the "stamp, stamp, stamp" of marching feet, a new generation of citizen-soldiers qualified for veterandom. The few Regular Army troops knew the military life—they had chosen it. But now high school boys and clerks who had joined National Guard units or had been "caught in the draft" and inducted into the National Army units were gaining uneasy eligibility as veterans.

And in the time warp between the first proud parades to troop ships and subsequent war-weary trudging to final, horrific battles, members of the A.E.F. had gone through some remarkable, often devastating, changes.

At home they had had the opportunity, perhaps not fully appreciated before, of pursuing their individual goals according to each individual's ability, ambition, and the occasional luck of the draw. But in the service they had sought to remain alive in the midst of destruction. For many, these experiences would haunt their fitful sleep for years to come.

Many of them shared the bewildering transformation from hometown to front line without having fired more than a few rounds in their rifles. There were those even who found themselves cleaning the manufacturer's grease from their Springfields only after they had taken up rat-infested residence in trenches separated from the enemy by only a few yards of no-man's-land. Hurrying to review a manual of arms, they likely would suffer their mistakes in a predawn raid.

Much of the original jauntiness had evaporated from the A.E.F. long before Sgt. Joyce Kilmer, a well-known poet, was killed on August 1, 1918, near the Ourcq River. Before the war, one of the most famous of Kilmer's unaffected iambic tetrameter verses had celebrated the simple wonder of a tree. But he and his compatriots would witness bombardment that typically in a few hours of concentrated shelling could destroy township-sized areas of once serene woodlots.

It was a war on the emotions as well. Those who were ordered to the front lines wearily and warily approached the horizon marked by the red glow of bursting bombs. No longer merely lyrics from the "Star-Spangled Banner," the sight before them had never before been seen in the massive proportions that buffeted their senses and threatened their sanity. For certain, any illiterate doughboy who in the gloom of a winter fog had become separated from his squad in no-man's-land or whose lungs had been set aflame by chlorine gas could improve on Dante's description of Hell.

The majority, of course, lived on in the stale, stifling aftermath of the major battles, aiding stricken comrades and at times being transfixed by the blank stares of those unhinged by the enormity of it all. Those especially who had been at the front had absorbed, as through their pores, the reality of the valley of the shadow of death. Those toward the rear who had been set to digging graves "row on row" had that frame of reference for the awful totality of what had happened.

Because of their common experiences, those who served in the military in Europe and the United States in 1917 through 1919 automatically became members of an immense fraternity. They had seen the worst and, in the case of lifesaving heroics, the best of which mankind was capable. They had acquired a viewpoint. Whether it intruded on their daily actions or remained brooding in a corner of the mind, these men and women would return home changed.

The removal, moreover, of four million people from civilian life within a few months' time, half of whom were sent across the ocean, affected the nation in ways that had not been adequately anticipated. During demobilization, the special needs of many for rehabilitation went far beyond that of the inflation-besieged sixty-dollar chit they received for a new suit of clothes, which at that point was the nation's thanks.

What they needed, they agreed, was an organization born of common experiences and dedicated to addressing postwar needs. A few visionaries with considerable ground support planned exactly that.

Thus an inevitable Great War veterans' organization was about to be formed. Its dynamism would mark American history.

BEGINNINGS

PARIS

JANUARY 1919

Four line officers of the American Expeditionary Forces met in Paris in late January 1919 to renew acquaintance. Each had led battalions or regiments into battle. They could count seven wound chevrons on their wool O.D. uniforms. Theodore Roosevelt, Jr., (1st Division) whose father, the 26th President of the U.S., had died earlier in the month, reminisced with Lt. Col. George S. White, (ex-41st Division, attached to G.H.Q.), a confidant of his father from the Spanish-American War and an editor of the *Portland Oregonian.* Present also were two other friends closer to Roosevelt, Jr.'s own age: Maj. Eric Fisher Wood, 88th Division, a former architecture student and American Embassy attaché in Paris, who had witnessed the first horrific weeks of the war and Lt. Col. William J. Donovan of the 69th, New York City's "Fighting Irish," who had made a name for himself during the war.

The four talked, of course, of mustering out and of their expectations for life after the army, subjects dear to hundreds of thousands of other citizen-soldiers as they eagerly awaited orders for transport home.

By the time the Armistice was signed, 1,981,701 American soldiers had "crossed the pond." They had marched off from the farms, towns, and cities of America to the strains of George M. Cohan's 1917 tune "Over There." Now they were impatiently waiting to return home. As far as they were concerned, the chorus of the familiar song, the part about going home when "it's over over there," spoke their minds precisely. They repeated the ironic variation of a quote incorrectly attributed to General John J. Pershing: "Lafayette, we are *still* here."

Though only an armistice had been signed instead of an actual peace treaty, the Kaiser had been defeated and the French nation saved from the threat of domination posed savagely and successfully by the dreaded, well-oiled war machine of the Boche. Thanks to the Yanks, the map of Europe had not been altered as drastically as Wilhelm II had once fancied.

The four officers discussed another popular subject: Other wars had spawned associations of veterans, for example, the Grand Army of the Republic, the United Soldiers of the Confederacy, and later the Spanish-American War Veterans. Was the "Great War" to have one? What form should such an organization take? It dare not, surely, be as political as the old G.A.R. What could it be if not merely fraternal and reminiscent?

One apparent need cried for resolution. At the close of the war, American citizen-soldiers were particularly sensitive to developments at home that seemed to endanger the values for which they had risked their lives and for which their less fortunate friends had lost theirs. The hue and cry over Bolshevism was particularly disconcerting. Victorious soldiers placed renewed value on that for which they had fought, and "Red" extremists (their number often a matter of wild speculation) seemed bent on inciting riot and turmoil.

It had been irksome enough that the A.E.F. had had to shoulder a greatly increased burden when the Bolsheviks, coming to power after the Russian Revolution of 1917, had made their own separate peace with Germany (with the Brest-Litovsk Treaty in March 1918) and thereupon had withdrawn from the Allies. This move had freed numerous German divisions from the Russian quarter, which were then thrown against the Western Front.

After the Armistice, A.E.F. members were made to engage in military maneuvers that seemed to them to be merely set up to occupy their time. And while they languished under a military regimen, they read of the Bolsheviks who were said to be at work in America in the mill and factory towns and big city industries, creating disturbances and causing other problems.

Shouldn't soldiers and sailors join together as civilians to uphold and protect the traditional values unique to America? If such a battle royal between forces for good and evil should occur, as the more animated among them foretold, would not a veterans' organization provide a counterbalance?

Organizations were already making some headway. In Europe, the "Comrades in Service," A.E.F. Chief Chaplain Charles Brent's brainchild, had been gaining members since the Armistice. Having received the approval of President Wilson and the tolerance of General Pershing, the Comrades was the nearest thing in the A.E.F. to an official veterans' organization. Bishop Brent had utilized his chain of communication with chaplains serving all units, down to company level, to register several thousand members.

The Comrades in Service, by its own definition, was The Company Club of the A.E.F., the future veterans' fraternity for all men who honorably wore America's uniform during the first World War. The Comrades had adopted as an emblem a colorful red, white, and blue shield on which appeared both the Star of David and the Cross placed above a Scripture verse from Nehemiah (4:18): "For the builders, every one had his sword girded by his side. . . ."

Lyrics of the Comrades in Service song "Our Fraternity" pointed out that the "Service" was both military and civilian: "There's a club to keep us cheerful/Help to pass the time away/It will tie the boys in France together/Till we all sail for the U.S.A./After that, we'll keep together all men/Who have served the banner of the free/Still to work as true Comrades in Service/In our future Fraternity."

But as the four officers meeting in Paris noted, Comrades in Service had an official aura about it. It had been organized "from the top down," as George White put it. Absent, another argued, was the effervescent camaraderie and, especially, the unmistakable leaven of democratic spontaneity which, it was assumed, would enliven a soldier-originated organization.

Roosevelt and the others employed the facile "what if" to their conjectures. If such a doughboy-inspired movement could be set in play, would it not be the ticket for attracting those who refused to become members of the Comrades? To this question, the answer being heard was "Yes!"

The subject was brought up again at similar confabs in the next few days as a running discussion evolved. The four agreed that there were probably insurmountable difficulties attached to such a grandiose venture, since it would be thrown open to all qualified persons regardless of military class. Thus in the conceptual stage the proposed organization was admirable though problematic.

At one point, White spoke of the difficulty of even attempting to lay the groundwork necessary for beginning such an organization while the troops in Europe were still bound by military rules and regulations. Travel, for example, was restricted. The troops were spread from the Rhine to the Mediterranean. Communication with the many units of the military forces, for unofficial business such as this, was all but impossible. Many a difficulty came with arranging a large meeting of military personnel for the purpose of organization. A better time for such a meeting, White said, was when the former soldiers had returned to the States.

But he and the others argued also that if one were to organize veterans into a great patriotic and civic organization, no time should be lost. They had heard that many "dues grafters" in the States were already scheming to exploit the returning doughboys. White told of a veterans' organization recently begun in Oregon. He distrusted its motives and regarded it as little more than a dues-gathering scheme to benefit the founder, one, White had heard, who had not even been in the army. As they all knew, numerous other organizations were springing up in the States, even in Europe.

There was also the matter of returning soldiers being set upon by those out to get what little cash could be had. They had heard that when soldiers disembarked in New York or elsewhere, they left themselves open to sellers of Great-War–related gimcracks, commemorative inanities, and other nickel-and-dime fobbery.

If this were not bad enough, others of far more fraudulent intent took advantage of former soldiers attempting to find work. These charlatans were congregating around soldiers in alarming numbers with get-rich-quick scams or promising shortcuts to employment, always at a price.

Roosevelt, White, Wood, and Donovan noted, also, that cheap buttons identifying the wearers as former soldiers were being sold indiscriminately. This cheap gimmick played upon a soldier's desire to demonstrate membership in a brotherhood of fellow veterans. Some meaningful, tasteful symbol of service should be designed and distributed systematically, the four believed.

Soon after the meetings of the four officers in Paris, Lt. Col. White was transferred from the command of a regiment to General Headquarters at Chaumont, where he was made Chief Personnel Officer of the A.E.F. In early February, Roosevelt, while visiting White, noted that among White's duties was that of maintaining the personnel records of the entire A.E.F., so Roosevelt once more returned to the subject of a veterans' organization. Another occurrence during Roosevelt's visit proved to be even more fortuitous.

General Pershing asked to see the son of the former president. The general, it seemed, was perturbed by reports of morale problems among the troops. These reports were true enough, but to White, Wood, and others it appeared that Pershing refused to believe such problems could exist in his army. Spoken of now by many as a possible presidential candidate, Pershing was indeed concerned with rumors of poor morale.

Pershing met alone with Roosevelt, wishing, it seemed, to glean something from political instincts. When the general put the question of morale directly to his guest, Roosevelt regarded the moment as propitious. He therefore neither denied nor confirmed that there were widespread morale problems. Instead, he used the question as a springboard for presenting his and his three friends' ideas.

If the general wished to clear the air about the army's morale, Roosevelt suggested, he might call a "morale conference" at which representatives of the civilian-soldiers from the far-flung units of the A.E.F. could be heard on the subject. Behind the smiling contours of his wide, boyish face, Roosevelt was thrilled by the realization that he might be about to receive official sanction for a gathering of A.E.F. representatives to whom he might present the concept of a veterans' organization.

Not wishing to lose the momentum created by this unexpected opening, Roosevelt remembered White's access to personnel files and volunteered himself and White to compile, for such a conference, a list of likely candidates to be presented for Pershing's approval.

The general agreed. Roosevelt returned to White with the news. White managed to get orders telegraphed to Eric Fisher Wood to join them, and the three set about compiling the list. White managed to contact Donovan also; however, because Donovan was then on duty with the occupation troops in Germany, his travel orders arrived too late for him to join the other three.

The three "suggested" some thirty names to Pershing, including ten company officers as well as enlisted men. Pershing cut the list to twenty, all field grade officers but one. Captain Ogden D. Mills, of the Paris Command, came thereby to be included; it was he whom Lt. Col. Fred Taylor Pusey, Chief Quartermaster, 28th Division, also on the list, would call "the Thomas Jefferson of the Legion's constitution." Others who made the final list included two colonels, fourteen lieutenant colonels, and three majors, representing ten combat divisions, G.H.Q., and several Service of Supply (S.O.S.) sections. In this fashion, Roosevelt and his cohorts came by their first truly concrete achievement in what had begun as an imaginative exercise for guessing at the nature of a future veterans' organization.

Compilation of the list related directly to success for the organization. Wood, for example, had recommended Lt. Col. Bennett C. Clark of the 86th Division as a conferee, and his name survived Pershing's cut. Wood and Clark had arrived in France in the spring of 1918 as field officers of infantry and had been classmates at the Command and General Staff School at Langres. Since then they had become friends serving as G-1 and G-2 respectively of the 88th Division.

But Clark's inclusion served more than friendship. Before long, joint references to Roosevelt's name and that of young Clark would serve a very useful purpose. With a presidential election nearing in 1920, the names of these two appearing in news accounts about efforts to start a veterans' organization and in early public relations pieces helped greatly to dispel the presumption of many that politics lay just beneath the fraternal guise of this effort to organize soon-to-be-former soldiers.

Young Roosevelt had been touted as the reigning heir to his father's robust Republicanism, perhaps even to playing the maverick role of the irrepressible Teddy's Bull Moose in the staid political china shop. Young Clark, meanwhile, as the true son of his father "Champ" Clark —"Ol' Hound Dawg" of Missouri, Democratic Speaker of the House of Representatives, once a presidential contender—was billed as a rising star among those of that political persuasion. And so these two proved a worthy political counterbalance when appearing on the playbill of the budding organization. They would become the most visible and best known champions for the cause.

With Pershing in possession of the list, the wheels of G.H.Q. meshed, producing special orders issued to the twenty elect telling them to report to the Y.M.C.A. headquarters in Paris ("travel enjoined is necessary in the Military Service") there to meet at 10:00 A.M. on February 15 with a few senior generals from G.H.Q. and for three days to consider and advise upon the question of morale.

During the working days, then, of February 15, 16, and 17, the twenty handpicked representatives of the A.E.F. met with the Regular Army men picked by Pershing himself to discuss the scope and solution of the morale situation. They hammered out a series of recommendations for their commander so as to alleviate the discontent of hundreds of thousands of soldiers with little to do but routine, wind-down, military duties. First, they asked that G.H.Q. share with them information about a policy for demobilization. In this respect they advised that the schedule for home-bound troops follow the order in which the men had arrived and that it be published soon. They recommended that there be fewer restrictions and that more be done to grant promotions, many of which had been stopped on November 11 with the cessation of hostilities. They also asked that the number of divisional maneuvers and "terrain exercises" be reduced.

But on the evening of the first session, beneath the chandelier in the dining room of the Inter-Allied Officers Club, a century-old home on fashionable rue Faubourg St. Honoré and diagonally across the street from the Y.M.C.A. facility, the twenty A.E.F. men came together by personal invitation of the gregarious Roosevelt to form, as one put it, "the G.A.R. of the World War."

The dinner began at 7:00 P.M.; afterward Roosevelt launched into the subject of a postwar association of veterans. He admitted (as White recalled several years later), "It is a nervy thing for us, as a self-appointed committee, to set about such a thing. But someone has got to do it and it ought to be done as soon as possible for the good of the men and for the good of the country."

One among the twenty, hearing Roosevelt's general concept and having his own idea of the usefulness of such an organization (White refrained from naming him but said "he ranked all the rest of us"), demanded that a poll be taken to ascertain how many present favored universal military training and the establishing of a larger army than the country had previously seen.

This demand, coming when the organization was barely conceived and long before it could be born, brought several protests. William Donovan, whom his three friends, of course, had chosen to represent the 69th, protested. It was enough of a challenge, he said, to get a veterans' organization started without its being saddled with position statements sure to attract immediate confrontation. Donovan expressed an important tenet—one often repeated—that nothing permanent should be enacted until the organization was set to function back in the States as representative and democratic.

As White put it later, "The founders were to concern themselves with the details of organization only. What we set out to do was to establish an organization of returning soldiers for their benefit, to be conducted by them as soon as the details of organization had been worked out and the organization was large enough and representative enough to reflect the common opinion of the majority of those who had served in the war."

White felt that great steps toward that goal had been taken at the dinner meeting on February 15. "When the meeting adjourned [about midnight], the G.A.R. of the World War consisted of a date for a general caucus at Paris [set, ambitiously, for March 15th, only a month later], the promise of every man present that he would do everything possible to get the word out over the A.E.F., and a working force consisting of Eric Fisher Wood of Pennsylvania, Ralph Cole of Ohio, and myself."

White explained that each of the three had his duties: "Wood and Cole were to send written notifications to all divisions and S.O.S. sections and supply information to the European and American press, while I was to work the field by personal visits to the various combat divisions. Cole dropped out after the meeting that night, while Wood, by his untiring energy and initiative, did a really big piece of work in getting the Paris Caucus together."

On February 16 and 17, the twenty met at the club during off-duty hours, late afternoons, and evenings to continue the work. Somewhere during their deliberations, they became "the Temporary Committee of Twenty." Roosevelt was made chairman; Wood, secretary and ex officio vice-chairman.

Roosevelt was urged to return to the United States to lend his energy, charisma, and name, with the express purpose of promoting a caucus in America to match that planned for Paris in what was already being called "a movement." He had been wounded badly late in the previous summer though he had remained in command of an infantry regiment until the Armistice; and he had in hand his S.C.D. (Surgeon's Certificate, Disabled), enabling him to return home nearly at will. He left for the States shortly thereafter. Others of the twenty were urged to follow Roosevelt back to the States as best and as soon as they could so that they might aid in advertising the organization there. Ten of them actually managed to get themselves sent home early enough to attend the U.S. caucus, which would be scheduled for early May.

Wood remained in Europe to arrange for the A.E.F. caucus in Paris, which would provide the first public forum for discussion of and reaction to the proposed organization. The others, while yet in Europe and upon returning to their units, were to promote the concept generally. Specifically, they were to recruit delegates to the meeting in Paris.

For a time, White and Clark helped Wood while the two were still in France. For clerical work Wood relied on enlisted personnel at 88th Division headquarters. This unofficial army work was supervised by Field Clerk Edward L. Bladel, later Assistant Secretary and Treasurer of the Paris Caucus partly because, it was said, he was the only stenographer there.

Roosevelt, before leaving for America, had scored another coup. Stopping by G.H.Q. again, he and White prevailed upon General Van Horn Mosely and Intelligence Chief General Dennis Nolan, both of whom had attended the morale conference, to push for granting leaves for delegates to the Paris meeting.

This latest achievement was not without its touch-and-go moments. After the mid-February meeting, Wood, with editorial help from White and Clark, dutifully prepared an announcement of the Paris meeting and in late February widely distributed copies to about two thousand officers and enlisted men. The mimeographed form, which the *Stars and Stripes* of March 14, 1919, called "an invitation," thus became the first official document actually produced by the as yet unnamed veterans' organization.

The appearance of this invitation, however, coming before General Pershing had been alerted to its publication, rankled the general, as Wood soon found out. "Pershing was furious," Wood recalled. "He considered this a transgression of his rights." Several of the Committee of Twenty were summoned to the general's office, Roosevelt, White, Donovan, and Wood among them. The word "Urgent" had been stamped prominently and threateningly on the summons.

The meeting with the general was stormy, but in the end he agreed to not oppose the caucus in Paris. Donovan was said to have informed the general indelicately of the obvious—that the war was over and that Pershing might consider the National Guard and National Army units at least as men who had done their jobs and who now were waiting none too patiently to go home.

At that point, Wood was emboldened to ask that an order be given to all divisional commanders to allow delegates to attend the caucus. To this the general also agreed, but reluctantly.

The result was order M495. Appearing over the signature of Brig. Gen. Robert C. Davis, Adjutant General of the A.E.F., it was directed

"To C. G. 1st (2nd, 3rd) Army" and called for notification to be given to division and other commanders that "requests of officers for leave to visit Paris to attend committee meeting called by Major Wood for March 15th should be granted." Though only an order like reams of others churned out on the Army's mimeograph machines, this one became the third significant document, after (1) the order for the February morale conference and (2) Wood's announcement of the Paris Caucus, in an evolving archive of the American Legion's development.

Wood's call for the Paris Caucus was an important composition; it set forth a clear and appealing description of what he and the others had advanced for several weeks.

In it he explained that the officers who "happened to be together for an official purpose" in Paris in mid-February "had long shared with thousands of other soldiers of the American forces the hope and desire that the officers and men who are about to return to civil life after serving in the present war, whether with the combat units or in the S.O.S. or at home, might sooner or later be united into one permanent nation-wide organization similar in general character to the Grand Army of the Republic or the United Soldiers of the Confederacy and composed of all parties, all creeds, and all ranks who wish to perpetuate the relationships formed while in the military service."

In the "several meetings . . . during the recesses between their official conferences," Wood explained, the officers planned an assembly of representatives of the military units of the A.E.F. To that meeting recipients of the announcement were being invited.

Wood's call for the caucus alerted recipients, "You were suggested by [the one named] as being a proper representative of the [military unit] as well as of the territory from which much of its personnel is drawn, and I have been officially instructed on behalf of the Temporary Committee to invite you to avail yourself of a three-day Class C leave to Paris as provided for instance in Par. 2, G.O. 14, G.H.Q., c.s., in order to act as a delegate to the impending Caucus."

It was to be a working conference. Those who accepted the invitation would adopt a "tentative" constitution and plan for "a great convention . . . next winter in the United States."

The invitation was all-inclusive. In addition to those to whom the announcements were addressed personally, announcements in the newspapers stated, "Any officer or enlisted man not invited who is in Paris at the time of the meeting is invited to be present and to have a voice in the meeting."

Wood was also careful to state the A.E.F.–U.S. connection: the Temporary Committee, "through the Training Camps Association," had already alerted ex-servicemen in the U.S. of a state-side caucus to be held in April (an overzealous scheduling that did not materialize).

Lt. Col. George White occupied a vantage at G.H.Q. from which to observe that the nerve center of the army was rather "a mild, if somewhat academic sort of institution." He had no doubt that "some of its personnel had their own ideas and hopes as to just what the organization of veterans ought to be and ought to do." Yet he insisted "as a hard fact" that G.H.Q. "had no voice or part in directing the course of the American Legion." Though there were some roadblocks and the usual red tape, there were many instances, he said, of permission from the higher command for leaves and a more or less "liberal attitude toward those who asked [for] time off for committee work and executive sessions." Such support greatly aided the work of organizing.

If G.H.Q. was an "academic institution," neither enthusiastic nor antagonistic, the men of the A.E.F. themselves needed convincing that this would-be veterans' organization was worth their while.

As soon as the announcement for the Paris Caucus was made, criticism came from those who suspected ulterior motives. There were many complaints. "What is the army trying to pull off on us now?" "What kind of political scheme is this anyway?" "Is this a scheme to elect Pershing president?" "Is the General Staff trying to organize the soldiers for some militaristic purpose?"

Though White's position at G.H.Q. had been a boon in the early stages of organization, his arrival at the 26th Division while promoting the upcoming caucus in an automobile bearing the distinctive G.H.Q. red, white, and blue circle had at once put some on the defensive. He longed to tell them that his use of the auto had called for some hoodwinking of G.H.Q.; the very orders under which he was traveling then were "rather ancient." At that very time, "My greatest fear on that trip was of some too inquisitive M.P." finding him out and sending him back, embarrassed, the job undone.

Morale had been especially low in the 26th. It had been the first National Guard unit to arrive, had suffered more deaths and wounds than almost any other unit, and now they were convinced they were languishing unnecessarily in Europe instead of being sent home as they felt they deserved.

White was allowed to explain to division leaders that representatives of National Guard and National Army units had attended the morale conference and had favored the caucus planned in Paris. He sought to assure them that the intentions of the organizers were democratic, nonpolitical, and especially non-Army ("All of us in the movement are citizen-soldiers"). White's persuasiveness prevailed. The 26th would be represented by the largest delegation at the Paris Caucus, as it would be also at the national convention in the United States eight months later.

Many responded favorably to the promotional work by White, Wood, and the others. Lt. Col. Franklin D'Olier, on the General Staff at Tours as well as being one of the original Temporary Committee, had assured Wood that S.O.S. sections from Nevers to Marseilles would send representatives.

Wood and the others pondered the question of how to convince enough people that the cause was worthwhile. There were too few people actively involved—merely the twenty from the morale conference—to recommend personally those who should come. The method that Wood used to find more potentially interested people was to ask the original twenty to send pleas for help to people known to them, asking them to supply the names of twenty or more others. Wood's Signal Corps/U.S. Army telegram of February 20 to Maj. Gen. Edward Buxton of the 82d was typical of eleven others he sent that day. The caucus (which he was calling "the Liberty League Caucus") "must be as large as possible," so would Buxton please "send immediately not less than twenty names. . . . Send forty names if possible. They need not be confined to your organization."

Meanwhile, Wood was concerned about the number of those responding and about the details involved in arranging for the meeting. Four days after sending the telegrams, he wrote to Col. John Price Jackson at the Paris Command for help in locating a meeting place. He asked Jackson to find a "hall comfortably holding three hundred persons where this meeting may be held." Like a true visionary he had chosen to muse upon what might be, while leaving tactics to the last. Better late than never, he now needed Jackson to provide the meeting place. Thanks to Jackson, Wood could announce the location of the American Officers Club when he sent out his notice of the caucus.

When hundreds of written acceptances came across Wood's desk at the small office quarters he was using in Room D, 4 Place de la Concorde, he and the others knew that the turnout would far exceed expectations. Now the worry was not whether anyone would come but rather where they would put them all?

On March 3, Wood cabled Roosevelt in New York City that there was "every prospect of a large and successful caucus." As if to prove that he was remaining true to the spirit of their original conversations, he added, "Am inviting enlisted men."

The Paris Caucus: March 15–17, 1919

The *Stars and Stripes* on March 7 carried a front-page announcement of the big event to come: "Veterans of A.E.F. In Liberty League" (Wood's choice for a name). The "Conference on Organization . . . In Paris Beginning [the] 15th" would involve "definite steps" for organizing a veterans' association.

The concept for such an organization, the article declared, had grown out of a recent meeting "of a score of National Guard and National Army officers" who, White, Donovan and company must have been amused to read, "chanced to be on official business" in the city.

Wood, for his part, continued to keep the "chance" sense of spontaneity alive in his subsequent presentations about the after-hours sessions during the morale conference; for spontaneity was also conducive to the kind of democratic movement that he and the others hoped to see started. Granted, an open announcement of a meeting in Paris would attract many who would come for less serious minded pursuits than the founding of a veterans' organization. (Those who succumbed to the pleasures of the city and did not attend all, or any, of the caucus meetings were later said to have lost "the Battle of Paris.") Nevertheless, he and the few others making plans for the caucus no doubt wondered about the truly representative nature of the upcoming gathering.

After the deluge of acceptances Wood began looking for a larger meeting hall. He informed Capt. Ogden Mills by telegram, "Col. Jackson and I arranged for the use of the Cirque de Paris during the daytime of Saturday and Monday and probably also Sunday. This has a capacity of over two thousand. . . ." He retained the use of the American Officers Club "with its seating capacity of about two hundred and fifty as a meeting room for larger committees. . . ." He asked Mills to arrange "for two additional committee rooms each seating upwards of fifty people." Worrying earlier about a disappointing turnout, the concern now was for adequate accommodations. "We should increase the number of bedrooms engaged from two hundred to four hundred." Now, too, he told Captain Mills, "The idea of giving a luncheon on the first day will have to be foregone."

The Cirque de Paris, which during the war had been leased to the Y.M.C.A., was one of several popular places in the city offering inexpensive family entertainment, such as traveling circuses and occasional vaudeville. The site, situated on the Avenue La Motre-Picqet, was centrally located and had recently been booked for the finals of the A.E.F. boxing championships, an event second in attendance only to the upcoming Inter-Allied Games.

This polygonal amphitheater had one ground floor of about eighty feet across surrounded by slightly raised box seats. A balcony or gallery circled the arena. A corridor at the back of the boxes served also as standing room. An elevated stage had been erected on one side for the presiding officers of the meeting. The playhouse, as some called it, had been decorated with red, white, and blue bunting, patriotic colors common to both the United States and France. Placards bearing division numbers and other designations marked seating sections set aside for the various military units which, it seemed assured, would be well represented.

And come they did. From Calais to Marseilles, from Rengsdorf to Belfort. Singly, in twos and larger groups, they came from almost every combat division and S.O.S. section in France, Belgium, England, Luxembourg, and Germany. They arrived on late-night trains, in limousines, flivvers, motorcycles, and from hitchhiking on army trucks and other conveyances.

Those who came without personally having received an invitation invented cover stories and scrambled for the means of getting there. Maj. Humes Galbraith had heard Lt. Col. Alvin Owsley and "other politically inclined Texas comrades" at 36th Division Headquarters speak of an "after-the-war G.A.R. type civil organization of veterans." To a group there, Owsley had read the memo from G.H.Q. explaining that some division personnel could be detailed as delegates to a meeting in Paris for that purpose. Even though the delegates from the 36th had already been chosen, Galbraith determined to go.

Not unlike many others, Galbraith's interest in the caucus was rewarded with an assignment. Officially he was permitted to go to the Paris headquarters of the *Stars and Stripes* to straighten out a subscription snafu for a disgruntled Red Cross worker. Galbraith joined the others from the 36th who went to town "in a White machine gun truck, the fast ones." Once in Paris, he took care of his official business, then went to the Cirque de Paris.

Like Galbraith, many came to Paris because they were curious about the forming of a veterans' organization. Others happened in on the spur of the moment. Thomas Keating, a Spanish-American War veteran, was among fifteen or so from the 69th Coast Artillery, "all out for a lark," who wandered into the Cirque de Paris and attended much of the first session as spectators. Though he didn't stay for the entire caucus, Keating was impressed with what he had seen (enough so that when he arrived back in the States, he joined with some who were forming one of the earliest Legion posts in Detroit). Though some later remembered having signed attendance slips at the caucus, George W. Munroe saw "no evidence of registration at the caucus. As far as I could see, anybody who happened to wander in could sit down and take part. It was somewhat of a madhouse. When I reported to the Cirque de Paris, I presented my travel orders to the soldier on duty at the door and he looked me over, handed them back, and directed me to the section reserved for the First Division. After that I came and went as I pleased. I am sure that a great many of the accredited delegates never showed up at the session at all; in fact, some of them never knew where they were held, as they had a chance to take in the sights and excitement of Paris and they went to it."

Munroe, who was but "a bewildered buck private," had been picked to attend the caucus. "It came out of a blue sky, and I did not know what was going on until it was all over and then we did not know whether anything was ever going to come of it [the Legion]. In fact, it was a year before I was convinced that the Legion was going to be worth anything."

For some it was a time of reunion, and for no one more familial in nature or symbolic of the old-age and the new-age military present in France than Captain Theodore Davis Boal of the Cavalry and his son Captain P. L. Boal of the "Air Service." The Boals sat together proudly as, at one break in the proceedings, the official photographer took a group picture of the caucus.

The caucus was scheduled to begin at 10:00 A.M. on Saturday, March 15. The hour came and went. Confusion ruled. Although they had the best intentions, the organizers had no experience in conducting such meetings.

At 2:45 P.M. a French orchestra hired for the occasion, which had struggled through a series of American patriotic tunes, finally hit upon "Dixie" and the crowd responded with a spontaneous joining in on the lyrics. Ten minutes later, Eric Fisher Wood called the caucus to order.

Though he and the others were not sure as yet in what manner the business at hand was to proceed, Wood, as chief spokesman at this point, began the caucus with what would be an often repeated explanation—that what was about to transpire was temporary.

In fact, redundancy became a kind of caucus motif. Wood explained that he served as "Temporary Secretary of the Temporary Committee, in the absence of Theodore Roosevelt, Jr., Temporary Chairman of the Temporary Committee."

In his opening remarks, Wood tied the repeated references to the temporary nature of the work at hand to the democratic intentions of those who first discussed the founding of this veterans' organization. He did this by giving a brief description of how the twenty A.E.F. officers had come together to discuss such a thing.

The rendition he gave was remarkably, if necessarily, humble. Wood had but to speak a few sentences before White (said to be serving as floor leader for the twenty originators from the February meeting) and other privileged insiders could tell that he was resorting to his experience as a former diplomatic attaché. Wisely he chose not to divulge publicly at this time the improvisational aspects of the early work by himself, Roosevelt, White, and Donovan. As he told it now, it all evolved by near accident.

"Early this year," he said, "it was decided by G.H.Q. that it would be advantageous to get in personal touch with the point of view of the citizen-soldiers of the A.E.F., with drafted men of the National Army divisions and with the volunteers of the Militia divisions, as well as with their respective reserve and national guard officers.

"In order to bring this about, G.H.Q. decided to hold each month until further notice a meeting of some twenty or thirty National Guard and Reserve officers of field rank in order to obtain from them an expression as to the wants, inclinations, and needs of the nonprofessional soldiers who constitute the vast majority of the present American army."

Wood gave a brief overview of the official work done at the morale conference in February, then returned to the story line of the after-hours work of the twenty (whom he, Roosevelt, and White, of course, had chosen to attend), all of whom "entertained a feeling that had been shared for some time past by a great number of the members of the army."

Perhaps with a wink at White, Wood explained that the twenty "inevitably fell to discussing among themselves the want and need for a proper association of the veterans of the Great War."

Those A.E.F. officers reasoned that several previous attempts had failed, either because the initiators had some personal aim in view, or because they were insufficiently representative of all classes and units of the army. Several attempts failed because the initial membership was limited to one unit or section of the country, or to one stratum of the A.E.F., as, for instance, one movement composed solely of officers.

They understood that one of the principal obstacles to the proper initiation of such a movement was the assembling of a gathering of individuals who would be even approximately representative of such a vast aggregation as an army of four million men. Therefore they discussed with growing interest the various steps which would be incidental to the formation of such an association, as well as the difficulties incidental to each step.

"Upon comparing notes," the officers found that they knew "prominent leaders both in civil life and from a military point of view" who were "representative of the whole A.E.F. and of all units, ranks, services, corps, and classes thereof." It therefore occurred to them, "as a natural conclusion," that if these persons were gathered together in the "only such gathering . . . during the life of the A.E.F.," they would form a "competent" assembly to "take at least the preliminary steps for the eventual formation of a great association of the Great War. . . ."

And so "their united presence in Paris constituted an unusual opportunity to initiate such an organization; an opportunity which was unlikely to be repeated and which [they] ought not to let slip." So spontaneously were they gathered and found to be in agreement, Wood continued with his preordained version of the scenario, that they "constituted themselves as a temporary committee to take the necessary steps for gathering together from the whole A.E.F. a body of several hundred officers and men who would be of a character to command the confidence and support of all units and all states, and who would be sufficiently representative to properly act as . . . a caucus for the discussion and formation of tentative arrangements which might result in creating a satisfactory permanent organization, [and here he even interjected a potential name for it] the American Veterans of the Great War."

As Wood now summarized it, that was how, and why, those in the audience had come to be together this day.

Wood then turned to the practical matters at hand. He recommended three steps for the caucus to take. First, it should set up "a definite machinery for the holding of a convention next winter in America." He spoke briefly about the "convention," to which delegates should be chosen "from units or territories on some basis of proportional representation" so that they might be "in every way competent to decide the purpose of the organization."

While this was the "primary and principal object of the [present] caucus," it should also adopt "a tentative name for the organization." And it should draft "a tentative constitution that could later be adopted, modified, or rejected" by the subsequent national convention back home. If not a full-blown constitution, then at least a preamble might be composed, which "while it more or less fixed the spirit of the new organization, still left the working out of detailed plans to the convention," much like the relationship that, architect student Wood explained, "the architect's original design or sketch bears to the working drawings in accordance with which a building is eventually erected."

The Temporary Committee, Wood reiterated, did not consider itself, or the present caucus for that matter, to be "competent to decide any definite policy or policies for the Government or adoption of the organization." That, as a now common refrain, was to be the province of the national convention.

This was not to say that among the original twenty, and during the initial brainstorming session about what the organization should be, there were not those who quickly gauged the potential power and political clout that a large and all-inclusive veterans' organization could possibly bring to bear eventually. Wood acknowledged that there were those among the original circle of twenty who proposed, and saw passed, resolutions that as individuals they "deemed vital to the welfare of their country."

But again he stated that the Temporary Committee had quickly agreed that it was not representative enough of all the military forces to take action that would commit the eventual organization permanently to any specific policy.

Wood reported that Temporary Chairman Roosevelt had already left for the United States to continue the work there, particularly to arrange for "a similar caucus a month hence in America to be attended by officers and men representing the troops now in the States" (both those who had returned from Europe and those who had been "denied the great privilege of coming to France to fight the Germans"). That caucus, too, was to provide delegates to the national convention scheduled for later in the year.

With that, Wood stepped down as Temporary Secretary, leaving "all further problems to the decision of this caucus which we have so boldly called together."

A delegate from the Paris Command, Maj. Richard C. Patterson, Jr., made the motion, seconded by someone from the 28th Division, that Lt. Col. Bennett C. Clark act as Temporary Chairman of the caucus. Clark was elected unanimously, as was Eric Fisher Wood as Temporary Secretary. Following that, the use of the rules of the House of Representatives was moved and seconded, the only change being that instead of the one-hour debate rule, one for five-minute debates was substituted.

Since there were more in attendance from some divisions than others, it was decided "after lengthy discussion" that each delegation would be given one vote; hence, one vote would be recorded from each division, each army and its corps troops, each S.O.S. section, the G.H.Q., the S.O.S. Headquarters, the Paris Command, and one each to the units serving with the French. There being "divisions of opinion" on this method, a "standing vote" was taken, in which 279 favored vote by delegation and 72 opposed it, with "many not voting." (Thus occurred one of the few counts of those in attendance, though it was a fairly inconsequential tally since not everyone cast a vote nor registered their attendance otherwise.)

Captain Ogden Mills of G.H.Q. then made the motion for four committees to be formed to work on the organizational "steps" that Wood had listed earlier. Thereupon committees of fifteen persons each for "Convention," "Permanent Organization," "Constitution," and "Name" were formed. After chairmen were named, the caucus recessed from 5:20 to 5:50 for the chairmen to form their committees.

Again the motion was made for approval and endorsement of the actions of the previous Temporary Committee, but again no vote was taken. Instead, a motion was made for the appointment of a committee of five to "wait upon the President of the United States and invite him to address the caucus." President Woodrow Wilson had arrived in Paris the day before, on March 14, for the second round of peace negotiations.

No sooner had the motion been made, however, than one was made for adjournment. That motion, following ingloriously on the heels of the first, made it appear disrespectful to the president in news reports in the States where that episode was made to overshadow the serious and constructive work done at the caucus.

At the caucus, too, the sequence of motions caused great consternation among the leaders of the caucus, who then ordered the resolution and the vote expunged from the record. According to George White, this was an attempt, which failed, to keep the press from seizing upon it. (Eric Fisher Wood would be criticized later for not including in the official minutes all the pithy remarks and cantankerous exchanges between officers and the few enlisted men.)

Before adjournment, the four committees were instructed to meet on Sunday to pursue their various charges and to report to the caucus on Monday. Thus began the Legion's tradition of deliberations by committees charged with specific duties for drafting resolutions.

Chairman Clark called the caucus to order at 9:25 A.M. on Monday, March 17. Temporary Secretary Wood, in reading the minutes of the Saturday meeting, reminded those in attendance of the unfinished matter about inviting the president. The motion, repeated that morning, carried unanimously, and the chair appointed five for the mission: Pvt. Harold W. Ross (later editor of *The American Legion Weekly* and later still a founder of *The New Yorker* magazine), Sgt. John T. Winterich, Brig. Gen. William G. Price, Brig. Gen. John H. Sherbern, and Brig. Gen. A. A. Allen. This unlikely grouping of rank left the room at 9:40 "to seek the president."

Clark then informed the caucus that he would be absent from his duties temporarily to attend a conference at G.H.Q. He turned the chairmanship over to Lt. Col. Thomas Miller of the 79th Division. By House rules, Miller became chairman pro tempore.

Clark's choice of Miller was not made at random. Miller, an early trainee at the Plattsburg Training Camp, had served in Congress before the war and knew Clark's father, the Speaker of the House.

Miller called the caucus to order. With no gavel at hand he rapped the table with an 1879 silver dollar that he carried always with him. When a brigadier general rose to question Miller's right to occupy the chair, the colonel coolly told him to take his seat. The former congressman suggested that the four committees report back-to-back before the reports were discussed by the delegates, since each report would likely relate in some say to the other three.

The committee to recommend a name for the organization reported that they had considered twelve names: Comrades of the Great War, Veterans of the Great War, Liberty League, Army of the Great War, Legion of the Great War, Great War Legion, the Legion, the American Legion, American Comrades of the Great War, Society of the Great War, the Great Legion, and American Comrades. Of these, the committee (now reduced to eleven members with the absence of an S.O.S. colonel and three sergeants from the Paris Command) narrowed their selection to five names, which they now recommended to the caucus in descending order of choice, from "Legion of the Great War" down to "American Legion."

The committee on a constitution reported next. Lt. Col. Lemuel Bolles read the report, which included the draft of a preamble:

"We, the members of the Military and Naval Services of the United

States of America in the Great War, desiring to perpetuate the principles of Justice, Freedom, and Democracy for which we have fought, to inculcate the duty and obligation of the citizen to the State; to preserve the history and incidents of our participation in the war; and to cement the ties of comradeship formed in service, do propose to found and establish an Association for the furtherance of the foregoing purposes."

Bolles spoke then about eligibility and about the eventual scope of a "national organization with subsidiary branches" in states, territories, foreign possessions of the United States, and foreign countries where members wished to organize.

State organizations would be autonomous "except that the requirements and purposes of the permanent national constitution as adopted shall be complied with."

Officers of the organization were to have the titles of president, one or more vice presidents, a secretary, a treasurer, and a board of directors.

Representation was to be based on the actual enrollment of the "subsidiaries" at all conventions.

The convention committee brought two reports: The majority report of the convention committee was read by Wagoner Dale Shaw of the 88th. November 11, 1919, at 11 A.M., was recommended as the date and time to convene a national convention. The place was to be chosen by a joint meeting of the Executive Committee of the organization acting with a similar committee in the United States (he spoke of two different "organizations" at this point, that originating in Paris and that to be formed in the United States.)

It was important, he said, to hold the convention as soon as possible before 1920 since that was a presidential election year "when the purposes of the organization might be misconstrued and an attempt made to involve it in party issues. . . ."

The minority report of the convention committee addressed the matter of representation in the States with much more detail than had that of the majority, calling for "a strictly local . . . basis" for representation, beginning "in the smallest political subdivisions of each state or territory" where delegates would be elected to county conventions, then to state and finally to national conventions. The national convention was the goal to which all pointed, it said, so no "permanent or representative organization or attempt [of] any expression of policies in Europe" was desirable. The focus was on future action in the United States. The minority report also called for "a campaign of education" (not otherwise described).

The committee on permanent organization, too, stated the need for representation to be based on "territorial considerations rather than [military] organizations" and so it recommended an executive committee of fifty, half commissioned officers and half enlisted men. The committee then submitted a list of names for an executive committee.

When the reports of the four committees had been read, attention was turned to action from the floor. Someone moved that the report on a proposed name be laid on the table. It was seconded and carried.

At that point, the five who had been sent to invite the president to speak to the caucus returned to report that they were unable to see Wilson, but added that "the president would send his reply to the caucus." (The reply arrived too late to be included in the proceedings of the caucus distributed to those who attended.)

When Wood reread the report on the constitution, one attendee moved that it be adopted. Bishop Brent, Senior Chaplain of the A.E.F., seconded the motion, and then asked to speak. By motion, seconded and passed, Brent was allowed to take the platform.

The bishop said the army was not merely a body, but possessed a soul and a conscience, and those aspects he was happy to find were represented "in the report of your committee." Earlier, he said, he "was fearful . . . lest you should create a great mechanism without adequate purposes." But his fears "have been wholly allayed and I see in the report . . . the ideals not only of the army but of the nation adequately expressed, and I wish to tell you gentlemen that so far as I have any ability to promote this great movement, I give you my most hearty support.

"I believe that the army of today, when it goes back to citizen thinking and citizen acting, will be capable of contributing to the commonwealth of the United States as will change the character of the whole country and lift it up to a higher plane of political, industrial, and religious life."

As for the Comrades in Service, which he headed and which had worked to "promote the various ends that are so well expressed in the committee report," he and his cohorts "are prepared to contribute to this army-wide organization [the concept of an American Legion]. We are entirely loyal to your principles and methods of approach and we are quite willing to forego any attempt to make an organization which might become a rival to you."

Indeed, the bishop would help "between now and the time of demobilization" because "there is a great opportunity for us to promote the principles which actuate you. We have already a temporary and provisional organization for the promotion of such principles, the creation of better citizenship along the lines so well expressed. We would like everyone who can to give support to that which we are endeavoring to do, while we ask all who come in with us to be prepared to throw in their lot with this organization when it is perfected in the United States."

Following Brent's remarks, a lengthy discussion was precipitated when a delegate from the 81st (North Carolina, South Carolina, Florida) raised "the race question, holding that negro troops should be excluded from membership in the organization." No further action on this matter was entered in the minutes.

By motion of one from the Paris Command, thanks were given to Bishop Brent for the goodwill and support that he fostered on behalf of the Comrades in Service. The measure carried unanimously.

Finally, on the motion of Lieutenant Colonel Bolles, the previous work by the officers of the Temporary Committee was approved, endorsed, and commended.

The motion to lay the name committee's report on the table was then reconsidered. In the free-for-all discussion that followed, the name American Legion was said by one (some say it was Medical Sergeant Alexander Woollcott, later of literary fame) to have an aura of "the silk stocking" about it. There were immediate objections. In some accounts it was a colonel, in others a sergeant, who observed that he had never noticed any aversion on the part of doughboys to silk stockings, especially those worn by Parisian ladies of the evening.

More names were suggested, including American Crusaders and Legion of the Great War. The delegates from G.H.Q. still favored Comrades in Service.

Earlier, Maj. Thomas R. Gowenlock, who would recall that Roosevelt, Jr., had mentioned the need for a veterans' organization early in the war, had been part of a discussion at the *Stars and Stripes* office about a name for the new organization. His proposal of American Legion prompted others to cite a host of legions: the French Foreign Legion, Roman legions, Thundering Legion, the Tenth Legion, the Theban Legion, the Legion of the Lark, The Legion of Honor, Loyal Legion, the Louisville Legion (the old First Kentucky, from the Mexican War forward).

No one, according to Gowenlock, mentioned the American Legion of Benedict Arnold. Someone did refer to there being an American Legion organized in 1914 in preparation for the war many saw coming. That temporary organization, for which Roosevelt, Jr. had been chiefly responsible, was said to have enrolled 35,000 and had published several issues of a magazine before being absorbed into the Council of National Defense in 1916. Someone else mentioned having heard in the summer of 1916 about recruiting banners at Fort Francis, Ontario, advertising for American volunteers to "Join the American Legion" of the Canadian Expeditionary Force's 97th Overseas Battalion.

One who supported the name American Legion reportedly said that his outfit had fought alongside an outstanding legion, otherwise unidentified, and the designation of American just seemed essential. Another liked the name "American Legion of the Great War" because the initials were also those for Abraham Lincoln and George Washington.

It seemed for a while that the caucus would disband without giving a name to the organization it had founded. Richard Selye Jones of the *Stars and Stripes* was credited with saying that, for reporting and promotional purposes, the organization surely needed a name. Hearing that, Col. W. McD. Rowan (brother of Captain Andrew Rowan, famous for having carried "the message to Garcia" in the Spanish-American War) encouraged John W. O'Conner, another newspaper man, to endorse the idea by calling for a temporary name. O'Connor suggested American Army Association (forgetting all about the navy) but stated that he hoped the permanent name would eventually be the American Legion.

The matter of temporary versus permanent names was debated, during which time it was said that whatever name was now publicized would no doubt stick with the public.

In the printed minutes of the caucus, Maj. Maurice Gordon of the 36th (the "Lone Star Division," although it contained Oklahomans, too) was recorded as having made the motion that " 'American Legion' be adopted as the temporary name of the organization." His motion was seconded and carried unanimously.

In the last twelve minutes of the caucus, the secretary was authorized to publish the names of the now current Executive Committee and thanks were given the Y.M.C.A. for the use of the Cirque de Paris. "In the absence of further business," the meeting was adjourned at 5:27 P.M.

With haste and heart, the spirited gathering of citizen-soldiers had launched a vessel of new design. It was an amateurish effort, buoyed by youthful intelligence and trimmed by a touch of mature counsel. There was much to be learned. But at this point, momentum was everything.

In the waning minutes of the caucus, as Donovan and White stood in the foyer of the building, congratulating themselves on the success of the event and on their freedom from further responsibility for the organization other than spirited membership, Bennett Clark came to them with the news that they were being "put up" as president and secretary of the organization.

"Not a chance," the two chimed in unison. Both were leaving Paris for their home stations and wished to accept no further official duties. Donovan was taken at his word, but White was once again tapped for a position of leadership. His admirer Eric Fisher Wood later said of the "valued friend and adviser to Theodore Roosevelt, Sr." that the Oregonian "was much looked up to by the others" as the "real brains throughout the formation of the Legion." Wood, Roosevelt, Jr., Donovan, and Clark, all younger than George White, "willingly accepted the guidance of his snaffle rein. He made the bricks they threw; and indicated what heads they were to be thrown at."

That evening the new Executive Committee held its first meeting and elected Spanish-American War veteran Col. Milton A. Foreman of the 3rd Division, a Chicago lawyer, as chairman. George White was made secretary; Major R. C. Patterson of the Paris Command was named assistant secretary. The next morning White and Foreman met for a postcaucus appraisal of just what had been accomplished. Wood's high praise of White notwithstanding, White himself gave Foreman credit for having "a truly remarkable vision of the future course of the American Legion. He saw into the future of the organization as clearly as many men now observe into its past."

In White's view, "As near as we could calculate tangible assets, we possessed a pile of resolutions, the tentative name 'American Legion,' and a responsibility to do something along lines which we must determine upon and promulgate."

If awed and amazed by their responsibilities, the officers of the organization were not at a loss for lofty statements of purpose. When Milton Foreman composed credentials for Eric Fisher Wood, recently arrived at "the Yale Club, Vanderbilt Avenue, New York City," to present at a meeting in America scheduled for April 12 (but which did not occur) he spoke of "an association . . . which will be the most potent and dependable force in our country in the development and promotion of the principles as set forth in our preamble as well as of the greatest benefit and enjoyment to its members."

On the second day after the close of the Paris Caucus, White wrote to Roosevelt on March 19 on his G.H.Q., A.E.F., letterhead, "Reactions have been mostly very good. The meeting itself was successful and wholesome." The most promising feature, he thought, was "the free expression of opinion on the part of all concerned and the earnest manner in which any plans that might have been made toward a 'program' were swept aside and the meeting taken possession of by the whole caucus."

"The outstanding feature," he wrote, of the post-caucus meeting was "the presence for the first time of an adequate representation of enlisted men. At the Paris Caucus, the new Executive Committee was formed which gave equal representation to the enlisted men, who were poorly represented at [that] caucus itself."

But a nettlesome problem in that regard persisted. "The difficulty seems in getting the enlisted men to Paris." He and the others would be trying to get them ordered there for an early April meeting. If those efforts failed, "several of us will advance the necessary funds for their expenses, as it is manifestly necessary that they be present and have full voice." He was making a "telegraphic canvass," he informed

Roosevelt, of delegates to ascertain who would be present. He was urging all to attend.

White wished Roosevelt well in making the U.S. meeting as successful as that in Paris. After all, could the American caucus be less so? With the energetic and effective Theodore Roosevelt, Jr., and others like the recently returned Wood working to that end, a gathering of veterans at home promised to be another advance in the fortunes of the Legion. White hoped that "the movement will assume such proportions as to prevent the origin of rival organizations of questionable character."

In summation, the work was "going smoothly." "Favorable sentiment for the new organization has developed rapidly. All prospects are for its complete success."

The Aftermath

The *Stars and Stripes* of March 28 carried the first piece of publicity after the Paris Caucus under the name "The American Legion."

It began with a brief background note: "The A.E.F. as a whole—doughboy, colonel, and general working together—organized the American Legion this month as its postwar association. It likewise rests with the great body of the A.E.F., and not with any particular committee, to determine the scope of the work and carry forward the objects of this association.

"To continue with success the work already launched will require the personal cooperation of every soldier in every organization now in France. When we return to the States it will be equally important to have a nucleus of men in every community who will take the lead in their particular local organization.

"For this reason, the committee desires to obtain immediately the names of all officers and enlisted men who are interested in promoting their particular company or community organizations. It is requested, therefore, that every soldier in the A.E.F. who is personally interested in having a part in completing the final organization of the American Legion send in his name and address to the Secretary of the Executive Committee. The committee will then send him all information as to what has been done so far and keep him informed of future steps taken. The writer should state his name, rank, present organization, and present A.P.O. number; in addition, home address, town, and street number are requested.

"Communications should be addressed to Maj. R. C. Patterson, the American Legion, Room 4B, 4 Place de la Concorde, Paris. The success of the American Legion thus far is a result of the enthusiasm with which the entire A.E.F. has assisted in its preliminary organization. The assurance of its future will, in the same way, rest on the individual work of every soldier in France." It was signed, "L. R. Fairall, Publicity Committee."

The reference to "doughboy" in the lead sentence of the announcement was no accident. The most difficult criticism to counteract, in spite of its untruth, was that the organization was for officers only. True, the large majority of those who attended the Paris Caucus were officers, but as George White and others pointed out, officers simply had more mobility. He and the others most closely involved in the organizational work pointed out continually that when the call for representation went out, enlisted men would be welcomed. It was also pointed out more convincingly that the Executive Committee of One Hundred was numerically equal, officers to enlisted men.

George White placed an announcement in the European edition of the April 5 (Saturday) issue of the *New York Herald,* detailing a "meeting of the Executive Committee on Monday [April 7] at the Officers' Leave Bureau, 4, Avenue Bagriel, Paris, at 10:30 morning and 3 P.M. Colonel Milton A. Foreman of 33d Div. will preside." This was to be the last meeting of the A.E.F. Legionnaires while they were still in Europe.

For this meeting the goal was for one officer and one enlisted man from each unit to be present, a truer representation of military men than had attended the Paris Caucus. White had said that the Legion was the miracle worker that swept aside rank once civilian considerations were being dealt with. This was the chance to prove it.

The publicity piece apparently was well received. Generals who had snubbed or otherwise ignored the initial efforts of the organizers were now inquiring about how their units might be represented.

Leaves of absence for the April meeting were authorized by G.H.Q. Though army transportation was denied, army telegraph lines were used openly for notices and other Legion messages. Brigadier General Robert C. Davis of the Regular Army and Adjutant General of the A.E.F. was often credited with being particularly lenient in his attitude toward the use of the telegraph and mimeograph machines by Legion organizers.

The nearest thing in the archives of the Legion to official minutes for the April 7 meeting is George White's letter to Roosevelt, dated April 13. On letterhead paper of "General Headquarters, American Expeditionary Forces," George White reported on the meeting six days earlier, giving "some of my impressions of the meeting and of the 'situation as a whole.' "

He assured Roosevelt that the meeting was "truly representative" in that each combat division had sent one officer and one soldier and all those eligible were on hand "excepting Base Sections 5 and 7." This time, also, unlike at the first public meeting, the seven Regular Army divisions were represented, as were troops in England and Germany.

The popularity of the fledgling organization had been sustained,

White indicated. Though G5 had refused to issue orders for the enlisted men to attend the meeting ("after having informed me that such orders would be issued"), the men came at their own expense.

The meeting was "harmonious," and business transacted had had "a helpful effect on the entire movement." As for organizational matters, "the temporary officers were made permanent, pending the general convention in the United States. . . ."

White admitted surprise at both the growth of the movement, which "the headliners say has 'spread like wildfire,' " and "the small volume of friction." But he repeated the caution often expressed during the early months: those in leadership and official roles must take "no action looking to the development of the Legion except along the broadest lines, with due consideration for the several schools of thought now prevalent, and [they should] be keeping in mind at all times in every phase of the work that we are concerned at this time with nothing more than providing the machinery upon which a spontaneous getting-together of all those who served can be effected."

Referring to an earlier cable from Milton Foreman to Roosevelt telling of the appointing of a liaison committee that would represent the A.E.F. in the United States, White explained that the selection of Col. Bennett C. Clark as chairman was deliberate "as representing one school of thought in the movement" since "I believe you represent the other school." (If White meant something other than that the two were well-known members of opposing political parties, he did not say.)

The Executive Committee, White explained, had been enlarged, "to embrace several members I thought should be added to the work." One such addition was Capt. Ogden Mills, Jr., who had "proved to be a remarkably clear thinker and a very forceful speaker at the initial caucus." Mills had his detractors apparently, but White dismissed their criticism as "minor petty enmities" that were well offset by the man's "work and his judgment." It may have been that the wealth of Mills's family put off some who were particularly conscious of the common doughboy image that Legion organizers had projected as representatives of the organization they were establishing. The Mills family had loaned their lavish Paris home to General Pershing when he had been headquartered in Paris in 1917.

The easiest and perhaps most appropriate comparison of the Legion to some known quantity, he said, was to refer to it as "the new G.A.R." And the most convincing statement as to how the Legion had evolved, he had found, seemed to be that "it is being formed by the army itself, to be directed by [servicemen] after they have left the service" and have had a convention where "they will be fully represented by their elected delegates."

As for the matter of membership eligibility, White was thankful, he said, for not having heard "of a single resentment" in Europe about "uniting with those who saw service in the United States." He had heard those, however, who did not want to extend Legion eligibility to Red Cross and Y.M.C.A. personnel. In fact, he regarded this as "an extremely dangerous subject," something to "keep entirely away from as a matter to be settled, if it comes up at all, at the main convention."

Newspapers in the United States, as a sidelight to the biggest story of the time—the end of the war—speculated about the formation of a large organization of veterans. Knowing of Roosevelt's efforts in the United States for the Legion, journalists were sure that a large group of veterans organized for whatever purposes would not fail to have a political impact.

In this light, the *Chicago Tribune* on April 8, dateline Paris, focused on one of the "lofty aims" expressed by those meeting in Paris—that of the need for civic-mindedness—and proclaimed, "One of the ideals of the new G.A.R. will be to fight for good government. (Will keep unsullied)."

And, in the confines of the column inch, it was an easy step to the assertion that the Legion, even as it was being born, had been imbued with appreciable political clout. In the journalistic penchant for adding active verb forms to suppositions, subheadings about the April meeting in Paris announced: "American Legion Sounds Warning to Politicians." "Solemn Warning to Erring Political Parties Was Sounded Yesterday by the Executive Committee of the American Legion."

What substance there was for the supposedly stern nature of the proceedings that day may have been derived from a statement by Brig. Gen. William G. Price of the 28th Keystone Division. "It would be unfortunate to place the American Legion in competition with political parties," Price was said to have remarked. "But [the Legion] will uphold what is right so firmly and forcefully that whatever party is wrong will learn to fear it. It is the brotherhood of men who have realized thoroughly their responsibility to the nation. Those who have been over [in Europe] are going back [home] with altered ideas about many things [and] will fight for those ideals they have been taught to hold dear."

The Legion's message, Price was quoted as saying, "is like the Monroe Doctrine—not a law but a respected principle. The Legion is to be the Monroe Doctrine of decency." Similarly, Bennett Clark reportedly stated that the Legion should not allow any clique to control it.

So, already, the Legion was beginning to be judged on its political potential. There were, of course, a few instances in which Legion organizers had encouraged such a view.

The Legion's own public relations materials had referred to the Legion itself as the new G.A.R. Since the G.A.R. had been unabashedly political, it was assumed by many that the Legion would be the same. Also, with presidential electioneering already in 1919, it was a fact that political connotations and guessing games would attend such a joining together of a large number of people. The presence of Roosevelt and Clark as easily recognizable and visible personages associated with the veterans' movement was certain to raise speculation. In the current political frenzy both were seen as progeny with whom their fathers' entourage would surely join at the slightest encouragement by the two offspring.

The time remaining to the Legion in Europe was not wasted. Bishop Brent's public commitment to aiding the Legion, even to the consolidation of the Comrades in Service with the Legion, was being born out in practice. Originally, Brent's chaplains, in reportedly enrolling 60,000 Comrades, had been assisted by G.H.Q., which had authorized the assignment of one line officer and three noncommissioned officers in each division to promote this post-Armistice fraternal association that emphasized good morale and citizenship.

Now, with the understanding the chief chaplain recently had fostered with the Legion, the officers and NCOs formerly enrolling members in the Comrades would continue to do so, but the newly enrolled Comrades would be told that their current membership was to be continued, after leaving Europe, in the American Legion, which had the aim to perpetuate in civilian life the comradeship and spirit for service for the nation, too. The Comrades would continue in existence while there were forces yet in Europe but would not be continued in the States.

White was familiar with the army's large output of manuals and other materials, often in runs of hundreds of thousands, on such workaday matters as the recent four-page leaflet on the treatment of mange and one on the proper use of dubbin for dressing leather. He had been told, he said, that there was at least a possibility that the Legion's pamphlet could be printed on an army press.

White and Foreman, whose vision for the Legion White greatly respected, once sat up all night "reducing the American Legion to paper." Their manuscript was finished when reveille sounded.

White presented the manuscript to the higher command at Chaumont. When it was handed back to him with a request for specifications about the number of copies wanted, the overall size, and the width of the margins, he took this to mean that it would be printed, and he found an enlisted man who had been a printer before the war to help him provide the specifications requested.

Several weeks later he heard from the assistant chief of staff. "It is not believed expedient for the Government to publish this unofficial matter." Fuming, White had five thousand copies printed in Paris. Legion Assistant Secretary Richard Patterson distributed these copies throughout the divisions and S.O.S. sections.

The purpose of the pamphlet, as was stated therein, was "to get into the minds of all who saw . . . service that they shall form their own organization, subject to their own direction and shaped according to their own wishes. All organization work so far is tentative [for] the creation of the necessary foundation."

It was also stressed as in previous advertisements that membership in the Legion was all-inclusive and that the organization claimed an ambitious priority: "Every member of the A.E.F. is automatically a member of the American Legion, and no action is necessary at this time in order to attain membership. No membership campaign is being undertaken or is authorized. . . ."

The matter of membership, it was explained, would be taken up in a more systematic and permanent fashion once the soldiers had returned to the States, where "state, county, and city units [of the Legion] will be initiated."

This read-and-pass-it-on introduction to the Legion, along with the word of mouth campaign by individual workers, helped alert many to the origins, activities, and goals of the new organization.

"Policies, not Politics"

Theodore Roosevelt, Jr., had left France before the Paris Caucus and, employing all his many resources to good effect, had spent an active and productive two months in the United States promoting the first U.S. caucus of veterans. In March through May he called upon governors, mayors, and others while he encouraged statewide caucuses of world war veterans to prepare for an American caucus. The Legion, he promised, would keep alive the principles of justice, freedom, and democracy for which they had fought.

The influence of Roosevelt was large and effective. He traveled the country, exerting his personality and prestige for the Legion. He was the public figure; Wood, White, and the others were the journeymen organizers fresh from the Paris Caucus and other work in Europe.

Soon after the April 7 meeting in Paris, several newspapers carried an account similar to that in the *Chicago Tribune* of April 10 telling of the plans for a caucus in St. Louis (a Wyoming Legionnaire wrote Roosevelt that he hoped the convention site "would be somewhere west of the Hudson") scheduled now from May 8–10. All contained quotes by Roosevelt about the aims to develop a tentative constitution and a system (eventually the state conventions) whereby all could participate in the election of delegates to a national convention. Half of those elected in the states, it was stressed, should be enlisted men.

Roosevelt and a few others set up a temporary office in New York City. They named chairmen in each state on the authority of the Paris Caucus and continued to publicize the Legion as best they could.

Roosevelt was joined by his brother-in-law, Dr. Richard Derby, along with Cornelius Wickersham, Henry Fairfield Osborn, Granville Clark, Leslie Kinkaid, and R. B. Beers. Eric Fisher Wood and Franklin D'Olier were also present, having returned to the States shortly after the Paris Caucus. George White also returned home in early May to add his considerable influence to the important steps ahead—the U.S. Caucus and the national convention.

The New York office, during this time at 19 West 44th Street, was the place where the flame was kept. Here the principles of the Legion were voiced daily by the staff. Here was compiled a growing file of statistics received periodically from the states or requested by national officers for their work.

Having determined not to control the Legion themselves, the national officers worked at making it large enough and truly representative of American veterandom, so that it could not be controlled by factions, blocs, and cliques. They waited now for the caucus in St. Louis to speak.

THE VETERANS MEET IN AMERICA

May 8 – 10

Six weeks after the Paris Caucus, the stateside version of an assembly of veterans took place in St. Louis, the first such gathering in a movement that, eight months later at a national convention, would number 700,000 members.

The founders in Paris came from military units varied in their duties and origins. The founders who met by the Mississippi River in early May were largely those who had served stateside. Several listed themselves as students; only one on the official list of delegates reported having no occupation at the time of registration.

From Colorado, for example, came a railroad conductor, a chef, two lawyers, a letter carrier, a grain dealer, a Linotype operator, a tire salesman, and an undertaker. Illinois, a strong Legion state from the beginning, sent 112 delegates. Except for the twenty-five lawyers, these veterans, ranging from privates to colonels, worked at an assortment of occupations nearly as numerous as the state's delegation.

Temporary Secretary Eric Fisher Wood had returned from Paris about April 1 and had worked nearly full-time on arrangements for the caucus. Bennett Clark was present also, as vice chairman. As one of several who had arranged to be home, he was particularly helpful to Roosevelt in naming those capable of beginning state organizations. Clark and White helped in hammering out policies and making diplomatic overtures to other veterans' organizations. Donovan, D'Olier, and Buxton also aided in this area. At the caucus in St. Louis, White was again floor leader.

The work for the Legion that had been done in Europe was represented at the St. Louis Caucus by the fifteen representatives of the Paris Caucus headed by Bennett Clark. This time the group included Roosevelt, of course. Together they determined that the American Caucus should name a chairman, secretary, and executive committee of one hundred to match the committee appointed in Europe. The two committees were then to join and to generate another set of temporary officers who would officiate in limited capacity until the charter convention in November.

The meeting in Paris had been a tentative, exploratory affair, a unique respite from military discipline, at least within the confines of the Cirque de Paris, in which equal treatment was extended to all in order to conduct the business at hand. There the caucus officers, though having to quell occasional outbursts, had performed their duties in a manner that favorably impressed those who heard them. While the floor was actively involved in the vigorous give-and-take of deliberation on a few key matters of organization, the presiding officers provided enough leadership so that the caucus could accomplish something of importance.

But at St. Louis, after the participants had had a few weeks to read accounts of the Paris Caucus, to see conditions in the United States that needed addressing, and to look to the future, they brought to the American Caucus a democratic initiative that would not be denied. The floor at the St. Louis gathering would also be an active arena. And the leadership this time would not only have to be capable of conducting a large convention, but also be capable of following through with what this caucus demanded of them.

In the six weeks since the Paris Caucus, the Temporary Committee had learned how to arrange for a caucus in ways that would continue the democratic origin of the organization. One move especially saved the Temporary Committee the onus of exercising too much control and influence on the upcoming proceedings. Roosevelt telegraphed each of the state organizations, themselves only weeks old, and requested that one delegate from each state be sent to St. Louis three days before the opening of the caucus. These forty-nine delegates (one from each state and the District of Columbia) would then constitute an Advance Committee that would offer advice on the committees that should be formed and make recommendations for the program.

(A few independent organizations had sent representatives to the caucus, including the American Army Association, the World's War Veterans, American Service League, Camp Perry Instructors' Association, and the Missouri Officers' Association. Of these, the American Army Association and the World's War Veterans, though having been formed before the Legion in Paris, agreed to "amalgamate" (Eric Fisher Wood's word) in the American Legion. The Temporary Committee, in deference to this voluntary decision by the two predecessor organizations, invited each to send twelve delegates-at-large.)

The work set out for the caucus was largely that decided upon by the Advance Committee, and when the caucus was so informed, it was to a greater democratic effect than had it all been spelled out by the few on the Temporary Committee, well intentioned and well respected as they were. A roster of the committee titles created by the Advance Committee indicated their intentions to conduct business on the full gamut of organizational matters: Credentials; Temporary Name; Organization; Resolutions; Constitution, By-Laws and Declaration of Principles; Next Meeting Place and Time; Publication; Emblem; Permanent Headquarters; and Finance.

It was the Advance Committee that also recommended that each committee should be made up of one member from each state (when possible) and that an Executive Committee be comprised of two members from each state.

Obviously the U.S. meeting would be more accessible to journalists and was therefore easier copy than the Paris Caucus had been (though the latter had been widely reported). Americans, quick to organize, and at the same time quick to question the motives of others engaged in the same process lest they assume too much power, watched with interest as reports of the activity there appeared in the press.

Both Roosevelt and the new American Legion were much in the public eye. Having spent much of his life in the entourage of a world-famous man, Roosevelt was keenly aware of public scrutiny. He also had definite ideas about what this organization should become, and how it should be perceived by the public it professedly wished to serve.

There was no mistaking the good fortune of the Roosevelt name being associated with the new veterans' organization. Serious members hoped, organizers assumed, and many in politics and elsewhere anticipated that the Legion itself would soon acquire appreciable name recognition. What was about to transpire at this caucus would do much to assure that.

So one of the main attractions at St. Louis was the presence of the temporary chairman. Obviously the family name had its own lasting mystique. When on May 8 the affable Theodore Roosevelt, Jr., called the American Caucus to order at 2:45 P.M. in St. Louis's Shubert Theater, he used a gavel fashioned from the rudder of the steamship *Roosevelt,* which had carried Admiral Peary on his explorations of the North Pole.

Before the echo of the gavel had faded, the mood of the caucus was apparent. In less than twenty-five words, Roosevelt greeted those assembled and called them to action. They needed a permanent chairman, he said, and he opened the floor for nominations. There followed immediately a raucous display of adulation for the one man who to most of those present personified the organization they had come to advance.

Just as quickly, the man in the spotlight demonstrated his intent to dispel the persistent rumors that all his organizational labors on behalf of the Legion were but a ploy to raise support for his alleged political aspirations.

So when Jack Sullivan of Washington nominated "the worthy son of a worthy sire—Theodore Roosevelt, Junior," the nominee immediately asked that his name be withdrawn. But first he had to wait out a rowdy show of favor and affection punctuated with much cheering and applause.

Even in the staid medium of the verbatim minutes much of the excitement of the moment can be seen:

> Roosevelt: Gentlemen, I would like to speak in regard to that nomination myself. (Cries of "We want Roosevelt"—"We want Teddy.")
> Roosevelt: Gentlemen, I wish to withdraw my name from nomination. (Cries of "No—no!" and there was a "prolonged disturbance.")
> Roosevelt: I wish to withdraw my name from nomination for a number of reasons. The first is that I want the country at large to get the correct impression of this meeting here. We are gathered together for a very high purpose. I want every American through the length and breadth of this land to realize that there is not a man in this caucus who is seeking anything for himself, personally, but that he is simply working for the good of the entire situation. I believe furthermore that what we want here is someone who has been connected with the movement only since it started on this side; someone who originates from this caucus."
> (Cries of "We want Teddy" drown out a motion to close the nominations.)

Roy C. Haines, a delegate from Maine, attempted to take Roosevelt at his word and after heartily complimenting the caucus's first choice, he nominated a Texan, Col. Henry D. Lindsley, a former mayor of Dallas and an officer trained at Plattsburg before serving for a year in France as the chief officer in charge of war risk insurance matters.

Though Lindsley's nomination was seconded, and even "thirded," there were still shouts of "We want Teddy." Soon the entire caucus rose to its feet. One from Idaho seconded Roosevelt's nomination, another moved that the nominations be closed. This was seconded, forcing a runoff between the two nominees. One rose to say that it would be a mistake to take a "no" from Roosevelt.

Roosevelt again declined. Again "The entire body rises and cries, "We won't take 'no.' We won't take 'no.' "

Roosevelt pointed to Lindsley as "the only one candidate before the convention." He was adamant. "I am sticking to it, I withdraw my name."

It was moved that Roosevelt give the chair to Bennett Clark temporarily while the election process continued. Clark stepped in as acting chairman and immediately stated that Roosevelt should accept the nomination and if he didn't he "should be made to take it." Once again the caucus rose to its feet.

The reason for Clark's gesture was soon apparent. By allowing the many who wanted to elect Roosevelt another chance to demonstrate their wish, he showed that there were some who wished to abide by the favorite nominee's wishes to have his name withdrawn. Though an obvious first choice, there could be no unanimous vote for him since many now also wished to honor the nominee's decision not to run.

Clark then explained that Roosevelt had told him when he took the chair that he absolutely would not accept the nomination. There was also the matter of the other nominee. "He refuses to enter into a contest with Colonel Lindsley in any way," Clark stated for his famous friend.

Finally, Jack Greenway of Arizona spoke. He knew "this Roosevelt outfit," he said. He had "followed [Roosevelt's] father through Cuba," and had observed Teddy, Jr., at Cantigny and on the Toul Front. When both father and son said no, they meant no!

Greenway's summation of the circumstances, and his invoking of the family name to prove the resoluteness of the temporary chairman's intent not to become a permanent officer, convinced the caucus to consider other nominees. Greenway also implied that Roosevelt might consider the leading role at the November convention "after all the boys come home." With this the calls for Roosevelt to assume the chair dropped off, at least in volubility.

Texan Henry Lindsley came forth to say that Roosevelt was his first choice, too, but that the caucus should elect a chairman and begin conducting business right away.

The temporary secretary called the roll and the delegations announced their votes. Lindsley won, Sullivan asked that the vote be recorded as unanimous, and the new chairman was handed the gavel.

Roosevelt then nominated Sullivan as vice-chairman and the former sergeant was voted in unanimously. Sullivan rose to reiterate that "this fraternity" was one of doughboys with a common password to action: "the Red, the White and the Blue." The minutes recorded "prolonged applause."

Eric Fisher Wood was elected unanimously as secretary. Over cries for "speech, speech," Wood rose only to ask that business be expedited. Two nominees were then introduced for the position of sergeant-at-arms and both were elected. Moments later they were pressed into service when a delegate "appeared unexpectedly upon the stage" and attempted to speak.

After the offending delegate had been "interrupted" and "escorted from the stage," one who had been awaiting recognition from the chairman during the incident observed that, "We did not come down here for a vaudeville show, or to be entertained by some drunken boob; we have plenty of them back home." His comments were met with "violent applause."

Secretary Wood then spoke about the appointment of committee members. He explained that the Temporary Committee had determined that the caucus should be "programmed" by an Advance Committee to help equip the three day caucus to conduct all the business it must. That advance group had recommended the committees for which Wood now solicited members. The caucus recessed then for thirty minutes while delegates selected committeemen.

Hamilton Fish of New York suggested that since the navy had largely been ignored in the nominations so far for Legion officers, that two more vice-chairmen be elected and that both should be navy men. The idea met with the approval of the caucus. After a spirited round of nominations, "ordinary seaman" Fred Humphreys, a student and hotel clerk from New Mexico, was elected second vice-chairman. Addressing "gobs, soldiers, and marines" he promised to do his duties in the best way a "deck-swabbing sailor" could.

The election of a third vice-chairman was put off until the next day, and the caucus was adjourned.

That evening the caucus was invited to the Missouri Athletic Club by the Confederate Veterans, the Grand Army of the Republic, and the United Spanish War Veterans, who, the chairman had announced, "want to feel that this great new organization which is having birth in the United States today is hand in hand with them." He urged all the delegates to attend to show their elders, "We are with them in common purpose upbuilding the United States . . . and upholding the principles for which we fought."

The meeting on Thursday had been that of an organization of bounding energy, strong in fraternity, reveling in good-natured give-and-take while electioneering for a chairman and vice-chairmen and while awaiting appointments to the numerous committees.

Friday's meeting was different. A few minutes into the afternoon session (the morning was devoted to committee meetings) it was obvious that ritual and historical reflections were far down the list of things that animated the organization.

Though occurring primarily as a planning session for a national convention later in the year, the caucus was forced to consider present and troubling issues.

On this memorable afternoon, the caucus observed a silent and sobering memorial for the war dead, confronted the I.W.W., accused the mayor of Chicago, William "Big Bill" Hale Thompson, of being unpatriotic and refused to hold its convention in that city, took the dare to "teach 'em what it means" when the name "the American Legion" was faulted by one as being amorphous and otherwise unsuitable, determined to vigorously promote Victory Loans, and, in general, engaged in vigorous debate on the matters at hand.

There were significant hints about what could be expected from the Legion in the future. In the short time between the presentation of the concept in Paris and the convening of the veterans on the Mississippi River, a unique vitality had begun to take on definable proportions.

The life cycle of the organization had progressed quickly from infancy to adolescence. So far no policy statements had been formulated. That wasn't the province of the caucuses, anyway. But there were emerging now certain attitudes and reactive tendencies—abstract qualities, to be sure—which nevertheless would prove to be fairly dependable indications about what would emerge eventually as the characteristics of the Legion.

The Friday full-caucus session began with the election of a third vice-chairman. In a genuine enough show of respect for those currently fighting their way back to some measure of health, the nominations included Idaho marine private Jack Tupper, a Distinguished Service Cross holder, wounded twice at Château-Thierry and for the past nine months a patient at a hospital in Washington. Tupper's nomination joined that of three others—Maj. Henry Leonard, said to be "a veteran of four wars" and now retired from the Marine Corps; Pvt. Philo C. Calhoun, a lawyer who asked that it be announced that he "is not an overseas man;" and former marine sergeant James C. Wooly, who worked as a newspaper reporter in Salt Lake City. Calhoun, the stateside soldier, won with 416 votes and pledged service worthy of the office.

Next, the report of the Credential Committee, which followed the election of the third vice-chairman, touched off the Legion's first official salvo at the International Workers of the World (the "wobblies" so noted in derision) when it refused to allow voting privileges to another independent group, the Soldiers and Sailors Council headquartered in Seattle, thus excluding the council from the caucus.

The representative of the Soldiers' and Sailors' Council, Sergeant Sherman H. Curtin, asked to speak, and over cries of "No! No!" the chairman reminded the caucus, "We are here for a fair deal."

Curtin took the stage to explain that, unofficially, he represented the "conservative element" of the council, which he had joined to "throw out those I.W.W.'s." He asked the help of the Legion in doing that. He stated that all the offices of the council except one were held by those who felt as he did and that he had taken it upon himself to rewrite the constitution of the council to reflect the one hundred percent Americanism stance as he understood it to be developing within the Legion.

When questioned about the council not allowing former military officers as members, Curtin refused to give a definite answer. He was "not here . . . to be prosecuted," he said. He did respond, however, that though the charge was "true in letter," it was not true "in spirit." This, as recorded in the proceedings, brought "disturbance, hoots, etc." from the caucus.

At this, another from Seattle rose in defense of Sergeant Curtin, stating that "in a recent demonstration for Bolshevism in Seattle," the sergeant "had commanded a machine gun company on the side of right and law and order."

A member of the Credentials Committee interjected that while Curtin was admittedly doing what he could to clean up the council, he nevertheless represented a minority of that organization. "But we can lick the majority," Curtin responded. The caucus applauded his resolve.

Captain C. B. McDonald was then called to speak as one who had once headed the "Intelligence Department" at Camp Lewis in Washington State and "knew the history" of the council. McDonald impugned the council and insisted that if Curtin wished Legion membership "let him cut loose from [the council] and come into this organization."

That was the attitude of the caucus also, and the Credentials Committee's report excluding the council was adopted, whereupon it was noted that "Sergeant Curtin leaves the hall."

While the chairman of the Committee on Name made his way from the gallery, the secretary read the report of the Committee on Emblem. That committee had decided upon a contest that would place before the national convention ten designs from which they were to select one. The four best entries were to receive cash prizes.

Some of the same zeal for Americanism that had been demonstrated vividly in the matter of the I.W.W. spilled over to the next topic—a name for the organization.

When Roy Wood of Arkansas reported that the committee on name recommended "the American Legion of World's War Veterans," Wickersham of New York moved that the name be shortened to "the American Legion." Lieutenant Colonel Cochrun of Ohio seconded the motion. On the question, another delegate from Ohio objected that the shortened name did not sound like an organization of soldiers. Acknowledging that the shortened name would no doubt be chosen, he complained that it was "not comprehensive enough."

But one from Florida piped up, "We'll soon show them what it means," and the caucus agreed. Another complimented the wisdom of those at the Paris Caucus who set in play the temporary name; he desired to keep the name in honor of them. The American Legion as a final name it was.

In Paris the Temporary Committee had understood the need for spreading the word in promoting the Legion, so, too, those in St. Louis wished to keep up the momentum by well-phrased and well-placed announcements and other bulletins. The Publicity Committee from Paris had been the only committee other than the Executive Committee to be charged with a continuous duty. The chair now appointed three newspapermen—G. S. Wheat of the *New York Herald,* U. J. Bell of the Louisville *Courier Journal,* and L. R. Collier of the Pocatello, Idaho *Tribune*—as the Permanent Public Relations Committee to work until the fall convention.

With the next item of business, the Legion for the first time called upon all America to join together for a cause—the payment of war debts through subscriptions to the government's Victory Loan program.

The resolution that the Resolutions Committee now presented asked that all citizens subscribe to the Victory Loan program so that funds would be available "for the completion of our war enterprises," a euphemism for the unpaid debts of the war. Americans should "show to the world their sincerity of purpose" in finishing the job in which the soldiers and sailors had done their part. And so with this the Legion began a tradition of publicizing what war costs in real as well as human terms.

From this show of civic mindedness, the delegates again were riled up by accusations of un-Americanism. When the Committee on Next Meeting Place recommended Chicago as the site for the convention in the autumn, there erupted a louder protest than the one caused by the mention of the I.W.W.

The committee had met "in a very quiet, orderly and gentlemanly manner," the chairman explained, to decide upon a place "for the best interest of the organization" and not of any one locality. But no sooner had Chicago been mentioned than it was moved that that city be dropped and Pittsburgh be considered instead. Then came the motion that the matter be deferred until the next day. When that move failed, another moved for a half hour recess, which also failed to carry.

The problem created with the suggestion of Chicago for a convention site was soon aired. When no other seemed ready to jump into the breach, one from Massachusetts spoke first about the real underlying difficulty. Pointing to the "placarding" of the hall with signs saying "American Legion, Chicago wants you in November," Col. J. Herbert complained that he felt it was his duty to "rebuke any city or representative of any city for un-Americanism during the time when the soldiers of that city were offering their lives in defense of the world." Had the signs said "Chicago's soldiers want you," the response might have been different, Herbert said. But given the reputation of the city's mayor for making remarks reflecting poorly on the American war effort, he for one objected openly to Chicago as a choice for the convention.

At that point the report of the Committee on Next Meeting Place came aground. Speaking for an estimated 750,000 veterans from that state, the chairman of the Illinois delegation protested the lambasting of Chicago's Mayor Thompson as an insult to the patriotism of Illinois soldiers. When those from Massachusetts reiterated that their objections were to Thompson and not the soldiers and sailors of the city and state, their Illinois brethren explained that the mayoral contest, which took place while the soldiers were off to war, had developed as a three-way race that weakened the opposition so that Thompson, not a majority choice it was said, gained the office nearly by default.

But other cities were then suggested and a roll call vote was taken. Louisiana voted for Chicago so those delegates could "go there and tell Big Bill Thompson to go to hell!" Michigan and Nebraska voted for the windy city, "in justice to the soldiers of Illinois." Oklahoma, however, "in justice to the soldiers of Chicago," voted for Minneapolis.

It was decided that the two cities receiving the most votes would be placed in a runoff contest. Thus Minneapolis and Pittsburgh became the choice for the next vote, with Minneapolis winning 573 votes to 456 for Pittsburgh. Minneapolis it was, then, for the first convention. A resolution was adopted that stated that the objections to Chicago were based on the presence of an objectionable public official and did not in any way impugn the patriotism or lessen the sacrifice in service of Illinois soldiers.

After that the caucus was adjourned to meet Saturday morning.

Not all were free to go. Members of the Executive Committee were reminded that they had a meeting at the Hotel Statler at 8 P.M. There they discussed the mechanics of conducting business at the caucus. But it was also an important meeting for another reason. As they sat there that evening after a day and a half of observing their comrades in caucus, a clarity of purpose apparently was revealed, as if some door had been opened before them.

As Chairman Lindsley reported on Saturday, the committee not only crystallized "the purpose of this caucus," but also attempted to call up "a foresight into what [the Legion] is going to mean not only to these four millions of men but to the people of the United States for the next half century."

Apparently the group came to a more confident and clearer view of the purpose for this ambitious venture on which they had come. Particularly, it was understood that the development of the Legion should not be rushed, but that its present momentum should not be lost. The chairman, and others, spoke now of the "spirit" of this new organization as something that must be taken back to the states and nurtured in preparation for the national convention that would officially launch the Legion. A sense of opportunity seemed to be a fundamental element in that "spirit" of which the chairman spoke. Opportunity meant that constructive, positive solutions could and must be fashioned by a new organization in the face of disquieting problems—a nation undergoing many changes and veterans needing rehabilitative help.

The spirit of which the chairman spoke was conciliatory, also. An Illinois delegation spokesman rose and told of a change of heart his group had experienced after taking the Massachusetts group to task for objecting to Chicago as a convention site. He now wanted the New Englanders to know that the Illinois men held no grudge but instead, after "cooler deliberation," admired the patriotism that had prompted their brethren to object to Chicago's mayor. What was emerging, this delegate said, and many others agreed, was a sense of belonging to the American Legion and less regional rivalry, which had prompted some of the defensiveness of the previous day.

That grand opportunity which was part of the "spirit" had its day-to-day tasks. As Russ Simonton of Washington put it, "When we pack our troubles in our kits and go home, the real burden begins. . . ." He cited "a half dozen or so" new organizations in his state which were in the process of forming. One, headquartered in Seattle and called the American Legion of Liberty, already had about 10,000 members.

"It has occurred to us in Washington that if possible this caucus in Saint Louis should apportion such authority to the largest existing organization. Thereby the work of these various organizations is preserved; it would be possible to take them over lock, stock, and barrel and to protect their work."

Call the completed business of this caucus temporary if you want, it was said, but it must speak to the situation out in the States. And though it can be changed somewhat later, there must be substantial organizational work done; there were many who awaited direction now from the Legion.

John MacVicar of Iowa spoke of the twenty-one separate war veterans' organizations in his state, many of which "have held in check as far as further development until our return." Whereupon, "It is expected of us to have a definite program that we can put immediately in force. . . . We cannot wait until the November convention makes our program permanent, or before developing along permanent lines in our state."

Those other organizations were looking to the U.S. caucus for guidance, MacVicar said. "If we can take something definite to these men, they will all organize immediately under the American Legion. We cannot hold in check the various elements until November."

A. M. Phillips, Jr., of Connecticut, agreed. The employment of veterans there had been "one of our biggest problems—putting them back in their jobs." His own delegation, he said, had been engaged in just such an effort "for several months." These efforts, which he described as having been done by "relief committees" in "posts" (though the timing he indicated would predate the Legion) were aimed at finding jobs. "We go to the chairmen of the Manufacturers Association in each town, and the Chamber of Commerce, and the various merchants' associations, and the Rotary Club, and say, 'We are trying to see that the soldiers and sailors in this community are satisfied. We do not ask favors. We simply ask cooperation, and every time the soldiers and sailors come to us and say they want jobs or that they have sickness in their family, we telephone the Chamber of Commerce and pass [along] that man's name and we have been very successful. The post relief committees have even handed checks to some as a loan."

A Connecticut delegate then recommended that "a temporary state committee be gotten together as this caucus may see fit and . . . given authority to grant charters to individual posts that apply." The veterans in his state were saying "if you are working for jobs, we will join; if not, we will work against you."

Another repeated the concern. "The American gob and doughboy want to know something. And we are striving to hold them off until we get back from St. Louis. We must carry something back of a permanent nature."

The discussion now moved to the nature of that "permanence" of which the last delegate had spoken. Caucus chairman Henry Lindsley now spoke, stating that it was his understanding that "this will be a fixed organization resulting out of this caucus in everything except the permanent offices." The caucus "will select a general chairman who will perform the functions of this organization. It will have a home in Washington or elsewhere and in every way there will come out of this organization a growing concern, so that those men who are still on the other side will not be able to say that there was a completed organization" in which they had no voice. "That was my understanding, that there would be no weaknesses, but strengths to hold this machine together."

Roosevelt concurred. "I think we are arriving at that rapidly. However, I believe that we should not have any national offices and that the people who have not been able to express their opinions shall go into the November 11 convention as members of the organizations which are going, but they will come in there with the firm feelings in their mind that they have an expression as to who shall be the officers of the organization and that they have the power to amend, reject, or accept all action up to that time. Now, as a matter of fact, they won't amend or reject but very little of it. It will probably go right straight along, but they must have the feeling that they have the power to amend it if they wish."

Luke Lea of Tennessee expected the adoption of the constitution the next day to enable state organizations to be created from which delegates would be chosen for the November convention. So, the only matter left incomplete was the final form of the constitution and the election of the first national officers.

MacVicar reported that those in his state had anticipated that and had already selected two members from each congressional district for a state executive committee (plus two at-large members). The state also had a temporary secretary, chairman, and vice-chairman. They had also designated Des Moines as their state headquarters. The Iowa delegation planned meetings of their own while yet at the caucus to further organize their state.

On Saturday the delegates were convened at 10:30 A.M. to hear more committee reports. The Publications Committee recommended that the organization initiate a national Legion publication to be its "exponent of Americanism," presented in a nonpartisan, nonsectarian memorial "to that other legion of those who did not come back."

The Finance Committee assessed all members two dollars for an enrollment fee, and set the annual dues at two dollars, to be collected on or after the eleventh day of November each year. Forty percent of the enrollment funds in this arrangement could then be requested by the State Executive Committee, just as the National Executive Committee received up to twenty-five percent of the annual enrollment funds (the remainder, apparently, to be retained by the local posts). Deemed a matter for the Constitution and By-Laws Committee, the entire matter of finance was referred to that committee.

The matter of a permanent headquarters was deferred to the November convention. The committee responsible for that recommendation had suggested Chicago, but the choice did not raise the raucous objections that had accompanied the earlier mention of the city as a convention site.

The Committee on Resolutions then read its report. The "First paragraph, General Principles and Creed" was set aside on the motion of Hamilton Fish of New York to be considered after the caucus had heard the report of the Constitution and By-Laws Committee. Attention was then given to the "second paragraph" proposing vigorous support of the Victory Loan program.

Paragraph three dealt with the matter of conscientious objection to military service, particularly the misuse of that provision in federal law by a group which had once been convicted, but later pardoned with full restitution by the federal government. What was especially objectionable to those assembled was the seeming success of the I.W.W., the International Socialists, and other "anarchists" who had lobbied long and effectively for the release of those convicted.

This resolution not only registered the Legion's displeasure on this matter, but also requested Congress to investigate the pardons as a possible misuse of the 1917 Federal law regarding conscientious objection to service in the military.

At this point another Legion tenet began to emerge. When the word *request* was read, relating to how the Legion should approach Congress on this matter, one rose and moved the word be changed to "demand."

"We are a body large enough and representative enough and powerful enough to tell Congress what we want," he said. His assertion was met with applause and cheers. The point of the word change was not to be missed. The Legion, cautioned often already to remain apolitical itself, was well on its way to gauging its potential for political clout. During the caucus, a representative of the *St. Louis Post-Dispatch* tried to survey the delegates on how they intended to vote in the next national election. The caucus as a body said no to the survey. But now a particular assertiveness had been expressed regarding the lobbying of Congress; it would become the rule rather than the exception when dealing with the federal legislative branch.

The next resolution dealt with the "alien slackers," about whom much would be said in the future. Such "counterfeit Americans" were said to have used their alien status as protection against military service while they continued to reap the benefits of wartime employment in the nation's mills, factories, and shipyards. Allegedly, these aliens used a 1918 amendment to the Selective Service law, which allowed them to revoke their earlier requests for citizenship, rendering them exempt from military service. For these, the Legion demanded no less than immediate deportation (and "for all times").

Private M. L. Sosnin of Louisville, noted in the printed proceedings as being "on crutches, having lost a leg in France," spoke, and the stenographer attempted to represent his speech pattern: "I vass born and raised in Poland, but game to this country and enjoyed all the freedom of the American constitution. At the age of thirty-seven I left my business and my family and fought for this country." Those "not wanting to fight for the greatest of all flags . . . I say, 'Damn him, kick him out of here!" He was applauded soundly.

In this matter also, like the previous, the resolution was changed to demand action from Congress instead of merely requesting it. One at this point spoke for objectivity in the matter.

Cole of Ohio, who spoke now of the "militant Americanism" he was witnessing at the caucus, remarked that as assistant adjutant of the 37th Division he had witnessed thousands of aliens who did pledge fidelity to the United States Constitution and who joined the military services. These, he said, should be commended.

The Resolutions Committee continued, this time referring to the issue of respect for the uniform. "Unscrupulous firms and individuals have taken nefarious advantage of popular sentiment by utilizing men in uniform ('those who . . . have forgotten the respect due the uniform') as peddlers and sales agents." The Legion went on record as being opposed to such practices and called on state and local organizations to do what they could to stop it.

The next resolution was one that could be expected to arise in a job-poor, land-rich nation with a large agrarian population but where thousands of veterans needed opportunities to establish themselves in gainful employment. Paragraph six of the committee's report proposed "presenting to discharged soldiers and sailors an opportunity to establish homes and create for themselves a place in the field of constructive effort" by means of land reclamation of "arid, swamp, or cut-over timber lands [which] is one of the great constructive problems of immediate interest to the nation."

Since one reason the Legion was formed was "to take an energetic interest" in promoting "the happiness and contentment of the people" and "to assist men of the army and navy in solving the problems of wholesome existence," the Legion now endorsed those plans and urged Congress to act favorably and quickly to implement the plans. The Department of the Interior and the Reclamation Service had already publicized plans for reclamation.

But such a move only hinted at the plight of veterans needing jobs. Paragraph seven of the report protested employers' refusal to rehire ex-soldiers and called for veterans to be given preference when new jobs were created. Some new jobs could be created by the government in "internal improvements" programs (not otherwise defined), it was said.

Before its passage, this resolution was criticized by one who worked in an employment service, as dealing only in generalities. There followed a discussion of specific cases of failure of promised reemployment in education and municipal jobs. Another, attesting to the job placement failure of the United States Replacement Bureau, stated that veterans should take care of veterans, recommending that Congress should be required to aid the Legion in taking care of the problem. Yet another, who had served on a Resolution Committee subcommittee to consider this very problem, stated that the Legion should create an employment bureau of its own. This resolution, he said, general though it may be, was all the organization needed to do just then. With that the original resolution carried.

The next resolution called for an extra six months pay of thirty dollars a month for all ex-servicemen for the "financial sacrifice" they had suffered in serving in the military while others at home retained consistent employment.

This resolution would serve as the first official instance of the Legion's entering upon the "adjusted compensation"–"bonus" issue. Caucus Chairman Lindsley, as one who was capable of comprehending the large-scale view of this issue, reminded the caucus of the weightiness of this resolution and asked for more consideration before allowing motions for its passage.

Roosevelt, too, spoke up at this point and told of a disturbing instance on his train ride to St. Louis. He had heard one of the passengers remark: "Young Teddy . . . is going to St. Louis to get the men together to sandbag something for them out of the government." That most assuredly was not the purpose of the caucus, he said. While "we want everything which is right for us to have," he was determined "to put something back into that government, instead of subtracting something from it." He was applauded. "Think about that," he urged, and was applauded again.

With that the caucus "laid the resolution on the table," which, under the rules of the House of Representatives governing the caucus, meant the end of the resolution, at least at this point.

"Gentlemen, you have done a very big thing," Chairman Lindsley said.

The ninth paragraph of the Resolution Committee report was another resolution relating to payment for ex-servicemen. At issue was the provision for Regular Army personnel to get two-thirds pay upon retirement if they were disabled in the service while National Guard and National Army personnel got only their War Risk Insurance. The resolution carried handily. Before it was put to a vote, one moved to include women who had served in the military as being among those to be included in this resolution.

The next resolution was about War Risk Insurance, a prime subject of concern among veterans and from this point a major Legion concern, as well. There were few people more qualified to speak about it than the caucus chairman, who was at that very time director of the Bureau of War Risk Insurance.

One objection to the program was that soldiers were being discharged in large numbers and many were not being told of all the provisions of the insurance and therefore were losing out on benefits. The resolution called for the Legion Executive Committee to meet with the War Risk Insurance Bureau to arrange for a program of education to alert veterans to their rights and benefits under the War Risk Insurance Act.

The resolution recommended that the bureau allow veterans to elect a onetime payment upon the maturity of their insurance instead of the annuity already set up, and that the insured should be able to name their own beneficiaries, even if they were not family members.

The chairman turned the chair over to the first vice-chairman while he spoke at length on the resolution. He recalled a conversation he had had with officers and enlisted men in Europe the year before, at which time he remarked that if there was no other reason for a veterans' organization to be established, the promotion of understanding about veterans' insurance was a good enough reason. He had served as an official of the insurance program in Europe and upon returning to the States was asked by Treasury Secretary William Gibbs McAdoo to reorganize the bureau in the States.

Lindsley stressed the long-term value of the insurance as opposed to its short-term benefits. He depicted the immensity of the insurance program with the government being "the greatest insurance institution in the world" to which "39 billion dollars in applications" came during the mobilization of the army and navy. This was an average of $9,000 per man, and over ninety percent of those eligible did apply for this insurance at a savings of ten to twenty percent over all other insurance programs, a savings made possible by the tax money that went to administering the Bureau of Insurance.

On June 1, policy holders could elect "to continue the present term insurance for five years (after a date the president would set for the end of the war), or to convert to ordinary life, limited payment life, or endowment insurance.

Lindsley urged those present to take the message to all others to hold on to their War Risk Insurance, and to maintain only that insurance amount that they could afford. And he asked for them to help him and others to keep politics out of the Insurance Bureau.

The plight of the disabled veteran was addressed next in a resolution that cited 60,000 who had been incapacitated by war wounds, and another 140,000 who were "more or less disabled," and this in addition to 100,000 who had suffered some disabling injury during initial training.

Many of this substantial number, it was said, would need encouragement for joining the Legion. The resolution recommended that an effort be made by the Legion to establish a disabled veterans' "division," to draw in those persons as members.

But many at the caucus objected to what appeared to them, or could be so taken, as a special class of membership—the disabled. On that point alone, the resolution failed adoption.

The final resolution presented at this session (and the last of the caucus) was for the presentation of all the preceding resolutions to every representative and senator in Congress.

The caucus then officially thanked the War Camp Community Service, which had given away tickets to performances at the Orpheum Theater next door (whose jazz band had performed for the delegates that morning) and for "other services."

On this note, the caucus was adjourned for lunch.

The delegates were reconvened at 2:50 P.M. All the talk earlier in the day about economic issues relating to veterans caused someone to remember that the Legion had no treasurer. Maj. Gaspar G. Bacon, a lawyer from Jamaica Plains, Massachusetts, was nominated and elected to serve during the caucus.

The Committee on Constitution, By-Laws, and Declaration of Rights made their report at this point for a constitution that would be in effect until the November convention. They presented the preamble, which was adopted, as was the name "The American Legion."

Membership eligibility was established, requiring military service to have taken place between April 6, 1917, and November 18, 1918. The Legion's political nonpartisanship was established by the "Article II [two]—Nature" which stated that it "shall be absolutely nonpolitical and shall not be used for the dissemination of partisan principles, or for the promotion of the candidacy of any person seeking public office or preferment. No candidate for or incumbent of a salaried elective public office shall hold any office in the American Legion or in any department or post thereof."

Article Four established the annual National Convention as the legislative body of the organization, and spoke to the composition of delegations to that body, as well as vesting the executive authority of the Legion in the Executive Committee.

Next, the state organization was defined, as was the local unit, called at this point a "billet." But a chief yeoman from New Jersey was joined by a colonel from Arkansas in objecting to "billet," suggesting "post" instead. Billet, they said, was a French term not yet a part of American vernacular, had no relevance to the navy or to anyone who did not serve overseas. Furthermore, the word was not otherwise "dignified," as "anyone who slept in France will testify," and, since it meant a place to sleep, it was not appropriate for the American Legion, which "is not going to lie down and sleep." Others agreed. "post" was chosen handily over the discredited "billet."

At this point the first paragraph of the Resolutions Committee's report—the resolution about "general principles and creed"—was reconsidered, having been put aside for that purpose. With the passage of a preamble, the paragraph was deemed superfluous according to Hamilton Fish of New York, who had chaired the committee that had drafted the preamble. His motion was seconded and carried.

Hearkening back to the matter of local organizations, particularly that posts were not to be named for living persons, delegates from two locales—Washington, D.C., and New York City—spoke about embarrassing circumstances relating to the naming of local posts. In the first, "Pershing Post No. 1" had already been established, and in New York several posts had been named for persons still living.

But they were told that the matter was larger than their specific situations, embarrassing though they might be in renaming the posts. "We know positively that in due time those things [the naming of posts for living persons] would be used to at least a certain extent politically," Private Hugh Haugherty of Enid, Oklahoma, said. "There is no question on that." Find some other way to honor Pershing and the others, he advised. "Keep out every possible way of letting this organization be used in politics."

As the delegates began to sense the final moments of the caucus, they voted to cable greetings "to our comrades who are still overseas."

Roosevelt, Jr., asked to be heard. The caucus, he said, had impressed him like no other event in his life. This large group had thought and acted for itself, adopting resolutions, then "rethinking" them, some of which were actually "redecided," and done so "right." His only regret was "that my father could not have been alive . . . to see the action of this body of Americans."

On a motion from a seaman from New York, the caucus rose for one minute of silence for "the greatest statesman that this nation has ever produced—the president who defied Wall Street and every other combination—Theodore Roosevelt."

Before presenting the motion for adjournment, Chairman Lindsley offered a succinct summation: "This is a momentous gathering; this is a spendid close."

Two last-minute occurrences spoke volumes for the immediate future. The chairman reminded state delegations that the Executive Committee would be in touch with them, and he asked that the Publications Committee meet at 4:45 P.M. to work on the Legion's chief publicity organ, its own print voice.

The work at St. Louis had been completed. There was a summer of activity ahead at national headquarters and in the field at posts and at state organizations. And all looked now to Minneapolis and the first national convention.

THE SUMMER OF 1919

On May 31, Richard Patterson, "Assistant Secretary of the American Legion in France," was lonely and overwhelmed. He wrote from Paris to Lindsley, "Chairman of the American Legion in the U.S.," to report on Legion activity in Europe. Both Milton Foreman and George White had been back in the states for several weeks. The assistant secretary, along with Ogden Mills and a stenographer, was trying to handle the "hundreds" of inquiries and other correspondence about the Legion "on this side of the water." For that, Mills "has a little of the Legion's money in the bank turned over to him by Lieutenant Colonel Wood when he left and has all the original records of the formation of the American Legion in France."

Patterson asked for instructions "for the conclusion of the Legion on this side." White's pamphlets were yet to come off the press and Patterson awaited them as the largest and last distribution of information about the Legion to the A.E.F. (while it was still in Europe.)

The assistant secretary added his approval of the choice of leadership of the Legion made at St. Louis. Roosevelt "was quite right in not allowing himself to be made head of the Legion in the United States."

If Patterson was feeling somewhat isolated, the work of organizing in the United States offered the opposite challenge. During the American Caucus just adjourned, the Executive Committee had heard several members report on activity in their states. Much had been accomplished. And the fervor with which the Legion had begun on the local level only mirrored social changes occurring in the United States after the war.

The moments following the cessation of hostilities were widely hailed as the threshold to a new age. New energies and capabilities, it was promised, would spring forth, set free from the strictures of wartime.

The first loud hurrah of the Roaring Twenties came upon hearing the report of the Armistice. The nation rushed exuberantly into the decade, and that without even waiting for the doughboys and gobs to arrive home. This flurry of post-Armistice celebrating was epitomized in the often heard story of a doughboy's last letter from his Suzy, received while he languished in France awaiting transport, in which she informed him that in all the wild celebration of the war's end she accidentally had married someone else. A more real and troubling ramification, of course, would be the desire of the nation to get on with life without wishing to look at the disabled and others of the war who needed rehabilitation.

Truer to form than the stock lament of the accidental marriage for depicting the rush to change was the inauguration of the golden age of long distance aviation following the war.

The flight that set the record for transatlantic flight was that of British Royal Air Force Capt. John Alcock and Lt. Arthur Whitten-Brown in a Vickers Vimy, a large biplane (wings of 67 feet, 2 inches on a plane 43 feet, 6 inches long) that had first been tested in November 1918 as a long range bomber with a flying speed of one hundred miles per hour and suitable for attacking Berlin.

On the airstrip at Lester's Field near St. John's, Newfoundland, on June 14, 1919, the Vickers carried a crew of two instead of the originally intended three, and with the 2,476-pound bomb capacity converted to extra tanks for a total of 865 gallons of fuel, the two 360 horsepower Rolls-Royce Eagle VII 12-cylinder liquid cooled in-line V's were revved for the 1,933 miles of sea to Clifden in Ireland. At 16:12.5 Greenwich Meridian Time the plane was off, chasing an aviation record.

Sixteen hours and twelve minutes (15 hours and 57 minutes coast to coast) after takeoff, the Vickers was set down unceremoniously in a bog in County Galway.

But as a reference point for portraying the postwar rush toward modernity, had the converted Vickers been several hundred miles south when it fairly skimmed the ocean waves, it would have risked being impaled on the bow of one of the many transport ships just then bringing hundreds of thousands of American doughboys home from the Great War for their own conversion back to civilian life.

Twenty-four cruisers and battleships reportedly had been pressed into service to bring the troops home over the 6,087 nautical miles from the largest debarkation port at Brest, France, to Hoboken. Other craft, such as the 950-foot *Leviathan,* among the largest afloat, had been converted to transport duty. That ship alone brought back a record 14,300 persons on its fifteen-day, six-hour round trip. British ships, too, were employed (at a cost of $81.75 per man). In May, the navy had brought home 333,000 veterans, and in June another 340,000.

It would be slightly more than a year after the Armistice before all the American troops had been brought home. War Secretary Baker announced that the demobilization of the combat troops should be completed by the end of October. Actually, the last transport left France in mid-November, fully a year after the Armistice.

Many of the wounded and sick were made to remain in Europe for their period of convalescence, because there were not enough beds in the States to accommodate the large number of military personnel needing them. At the Armistice there were 192,844 hospital beds available for the A.E.F. (the greatest number of patients at any one time was the 190,564 hospitalized as of November 7, 1918). There had been 153 base hospitals, 66 camp hospitals, 12 convalescent camps, 21 hospital trains, and 6,875 ambulances. There were no similar accommodations for them back home.

Structural changes had allowed the Vickers Vimy to assume a new role, to point the way to a new usefulness. The nation that now entertained a breathless interest in such things, however, was not particularly hospitable to the returning A.E.F. Ex-service personnel were about to experience remarkable changes in the nation they had departed a year before. Resumption of former lives and life-styles was not to be for many. They would need help.

While soon-to-be ex-servicemen walked down the gangplanks of the transport ships and still more were on the high seas coming home, the national officers of the Legion met in their New York headquarters and daily discussed the many topics and issues that their organization had pledged itself to consider and act upon.

In a day of local opera houses where opera rarely played but lecturers with lantern slides did, and high school oratorical contests drew cheering crowds, the incorporating of a "Speakers Division" into the Legion's national program of publicity was not fanciful but expected. Veterans speaking to veterans, face-to-face, was of course the most effective way to get the Legion message across.

That was the job given to the fifteen "strong speakers" selected on May 30 as the "Speakers Bureau" to take charge of that many "zones" of the country for the purpose of spreading the word by personal presentation. As one explained, "Readjustments in social and labor conditions are taking place, and it is a very vital function of the American Legion to show to the meetings of men getting together for organizational purposes not only why it is to the interest of all to become members of the Legion but also the great part which the Legion does play in national affairs."

It fell to the Joint National Committee of Thirty-four to maintain a national vantage from which to direct the organization. That committee met for the first time in early June to continue what its predecessors had begun. It had before it many discussions about the issues only hinted at in Paris and that had been put off at St. Louis until the national convention. The first national convention was the next milestone for which to plan, and that was but a few weeks away. Much needed to be done, and many administrative matters (rather than the setting of policy) needed attention.

Immediately, for example, there was the important matter of where to locate the national office. Roosevelt had recommended Washington, D.C., knowing that the seat of government had much relevance to emerging Legion interests and concerns. He didn't push the matter, however, and even recommended that the address in New York City be kept at least until the convention convened, since the address was known out in the States.

The Legion's office quarters in New York occupied 12,000 square feet, which housed the magazine publishing office and the seven "divisions": office department, finances, public relations, state organizations, war risk insurance, employment, and speakers division.

The office division required the most space for the files, the mailroom, printing, storeroom, and personnel. At this point, the files chiefly included correspondence, a card index of all state officers and their executive committees, and all the members.

Even with this diversification of effort, the headquarters staff was not moving fast enough for the action out in the field. "The organization has been so embryonic up to this time," Chairman Lindsley reported to the committee during a two-day meeting (June 9–10), its first after the St. Louis Caucus. "There has been considerable pressure . . . from some of the states who need assistance greater than this committee has extended to them and directs to them."

This meeting of the Committee of Thirty-four was important as a sounding board for "the thought and views of all who attended the Paris Caucus so that in no single instance would the wishes of those who inaugurated the movement 'Over There' be other than carried out by those on whom is entrusted the responsibility for the work here."

The first matter discussed in the "informal discussion" that the chairman convened at 2:45 P.M. on Monday afternoon, June 9, was membership eligibility, said to be a much confused topic out in the States.

Since it had been the majority opinion at the St. Louis Caucus that Red Cross workers were to be excluded from membership, how about the members of the merchant marine? While that was normally a private service, the members of the Overseas Transport Service had all been enlisted men. How about those discharged for physical incapacity (different from physical disability)? Many were drafted but were in a cantonment only long enough for a physical exam (they still qualified for the sixty dollar bonus, one said). Tom Miller suggested that only those who qualified for a campaign badge be considered for membership.

Since it was agreed at the outset that all these matters would be discussed more productively and conclusively at the national convention in Minneapolis, the subject of eligibility was eventually referred to a committee. But not before the discussion included the suggestion for an auxiliary organization for mothers, wives, sisters, and daughters of Legionnaires. The suggestion had already been voiced in many states, it was said. D'Olier cited a strong feeling nationwide that if the women were encouraged, it would materially strengthen the formation of posts in some towns. In fact, it was the opinion of one that auxiliary units "are absolutely necessary for the creation, the life, and the maintenance of interest in more than seventy percent of the posts." The associate members of the G.A.R. had greatly aided that organization, he said.

Others thought the cart had swung around ahead of the horse. If the Legion is not officially organized itself, how can it take in auxiliaries? Others, though, said that women's auxiliaries would help in that process. Besides, they added, the question is already being posed by many states and already several auxiliaries are in the process of forming. One site in particular, the 308th Infantry organization in New York, had notified the national office that it would come into the Legion if the women came, too, but only if they were allowed to come in. Some of the group stated that when during the war they wanted socks and other items of need, it was the women's auxiliaries more often than not that sent them. Without the help of the women, all the strawberry festivals and other money-making projects would be lost, this one said.

Hand in hand with the matter of membership eligibility came the establishing of posts. That was the most important work at present, D'Olier said. With many troops still located at military installations in the United States and Europe, the subject of establishing posts there and on college and university campuses was discussed next.

Roosevelt moved that posts at such sites "where the membership may not necessarily be permanent, be encouraged and fostered." If the veteran was now at the Brooklyn Navy Yard but lived in Wyoming, he would otherwise not have a voice in the Legion, since he was away from the post in his home town. It was a practical matter to allow him to be active in the Legion where he was now.

Posts, however, should not ever come under "definite military discipline or government supervision," another said; nor should that occur at institutions of higher learning. "That is organizing along special and distinct lifelines and is contrary to the spirit of the organization. They ought to join the nearest post."

But saying where posts may *not* be formed seemed un-American, one replied. If one is on a campus, or a military base, that is one or two among thousands "and will not unduly influence the whole organization."

Franklin D'Olier, who chaired the Legion's Division on State Organization, wanted as many posts as possible, wherever they may be located. That division, he reported, had relied heavily on a packet of information sent recently to state organizations, which had contained the Legion constitution (carefully labeled as temporary, he assured those gathered), the resolutions adopted at St. Louis, a list of state officers, a notice to potential members, and suggestions for organizing posts and state organizations. There was also a letter about War Risk Insurance and one requesting the appointment of a state employment officer. "It is felt that the two main things which we have to offer are, first, assistance in securing positions [employment], and, second, assistance in reference to War Risk Insurance." The division was preparing another mailing, which would include a questionnaire and a "little catechism on what is the American Legion."

While "we wanted to get everything nearly uniform as we possibly could," the autonomy of the local and state organizations had been encouraged. "Home rule is the keynote of the whole situation."

Roosevelt's motion carried for establishing posts where members away from home wanted them.

As for the matter of nonresidents, it was advised that posts allow nonresidents to join, and that divisional, regimental, and other military unit posts be established.

But, one said, this would make it possible for a veteran to join two or more posts. What then would happen to representation at national conventions? Eric Fisher Wood added that if members could join more than one post, "politicians will join them all."

The importance of organizational methodology was stressed by another. In New York, he said, posts elected county representatives for the state convention. But in Pennsylvania, "we feel we should get as near the hometown meeting as possible." So, thousands of delegates attend, constituting direct representation of each post, "because the state convention is going to be the great thing for the greatest number of posts."

While fifteen members was the minimum for forming a post, how large could a post be? Again, there were wide-ranging opinions. In New York, D'Olier said, the maximum was 5,000 members. J. F. J. Herbert of Massachusetts favored larger posts, even one per state perhaps, thereby "avoiding the rock of factionalism and cliques." G. E. Buxton of Rhode Island told of intentions there for the state's 11,000 members to form one large post. But, one asked, how do you find meeting facilities large enough for such a post?

On another matter, D'Olier asked, "Does this committee have the right to commit the national convention" to charters that National Headquarters issues?

"Certainly," Chairman Lindsley replied, as long as the state organization has approved it.

This was the reply desired by D'Olier, who added, "There is nothing which we have sent to the states so far which binds the states at all. Everything is in the nature of a suggestion. If we pass this motion now, the only thing that we bind the states to is to the National Constitution. The question comes to my mind as to whether it is advisable to start now giving definite rulings to the states. It seems to me we should let the National Convention decide this thing."

For many weeks—from January when Roosevelt and the others met in Paris, through the Paris meeting and the promotion of the Legion throughout the A.E.F. in Europe, and then during the St. Louis meeting and thereafter—the task of publicizing the Legion had occupied much of the organizers' time. The St. Louis Caucus had given the go-ahead to publish a Legion magazine. The permanent Publications Committee appointed by the St. Louis Caucus had determined that a magazine must be produced weekly.

A fourth of July first issue would gain much publicity as a patriotic gesture. Up-to-the-minute news, if submitted on Tuesday, could appear in print on Wednesday and be mailed that day. The beginning budget, the committee decided, should be about $100,000 for a proposed circulation of 65,000. Estimated cost of paper, printing, binding, and distribution of that many copies was somewhere between $3,000 to $4,000 each issue. One stated the belief that "advertising prospects are amazing" and that the venture would eventually pay for itself.

The primary purpose for the weekly publication, of course, was to get the word out about the Legion and at the same time prove that the organization was moving ahead and serving its members. Distribution, then, was a key consideration. Individual subscribers would account for about 10,000 copies, and another 30,000 copies would go in bulk packages to state organizations.

The Publications Committee visualized the weekly magazine in 35,000 reading rooms and libraries in America. Another 5,000 would go to newspapers, 6,000 to Congress, 12,000 to the troops on the forty transport ships arriving from Europe weekly at this time, and another 2,000 copies would be distributed widely in Europe.

As the primary print voice of the Legion, the magazine should contain "lively materials with pep and push." The first issue had already been roughed out: brief greetings from each state governor to show bipartisanship; an article by Ole Hanson, mayor of Seattle, on Bolshevism; one on what an ex-soldiers' organization could mean to veterans;

something from Sergeant Alvin York; an authoritative article on War Risk Insurance; an article on the formation of the G.A.R., since that was the most often mentioned comparable organization; a story on demobilization; and one on the rehabilitation of injured soldiers.

Though the Publications Committee had not yet found the editor it wanted, the search was under way for someone "nationally and internationally known." The Legion's own George White was finally asked to sit in temporarily.

More basic even than a national print voice was the attainment of financial resources with which to carry on the work. The Finance Division reported that about $10,000 had been taken in at the St. Louis Caucus, he said, of which $8,000 had been spent. The Legion needed some way of raising funds until the $2 annual dues (of which 25¢ was to come to National) began coming in. (The $2 dues mentioned at this time would eventually be dropped to $1.) National currently needed, it was said, about $250,000, which included the cost of sending representatives of the Speakers Bureau around the nation.

The organization presently had credit arranged up to $10,000, which would see it through the next two weeks. The magazine, it was said, could either be a financial failure or a tremendous success. It could even make money by the end of its first year.

One suggested $250,000 to be entirely provided by members of the Legion, avoiding large donations from any one man or any one interest. The donations would be on the basis of loans that the Legion would repay. That way, the Legion could be self-supporting from the start.

But should the drive be directed at members only? Roosevelt remarked that "it is poor policy to milk the same cow too quickly in succession."

Roosevelt moved that contributions (he called them "underwritings and subscriptions") be accepted from anyone "who sees the good of the Legion for the country." While there would be no maximum, small sums would be particularly sought. As in most instances when Roosevelt spoke, the motion carried handily.

On a par with the slick professionalism expected of the Legion magazine, which would be called *The American Legion Weekly,* the Publicity Division reported that Luke Lea, former publicity director for the Red Cross during the war, and before that a U.S. senator and newspaper editor, would now look after the Legion's image. (When Lt. George Wheat, who would write the first (1919) overview of the Legion's origins, moved from public relations work to the *Weekly* staff, the publicity slot was vacant for awhile.)

Public relations was aimed as much at counteracting negative criticism as it was at convincing veterans about what the organization could do for them. As one national committeeman explained, the purpose of the current public relations work was "to allay the suspicions, to answer criticism and prejudices that have arisen about the American Legion."

The work followed the Red Cross plan: decentralization, with the emphasis being on local organizations generating and disseminating news about their purpose and activities. The committee encouraged the Public Relations Division to project the views and work of the national officers, as well. Many believed that there had not been enough news about the Legion in the press so far.

The committee next considered the reports of the two divisions of National Headquarters, which had the responsibility for matters soon to become known as fundamental Legion advocacies.

C. F. Sheridan spoke about War Risk Insurance work. He reported that a "war risk officer" had been appointed in each state who would see that each post appointed a volunteer to work with War Risk Insurance matters and find answers for the many questions veterans had about this national program. The most pressing problem, he said, was the correct and proper filing of claims. While routine questions would be handled by this state officer, more difficult cases would be forwarded to the War Risk Division at the New York office, where there were "two or three men from the [War Risk] Bureau who are familiar with that kind of work." Also, "zone finance officers" were in place, "looking at Liberty Bonds, back pay, bonuses, and additional travel pay," about all of which veterans may have questions.

The second area in which the Legion was becoming an advocate for veterans was that of employment. Particularly in the larger cities, much more so than in rural areas, there were many dissatisfied ex-service personnel, and "the Legion is perhaps the only one which can get to them and can get them employed." A few days before the meeting of the Committee of Thirty-four, state organizations had been sent a telegram from the Legion's Employment Division asking them to appoint a state employment officer to answer questions at the local level and to function as liaison with the national office. So far, seven states had complied. But as Employment Division Chairman Richard Derby told the Executive Committee, during the previous six months, "There has been a number of agencies in the field, principally welfare organizations, doing reemployment work. So we felt that it was not advisable for the Legion to institute a new organization to carry on employment work among the returning soldiers."

Derby had spoken with both the National Catholic War Council and "Col. Arthur Wood's organization, which is a group of officers operating for the War Department . . . [in] . . . coordinating reemployment work throughout the country." He had learned that "at the end of three months' time the employment question will have passed an acute stage." But during that time, it was important that the Legion enter the scene.

Colonel Wood, for example, wanted the Legion to help "as soon as possible" so it could "take over his work" and he could "close shop and go out of business." Other groups were willing to cooperate also. The National Catholic War Council, the Y.M.C.A., War Camp Community Service, Jewish Welfare Board, the Red Cross, the Salvation Army, U.S. Employment Service—all had agreed to send to the Legion lists of the names of their representatives all over the country.

Those having the most difficulty finding work, Wood said, were the unskilled laborers who had acquired new responsibilities after the war —principally young families—and who now didn't want to return to their prewar eighteen-dollars-a-week jobs. And, Wood added, it was not only "comradely advice and direction" these men needed. Communists were preaching "undiluted discontent" among laborers; unemployed soldiers and sailors were a "seedbed" of discontent.

Perhaps, Wood suggested, the Legion should raise funds to help veterans financially until they find jobs, and perhaps even aid in financing new homes for veterans. He had approached the U.S. Treasury Department with such a suggestion but had been told such a thing "is not sound." (Readers privileged with foreknowledge will note in this suggestion by Wood a presaging of the Legion's appreciable involvement twenty years later in the establishment of the G.I. Bill of Rights.)

One matter of importance before the November convention was that of obtaining a charter for the Legion. When the session at National Headquarters on Tuesday, June 10, began at 9:15 A.M., the charter was at the top of the day's agenda. Two points regarding a congressional charter received serious consideration: the need to stay clear of politics, and that for a clean reputation. Both, Tom Miller said, were absolutely necessary to get a charter and the accompanying approval from Congress, which august body had previously so honored only the Red Cross, the Boy Scouts, and possibly soon the Roosevelt Memorial Association. Should there be any friction and debate caused by the Legion's request for a federal charter, Miller said, the effort was thereupon doomed.

One asked whether the Legion, though favored with a prized and impressive federal charter, would be limited in its ability to alter its course when necessary. Miller explained that while a charter from Congress would mean that the Legion existed by statute of the United States and was thereby protected from possible abuse by future leadership, it did mean that it was restricted to the activities and conditions contained in that charter.

Indeed, the grant of powers given in the charter should receive the best attention, he said. He suggested that those who would soon draft the charter should rely primarily on the resolutions passed at Paris and St. Louis.

But there should be more than that included in the text of the charter, Bennett Clark said. And the son of the famous Speaker of the House of Representatives here appeared nearly clairvoyant. For the fine list of resolutions to which Miller had just referred did not include, he said, an "emphasis on the function of promoting social or industrial reform." In the future, even a generation hence, a function of the Legion may be "to enter this field in a nonpolitical and noncontroversial" manner. In fact, Clark was sure that "in the long run . . . this organization will find that . . . one of its great functions [is] to take up such matters as national education, to suggest greater support to education in general, that it might make certain recommendations about better housing, better agriculture, loan societies, employment exchanges, and many things in that great field where the government aims to promote social welfare, things, of course, that on the whole would not be within the range of parties and politics at all.

"This association has got to get down to outlining a series of constructive and permanent policies that will put the organization on the map permanently as a national institution. It can't live forever on the social benefits to its members or on perpetuating incidents of the Great War. It will have to stand for some great national movement, and have settled policies in which the entire country is interested."

Thus in one impressive, sweeping projection, Clark foresaw the many program areas into which the Legion would someday move. Regardless of the Executive Committee's wanting, indeed being ordered, to put off as much as possible until the November convention, more of substance must be written into the charter language, Clark said.

Tom Miller, if less philosophical, was not wanting in pragmatic advice. He again emphasized that the decision to enter the halls of the Capitol with the request for a charter for the Legion should not be made in ignorance of the likely reaction there. "Washington today is made up of cliques, and cliques that are suspicious of one another." He told of attempts at the last session to form three or four hybrid organizations to include men who fought in the Great War. But these efforts "were held down" by some congressmen for being "mostly semigrafting organizations that wanted to get a few dollars from each man a year, and with highly paid officers."

"We are starting out clean," Miller said. "No other bills have been introduced to date for any organization like ours." Success, he added, would come only when those on both sides of the aisle delineating the political persuasions affecting much of the nation's public business had been convinced of the Legion's worthiness.

Former congressman Miller had a few tips to offer. "Congressmen will want to know if we had the great enlisted man represented at the two caucuses." The committee agreed that the incorporators of the Legion should be those who attended the caucuses. Of these, Miller continued, congressmen will check for those in their states. Those on the list "must be on friendly terms with the congressmen and senators."

Miller stressed the point, telling "how touchy the Capitol Hill bunch are. . . . Most of us have not been in politics [himself excluded], so we haven't political enmities. But if any of you have, let me know so I can prepare myself for it. Even to the extent of taking your name off the incorporating list if you have made political enemies who might keep the Legion from getting its charter."

William Price recalled the G.A.R.'s exceedingly political nature and called the Legion "as conceived, the Monroe Doctrine of decency and good citizenship," an "intangible" that could be read by congressmen any way their particular bent might dictate. He advised that the text of the charter should explain clearly and convincingly that the Legion stood for "all things that are best in citizenship and government." In this way, neither political party would wish to object, yet both would be aware that the Legion was closely observing their actions. "It might be well to have that dangling over the heads of some of them."

In this connection, Tom Miller referred to the clause in the proposed charter assuring that the Legion would not back any one individual politician in a partisan sense. Secretary Wood asked if that "would prevent us from going after Mayor Thompson of Chicago [and] cutting a spoke out of his wheel?" In St. Louis, the caucus had gone on record as opposing Thompson on grounds of un-Americanism. Such a blast from the Legion would surely affect the man's political fortunes, Wood reasoned. Did such an attack on an officeholder constitute entering politics?

Bennett Clark, himself no stranger to the political arena, answered that he thought that that clause in the charter should be revised to allow the Legion "scope for criticism or attacks if necessary on disloyal people." But as for politics, the organization should be prevented from saying who should be elected or defeated. That kind of political activism "would wreck the organization."

Eric Fisher Wood counseled that a statement such as Clark's could be left out of the charter but included in the Legion's constitution.

Following the meeting of the Joint National Committee of Thirty-four in early June, national officers met nearly daily at the New York office throughout August, September, and October. With an estimated 353,000 members nationwide less than a month after the first American Caucus, the Executive Committee had much instructing and directing to do.

In Washington, Tom Miller and Luke Lea, teamed as the Legion Legislative Committee of two, pursued a charter for the Legion. They also took an active interest in what Congress was considering and debating that in any way directly affected veterans.

And there were many legislative developments in which Legionnaires had an interest, ranging from changing the law that did not allow the War Department to loan rifles and furnish blank ammunition for post memorial ceremonies to matters related to large-scale veterans' benefits. In mid-September, the Legion heard from Congressman John J. Rogers of Massachusetts about his bill authorizing the Secretary of War to loan army rifles to posts for funeral ceremonies of deceased veterans. National Executive Committeemen were asked for their opinion about the propriety of sending letters to each congressman stating the Legion's endorsement of the bill. In August it was suggested that Miller and Lea look into the many similar proposals for legislation, such as were in practice or were pending, in Canada, New Zealand, Australia, and England, regarding the widely discussed and hotly debated issue of bonuses to discharged soldiers.

The Executive Committee also recommended that the states support the Sweet Bill, which would change some conditions of War Risk Insurance to veterans' liking.

But while the Legion wished its general attitude about select bills to be known in Congress, the majority of the Committee of Thirty-four advised, whereupon it became the position of the committee, that the organization not take any official, publicized stance until after the national convention.

From discussions among the Executive Committee itself there issued some suggestions for dealing with Congress. It was suggested at one point that letters be sent to all congressmen alerting them to the Legion's one-hundred-percent Americanism resolution, a move which, it was added, should be taken by all posts as well.

In early October one of those touring the country for the Legion asked for permission to address a convention of bankers in New Orleans "on the principles of the American Legion." Permission was granted, but the speaker "was not to enter into any controversial points."

And when a Legionnaire in Frankfort, Kentucky, complained to National Headquarters that a representative (unnamed) from that office was taking part in "controversial matters" at state Legion conventions, the Executive Committee wired two representatives of the Legion touring the South to have them defuse if they could any references to a supposed stance by the Legion on states' rights, one "controversial matter" to which the informant had referred.

At this time also, Franklin D'Olier, Lemuel Bolles, and Dr. Richard Derby were appointed a committee of three to draw up resolutions for the next meeting of the Executive Committee to deal with the question about Legion officers now holding or who would run for public office. For the present, however, the state organizations were advised to take care of their own problems in this area.

On another matter, the Legion was often said to have a militaristic aura about it, an opinion generally voiced by outsiders. To counter that criticism, it was resolved that the chairman should issue a statement based on the new constitution being prepared by Eric Fisher Wood that would define the status of the Legion as a veterans' organization that considered and treated its members as civilians.

When headquarters staffers in New York City heard of references to the Legion in the *Congressional Record* regarding opposition to the World War Veterans organization, they began subscribing to the *Record* for reference use. Similarly, the Legion notified the Anti-Saloon League that though National Headquarters had not taken a position for or against Prohibition, it was "entirely proper" for state and local Legion organizations to suggest what their delegates to state or national conventions should do in this area. (Prohibition would become the law of the land with the passage of the Volstead Act, which would go into effect in mid-January 1920.)

When the Martins Ferry, Ohio, Post Number 38 inquired in late September about the Legion's stance on the national steel strike, they were told that no action had been taken at Headquarters and that the subject was but another one with which the National Convention would have to deal.

The Military Training Association also sought information on what they assumed was Legion support for a military service bill. They were told that the Legion did not at present back any specific measure. In a more direct action, the Executive Committee required Chairman Lindsley to resign from the Universal Military Training League's Advisory Committee so there would be no misunderstanding about the Legion's current desire to remain clear of that issue. (This was perhaps another way to discredit the often heard criticism that the organization had militaristic overtones. Later, the Legion would come out strongly for universal military training, what with the lessons of unpreparedness for World War I a matter of recent memory, as both a deterrent to war and necessary survival insurance for future citizen-soldiers.)

So adamant was Headquarters about clarity on this matter that it issued a bulletin to the states assuring them that no official position had been authorized, that the use of the Legion's name by various organizations promoting universal military training had not been authorized, and that in this matter especially, posts should not allow themselves or their members' names to be included on mailing lists compiled by others promoting the subject.

Senator James R. Wadsworth, active in the field of "soldiers legislation," was informed that on that subject the Legion "has not assumed any position . . . at this time and no one is authorized to speak for the Legion on this question" in spite of the existence of the Legislative Committee. Wadsworth was informed that the matter would be treated at the Minneapolis Convention, and he was welcomed to send any of his committee members there to meet with Legionnaires about this important matter. At that time also, the Legion would not adopt a position on the League of Nations; this was said to the many inside and outside the Legion who asked about that topic of current interest and importance. Nor would Headquarters comply with the request received in early October for a referendum of Legionnaires on the question of the League of Nations. The immensity, meaning also expense, of the proposal was also cited.

In at least two instances, however, the Executive Committee either supported or opposed legislation despite what Senator Wadsworth had been told. When Senator Charles F. Curry of California introduced a bill that would give honorable discharges to all those earlier who had been excused from the draft, a special committee composed of Lemuel Bolles, Dr. Richard Derby and J. F. J. Herbert clarified the Legion's stance, whereupon Curry wrote in mid-September to thank the Legion for pointing out "defects" in his bill and to say that he was withdrawing it.

Similarly, Congressman Rogers of Massachusetts informed the Legion that he had introduced a bill for the investigation of the Federal Board of Vocational Training. Rogers was told that the Legion favored his bill, would follow its course closely, and if it were passed would work for its implementation.

That particular move had been proposed by an Executive Committee subcommittee, the Committee to Propose Soldiers Beneficial Legislation, a forerunner to the Legion's later, large-scale rehabilitation initiative. The Soldiers Beneficial Legislation group was currently wrestling with the wide-ranging needs of returning citizen-soldiers and was developing a clearer view of the immensity of the problem, and consequently the cost of solutions.

Chaired by Bishop Brent of the Comrades in Service, and including Theodore Roosevelt, Jr., George Springmeyer, Tom Miller, Dr. Richard Derby, R. M. McCracken, and Lemuel Bolles, this high-powered group of Legionnaires was currently pondering several congressional bills for veterans' benefits.

At one session, the discussions of the Beneficial Legislation Committee included an overview of a bill proposed by Springmeyer, suggested also by Senator Irvine L. Lenroot, that sought to establish a ten-month educational program for ex-servicemen seeking occupational development. When another asked if ten months was enough, Springmeyer replied that he was thinking primarily of those men who wanted to learn a trade—carpentry, blacksmithing, electrical engineering, and so forth. Extending the training over a period of years "would tend to make a man loaf," he said.

There was a need to know what was happening in the nation in regard to veterans' educational and employment status and goals. This subcommittee suggested a survey of Legionnaires for that purpose. One said he was told by an ex-serviceman selling newspapers on the street corner that he was making ten dollars a day and therefore desired no better job. Other veterans seemed to expect to find higher paying jobs even though they had outdated or otherwise limited job skills.

It was still widely assumed that veterans had little confidence in existing government programs because of alleged incompetency, for example, at the Bureau of War Risk Insurance. The Executive Committee heard the suggestion that when congressional bills sought to create additional agencies and boards, staffing should be by veterans exclusively.

Bonuses for veterans was a hotly debated issue nationwide and the subcommittee dealt with it, also, suggesting that a compromise measure be developed in which each soldier be given a certain amount of money on credit, which would then be applied as periodic premiums on his War Risk Insurance. Or, in lieu of a cash bonus, each soldier would be given a paid-up policy of $1,000.

The subcommittee nurtured the hope that since there was not likely to be only one system for dealing with soldiers' legislation, a variety of bills should be proposed to cover the many aspects of the subject. The key, it was agreed, was in coordination, perhaps by a congressional committee, of the various measures that should and would emerge to meet the wide-ranging needs of ex-servicemen.

The New York office heard many times, of course, about local situations involving mistreatment of ex-soldiers. Many replies were received about specific instances of need, especially after the office sent out a bulletin in August suggesting that states survey local posts about the needs of wounded soldiers. From Texas came a letter from a patient in an army hospital there who protested the treatment he and others were receiving. The Executive Committee took this instance so seriously as to take it to the Surgeon General, asking for an investigation of the site and the specific alleged problems.

To be expected, there were many questions directed to National Headquarters about the upcoming national convention. When the executive committee of the Ohio Legion asked, for example, about the authority of a national nominating committee, they were told that since it was "purely advisory and having a representative on it from each state, its advice will be of value to the convention. But this does not in any way prevent nominations from the floor. We heartily concur that for the Nominating Committee to have powers beyond those expressed would be thoroughly undemocratic and un-American."

During the summer of 1919, the emerging strength and consistency with which the Legion would pursue its work for veterans' rehabilitation could be seen evolving from the discussions of the Executive Committee during the pre–national convention months.

So, too, were positions on national defense and foreign relations beginning to be formulated (though not yet to the same extent as that of "soldiers' legislation"). In August it was suggested that "with a view of getting the fullest expression with regard to the military policy of this country . . . a bulletin should be sent out to the various posts suggesting that a free discussion be given on the subject of military service and that a syllabus covering all the points which should be considered be made a part of the bulletin."

Such was the confidence of those manning the New York office in the expertise of the Legion's membership on the subject that they began looking for servicemen and ex-servicemen "conversant on military affairs" to attend an informal meeting on October 16 "to discuss the future military policy of the U.S."

Foreign relations also became a subject of discussion in September when the Illinois state organization offered a resolution protesting the refusal of the British government to issue passports to some Chicagoans who wanted to visit British colonial possessions for business purposes. Aiding the Allies during the war, it was reasoned in the resolution, should yield some considerations in the marketplace.

For the summer and fall, then, of 1919, the New York office of the Legion, admittedly temporary in its authority, housed and sheltered the emergent identity of the organization.

Those who had not witnessed personally the competence of the caucus in St. Louis and how that gathering had launched the Legion "movement" in the United States may have been surprised by the polish and heft of the first issue of *The American Legion Weekly* on July 4, 1919.

With the scheduling of the first national convention on November 11, the anniversary of the signing of the Armistice, the Legion had begun a tradition as keeper-of-the-flame for patriotic holidays. The *Weekly,* as it quickly came to be called, would continue that practice with the appearance of the first issue on July 4. An editorial entitled "The Spirit of the Legion" claimed that the magazine's appearance on that day was indeed appropriate, for "The principles and ideals of that epochal document in human liberty are those of the American Legion, which *The American Legion Weekly* represents."

In this fashion, the *Weekly* "sets upon its way . . . a spontaneous expression of purpose by those millions of Americans who helped crush autocracy."

Legionnaires were bound together by life-changing experiences.

"Out of their common experiences through the dark months of the war has grown a comradeship and a patriotism which are vitalized by their organization into this single concrete force which will stand always as a barrier against the forces of greed, ignorance, and chaos."

Furthermore, "The American Legion is the epitome of that Americanism for which it stands. Its voice is the majority voice of its members; its will the will of many. Spontaneous in inception, it has been democratic in its development. There are no titles recorded on its rolls. It is free of rank, of cast, and of partisanship. If it seeks in a full measure to serve those who were in service, it seeks in fuller measure to serve America."

(At first, the magazine was under the direct care of the Committee of Thirty-four and was published in New York. When the printers' strike occurred there and many magazines were forced to cease publication, the *Weekly* was moved to Washington, D.C., in early October 1919.)

The *Weekly* pointed the way to strengthening the movement. An article in the first issue, "From Now Until Then" (until National Convention time), urged Legionnaires to enroll new members; organize posts in the states; hold state conventions; and elect delegates to the National Convention.

In addition, Legionnaires were urged to inform former service people about the Legion's aims and progress; see that the Legion was presented to the American people in its proper light; keep local posts free of participation in partisan politics; explain War Risk Insurance to those who did not know their rights and privileges under the War Risk Insurance Act; fight Bolshevism and ultra radicalism; put wounded and disabled men in communication with the "Rehab Department of the Government at Washington."

And it didn't stop there. "Try to stop unscrupulous firms and individuals from taking nefarious advantage of popular sentiment by utilizing men in uniform as peddlers and sales agents; publicize the demand of the St. Louis Caucus that Congress immediately enact a law to deport alien slackers as well as every naturalized citizen convicted under the Espionage Act."

The front cover of the first issue was an enlarged reproduction of General John J. Pershing's congratulatory telegram to the Legion. "Black Jack" Pershing's name was the most celebrated in the land. His picture and message on the cover of the first issue of the *Weekly* symbolized victory and comradeship unmatched by the popular obsession with renaming streets, parks, and chrome-plated railway passenger cars after the general.

The array of advertising in the first issue also reminded ex-servicemen and women that they had indeed returned to the land of opportunity and free enterprise. Those who had taken off their "tin lids" and were dressing in "cits" again found they could also exchange their puttees for "Boston garters," their reveille rations for "Washington Crisps" ("the perfect toasted corn flakes").

The *Weekly*'s primary purpose was not to make money. "This magazine is nobody's striker. It is not a commercial enterprise. It doesn't have to make a cent for anybody. It is the Legion's—your—property. Any profits go to the Legion, to you." Its start was "modest and it is trying to build with the [growth of the] Legion. It has to do this for its capital is limited."

With every issue, the audience increased. Originally produced in a run of 12,000 copies, the twelfth issue claimed 175,000 copies in circulation. Seven issues later, the week before the national convention in early November, 300,000 copies were distributed. But while newsstands were selling out of copies (". . . no publication in America has been so widely quoted in the press as the *Weekly*"), the subscription price for members of one dollar per year had resulted already in a shortfall. "It costs 3.92 cents per copy to publish and deliver the magazine. For this service the Legion member pays less than 2 cents (.0192). In view of the present prices for labor, paper, and other materials this necessarily [has] meant a loss on subscriptions." It would be left to the Publications Committee meeting just before the national convention to worry over.

For the remainder of the summer and fall of 1919, the *Weekly* continued to appear. In spite of a financial shortfall, the *Weekly* was the acknowledged publicity backbone of the Legion. No other means could be devised at the time for reaching so many people and for greeting them four times a month with news of the Legion's great growth.

Specifically, as stated in the tenth issue (the first with a color cover), the *Weekly* "intends to represent in vigorous fashion those ideas of economic, political and social reform and readjustment which the Legion members are going to insist upon." This required a "mission . . . of keeping the men formerly in service advised on matters pertaining to their organization, on legislation affecting their interests, on national affairs, and to meet their demands for a publication devoted to those subjects in which they are interested."

Publicists were never at a loss for high-minded statements of purpose for the organization, and the *Weekly* was the means for getting the message across. The first issue explained that the Legion was "something more than a veterans' organization to promote reunions and social gatherings; something more than an organized effort to get something out of the government for service rendered. The American Legion is dedicated to the high purposes of putting something into the government because of a zealous desire to continue to serve after the uniform has been laid away. It aims to crystallize for peaceful achievements that spirit which brought America into the war and then sustained America in fighting through the war as she did fight."

More to the point, the Legion existed to aid the individual veteran, as exemplified by an announcement that ran in several successive issues: "Attention! Have you had any trouble with your: War Risk Allotment or Allowance; Quartermaster of Navy Allotment; Compensation; Insurance; Liberty Bonds; Bonus; Travel Pay; Back Pay? The American Legion is ready to help you straighten out your accounts. Write or tell your troubles to your state war risk officer of the American Legion. Write in care of your state secretary." Each issue contained a list of state officers for the convenience of the veteran.

The contents of the *Weekly* quickly set it apart from other magazines at the time. Statements of purpose and self-praise aside, the mix of content which the *Weekly* staff decided upon included articles about the war, the returning veterans, the needs of the veterans reentering civilian life, army and new-civilian life humor.

Overall, a tone of expectancy was maintained by the many references to the upcoming Minneapolis Convention. It was assumed that all the troops would be home by then.

The *Weekly* included news on federal legislation. The Legion had been organized to aid in the successful readjustment of citizen-soldiers to civilian life and there were now many veterans-related bills in Congress.

After the war, numerous bills were introduced proposing various forms of veterans' bonuses; loans for homes, businesses, and farms; and other measures which claimed beneficence for veterans. Confusion had resulted. There were a few truly worthwhile measures being considered. But there were many others which, though appearing to be helpful, were actually veiled methods for exploiting veterans.

In early September, readers were informed by the *Weekly* that the Legion "was watching Washington." In the "convention number" (November 7 issue) of the *Weekly* an article headed "Congress Waits for Legion's Voice" stated that key legislation that would affect veterans had been tabled in Congress until the Legion had spoken at the Minneapolis Convention.

One of several Legion slogans often referred to in the magazine was the well-known "policies, not politics," a maxim favored by Teddy Roosevelt, Jr., who elevated it to an essential Legion rubric. As had the early organizers, the *Weekly* staff now sought firmly and permanently to etch the fine line separating the extremes of this engagingly alliterative polarity.

The September 12 issue spelled it out. Was the Legion to have nothing to do with politics? "It will have a great deal to do with politics. [The Legion] will take cognizance of what is sound practice and what is not sound practice in the political readjustment of the country. Its members are not going to wink at political flabbiness and political rottenness. Nor are they going to temporize with public servants or would-be public servants whose Americanism is found tainted with suspicion. The word has gone out to the 3,500 posts. . . ."

On the cover of the July 11 issue there strode a heroic figure in military uniform signifying the American Legion closing in on a wild-haired, wild-eyed figure who crouched beside a columned facade labled "American Institutions." In the miscreant's hand was a bomb.

The Legion's early attention to Americanism took many forms. One of the most adamant was the cry against Bolshevism as an ideology, as a disruptive force in American labor and education, and as a so-called solution thrust upon returning servicemen that sought to take unfair advantage of real enough problems caused by hundreds of thousands of former military personnel returning all at once to civilian life.

The *Weekly* also spoke out against those who had refused military service by surrendering their application for citizenship, but who remained to collect high wartime wages. These were the often lambasted "alien slackers."

The first issue of the magazine had called for Legionnaires to fight Bolshevism and "ultra radicalism." The second issue included an article by Ole Hanson, the mayor of Seattle, about his first-hand experience with labor disruptions on the West Coast. The ever-popular Theodore Roosevelt, Jr., wrote an article for the August 8 issue in which he set out his own views on Americanism.

On the cover of the August 15 issue, the Legion was portrayed again in military uniform and as the "big brother" of the Statue of Liberty, while a Bolshevist, a Wobbly, an alien slacker, and a "propagandist" retreated to one corner of the page.

News items from the states sometimes showed the Legion concept of Americanism at work on the local level. The September 19 issue reported that local Legion "support of the police in their battle against disorders and riots attendant on a strike was voted by the Allegheny County [Pennsylvania] executive committee when Pittsburgh was suffering from such trouble recently. Employers and strikers fell in behind the Legion with avidity, and no action on the part of the members was necessary."

Though the *Weekly* obviously aspired to much more than the mere broadcasting of fraternal chitchat, there were recurring features that warmed the heart, tickled the funny bone, offered encouragement, or informed readers of some war-related development.

In the November 7 issue of the magazine the picture of a new ship launched at Camden, New Jersey appeared. The ship measuring 525 feet with a 50-foot beam had been christened *The American Legion.*

MINNEAPOLIS CONVENTION

NOVEMBER 10 – 12, 1919

When Henry D. Lindsley was elected chairman of the St. Louis Caucus, he did not know he would subsequently be giving to the Legion all of his time during the summer and fall of 1919. But when the National Executive Committee, or N.E.C. asked him to go to New York and do just that, the former Dallas mayor had complied.

When the preliminary caucus of the Advance Committee met at 11:00 A.M. on Saturday, November 8, at Minneapolis, the first order of business—the financial condition of the Legion—was one which had been for Lindsley and the others of equal concern as to the more time-consuming task of publicizing the Legion around the nation in preparation for the national convention.

Treasurer Gaspar Bacon passed around copies of a consolidated general balance sheet of the national headquarters and a statement of revenue and expenses for June through October. Section seven of the Legion's crisp new charter required it to assume the previous unincorporated organization's debts. What had it inherited in that agreement?

As assets the organization had cash on hand in the bank, accounts receivable primarily consisting of money due from state organizations for the sale of the Legion's official buttons, and $36,000 consisting of unpaid state assessments, money from news dealers for copies of *The American Legion Weekly,* an inventory of print paper and manuscript articles for upcoming issues of the magazine, a supply of buttons, and a deposit with the post office required for magazine distribution. Exhibit "A" then showed $91,000 in the bank and other assets "immediately cashable" aggregating $16,000.

Exhibit "B" however was a stunner—a net deficit of $134,000 due to overruns in publishing the *Weekly* and a total of $257,000 worth of notes taken out for operating capital. Very quickly the Advance Committee saw that though the craft which had been launched was moving ahead, it was listing alarmingly. The balance sheet told the story. Bacon stated the obvious: it had been "very expensive to operate the *Weekly.*"

As for the operating funds, "When we started and opened headquarters in New York, we had to have some funds. There was not any money coming in from state assessments, of course, it was too early in the game. Our first plan was to go out and try and borrow from individuals. . . . We didn't want to go out and beg . . . so we decided to borrow in the form of subscription receipt . . . to be paid back when and if funds were available and with interest at 6%." It had always been the intention, he said, to recommend that the upcoming convention follow through with these borrowing agreements already undertaken on its behalf.

At first, "We borrowed about $10,000 on that basis, a very small amount considering what we had to tackle. So the subcommittee of the N.E.C. authorized the chairman of the National Finance Committee—Mr. Prentiss—to borrow on the notes of the Legion [most for one year] enough to keep us going. He appointed assistants in the different parts of the U.S. and asked them to raise what he and we all considered was a fair share for each of the states." The apportionment was made according to membership in the states, with attention given to "a pretty equal distribution" around the nation. Actually, Treasurer Bacon explained, not every state was contacted. The fund drive "went on the basis not of states but of Federal Reserve Districts and we tried to apportion it in those districts."

The method called for state organizations to find those among its members (and "friends of the Legion") who would cosign notes with the Legion. Quotas were given the states for the amount they were expected to raise. The Legion headquarters then sought the actual loan from financiers.

In this fashion, members in New York provided signatures for $100,000. Those in Ohio and Pennsylvania signed for $25,000 worth of notes in each state. An Ohioan interjected that the money from that state had been raised in "honor loans of not more than $250" from any one person. To one, the method of raising the operating funds should have been publicized more to offset criticism that "the Legion has been financed by Wall Street."

Obviously then, one of the convention's chief tasks would be to decide on the future of the *Weekly* in the "movement." But even though the committee should properly pass the matter to the convention, or at least to the Committee on Finance, former congressman Tom Miller of Delaware recommended that the present group buckle down and make some hard decisions rather than have the entire matter dealt with on the floor of the convention. The national convention would last only three days, he reminded, and there were many other items of business with which to deal.

Chairman Lindsley explained that the magazine "has never been adequately financed with working capital." That financing, in fact, had not been attempted. Nor did the overrun go for high salaries. Editor George White "gave his splendid energies, and he worked without real salary, merely for the amount of his expenses. He used underpaid men who were willing to serve during the formative period." But certainly if the *Weekly* was to go forward, "all that must be considered in budgeting for the coming year."

The magazine had potential to make money, Lindsley said. He had been told "by publishers that a magazine of 1,000,000 circulation is worth a million dollars. It can make money for the Legion if the members support it."

A delegate then raised a key question. If the magazine represented such financial potential as the chairman had indicated, why not charge more for it and thereby raise the revenue to operate the entire organization? (A per capita charge of twenty-five cents had already been levied the membership for the magazine.)

No one doubted the value of the *Weekly* to the Legion. As delegate Mathewson of California said, "The *Weekly* must be in the hands of every member." So, he continued, "Have the states subscribe for every member. If the Legion can really be financed by just the *Weekly*, then the magazine must get all the support it deserves, for it can liquidate the present indebtedness. We must have the magazine; it is the life of the organization." The advertising space sold by the magazine, he had been told, "is worth twice what is being charged."

Myers of Indiana was among the first to suggest a method that would receive much discussion in the coming hours. Why not combine the national dues with the magazine subscription? Someone else suggested an increase to $1 for the total dues amount.

Another expressed the same idea, that the *Weekly* be made a part of the dues for membership and not just left for the men to subscribe to or not. He had heard that "85% of ex-servicemen dropped their War Risk Insurance because of carelessness or forgetfulness." Subscriptions to the *Weekly* could suffer from the same tendency.

But, another observed, state conventions had already met and dues had been set, and they would not meet again for another year. Furthermore, as a Montana delegate reported, "The strength of the American Legion ultimately rests in the states. The national organization will be just as the chairman has suggested—a correlating body. The force of the Legion is in the states where the rank and file reside and where the personal element will be felt. That makes it necessary to have state papers."

State papers, therefore, were yet another expense for the members. And since in Montana the annual dues of seventy-five cents were hard enough to come by, and there were but 5,000 members out of 40,000 ex-servicemen, most all of whom "are not fixed well financially," any additional expenses were not likely to go over with members and certainly would inhibit new members. The Westerner would rather "have more members and less money than more money and less members."

Though there was a variety of dues schedules reported in the states, from the seventy-five cents in Montana to five dollars for one post in the Washington, D.C. area, some said that they had tapped all the resources and interest in their particular state and any increase in dues likely would cause them to lose current members and certainly would discourage potential members.

But, one said, those who object to more money being assessed "have not grasped yet what the Legion really is" for "there is much more to be done," and, therefore, he implied, more expenses to incur.

Another stated that when he left for the convention he told the local organizations that he was going to the convention "to participate in making the laws of the organization, and whatever those laws were the locals would have to abide by them." One, less philosophical, hit the target squarely: "We are in debt and we want to get out of debt. We must deal with the problem." Raise the dues, he said.

Weekly editor George White then spoke. Drop the idea of the magazine being included in the increased dues of $1, he said. For one thing, no magazine costing less than one dollar a year would be accepted for mailing by the Post Office Department. Even if the entire dollar from each member went toward the magazine, there would be a loss of $30,000 an issue figured on one million copies. "The success of this thing depends entirely on advertising."

Even if the magazine could be part of one-dollar dues, "it can't go out to people outside the Legion for less than ten cents a copy. There is a loss; it costs four cents per copy roughly to get the magazine out at the present time and it goes to the individual for roughly two cents, so on every hundred thousand we lose $2,000. That has to be made up by advertising."

Nevertheless, "the prospects for success are excellent for this publication." He suggested switching to a cheaper grade of paper and raising the price for nonmembers to ten cents (current newsstand sales were 100,000 per week, he said). The cost would be reduced "materially" he agreed, if, as one suggested, the magazine were published twice a month instead of weekly. But, in his opinion, if published less often, the magazine, "would lose its force as the national spokesman of the Legion."

The recent article on War Risk Insurance in the November 7 convention issue was itself a good way to get more members and subscriptions, he said. White explained that the convention issue had thirty pages of advertising and as "a rather expensive magazine printed on super-calendar" paper was not a fair example of the magazine's normal appearance.

During the discussion on this subject, there continued to be many testimonials for the value of the *Weekly*. As one said, it "is the most important voice of the Legion . . . reaching members and also entire communities." The magazine "helps to mold opinion for the American Legion."

A delegate from South Dakota said, "You can't hire doughboys for less than five or six dollars a day, and the magazine [subscription] is worth a couple of hours of their work time."

In an afternoon session reconvened at 5:25 P.M., the Advance Committee returned to the motion remaining from the earlier session for the magazine subscription to be joined with the national dues for a total charge of one dollar per year.

An Oregon delegate said that he had asked Legion members what the Legion is and "they don't know. The *Weekly* is the best educational tool the Legion has. Keep it and combine it with the dues," he advised. "They sign up in the Legion and don't know what a fine organization it is. So make sure they get the magazine and learn about the Legion. That is the way to a stronger and more effective Legion." Another called it "the mouthpiece of the Legion." One who claimed credit for forming nearly one hundred posts and who "knows the local scene," wanted the *Weekly* in every member's home.

Foreman of Illinois said, "We haven't the monopoly of the intelligence or judgment or discretion." So, let the convention decide as it must anyway, he counseled. But a motion was made and seconded: the matter of dues and *Weekly* subscriptions would go to the delegations from which would come a resolution ready for assignment to an appropriate committee.

The matter of the Legion magazine was a warm-up exercise. Lindsley explained that they had been called together "so that the heads of the various divisions of this country and abroad could determine a tentative program" to submit to the proper committees, which would be appointed at the convention "with the recommendation that that program—I am speaking of machinery now—be adopted."

In observing that there was not to be a nominating committee, a delegate from Rhode Island stated, "One of the most important things . . . is who is going to be the head of it next year. We know in conventions of this kind some hot air artist is likely to put something across." He knew that when his delegation arrived they were going to ask who was slated for the top role next year and he would have to say, "I don't know, it will be up to the floor of the convention." This possibly would not lead to the best man being nominated or elected, he said.

By his calculations, perhaps fifty to ninety percent of the delegates coming had not been to the St. Louis caucus and had no experience in such matters. He wanted candidates for the top offices to be better known to the membership. He didn't want a slated ticket as such, but he felt that at least some discussion should be had among the Advance Committee as to who might be put up as candidates.

Delegate Warren of Louisiana objected, however. "I can't think that it is the spirit of this organization to put any man in the office that would seek that office. If he conducts a campaign, we in Louisiana will not vote for him."

But that wasn't what the New Englander had in mind. He was not pushing for nominations, he said, but he wanted the delegates to know more about some of those who would be good for the office. He didn't want to vote for "the one who comes and says 'I want the job.' "

Before adjournment the Advance Committee acted on another important matter: delegate Fuller of Minnesota moved that there be an Executive Committee during the convention made up of the chairmen of the various divisions of the Legion to which could be referred matters of importance during the deliberations.

He pointed out that "the N.E.C. which met during the St. Louis Caucus saved the day many a time from being busted wide open. There were a great many important questions of policy which were shoved down to that committee and which were so wisely decided there and in the most amicable frame of mind." Should not this convention have such a group as a sounding board? It was agreed.

The hundreds of delegates and alternates arrived for the first session of the convention on Monday morning. As news reporters checked the proximity of the telephone and telegraph facilities set up for them in the auditorium (some had accompanied state delegations to report to the folks back home), Henry Lindsley called the conventioneers to order at 10:30 A.M.

Dr. Cyrus Northrop, president emeritus of the University of Minnesota (and a "grand old man of the [Old] Northwest") gave the invocation. Next, Minnesota's Governor Burnquist welcomed the delegates. He was impressed and thankful, he said, that, "In this day when old empires are falling, new nations are being born, and the fundamental principles of the American republic are being attacked, you advocate the upholding and the defending of the U.S. Constitution." His short patriotic speech, composed primarily of commentary about the Legion's preamble from the St. Louis caucus, was interrupted by applause nine times.

The governor also referred to the Minnesota legislature having passed a bill granting ex-servicemen fifteen dollars a month for military service. It cost the state about twenty million dollars, he said, but it was an entirely appropriate expense. Many cheered; those who did not cheer would take the other side in debates to follow, arguing a bonus "handout."

The mayor of Minneapolis was the next to welcome the conventioneers. He spoke about the readjustments with which they were struggling. Their attendance at the convention, he was encouraged to observe, meant that they were continuing their service to the nation "not in petty politics but in civic life." He berated the "slackers" who refused to defend the very system of freedoms they had come otherwise to enjoy by renouncing their citizenship applications for the duration of the war. All right-thinking citizens should closely examine the immigration laws of this land, he urged. Following the mayor, the French ambassador to the United States read a cable of greetings from Marshal Foch.

After these luminaries spoke, Chairman Lindsley introduced a few Legionnaires who had been of special help at national headquarters: Eric Fisher Wood, Dr. Richard Derby, Franklin D'Olier, and "three who went throughout the country preaching the Gospel of the American Legion": J. F. J. Herbert of Massachusetts, J. W. Inzer of Alabama, and the inimitable Teddy Roosevelt, Jr. The chairman assured those gathered that it was in the states (and in the "foreign possessions") where the Legion would become "the greatest power in American life."

For the present convention, Lindsley said, there was "no set program" but rather "a tentative outline." He hoped there would not be a time "when the American Legion will follow any set program prepared by anybody." Organizing the "mechanics" of a convention was necessary, he continued, but this was an "unbossed organization." The delegates cheered, as they did when the chairman said, "There will never be a nominating committee of the Legion but every officer who is elected by a convention should be nominated from the floor."

The chairman now listed the committees established to consider the wide variety of issues that the Legion would address. Of these, three were permanent and had been working already (Credentials, Rules of the Convention, and Officers of the Convention—these being necessary to the organization of the convention itself). The others would function only during the convention: Emblem, Eligibility, Auxiliaries, Political Restrictions, Finance and National Dues, Constitution, Legislation, Next Meeting Place, Permanent National Headquarters, Post Activities and Memorials, Employment, War Risk Insurance, Beneficial Legislation, Military Policy, Anti-American Propaganda, and Resolutions.

(There were some "consultants" present, also, who were there to provide specialized information on important topics. These "the committees can use as they need. But they are here only for information" and not as salesmen for any one point of view or special interest.)

The chairman next engaged in some scene-setting for the serious nature of the business at hand by reminding the delegates of an impressive feat. Even before the final peace treaty ending the Great War had been signed officially, the Legion had acquired a stamp of approval from Congress. And even as that process was under way, the Legion had affected national legislation by supporting an alien slacker deportation bill, aiding the progress of the Sweet Bill, pressing for the investigation of the Board of Vocational Training, urging action on the bill giving civil service preference for federal positions to honorably discharged soldiers and sailors, and making veterans' needs known so that the Lenroot Bill—providing nine months of educational benefits to ex-servicemen—could become a reality.

In the same light, the Legion could be proud of something it didn't do. It hadn't been a part of what the national leaders and, it was assumed, the majority of members believed to be a mercenary agitation for the various cash bonus measures put forth by those who wanted a cash handout immediately.

The chairman continued. "There will come before you here a vast number of problems." He listed, among others, the nation's military policy; War Risk Insurance; the proscription of active political involvement; the nation's industrial situation (the Legion "will not take part in any confrontations between labor and capital"); and the need for law and order in these troubled times.

Legionnaires come from every part, party, and class of America, he said. And though consisting of workers and those who employ workers, cooperation must rule the day. "We should not dodge any issues," he said. Congress was watching, listening, and waiting for the Legion's viewpoint (certainly some indication at this juncture of its real potential for exerting political pressure).

The one hundred men of the Advance Committee had met on Friday and the most important thing to come out of that meeting, he said, was the enthusiastic "spirit of convention and how that goes out to the nation. There is no mistaking the power of the American Legion."

The delegates happily agreed. They were complimented for working diligently in the states and for being a constant source of inspiration to those at National Headquarters. "When there came a time—and there were many—when we were rather uncertain of how the Legion was going, from every part of this land there came the voices of those who let us know that in their particular states or places the spirit of the Legion was alive."

The chairman wished to impress upon the delegates that the work of the various committees, while done in closed rooms with but one representative from each state, was, nevertheless, of national importance. They should not be afraid to make recommendations. "You have the power, a power so great that it rests with you as a tremendous responsibility. This is a momentous convention." Those gathered were representing five million (Lindsley in the ascending rhetoric of the moment said they *were* actually the five million) who had been involved in the war effort. And, among other momentous actions, they were going to "put the heel of condemnation" on everything that was unpatriotic and un-American.

"Everything that comes before you must be disposed of, not acted upon affirmatively necessarily, but not postponed. The American Legion has found itself. The American Legion has its stride. The American Legion recognizes its power and its responsibility to the people of this country, and in this convention the American Legion will, I am sure, meet every situation as Americans would have those situations met." For this the stenographers transcribing the proceedings noted "prolonged applause and cheers," as they would for numerous other demonstrations of enthusiasm throughout the next three days.

The chairman then announced the report of the Advance Committee. The order of business for this first session was announced. First would come the report of the Committee on Credentials, then that of the Committee on Rules and Permanent Organization. The election of convention officers would follow.

But while these two committees now conferred momentarily, the reports of the secretary and the treasurer were read.

Following the election of officers of the convention, the Advance Committee had recommended adjournment until the committees were ready to report.

During this time also, Vermont received the N.E.C. banner for having the greatest percentage of its quota in the million-member drive. Actually, Vermont boasted 165 percent, representing well over half again as many members as it was assumed the state could enroll.

Before adjournment for committee work, the report of the Committee on Officers of the Convention was read.

The Rules Committee recommended debate be limited to five minutes per speaker. Then committees were assigned meeting rooms. The women present who were acknowledged as "delegates, alternates, or delegates-at-large" and who were interested in forming auxiliaries with other women, were invited to meet with the Auxiliaries Committee.

The delegates then sought their counterparts on the many committees for an afternoon of deliberations, the activity which would come to characterize an important aspect of future Legion volunteerism.

Before being adjourned at 1:50 P.M. and stepping into the Minneapolis winter outside, the Advance Committee was reminded, "We are making history in this hall."

Immediately after the convention was called to order on Tuesday at 9:40 A.M. and a telegram of greeting was read from General Pershing, the chairman interjected a personal note. He would not be a candidate for the chief leadership role after the convention, he said. For the past six months he had been "head" (his word) of the Legion. It had been a singular honor, but he was determined to prove his belief that the organization should never be led by the same man in successive terms.

After that, Tom Miller reported on the work of the Legislative Committee authorized in June. Not only did he quickly recommend the obvious—that the work continue—but called for similar efforts for state-level legislation to be undertaken by state Legion organizations.

The Legion's proposal for a federal charter was introduced on June 2, he said, and it became law on September 16. The "rapid passage through both houses" had shown the "significance of the strength of the Legion" as seen by national legislators.

When the St. Louis Caucus told Luke Lea and Miller "to go after alien slackers," he had a Legion bill introduced for the deportation of naturalized citizens or aliens convicted under the Espionage Act of 1917. This Legion-inspired measure has passed the House and had been favorably reported by a Senate committee.

As for the slackers who withdrew their first citizenship papers when called upon to serve in the military, a bill had been introduced "and properly advanced through public hearings," but due to its "purported infringement of treaty rights the State Department has opposed the enactment of it."

The bill amending the War Risk Insurance Act had passed the House as the Legion wanted and was pending before the Senate Committee on Finance.

The Legion's legislative committee had also looked at "the treatment of disabled soldiers and the deplorable conditions existing in connection with this matter." Miller gave no details.

In addition to this investigative work, the Miller-Lea committee had obtained amendments "to the proper bills which provide that Civil Service preference be given to honorably discharged soldiers, sailors, and marines in federal positions throughout the country." For officers and enlisted personnel who served in the war and who were disabled, the two had also pushed for retirement benefits comparable to those who retired "under the regular establishment." Finally, they had worked closely with the War Department in matters of reemployment of ex-servicemen.

The report of the Committee on Next Meeting Place prompted a spirited regional rivalry. Cleveland was eventually chosen, a city with a five-hundred-mile radius wherein lived more than half the population of the United States. Eighty-three passenger trains a day arrived in the city, a fact that assuredly would expedite convening. To sweeten the pot, the Ohio delegate and chief boomer for Cleveland promised that the city would raise all the money needed "to defray the expenses of such entertainment as your Executive Committee will prescribe."

Not long into the competition, however, a Texas delegate took the floor to complain about the way the convention site was being chosen. The N.E.C. or some such group should decide on the city, he said, and only after a written guarantee had been received from the winning city and some Legionnaires had visited the city to check it out.

The chairman interrupted the business at 10:58 A.M. "Gentlemen, one year ago at this time the world was in expectancy of the cessation of hostilities in the greatest war in all history. We are approaching the moment when the world ceased that great conflict, the result being a victory for democratic peoples all over the world.

"I am going to ask every delegate here to rise and bow his head or her head in silent prayer as that moment approaches, thinking of what it has meant to the world, what it means to our country, and particularly thinking of our comrades who on the other side gave their lives not only that the world might be safe but that we as a nation might continue to live as a free people. And our hearts and our prayers should go to those who are bereaved throughout our land and because these men—our comrades—went there and gave the supreme sacrifice."

The delegates rose and for a few moments the entire hall was silent as the largest assembly in the nation of eyewitnesses to the war contemplated the significance of this first Armistice Day.

Following this, the Committee for Selecting a Permanent National Headquarters reported that Minneapolis was the choice of the majority but not the unanimous choice. Furthermore, when a motion was made to make it unanimous, that failed, also. Therefore, the convention was asked to take up the matter.

From the floor, others suggested cities of their liking. Two delegates, from Kentucky and Tennessee, spoke for Indianapolis, saying that they wanted national headquarters there because it was the center of the nation and was accessible. If located there, "The lowest buck and gob can come to National Headquarters." Furthermore, "It will not be overshadowed or be an annex of any other institution" (implying perhaps that there was nothing else in the Hoosier capital that would attract more attention). The implication, real or not, was not objected to by any natives of the state.

Next, a delegate from the District of Columbia rose to engage in the running argument about the advantages versus the pitfalls of being located in the nation's capital. Washington was "a place of political corruption and rottenness, some have charged," he said. But though it had been said "that placing the Legion headquarters in Washington, D.C., would corrupt it, think instead to changing Washington rather than fearing that Washington will change the Legion."

A delegate promoting Kansas City, Missouri, noted that the city had recently raised two and a half million dollars to construct a building in honor of the war dead. The American Legion would be an ideal occupant of that building, he said.

Three from Indianapolis, Walter Myers, Dr. T. Victor Keene, and Robert L. Moorhead, urged the delegates to vote for their city, a rail center.

With those choices before them, the convention voted. The first round gave Washington, D.C. 282 votes and Indianapolis 226. These two top vote getters were then engaged in a runoff. Indianapolis emerged with 361 votes, though 323 of those voting would have the Legion brave the avowed corruptions of the nation's capital.

Before adjournment at 12:55 for lunch, the convention was instructed about the parade scheduled for 2:00 P.M. Reminiscent of their former temporary occupations as doughboys, gobs, and marines, they were told where to "form columns of eight" before taking their places in the parade. They were then released to don the new uniforms they had received when they were discharged from the armed services. Once again they would march en masse, and even the weather would remind them of a season in France, for Minneapolis was in the throes of a winter blizzard.

When the afternoon session reconvened at 4:10 P.M., the esprit de corps of the young men from every state in the nation, heightened no doubt by participation in the parade, was memorably shown when a delegate from New Jersey brought forward the American flag that, it was said, was the first to be taken "over the top" in the war at La Belle in 1914 by an American with the Canadian forces. The American soldier who had carried the flag originally, Martin Wallberg from Westfield, New Jersey, had died in the charge. His mother had asked that it be unfurled here in the presence of others who had served and who had returned. The flag, therefore, represented the 83,000 battle casualties who had not returned and another 40,000 who had died from other causes.

Then the business at hand was resumed. The Emblem Committee reported on its deliberations on the design of standards for national-, departmental-, state-, and post-level use. An official Legion button had been adopted, as had the slogan—"One Hundred Percent Americanism." The committee also urged that the Legion publish a ritual covering all national, departmental, and post ceremonies. A standard membership card patterned after the Elks was also recommended. Finally, the committee reported on the competition for a national emblem, which had been arranged for at the St. Louis Caucus.

Delegates listened closely to resolutions read next by the Committee on Employment treating the pressing problem of veterans' unemployment. The first "whereas" spoke volumes. "Considerable numbers of discharged service men are not placed in employment suitable to their abilities and needs and large numbers are in need of help and information regarding many matters other than employment." Posts and departments, it was said, should aid in setting up Service and Information Branches (as part of the War Department's efforts) and Congress should appropriate funds to continue the work. Furthermore, those working in such agencies should be veterans themselves.

What's more, the Legion should encourage national, state, and local welfare agencies that maintained services for veterans "to continue their activities during this present period of uncertainty and unrest." Each post should see to it that no member was unemployed.

The second resolution would continue the work: "Government even more than private employers owes an obligation to its discharged servicemen and women for jobs." These persons are employable because "military experience and training make them better able to render loyal and efficient service in public employment."

At the same time, the Legion urged veterans to "uphold the highest standards of government service and to avoid fostering the claim of the unfit and the undeserving under cover of patriotism," though for certain, "government in Civil Service should make places for veterans and their widows to work if they are qualified."

And that was the third expectation: that disabled veterans should have "absolute preference for appointment in any Civil Service position for which their physical disability does not otherwise disqualify them."

Someone pointed out that the Legion itself, on the national, state, and local levels, was not always the best example in hiring veterans for its many jobs as clerks, typists, and stenographers. How can we go to employers and encourage them to hire qualified veterans, this one said, if the Legion fails to find and hire those of their comrades who can do that work?

Before the Employment Committee finished its report it was advised by one to "include the women in the wording of the resolutions," the text previously referring to "servicemen" only.

The report of the Committee on Post Activities and Memorials began a long exchange about a proposed addition to the national constitution of the Legion in which the merits and implications of the words "partisan" and "political" were debated.

The proposed addition was read: "While requiring that each of its members perform his full duty as a citizen according to his own conscience and understanding, this organization shall be absolutely nonpolitical [hence the insistence by some on "nonpartisan," and thence the debate] and shall not be used for the dissemination of partisan principles or of the promotion of the candidacy of any person seeking public office or preferment; and no candidate for or incumbent of a salaried elective public office shall hold any office in the American Legion or in any branch or post thereof."

"The Legion can do a lot of good if it stays out of politics," one said, crytallizing the sentiment of many. "The potential power of this organization must not be exhibited."

The motion carried, and the session adjourned at 6:45 P.M. for the evening meal.

The Tuesday evening session was called to order at 9:00 P.M. by Chairman Lindsley, who by this time was complaining of hoarsness (as soon would Eric Fisher Wood, too) as he read aloud several telegrams from posts around the country reporting Armistice Day activities and the enrollment of new members.

One rose to complain that the newspapers were referring to delegates by their military titles, and since "the Legion has gone on record many times as being against that," he wanted the convention to request that the journalists comply. His motion was seconded quickly and carried unanimously. (The chairman also related the complaints of several about pickpockets encountered on the streets.)

When the Committee on Auxiliaries recommended that a women's auxiliary to the Legion be established, a lengthy debate ensued over just who should be permitted to join. That such an organization would be beneficial was not doubted. But the pondering of an appropriate membership rehashed all the past debates about who was eligible for Legion membership. The challenge was to include as many as possible without diluting the meaning of membership.

There was no disagreement about two items that followed: the willingness at posts to serve as collection points for the Roosevelt (Sr.) Memorial Fund and for the sending of a message to President Wilson wishing him well. Wilson, gravely ill, had returned to Washington after a nationwide tour, during which he attempted to present to whistle stop audiences the peace treaty that he had effected in Europe, but which Congress had rejected. On October 2 he had collapsed, the victim of a cerebral thrombosis.

For those who had perceived this young organization's potential for making an important, constructive impact on the nation, the report of the Committee on Military Policy contained some interesting thoughts.

This committee, containing many former military officers and a respectable representation of privates, as well, had developed a serious, long-range view on matters of national military strength.

It was the committee's view that, first, a large standing army was expensive and un-American. "National safety with freedom from militarism is best assured by a national citizens' army based on the democratic and American principles of the equality of obligation and opportunity for all."

Second, it favored universal military training not "under military control." Its third point followed the second closely: it was strongly opposed to compulsory military service in peacetime.

Fourth, since in their recent memory there had been "a bitter experience" with unpreparedness for national defense, what with "the lack of proper training on the part of officers and men," the committee called for "an immediate revision of our military system and a thorough housecleaning of the inefficient officers and methods of our entire military establishment."

With the images of military camp and front lines fresh in their minds, these delegates reiterated their strong favoring of "a national military system based on universal military obligation to include a relatively small Regular Army and a citizen's army capable of rapid expansion sufficient to meet any national emergency on a plan which will provide competitive and progressive training for all officers, both of the Regular Army and of the citizen forces."

Furthermore, "We believe that such a military system should be subject to civil authority. Any legislation tending toward an enlarged and stronger military caste we unqualifiedly condemn."

Fifth, "The national citizens' army which should and must be the chief reliance of this country in time of war should be officered by men from its own ranks and administered by a general staff on which citizen-soldier officers and Regular Army officers shall serve in equal number."

Listed as "5 1/2," and no doubt hearkening back to all the times they had sought cover from the increasingly dangerous enemy "aeroplanes" in France, was the recommendation "that Congress pass such legislation as will make the U.S. Air Service a separate and distinct department of our system of national defenses, under control of a member of the president's cabinet appointed for that purpose alone."

In their sixth statement regarding the nation's military policy, the committee favored "the continuance of training camps for the training and education of officers to serve in case of national requirement. We recommend that military training in high schools and colleges be encouraged. The National Citizens' Army should be organized into corps, divisions, and smaller units composed in each case of officers and men who come from the same state or locality for the preserving of local designations as far as practicable." The seventh point was that the National Citizens' Army should be "trained, equipped, officered, and assigned to definite units before rather than after the commencement of hostilities."

Eighth among the committee's recommendations was that "the selection and training of men for the National Citizens' Army should be under the local control and administration of its own officers, subject to general national regulations."

Finally, the ninth point was that "a committee of seven be appointed by the Executive Committee of the Legion to consult with and advise the military committee of both houses of Congress as to the working out of the details of organization and training of the future army and navy of the U.S., using as its basis the resolutions accepted and adopted by this convention."

This session was adjourned at about 10:30 P.M.

The news the delegates heard when the Wednesday morning session convened at 9:15 A.M. was shocking.

With the sounds of the gavel still echoing in the hall, the chairman introduced the Attorney General of Washington State, Mr. Thompson, who spoke immediately of "an outrage that is almost beyond comprehension."

Thompson then read a telegram "from our representative in the city of Centralia, Washington." If previously there had been any hint of uncertainty or unfocused attention about the often-touted one hundred percent Americanism, the news Thompson now read about an event on the West Coast that had occurred the preceding afternoon would provide a vivid example to point to when arguing for patriotism of that absolute quality.

From the Olympia, Washington post came a message of alarm, its immediacy stressed by the clipped phraseology sped along the telegraph wires. "This afternoon in Centralia, American Legion Parade fired on from I.W.W. headquarters. Three [actually four] former soldiers including Warren Grimm killed. Three other former soldiers, including Dale Hubbard, sons of lumbermen seriously injured. No provocation. 13 I.W.W. in jail." The telegram ended with a curious postscript: "Start something."

To a stunned audience sitting in silence, Thompson read a second telegram.

"At 9:30 [P.M.] town quiet, possee rounding up Wobblies from list captured at headquarters. Bill Scales [post commander] in command. Local Post urges law and order on part of Legion men. Civil authorities have situation well in hand. One man has been hanged. Sixteen in jail but no positive evidence of killing on their part. Government has ordered out Tacoma guard. Christensen assisting prosecuting attorney. [signed] Fullerton."

At this the delegates applauded and cheered, breaking their momentary silence of disbelief with a soldier and sailor's response to what now was apparently judged to be heroic action. Immediately the Washington delegation asked that sympathy be expressed by the convention to the families of the slain Legionnaires. They commended William Scales for preserving law and order. The New York delegation seconded these "100 percent American resolutions." An acquaintance of Warren Grimm was heard to say that the young former college student had "just returned last Thursday" from Siberia.

Grimm had been a member of the infantry regiment sent to Archangel in an effort to create a White Russian counterrevolution to do battle with the Bolsheviks. Now, having survived the rigors of that bizarre sidelight to the war, young Grimm had been gunned down in his hometown.

As the news of the event in Centralia was flashed across the nation, the conventioneers in Minneapolis were no doubt struck by the coincidental nature of the occurrence. For months now, Legion spokesmen and the *Weekly* had been condemning disruptive acts of un-Americanism. Now as the delegates were gathered to discuss this and other issues, this painful object lesson was thrust upon them.

Those on the podium tried to continue conducting a convention with the discipline that had seen them through service in France.

In a motion reminiscent of the practice at the front line of filling the ranks after the loss of comrades, Lindsley read a congratulatory message that referred to the current membership drive. The telegram ended with the challenge to go "over the top," a phrase that once quickened those who heard it in the trenches and now was a part of postwar slang.

Another telegram called for a "rededication to American ideals, traditions, and principles." The Legion, it said, "is civilization's best insurance policy." Though inspirational in its intent, this message coming closely after the news of the murders of the four Legionnaires in Centralia no doubt reminded the delegates that the ensuring of civilization was an expensive calling.

The spitefulness of coincidence continued. The next committee scheduled to report was that on anti-American propaganda. Their first resolution, composed before the news arrived from Centralia, cited a "growing tendency toward lawlessness and disorder in this country . . . numerous riots in various localities and . . . the nefarious activities of a small minority of anarchists and traitors." The text of the resolution invoked some staunch Legion principles: liberty, maintenance of law and order, upholding of duly constituted governmental agencies, and the defense of the flag.

The Legion, the resolution continued, stood "ready to fight the enemies of the Republic within our gates as we did to face the foes without." Not only was it necessary to "talk Americanism," but it was necessary to act. And the action called for was for Legion posts not only "to tender and volunteer their services to maintain law and order in time of public crisis," but to "make preparatory plans for such instances of service."

But even with the image of Legionnaires in far-off Centralia standing guard against retaliatory mob action in their little town, a delegate now objected to the insistence that the Legion, in effect, assume police powers. "Is this a civilian organization or one organized for the primary purpose of aiding the National Guard? You must remember that we have at present no more than one-eighth the membership of the soldiers of the U.S. If we continue on a basis like that, we will antagonize them. I feel we are making a serious mistake. I believe this is no time to take a step in that matter."

Another delegate expressed similar misgivings. While the resolution "has the right idea," he said, it "is drawn rather amateurishly and therefore can be used for purposes other than the good one intended. With it we can be called to put down any disturbance for whatever reason. It goes too far. We stand by our constitution and bylaws and all the tenets and oaths of our organization for law and order and Americanism. If we have not made that already manifest to the country we never will be able to. We have done it in times when it was necessary to go to war to do it; we have had to do it ever since we have been back here in peacetime. We stand ready to do it now and we do not need this resolution."

To a delegate from Washington state, however, the previous two protests were made in "the spirit of compromise, and the American Legion will not compromise with wrong."

Another spoke up for the resolution. "The elements of disorder and anarchy are never afraid to assert themselves; the elements of right and law and order should be equally independent, fearless, and regardless of whatever comes."

But the wording of the resolution was objectionable to still others. "If this resolution passes, we will have dedicated ourselves to a military policy." The Legion was living in a glass house; few others would join if the organization appeared to take such powers upon itself.

Were labor strikes to be considered thus? How did one define "public crises" as mentioned in the resolution? As one reminded, sixty-five percent of ex-servicemen and -women had not yet joined the Legion. They would not if they saw such a measure adopted as Legion policy. "This resolution is not in accord with the spirit of the American Legion's preamble. The Legion has been charged in this part of the country as being the tool of the capitalists and being financed by capital to put down the laboring man. Many won't come into the Legion because the Legion has the reputation of being against strikes."

When one rose to read aloud the second article from the draft of the Legion's proposed national constitution, that about the Legion's being "a civilian organization" in which "membership . . . does not affect or increase the member's liability for military or police service," many in the hall applauded.

The delegates listened attentively when New York delegate and Legion founder William Donovan spoke. "The essential evidence that this organization must contribute to the country at this moment is sanity and clearheadedness. Some expression of our opinion on the shooting of these members of the Legion yesterday should be taken. But a resolution such as this goes too far and should be redrafted."

Finally, a member of the Committee on Resolutions, whose group had met until 4:00 A.M. that morning pondering just such matters as one of 300 resolutions, recommended that the resolution be referred to the Committee on the Constitution, which had drafted in Article Two a statement which dealt with the same subject. A subcommittee of the Constitution Committee was called into immediate session in an upstairs meeting room.

Meanwhile, the chairman of the Resolutions Committee continued to read the Americanism resolutions which his group wished the convention to consider. First, the creation of a national Americanism commission was urged. The next one called for public and private schools to devote ten minutes a day to patriotic exercises and for the flag to be kept raised over the schools "weather permitting." This resolution was referred to the Committee on Legislation.

Sixteen more resolutions were read, comprising a range of applications of the Legion's brand of Americanism.

At this point, the report of the Finance Committee was interjected into the schedule. This committee presented both a majority and a minority report. The first called for annual dues of one dollar "as are now constituted under the Constitution of the Legion," twenty-five cents for the national, twenty-five cents for the state, and fifty cents for the local post.

The minority report called for one dollar "national dues" (in addition to state and local dues not here specified) so that (1) members could continue to get the *Weekly,* (2) National Headquarters could be financed, and (3) the current indebtedness could be liquidated.

These reports generated much discussion and, in the end, the minority report was rejected by "about eighteen votes." This started another round of debate about the means for allowing the organization to continue with a magazine and a group of national officers. After a roll call vote, the minority report was rejected.

Though the chairman of the Finance Committee again spoke for the total one dollar dues, George White asked the convention pointedly, "Do you want a magazine or not?" With cries of "We do!" he continued. "You cannot have the magazine . . . on the conditions laid down in the majority report." There then was a vote taken on a motion to reconsider the previous vote. After the second roll call vote on the dues, the minority report was accepted 384 to 300.

Now came speeches from the commanders of the Grand Army of the Republic and the United Confederate Veterans. Ex-governor Samuel Van Zandt spoke for the G.A.R. Representing those like himself "whose work is about completed," he spoke to them about the passage of time. "Gentlemen of the American Legion, I envy you the privileges and the years of usefulness that lie before you. Each generation must furnish its own torch-bearers of freedom, and it avails nothing what former generations have done. . . . Our faith is supreme in you, and if you fail, America dies."

When he was finished, Chairman Lindsley reported that the U.C.V. commander, a fellow Texan, had been unable to attend but that he had recommended that Van Zandt speak for U.C.V. as well. Van Zandt quipped that he could well speak for the South since his winter home was in southern Florida, but also because "General Lee was an American General," a conciliatory remark that was loudly applauded.

After a commendation from the convention to the Boy Scouts who had helped with numerous chores during the convention, the delegates were recessed at 1:43 P.M. for lunch.

At 2:45 P.M. they were again in their places and the last session began. With accounts of the Centralia murders much in the news, many delegates read newspapers as Chairman Lindsley took the podium. He asked them to put the newspapers aside so that they could continue with the pressing schedule of business. He had been informed, he said, that the Pullmans were needed back in Chicago, and that if the convention went on too long, that means of transportation home would not wait.

Secretary Wood read a few telegram greetings to the convention: from farmers; from the Service Star Legion in Indianapolis made up of mothers, wives, sisters, and daughters "in the service of their country in the world war" who welcomed the Legion to Indianapolis, and from posts in Dunson, Texas and Jamestown, North Dakota announcing membership drive results.

Next, with the report of the Committee on Beneficial Legislation, the convention heard the substance of what at this point was the forerunner of the Legion's advocacy for veterans' rehabilitation. In this area, the Legion recognized the obligation of the federal government to those who served in the war, but declined to go on record for a particular cash bonus.

Since none of the land and home aid bills before Congress currently impressed the committee as being adequate for the situation of ex-servicemen, it recommended that an American Legion Home Founding Act be enacted, an omnibus measure including (1) reclamation of unproductive lands by the government for settlement by veterans, (2) the development of rural communities by government loans, and (3) loans for purchasing or developing farm and city homes.

Disabled veterans now in hospitals were said to deserve at least fifty dollars a month upon being discharged and until they received their War Risk Insurance payments or those from the Vocational Rehabilitation Act of 1918. Veterans with tuberculosis were due seventy-five dollars a month, the committee said. Also, all disabled veterans should be permitted to go to the best hospitals and be treated by their own doctors if they so desired.

Furthermore, the compensation of eighty dollars a month already allowed in the Vocational Rehabilitation Act should be increased to one hundred dollars and that act should be enlarged to include all disabled persons. The Sweet Bill (H.R. 8778) should be passed immediately, the committee said, but with the amendment called for by the Legion for a higher family allowance than the War Risk Act currently gave.

The Legion's national legislative team was asked to investigate all complaints made about the War Risk Insurance Bureau and the Federal Board for Vocational Education.

Finally, Congress should equate all ex-servicemen in matters of retirement with those of the Regular Army.

This report, which a Michigan delegate called "quite a collection," prompted a lengthy debate about the ever-present controversy regarding "the bonus." One said he didn't want a one-shot handout that would be too quickly gone; he wanted work. The response in agreement indicated that he apparently spoke the mind of many.

That subject had been hotly debated ever since members of the A.E.F. had begun returning to the States and the former soldiers and sailors were handed their ticket home and sixty dollars for a new suit of clothing as the government's fond farewell. From that point on they were on their own except for a few recent measures for vocational education or small stipends for some disabilities.

As occurred any time the matter was discussed, a lengthy debate ensued on the floor of the convention about the great disparity between servicemen's pay and that of those who remained at home in the job market during the war. This always brought forth charges about "lounge lizards" who stayed home and profited by the high wartime wages paid to employees of the railroads and the mines, and in shipbuilding, munitions manufacturing, and other industries. Indeed, there was much bitterness about the pay differences between "the boy who fought and the boy who feathered."

For certain, there did seem to be an appreciable need for an adjustment, hence the term "adjusted compensation," an expression vulgarized in the tyranny of the column inch to the more vociferous catchword "bonus." Many objected to bonus giveaways and bonus thinking as being beneath the dignity of their sacrifice in the war. Others needed the cash in their pockets now.

Actually when "the bonus" was debated, there were three general camps: those who wanted the bonus whether it was called a handout or not, those who wanted neither cash money bonus nor an "adjustment," and those who said the whole matter was one Congress alone should settle. As in St. Louis, but more so here in Minneapolis, all three opinions were present in force.

Even so, the dire predictions made by many inside and outside the Legion about the issue of the bonus being sure to disrupt greatly if not rend the convention and hence the Legion did not prove correct.

Though the debate was spirited and not many minds were changed about how the issue should be resolved, the convention dealt with the subject of a bonus by entertaining an amendment to the Beneficial Legislation Committee's report, which called for "a dollar a day or more" for all days served in the armed forces during the war.

The discussion that followed had all the vim and vigor of the usual three-way pull. While some favored a dollar-a-day gesture by the government indicating that their wartime service was appreciated, others said any attempts at gaining a bonus were akin to putting a cash value on their military service. "Let us not inject another word in our preamble by making it '*me,* God, and country,' " one said.

Finally, and with the Pullmans waiting, a delegate from South Dakota moved for the adoption of the report just as the committee had read it. On a voice vote, the report of the Beneficial Legislation Committee was adopted.

The report had stated simply that the federal government owed the veterans an obligation, but that the Legion at this point did not favor "a particular cash bonus." The convention, whose voice Congress was said to be awaiting, had just thrown the matter back to the government for action.

The debate on the bonus would surely be continued on the trains going home and in the states. All knew the subject was long from being settled. (Even the most prescient, however, could not foresee the clamor that would arise a decade hence when the nation found itself in the grip of an economic depression and the bonus matter, with a congressional act on the books, would be an even more divisive and disruptive issue.)

With the bonus matter shelved for the time being, the Anti-American Propaganda Committee took a swipe at socialism, calling it "a revolutionary organization formed for the purpose of abolishing the right of the individual to own and inherit property and making farms, mines, factories, and railroads community property without compensation to their former owners." Socialists had "for a quarter of a century preached their doctrines from the soap boxes and sugar barrels of every city in this country." A. C. Townley, in 1914 the head of the Socialist Party, came in for such criticism being "now under sentence for disloyalty to the government" and who "is now working on the farmers of the nation" even after failing, it was said, to convince the farmers of the Northwest of the same doctrine.

The chairman of the Committee on Eligibility reported that his committee had reconciled its minority and majority report (the latter had been adopted by the convention) and was now of one mind on the formerly disputed topic of who might join the Legion and, consequently, any auxiliary groups. The new version was read and adopted.

Before the convention could vote on the officers for the coming year, the Constitution Committee was asked to report, since the election of officers was dealt with extensively in the constitution. Luke Lea read the report, actually the constitution itself, which had been the subject of two days and nights of what Lea called "quite a small convention" itself amid the larger forum.

The delegates then adopted Article VI, setting forth the establishment of national officers so that elections could be held. (A constitution for the Legion was eventually adopted without further discussion.) The roll was called for nominations. The chairman of the Arkansas delegation nominated Franklin D'Olier of Pennsylvania for national commander, one who had been working at the New York office since the St. Louis Caucus.

New York delegate Hamilton Fish nominated Hanford McNider of Iowa. Fish said his nominee was the only one "who did not have his friends campaigning for him before this convention met and while the delegates have been assembled here."

When E. Lester Jones of Washington, D.C., was nominated, a delegate objected because Jones "already had a civil job as head of the Coast and Geodetic Survey." Another delegate shouted that the job was "not elective," so the nominee's name was allowed to remain.

A Kentucky delegate nominated Emmett O'Neil of that state, who had joined the French army and later the American army when the A.E.F. landed in France. O'Neil, a lawyer, was credited as being the one who "drove the red forces out, and helped to drive from the pulpit in Kentucky a man [not named] who under the cover of religious teachings was preaching . . . Bolshevism."

The Texas delegation nominated its own Henry D. Lindsley, who summarily declined, repeating his statement earlier in the convention that, having served in the leadership capacity he had for the previous months, he could not continue, for "the American Legion is now so much bigger than any one man . . . that there will never be a time . . . when it will be necessary to even think of reelecting a national commander who has served this organization." This compliment on the democratic intentions of the Legion and its growing importance to the nation was roundly applauded.

The roll call on the election of a national commander resulted in Franklin D'Olier being elected on the first ballot. Asked for a speech, the new national commander said simply, "We came here for work. Let us keep on working and not listen to speeches. Thank you." Though an annual salary of $6,000 had been authorized, D'Olier refused it, choosing instead to serve without compensation and to pay all his own expenses as he had in the past.

At this point, Chairman Lindsley was honored by being named the first past national commander, and a cheer went up: "What's the matter with Lindsley? He's all right. Who's all right? Lindsley!"

The nominations and election of vice-commanders followed; and while the votes were being tallied, the Committee on War Risk Insurance reported. Calling " 'War Risk' a good name with a bad history," the committee called upon Congress, the Legion, and the War Risk Bureau to work together to see that veterans received the compensation due them. The resolution was adopted.

When the votes for eighteen nominees for vice-commander were announced, five winners were named: Allen Tukey (army) of Nebraska, James J. O'Brien (navy) of California, Joyce P. Lewis (marines) of Minnesota, Alden R. Chambers (navy) of Massachusetts, and William B. Follet (army) of Oregon. New Vice-Commander Lewis appeared in a wheelchair, disabled from attempts to save his brother from machine-gun fire at Belleau Wood. His hometown post in Long Prairie, Minnesota, had been named for the brother, William T. Lewis.

For national chaplain, the Reverend Father Francis A. Kelly of New York, winner of the D.S.C. for service with the 27th Division, was elected over John W. Inzer of Alabama, with 411 votes to 246.

The ever-popular Teddy Roosevelt, Jr., spoke for Father Kelly. When the perennial Legion favorite rose to speak, there were cries of "We want Teddy!" When told to go "In the stall!" Roosevelt replied, "If I may drop into the vernacular, isn't it a damned particular convention. If you don't believe it, take my authority."

It was now approaching 9:00 P.M. In order to accommodate those hurrying to the Pullmans, the chairman asked for a motion to set the date of the next convention. The body chose the "third Monday in September 1920."

At that point the Resolutions Committee resumed its report with a resolution calling for "the collection of war photographs, equipment and such other paraphernalia of war as would preserve our knowledge of the Great War for all time." Another expressed the desire to leave the bodies of fallen comrades in France, except for those whom families wished returned. For the remains left in the cemeteries in France, the U.S. and French governments should cooperate to create and maintain the cemeteries, this one said.

"Absolute rank" was recommended for nurses who had served in the trying and dangerous times in Europe. Based on the reference in the preamble to obligations for service in the communities, a resolution was read calling for a national committee to be appointed to survey the various types of community service proposed by "noncommercial, nonpolitical and nonsectarian" organizations so that the Legion could learn how it might help and thereby become "a power in every community" for similar service.

It was resolved that those same communities not be the site of "German opera, instruction of German in the schools, public performances of German or Austrian performers, and any other act which tends to minimize the German guilt."

The Legion, through its posts, should search for the widows and children of "our deceased comrades" and to extend to them "such care and assistance as may be within their power."

One resolution sought to deal with labor unrest and "all the disputes now interrupting the peaceful pursuits of the nation." It was recommended, therefore, that the Legion go on record as deploring and condemning strikes by police and firemen, as well as "all employees of the nation, states, and municipalities to whom are committed the protection of life, order, and law. . . ."

Furthermore, since "disturbed conditions growing out of the World War are apparent in various countries and . . . have appeared in the U.S. through the activities of persons of undemocratic tendencies," behavior that is disrupting "manufacturing, labor, and social interests," the Legion now called on all parties involved to acknowledge "the rights of the people as a whole to demand a lasting settlement" of the various and many disputes.

On another matter, a resolution called for "full rights of citizenship" to be given Native Americans who honorably served in the armed forces.

Without fanfare the convention was adjourned at 9:20 P.M.

One year to the day since the end of the war, the gavel had first sounded at this national convention. In the previous months, hundreds of thousands of citizen-soldiers had returned to civilian life. But, scattered as they were across the width and breadth of the nation, they remained an unassimilated segment of that larger population.

Now when the gavel sounded for the last time, the delegates representing veterandom in America had in hand an agenda for action and a system for recognition: they had their resolutions and they had their Legion posts as the bases from which to serve and from which to speak on the needs of their peers.

It had been hammered home during the convention—from the podium, in the many deliberations over the many resolutions, and in the general atmosphere of serious concentration on the solving of problems—that (1) there was now a veterans' lobby with which to reckon and (2) the "citizen" component of the "citizen-soldier" was as demanding and essential a responsibility as had been insisted upon by "Black Jack" Pershing of his soldiers and admirals of their sailors.

In this light, the closing of the convention implied the official beginning of a new-age movement for veterans' rights and benefits and for a commitment to peacetime service to the nation.

The principles of the organization were no doubt the subject of lengthy discussions on the trains and other conveyances home. To all those favorably impressed with the conduct and results of the first national convention, membership as American Legionnaires had special significance.

Not only would the nation soon hear much more about what care and other consideration were due to American veterans, but also at no other time in the history of the republic had so much attention, outside Congress, been focused on the meaning of citizenship.

What had transpired in the convention hall in the presence of hundreds of delegates would be magnified in the ripple effect of both press coverage and the enthusiasm displayed back home at the posts for what could and should be done by the organization.

The convention was a product of the times, as much so as it was the manifestation of a new generation of veterans. The news from Centralia, of course, had been disquieting. If nothing else that transpired during the convention had done so, that event alone would have pushed the adolescent organization into adulthood.

Otherwise, it appears that delegates left in good spirits. They had come to take the measure of their new organization. They were, it seemed, generally satisfied. One of Roosevelt, Jr.'s favorite departing images was of the delegate who, as if memorializing a departed comrade, jumped to a bench at the Minneapolis railroad station and with hat clutched to his chest pleaded: "Comrades, let us take off our hats and stand for one minute in reverent silence in memory of those resolutions that died in committee!"

The many resolutions that had survived required action, but this was an action-oriented group. The decade of the 1920s lay just ahead. For a new, vigorous, and unafraid organization, the fun was just beginning!

FOUNDERS

For all their concern about and successes on behalf of the common doughboy and gob of World War I, the first few men who came together to discuss the founding of The American Legion were themselves an uncommon lot, not average in any sense.

They were a hyphenated lot; among them, one would find a lawyer-soldier, a writer-soldier, an architect-engineer-author-soldier, a lawyer-soldier-military intelligence guru, a big city mayor-banker-soldier, and, perhaps most notably, the bearer of a famous name whose vita included the most amazing variety of all, and who died a soldier.

Eric Fisher Wood *was at the Ecole des Beaux Arts in Paris studying architecture, when in August 1914 there came the quick succession of declarations of war among the principal European combatants of the First World War. As a volunteer attaché at the American Embassy, he had witnessed the first blows on the anvil that would reshape much of Europe. Later, he joined the American Ambulance Corps for a few months. Back in the States, he was vice-president of the National Security League from 1915 to 1917, and for a year in 1915–16, he was on the Plattsburg Training Camp Executive Committee, a camp where earlier he had entered as a private and emerged as a first lieutenant.*

Returning to Europe, he served in the British Army with the rank of major, during which time he was wounded by gunshot and shell at Arras on April 9, 1917. When the United States entered the war, Wood was commissioned a major in the U.S. National Army on August 14, 1917, and was made assistant chief of staff (G-2) for the 88th Division. Close to the action once again, he was injured by poison gas during the Meuse-Argonne offensive.

With all this happening, he still found time to write. His Note Book of an Attaché *was published in 1915,* The Writing on the Wall *in 1916, and* The Note Book of an Intelligence Officer *in 1918. He also contributed articles to* Colliers, Saturday Evening Post, The Forum, The Outlook, Century, The London Times, *and other publications.*

After the Armistice, Wood served as the first temporary chairman of the Paris Caucus and Secretary of both the St. Louis Caucus and the

Minneapolis National Convention. He was fond of pointing to his introductory remarks opening the Paris Caucus as containing tenets nearly identical to those in the "preamble" to the Legion's constitution.

Wood's military career would continue to World War II. A brigadier general in December 1940, he was in active service from 1941 to 1945. He would win the Legion of Merit, the Purple Heart with oak leaf, and the Croix de Guerre, in addition to earning twenty ribbons and ten battle stars over the course of his military career. He was also a principal partner in the engineering and architectural firm that designed the Warren G. Harding Memorial at Marion, Ohio. Wood was named past national commander in 1955.

George Ared White *volunteered for the Spanish-American War, riding with the Utah Cavalry as a bugler. He remained in military service until May 1903, emerging as a first sergeant. Traveling through Oregon in 1904, he stopped in Portland on his way to Washington state to look for newspaper work and, witnessing the deaths of several people when a bridge collapsed over the Willamette River, he hurriedly asked to report the event for the Portland* Oregonian.

When the United States entered the war in Europe, White was adjutant general of the Oregon National Guard. White was a major by the time his Third Oregon was said to be the first National Guard regiment in the nation to be readied for service when the call to arms came. The Third was given a berth in the 41st Division (troops from Oregon, Washington, Idaho, Montana, and Wyoming), and White became a colonel connected with G.H.Q. of the A.E.F.

White arrived back in the States in May 1919; in New York in mid-June he was encouraged by Roosevelt and the others to continue the Legion organizational work he had helped with in Europe. According to a public relations piece "to be released on or after Sunday, August 10, 1919 . . . White is also in full charge of The American Legion Weekly *magazine as temporary editor and general manager." The* Weekly *at the time had a circulation of 100,000.*

Actually White did more than head up the Weekly. *He also sat in on meetings about "national organization problems" as he called them, until the middle of each day, after which he edited and managed the Legion publication during the afternoon and evening. He called on his many acquaintances in the newspaper business to help publicize the Legion; he also traveled, spending as much time as he could spare from his other duties to go to Washington, Chicago, and other major cities in the interests of the Legion.*

After his return to Oregon, White rejoined the National Guard and took on a major reorganization of the unit. He also continued to write, under the name "Ared White," and published stories of spies and other adventures set during World War II, including The Spy Net, Agent B-7, *and* Seven Tickets to Singapore. *His* Attack on America, *a military exposé of the vulnerability of the nation's defenses, made the point that America's West Coast, possibly, and, more certainly a little known outpost—Pearl Harbor—would be threatened by hostile action from Japan. (The attack would come just fourteen days after he died in November 1941.)*

Theodore Roosevelt, Jr., *was fourteen when his father was elected the twenty-sixth president of the United States. Educated in public schools and at Groton and Harvard, he exhibited much of his father's bounding energy and varied interests. But rather than politics, he chose business and periodic stints in the military.*

His interest in the military preparedness of the nation led him to help originate the Plattsburg Training Camp. He entered the service in April 1917 as a major, and was assigned duty as an instructor. In June he went to Europe with the 26th Infantry, 1st Division, as a battalion commander; he later commanded the regiment. He was wounded and gassed at Cantigny and shot through the left knee at Soissons. On September 13, 1918, he was made lieutenant colonel. After being discharged in March 1919, he devoted much of his time for the next several months to publicizing and promoting the American Legion.

When asked to describe the American Legion in one sentence, Roosevelt replied that it was "composed of men who intended to justify in time of peace the title of servicemen earned in the war."

After the Minneapolis Convention, he was a member of the Committee on Civil Service Preference in 1921; of the Committee on Distinguished Guests during the Foch tour of 1921; and of the National Defense Committee in 1927.

Later, Roosevelt was assistant secretary of the navy, 1921–23; led two expeditions into Asia for the Field Museum of Chicago in 1925 and in 1928–29. Later, he was governor of Puerto Rico (1929–33), where he organized village council meetings to promote democratic methods of dealing with problems. In later life, his civic work included stints as vice-president of the Boy Scouts of America and president of the National Health Council.

Roosevelt would maintain his Officers Reserve Corps commission and be ordered back to active service April 22, 1941, as a colonel with the 26th Infantry, 1st Division, the same as with his World War I service. As a brigadier general, Roosevelt would witness the military campaigns in Tunisia, Sicily, and Italy. At Normandy he was the first general to land on D-day, at Cherbourg Peninsula. He died on July 12, 1944, of a heart attack while resting in the captured German truck that had been turned into a mobile office for his use. Roosevelt was named past national commander in 1949.

Columbia-educated **William Joseph Donovan** *(A.B., 1905; LL.B., 1907) was born in 1883, a native of Buffalo, New York. While practicing law, he also helped in 1912 to organize Troop I, New York Cavalry, of the National Guard. He worked in Polish War Relief Service in 1915, then resigned in 1916 when his National Guard unit was mobilized for service on the Mexican border.*

Donovan was assistant chief of staff of the 2nd Division when he was promoted to major and later brigade adjutant of the 51st Brigade of the 2nd. Soon thereafter, he went to Europe as commander of the First Battalion of the 165th Infantry, the old "fighting 69th" of the 42d Rainbow Division. Somewhere along the line he had been tagged "Wild Bill." Promoted to lieutenant colonel in September 1918 and to colonel in March 1919, Donovan received the Distinguished Service Cross in July 1918. He was wounded for the second time during the battle of the Meuse-Argonne and earned the Medal of Honor. Later he would win the Distinguished Service Medal. Though he was unable to meet often with the others in Paris because of his duties with the occupation troops in Germany, he did attend the Legion's Minneapolis convention and worked as a floor leader there.

In 1924, President Coolidge made Donovan deputy assistant to the attorney general to head up the Anti-trust Division; he quickly gained a reputation for protecting the public interest with style and success.

In 1941, Donovan would become the nation's chief spy-master, organizing the the forerunner of the C.I.A., the Office of Strategic Services. A close associate, Ambassador David Bruce, would later say, "His imagination was unlimited. Ideas were his playthings." That attribute may have prompted his interest in the formation of the Legion. William Donovan died in 1959.

By the time the United States joined the war in Europe, **Henry Dickerson Lindsley** *had been mayor of Dallas, Texas (1915–17), then a city of 200,000. He also gained a reputation as a banker, the president of a life insurance company, and the director of several financial and industrial enterprises in Texas and New York. Sometime during this period of his life, he spent a year in Europe studying municipal governments and eight months in Asia studying religion.*

Lindsley, the only one among the original founders who did not attend college (but who became a founder of Southern Methodist University), attended the Citizens Training Camp at Leon Springs, Texas, before the war. He also attended the second officer's training camp at Plattsburg, New York. On December 8, 1917, he was commissioned a major of infantry, one of sixteen among three thousand to receive the appointment and, once ordered to France, was made chief of the War

Risk Section of the A.E.F. He was made colonel in August 1918. He received the Distinguished Service Medal and eventually the French Legion of Honor, Officer of Public Instruction Order, and the Belgian Commander of the Order of the Crown.

After the war, Lindsley became director of the Veterans Bureau in Washington, D.C. His chief service to the Legion came from his being made chairman of the St. Louis Caucus and entrusted with the same job for the Minneapolis Convention. The oldest of the original national officers, Lindsley brought maturity and sage advice to the new organization. Later service to the Legion included the chairmanship in 1927 of the World Peace and Foreign Relations Committee (the year before he had been American vice-president of the Federation Interalliée des Anciens Combattants (FIDAC, or Allied Veterans Federation).

But it was his guidance and sense of order and fairness at St. Louis and Minneapolis for which he chiefly would be known. For those qualities and his other service, he was given the first "Past National Commander" title at the Minneapolis convention in recognition and thanks for the previous weeks of vital service to the Legion movement. Lindsley died in 1938.

Bennett Champ Clark, *born 1890, was the son of the well-known Champ Clark of Missouri, the longtime Speaker of the House of Representatives, and had also practiced law in Washington, D.C. since 1914. Educated at the University of Missouri and George Washington University, Clark brought many valuable talents to the job of presiding over the Paris Caucus, none more so than his experience as the parliamentarian of the U.S. House of Representatives from 1913 to 1917.*

In 1917 he had joined the class of the First Officers Training Camp at Fort Myer, Virginia, and was commissioned captain. Back home in Missouri, he was elected lieutenant colonel of the 6th Missouri Infantry. When that unit was called up in August 1917, he became lieutenant colonel in the 140th U.S. Infantry. Later, he was transferred to the 88th Division as Assistant Chief of Staff, G-1. Another transfer took him to the 35th Division in the same capacity. He became colonel of the infantry in March 1919.

After the war, Clark served as vice-chairman of the Legion Executive Committee at St. Louis, and as a member of the Constitution and Military Affairs committees. Later he was a director of the Legion Publishing Corporation; a National Executive Committeeman (1922–23); a member of the Committee to Investigate War Chest Funds in 1923, and of the National Finance Committee that same year. He was named a past national commander in 1926.

Bennett Clark's lasting contribution to the budding Legion was his vision for what it could and must be, expressed early before the organization set its attitudes and outlook.

Thomas Woodnutt Miller, *born in 1886, was a Yale graduate, the son of Delaware governor Charles E. Miller. In 1913–14 he was Delaware's Secretary of State in his father's administration but resigned to run for Congress, winning a seat as a Delaware representative-at-large.*

While a congressman, Miller attended Plattsburg Training Camp in 1915. He was defeated in 1916 by 153 votes for a second term as a U.S. representative. When war was declared, he enlisted as a private in an infantry company in July 1917. From corporal he was commissioned in the 114th Infantry, and in the spring of 1918 he was at Fort Dix awaiting orders to ship out when he was refused active service because of impaired eyesight. He had earlier been refused entry into the First Officers Training Camp in Virginia after a physical exam. After the second refusal, he persisted and was given a nonphysical exam after which he was commissioned captain in the Signal Corps. He soon became a major of ordinance. Attempting to join combat troops, Miller was assigned to the 79th Division as an ordnance officer and sailed for France.

Miller went to Paris in March 1919, eager to learn more about the formation of a veterans' organization. He was tapped to preside over the caucus in the temporary absence of Bennett Clark. Back in the States, he was the ideal person to head up the Legion's quest for a congressional charter and to guide the organization's growing interest in federal legislation. In Washington, which he knew well from his earlier days as a shorthand and typing clerk in the Federal Bureau of Census and then as the youngest congressman in town, he, Luke Lea, and John Thomas Taylor lobbied Congress for the Legion.

Miller was also the Delaware N.E.C. representative from 1919 to 1928, the first of a long series of departmental and national offices held over the next several decades, including departmental commander of two states: Delaware and Nevada (his residence after 1933), and thence NECman of Nevada. In 1921 he was appointed by the president to serve on the committee that created the Veterans Administration. His troubled tenure as alien property custodian of the U.S., 1921–25, embroiled him in controversy that resulted in a federal prison term for him, later revoked by the government with full restitution given. After moving to Nevada, Miller supervised C.C.C. camps in the region and helped originate the Nevada state parks system.

During World War II he chaired Nevada's Veterans Coordinating Committee and sat on the Nevada State Council of Defense. He was appointed past national commander in 1968 at the New Orleans National Convention.

"BENEFICIAL LEGISLATION"

ESTABLISHING VETERANS' REHABILITATION STANDARDS

1919 – 1924

"Three fourths of 'grit' is 'git.'"
(Former doughboy undergoing rehabilitation in 1919)

The gavel for adjournment at Minneapolis had sounded. Pronouncements by the earlier caucuses had been transformed into programs, and aspirations into assignments.

Though planned as an organization of common citizen-soldiers, the Legion had been prompted and publicized in France by a few affluent officers. Now, after several months of organizational work back home in the States, Legion membership rolls included several thousand former doughboys and gobs, and their opinions on select issues of national importance were on record.

The Legion's officers now had specific goals: aiding physically and economically disabled veterans; promoting patriotism; emphasizing the need for a national military policy in the postwar age; and, in general, acknowledging the responsibilities of citizenship on the local and national scene. Now the real work must begin.

The National Executive Committeemen remained in Minneapolis on November 13 for a postconvention meeting, the first for this administrative body. Henry Lindsley, just regaining his voice after having gone hoarse the last day of the convention, looked into the meeting.

He was still enthusiastic about what had been accomplished and what was promised for the future.

"The Legion has done more than anything since the Civil War to tie our country together and to absolutely secure to us and to our children's children the benefit of constituted government in the United States." The Legion was bound to become "a great force in American life."

Politicians, according to Lindsley, were taking note that "nonpolitical as this organization is, and as it will remain, it has set a standard for those who are going to occupy places in the public life of this nation. . . ." Those in either party unable to abide by the standards the Legion was calling for "are going to be retired to private life." The Texan's remarks were applauded.

The convention had provided an official answer to the question posed by Congress: "What do veterans want?" Ostensibly awaiting an answer, that body took no decisive action, even though national legislators had introduced a patchwork of veteran-related measures. Although the Legion had not stated a specific dollar figure for the adjusted compensation—the misnomer "bonus"—it could speak now with a unified voice (at least officially).

Henceforth the mention of the Minneapolis Convention would signal an impressive mark of achievement.

National Commander Franklin D'Olier suggested the name of Lemuel Bolles of Washington as the new "secretary" after Eric Fisher Wood begged off, citing work commitments outside the Legion. Bolles was a selfstarter, a trait typical of many who had associated themselves with the Legion. He had served for fourteen years in the Washington National Guard when in September 1917 he entered service in World War I. Two months later he was in France; two years later he was discharged as a lieutenant colonel, having served on the general staff. Bolles had contributed to the Legion Constitution drafted in Paris and did much of the logistical planning for the first national convention.

D'Olier asked that the meeting be informal. He spoke of the immediate future. Having spent every working day for the last six months as head of the State Organization Division at the temporary New York headquarters office, his vantage at 19 West 44th Street had given him a unique perspective. "I think I see pretty clearly what a big job there is ahead of us.

"The Legion is successfully launched," D'Olier said, but "we have really only just begun to scratch the surface. We have an enormous task ahead of us." Starting out with a membership of approximately one million, committeemen must help "consolidate our position, and having done that to go forward and get a very much larger percentage of the four million potential members. . . ." He pleaded for the committeemen to spend all the time they could spare for Legion work.

Money was a problem. The Legion magazine had a voracious appetite for funds, appeased so far by loans. In contrast, the small (as yet) National Headquarters had required far less money to operate. The only real assets currently were $50,000 in the bank and about $40,000 due from states for the popular Legion membership buttons. This was the meager wherewithal on which "National" would attempt to make do until the one dollar annual dues began in January 1920.

D'Olier reaffirmed the decision of the previous temporary officers that the Legion would not accept any "subscriptions," meaning donations, from anyone but would look instead toward the time when the organization could "stand on its own bottom." Money had been borrowed with the understanding that loans would be repaid when the Legion began producing revenue, money that was expected to come largely from the *Weekly*'s proceeds.

Meanwhile, while awaiting the long-promised revenue from the *Weekly,* the loans were weighing heavily. Galbraith of Ohio urged the appointing of a finance committee to look after the $250,000 in outstanding notes due to be paid soon. The talk about accounting, and accountability, reminded others that posts were using widely varied and otherwise uncoordinated methods of bookkeeping. That situation needed to be addressed.

D'Olier complimented the two-man Legislative Committee for work they had done for the Legion. Tom Miller was a former congressman and had been chairman pro tempore of the Paris Caucus. Washington lawyer John Thomas Taylor was on his way to becoming one of the most effective, if eccentric, lobbyists of his time.

Even before the first national convention, these Legion spokesmen had emphasized the government's obligation to care for World War veterans disabled totally or temporarily and for their dependents. They had begun to make this point by agitating for more efficiency in the three agencies dealing with veterans' affairs: the War Risk Insurance Bureau, the Federal Board for Vocational Education, and the Public Health Service.

During the summer, Miller and Taylor had lobbied for legislation that became public law, allowing disabled veterans to be placed in occupational training and to receive training pay regardless of the compensation due them as judged by the War Risk Insurance Bureau. Previously, a red-tape rigmarole had kept many from receiving the training while they awaited a judgment from the War Risk Insurance Bureau. Near the end of the year, Miller and Taylor tried to help tuberculosis patients draw their small military pay allowances while these veterans awaited entry into the Federal Board for Vocational Training program and its temporary compensation.

After the convention, the primary attention of the Legislative Committee was directed at the Sweet Bill (H.R. 8778) and the Wasson Bill (H.R. 10365). The first, in its current form, provided for increased compensation for disabled veterans (eighty dollars per month instead of thirty dollars), and death payment in one lump sum or in thirty payments, the choice being up to the insured. The range of beneficiaries was also increased.

The Wasson Bill, which would be bandied about for another year, would authorize the War Risk Insurance Bureau to set up fourteen regional offices, to advertise the bureau's services and veterans' rights, and to allow the payment of premiums at local post offices for convenience.

Miller and Taylor were attuned to fellow Legionnaires in the field who reported on whether hospital facilities offered the unique treatment needed for war injuries and who sought to expose the ongoing shell game of statistics about the actual number of beds.

Public Health Service hospitals, for example, were often not equipped or staffed to deal with mental and nervous disorders. Also, tuberculosis patients were often shunted about, seemingly with little regard to their condition or requirements for treatment. Meanwhile, TB sufferers were flocking on their own to the Southwest and simply appearing unannounced on the doorsteps of the few government hospitals in that region.

In addition to scrutinizing the post-Armistice flourish of sundry veteran-related bills emanating from a congressional popularity contest in this field (not altogether unmixed with the sincere efforts of some in public office), Miller and Taylor had been directed to focus on three important areas in which the Legion might draft legislation: that for benefiting those disabled in the service; that for establishing a national military policy for preparedness based on what had been learned the hard way during the recent war; and that for bringing about "a better Americanization of the fabric of our society," as D'Olier described it.

When the N.E.C. members left Minneapolis, they were justified in thinking that they had participated in an important rehearsal for yet another vital Legion function—the National Executive Committee, the Legion's governing body between national conventions.

Volunteerism in the Legion had already acquired a few noteworthy characteristics, principally the American concoction of equal parts idealism and industry. The concept-oriented, blue-sky thinking of the founders had been taken up now, as they had hoped, by their young, energetic, action-oriented counterparts. There was also more than a sprinkling of veterans a few years older who had left established positions at the declaration of war and who had now returned to professions that were useful to the Legion's purposes. Whatever the organization needed in the way of expertise and counsel on the national level, as well as at local and state levels, could be found among its growing membership. Already a depth and breadth of membership had developed.

At "National," which capped the pyramid of what was often referred to in these early years as the Legion "movement," volunteerism was, of course, a familiar topic. "About three weeks before the convention," D'Olier now remarked, "we were talking about upon whom the responsibility in the Legion could be fixed during the year, and we talked about all kinds of people, and name after name was suggested. Some said, 'Well he won't do," or 'He can't do it,' and I made the unfortunate remark that the Legion has grown so strong and . . . means so much to the country that a man's personal judgment and his personal preference or wishes shouldn't be considered. If he is needed by the Legion, he must be drafted. I think that is the way we will be able to get the work done."

D'Olier joked about the heavy workloads awaiting volunteers and staff members. "I have found in all American Legion work that if any man had had any idea of what he was going to do, he wouldn't have gone into it in the first place."

The paid staff members who maintained the Legion's temporary National Headquarters in New York during the summer of 1919 had experienced times of exhilaration resulting from the heady success of the organization's quick growth. There had also been bouts of confusion and disarray as, relying on correspondence and telephone calls, they tried to imagine what was happening in the rest of the country.

During the convention in Minneapolis, the few national leaders had been buoyed by the rousing enthusiasm of the delegates from across the nation who had paraded triumphantly in a snowstorm and who had attended the marathon sessions in meeting rooms and on the convention floor (twelve hours the final day).

But after the last shout of affirmation and the comradely repartee had been lost in the bursts of steam from the locomotives pulling the Pullmans out of Minneapolis, the weight of maintaining "National" for the next several months fell to D'Olier and the small national staff. Immediately he began planning to move the National Headquarters to Indianapolis in mid-December.

In New York, D'Olier continued to gather volunteers to man the committees that the convention had authorized and charged with responsibilities. From those whom he approached about accepting staff positions or the time-consuming volunteer work, he often heard, he said, "That is all very fine, but I can't do it."

As he explained at the time in an issue of the *Weekly,* "It is not hard for some to go to war when the vision of the world is centered upon the warrior in uniform. It is harder to fight the quiet and less spectacular fight for those same ideals at home and in the ordinary walks of life. Yet that is what the Legion proposes to do, and what it will do."

When speaking before other organizations or audiences who welcomed him as the chief spokesman for a new and vigorous organization often in the news, D'Olier spoke of the Legion as being well on its way to becoming "a constructive influence during these days of national readjustment" after the war. Such a role was derived from three basic needs.

First, "mutual helpfulness whereby all our comrades who have been handicapped in mind, body, or position through service to their country may receive that liberal consideration which they have reason to expect from a grateful and patriotic nation."

Second, "protection for our country from foes without. It will be our endeavor to assist in the adoption of a military policy which will make it safe from future aggression and yet a policy which will be truly democratic, truly American, just, and equitable to the entire country."

Third, "protection for our country from foes within. Our stand for 100 percent Americanism will be virile. As soldiers . . . and now as civilians . . . with an ever keener sense of the responsibility of citizenship, we shall not hesitate. Now our orders originate from the Constitution of the United States as expressed through the duly constituted agencies of national, state, and local government. [We will] support civilian authority [and cooperate with the 100 million loyal and patriotic Americans to promote 100 percent Americanism."

From the beginning, however, it was the first of these "basics" derived from the Legion's preamble—that of veterans' rehabilitation—that was the dominant concern.

Work in this area had begun even before the Minneapolis Convention. The St. Louis Caucus had resolved that a "War Risk Division" be created at National Headquarters. A few days after the caucus, Charles Sheridan was named national war risk officer. The division was named for "war risk" because at the time it appeared that its principle work would be with the War Risk Insurance Bureau. It could have been called simply the Service Division, Sheridan explained, since it dealt with every government office in Washington, with various state and city government offices, and with private individuals and service organizations throughout the country. Sheridan soon hired a few others to help him in the work.

At that point, also, each state Legion organization was asked to appoint a War Risk Insurance officer for the state as well as local war risk officers at each post. On June 18, War Risk Bulletin 1 was sent from New York City instructing the departments in the proper manner of handling that kind of work. State war risk officers were instructed to take up the ordinary or routine cases directly with the proper government office. The extraordinary or difficult ones they were to refer to the National War Risk officer. In this way, large-volume case handling was organized on the state level and a highly specialized service at "National" for especially difficult cases.

In mid-August 1919, Legion representatives had been invited by R. G. Cholmeley-Jones, director of the U.S. War Risk Insurance Bureau, to a conference of organizations directly interested in such matters. There the director had unveiled his plans for a nationwide campaign "to facilitate adjustment of [veterans'] allotment and allowance accounts, compensation and claims, and reinstatement of lapsed or canceled insurance"—in effect, to revamp the much criticized contact work between the bureau and veterans.

Charles Sheridan and J. F. J. Herbert attended for the Legion. Other organizations represented included the American Red Cross, American Library Association (Library War Service), Jewish Welfare Board, Knights of Columbus, National Catholic War Council, National Council of World War Veterans, National Tuberculosis Association, the Salvation Army, War Camp Community Service, and the Y.M.C.A.

The director's plan called for the home service sections of the Red Cross to receive all inquiries by veterans about such matters and, thereby, serve as a clearinghouse for War Risk Insurance matters among the members of the various veterans' organizations.

In practice, the veteran claimant's inquiry would come to the nearest Red Cross Home Service Section, which would in turn transmit that inquiry to its Washington office for delivery to the War Risk Insurance Bureau. Uniformity, speed, and the prevention of duplication were the chief goals of the bureau's plan. Those veterans needing immediate medical care were to be referred directly to the Public Health Service.

By October 1919, the Legion's War Risk Division, with its complement of state officers, had achieved some noteworthy successes: upward of $15,000 for war risk allotments; $2,000 in claims against the U.S. Army; $1,500 in allotments made through the Quartermaster Department; $1,500 a month compensation payments being made because of Legion intervention; $10,000 worth of Liberty Bonds; $200,000 in War Risk Insurance secured awards; and the release of five soldiers from prison. The division had even located the service-related lost baggage and effects for upward of one hundred individuals.

Just five weeks after the convention, D'Olier performed what he referred to as the first official act of his administration by calling the state commanders to Washington, D.C. on Monday, December 15 for three days of determining what legislation the Legion would support for aiding disabled veterans. What resulted was the precursor of the Legion's subsequent all-important Washington Rehab conferences.

State commanders critiqued the performance of the agencies. The conferees attempted to sift from the many bills being offered on Capitol Hill those that truly addressed the proper protection of the disabled man and his dependents. They discussed what should be done to make War Risk Insurance more appealing to those who still held policies and to the many who had allowed theirs to lapse.

Tom Miller and John Thomas Taylor, the Legion's legislative duo, also attended. Before, when they had approached elected officials on the Hill, they had found "soldiers' legislation" subordinated to issues said to be more "timely," such as the issues featured daily in the press. There was the current process for returning the wartime federalized railroads to private ownership. The League of Nations was also much in the news (Congress had rejected President Wilson's reasoning and finally his pleas for joining this new forum for international debate).

Miller and Taylor sensed that the gathering of Legionnaires in the capital was about to make legislative history, because the trek of the conferees to the Hill, planned to take place during the conference, was a novel approach designed to impress Congress with the urgent need for decisive action on veterans' issues.

It should be noted that this first "Rehab Washington Conference" was aided financially by the War Risk Insurance Bureau whose director, R. G. Cholmeley-Jones, had once again, as in August 1919, invited the Legion to participate in a conference of veterans' groups and the governmental agencies that dealt with veterans' benefits. (The bureau paid the travel expenses for the representatives of the various veterans' organizations to come to Washington.) Cholmeley-Jones, it was said, had made the invitation against the advice of some inside the agency who feared that criticism by the Legion following the previous conference would erupt into a heated exchange. The director, however, was a Legionnaire, and he chose to follow his own counsel.

When the Legionnaires attending the conference assembled for their own meetings, D'Olier was favorably impressed immediately by the apparent quality of work the state commanders and their adjutants had done in their individual departments and, particularly, by their attitude about the work that lay ahead. They showed, he said, "the most wonderful spirit you ever saw in your life . . . they worked so hard, they thought so clearly, they played so fairly. . . . They had just one idea in their mind—the good of the Legion."

Here it is important to note that as significant a role as the National Executive Committee had come to play, it was the state commanders who were called to the conference in Washington in mid-December. Though the N.E.C. was the functional heir of the earlier, temporary, between-caucus governing entity, state organizations were in place now, properly elected and officially sanctioned to represent individual veterans who were making claims. Thus, in little more than a month after the first national convention, the local, state, and national elements of the organizational structure were already working together effectively.

The governmental agencies, too, D'Olier reminded the conferees, had been formed on good principles. But they had been hampered by the enormity of their respective tasks, by the entrenched bureaucratic penchant for red tape, and, of course, by generally inadequate enabling funds from Congress.

The first day of the conference was given to a review of the Sweet and Wasson Bills then being considered in the Congress.

There was criticism in abundance of the governmental agencies. For openers, there was an original idea—the concept of a new governmental bureau encompassing the three veterans-related agencies (an early mention of a Veterans Administration–style superagency).

The conferees agreed that federal War Risk Insurance was still the best insurance value possible for veterans. Though veterans had been advised before by the Legion to renew their policies and convert term insurance (that issued during the war) into permanent policies, the large majority of the original policy holders had allowed their policies to lapse. The Legion blamed the War Risk Insurance Bureau for poor service that discouraged former policy holders and for a lack of willingness to publicize effectively the long-term benefits of the insurance.

Also, the state commanders wanted the bureau to bring its services closer to the people by establishing regional offices. To ease the process of policy premium payments, many called for local post offices and rural delivery carriers to accept and process the remittances.

The Legionnaires reiterated their qualified support of the Sweet Bill, which would more than double compensation to the disabled and add other attractive features to the government insurance program. Though the Legion was not completely happy with the bill, its recent passage by the Senate Finance Committee and its slating for consideration on the floor of the Senate was encouraging. Additional amendments would only slow down the process, it was said. (The bill as passed, however, did reflect appreciably the mandates of the Minneapolis Convention. The drafters and the redrafters of the bill presumably had heard and heeded the Legion's expertise and concern.)

The Federal Board for Vocational Education received the most criticism. While the law guiding it was called adequate, the agency itself was said to be incompetent. Though three cabinet officers sat on the board, internal wranglings were said to greatly impede the agency's operation.

Marquis James's first assignment with the *Weekly* had been the writing of two articles (for the September 19 and 26, 1919 issues) criticizing the Federal Board. He had dared to make a purely fictional reference to a shake-up at the board, writing that, "The report is current about Washington that the premises of the . . . Board . . . are due for an official housecleaning, and some imminent heads are going to fall." For increased distribution, a shortened version of the article was released to newspapers. James later admitted that the insinuation about an impending shake-up at the board was "a piece of journalistic audacity that worked," causing the board to engage in some self-examination. That was necessary, as James described it, because the board had "the worst record, the least excuse for it [and] behaved with very bad grace."

James had faulted the board mainly for the dismally small number of veterans placed in gainful employment. The federal government had passed the original Vocational Rehabilitation Act on June 27, 1918, creating the Federal Board and appropriating $2,000,000. Not many wounded veterans had returned as yet in those days, and the board had had some leisure during which to organize and prepare. But the wounded began being discharged from whatever hospitals were available, and there was, James continued, an unnecessary delay before they were taken into the training program. Though the law implementing the board had been revised, the board did little to relieve the situation, he charged.

As for the Treasury Department's Public Health Service, inadequate funding and facilities were cited as that agency's chief problems.

On the second day of the Washington conference, the Legionnaires adjourned at 10:00 A.M. and went en masse to the Capitol and the Senate and House office buildings to impress upon their senators and representatives the need for the Sweet and Wasson Bills to be passed.

They had been told by Tom Miller to "be specific and be firm." Apparently they followed his advice to the letter. Capitol Hill, by many accounts, had rarely, if ever, been approached by more resolute people in such numbers and manner.

On Tuesday evening several elected officials hosted a dinner for all delegates to the conference in the House's basement restaurant. The Legion on its own invited several disabled men from the Walter Reed Army Hospital in Washington. The presence of these veterans made unavoidably visible to the politicians the various disabilities with which thousands of other veterans struggled daily and which impoverished them.

"These men are only twenty minutes from your Capitol," the national legislators were told. The stricken guests, an infantry corporal, a private, a tank corps sergeant, and the others, were asked to tell of their difficulties, in addition to their physical condition, that they now faced in receiving what few benefits were available to them.

Wednesday morning the conference continued, but in the afternoon, Senator Smoot, chairman of the Senate subcommittee dealing with veterans' affairs, sent for D'Olier to discuss the rewritten amendments upon which the committee at this point had agreed. Two days later, the Sweet Bill, whose sponsor himself was said to have despaired of its reaching the Senate floor before the Christmas recess, was not only brought forth, but it also passed, increasing benefits from thirty dollars to eighty dollars per month for total disability. The next day, Saturday, the House passed it, also. Now the Legion's Legislative Committee could concentrate on the push for the Wasson Bill.

The Legion savored its first legislative victory in the same Congress that had chartered it only three months earlier.

On the heels of the Washington Rehab Conference came a meeting of the N.E.C. on December 20 in Indianapolis.

The first order of business was the election of a national treasurer. D'Olier had appointed a temporary treasurer, Gaspar Bacon, out of necessity, he said, though he acknowledged he hadn't the authority to do so.

Robert H. Tyndall, vice-president of a local bank, was nominated and quickly voted into office.

He spoke encouragingly about the possibilities of securing a $100,000 loan locally. At dinner Saturday evening he and D'Olier reviewed the entire Legion situation, looking to the loan to enable the organization to continue until it could begin to sell the preferred stock of the magazine. That stock, it was hoped, would repay the loan in addition to earning another $150,000 to turn back into the magazine until increased circulation and advertising volume made it self-supporting. If enough preferred stock could be sold during the spring and summer of 1920, the committeemen were told, the entire $250,000 borrowed during the summer of 1919 could be repaid. As before, it was assumed that the magazine's financial star was well on its way to a proud and profitable zenith.

(A few days later, however, D'Olier learned that the loan Tyndall had hoped to secure had not come through. Also, a $20,000 loan arranged by Lemuel Bolles was soon due. D'Olier met with Roger Winthrop, new chairman of the Finance Committee, and handed him the job of raising money.)

The growing national organization generated other items of business. One of the most heartening was the report by Dr. T. Victor Keene of Indiana about the state legislature of his state, along with the city of Indianapolis and the county government there, having promised to build a National Headquarters building for the Legion. In the meantime, the Indianapolis Chamber of Commerce had arranged for temporary quarters for the Legion in the Meridian Life Building and was even paying the rent.

The Legion's first full year began January 1, 1920, and one New Year's message to D'Olier indicated that one of the tedious suspicions about the original intentions of the organization was still in evidence. Dr. F. A. Cogswell of Leona, Kansas, in sending his wishes for a happy New Year, noted, also, that he had found "quite a lot of Kansas privates and noncoms who refuse to join the Legion, saying they believe it was organized at the instigation of 'big business' and national political leaders."

The national commander no doubt sighed wearily at yet another assumption that politics was corrupting the Legion. But D'Olier could affirm that the Legion had already taken the doctor's good advice to act definitely in the interest of securing justice for the common soldier and to "act so plainly and forcibly that no one can doubt its honesty and fairness." In looking over the schedule of meetings for January, for example, he saw the evidence of the Legion's already varied interests: the Military Policy Committee was scheduled to appear before the Military Affairs Committee of the House of Representatives on January 14–16; the Americanism Commission would meet on January 19 with state Americanism chairmen; and the Land Settlement and Home Aid Committee would gather in Washington, D.C. to be on hand when on January 14 governors from western states met there to discuss land reclamation. In each of these activities, rank and file veterans were either represented, enlightened, encouraged to act on the responsibilities of citizenship, or bound to benefit by changes recommended for the good of the nation.

The next month the N.E.C. was called together again on February 10 in Indianapolis to consider the faltering Legion finances and the *Weekly,* two subjects inextricably intertwined in these early months.

D'Olier began with a bit of levity. He recited a few of the requests made of him as national commander, indicating the national stature to which the position had been raised. For example, he had been asked by the press for "a statement on organized labor, just as though I could reel it right off"; by others to help decide the Jack Dempsey case (the prizefighter was being criticized for not serving in the military during the war); and by a woman (unnamed) to lead prayer meetings throughout the country. He respectfully had declined in all instances. As for the prayer meetings, "My experience in the A.E.F. had not particularly fitted me for such duties. . . ."

Before the discussion turned to the strain on the treasury caused largely by the expenses of publishing the *Weekly,* D'Olier introduced a topic that was compellingly coincidental.

During the war, the National War Work Council of the Y.M.C.A. had amassed a deficit of a million and a half dollars in selling various commodities at military PXs or canteens. The Y.M.C.A. had not been expected to make a profit in its endeavors in this field, yet charges of overpricing had been leveled and considerable bad feeling had been generated.

Now, many months after the Armistice, an unexpected windfall had come to the Y.M.C.A.: the costs of delivering the goods to the cantonments—the charges paid by the "Y" to the federal government for carrying the goods in transport ships—had been refunded in the amount of $500,000.

What to do with it? Those heading the Y.M.C.A. knew that the money should be refunded to the soldiers of the A.E.F., but that organization had been disbanded. Perhaps, some said, the funds should be awarded to the American Legion as the largest veterans' organization growing out of the war for use in helping the disabled of the war. Would the Legion accept the $500,000 and apply it in some way to the benefit of disabled veterans?

D'Olier had requested a letter from the Y.M.C.A. explaining in detail how the refund had occurred. National committeemen rose to speak for or against accepting the money. Immediately some wanted to accept the money and put it into a trust. But others were mindful of criticism by those who charged that their organization, as one said now, had acquired funds "from Wall Street to start up." He warned, "If we take this money, the criticism will escalate, so be prepared to defend it." Someone reminded the group that it was still being said that the Legion was "a rich man's club."

As another put it, "The first cry that would come from the opponents of the American Legion is that the Y.M.C.A. is conscience-stricken and appeals to the Legion, which is representative of the capitalistic monopolies, to help them out of the situation, and so they tendered them a half million dollar heart balm." Someone else added, "Let it out that we have received the money and we'll be swamped with requests for help."

One, apparently entertaining a truncated view of the work ahead for the Legion, said that putting the money into a trust would simply be "tying it up for five years, and the best part of our work will be done before that time comes around."

D'Olier disagreed. He introduced a draft of a resolution to accept the money, a resolution he had prepared a few minutes before the meeting. It was adopted, the Legion's first trust was soon formed, and the first use of it was to retire $257,000 worth of notes at six percent interest that had been endorsed by Legionnaires across the nation in the summer of 1919 when the temporary officers raised the first operating funds.

Other topics were considered. For example, was there to be a "Field Department?" Some said such a service was needed to provide consultation to departments and posts. Others, the majority, voted down a proposal for establishing such a function at this time. The idea, however, had been planted and would reappear.

Another matter emerged as the most controversial legislative effort so far and one that would remain so for years to come. The topic again was "beneficial legislation," but the ensuing debate signaled the emergence of a long-running debate over what economic benefits were due to veterans.

The vehicle for the deliberations was the first detailed presentation in substantive form of the Legion's soon-to-be-famous "Four fold [later five] Optional plan" for compensating veterans for time spent in military service. This was the "adjusted compensation" issue, shortened improperly, its advocates would consistently maintain, to "the bonus." (Some posts fined their members ten or twenty-five cents each time they said "bonus.")

When D'Olier mentioned the word "bonus" in his introductory remarks on land settlement and home aid—two other potential benefits often discussed—a committeeman remarked that previously he had supposed a bonus was a reward given in addition to one's regular pay. Used in that sense, he objected to the word.

But he had changed his mind "after I had been home for some time and learned more of actual conditions. . . . I found that men were returning home busted while others who stayed at home had their jobs and the chance to accrue very large savings balances." He decided then that a "bonded bonus" of fifty dollars per month for "the average eight months most spent in service" would be a suitable benefit.

"Can we believe those who tell us the country can't stand another bond issue presently?" one asked. Another recommended that they "must go to Washington to push for [a bonus]. The morning paper says the Wasson Bill has been thrown over the transom."

There began then a review of the action of the Minneapolis Convention in putting the matter back in the lap of Congress. Several saw that as a weak response. "The majority of men, you'll find in talking with local or state officers, will say, 'What about our bonus?' So you see where their interest lies," one said. And as for a "reward," they didn't mean a bonus in that sense. "They believe they are entitled to it [as] equalization . . . with those who stayed home."

Indeed action was called for, several said. As one put it, "All eyes are on the Legion meeting now. The World War Veterans [which reportedly was demanding federalization of some mines and other industries to employ veterans] is competing with the Legion for the favor of the rank and file. We are accused of being an officers' organization. We are nearly that. We have been accused of being highbrow, and we are." The Legion must do something "Today!" he said, to prove that it was working for all veterans. But another said that when one looked at the Legion's public statements about "service to comrades and service to country" that didn't seem to allow for strapping the nation with an "overburdening bonus."

The discussion turned then to a finer point of Legion governance. Was it permissible for the N.E.C. to expand and improve upon a national convention policy when that supreme body had merely repeated the belief that Congress was responsible for formulating veterans' compensation legislation? While several said no, the majority favored the view that the N.E.C. had full power to act for the Legion in the interim between conventions. Congress had failed to act in the four months since the convention. The N.E.C. should act, it was concluded.

D'Olier appointed a three-man committee to draft a compensation resolution. When the three reported back, their resolution included a call for a fifty dollar bond for each month of military service. The majority approved; the resolution passed.

This move, as in the area of benefits for the disabled, had been hinted at in the summer of 1919, when the Temporary Executive Committee was hammering out potential policy.

The Joint National Executive Committee of Thirty-four had resolved on August 12 that a committee chaired by Bishop Charles H. Brent, former head of the A.E.F.'s Comrades in Service, and which included Tom Miller and Theodore Roosevelt, Jr., would draft veterans' "beneficial legislation" with a distinct American Legion viewpoint, even though Congress was awash with veterans-related bills of all sorts.

When the Committee of Thirty-four appointed a Legislative Committee, Congress, also, had in hand a much ballyhooed petition, said to have over six million signatures, that demanded a bonus of six months' military pay for every veteran.

The ever-popular, newsworthy "bonus" (outright bonuses had been granted by several states) had been dealt with already at the St. Louis Caucus. There a resolution calling for a bonus was offered, and a delegate apparently speaking the mind of the caucus moved to lay it on the table. Not a single vote was cast to keep the "bonus" proposal alive. The consensus was that the time was not right. Better to wait until after the general demobilization of troops, it was said, so that all the former A.E.F. personnel could voice their views on the matter.

Many in Congress, however, continued to introduce bonus bills. In late August 1919, Tom Miller had reported a list of eighteen House bills pending, all of which included some mention of a bonus. A few days later, he reported another thirteen House bills, ten of which had been introduced by the Wisconsin delegation of ten representatives acting as one for this matter. During the 2d Session of the 66th Congress, ninety-one bills and five resolutions proposing some form of "soldiers' bonus" or adjusted compensation were introduced, most by individual congressmen.

During the summer of 1919, posts were urged to discuss the matter in preparation for action to be taken at Minneapolis. The bonus question could be settled there, it was supposed. In the meantime, the Joint National Executive Committee had purposefully held hands off the bonus matter.

Many in the Legion favored a quick cash bonus. Before the convention, several posts called for a referendum vote to be taken of the membership nationwide. The Minneapolis Convention had pondered the issue and had adopted a policy that emphasized the federal government's obligation on that score and, therefore, the expectation that Congress would act to carry out that responsibility. The convention passed two resolutions under the heading "beneficial legislation," those for land settlement and for "adjusted compensation."

Now in February 1920, the just-appointed three-member Beneficial Legislation Committee had brought in the fifty dollar bond resolution approved by the entire body. With that action the N.E.C. adjourned its early February meeting, primed to take up the same subject next month, knowing that there was not unanimity of opinion on adjusted compensation or even on the authority of the N.E.C. to be considering such a plan that had not come directly, etched in stone, from the national convention.

To D'Olier the differing opinions just expressed by the Executive Committeemen on "the bonus" was an object lesson. He counseled staffers and volunteers against taking the "big stick" approach by insisting that those who did not hold with the majority opinion should nevertheless fall in line. It was his way of walking the thin line between national and local authority. For that issue—the separation of powers—would surely appear in other debates (concerning revoking the charters of errant posts, for example) just as it was obviously going to suffuse the debate on adjusted compensation.

A few days later, the new Beneficial Legislation Committee and the former Land and Home Aid Committee (the two hereafter joined and given the title of the first named above) met on February 16 in Washington, D.C. with the National Legislative Committee and recommended a plan with four optional features for compensation, the "Fourfold Optional Plan."

The four options were (1) land settlement possibilities in all states, (2) aid to encourage the purchase of homes in the city or the country, (3) vocational training, and (4) an adjustment of compensation based on length and type of service for those who did not choose one of the first three options.

When on February 26 the House of Representatives decided by resolution that all "soldier related" measures, particularly those having to do with any adjustment of compensation, would be referred to the House Committee on Ways and Means, a hearing was scheduled for March 2 to March 24 on the many measures having in some fashion or other to do with veterans' affairs.

On the first day of hearings, D'Olier presented the Legion's fourfold plan to the House committee chaired by Joseph W. Fordney. From this point forward, the Legion's compensation concept, redrafted and revised during the next few Congresses, would be linked in support and even name with Representative Fordney.

Earlier, the Legion's Land Settlement and Home Aid Committee had as part of its assignment, obviously, the investigation of land reclamation and settlement as a primary compensation for veterans of the World War. It was a likely option to occur in land-rich, land-of-opportunity America. (From the historical perspective there beckoned the precedent of Revolutionary War veterans having been given land claims in payment for their military service.) At this point still, in early 1920, the consideration of this option continued to be a part of every draft of the Legion's adjusted compensation bill.

It was a popular idea. *Call of the Canyon,* the 1921 novel by Zane Grey, the prolific writer of romantic western fiction, featured a broken and dejected former doughboy who fled to the wide-open spaces of the Southwest to heal both body and mind. (For good measure, the cast of characters also included the ex-serviceman's fiancée, whose concept of patriotism underwent an enlightening change, a war buddy who lay dying in a veterans' hospital, and even a profiteer-slacker.)

"Shell-shocked and gassed, a wreck of his former sterling self and in many unaccountable ways a stranger . . . cold, silent, haunted by something," the fictional combat veteran, a composite character representing the plight then of the American veterans of the World War, had had heaped upon him a catalog of woes and physical disabilities resulting from his wartime service.

Moody and uncommunicative, he, nevertheless, was made to speak occasionally to the reader about "the chaos I've wandered through since the war." For a few critical months, unable to work, he struggled desperately to survive, a tormented time during which he was chiefly "concerned with keeping my body from the grave and my soul from hell."

His embittered view of America was not uncommon among fellow veterans. "My old job was not open to me, even if I had been able to work. The government that I fought for left me to starve, or to die of my maladies like a dog, for all it cared."

Zane Grey did not have his depressed doughboy consult the American Legion. Instead, he took him, characteristically, to Arizona, the land of the tumbling tumbleweed. There, with lungs weakened by gas and hemorrhaging, the ex-serviceman sat for weeks on the porch of a boardinghouse and breathed the dry desert air scented by cedar and pine. There he was eventually reborn, regaining his "spirit" (and his virility, the reader was cautiously assured).

And so there was healing, it was assumed, in the western environment, a region about which one first thought when land settlement was mentioned. Land for the asking! It was a dream of many young veterans.

The Legion's compensatory "option" of land provided for the division of large tracts of land into smaller tracts to be sold as farms to the ex-servicemen, the purchase price for which was to be paid in installments extending over several years. The plan, also, called for loans for improvements and livestock. The concept interested the governors of western states, who foresaw a productive influx of revenue-producing landowners. (The option included "reclaimed" land in the East and elsewhere as well.)

Compensation in land had been popular with national legislators, as well. The plethora of veteran-related bills produced by the 66th Congress included many in which was mentioned some form of land benefits.

A second option of the fourfold plan was that of "home aid"—loans for purchasing homes. In this choice, the veteran could receive from the government a partial payment on a city or rural home or for improvements to a home already owned, a figure based on a sum for each day spent in military service.

The third choice was the option for vocational training, with money to support the veteran and his family while he was in school. The amount of this benefit was tied to the length of the veteran's time of service.

But it was the fourth option, the misnamed "cash bonus" payment based on duration of military service, which was actually less generous dollarwise than the first three options and which caused the ensuing long-running furor over how much monetary compensation each veteran was to receive (and even why).

Before, neither Congress nor the Legion, each for its own reasons, had supplied the dollar details of a cash-equivalence for this option. But at the meeting of the Legion committees on February 16, actual compensation figures were devised: $1 a day for home and $1.25 a day for foreign service, with maximums of $500 for all home and $625 for home and foreign service combined.

Actually those figures were low according to many. Hanford MacNider, for example, the state commander of Iowa and a banker before and after his military service, figured it this way: The average enlisted man (age 24) had earned $25 a week, or $1,200 a year at the time he went to war. In the service he was paid $30 a month ($360 per year), "board" rations at 50¢ a day ($182.50) and $50 worth of clothing, for a total of $592.50 combined salary and allowances.

The difference between that figure and his average prewar yearly earnings was $607.50, which MacNider called the price the American soldier had paid "for the privilege of serving America" for one year.

And even if one disregarded the possible cost to one's health, the year had been lost for job advancement (or even retention), and the inflationary effect on the dollar, which was worth one hundred cents when the veteran left home made it worth about forty cents when he returned to civilian life.

This startling fact of economics was driven home forcefully, MacNider reminded, when the discharged ex-serviceman took the sixty dollar clothing allowance he had received upon mustering-out and headed into the clothing store on Main Street. Chances were that the attire with which he emerged was not nearly as spiffy as he had first hoped. Furthermore, outfitted in civvies a bit disappointing in quality or quantity, the ex-serviceman's search for gainful employment was likely to be long and frustrating.

Land settlement, home aid, vocational training, or adjusted compensation based on length of service—this was the Legion's four-point plan, devised because Congress had failed to produce one.

When the N.E.C. next met on March 22–24 in Washington, D.C. the "beneficial legislation" on the agenda was again the "Fourfold Optional Plan" to which D'Olier, in appearing before the House Ways and Means Committee three weeks earlier, had already committed the Legion.

The entire first day of the March N.E.C. gathering was spent on the topic. Anticipating disagreement, D'Olier referred to the N.E.C. meeting in December at which members had debated benefits for the disabled. "In spite of great differences of personal opinion . . . a compromise was finally reached and then unanimously backed by everyone, and the American Legion presented such a unified front to Congress and spoke so positively that work started [on a] Monday morning actually resulted in legislation passing both House and Senate by Saturday morning."

But one couldn't count on the same amount of empathy associated with plans to aid the pitiable circumstances of the more visibly disabled to work for adjusted compensation. Also, the pro- and anti- "bonus" lines had long been drawn, from the earliest days when state bonuses had come into being.

The first three options of the plan were fairly straightforward and not remarkably controversial. But the hubbub over the fourth option —that with the nettlesome moniker "cash bonus"—proved to be the first real test of the Legion membership's ability to disagree agreeably among themselves without their new organization being rent asunder by factions. Many inside and outside the organization were saying now that the bonus brouhaha would make or break the American Legion.

D'Olier pleaded the rule of the majority. A realist, the national commander never expected the Legion "to be absolutely unanimous on any subject except where real Americanism is concerned any more than I expect the country to be unanimous on any subject. . . ."

But, "The American Legion cannot fulfill its mission without organization and organization cannot be efficient without tolerance being shown by all. I personally have such confidence in the soundness of the judgment of the majority that I am always willing to accept their decisions, not merely because I respect the right of the majority to rule but also because I recognize the fact that the majority are almost always right."

Once again the Minneapolis Convention was referred to by those who favored the bonus as "a bonus convention" since the overwhelming majority of those first delegates favored adjusted compensation (though they turned to Congress to define it and act upon it). Most agreed also that the mood at the convention was one of hopeful anticipation that Congress would act and that a bonus of some kind would be the result. Therefore, the N.E.C. now had the responsibility to remind Congress again of the matter of adjusted compensation, since that body had recently done only half the job by passing the Sweet Bill for the disabled veterans, as deserving and overdue for that consideration as those recipients were.

Those who were against the bonus and also the N.E.C.'s action in the so-called "follow-through" of a convention mandate continued to voice their opposition. D'Olier welcomed their remarks. He "would rather run the risk of impairing the right of the majority to rule than . . . even indirectly interfering with the right of the minority to free speech."

The debate that followed included all the now familiar pros and cons. "When the war was on," Frederick Galbraith of Ohio said, "all the people placed their hope and faith in the servicemen, in their patriotism, their ability, their prowess, their strength, and believed them to be honorable citizens. Now that the war is over, and they need compensation for their losses even to a small degree, they are said to be selling their patriotism, selling their service, draining the treasury. They haven't been called 'grafters' yet, but that too is probably coming."

Some pointed again to wartime compensations paid out in the form of civilian bonuses, allowances for those in the Spruce Service, profits made by those in munitions factories, and compensation allowed to manufacturers.

One recent telephone survey of randomly selected posts from across the nation conducted by National Headquarters showed ninety-three posts for and thirty-one against the bonus plan. The committeeman from Minnesota referred to the ninety percent favorable opinion there, a state which was among the tops in the nation for the percentage of Legion members among the state's total World-War veteran population.

But an Indiana post wired notice during the meeting of its opposition to the bonus: "[The] Legion as an organization should not ask for this bonus. Only in proportion as its motives are unselfish will the Legion serve as the greatest single influence in American social and political life now and in the future. From the instant the American Legion falls from its high and patriotic plane, its influence will wane, and we shall see the beginning of the end of the cleanest and soundest single influence in America." (From within the Legion, opposition to the bonus was usually twofold—that it would bankrupt the nation and, as the telegram above indicated, that military service was an obligation and not due cash bonuses.)

Perhaps, seeing the set jaws and straight backs of bonus opponents sitting before him, D'Olier invoked the spirit of the Paris Caucus. "Don't lose sight," he said, "of the fact that we are American citizens first and what we decide must also serve the U.S. as well as veterans."

After an open debate during which all arguments for and against were reiterated, the chair called for the "sentiment" of all the forty-seven states represented, asking the committeemen to speak in their representative rather than personal capacity. In the spirited roll call that followed, the committeemen responded with vigor and conviction. Several indicated that they had conducted polls of varying scopes among their constituents about the "adjustment" issue. Most said that at home the members preferred a cash bonus.

Others pointed at rifts among some Legion state officials and their memberships. In California, for example, when Dr. David P. Barrows, president of the University of California and state commander of the Legion, came out against the bonus, California Legionnaires opposed him and declared themselves for the bills that the National Legislative Committee were lobbying for in Congress.

After hearing several such exchanges of opinion, D'Olier estimated the "sentiment" to be four-to-one in favor of the Fourfold Plan. The minority, however, was vocal and persistent. As the committeemen adjourned for lunch, D'Olier, the ever-hopeful conciliator, reminded them of the group picture to be taken in front of the hotel. Though they may have tried for appearance's sake at least to look agreeable for the photographer, the deliberative N.E.C. had much more wrangling to do before it could stand in official support for, if not in total agreement of, legislation encompassing the Fourfold Plan.

When they reconvened at 2:15 P.M., Milton Foreman from Illinois spoke, desiring that they all stand back and gain a wider perspective of the matter. The discussion, he said, should rightfully include welfare work for the wounded, the insane, and the tubercular along with the four-point bill. "Before we commit ourselves to a program needing large sums of money for sound men, we need to find out how well these people who require our care are being taken care of, or not, by the government." These persons, Foreman said, "are the Legion's direct responsibility."

Tom Miller assured Foreman and the others that the Legislative Committee was taking the "affirmative action" for which Foreman was calling. The former congressman from Delaware also explained that legislation in the House was absolutely under the control of a five-man Republican steering committee that held fast to the power to call up or deny any bill for a hearing, especially those concerning appropriations of money. That committee, Miller said, "has more influence than it is intended to have under our system of representative government."

For that reason if for no other, Miller explained, the conservatism of that powerful clique must be challenged and adjusted compensation was the issue at hand with which to do it. (In this instance and others, Miller was not shy about lambasting fellow Republicans if, in his view, they threatened Legion policies or insulted Legion ideals.)

Reluctantly for some, the N.E.C. at its March meeting approved the "Fourfold Optional Plan." In the next few weeks the plan was drafted as a legislative bill. Introduced in the House as H.R. 14157 by the chairman of the Committee on Ways and Means, Representative Joseph W. Fordney, it was passed on May 29 by a wide margin of 289 to 92. Sent then to the Senate, it was referred to the Finance Committee.

The bill included provisions for (1) adjusted pay at the rate of $1 a day for home service and $1.25 for foreign service to maximums of $500 and $625 for home and foreign service; (2) vocational training aid; (3) farm or home aid; and (4) land settlement.

In the process of rewriting the bill, sponsors added a fifth option, that of "adjusted service certificates," actually a paid-up twenty-year endowment insurance policy with attached loan values. As before, large financial and industrial interests came out in opposition to the bill.

In late September 1920, the now fivefold plan was endorsed by the Legion's National Convention in Cleveland. On September 13, presidential candidate Warren Harding, senator from Ohio, came out in favor of the bill in the last few weeks of the political campaign.

New National Commander Galbraith called a meeting in Washington soon after the convention to consider the plight of those disabled veterans still caught in unsatisfactory circumstances created by bureaucratic malaise or their own ignorance of benefits available to them.

Galbraith also looked to the antilabor label placed on the Legion from the earlier period of strikes and other labor-related disruptions in which the Legion had acted to assure public safety, and sometimes individual posts had committed themselves to antistrike conduct.

He had welcomed Samuel Gompers's "declaration of principles on behalf of the American Federation of Labor," which had been sent to him by the labor leader in an effort to keep communication and understanding open between their organizations. Galbraith had answered that Legionnaires could find nothing therein with which to object, and thus could and should subscribe wholeheartedly "to every word."

At this point, National Commander Galbraith looked also to the internal affairs of the Legion. Galbraith insisted on an efficient staff for the divisions, compliance with budgetary constraints, a harmonious (even "pleasant and agreeable") working atmosphere, and salaries comparable to abilities and duties. "Contentment and mutual appreciation promotes efficiency in any force."

Finally, "No member of the national organization must lose sight of the fact that the real work of the American Legion is being done by the members of the posts and departments [the name given to state organizations of the Legion] and that they need all the help, encouragement, and sympathy it is possible to receive from their national headquarters. It is impossible to lay down binding rules to fit all cases. Let each case be decided upon its merits and the decision given with a view to helping our comrades rather than hampering them with an unsympathetic construction of hard and fast rules."

The 66th Congress reconvened on December 2 for a third session. National Legislative Committee Chairman Gilbert Bettman and Committee Vice Chairman John Thomas Taylor immediately arranged to appear before the Committee on Finance of the Senate to urge once again for the passage of an adjusted compensation bill.

Not much was to happen, however. "Political expediency demanded that Congress delay action upon the adjusted compensation bill," was how Taylor described it in writing. In person he was champing at the bit for action that did not come. The bill died when just before adjournment it was brought out by the Senate Finance Committee too late for a recorded vote.

In late January 1921, John Thomas Taylor complained of having become "a first-class correspondence clerk"—his "in" and "out" boxes were piled high as he promoted, explained, defended, and reported on the five-point optional plan to congressmen, to the press, through bulletins to the posts, to other organizations, and to those industrial and other associations whose opposition was getting large play in the press.

The activity of which the Legion's ebullient lobbyist both complained and boasted impressed National Commander Galbraith with the thought that the contest was soon to be won. The senator from his home state of Ohio was now the president-elect, and it was assumed that he sought to accommodate some form of veteran compensation. Also, the Legion's current compensation bill had recently passed the House in almost the same form in which the Legion had delivered it and with the addition of the fifth option—adjusted service certificates.

Thus encouraged, Galbraith could concentrate more on the other branch of the Legion's twofold rehab program—that regarding the disabled. He decided at this point that what the Washington office needed was a first-class service bureau, connected to the Legislative Division, so that more could be done to process veterans' claims that were being sent in from the field. He told National Legislative Committee Chairman Gilbert Bettman, another Ohioan, in late January, "We are not getting the results we should because most of the work is done by correspondence from Indianapolis, by visits of department men to the government bureaus, and by H. H. Raege's [rehab staff member's] visits now and then to look up cases."

To head up this new service, Galbraith wanted a man with "vision and industry" to record and pursue each claim. That, of course, called for more money, about $500,000, he guessed, which he hoped to find "in the most dignified way possible, but it must be procured."

Another goal for which the Legislative Committee worked—the consolidation of the three governmental agencies dealing most directly with veterans' benefits—also seemed to offer promise. Such a move, in fact, seemed to be much in line with the incoming Harding administration's plan for reorganizing bureaus and departments in Washington to save money and increase efficiency.

So Bettman targeted the Rogers-Capper Bill for attention, particularly negotiating the objections of certain influential congressmen to that bill so that a consolidation plan acceptable to the Legion could be handed to the new administration.

Before long the sponsors of the fivefold optional compensation bill found themselves worrying more over the attitude of the new president. Warren Harding, when campaigning for the presidency, was heard occasionally to refer favorably in his good-natured way to veterans' measures. As president, however, in spite of election campaign rhetoric, Harding had quickly assumed officially the anxious demeanor of a man greatly worried about the status of national revenue. Now he was found to have little to say about veterans' affairs unless pressed by veterans' advocates. When thus cornered, the president reaffirmed his interest, but asked them to wait until later to have costly veterans' bills enacted. Just how much "later" he was unwilling to say.

Soon, also, it was assumed by the Legion that not only was Harding absorbed in the tax issue, but he also was not getting the best and fullest information from his staffers, advisers, and other insiders about the optional choices of the Legion's bill. Among the ever-present gallery of observers in Washington it was said now that what was formerly assumed to be the president's conviviality was actually a good-natured inattention to, or even a fairly constant confusion about, complex matters of state.

The measure of Warren Harding was being taken; for The American Legion, the presidential honeymoon was quickly coming to an end.

Harding, to his credit, did apply the power of his office in April 1921 to a close look at the plight of disabled veterans by convening a "Committee . . . to Investigate the Administration of the Law in Caring for the Crippled and Impaired Soldiers of the Late War." (Even before that, Harding had requested the Legion to state its position on legislation for disabled veterans. National Commander Galbraith had responded on March 17 with a brief overview of what he hoped to see accomplished for them.)

In addition to the chairman, the well-known Charles G. Dawes, first director of the Bureau of the Budget (1921) and later Calvin Coolidge's vice-president, the committee included labor leader John L. Lewis, four doctors representing the Treasury Department (Doctors Frank Billings, Pearce Bailey, William Charles White, and John G. Bowman), Henry S. Berry, Mrs. Henry R. Rea, Miss Mable Boardman, T. V. O'Connor, and Dr. C. E. Sawyer (representing the president).

The Legion, too, was represented on the investigative committee and used the opportunity to advance the concept of consolidating the three government veterans' agencies into one all-encompassing veterans' bureau.

Those so chosen were National Commander Frederick Galbraith, Past National Commander Franklin D'Olier, Thomas Miller (now Alien Property Custodian), Theodore Roosevelt, Jr. (now Assistant Secretary of the Navy), and Milton J. Foreman. (The committee would also hear testimony by Abel Davis of the Legion's Hospitalization Committee.)

Chairman Dawes set the tone for the committee's work. "We know the conditions and they are deplorable. There are insane ex-soldiers in the jails and poorhouses of the country while hospital beds remain empty. The thing is to find a remedy. We will stay in continuous session. The soldiers while on the other side worked all night. Instead of going out to dinners and coming back the next morning blinking like a lot of mesmerized toads, without energy, let us stay in session until we get through." He also said that there was to be "no muckraking." Instead, the group would look to positive solutions.

Dawes called on Galbraith to give "an overview of the general situation." The national commander quickly reiterated the three primary requirements for successful rehabilitation. The "discharged veteran must be afforded medical treatment and hospital care as long as his physical condition can be improved thereby; cash compensation for the financial loss his disability occasions him and his dependents; and vocation training to enable him to overcome as far as possible the vocational handicap imposed by his disability."

Galbraith reviewed the establishment of each of the three agencies dealing with veterans and what each purported to offer: the Public Health Service ("functioning as an agent of the War Risk Insurance Bureau"); the Bureau of War Risk Insurance (financial support), and the Federal Board for Vocational Education (for vocational training).

The three had begun at different times and had developed independently, he said.

But the system was not working. "The War Risk Insurance Bureau is in Washington and is not permitted to go out and search for the men." Decentralization, therefore, of this agency was essential. Also, the bureau "has no facilities, no hospitals, no medical staff . . . all that is delegated to the Public Health Service, which is overburdened." Finally, the Federal Board for Vocational Education, he charged, had done little so far to train sizable numbers of veterans.

"To receive the three benefits which always should be continuous and often simultaneous, the disabled man must transfer from the jurisdiction of one organization to that of another. Attending each transfer is a hiatus when the veteran is under the wing of no agency and consequently without either medical care, financial support, or vocational training." Currently, he said, there were 91,000 cases being dealt with, 10,000 of which were more than nine months old.

To the credit of the Legion, Chairman Dawes readily agreed to have the National Commander do much of the questioning of those the committee consulted. Galbraith quickly focused on those issues that the Legion had been working on for nearly two years.

On the need for new hospitals, the committee heard a doctor explain, "The hospitals in the country are now so distributed that even if you had autocratic power you could not find hospital beds where you want them for existing patients. They do not exist."

Many of the existing hospitals were little more than former barracks, cantonments of green wood and "beaverboard" with wooden underpinning. Fires had occurred at several of these sites. At other places, civilian hospitals had been given over to the military during the war, and now the operating boards of several of these sites had notified the government to quit the premises.

Dr. Lamkin of the Federal Vocational Board emphasized the importance of eventual government appropriations for more doctors at government hospitals being sufficient to hire "the best" talent available. Apparently that had not been the actual practice before. (Here another eventual Legion initiative may have been born, or further encouraged, during this discussion: action to aid medical education for the unique needs of veterans.)

R. G. Cholmeley-Jones, speaking for the War Risk Insurance Bureau, reported that the workload there was increasing. "I attribute part of it to the fact that men are now taking an intelligent view as to their rights, and also to the fact that they have been trying to bear up under the diseases from which they are suffering, not wanting to apply for hospitalization or compensation, but as they become more seriously affected by their injuries and diseases, they are compelled to make application. Then, too, it can be largely attributed to the work being done by the volunteer agencies in the field in acquainting the men with their rights."

Some 600,000 service persons had been discharged with some percentage of disability, it was said. Yet well over half of them had allowed their government insurance to lapse. That, too, was a problem that needed addressing.

Galbraith outlined ways in which the Legion could help in distributing payments for the disabled and dependents. "Would anyone know any better who went into the service from a little town of 200 than the men living in that town? Wouldn't they know more about the general condition of the health of their buddies than anyone else?" He cited problems existing concerning disability ratings and personal contact with veterans as proof that something needed to be done and as evidence of the Legion's availability to help.

Cholmeley-Jones added that the Legion might look to the problems of cheating on claims. "During the war and to this date there have been about 100,000 questionable cases where statements were probably not correct."

The committee viewed an organizational chart for the proposed veterans' rehabilitation agency. Chairman Dawes, the Legionnaires, and others discussed an illustrated, interlocking system of job titles and functions incorporated in a proposed new veterans' bureau.

At the end of the second long session of the committee meeting, Chairman Dawes appointed a subcommittee to write the report for the larger group. For this task he appointed Rea and O'Conner, in addition to Galbraith, Foreman, and Roosevelt of the Legion. Before adjournment, Galbraith and his cohorts presented a resolution that the $18,600,000 appropriated by the 66th Congress "for building new hospitals and enlarging existing ones be utilized for the purpose without delay." The resolution passed.

On the morning of April 7, the full committee met again to view the report. Chairman Dawes motion was seconded and adopted for Galbraith to handle the publication of the report in the press. Then the committee went to the White House to present the report to the president.

Two weeks after the president's conference, a printed broadside bearing Galbraith's signature and addressed to "Fellow Americans" explained, "Last January the Legion brought to your attention shocking conditions about the rehabilitation of disabled veterans. The press and people were aroused. Congress met and considered five bills approved by government experts and congressional committees. But legislative logjams in the dying days of the 66th Congress prevented passage of all but one of these bills. The four failed bills must be passed. President Harding has named a committee to study the situation and that group has reported; its recommendations have been included in the presidential message to Congress.

"The Legion is summoning its 11,000 posts and 2,500 units of Women's Auxiliary to petition Congress for quick passage of these bills. At the next meeting of your organization, read and sign the enclosed copies of the memorial and mail it to your congressmen, senators, and one copy to the American Legion.

"The bands have stopped playing, the battle flags are furled, but action needs to be taken to aid the veterans."

In mid-May, the N.E.C. created a national Hospitalization Committee chaired by Gen. Abel Davis of Chicago to help the Public Health Service extend service for sick and wounded veterans.

A few days after the investigative committee delivered its report to the president, calling for a new bureau to handle veterans' affairs, Joseph W. Fordney, chairman of the House Ways and Means Committee, introduced on April 11, 1921, into the first session of the 67th Congress a bill, H.R. 1, for adjusted compensation. The bill was basically the same as that reported by the Senate Finance Committee in the preceding session. The next day, Senator Porter J. McCumber introduced S. 506, the House bill of the earlier Congress as reported to the Senate.

Hearings before the Senate Finance Committee began on June 2. Taylor, Bettman, and Galbraith appeared before the committee. Senator McCumber, the chairman of the committee and the one in charge of the bill, struck out the provisions for land aid and settlement. The Legionnaires consented in order to move the bill with its remaining provisions ahead. Once again, opposition came from the U.S. Chamber of Commerce.

Less than a week later, the Legion membership was stunned by the news flash coming out of Indianapolis on June 10 about the death of National Commander Frederick Galbraith in an automobile accident. He and Milton Foreman were being driven to the train station late at night by Americanism Director Henry Ryan when their roadster slid off the road and down an embankment at 16th Street and Indiana Avenue. Galbraith, who had survived a ship fire at sea and enemy gunfire in France, was pronounced dead of a skull fracture at the scene. Foreman and Ryan were hospitalized. At the train station, William Q. Sutliffe, Adjutant of the Illinois Department, waited with the luggage of the national commander and Foreman; there had not been room in the car for him, so he had gone in another automobile to meet them there and board the 12:30 A.M. train to Chicago.

Franklin D'Olier was asked to return to take over until a successor to Galbraith could be named. In the meantime, the Galbraith funeral took place amid much public attention and an outpouring of sympathy to his family and the Legion. His body lay in state at Cincinnati, the standards of the Cincinnati Bentley Post, the Indiana, and Ohio departments, and the national organization at the four corners of his casket. In towns throughout the nation where there were Legion posts, standards were draped in black for thirty days beginning June 9. Legionnaires and others observed a few moments of silence as Galbraith was laid to rest.

On June 14, Vice-Commander John G. Emery of Michigan was elected by the N.E.C. as the third national commander. A veteran who had been wounded in combat, Emery said, "If I ever needed anyone's prayers, it is now."

Emery's attention was soon turned to national legislation when the Senate Finance Committee reported out the Adjusted Compensation Bill on June 20. When on July 5 the bill was designated "unfinished business" by a vote of 46 to 4, it was assured a place on the legislative calendar. The vote whereby the bill was given that status pleased John Thomas Taylor; because it indicated that the Senate genuinely wanted to deal with it decisively.

But the opposition outside the government, most notably the Industrial Conference Board and the U.S. Chamber of Commerce, continued to work for its delay. The Harding Administration, too, stepped up its pressure on Congress to defeat the bill. On July 6, Secretary Andrew W. Mellon sent a letter to the Senate urging that the bill be defeated. Its passage, he said, would impose an "intolerable" burden on the treasury.

Mellon's letter did not have the effect he desired. Senate compensation advocates stood firm. But those who agreed with the secretary approached the president for some tactic which would again stay the bill.

When Taylor next reported to Emery, he was obviously agitated. In characteristic grandiloquence, but with more than a tinge of combativeness, he assured Emery of his duty-bound single-mindedness, that he was "diplomatic and conservative" until in the heat of the fight, and then, "I intend to fight until the last whistle blows . . . [using] . . . the most vigorous methods I know, and . . . every weapon at my command." When given an assignment, Taylor reveled in carrying it out. "I will not backwater one inch unless instructed to do so by the N.E.C. or the national commander, and I will not be influenced by suggestions from Legionnaires, no matter how influential they might be . . . if their suggestions in any way interfere with our legislative program."

Finally Taylor explained the cause of this particular display of pique—he had just learned that Senator Boies Penrose moments before had moved for recommital of the bill ("at the request of the president, I presume"). If the bill was lost even temporarily, Taylor was prepared to "start the fight immediately in the House. We must not fail!"

In the House, however, Fordney was "going right ahead with the bill," regardless of what the Senate did. If the bill survived the House, and was sent back to the Senate before October, passage might be possible, according to Taylor. He reasoned, "A bill which has already passed the House and which has come so close to a vote in the Senate cannot ultimately fail, even if opposed by the Executive Department." In the meantime, he was hoping to get the second Sweet Bill, for joining the three veterans' agencies into one, through in a few days.

But on July 12, the president had appeared before his former colleagues in the Senate to reiterate his Treasury secretary's claim that the national coffers could not stand the strain of an adjusted compensation act. He asked that the bill be sent back to the Finance Committee.

The president's plea to the Senate, coming this early in his term, was heeded by his majority party, and the bill was recommitted by a vote of 47 to 29. When Congress adjourned, the bill died.

Taylor called it a fight between "Main Street and Wall Street." He blamed the U.S. Chamber of Commerce, Mellon, the president, and "a hostile press" for the bill's defeat. He cited Representative Fordney's article in the *Weekly,* in which the chairman of "the greatest committee in the House," Taylor said, and "one of the oldest and most influential members of the House" predicted that the bill would eventually pass.

While the chances for an adjusted compensation law dwindled during the summer of 1921, the Legion's efforts toward the consolidation of the three principal federal agencies dispensing benefits to veterans was rewarded.

The second Sweet Bill, largely on the strength of the presidential investigative committee's recommendations, became law on August 9, 1921, consolidating the War Risk Bureau, Federal Board for Vocational Training, and Public Health Service into the Veterans Bureau. The implementation was actually based on a series of amendments to the War Risk Insurance Act. President Harding appointed as director Charles R. Forbes, a chance acquaintance the former Senator Harding had met in Hawaii on a congressional fact-finding trip. Forbes had been director, also, of the War Risk Insurance Bureau since April following the hospitalization of R. G. Cholmeley-Jones (said to have been due to fatigue caused by the immense workload placed on that agency during and after the war). For certain, the American Legion, as a chief promoter of this consolidation, took a keen interest in the new Veterans Bureau's subsequent operation.

Abel Davis, Legion Rehabilitation Committee Chairman, and A. A. Sprague, the acting Federal Fair Price Commissioner for Illinois and now also new National Commander Hanford MacNider's own representative to the bureau, met with Forbes in mid-November to personally introduce Legion concerns and complaints. Already there had been reports from the field that political appointments had been the order of the day at some bureau facilities.

Earlier, the commander of the Department of Kentucky had specified instances of questionable appointments in his state. A month later, the Kentucky commander detailed more complaints. Soon there would be others from around the nation.

The Legion's own Lemuel Bolles had taken a look at the Cincinnati District of the new bureau and reported that "political appointments have not only been numerous in this the 7th District, but some of them were set sixty days prior to the passage of the Sweet Bill, which created the positions."

Bolles pointed out one senator who, "from all information, is the most vigorous prosecutor in this respect and has been very successful in placing his constituents with the bureau office in Indiana. I do not know that the 7th District is any different from others."

Before long there was more evidence that the Veterans Bureau was a dumping ground for job-seeking constituents of politicians. Legion founder Odgen Mills, now much involved in national Republican party politics (particularly in the party platform formation that led to victory in 1920), counseled against making too much of the commonly heard assumptions about offenses being committed at the bureau without real proof. Be aware, he said, that many of the men already in charge of the regional offices of the three former agencies now joined together as the Veterans Bureau are Legionnaires. That fact, emphasized negatively, could be used to embarrass the Legion, he warned.

But National Headquarters also learned that Legionnaire Congressman Louis Frothingham of Massachusetts, who had already declared himself for adjusted compensation legislation, was going to read into the *Congressional Record* a list of rentals paid by the Veterans Bureau for offices whose expenditures he considered exorbitant. An official charge of mismanagement of the bureau was already taking shape.

By mid-September it seemed to National Legislative Committee Chairman Bettman and others that Harding's postponement of the adjusted compensation bill by having it recommitted to the Senate Finance Committee was little more than evidence of a real determination to scuttle the bill altogether. Even bolder opposition was expected. Pro-bonus publicity from outside the Legion had taken a downturn, it seemed. "A good part of the press [is] opposed to adjusted compensation, and it is hard for our side to get newspaper notice," one observed.

Even the occasional unsolicited pro-compensation publicity could cause some concern. National Headquarters staffers no doubt wished that the recent references in the *Chicago Tribune* friendly to the cause had not made so much of the assumption that the fight for adjusted compensation was a do-or-die contest for the Legion.

Though overplayed in the *Tribune,* the insistence on the importance of the outcome of it all was, indeed, correct in that the failure of the adjusted compensation bill to become law could hurt the Legion's claim to be an organization for all veterans and not the disabled only.

The 1921 National Convention continued the practice of Legionnaires meeting once a year to form the primary governing body of their organization. Vice-President Calvin Coolidge addressed the delegates, as did others of more direct interest to the Legion, such as George L. Berry, representing the A.F.L. as president of the International Printing Pressmen's Union (and a member of Hawkins County Post No. 21 of Rogersville, Tennessee). Berry often served as chief liaison between the Legion national officers and organized labor.

It was a time also for honoring the leaders of the Great War. Marshal Foch and General Pershing entered the convention hall on the second day of the convention to the singing of the "Marseillaise" and the "Star-Spangled Banner." The day before, Gen. Armando V. Diaz of Italy and Lt. General Baron Jacques of Belgium had addressed the convention. The Montana delegates presented Foch with a wildcat kitten, and the aged marshal was made a member of the Legion. His speech was reread in English by Legionnaire Francis Drake of the Paris post. Following the convention, Foch was conducted on a 20,000-mile train tour of the country, accompanied by D'Olier and new National Commander Hanford MacNider.

Beyond the ritual and pomp, however, was a national organization eager to deal with matters of real importance. By now delegates to Legion national conventions were voicing their concerns and making resolutions on such topics of national importance as aliens, aviation, civil service, land use, naval military policy, education, immigration and naturalization, and public health, in addition to the organization's own specific interests of medical care and economic compensation of veterans.

The American Legion had become the expected convener of information and the expert about a most ambitious and varied collection of concerns. And the annual event of the Legion national convention was quickly coming to accommodate both a patriotic pageant of reknown and the working model of an American phenomenon—a democratic assemblage focusing on the issues of the day.

As to be expected, with the spotlight of the national press focused on the Legion in Kansas City and particularly on the subject of adjusted compensation for veterans, opposition in the form of warnings about the disastrous effect the bill would have on the treasury surfaced again. Legion publicists sought attention-getting ways of countering the criticism of anticompensation forces. National Commander MacNider provided a publicity coup when, immediately after the convention, from the special American Legion train taking Marshal Foch around the nation, he issued a communiqué stating that his father, C. H. MacNider, director of the Federal Reserve Bank of Chicago, did not believe that adjusted compensation would be disastrous to the nation.

Having helped appreciably in seeing three government veterans' agencies consolidated into the Veterans Bureau, the Legion now moved to form its own advocacy mechanism for veterans' rehabilitation. In December 1921, the National Rehabilitation Committee was organized. Albert Sprague was appointed the first chairman. The committee was composed of two groups: professionals, including physicians and educators, and volunteers who had demonstrated their interest and competency in the rehabilitation of veterans. District committees were organized corresponding in number and location to the fourteen districts of the new Veterans Bureau. Legionnaires on these "working committees" were assigned to investigate the treatment of nervous diseases, tuberculosis, medical and surgical cases, vocational training, and compensation and insurance.

The Legion's Rehabilitation Committee had been preceded by an active rehabilitation initiative beginning even before the first national convention, and it had focused on medical benefits. But it was pointed out at this juncture that the new Rehab Committee should look to the area of vocational training as the best way in which to be of aid to the new bureau.

Rehabilitation, for those formulating policy for the Legion, included economic considerations chiefly related to employment. In early 1922, 110,000 veterans were in vocational training and another 45,000 were expected to enroll. Local Legionnaires who were already employed were told that they could help in three ways: inspect the quality of government training and how that training was supervised; bolster the attitude of those enrolled in training toward their own rehabilitation; and aid the community to absorb graduates into its industrial and professional life.

In part, perhaps, to try to offset some of the criticism for proposing costly legislation, the Legion began a nationwide campaign involving two tactics for publicizing the official Legion view of the matter: presentations before local chambers of commerce and a nationwide "Service and Adjusted Compensation Drive" to gather information about veterans' medical needs and their preferences for compensation.

In the first phase, local Legionnaires were asked to enlighten local chambers of commerce (of which many were members) in their towns and cities about the options of the proposed adjusted compensation measure and to dispel the charge of treasury raiding, created, the Legion said, by half-truths and worse. In this way, it was hoped, the Legion could influence a positive response on the U.S. Chamber of Commerce's referendum.

Many Legionnaires reported to National Headquarters about their experiences with the local chambers of commerce. While some were met with entrenched opposition, more reported success. Not unexpectedly, there were those Legionnaire businessmen who reported to National Headquarters on local chamber of commerce letterhead paper that their own chamber had no intention of subscribing to the U.S. Chamber's criticism of the adjusted compensation bill and of the Legion.

The addresses on the notices confirming procompensation chambers of commerce sent to Indianapolis read like an American gazetteer: Adrian, Michigan; El Dorado, Kansas; Los Angeles; Marion, Ohio (the president's hometown); Des Moines; Omaha; Portland, Oregon; Seattle; Brainerd, Minnesota; McKeesport and Bedford, Pennsylvania; Oklahoma City; and so on around the nation.

One of the more impressive reports of success involved Legionnaire J. R. McQuigg, a past Ohio department commander and president of the Windermere Savings and Loan Company of Cleveland, who had already taken credit for adding that city's chamber of commerce to the proadjusted compensation roster. But when he reported that his talk before the Pittsburgh chamber of commerce met a similar response, National Adjutant Lemuel Bolles was moved to view it philosophically.

Saying that McQuigg had "carried the war into Africa" for having preached the Legion message in the hometown of Treasury Secretary Mellon—"bearding the lion in his den" as he put it—Bolles then stated a Legion truism: "This is simply another evidence that the American people are essentially fair, no matter in what walk of life they may be, and that all in the world that is necessary to win in our fight for adjusted compensation is that the great mass of American people understand the merits of the bill."

Bolles's expression of faith in the American people was a characteristic of that undefined but often evoked phenomenon: the Legion "spirit."

At first glance, the "spirit" of which Bolles and others present at the founding of the Legion spoke might be passed off as a fraternal cliché. But as innocuous sounding as it might appear to the uninitiated, that "spirit" was an essential ingredient for animating the organization's psyche, composed of equal parts of an intuitive sense of propriety (as in the Legion concept of Americanism) and a fetching, fresh-faced naïveté that said that just because things were one way now didn't mean that they must always be so.

Bolles and others who trod unafraid among feelings and concepts apparently believed that whatever the issue at hand, if only the Legion's message was well stated and broadcast widely enough, the nation would embrace it since the Legion, this reasoning continued, was actually speaking the mind of the country, anyway. (Debate in the N.E.C., correspondence files extant from the Legion's first few years, and other sources all imply this belief in the rightness of the Legion's mission and message.)

As Bolles knew, such philosophical ponderings should not take the place of direct actions, and so the second phase of the Legion's current campaign to change minds about adjusted compensation involved gathering up-to-date information from the membership about how the provisions of a compensation law would be used by veterans. Such an activity could also include a survey of current needs among veterans who were still having difficulty with claims made to the new Veterans Bureau.

For this purpose, MacNider and the others organized the Service and Adjusted Compensation Drive, which was authorized by a meeting in January 1922, of national committeemen, state commanders, and adjutants. This campaign would eventually include the personal distribution of over four million questionnaires by teams made up of a Legionnaire and a member of the American Legion Auxiliary going, it was intended, to the home of every veteran in the United States. Instruction sheets encouraged the canvassers to "Get every buddy cared for who wants and needs it."

One of the main purposes of the survey was to prove wrong the opposition's contention that almost all of the veterans, if given the chance, would opt for the cash payments. When Hanford MacNider was Iowa department commander, he had initiated just such a survey. The "Iowa Plan" had proven that not all veterans wanted the cash bonus. It also netted 18,000 new members. While survey volunteers were cautioned against speaking of or using the survey simply as a membership drive, that aspect was indeed a worthwhile corollary.

Soon after the survey was authorized by the N.E.C., National Headquarters took a quick and selective poll of a few departments and none too surprisingly found that the options chosen from the fivefold choices related directly to the economic conditions of the area being queried. It was guessed from the results of the poll that nationally less than one-half of the veterans would opt for the "ready money."

The nationwide survey also provided, as a byproduct, a good test of the ability of Legionnaires in the field to work together effectively. Department vice-commanders were to supervise the survey in their congressional districts, aided by district committeemen who were to oversee the work of county chairmen, who, in turn, helped direct post commanders whose post members, with the help of Auxiliary members, conducted the actual survey.

In early 1922, Secretary Mellon once again took his anticompensation campaign to the House of Representatives. On February 2, he appeared before the House Ways and Means Committee and told them that the Treasury was operating at a loss already. The deficit for 1922 would be $24 million; for 1923 he estimated a loss of $167 million.

Sensing that the doomsday rhetoric of the nation's chief fiscal officer might sway House members, Legion leaders met with leading representatives and with the president, eventually agreeing with the chief executive that the cash feature of the bill be restricted to veterans who would be entitled to fifty dollars or less. Also, the land settlement provision was dropped from the current version of the bill. A new option was added: veterans were to be allowed to borrow on their insurance certificates. So three options remained: home and farm aid, vocational training, and paid-up insurance.

On March 23, the bill passed the House by a whopping 333 to 70 votes. Immediately both sides began exerting pressure on the Senate. By the end of June, the Legion and others were poking fun at a Treasury year-end report that showed a surplus of $313 million rather than the deficit of $24 million about which Mellon had warned earlier. The secretary's $337 million "pencil error" was touted far and wide as either an unconscionable mistake or a deceitful attempt at misleading the public about adjusted compensation. Legion publicity also sought to remind readers of the Mellon family's industrial holdings in war-reminiscent and profitable commodities such as aluminum.

The Senate voted on August 31. By a vote of 47 to 22 the bill was sent to the president for his signature. Twelve veterans' organizations, ranging from those of Civil War veterans to their counterparts of the World War, urged him to sign. Instead, on September 19, as expected, he vetoed it. The country could not afford it, he said.

Back in the House, where it was known that the veto could be overridden, the bill was passed again, this time by a vote of 258 to 54. But the Senate's vote of 44 to 28 was four votes short of the two-thirds required to nullify the veto. The president had won, if narrowly, and adjusted compensation—now drastically *adjusted* and with no cash *compensation* cited at all—had been sidetracked again.

All the while the drama in Congress had been unfolding, leading to yet another delay in achieving adjusted compensation, the Legion had continued to assume, as a bulletin from National Headquarters stated, a "constructively critical attitude toward all officials and departments of the federal government having to do with the hospitalization and rehabilitation of war veterans." That meant, of course, a continuing close watch on the Veterans Bureau.

Some good reports were mixed among the mounting suspicion of political patronage and mismanagement at the bureau. In April 1922, the bureau's "clean-up squads" clearing the decks of outstanding claims were said by Legionnaires on the scene to be honoring Legion claim submissions. Decentralization of records, a necessity of immense proportions, was also said to be under way.

Near the end of April, it appeared that the bureau, though not officially, had, in effect, set up a special division to consider cases rising from the Legion's nationwide Service and Adjusted Compensation Drive just then getting under way in the majority of the states. Also, Director Forbes took the time to answer in writing a long list of questions posed by the Legion's National Headquarters.

Before the increasingly troubled four years were over for the Harding administration (the president died in his third year in office on August 2, 1923) several crises of confidence came to light, some to become full-fledged scandals precipitated by cronies in the "Ohio Gang," the president's inner circle.

Among Harding's associates, old friends and new friends (such as Charles R. Forbes) were those who if not exactly in the rogues' gallery of grafters nevertheless had idiosyncrasies that made them memorable. Among this administration's cast of characters briefly treading the boards of the Washington political stage was the president's personal physician from Marion, Ohio, Dr. Charles E. Sawyer, whom the amiable but increasingly put-upon Harding had made a brigadier general in the Medical Corps in the most blatant penny-opera fashion.

In fairness, it should be noted that Sawyer was assumed generally to have distanced himself from those who had gravitated to the president for other than honorable reasons.

The diminutive doctor was, however, a favorite foil for editorial cartoonists. As his critics tittered, "General" Sawyer, gussied and dour, seemed well on his way to becoming a U.S. public health czar when his friend the president appointed him "coordinator" of the Federal Board on Hospitalization. His tenure as the president's personal representative on matters associated with public health and welfare would be stormy. Many charged that the doctor had been elevated well beyond his competency.

Though Dr. Sawyer had set the Legion's teeth on edge by his penchant, in its view, for uttering offensive non sequiturs, some credited him for his part in promoting, if not helping to design, a plan for a new cabinet-level social-service department.

On this proposal, however, even those who gave him points for honesty, in contrast to some of the other card-playing chums of the president, judged the doctor's attempts at meddling in the executive branch as being simplistic and his proposal unworkable. In this arena he found himself at loggerheads with the Legion.

Dr. Sawyer had appeared early in the Harding Administration at hearings in April 1921 before the Senate Committee on Education and Labor and, in conjunction with Senator Kenyon, had presented the concept of a new cabinet-level agency—the "Department of Social Welfare" or as the follow-up of the president's campaign promise.

This new federal department, Sawyer said, should "bring together into one many of the bureaus, sections, and divisions of the government that are now apparently without favorable attachment." The free-floating agencies without proper "attachment," he said, were those of public education, public health, immigration, and the Federal Board for Vocational Education. These should be joined with agencies dealing with veterans' benefits to constitute the new "welfare" department to be overseen by one secretary with assistant secretaries overseeing the individual entities to be joined.

The divisions of this new federal department, the doctor explained, would be entitled Education, Public Health, Social Service (to include a "woman's bureau") and the Veterans Service Administration (for the administration of all veterans' benefits).

A disagreement between Sawyer and the Legion over such a combining of veterans' benefits with these other programs had been removed when the second Sweet Bill was enacted a few months after the doctor first unveiled his "Department of Social Welfare."

But it was as Harding's personal representative on the Federal Hospitalization Board that Sawyer was again at odds with the Legion for his refusal to allow congressional appropriations to be used for their intended purpose—to build government hospitals for disabled veterans.

Seeing disabled veterans languish for want of hospital care, the Legion protested vigorously during the summer and fall of 1922. The ongoing confrontation between Rehab Committee Chairman A. A. Sprague and the president's own doctor was often headlined in the newspapers. Sprague and the others became exasperated with Sawyer's interpretation of statistics in the continuing hospital bed count, which dredged up the tired assumption that a bed was a bed was a bed.

Why build hospitals when there were beds available in government hospitals, contract facilities to be had, and vacant government buildings to be converted to hospitals? Dr. Sawyer's frequent posing of this question brought down the full wrath of the Legion. Spokesmen for the organization said that they had explained all of that when pushing for the creation of a Veterans Bureau to coordinate the special-need facet of veterans' hospitalization and when helping to convince Congress to build more hospitals.

The 66th Congress had offered the bill commonly known as the First Langley Bill, and the president's signature on March 4, 1921, had created Public Act No. 384, which appropriated $18,600,000 for the provisioning of hospitals for veterans of the World War. The Secretary of the Treasury was, thereby, made responsible for the provisioning of these hospitals.

Appropriations from the second Langley Bill became available on May 11, 1922, and were to be expended by the director of the Veterans Bureau primarily for neuropsychiatric patients.

But from his position on the Federal Hospitalization Board, Sawyer had been able to delay the allocation of the funds of the two Langley bills.

One particular development around which the confrontation revolved was the doctor's letter to Sprague of July 12 which, when released to the press, was said by *The New York Times* to be an "astounding" indication of the doctor's apparent incompetence in meddling in matters beyond his ability.

In his letter Sawyer said that he was convinced that the peak of hospitalization of veterans had already passed (Sprague guessed it would be 1926 at the earliest). Furthermore, he was "opposed to the domination of people outside of the government forces in this matter." For "if the government is to be influenced by outside organizations, associations, or specialists' committees, we will continue to be in trouble."

When they first read that statement, national officers in the Legion undoubtedly were struck all but speechless. The doctor's assertion, of course, went to the very heart of the Legion's reason for being.

Perhaps the most poignant image of suffering veterans cited in the Sprague-Sawyer exchange was the warehousing, as the Legion charged, of about 5,000 shell-shocked veterans in contract hospitals which, it was said, did little more than collect the three dollars a day federal allowance that each veteran's confinement netted them. At the time, the Veterans Bureau's Committee of Neuropsychiatry agreed with the Legion that patients being confined in those circumstances should be transferred to government hospitals.

For several weeks the nation's press had reported the Legion's tussle with Sawyer. Finally, after a few national officers were permitted to see the president, the American Legion News Service (now supplying news copy weekly to nearly 10,000 newspapers) on September 27 announced, "After a conference with President Harding this morning, at which the president expressed his desire that any difference in opinion which might interfere with the best possible care of disabled ex-servicemen should be removed, Brig. Gen. Charles E. Sawyer met with Sprague and Doctors Lorenz and Salmo of the Legion, and they agreed 'for close cooperation between the Legion and the Federal Board of Hospitalization, which by executive order operates in its advisory capacity on all government hospital activities.' "

Sawyer professed complete agreement with a plan for removing veterans with mental diseases from contract facilities "at the earliest possible moment into government owned and operated hospitals." The Legion had won a skirmish, an appeasement in the longer running and more strenuous effort to get the hospitals built and equipped that Congress in the first and second Langley bills had already appropriated. The struggle would continue.

At its National Convention in New Orleans in mid-October, the Legion once again endorsed adjusted compensation. The new national commander, Alvin Owsley, was instructed to fight for the rebirth and eventual enactment of the plan. What hope there was for such a rebirth of the effort was unavoidably attached, oddly enough, to the impending, storm-laden fortunes of the Ship Subsidy Bill, over which a special session of Congress struggled from November 22, 1922, to March 4, 1923. Though that bill passed the House, a filibuster developed in the Senate so that all other legislation was held up. When the Ship Subsidy Bill was abandoned, all consideration of adjusted compensation suffered the same fate.

Owsley also inherited a now distinctly distrustful working relationship with Veterans Bureau Director Forbes, who did submit a ten-page report entitled "Hospital Data for New National Commander Alvin Owsley" in early November. The report in which he provided some hospitalization statistics that purported to show that the number of veterans being cared for was decreasing. Two days later, Forbes wrote a note to Owsley asking that the national commander try to keep criticism of the bureau out of the newspapers.

Before long, Forbes had been replaced as director by Brig. Gen. Frank T. Hines. Some earlier complaints of questionable leases and of misappropriated equipment and supplies now were said to be but the tip of an iceberg of mismanagement and outright theft in proportions hardly guessed at and never as yet seen before in a government agency. Forbes had gone on vacation in Europe but had returned to face federal charges. He would eventually be convicted and imprisoned. John Thomas Taylor had been appointed by the national commander to aid the government as requested in the ongoing congressional investigation of the bureau.

General Hines, in whom there was immediately more confidence and trust by veterans' organizations and others, had seen that almost all the contracts for hospital construction and renovation had been awarded up to the limit of the money appropriated by the first and second Langley bills. The Rehab Committee's most hearty efforts had been directed at promoting the bureau's hospital construction program.

The committee had also sent out the call for a survey of the threat of fire at all hospitals housing Veterans Bureau patients after learning of the fire at Ward Island, New York, in which some ex-service patients lost their lives. On a happier note, the committee agreed to order "radio outfits" for all Veterans Bureau hospitals for the entertainment of the patients. The need for occupational therapy was also stressed for those facilities with fewer than forty patients, the limit at which bureau policy cut off occupational therapy instruction. The American Legion Auxiliary, too, was organizing a hospitalization committee along the lines of that of the Rehab Committee, whereby an Auxiliary representative would be appointed for each district to serve as liaison with the Legion's efforts.

Another development at the Veterans Bureau was particularly pleasing. General Order 83-A had created a Cooperation Bureau, something the Legion had suggested long ago, whereby a cooperation section was created at every bureau office and subdistrict office, the duty of which was to coordinate the activities of the Legion with those of the bureau. Specifically, the cooperation officer was to be of service to service organizations such as the Legion, providing prompt and proper action when requested.

Other legislation had been pursued to some success. The third bill sponsored by Iowa Representative Burton Sweet had been passed in the waning hours of the congressional session before the spring recess and had been signed by the president. Though more ambitious originally, what had survived from the original bill was an extension of the time limit to three years for service connection on tuberculosis and neuropsychiatric diseases. Now after its passage, in one district alone, for example, 1,200 neuropsychiatric cases reportedly had been favorably adjusted.

The provision for tuberculosis, however, was "disastrous," according to Joe Sparks, the new Rehab Committee chairman. Though the time limit had been extended one year, the wording that had slipped through in the new act placed unreasonable demands on proof of ailment. The committee had gone to work to liberalize that provision so that the estimated 15,000 tubercular veterans not receiving treatment could be helped.

From March to October 1923, the Legion's National Legislative Committee planned an all-out campaign for next year. Taylor had prepared scorecards that showed that most of those in the House and Senate who earlier had opposed the adjusted compensation bills had been defeated in the recent congressional elections.

Conversely, most of those who favored the measure had been reelected. Majorities, then, were to be found in each chamber for overriding a presidential veto should the chief executive rely on that tactic again. The opposition, which Legion publicity again labeled "Big Business," resumed the alarm that tax reduction would be impossible if the veterans were compensated in the manner of the Legion's bill.

Predictably, for the fifth time the Legion's national convention meeting in San Francisco in mid-October endorsed adjusted compensation. A month later, Secretary Mellon, too, reiterated a surefire attention getter—tax reduction—as the prize if the adjusted compensation bill was beaten.

The final campaign for both camps developed in two phases. From mid-November 1923, to February 1, 1924, the opponents of the bill, which had the slogan "Bonus or Tax Reduction—Which?," inundated Congress with the heaviest barrage of propaganda ever visited on the national legislative branch.

New National Commander John Quinn readily admitted that his job was to get the bill passed. The Legion waited until February before unleashing its own brand of a letter and telegram blitz, complete with accusations that the opposition's show of force had been orchestrated by threats to the employment of those who did not support their employer's desire to shoot down "the bonus."

Quinn spoke at the Washington Press Club on the eve of George Washington's birthday and charged "some foolish executive" at one of Secretary Mellon's industrial sites with insisting that employees there write anticompensation letters to Congress or be fired. Quinn had scooped the newspapers; the accusation was featured prominently in headlines the next morning. Quinn, also, had defiantly proclaimed that the Legion would not be intimidated by such high-handedness. By specifying such an instance (it had been reported by a Legionnaire at the site), Quinn sought to help the public to visualize the opposition to the veterans' bill.

There was open opposition from the White House, also, now being voiced in the New England accent of Calvin Coolidge, who was already well-known for being as sparing of the nation's revenue as he was of talk. (However, he had signed a bonus bill when he was the governor of Massachusetts.)

But action in Congress looked more promising than ever before. By mid-March 1924, a compensation bill was passed in the House, again by an impressive vote: 355 to 45. Once again there had been revisions—this bill emerged without the original vocational training and farm and home aid details. The insurance provision alone remained among the original five options.

The Senate Finance Committee met on April 12 to decide which bill—that for adjusted compensation or that revising the national tax revenue—would be introduced on the Senate floor first. For the Legion it was much more than a routine matter of scheduling. If the tax bill was reported first, weeks of debate would follow and the Legion's bill was sure to be lost in the delay. That, in fact, was the plan of its opponents. But if the compensation bill was reported first, Legion strategists, scorecards in hand, believed it would pass the Senate with no more than twenty-seven negative votes.

After the Senate committee had met and decided on the priority of appearance of the two bills, a recitation of melodrama called "Taylor's Timely Intervention" went the rounds at National Headquarters, in which the intrepid Legion lobbyist, never one to shrink from employing the most dramatic tactics, was cast as the hero in a last-minute rescue of the imperiled adjusted compensation bill.

Dramatized for effect, the curtain was raised to show Taylor waiting along with a few newspaper reporters in an antechamber off the meeting room of the Senate Finance Committee. Beyond the door the committee members sat stiffly around a large mahogany table arguing over which bill would be reported out first.

As the hands of the clock above the marble mantelpiece crept toward noon, the witching hour when the committee was required to return to the Senate floor with its decision, Taylor sat impatiently in the antechamber. At 11:40, a clerk emerged and signaled to Taylor that the Legion bill would take precedence for introduction on the floor. Taylor sighed in relief. Two reporters rushed to the telephones with this unofficial news. Old hand Taylor remained and waited, as did the other equally seasoned reporters, for official confirmation.

Through the door left ajar the sound of debate continued. Taylor struggled to keep from showing the gnawing uncertainty that now alarmed him. Something had gone wrong! In less than ten minutes the clock would strike noon and the meeting would necessarily adjourn. If indecision remained at that point, it meant the tax bill would be dealt with first.

The clerk emerged again. Shrugging self-consciously, he looked to Taylor. "I guess I steered you wrong," he whispered hoarsely. "There is one holdout. They haven't actually agreed yet."

Taylor anxiously fidgeted for another five minutes. Then he approached the door. He asked for permission to speak to the senators. For once in his illustrious career, he stifled his tendency for table thumping and bombast. Instead, for a critical moment he tried mightily to project a calm assurance. Chairman Smoot gave him permission to speak.

With his hands held before him, giving him the appearance of supplication, but really to guard against flailing about in the grand gestures that were more his style, Taylor explained humbly and, he hoped, respectfully that already the nation and Congress had not only acknowledged the economic debt to the veterans but also expected that it be paid now. The proud and deserving veterans had waited five years. An honorable decision and one of long-lasting effect was now balanced on a pinpoint: would the compensation bill be reported out ahead of the tax bill? In a matter of minutes the committee's time for deciding would be over. Then, as if leaving the site of a tribunal of great consequence, Taylor stepped noiselessly and reverently back to the anteroom to wait.

A moment later the senators left the committee room. On his way out, Senator Smoot stated matter of factly, belying the inherent drama, that the Legion bill would be reported out first. The newspaper reporters hurried to file their stories. Taylor, man of action, stood for the briefest of moments to relish this brief episode in the four-year-long effort to gain veterans' compensation.

He was brought back from his reverie by the sound of the electric bell in the now empty committee room calling the senators to the Senate chamber. The procompensation decision had been made in the last sixty seconds before noon. Taylor resumed his air of importance and rushed off to wire the news to National Commander Quinn and Legislative Committee Chairman Aaron Sapior.

Now that the bill had survived the committee meeting, its appearance on the Senate floor was bound to cause more anxious moments for its supporters.

The Democrats, formerly opposing a cash option, now called for one to be added to the bill. The reasons ran from sincere desires to see veterans have that option, to less lofty politics in which such an amendment was instigated to cause the president to veto the bill (as he had already indicated he would) and thereby to lose the veterans' votes in the upcoming election. There were also Republicans who simply did not want a bonus bill of any sort to pass and who, therefore, also promoted the cash option to try to sink the bill.

Legionnaires from National Headquarters requested to see Democrats on the Senate Finance Committee and succeeded in gaining the abandonment of the cash add-on. Then miraculously, key senators who had bills of their own about to be debated yielded the right of way to the compensation bill. Suddenly all seemed in readiness for its passage at its scheduled appearance on Monday, April 21.

But the good news was short-lived. Senator Royal S. Copeland, Democrat from New York, announced that he would not be bound by the more cooperative spirit of the Democrats on the Finance Committee and would press instead for a cash amendment. He did just that on the 21st, and the day ended without the bill being agreed upon.

The next day brought more oratory, but again no decisive action on the bill, except for a leaning toward the Copeland amendment, which worried the bill's supporters. On the next day, Senator Oscar W. Underwood of Alabama spoke. Known for making few speeches and for the attention he received when he did speak, this senator, known to be antibonus, said he would vote for the amendment, but not for the amended bill. When at 3 P.M. the vote came on the amendment, it lost by a vote of 37 to 48.

That helped. After three more hours of debate on the bill, now consisting primarily of the insurance provision, once one of five options, the vote was 67 to 17 in favor.

Then came the wind-down to the "finish fight." On May 15, President Coolidge vetoed the bill. But the House the next day overrode the veto 313 to 78. On May 19 the Senate, too, voted. When the votes were tallied, the galleries in the Senate chamber erupted with the cheers of compensation advocates. The vote was 59 to 27 in favor. For several minutes presiding officer Senator Albert E. Cummins rapped for order. Word of the victory was flashed to Indianapolis, where the N.E.C. was meeting.

Back at the Washington headquarters of the Legion, John Thomas Taylor and his assistant, Edward "Eddy" McE. Lewis, rested from the last ten days of continually checking with fourteen senators whose votes seemed unpredictable or who seemed to be leaning against the bill. As it turned out, Taylor's scorecard was correct. (One senator had been queried just ten minutes before the vote.)

In Indianapolis, National Commander John Quinn, who had met with Coolidge earlier to ask that in the president's message accompanying his veto of the bill he not impugn the patriotism of the veterans, admitted to being one of those who had "tears streaming down our eyes" when hearing the news from Washington. He turned to National Chaplain Rev. Ezra Clemens of Minnesota and asked him to lead the assemblage in prayer. "That took the edge off," Quinn recalled. "And we started to holler, and that was that." The next day, the N.E.C. awarded a gold watch to John Thomas Taylor for his part in seeing the bill through and around a presidential veto to become law.

The cover of the *Weekly* for June 6 featured the well-known motif of the blindfolded figure of Justice holding a sword in her right hand and evenly balanced scales in her left over which illustration was a special-issue title, a direct, simple announcement: "The Federal Adjusted Compensation *Act.*" This issue of the magazine, a "complete manual of the new law," contained the text of the new national law, a detailed distillation in everyday language, and tables for computing the value of individual service credits and face values of insurance policies. There were also sample facsimiles of the application forms filled in to represent a real applicant: Private Thomas Richard Morris of Kennebec County, Maine, Serial Number 338,492, complete with the prints of the four fingers of Morris's right hand.

The Legion's role in the successful campaign for achieving the act was, of course, touted prominently. A sidebar to one of the explanatory articles transmitted the request of the army and navy that veterans not write to them, but read the *Weekly* articles and wait for the information sheets then being printed, which would accompany application forms. On the national commander's page, John R. Quinn proclaimed, "The Victory Is Won! . . . The Legion put it over." He welcomed "our non-Legion buddies" to submit their applications to local posts, which Quinn asked to be in readiness for the flood of paperwork. To the veterans who opposed adjusted compensation and particularly to those who for that reason had withdrawn from the Legion, the national commander referred to the majority of members who favored it, adding that "majority rule is the cornerstone of democracy."

Quinn still smarted from charges made during the adjusted compensation fight that the organization had but one purpose: conniving to raid the treasury.

Such an assumption, unfair and false, had some reason for being. The amount of publicity often required to get congressional action could impress the public with the appearance, at least, that the present concern was always the most sought after by the organization. Fortunately, the Legion had "other endeavors," Quinn explained. Much was still to be done in serving one's community and nation. He invited help. "Give us a helping shoulder at the wheel."

Though the original fivefold optional plan for compensation had been reduced to one provision, it was now the law of the land—a bird in hand worth several elusively on the wing.

All the while the adjusted compensation bill was taking the twists and turns to final enactment, there were other developments of importance to veterans' affairs.

One of the most important events in the decade of the 1920s for the American Legion was the establishment in February 1924 of the House Committee on World War Veterans Legislation. Not only was there now a congressional committee specifically created to hear veterans' legislation, but also the person named to chair it, Legionnaire Representative Royal C. Johnson of South Dakota, had an insider's view of the work to be done.

As soon as this House committee was formed, the Legion's Legislative Committee began coordinating the activity of other national committees that were drafting legislation to be presented to Johnson's new committee.

Even as the adjusted compensation contest was in progress, John Thomas Taylor and the others working closely with him began collecting all the amendatory changes that seemed necessary now that the existing veterans' laws had been in practice for three years or more.

Before the year was out, this amalgamation of corrections, additions, and other changes would come together as one statute establishing the rights and benefits of disabled veterans. Named the War Veterans Act of 1924, this cohesive policy of the federal government for the disabled of the nation's wars would be generated appreciably by the efforts of the American Legion.

THE AMERICAN LEGION EMBLEM

Even before the Minneapolis Convention in 1919, at which the Legion was first officially organized, the New York City temporary headquarters office of the fledgling organization dealt with the concept of designing, popularizing, and protecting what would become one of the most easily recognizable motifs in American history—the American Legion emblem.

On July 9, 1919, the Committee of Thirty-four issued a bulletin to the "State Organization Division" workers in the field announcing that on that day an official emblem button had been adopted and would soon be distributed so members could display their affiliation with the new organization.

The button was described as having a bronze center "made up of a small replica of the Discharge Button" issued to members of the A.E.F. during World War I, enclosed in a "narrow circular band of blue enamel containing the words 'American Legion.' " Ex-servicemen who had been wounded could wear a silver center in their buttons. The button was priced to sell at twenty-five cents. The Legion's Legislative Committee in Washington, D.C., the bulletin continued, was arranging to have the emblem copyrighted. The official seal of the Legion was to be an adaptation of this button-emblem.

Thus was begun a continual duty of the national headquarters, that of making the Legion's emblem a visible symbol of the organization, identifying not only the property on which it appeared but also signaling the public service–orientation of the many public activities in which it was displayed.

Immediately upon its design and announcement, the emblem was the subject of intense competition among firms wanting to manufacture the items of regalia for the new American Legion.

These firms "circularized" National Headquarters and also the posts incessantly to get their business. In many instances manufacturers used the emblem without the knowledge of or permission from National Headquarters. The emblem design was patented on December 9th of that year. Five days earlier, a restraining order had been granted by the Superior Court in Equity of the Commonwealth of Massachusetts against a company from publishing a song known as

"The American Legion March" and using a facsimile of the official seal of the Legion. Other injunctions followed in rapid succession.

There followed quickly, also, a series of announcements of items made available by the Legion's National Emblem office, which were becoming an important part of post and department functions. Many of these items depicted some aspect of Legionism: official Legion grave markers, silk or wool flags and banners for Memorial Day, lapel buttons fashioned after discharge buttons, an official Legion seal press, convention badges and souvenirs, department ceremonial badges, and official membership cards and receipt books.

Indicative, also, of the times was the announcement on December 8, 1921, of an "automobile radiator decoration" which was "an exact duplicate of the Legion emblem in colors, five inches in diameter and equipped with wire lugs for fastening to the honeycomb of the radiator." The radiator ornaments were also "especially well made to withstand the vibration that they will be subject to." A later announcement in August of the next year described "a smaller, neat, dignified Legion automobile decoration in full colors, 2½ inches in diameter, equipped with the same type of fastener as used on the various state automobile association insignias."

Emblem watermarked paper was offered on February 1, 1922, as well as membership buttons "in both midget and regular size" and "a real American Legion belt and buckle at last, made by Hickok, too!"

A Legion ring was offered first on June 23, 1922. In a non-air-conditioned era when during the summer members were likely to doff their coats on which were displayed their emblem buttons, they needed another method for displaying their membership, that is, if they weren't already using the official watch fob bearing the Legion emblem.

Summer was, also, a time for outdoor sports. In July 1922 it was announced that the manufacturer of Wilson athletic equipment would cut the price of its products to Legionnaires practicing for the preliminary tryouts prior to the National Athletic Meet to be held at the fourth annual convention at New Orleans. The next month the "standard American Legion athletic medal" was advertised "to foster and promote athletics throughout the entire nation." The announcement for this new product stated that the Legion, with its program for Americanism and fair play, "will dominate and be the controlling element in athletics." Such medals indicated that the recipient was the winner of a Legion sporting event.

Later that same summer, the first Emblem Division catalog was issued on September 6. One had not been issued before, it was explained, because "the expense heretofore [had been] prohibitive." Now also there were more items to advertise: official county banners (identical to the standard post and department banner except that the upper half was white and the lower half blue); goldplated membership buttons; a standard sixteen-inch No. 2 pedestal emblem lamp. The district organization banner was offered July 17, 1923, recently adopted by the N.E.C. as identical to county banners except for the wording. (At the convention the next year, each post and department appearing with official colors was awarded a silver flagpole band to help promote the appearance of colors at parades and other festivities.)

Thus the growth of the organization included a proliferation of items bearing what was to become one of the most familiar motifs in the country.

NATIONAL COMMANDERS, 1919 – 1924

The men who annually held the top office of the new American Legion in the early 1920s found themselves elevated immediately to national prominence. Their brief tenure in office was marked by the essential like-mindedness that reflected the spirit and purposefulness of the Paris and St. Louis caucuses and the Minneapolis Convention.

The first to hold that office was **Franklin D'Olier,** *who had attended both the A.E.F. morale conference dinner hosted by Theodore Roosevelt, Jr., and the Paris Caucus. D'Olier (Princeton, 1898) had worked at his father's company of commission merchants in Philadelphia until his war service. Commissioned in April 1917 as a captain in the Quartermaster Corps, he was sent to France in July, where he oversaw the salvage service for the Service of Supply, where his management skills earned him the Distinguished Service Medal.*

D'Olier was discharged in April 1919 as a lieutenant colonel on the General Staff and soon thereafter worked during the summer of 1919 as head of the division at the Legion's temporary headquarters in New York City, which was aiding the formation of state Legion organizations.

His year as national commander required precisely what this wealthy businessman could do best—to organize and exemplify a serious-minded group of young men who were capable, responsible, and energetic.

The overall Legion message, which ran a diverse gamut from Americanism to the care of disabled veterans, had to be presented with studied calm in a troubled time. This D'Olier apparently did well, rising to the occasion even though he was not by first choice a public figure and only by the demands of the office a public speaker.

Franklin D'Olier presented the Legion's viewpoint (even as it was being developed) by emphasizing the unique needs of veterans and the threat of radicalism. In a rambunctious era, D'Olier worked without bombast and with few demonstrations of anger or excitement. One who worked with him remarked that he had never seen D'Olier "hurried, worried, or flurried."

As with any new organization with an ambitious agenda, the Ameri-

can Legion sought recognition. This urbane, cultured, silver-spoon easterner, "Doly" to intimates, with his perpetually pursed lips and sly, self-deprecating humor, gave the Legion message substance and legitimacy just by allowing himself to be associated with it. His signature, along with that of Theodore Roosevelt, Jr., was sufficient to obtain a $10,000 note for the immediate needs of National Headquarters in the summer of 1919, before the Legion had come officially into existence and could generate any revenue of its own. His refusal of a salary enhanced his image as being someone who the office had sought rather than the other way around.

The first National Commander sought to represent the new generation of citizen-soldiers whose usefulness to the nation now as citizens was positive, selfless, and forward-looking. In the first year of the Legion's official existence, almost a million ex-servicepersons became Legionnaires.

Frederick William Galbraith, *looked the part of the no-nonsense national spokesman for veterans, many of whom in 1920 had waited too long for the government that had sent them to war to recognize and meet their needs as veterans.*

"Fritz" Galbraith had sailed the oceans, had in fact pursued two careers—as a merchant seaman on sailing vessels and as a successful businessman—before joining the First Infantry of the Ohio National Guard, becoming a colonel in 1916. As the 147th Infantry, this unit entered the World War, landing in France in June 1918. Assigned to the Baccarat Sector, Galbraith and his fellow Ohioans saw action in the St. Mihiel and Meuse-Argonne offensives and later in the Belgian offensive on the Scheldt River.

Galbraith returned home in April 1919. He had won the American Distinguished Service Cross, the Croix de Guerre of France, and the Croix de Guerre of Belgium. When veterans formed the Ohio department of the American Legion, Galbraith was elected commander. He also served as the N.E.C. man from Ohio and on the Legion's Publication Committee. Then he had the honor of being elected national commander at the national convention in his home state of Ohio at Cleveland in 1920. Previously, he had made himself known as an outspoken advocate for rehabilitation and for fiscal and managerial efficiency. As national commander he spoke convincingly about national-level concerns: radicalism, patriotism, veterans' affairs, public education, and national military policy. Like D'Olier before him, he continued the practice of giving expert testimony before congressional committees considering veterans' legislation.

He would have but eight months as national commander, dying "in the service of the Legion" (as the event would henceforth be acknowledged) in an automobile accident on June 9, 1921.

Described by his successor **John G. "Jack" Emery** *as having a "spectacular personality," Galbraith could rouse audiences, including the N.E.C., when he spoke about the Legion's strengths and its goals.*

But perhaps one of the most telling contrasts between Galbraith and Emery was exemplified by something that happened far from National Headquarters—in the work assignments each commander gave Legion staff persons in the field.

Galbraith believed the Legion's field representatives should be capable of motivating Legionnaires with inspiring speeches such as he often delivered, resounding with enough conviction to convince the general public as well of the rightfulness of the Legion's views.

John Emery, however, preferred to see that kind of inspirational work done by volunteers from the Speakers Bureau. Paid staff members, he believed, should help the departments and posts to acquire better accounting and budgeting practices.

Galbraith wanted orators; Emery wanted auditors. Emery moved to replace stump speaking in the field with instruction in fiscal practices.

Here, too, the different leadership styles served the Legion. Emery's priority had had the backing of Milton Foreman, for example, chairman of the first Executive Committee in Paris and, since the war, a respected adviser and chairman of the Legion's Finance Committee. As Foreman stated in the N.E.C. meeting in October 1921, the Legion "has passed the time where it can hope to maintain itself, its membership, its prestige, and its growth by mere enthusiasm. It must be organized on the basis of a purely business organization." Emery, most agreed, was the man to do that.

As a young businessman from Grand Rapids, Michigan, Emery joined the Second Officers Training Camp at Fort Sheridan, Illinois and went to France in December 1917, as a captain in command of F Company, 18th Infantry, First Division. He participated in the attack on Cantigny in May 1918, the second battle of the Marne, and a series of minor engagements. With the rank of major in September, he led the 1st Battalion, 18th Infantry, in the St. Mihiel and Meuse-Argonne offensives until being wounded on October 9 on Hill 240 in the Argonne near Exermont, when a shell fragment struck his elbow, nearly severing his arm. He spent the next five months in the hospital.

He, too, was discharged with decorations: the U.S. Distinguished Service Cross and the French Croix de Guerre. Emery rose in the ranks of the Legion through volunteer efforts, serving principally on the Legislative Committee that drafted the fivefold optional plan for adjusted compensation. When he was elected national commander, he was heading the city's committee to build a local tuberculosis hospital.

Emery attended several state conventions, urging disabled veterans to proceed with their claims for rehabilitation. In this effort Emery was aided by the Women's Auxiliary. Though at that point not yet an official organization (they had not had their first convention yet) the women of the Auxiliary did much to make a success of the "clean-up" campaign in which Legionnaires attempted to find and inform all disabled veterans of their rights under the current benefit law.

John Emery's four months as national commander came to a close at the Kansas City Convention with its massive turnout of Legionnaires, which attracted much public attention. This convention, notable also for the appearance of the European military leaders of the war, included as well a four-hour, four-mile parade watched by hundreds of thousands (the nation was coming to expect such a display) described by Armando Diaz, general of the Italian Army, as "the physical manifestation of a great moral force."

After John Emery's short tenure, **Hanford "Jack" MacNider** *of Iowa was elected at the Kansas City Convention, having served as a department commander and N.E.C. man. A Harvard graduate (1911, editor of the* Crimson*), MacNider entered military service as a private, then at the Second Officers Training Camp at Fort Snelling, Minnesota, he rose to provisional second lieutenant of infantry by mid-August 1917. In the meantime, he had served on the Mexican border with the Iowa National Guard. Early the next month he sailed to France with the 9th Infantry, 2d Division, serving as an instructor during the winter.*

Present at the Second Battle of the Marne, he eventually was awarded nine medals, eleven citations, and a wound chevron. Emerging as a lieutenant colonel with Occupation troops, MacNider had served as adjutant and later commander of his regiment before returning home in late summer 1919. He would often be referred to as the most decorated American veteran of the World War next to General Pershing.

Back home, MacNider joined the American Legion in Mason City, Iowa, and became post commander and then state vice-commander. Making himself known in national circles through his membership on national committees, he was elected national commander at the Kansas City Convention of 1921.

MacNider represented the Legion and the A.E.F. in general while traveling on the special train carrying Marshal Foch around the nation following the Kansas City Convention. With the duty of introducing Foch at the numerous stops made along the way, sometimes twenty or more daily, his brief introductory remarks, always the same, were quickly learned by the marshal's two aides, who used these opportunities to practice their English as they stood behind MacNider on the platform at the rear of the marshal's coach. Sometimes they practiced so loudly that MacNider had to speak louder and louder to drown them out. Once, to ease the monotony, he changed a phrase or two to throw them off rhythm. His little jest also confused the marshal, who likewise spoke no English and who listened in vain for his cue to rise and come forward for a bow. Thereafter, MacNider returned to his tedious repertoire and to the stereophonic feedback with a French accent behind him, which continued for the many thousands of miles he traveled with the train.

The trip also gave MacNider a chance to observe members of local posts as they led or participated in the local ceremonies honoring Foch. The train averaged a stop every quarter hour during the day for almost eight weeks. Though many were only "rolling stops" with the marshal saluting the hamlet, the Legion colors were often present. As Foch boarded his ship for home, he remarked through an interpreter, "You have something in this American Legion. It may cradle the future of your country."

After the ceremonial train trip, MacNider began a demanding itinerary of his own during his year as national commander, speaking in every state except two, averaging five speeches a day, and visiting many hospitals where veterans were being treated. Some 30,000 were then being treated for war-related injuries; it was estimated that a third of these were not drawing their rightful disability compensation.

The nation's rate of unemployment during MacNider's year in office was high, and ex-servicemen were often the ones hurt most. MacNider designated March 20, 1922 as American Legion Employment Day. By June 30, National Headquarters claimed to be able to verify that a half-million men (of the estimated 700,000 job-seeking veterans) found work through the campaign.

During his year as National Commander, MacNider was offered the Senate seat vacated by William S. Kenyon (who had been appointed as a federal judge) but turned down the opportunity, saying that he did not wish to abandon the Legion's leadership role. Keeping personal politics at arm's length during his year as national commander, MacNider later accepted a brief appointment as Minister to Canada.

MacNider often explained that there was no antagonism between the Legion and organized labor. He often quoted the A.F.L.'s leader Samuel Gompers, who called on local unions to work with Legion posts to form "pleasant relations." It was not lost on either man, of course, that the two organizations had hundreds of thousands of members in common.

The supposed trouble in the Legion-labor area, about which the press and others liked to speculate, MacNider explained, was invariably caused by "radical and irresponsible members" on both sides who "do not reflect the true sentiments of the bodies which they purport to speak for." Thus when Legionnaires were said to be strikebreakers, hired police, scabs, night riders, and just generally antagonistic to labor movements, the question one should ask first, he said, was: "Did it really happen?" followed by "Why is this assumed so readily to be national policy when no such directives or attitudes exist at that level?"

The fifth national commander of the American Legion was **Alvin Mansfield Owsley** *of Texas. A trial lawyer, Owsley was also a state legislator and then district attorney before attending the First Officers Training Camp at Camp Leon in Springs, Texas, when war with Germany was declared. Commissioned a major with the Texas National Guard, Owsley was assigned to the Seventh Texas Regiment. In July 1917 he went to France as battalion commander. Later promoted to lieutenant colonel with the 36th Division, he saw the fighting at the Aisne and Argonne offensives. In July 1919, thirty-nine years of age, he was discharged.*

Back in Texas he became assistant state attorney general and, as American Legionnaire, the first commander of the Arthur McNitsky Post at Denton. In 1920 he joined the ranks of national volunteers as assistant director of the Americanism Commission, at the time a paid staff position with an office in Indianapolis. In June 1921, he became Director of Americanism.

Known as an eloquent spokesman for the Legion's Americanism program (he once confided to an associate that he was able to look over the heads of his audience and, with remarkable aplomb, see his speeches page by page as on a large easel for him to read, edit, or rewrite at will), Owsley was elected national commander at New Orleans in October 1922. As an indication of the popularity of the American Legion, the schools of Denton, and the two colleges there, closed for the return a few days later of the town's favorite son.

Owsley's year was marked by the continuing problem of veterans' unemployment. He approached the Civil Service Commission for special preference in employing disabled veterans. He was an effective campaigner, too, championing the disabled as well as the compensation of all.

The first American Education Week had occurred in 1921 during Owsley's leadership of the Americanism Commission, and the third such event received his attention as National Commander. From that office, also, he was the first to recommend the Legion's long-running association with the Boy Scouts of America.

Owsley visited every state in the union, as well as Cuba, Panama, France, and Great Britain. He also attended the fourth Federation Interalliée des Anciens Combattants conference in Brussels. Viewed at the time as an important movement to keep Allied veterans of the World War united for world peace, F.I.D.A.C. received vital recognition from the Legion in Owsley's speeches. His legacy to the Legion, derived from his skills as a public speaker, was the ability to communicate Legion policies and programs.

John Robertson Quinn *joked that he had been elected at the San Francisco National Convention in 1923 because the conventioneers in the mood of the moment, drawn so far from their roots and caught up in the atmosphere of the far west, had elected a wild westerner as their sixth national commander.*

His jest overlooked the fact that they took eleven ballots to do it, however; so along with a genuine westerner as leader, they acquired a reputation for politicking on a par with delegates at the conventions of the major political parties.

Quinn was an honest-to-goodness cowboy raised on the 12,000 acre "Quinn Ranch" near Delano, California, settled first by his father, who had come from Ireland by way of Australia in 1868. The younger Quinn graduated from the University of California at Berkeley in 1912, and was riding with a cattle herd on the way to spring pasture in the hills when war was declared on Germany in 1917. Learning of it a month later, Quinn joined the Second Officers Training Camp at the Presidio in San Francisco, where he was appointed captain of field artillery. In France he commanded field artillery in the Meuse-Argonne offensive (defensive sector) and later served with occupation troops in Germany.

His long association with the American Legion began when he joined the Frank S. Reynolds Post No. 26 in Bakersfield, California. Later he organized the Merle Reed Post No. 124 at Delano. Rising to state commander in 1921–22, Quinn quickly became known as a firebrand for veterans' rehabilitation with his steady stream of complaints about and demands for proper hospitalization of veterans.

Quinn continued zealously to fight for the disabled as N.E.C. man the next year, serving also on the California Veterans Welfare Board. His ultimately successful efforts to get the California Veterans Farm and Home Purchase Act passed by the state legislature in 1920 helped make his reputation as a Legionnaire worthy of national notice.

It was this National Commander's good fortune to celebrate the passage of an adjusted compensation bill (the abbreviated yet appreciated measure that it was) over President Coolidge's veto. He announced the news at the N.E.C. meeting at National Headquarters, by coincidence coming in the midst of Watson B. Miller's report for the Rehab Committee. He also saw the House of Representatives create a Committee on Veterans Affairs during his year as chief spokesman for the Legion.

Quinn often said, "The Legion button is a war decoration, and one also for peace. Wear it." He displayed his button proudly on the first National Defense Day, a Legion-sponsored event for emphasizing military preparedness, on September 12, 1924 as he set out for the St. Paul National Convention. Before that he was privileged to speak at the groundbreaking for the first National Headquarters building in Indianapolis.

John Quinn remained active in the Legion's national affairs, serving as chairman of the Americanism Commission in 1924–25, a member of the National Child Welfare Committee the next year, and a director of the Publishing Corporation from 1925 to 1927.

THE LEGION AND AMERICAN EDUCATION WEEK

One out of every four doughboys drafted for the A.E.F. could not read the English language.

Government statistics showed that the United States ranked eleventh in the world in literacy behind ten European countries. At the rate of decrease at the time, illiteracy would continue to be a serious national problem for the next century.

Such a glaring handicap inhibiting an informed citizenry was not lost on those who met at the Paris Caucus when they discussed ways to be of service to their country after returning to civilian life. When at the St. Louis Caucus Legionnaires began considering ways to foster good citizenship, the problem of illiteracy during the war was not forgotten.

The Legion's national officers began discussions in 1919 with their counterparts in the National Education Association to formulate a plan to focus attention on public education. The idea agreed upon was the proclaiming of one week each year during which the public would be reminded of both the accomplishments and needs of the schools in their communities.

At their annual meeting in Des Moines, July 7, 1921, the N.E.A. board of directors welcomed "most heartily" and accepted "with great appreciation" the offer of the American Legion to "cooperate with the N.E.A. in securing for America a program of education adequate to meet the needs of the twentieth century . . . and which will make all, whether native or foreign born, good American citizens."

Furthermore, the N.E.A. adopted as its own a National Convention resolution by the Legion "that all teachers be American citizens (exchange teachers excluded); elementary and high school instruction be given in American history and civics; the United States flag be displayed at schools during school hours; and that the designated week focusing on education be observed in all communities." The N.E.A. also appointed a standing committee to work with the Legion's Americanism Commission throughout the year to carry into effect the program outlined.

The newly formed American Legion Auxiliary eagerly joined in. As

Mrs. Lowell F. Hobart, the Auxiliary national president, informed local presidents and secretaries of Auxiliary units in mid-November 1921, "This is our first opportunity to take part in any national movement" with the Legion. "Make this a conspicuous success."

In the Americanism Commission's bulletin of November 17, 1921, Commission Director Alvin M. Owsley announced that the N.E.A. had joined the Legion in sponsoring National Education Week December 4–10. The week's activities included Sunday church sermons on religious freedom and education. Local chambers of commerce and boards of trade were asked to request merchants to purchase advertising space to promote the needs of education during the week.

Motion picture theaters were requested to run slides with captions such as "The foundation of every state is the education of its youth" and "A cultivated mind is the guardian genius of democracy and when guided and controlled by virtue is the noblest attribute of man." Legionnaires, as well as Rotarians, Kiwanians, and others were encouraged to speak before school assemblies about citizenship. Newspapers were requested to print editorials and articles featuring National Education Week activities.

The Legion and the N.E.A. issued a joint statement regarding educational standards, requiring that no one be allowed to teach without at least a standard high school education of four years and two years of professional training. Furthermore, English, they said, should be the primary language for teaching, and school curricula should include instruction in American history and civics. Compulsory school attendance for a minimum of thirty-six weeks annually, also, was stressed (recent surveys had shown that of the 27 million school-age children in the nation, only 15 million were in daily attendance at school).

In speaking to the N.E.A. convention at Mechanics Hall in Boston on July 4, 1922, the Legion's "smiling, fighting preacher of patriotism," Alvin Owsley, said that the American Legion sought to build a nation and defend it, with education being a cornerstone.

American Education Week 1922 was jointly sponsored by the Legion, the N.E.A., and the National Bureau of Education. A more specific and ambitious program this year included themes for every day of the week. The subject suggested for Sunday was "For God and Country." Monday was "American Citizenship Day," followed by "Patriotism Day," "School and Teacher Day," "Illiteracy Day," and "Equality of Opportunity." On Saturday, "Physical Education Day," the primary focus was on the development of playgrounds. But also mentioned was the need to conserve the soils and other natural resources, and the need to develop forests and roads. A series of admonitions and goals was also publicized: "Children today, citizens tomorrow"; "A man of knowledge increaseth might"; "No illiteracy by 1927"; and "A sick body makes a sick mind."

The schedule for American Education Week was changed to Novem-

ber 18–24 for 1923. Like Harding before him, President Coolidge, too, issued a proclamation setting aside this week as a time for study of education questions by the people.

The bandwagon had begun to roll. By this time 150 other national organizations had joined in helping to coordinate activities in communities across the land. The joint efforts of the Legion and the N.E.A. to promote National Education Week would continue for several decades.

REMAINING RELEVANT

AMID THE ROAR AND THE CRASH

1925-1933

I

Adjusted compensation was now the law of the land.

On January 1, 1925, the so-called "bonus" certificates were issued. A loan clause allowed veterans to borrow on the certificates in two years, with maturity twenty years hence. Many organizations, colleges, and universities that had previously opposed adjusted compensation were now appealing to veterans to turn over their certificates as endowments.

For the American Legion the issuance of the certificates was a good object lesson at this stage of the organization's development. For despite the well-earned celebrations that occurred upon the passage of the act, the adjusted compensation enacted into law on May 19, 1924 was not all that had been hoped for, was not a matter of consensus even within the Legion itself, was still largely assumed by the general public to be a bonus, and would constantly be criticized by those insisting on economy in government.

It was a good time to ask how the Legion had fared after five years of existence. National Commander James A. Drain proclaimed in June 1925, "Every day there are more Legionnaires who understand 'Why the American Legion?' " It was a curious statement in light of declining memberships since 1920 (the trend would soon be reversed).

Perhaps he was speaking of his impression of the quality of the current membership.

The relevancy of the Legion in 1925, its stature and promise, were demonstrated impressively when the National Headquarters staff moved their offices from rented quarters in the Clalfont Building to the distinctive Indiana limestone structure anchoring one corner of the developing World War Memorial in Indianapolis. The state of Indiana and the city of Indianapolis had built the building as the Legion's permanent National Headquarters and had leased the building to the Legion.

That move marked the end, some insiders were saying, of the formative years of the Legion. The St. Paul National Convention in the fall of 1924, many believed, had ushered in a new era. The mandates of that governing body had been the most far-reaching and long-sighted so far. The arrival, too, of a new national adjutant at this point marked the first time someone to hold that office had come up through the Legion's organizational structure to the national level.

Iowan James F. Barton came to the job in 1925 from his duties as adjutant of a thriving department that had already produced a national commander (Hanford MacNider, 1921–22) and had gained national recognition as well for its excellent programming.

The job of national adjutant had grown. Legion founder Lemuel Bolles, the first to hold the office, had brought the brand-new Legion's official records in a dry goods box from the Minneapolis Convention in 1919 to the rooms loaned by the Indianapolis Chamber of Commerce to the Legion as its first quarters in that city.

Russell Creviston, who succeeded Bolles and who served in the job for two years (1923–25), had come to National Headquarters from Community Services, Inc. in Indianapolis through a loaned-executive program.

Community Services, Inc. was a nationwide organization during the First World War that performed some of the voluntary duties which in the Second World War were taken up by city and state defense councils, the U.S.O. and, eventually, the Federal Security Agency. Thus Creviston brought both executive ability and the community service concept to the Legion.

By the time Creviston had left, the Legion's Community and Civic Betterment Bureau, mandated by the San Francisco Convention in 1923 as another Americanism Commission responsibility, had become a storehouse of information for community and civic improvement that could be undertaken by local Legion posts.

With all due respect to the role of the national commander, it was often said that the national adjutant was the busiest man in the Legion. As executive officer and sometimes substitute commander, the adjutant ran what was becoming an ever-larger business organization, made speeches, and presided at meetings.

The domain in which Barton would serve included the Legion's major areas of advocacy and concern, the "basics": Rehab, the heartbeat; Child Welfare, the compassion for dependents; National Defense, the practical survival means; and the flag-bedecked Americanism.

The one thing these fundamental advocacies had in common was federal legislation—the need for it, the drafting, lobbying, and continued review and revision of it once enacted.

The Legion's lobbyist on the Hill was equal to the task. John Thomas Taylor's knowledge of Congress was encyclopedic. In January 1925, he once again boasted that several more politicians had met their congressional Waterloo. That point, he said, was not lost on those who retained their seats. Some of those who had been reelected "are starting in to play swaps now. They are starting in to dicker and say 'If I do this for you, what will you do for me?' "

Taylor described the work cut out for the current session of Congress. The St. Paul National Convention in 1924 had produced eighty-four resolutions that were subsequently compiled in Taylor's office into forty-two bills. That lot was then consolidated into fourteen bills, which were handed to senators and representatives friendly to the Legion to be introduced in Congress. These bills were composed primarily of amendments to the Reed-Johnson Bill, the World War Veterans Act (which when passed included fifty-one recommendations from the San Francisco Convention and which yet was considered to be in need of that many more changes), and the Adjusted Compensation Act.

"This is an economy congress, let there be no doubt about that," Taylor said; and it was dominated by Calvin Coolidge, who had just been elected president in his own right after having assumed the office upon the death of Warren Harding. The president, Taylor said, was exercising his influence for frugality just as he and his predecessor Harding had worked against adjusted compensation.

"They are having the same kind of breakfasts and dinners and suppers" as did the opponents of adjusted compensation. The current crop of national legislators was getting "the law laid down to them as to what they are to do and how far they are to go."

Taylor had adopted a lobbying strategy built upon a two-part legislative program. "We use our major legislative program as a sort of smoke screen," he explained to the N.E.C. in May 1926. "While [Congress is] busy quarreling about that, we manage to get through a very considerable portion of what we might call our minor legislative matters."

And when public support was needed, some proposal sure to grab public interest would be unveiled "to secure a certain momentum in all of the departments on the part of the Legion itself and to secure a lot of favorable comment by the press of the country."

Taylor added that all of this "gradually finds its way down through various channels to Washington and . . . cause[s] senators and congressmen to think perhaps the American Legion is a powerful political influence throughout the country." This process, it was hoped, would lead to the passage of bills desired by the Legion.

Getting laws passed did not excuse the lobbyist from the scene. One needed to keep a constant vigil to see that laws remained intact or that those that lost some important features during the last few minutes before passage were restored to the intended potency. The practice of amending existing laws was now a common practice by the Legion. Chief lobbyist Taylor, knowing the realities of life on the Hill —the customary compromise and the often last-minute alterations of legislation-in-progress—had adopted yet another two-step formula, this for dealing with the actual enactments resulting from his own successful lobbying.

It was necessary, he said, for new laws "to simmer down to the bottom to find out [their] defects" before pursuing the amendatory process.

In the spring of 1926, then, the major legislative program included several measures of chief concern: one to oppose—the Welsh Bill to remove R.O.T.C. from land grant colleges; and others to support—the Universal Draft Bill (Johnson-Capper Bill), and, collectively, all legislation for the disabled.

In addition to these matters of primary concern, the "minor" legislative program included a variety of interests and concerns: the promotion of airmail; the Columbia River compact of regional states for water apportionment; a supply of helium gas for the army and navy; and the restoration of the Robert E. Lee home at Arlington Cemetery, to name only a few. The Legion was also urging an appropriation in the current public buildings legislation for a national archives building to house World War records.

Taylor was careful to point out: "In our legislation we do not ask for money for the specific project. We ask for a lump sum appropriation. We present our testimony before the committee . . . and the director spends [the eventual appropriation] according to the testimony that has been presented to the congressmen in considering the authorizing of the expenditure." This left up to Congress the hard decision about specific sums for appropriations, allowing the Legion, properly, to remain free of the pork-barrel taint.

Just what was properly "basic" for the Legion, how the much publicized intents and purposes of the founders were to be exercised, and whether additions could be made were questions still being asked. Department conventions particularly, some said, listened to those who had some axe to grind, which all too often resulted in resolutions being sent to National Headquarters that were not "germane." Such was the "big funnel" approach to the production of resolutions annually handed to the National Legislative Committee for action.

There was so much that begged attention. The N.E.C. in January 1926 considered the pros and cons involved in the Legion's acting as an intermediary in the fray surrounding a coal strike in Pennsylvania.

National Commander Drain held a meeting at his room at the Indianapolis Athletic Club after a day's session at the N.E.C. on January 14 to consider whether the Legion should become involved in that dispute. It was decided that there would be no Legion involvement.

The Legion's rehabilitation function, by the very nature of the work to be done, by the way in which the work was being done, and by expectations placed on that operation, seemed poised to serve as the best example of what the Legion had accomplished so far.

National commanders fittingly attracted national attention while pursuing a busy speaking schedule as well as some large-scale project about which each felt strongly or which seemed to require special attention.

But Rehab Committee head Watson Miller regularly reported to state and national conventions and to the N.E.C. about a daily regimen that heaped on the shoulders of the Legion the brother's-keeper role for all disabled veterans.

If the national adjutant was the busiest man in the Legion, Rehab's Miller was the most harried. Rehab work, often exacting an emotional toll as well as presenting an immense clerical challenge, involved contacts with almost every executive branch department and national and local welfare organization in Washington, D.C., and throughout the nation necessitated by the Rehab mainstay—claims work in insurance, compensation, hospitalization, and vocational training.

Miller noted at this point that there had occurred some liberalization and extensions of the national statutes governing disabled men. Also, changes brought about by the enactment of the World War Veterans Act had caused the Veterans Bureau to set up a new claims division with seventy employees.

Miller explained the growing stature of the claims examiners at the Veterans Bureau, who were now next in importance to the doctors there because they fixed the legal, fiscal, and economic relationship of the federal government to the veteran being examined. They were also the persons with whom the Rehab staffers had most contact. (A group of them had just sent one hundred dollars to the Legion's Endowment Fund campaign.)

Also there was some promise apparent that the Legion's recommendation of more independence for the medical division of the bureau was being implemented by the director.

The new rating schedule in use was an encouraging development. It was, Miller said, "the most replete contribution to the bibliography of industrial disability which has ever been devised." Even so, and despite the fact that the new schedule increased the number covered, it was not likely to be accepted by the disabled because the amount each was to receive had not been increased substantially.

The schedule showed how 17 different parts of the body were used in 1,000 separate occupations. It measured 1,600 disabilities, with 9 ratings for each disability, dependent upon the occupational importance of that part of the body as determined in the first table.

In addition to the daily regimen, Rehab workers were reorganizing their work according to the decentralization under way at the Veterans Bureau. Miller also saw the need to expand the Washington, D.C. office work schedule to include a 24-hour service whereby department adjutants and service officers could quickly initiate claims and get current information on claims already filed.

The Rehab program in the field included full-time service officers for thirty-two departments and part-time service officers for another seventeen departments. From August 1924 to May 1925 the Washington, D.C. office had handled 7,700 letters and the field offices 22,500 letters, all relating to claims and other inquiries from veterans. In that year, $1,395,221 had been recovered in claims. There was now in place a national network for locating, advising, guiding, and checking on the progress of veterans in need of physical rehabilitation. "The Legion will always have to stand with the claimant to get justice and efficiency," Miller said.

Rehab at the Legion was as much an attitude as a vocation. As Watson Miller explained, "We always take the position that the federal government agencies charged with the relief of veterans should be operated not so much as business institutions but as relief institutions."

Miller was particularly troubled by the growth of mental cases among veterans. Though the TB case load seemed to be dropping off, it was because the disease was assumed to have an active life of seven years, and this was the seventh year since the end of the World War. "We are losing men to death more so than ever before," Miller said. "Men have gone out and tried to buck the game too hard and have broken down and come in to die." He praised the advisory aid provided by Legionnaire doctors William LeRoy Dunn of Asheville, North Carolina, and H. Kennon Dunham of Cincinnati, both TB experts.

A recent development at the Veterans Bureau was also troubling. The U.S. comptroller general had set up a "preaudit section" which, Miller charged, was tantamount to "case adjudication" since the new function impinged on decision-making rightly belonging to the director of the bureau. This, Miller contended, was in effect a new hurdle placed between the federal appropriation and the administration of that money for the bureau.

But the new office had the personal backing of the president. Assuming that the new section was there to stay, Miller was attempting to convince the comptroller that "veterans' laws are beneficial and remedial in character," rather than a mere rigmarole of do's and don'ts.

Legionnaires could empathize with fellow veterans who were disabled, but there was a special tenderness for the dependents of disabled or deceased buddies. Now another national network of Legion activity was growing along with Rehab.

The Legion's ambitious $5 million Endowment Fund drive, which began in 1924, was undertaken to benefit equally the Rehab and the new Child Welfare programs. National Commander John F. Drain had explained that the duties of the national commander included "contact" work and administrative chores. His own "contact" work had helped get the endowment campaign off to a good start. By midsummer during Drain's year in office, nearly $700,000 had come in, ninety percent in cash, the remaining in pledges.

Social worker Emma Puschner of St. Louis was hired in 1925 as the chief staff person in this field of endeavor, in which the Legion claimed impressive intentions. The first task was to collect information from the states about what work was needed. Child Welfare chairmen were making a careful investigation of minor wards of the Veterans Bureau.

The Legion had already acquired the Otter Lake (Michigan) Billet for orphans. Another small home had been opened at Clarksborough, New Jersey, and one to be called "Legionville" was being considered near Independence, Kansas, where a farm had recently been deeded to the Legion for that purpose.

But it became obvious quickly that the job of caring for orphans of ex-service personnel was a job too large for the Legion. Drain and many others believed that "National" should actually "restrain the natural inclination of those who are greatly interested in child welfare to rush off and construct a billet." Instead, "We should work toward . . . more absolutely certain connections of the orphan children with foster parents. . . ."

He had advised in June 1925 that "there should be a minimum number of billets . . . and a maximum effort to get every child adopted by foster parents at the earliest possible moment." He spoke of a time, a year or so hence, when no billets would be needed because the response of foster parents would be so great that all children would find "real homes."

By the middle of 1926, three Legion billets housed a total of seventy-two children in three states. Another forty children were being assisted financially while remaining with their mothers. Emma

Puschner supervised a growing number of volunteers who worked to have state and local laws changed to aid children.

John Thomas Taylor, meanwhile, continued to monitor conditions in Congress that affected all the legislation put forth by the Legion.

The situation there, he said, was "serious." First, "Congress feels that it has done enough and that the time is coming when we should shut down on our requests for legislation." Second, the fifty-five World War veterans in the House and the eight in the Senate, all of whom had aided the Legion cause in the past, were now reticent to do so when they found themselves opposed by other veterans for reelection. They sought a broader constituency, among whom the veterans' view was not always understood or appreciated. Also, "I see a rift in the clouds. I see the question of party politics coming up, a question which will involve soldier legislation the same as any other legislation." Finally, "Economy seems to have Washington by the throat."

In particular there were some Legionnaire congressmen who needed convincing on specific pieces of legislation. Ogden Mills, for example, Legion founder and first department commander of New York, was the only World War veteran on the House Ways and Means Committee. From that influential vantage he had fought adjusted compensation. But now that it was law, he reviewed the Legion amendments for changes in that area and after some argument agreed to sponsor the Legion bill for refining that landmark law. Taylor believed that with Mills and James Wadsworth of Indiana on the House Finance Committee as allies, changes in the adjusted compensation law could be made.

Taylor complained that "the more men who saw service that get into the House and Senate, the greater our difficulties become!" Also, "Veterans' legislation is becoming a partisan issue at the present time," with Democrats opposing bills introduced by Republicans and vice versa, with otherwise little regard for content or purpose.

John E. Rankin, for example, a Democratic congressman from Mississippi, was singled out as having "given us more trouble on the disabled men's legislation than anyone else. It is Rankin who is responsible for the way it has dragged along. He just talks by the hour."

Three hundred and sixty-four bills affecting veterans had been introduced in the current session of Congress, many of which had been drafted or acceded to by the Legion. Some, however, thought to be objectionable required as much effort to defeat as Legion-inspired measures took to get passed.

From 1919 on, Taylor reminded them, the Legion's Legislative Committee had written all its own legislation, not merely passing judgment and taking sides on bills that appeared in the Congress. Days spent in drafting the bills, conferring with government agencies, scanning the existing body of law, and rewriting could take weeks for each major piece of legislation. For Taylor and the voluntary Legislative Committee members it was a cumbersome process but by now the pattern.

By mid-1926, Taylor was reporting difficulty with the veterans' bloc that he claimed to have organized. Robert Simmons of Nebraska, a former department commander and now chairman of the bloc this session, was refusing to call the others together until Taylor backed off from the Tyson-Fitzgerald Bill, a piece of legislation that would give retirement benefits to disabled emergency army officers—the volunteer officers of the A.E.F. Legion bills had been passed to give retirement benefits to Nurse Corps members and to Regular Army officers retired before the World War.

Some wanted to reprimand Simmons with a resolution. Others prevailed, calling such a move bad diplomacy and policy.

To Taylor, however, the Volunteer Officers Retirement Bill was a matter of principle. "We have had that bill up since the St. Louis Caucus," he said. It had been twice passed by the Senate (where most of the problems occurred when Legion legislation was sidetracked or otherwise opposed) and was again being considered by that body. One senator who opposed it had just sponsored a bill to grant rank and retired pay to seventeen contract surgeons "who never had any military status of any kind. . . ."

That same bill (Tyson-Fitzgerald Bill) led the major legislative program in early 1927. It had been determined, additionally, by the 1926 convention that national defense measures would receive the most intensive effort of the legislative program this year. Taylor complained that organized pacifists, "great crowds" of whom met in Washington repeatedly, had "pushed our army and navy down to almost rock bottom" by fighting military appropriations. The Legion, he said, was the only organization that could combat that agitation.

The Legion's universal draft bill had been introduced before. Hearings were held. Later, both political parties included a universal draft plank in their platforms. But Taylor couldn't budge it from the Military Affairs committees of either house to be brought onto the floor for debate and action. Nor could he identify what was holding it up. There was the contention by labor groups that the bill would make it possible to draft laborers for some industries even in peacetime. That, the Legion said, was a gross and unwarranted misconception.

Though Past National Commander Hanford MacNider had been appointed assistant secretary of war in January 1926, he apparently had not had any great effect on the attitude of the department regarding a universal draft.

Taylor admitted that there was not much chance of getting a universal draft bill enacted. "We have used it mostly as a club to get through considerable other legislation. It is one of our big efforts and we will continue it as our big effort."

The big complaint, however, in the area of national defense was that though the National Defense Act of 1920 had stipulated a "six field army" plan for 280,000 personnel—the Regular Army, two National Guard armies, and three armies made up of Officers Reserve Corps members—it had never materialized. In fact, that figure of 280,000 had been whittled to less than 90,000 if one did not include the ten thousand persons outfitted in the new aviation program.

When the president did sign the War Department Appropriation Bill, he signed for an additional 4,998 men. "This increase was generally considered due to the influence of the American Legion," Taylor said. He also took credit on behalf of the Legislative Committee for the appropriation of over $39 million dollars for "civilian military activities:" the National Guard, Officers Reserve Corps, R.O.T.C., C.M.T.C., National Board for Promotion of Rifle Practice, and ordnance equipment for rifle ranges for civilian instruction.

As for the navy, the act of 1924 had provided for eight of the speedy 10,000 ton, 8-inch gun scout cruisers. Three of them had been cut from the shopping list. Roosevelt, however, former secretary of the navy, restored the order for the original complement of eight ships. But the navy still smarted under the confines of the postwar naval treaty of 1921 that determined that the United States and Great Britain would equalize the number of ships in each navy, with Japan agreeing to maintain three-fifths of the other two. This "5-5-3" plan caused the United States to scrap over 450,000 tons of existing ships or those under construction. Now, Taylor charged, Japan was actually ahead of the United States in construction of cruisers. Another conference of the three powers was set for June 1927.

The other matter of importance during 1927 was the poor reception by banks for the loan privileges of the Adjusted Compensation Act. On the first day of that year, veterans could borrow on the certificates. But only days later, the Washington office of the Legion received calls and telegrams complaining that banks were refusing to make loans on the certificates.

(To the amusement of the committeemen who remembered Treasury Secretary Mellon's ardent opposition to the Adjusted Compensation Bill three years ago, John Thomas Taylor read a letter from "Andy Mellon's bank in Pittsburgh . . . inviting the boys to come over to this bank and make their loans.")

Anticipating the reluctance of the banking community in many instances to accept the certificates, the Legislative Committee had already drafted legislation that would allow Veterans Bureau offices to make loans based on the certificates. The committee was relying on

Democrat Joe Robinson of Arkansas, a leader in the Senate, to put the bill through. Help was also promised by Edith Nourse Rogers, a Republican congresswoman from Massachusetts, who in the last two congressional sessions had acquired a respected reputation as a strong supporter of measures for disabled veterans.

In addition to Rehab and National Defense, the mid-1920s saw widespread interest in community betterment projects at posts. The Philadelphia Convention in 1926 had determined that each of the posts should assume at least one worthwhile, constructive act of service for the benefit of its community. At National Headquarters the National Community Service Division was designated to launch a campaign in December. First, in an inspirational phase, National sought to remind posts of the Legion's constitution pledge "to inculcate a sense of individual obligation to the community, state, and nation" and "to consecrate and sanctify our comradeship by our devotion to mutual helpfulness."

Here was opportunity for heroism, it was said, linked to the inspired charges by doughboys across the deadly no-man's-land. Community service was an activity that could and should remove any doubt as to the justification for the Legion's existence.

The second phase was for assembling informative material to help posts plan and carry out community-service projects. By late spring 1927, 1,706 posts had reported 120 varieties of activities involving a total of 130,000 Legionnaires.

The list of projects that accumulated at National Headquarters in 1927 was as long as the collective imagination of those at the local scene. At that point the sponsoring of Boy Scout troops led the list. Other activities related to local circumstance and size of posts: from equipping a general hospital to installing a public drinking fountain; from helping to clear the way for public buildings to be built to planting trees along highways; from promoting junior athletics to establishing public libraries; from providing baby clinics to sponsoring a "pig club" (not otherwise explained); from replacing a bridge to conducting regular market days for farmers.

In this age of "aeronautics" one of the most popular projects in which a post could engage was the building of landing fields and airports. At Boise, Idaho for example, the state's first modern airport was constructed in 1926 largely with the help of a pick-and-shovel brigade from the John Regan Post of that city. There a gravel bar overgrown by cottonwood trees and willows was transformed into an airfield so the city would not miss out as the intermediate stop on the newly established Elko, Nevada to Pasco, Washington route.

In 1926, the Legion again presented a national defense plan that included an air force as one of its integral parts and which, the plan stated, could be supported by the manpower and production capability of a commercial aviation industry. The plan also called for a contract system for extending the air mail; the building of lighted airfields; the dissemination of weather information; the release of surplus military aviation equipment for civilian use at reasonable prices; and the education of the public about the potential of commercial aviation.

The next year, Dan Sowers, director of the Legion's National Community Service Division, met with officials at the U.S. Commerce Department's new Aeronautics Division to present the Legion's idea of urging Legion posts in feasible locations to sponsor landing fields and airports. The department, Sowers reported, liked the idea.

With more and more aviators plying their trade in the great blue beyond, looking to keep to schedules but often blown off course by bad weather, another Legion aid to aviation was organized. In early 1928, National Commander Edward Spafford circulated a letter to post commanders setting out the latest community-betterment project—one for marking the name of every village and town for the benefit of pilots.

The specifications that evolved required that the name of the town be written in letters from twelve to fifteen feet high and of proportionate width to be visible from an altitude of 3,500 feet in optimum flying conditions. Also, the name was to be accompanied by an arrow pointing to the local landing field and the number of miles to that spot. It was the small town, Spafford pointed out, that needed marking so that pilots could return to their proper courses from which they occasionally wandered in fog or rain.

So it would develop that some part of the burgeoning commercial aviation business would be conducted from Legion-built airfields and with pilots being guided back on course by place names painted on rooftops by Legionnaires.

Promoting community improvement was a high order of civilian service to the nation. But now years after the founding of the Legion, the current chairman of the Americanism Commission, Frank L. Pinola of Pennsylvania, was still getting letters from Legionnaires saying, "I have just been appointed post Americanism officer. What am I supposed to do? What does Americanism mean?"

As Pinola explained in early 1928, apparently "Americanism," like "truth and beauty," was in the eye of the beholder. He cited a contest by a "leading magazine" to define Americanism that concluded that the word could not be defined. So, "We of the Americanism Commission have come to the conclusion that it is a subjective term; it means just what you choose to have it mean."

But the chairman of a national commission needed a more specific working definition than that. "Take the common denominator [of the variant connotations of the word], take an appreciation of the principles on which our nation is founded: loyalty and devotion to its institutions, and unselfishness, service in the promotion of the welfare and happiness of its people" and that would serve as a working definition for the purposes of the commission.

In particular, the Americanism Commission had turned its attention of late to the subversion most effectively portrayed by the murders in November 1919 of the four Legionnaires in Centralia, Washington.

In 1926 the American Legion Junior Baseball program was also begun on a national scale, and a national committee was formed to encourage posts to sponsor Boy Scout troops. Both these programs had the goal of helping boys to know the Legion and to teach Americanism. Baseball was the first of the two to gain wide recognition as a way to teach good citizenship through teaching true sportsmanship.

That program had favorably impressed the major league club owners, who gave $50,000 for the transportation costs of regional winners to the Junior World Series. The club owners' association was also paying to have a Pullman car sent to the town of the series winner to take them to the major league World Series of 1926. Legion publicists were pleased to learn that the son of famous big-league pitcher Walter Johnson was playing for a Legion team in Newark, New Jersey.

The pledge by Legion founders to keep the organization from becoming mired in partisan politics had been held to with impressive success throughout the formative years of the Legion.

But the application of that pledge was to many, now, as nebulous a concept as Americanism was to some. Committeeman Ferre C. Watkins of Illinois posed the question in May 1928 to start the current round of the debate. "Am I as a member of the N.E.C., holding or aspiring to no political office, stopped from expressing my opinion or taking some part in a political campaign?" Watkins reiterated the action taken at St. Paul in which "by all-embracing terms, every employee of the Legion, which means anyone acting in any capacity for the Legion, or an officer of the Legion in its national, departmental, or post organization, is absolutely prohibited from taking any part whatsoever in furthering the candidacy of any individual for office."

Watkins pointed to the fact that some committeemen were delegates to national conventions of the political parties. Rehab Director Watson Miller, for example, had been a delegate to the past three Democratic National Conventions.

Rufus R. Rand of Minnesota assumed that the framers of the Legion constitution intended that the possibility of the Legion's becoming an organization with "a distinct political destiny as a political party" be prevented rather than having it prohibit officers in the Legion from holding political office or aiding those who did.

Did the confusion over the matter require a review of the Legion constitution or of the resolution adopted at St. Paul? asked Volney

Diltz of Iowa. It was agreed that a committee would be appointed to study the question and that the national judge advocate would be a member.

Politics on an international level were also addressed, now, by the Legion in one of the organization's earliest demonstrations of interest in the nation's foreign policy. National Chaplain Gill Robb Wilson at the May 1928 N.E.C. meeting introduced a "Plan for Peace."

The Rev. Mr. Wilson had been asked by the national commander in January to report on the progress of the world toward peace, particularly toward the embracing of constitutional government.

The national chaplain charged that America had already lost the respect of much of the world, which had looked to it after the World War. He had attended the Peace Conference at Versailles "as an errand boy, as most aviators were after the war," and heard the pleas of small countries that looked to America for aid and protection.

But the role of the United States in helping to keep world peace had become "a political question here," and the nation, he said, had lost "that messianic leadership . . . the torch-bearing, in the eyes of the world."

The chaplain told of his own attitude when on the steamer home after the Armistice he was asked why he joined up. He had replied, "Just for the adventure." But after some thought he felt the need to search out some "moral purpose" for his military service. Before long he had decided that "I had to keep faith with our dead" by answering the question, "What did they die for?"

About that time he heard of the formation of the American Legion and was struck by the phraseology of its constitution, particularly the calls "To promote the peace of the world" and "To make right the master of might." Such statements, if believed, elevated the organization to a position of leadership with appreciable responsibility for contributing to world peace.

Since true, lasting peace couldn't be legislated once and for all, Wilson recommended that the Legion assume moral leadership. For the success of whatever was legislated, he said, "the people's spiritual level must be commensurate with the legislation."

The chaplain suggested a program for breaking down mistrust among nations. He recommended a student exchange among "first-class powers." He noted, "The preservation of values has many times been based on friendship."

Wilson then turned to a Legion standard: a strong national defense. If the Legion could promote a plan to assure the nation's safety and physical integrity, and could help create a nonpolitical, nonsectarian will among the populace to support that plan, then world peace would be greatly advanced.

No one had to convince Chaplain Wilson that the Legion was relevant.

II

In February 1929, the Federal Reserve Board aired its concern about the nation's burgeoning credit structure. Before the year was out, alarm bells clanged as those who professed to understand the "economic indicators" would point in panic to a ship of state about to go aground on the reef of speculative overindulgence.

The year began, however, with few other hints for the generally uninitiated that it would end with a "Crash." Most noticeably for the Legion, 1929 was the tenth anniversary for the organization, which viewed itself as an essential participant in the well-being of the nation and had adopted in the last ten years a varied agenda. So full had the agenda become, in fact, that the N.E.C. met four times in 1929.

This year and always, there was of course the long-running drama on Capitol Hill. John Thomas Taylor's report to the N.E.C. in January 1929 included his anticipation that the legislative program of the Legion would be carried along into the closing days of the session for the usual last-minute rush of activity to see a few Legion measures adopted.

He also recommended that the N.E.C. in May 1929 state itself clearly on the subject of pensions for veterans. When asked by a committeeman whether or not there was a move on in Congress to establish a pension system that would include political patronage, Taylor's answer was a ready "Yes."

He reminded them that when the Legion had worked for the passage of the Adjusted Compensation Bill, it had proclaimed its opposition to pensions. But even after that bill had passed, Taylor had been approached many times, he said, by congressmen and senators who said pensions were inevitable because so many veterans wanted them.

In fact, in Taylor's view, the Legion had already contradicted itself on that matter. He pointed to the recent resolution coming from the Child Welfare Committee calling for dependency pay for widows and orphans regardless of service connection. "That is pension legislation," he said.

The matter of the ever-larger resolution fest that seemed always to occur at national conventions was more and more a concern now among those who were subsequently saddled with them after the conventioneers went home. In November 1929 John Thomas Taylor urged cutting down on the number of resolutions. He joked about the influence of the N.E.C.: The San Francisco Convention had produced eighty or so resolutions. The N.E.C. had then suggested that fewer resolutions be produced. "That carried great weight with the convention at Louisville . . . because that convention adopted 102 resolutions." That convention had required that all resolutions for national legislation be referred to the Convention Committee before being taken to the convention.

One, of course, did not want to seem to be impeding the process whereby resolutions progressed from posts to department conventions and, then, to national conventions. But at this point the floodgates were apparently open wide, and the flow defied the feverish work by the available manpower for seriously considering all resolutions.

The answer provided by the N.E.C. in its last meeting in 1929 was to appoint a committee, chaired by Roane Waring of Tennessee later national commander, called the Committee on Legislative Program. This committee advised the adoption of John Thomas Taylor's practice of identifying major and minor legislative programs, but added a "deferred" classification for those resolutions that "should await action . . . until the major program has been disposed of."

Watson Miller joined John Thomas Taylor in complaining about the plethora of resolutions. Miller received some resolutions direct from departments. He more than ever had his hands full in seeking improvements in the way the Veterans Bureau dealt with veterans. He had asked his staff to produce at least one policy suggestion each working day. Some had proved impracticable, some of moderate use, and some of great importance.

The Legion had been trying to convince the Veterans Bureau to establish a separate medical division to upgrade medical professionalism there. Miller was happy to report that almost all veterans' hospitals employed medical personnel from outside the Veterans Bureau to aid the bureau's medical staff. This, he said, was desirable since it helped bureau physicians to remain current in the medical field.

Occasional "schools" had also been instituted in the hospitals, offering updated instruction in orthopedics, surgery, internal medicine, pathology, and bacteriology. The Bureau's *Medical Bulletin* was being distributed monthly throughout the system, carrying news of experiences and experiments. Physical and occupational therapy was being offered more often and "habit forming" classes were being taught at neuropsychological facilities.

One of the main problems Miller faced was that the Rehab service in general in Washington, D.C. was "admittedly crippled." The great growth of the "business" had for two years "threatened to exceed the manpower capacity of the office," Miller told the N.E.C. in January 1929. Also, the Rehab budget was the same as five years ago when "the business had just really begun."

Miller, and all national staffers, would soon learn what real hardship and economic handicaps could do to the Rehab function of the Legion.

When the bizarre news from Wall Street was heard in late October 1929, it was assumed by many that the matter would correct itself or that the federal government would cope somehow.

Postwar prosperity had peaked; the ride up had been bumptious, a roaring good time. But the stock market had just started to plummet down the far side of the peak; and the descent, soon to gain frightful momentum, would impart to an entire generation a fearful respect for economic causation.

A national organization such as the Legion, however, had the resources represented in its membership to see the big picture and to piece together the likely ramifications of the stock market crash. One thing was abundantly clear: great losses of money by some would soon be translated to the unemployment of many.

Less than a month after the first news of the crash, the N.E.C. considered plans for a new program called "Emergency Relief" to establish "State Emergency Relief Councils" through state legislative enactments and for continuing the organization of Emergency Relief Units at posts, expanding their usefulness by means of radio announcements, telephone follow-ups to job seekers, and then providing transportation to get them to job interviews.

Inspired themselves to belt-tightening, national officers were in a mood to reorganize for economy and efficiency. In the past, committees had sprung up whenever there was a job to do or a study to perform. There were now twenty-four authorized national committees, many with overlapping duties and many too large to work effectively, with the terms of committee members in many instances not fixed.

Now a new and shorter list of committees was devised, stipulating only those for finance, rehabilitation, child welfare, Americanism, legislation, national defense, publicity, F.I.D.A.C., censorship, trophies and awards, liaison with the Publishing Corporation board of directors, distinguished guests, and liaison with Rehab Committee.

Also, Section 2 of Article I of the National By-Laws was amended to state that the N.E.C. would meet in November instead of January for a savings in transportation funds.

For the Legion, any mention of jobs included the preference of disabled veterans (or their wives or widows) for available jobs through Civil Service. That had been a hard-won victory, one always tenuously held.

It was then to be expected that when the nation's attention was made to focus on all aspects of employment, the matter of jobs sought or filled by disabled veterans would be scrutinized in the light of current circumstances.

President Harding in 1923 had issued an Executive Order seeking to clarify the preferential rights of veterans. But problems had persisted, and in the waning hours of his administration, Coolidge had appointed a study commission that included Veterans Bureau Director Hines, Legionnaire Congressman Royal Johnson, and John Thomas Taylor. The committee heard from those complaining of the preference system and from those who favored it. Taylor reported that there was a movement afoot, he claimed, "to break down the influence of the American Legion so far as national legislation is concerned." In such a time of deepening "retrenchment" as the present, one method that would be used was to defeat legislation already on the statute books. Veterans' preference, he warned, was a likely target.

President Coolidge's Executive Order on March 2, 1929 had given able-bodied veterans five-point and disabled veterans ten-point preference on Civil Service examinations. Veterans who passed an examination with that preference were to be placed, together with their wives or widows, at the head of the eligible list. There was also on the statute books a provision for the protection of veterans' jobs in the Civil Service when any reduction in force occurred.

Nevertheless, the Washington Rehab office had been told that veterans were being dismissed from government jobs. Appeals could be made, but only to the division or bureau in which the problem had arisen. The new job ratings were the most common source of the difficulty, and they were usually sustained over the objections of veterans. The Legion had produced resolutions calling for both the Bureau of Efficiency and the Personnel Classification Board to be abolished and for the duties of the two agencies to be transferred to the Civil Service Commission.

But the problem persisted. Watson Miller had observed it for several years. "I am surprised," he said in May 1930, "that you get any veterans' preference . . . because my experience has taught me to believe that it is a declaration and not much more. You can get around it by many, many processes. We have had to fight for that constantly. We have not less than 5,000 cases of second-, third-, and fourth-class postmaster appointments in rural free delivery which appear to be violations of the law. We used to wear a path between the Legion office and the Postmaster General's office."

Veterans Preference was involved in roughly one-fourth of all jobs with the federal government. But the employment "downturn" as it was called antiseptically at the outset of the Depression had a direct and immediate effect on another Legion concern—adjusted compensation.

That recent legislative victory was a promise of partial reimbursement for ex-service personnel for sacrificing time and earning power in wartime service. Now with news that widespread unemployment was likely to come, veterans looked to the loan provision of their U.S. Government paid-up insurance as a wild card that should be played without delay.

It was not surprising, then, that not long after the crash, veterans began calling for prepayment in cash and for the full value of their certificates.

This movement, which was growing in number and intensity, ran counter, however, to the standard Legion stance of country-before-the-individual. It also pitted the Legion's Legislative Committee against all such bills now being pushed by legislators in Washington, some of whom were even considering raising the loan value of the adjusted compensation certificates as a post-crash measure. Much of the attention of Congress from April to July 1930 was spent with pension legislation. (This move for relatively quick action was precipitated more because of the threat of ever-increasing agitation for a full value cash-in than it was because of any particularly pro-veteran sentiment.)

The movement for a cash prepayment of the adjusted compensation certificates had actually been aided, philosophically at least, by the recent passage of five major laws pertaining to veterans, each one supported in whole or in part by the Legion.

One act validated 40,000 belated applications for adjusted compensation. One added 4,500 much-needed hospital beds for the disabled through new construction projects. Another authorized a study of the Legion's concept of universal military service. A fourth went beyond even what the Legion had asked: the Johnson Act provided immediate financial relief for 150,000 veterans who were unable to prove service connection in their individual cases of disability. That final development alone would have made the year 1930 remarkable for veterans' affairs.

But the one to which the Legion officially was most opposed (though certainly not by consensus) was the Disability Allowance Law passed in early July 1930, which awarded veterans $12 monthly for 25% disability; $18 for 50%; $24 for 75%; $40 for total disability.

This was the first of the real pension bills to be hurried through in these times of need. Not only was it wrong in principle, according to the official Legion view, but also the awards set new standards for inadequacy.

One law, however, met with cheers, particularly those of the Legion's Legislative and Rehab committees. By an act on July 3, 1930, Congress authorized the president to proceed with the consolidation of more government activities affecting veterans. Executive orders on

July 21 and November 4, 1930, brought together the activities of the Veterans Bureau, the Bureau of Pensions, the National Home for Disabled Volunteer Soldiers, and that function of the army surgeon general to furnish prosthetic appliances to disabled vets. The new Veterans Administration thus created was to be subject to the supervisory power of the president and the laws granting veterans' benefits.

The now customary method of convening the membership (in representative fashion) as a governing body became even more important when the funding of veterans' benefits would be seen in the context of a national depression.

To advertise the upcoming convention in Boston, the National Convention Committee organized a radio broadcast on September 18 aimed at reaching fifty million people. From 10 to 11:30 P.M. Eastern Standard Time, the National Broadcasting Company and the Victor Division of R.C.A. Victor provided technical assistance and funding for this national broadcast, which carried Legion addresses and musical programming.

The principle studio was at Boston's historic Faneuil Hall, where 1,000 Legionnaires sang Legion songs and World War refrains. National Commander O. L. Bodenhamer spoke from Chicago; other national officers spoke from Portland (in both Oregon and Maine), San Francisco, New York City, Florida, and Texas.

When the Legion met at their National Convention at Boston in early October, a year after the stockmarket crash, it was with an exhuberance that seemed determined to lift the nation's spirits with several days of convention pageantry. According to *Legion Magazine* staffer Marquis James, who had recently won a Pulitzer Prize for his biography of fellow Texan Sam Houston of Alamo fame, the convention this year, with an estimated attendance of 150,000, was the largest ever in the history of the nation. The *Boston Herald* called it "the spectacle of the century."

The thousands of spectators weary already of Depression woes were regaled by three parades: Massachusetts's tercentenary float pageant, the monkeyshines of the members of the Legions honorary "40 & 8" group, named after the small French railroad boxcars used during the war, each of which could transport forty men or eight horses, and the grand Legion parade which took all day Tuesday to pass in review. Schools and post offices in the Boston area were closed for the occasion.

Camaraderie was demonstrated by the 15,000 Massachusetts Legionnaires with their one hundred bands in their three-hour march past the reviewing stand. At dusk the float of Beckwith Post of Medford passed depicting Flanders Fields, the white crosses "row on row" among the poppies.

Fraternity reigned. Two Legionnaires from Kansas who roomed and marched together were also the opposing candidates for that state's gubernatorial election. Harry Woodring and Frank Haucke marched with the Sunflower State's delegation before returning to resume campaign trails at home. Democrat Woodring would emerge the winner the next month by a mere 251 votes. He would later be appointed secretary of war (1936–40) by President Franklin Delano Roosevelt. Kansas would also be honored in the election of the next national commander, Ralph T. O'Neil and the new Auxiliary president Mrs. Robert L. Hoyal.

Legionnaire Rudy Vallee marched with the party from Maine. Wearing the official white jersey with the silhouette of a green pine on the front and with a yellow cane, the popular radio crooner led the band from Auburn. Behind him others from Maine chanted the lyrics of a recent Vallee hit, the University of Maine "Stein Song."

A twenty-one gun salute announced the arrival of President Hoover, who to the 8,000 in the Boston Arena and a radio audience in the millions presented his standard talk about austerity necessarily preceding a brighter future that he said was sure to come. Ex-president Calvin Coolidge and Mrs. Coolidge came down from Northampton to attend the opening session. When introduced, the taciturn Coolidge waved off calls for a speech. By staying in character, the stoic New Englander played his part perfectly, to the delight of the audience. Sparing in talk as always, "Silent Cal" said simply, "You have paid your debt to Lafayette, but you still owe a debt to yourselves and to the United States of America."

For lasting effect, however, all the glitter and high-stepping on the parade route in Boston did not echo so long or reverberate so widely as the action of the convention. At this annual meeting the Legion's principal government voted to lay aside a proposal for immediate payment on the adjusted compensation certificates. The vote was a substantial 967 to 244. Amid a growing movement to the contrary, the convention had maintained a tradition of selflessness and service to the nation.

The Legion had enjoyed one of its most impressive victories in getting adjusted compensation legislation enacted. Now the official stance of the organization that had fought long and hard for realization of that benefit was that the adjustment of compensation should remain as 20-year paid-up insurance with the now current loan provision. (But as those of the minority opinion noted, it was action that could be reconsidered.)

Reconsidered it was when in January 1931 the N.E.C. met in special session. After one of the most notable debates in the life of the organization, the committeemen reversed the convention action and endorsed cash retirement of the certificates. They stopped short, however, of officially favoring any of the bills currently being considered in Congress for that purpose.

The Boston convention had said "hands off." So who called the meeting in January to reconsider the matter? National Commander O'Neil reminded the committeemen that while the convention had not authorized them to take action for the cash settlement, it had not forbidden posts from sending up resolutions for that very thing and that at the posts, it seemed, the sentiment was for the payments now in this time of ever-widening need.

O'Neil said he had received requests from fifteen departments to call the special session of the N.E.C. Before that, however, he may have primed the pump, he admitted, by sending out a letter asking for the opinion of departments. What he and the others found was that veterans feeling the bite of the Depression were responding to the loan provision of their adjusted compensation law. What did they do with the money they borrowed? A Legion survey reporting in May 1931 showed the most frequent uses were for paying off mortgages, bolstering small businesses, purchasing farm equipment and seed for crops, purchasing motor vehicles for business purposes, and paying doctor bills for themselves and their families.

One day after the N.E.C. meeting the Senate Finance Committee began hearings on adjusted compensation legislation. John Thomas Taylor observed the action on a bill under consideration by the House Ways and Means Committee for increasing the loan value of the certificates to fifty percent of their face amount. When reported out, the bill passed the House on February 16 by a vote of 363 to 39. From there it went to the Finance Committee of the Senate, then to the full Senate, where it passed 72 to 12.

Though the president vetoed it, before the month was out the bill again passed the House (328 to 79) and the Senate (76 to 17). At the end of two months the Veterans Bureau had made 1,175,593 loans (with another 50,000 pending) for a total of $680,032,000. The average loan was $377. But what the backers of the bill had assumed would be a thirty percent turnout of veterans applying for loans turned out to be three times that many, as the depressed economy continued to slide to new depths. This half-value measure would not stop the demand for full-value loans.

Many pointed to the N.E.C.'s reversal of policy, anticipated presumably even as the Boston National Convention had refused to sanction such a move, as a reason for the increased membership for the years 1930 and 1931. Some reiterated the notion that Congress, by giving partial loan value for the certificates, was actually trying to stave off the demand for full-value. Others observed that increased membership was more likely a natural tendency during times of upheaval to join one's fellows in an identifiable and organized mechanism for information and action. (Membership dropped for two years after 1931 and then began increasing gradually after 1934.) For whatever reason, more veterans were coming into the Legion, and "National" welcomed them as a constituency.

More members meant more grassroots support, but also more work, particularly for the Rehab function.

Watson Miller and his staff had been busy before. Now he readily admitted that Rehab had "bit off more than it could digest." But, "In a situation where equal service to all is difficult, many persons without much popularity and no friends seem to suffer delay. We do what we can to care for those who would appear to need us most." He added, "Much of our work concerns people who are not members of the Legion. We have found it impossible to put up bars as between types of effort or groups. It is my feeling that we shall have to continue to operate in respect of all reasonable requests for information or effort."

The thirteenth national conclave in late September 1931, meeting in Detroit, elected the youngest national commander so far, Henry Leonidas Stevens, and strengthened the effort of the National Employment Committee.

This convention also reversed the N.E.C. of January, largely on principle since congressional action had favored that which the Legion now once again officially opposed.

The press insisted upon calling the Detroit Convention the "beer and bonus" convention, the least common (and real) denominator for the two most confrontational, center-stage issues dealt with at the convention: the call to repeal the 18th Amendment, and the turnabout on the cash redemption of the adjusted compensation certificates. True, many of the Legion's most gifted and respected orators held forth in spirited exchanges marked by intelligence and emotion before an appreciative, and divided, audience that registered strong feelings. Hence the misleading moniker.

Regarding Prohibition, the convention delegates voted that Congress should submit the prohibition law to the states for repeal or modification.

The furor over Prohibition this time had begun in the Convention Resolutions Committee meetings before coming onto the floor of the convention. The chief justification for the repeal of the Volstead Act and for legalizing beer once again was "in the interest of furnishing added employment." Convincing or not to "drys" and moralists in general, that was the reasoning of the moment.

As had often occurred in the past, the raising of the Prohibition issue was challenged by one who cited the Legion's ban on nongermane matters. But National Commander Ralph T. O'Neil immediately turned to National Judge Advocate Frank E. Samuel, who said official consideration of the subject was not a violation of the Legion's constitution barring "the dissemination of partisan principles." When a roll call of the states was called, 1,008 delegates voted for repeal, 394 against it. The Legion now stood on a decision that had been recommended earlier by Past National Commander Savage who, at the time, failed to convince the organization to take his suggestion.

The other matter which would be given equal billing with the "beer" issue was the reconsidering of the N.E.C.'s action in January favoring the issue of cash payments for adjusted compensation certificates.

The official view now of the supreme governing body of the world's largest veterans' organization about adjusted compensation was for a return to the flag-and-bunting lexicon of country-first patriotism.

On this issue the convention realigned with the previous convention, calling again on Legionnaires to "refrain from placing unnecessary financial burdens upon national, state, or municipal governments and to unite . . . to the end that the war against depression be victoriously concluded and prosperity and happiness [be] restored."

A minority resolution reiterated the procash payment. Speakers for this view included Legionnaire Representative Wright Patman of Texas, who had led the campaign for the prepayment bill in Congress, the bill that late next spring would be called an incentive for the first Bonus Marchers.

Amid the oratory of Legionnaire congressmen, prominent lawyers, and others stood farmer and Legionnaire Wally Williams of Maryland asking to be recognized and who, many later said, tipped the scale for the majority report.

"I have my certificate stuck away and have not borrowed on it yet, although I am poor. I sold my wheat and can't pay my taxes but . . . I got my health, and I am going to borrow on that thing this winter according to the amount legally authorized when it was given to me and I am going to turn it over to the welfare association in my county, because I got a lot of neighbors who are a damn sight worse off than I am.

"Thirteen years ago this fall, October 14th, [National Commander] "Deke" O'Neil and I crawled out of a lousy trench and the regiment that we served in took that piece of ground where the Romagne Cemetery stands today, and when it was taken half of that regiment were killed or wounded. A comrade from my state lived, but lost both his arms. Another comrade from downstate took three hours to die, and left behind . . . a wife and a kiddie he had never seen. The Legion has had the esteem and affection and the love of the people of America because it has done the job of taking care of them, and on the day when we use our organized power to ask for a special privilege for ourselves and not for them the Legion loses the love that it has so richly deserved."

The roll call vote of 902 to 507 rejected the minority report. By acclamation the delegates once again adopted a majority report expressing the official version of the attitude humbly expressed by Wally Williams.

The dramatic debate over "beer and bonus" occupied more column inches and absorbed more printer's ink in the "extras" during convention time than all the other business conducted combined. Granted, both issues related in some fashion to members and nonmembers alike.

But so, too, did the most important action of the convention. This accomplishment was destined to be longer-lasting in its effect, more beneficial to more people, more undeniably constructive in its intent and eventual achievement, and, in the main, was more indicative of that phenomenon "Legionism" than the others.

For this item of business had to do with jobs: a nationwide effort to find employment or relief for jobless veterans. The recently organized National Employment Commission directed by Howard P. Savage had cooperated with the government's Employment Service, appointed State Employment Officers, and planned for post-level activities aimed at easing the problem of unemployment in the towns and cities of the nation.

Now this program was upgraded and reemphasized as the Legion's best hope of bringing its human resources to bear on the nation's plight. The program asked that posts (1) immediately seek out, or create if necessary, agencies for the registration and placement of the unemployed; (2) discourage "migration" of laborers from town to town looking for work; (3) help create work rather than relief; (4) create public sentiment for hastening to the building stage public improvements of federal, state, and local projects; (5) convince local municipalities to assume responsibility for local unemployment circumstances, with the goal being to alleviate the problems as best as could be done; and (6) convince both employers and employees to adopt the five-day work week of six-hour workdays to help involve more workers in staggered employment schedules.

Initiate, cooperate, and follow through—these were the watchwords for the employment program. Specifically, the goal was to make the winter durable for those needing jobs and who were desperate for food and clothing. National Commander Stevens presented the plan to President Hoover in early December along with the annual legislative program of the Legion. He also pledged the cooperation of the Legion's new mechanism for employment with that of the President's own new committee on relief and with the employment division of the Department of Labor. He listed the names of leaders in industry, labor, and transportation whose help and advice had been sought and who served as an advisory council for the Legion's employment program.

That group included the presidents or other key top officers of the

Pennsylvania Railroad, General Foods, Radio Corporation of America (RCA), Standard Oil, United Mine Workers, Brotherhood of Railway Trainmen, Anaconda Wire and Cable Company, Botany Worsted Mills, Continental Motors, Association of National Advertisers, Bancamerica–Blair Corp., and others, including those from the press. The worthiness of this venture had only one measure of success—the number of job seekers eventually employed.

One of the important things the Legion could do for a program of employment was to apply its practiced and often successful lobbying effort to getting appropriations for government programs seeking the same goals.

The Legion's legislative efforts were by now well-known. Other organizations sought Legion support and aid in getting laws enacted. Panaceas for the Depression were prevalent, running the gamut from employment insurance to the farmer who put in for the killing of every tenth cow.

But congressional appropriations were the key to success. That fact was demonstrated a month after the convention when the U.S. Employment Service under the Department of Labor established twenty-three offices that employed many veterans to help other veterans. In November the service reported finding permanent or temporary employment for 54,000 veterans. John Thomas Taylor said there should be twice the number of offices and multiples of the number reemployed so far. He led the push for a larger appropriation the next time around as part of the National Legislative Committee's charge for 1931.

The Detroit Convention had also adopted a plan for strengthening the efficiency of service officers on all levels. The "Minnesota Plan" had been developed and used in that department to admirable results. Presented to the December 1929 conference of department commanders and adjutants, the plan was largely the handiwork of past department commander Earl V. (Pat) Cliff, a N.E.C. man from Minnesota (1931–33) and later a Rehab Committee chairman (1936–37).

The Minnesota Plan included schools for post and district service officers that focused on the many aspects of claims work that most frequently caused problems for those making claims, and a review of techniques that other service officers had used successfully. The course work stressed gaining familiarity with the many forms used and information required by the Veterans Administration and the procedure for collecting all the correct information needed. In Minnesota service officers also resurveyed claims that had been rejected by the Veterans Bureau. They mounted a publicity campaign to educate, enlighten, and encourage veterans whose claims had been rejected or who had not made claims for lack of information.

The plan appealed to convention delegates, many of whom convinced department officials to replicate the work done in Minnesota.

The Boston Convention had adopted many constructive measures in addition to taking definite, if controversial, action on Prohibition and against the move to gain cash payments for adjusted compensation certificates. The destination of those mandates was the National Legislative Committee in which subsequent bills would be drafted for introduction into Congress.

New National Commander Louis Johnson, one of many lawyers who would occupy the office, recommended treating the legislative program like a jury trial: "Pick out the vulnerable spots of the opposition, take the opponent's case and analyze it, and build up your own case."

Face-to-face with congressmen and senators, John Thomas Taylor and others continued to press for a standing committee in the Senate to hear veterans' measures. (The House had established its Veterans Affairs Committee in 1924.)

But as members of the House or Senate would quickly and testily remind any Legionnaire who approached them about the needs of veterans, this congress had other irons in a fire that many said was already blazing out of control. The work ahead would require a strong heart and, for the times, not a particularly generous one.

In addition to the appropriations bills that needed to be hammered out for the operation of the government, there was an avalanche of controversial matters that required more attention than there was time to give: the national budget, unemployment relief, unemployment insurance, public works, economy proposals, Philippine independence (a holdover issue from the Spanish-American War), farm mortgage refinancing, war debt revision, railroad legislation, Muscle Shoals (the rapids in the Tennessee River later to be tamed by the Tennessee Valley Authority), bank reform, utilities regulation, stock exchange regulation, guaranty of bank deposits, price stabilization, postage rates, antitrust amendments, and new tax legislation, to mention the most pressing matters.

The catchword was "economy," a required prefix, it seemed, for the measures making up the deluge of proposals for relieving in whatever fashion the nation's economic depression. House and Senate leaders sent "economy letters" to fellow members in each house, asking for compliance with the president's suggestions for toughing out the nation's darkening circumstances. Each of the committees created in the previous two sessions to investigate "veterans' expenditures" had been called an "Economy Committee." There emerged the inevitable Economy Bill fashioned from many such bills.

Meanwhile, seeking to match and surpass the efforts of the Legion and others speaking for veterans, there arose the National Economy League, composed of those who worked vigorously to retain the tenets of conservative economic and political idealogy. N.E.L., as this organization was called, was said by its proponents to be dedicated to an "economic reconstruction." Harry Colmery, National Legislative

Chairman, had another name for it: "the speckled colt of the U.S. Chamber of Commerce."

III

Genuine "economy" considerations, along with the pontifications spouted by those who had long since opposed veterans' benefits, were taken up at the convening of the first session of the 72nd Congress in December 1931. A joint congressional committee, beginning December 9 and continuing until February 6, heard testimony on the benefits affecting disabled veterans. For the first time since the World War, opponents of the benefits also testified. The Legion was heard on January 11, 1932.

A tug of war soon developed among the many interested parties. In mid-April General Hines told the House Economy Committee that $80 million could be saved from the Veteran Administration budget. The next month the House on May 3 defeated Title IX of the Economy Bill, which would have cut $48 million from the bureau's budget, by a vote of 211 to 116. Two days later the National Economy League (N.E.L.) filed a brief with the president and Congress asking for at least $450 million to be cut from veterans' programs. A month later the Senate defeated Title VII of the Economy Bill by a vote of 63 to 14, a bill that would have cut another $48 million.

In September, with the Economy Bill still being debated in Congress, the U.S. Chamber of Commerce called for cuts totaling $403 million to be made in veterans' benefits. President Hoover's budget message in early December identified cuts of $127 million. A few days later General Hines recommended cuts aggregating $85,857,000 a year. Just before Christmas N.E.L. upped the ante to $457,065,354 worth of cutbacks.

So the year ended with the economic malaise deepening and solutions wanting.

The new year of 1933 would prove to be the darkest of the Depression. On January 2 the National Association of Manufacturers' Committee for Economy in Government issued a list of cuts totalling $411 million which it said could be made in the funding of veterans' benefits. The next day Representative Woodrum of Virginia, chairman of the Veterans' Subcommittee of the House Appropriations Committee, recommended a ten percent reduction in all direct payments made to veterans and their dependents, a total of $61 million. The following day a similar proposal (but for a comparatively lenient $8,570,000) was made by a special "economy committee" of the Senate Appropriations Committee.

In early January, also, there came the first proposals for cutting even into the benefits of those with unquestioned service-connected disabilities. One House measure would take a straight ten percent cut in all forms of World War compensation; the Senate version would reduce the compensation or pension of anyone drawing more than $1,000 a year (a sum only the disabled had so far achieved) by ten percent.

A month later the Senate adopted the Bratton amendment for a five percent cut in all appropriation bills. For the Veterans Administration appropriation of $946 million this would amount to $47.3 million. The Legion objected most vigorously to this amendment because of the requirement that the cut be applied only to administrative costs, which meant that since, as yet, V.A. funds for direct payments could not be touched, the cut would have to come out of the operating funds for hospitals. Legion spokesmen said this really amounted to a forty-three percent cut, which was likely to all but paralyze hospitalization.

The amendment was rejected by the House on February 21. In the meantime, however, Senator Smoot introduced a bill to eliminate all benefits except those for direct service connection; and Representative Menaclus Lankford of Virginia brought forth another of similar intent.

During this watch-and-wait year, the Legion had come to count on the seeming inability of Congress and the president to settle on a common objective. This apparent confusion and lack of coordination were said by some to be as big a help as was the Legion's lobbying efforts.

But in a state of emergency the time it takes to accept the inevitable is necessarily shortened. National officers, not alone certainly among national leaders and people on the streets, foresaw that the unraveling of the nation's economic fabric would surely include more than a mere move for drastic cuts in veterans' benefits.

Furthermore, the Democratic sweep of the nation's voting booths meant that though the House was still divided, there was someone now undisputably in charge whose "New Deal" would soon be revealed. Amidst a dramatic changing of the guard, the rumor mills of Washington churned out daily would-be scoops about how much veterans' benefits would be cut.

The National Legislative Committee's bulletin of February 25 gave credence to at least the higher-grade rumors that funding slashes were not only expected with the new administration but also would be sweeping.

The arrival of the Roosevelt Administration on March 4 was marked by a whirlwind of activity, actually the advent of a reformation in American federal government. Two days later F.D.R. closed all the banks for three days. On March 9 he called the expected special session of Congress. A new director of the Budget Bureau also arrived as a key person in the new administration. Trusted sources told Legion national officers that plans had already been laid for the bureau to set siege to veterans' appropriations.

John Thomas Taylor wired all department adjutants to call immediately on their congressmen and senators to register opposition to Congress "abdicating its constitutional responsibility by granting to the president authority to repeal or amend existing veterans' laws, without approval of Congress."

But the die had been cast. At the close of the first day of the special session of Congress, Roosevelt hosted a conference at 9:30 that evening at the White House in which an Economy Bill was drafted for immediate enactment. The next day his "economy message" was read to Congress. "It is too late," he said, "for a leisurely approach to this problem. We must not wait to act several months hence. We must move with a direct and resolute purpose now."

House Resolution 28 created a Special Economy Committee to report the Economy Bill, H.R. 2820, "to maintain the credit of the United States Government." As expected, cuts proposed for veterans' programs were wide and deep. Simultaneously, Senate 233 was announced, identical in text to the House bill. The Senate adjourned and its Finance Committee went into executive session. Legion spokesmen were granted an appearance before the Finance Committee on Saturday morning, March 11.

In the House, Tennessee's Representative Gordon W. Browning asked a caucus of Democrats to accept a twenty-five percent horizontal cut of veterans' payments as a substitute for the more drastic Economy Bill provision. His amendment lost, the caucus ended, and the House went into immediate session to hear House Report No. 1 and House Resolution 32, which provided for the rule to consider H.R. 2820 in two hours of debate.

Browning asked from the floor that his amendment be considered. It was not; the president's bill was passed 266 to 138. Legionnaires were asked now to concentrate their telegrams on the Senate where the twenty-five percent reduction measure would be introduced.

The senators debated for three days. On the afternoon of the third day, National Legislative Commission Chairman Ray Murphy of Iowa and John Thomas Taylor were permitted to see Roosevelt, who in 1925 had been chairman of the New York Legion Department's Endowment Fund drive, to lay before him the certain effects of the Economy Bill and to ask that should the bill be made law, the Legion would be consulted on the rules and regulations attending the law. The president assented and sent them to see the director of the budget, Mr. Douglas, who at their evening meeting similarly assured the two that the Legion would be consulted.

The Legion lobbyists then hurried to the action in the Senate, where they were successful in securing a few amendments to the bill from the floor. An hour after they had left the Budget Bureau the bill passed the Senate. The next day the House accepted the Senate amendments and voted 373 to 19 to pass the bill, a majority vote that sped the bill past conference consideration. The president signed the bill on Monday, March 20.

The system of benefits to veterans, including those for the service-connected disabled, had been cut $400,000,000!

National Legislative Commission Chairman Ray Murphy observed that "to have served [on that committee] in the year 1933 has been a chastening experience." He called the Economy Act "the disaster that the Ides of March and the few fateful days preceding and following brought to veterans and veterans' legislation." The Economy Act had virtually wiped out the World War Veterans Act of 1924.

Murphy struggled to put it all in perspective. "The salvation of our nation was the burning question. And in the dark days that followed the closing of every bank in the country, at a time when all that the founding fathers had envisioned for America seemed in jeopardy, in a crisis without parallel in time of peace, the Congress passed the Economy Bill."

Watson Miller spoke for the Legion function that had suffered a direct hit by the Economy Act fusillade. Appellate action undertaken for veterans had met with many fewer successes since March 20. Before, the recovery rate was about $490,000 a month. Since that date little more than $130,000 a month had been recovered. Yet, "our work is necessarily increased because of the March 20 Act" because the need rose in proportion to the cutbacks.

There was also the matter of alleged culpability for this turn of events. Ray Murphy responded to editorials such as that in the *New York Herald* (March 16) which asked, "Is the American Legion to live as a patriotic organization, or is it to end as a discredited combination of politicians and claim agents organized to trade federal doles against votes and membership dues?"

Murphy countered, "While we did not inspire or even approve of some of the former veterans' laws that made possible this condition, laws which no one can defend, it is not enough that we disclaim responsibility for their enactment. We much accept a further responsibility to recognize and guard against legislation of such character as certain to bring disaster upon veterans."

In that regard, Watson Miller cited one measure specifically. "Many felt that the Disability Allowance whose paternity the American Legion has many a time and often denied was the doorstep baby that had brought disgrace upon our house. As a result of such feeling by action of that convention [Portland] there was created a special committee now known as the Bodenhamer Committee to study the whole field of

World War veterans' legislation with a view to eventual elimination of such injustices and inequalities as it might find to exist. Unfortunately as has lately been revealed, this action was taken too tardily; it had neither time to avert the storm of criticism that has raged about our heads nor power to prevent the debacle that has befallen our truly worthy legislation developed through the years."

Recriminations notwithstanding, the cause for veterans' benefits had been dealt a stunning blow. Campaigners for the cause surveyed the damage. John Thomas Taylor, about whom General Pershing was said to have remarked at a postwar ceremonial event when observing him bedecked with World War medals, "It looks as though he has never known a day of peace in his life," for certain had known no peace during the months of congressional economizing zeal that culminated in the Economy Act.

Not one for making excuses, Taylor could point only to what had occupied much of his attention since the November 1932 presidential election—the resumption of a previously appointed joint committee for investigating laws and regulations relating to veterans' benefits. Taylor had not only to present detailed proveteran testimony, but also to counter the testimony of those who would axe established benefits and who now were backed by supportive public opinion.

While heavily engaged in that pursuit and even before the report of the joint committee was made, the Economy Act was suddenly upon him.

Watson Miller, who recently had said he felt a little like Sancho Panza to John Thomas Taylor's Don Quixote, now voiced exasperation admitting to no comedic relief.

"We must start anew; resell the Legion."

The N.E.C., jealous occasionally when it appeared that department commanders and adjutants were impinging on matters of policy, an N.E.C. prerogative, was nothing if not a forum for self-evaluation, even piercing self-criticism.

At this critical time, thoughtful observations were heard from a rising star among Legion orators. Harry Colmery, chairman of the National Legislative Committee and a man whose zenith with the Legion was yet a decade before him, spoke with conviction and emotion. Colmery's message was one of "much hindsight, a note of warning, and a note of hope as well." He spoke with clarity and objectivity.

"If we are to understand what has happened to veterans' legislation, we must be frank, we must express our opinions courageously, and if we are to profit by what has happened, we must know our own weaknesses.

"Let me say, again expressing a personal opinion, that the new law and the new regulations are by no means all bad. They cover a wide field, and considering the small amount of money set aside to cover that field, they do remarkably well. They recognize the duty of the federal government to care for the veteran, wholly broken in mind and health, financially unable to care for himself, whose disability is not traceable to service, who now receives a pension [though] pitifully small. They recognize the government's never-ending obligation to the veteran whose disability is service connected. They recognize obligation to widows and children. . . . They recognize certain presumptions as to disabilities appearing after discharge. In short, the new regulations form a broad base upon which to rebuild the structure of World War veterans' benefits. In building, let us hope we will not forget the lessons the past, even the very recent past, have taught.

"For years a hodgepodge of legislation pertaining to World War veterans has been enacted into law, all requiring vast sums of money. A tremendous body of regulations has followed. A Blackstone and a Solomon combined could scarcely have found his way through their labyrinth. Into these laws, and in their administration, have crept inequalities and injustices which we have, more or less to ourselves, admitted.

"For most of this legislation the Legion has taken credit, and received blame. Far into the night our convention committees have labored, and at last, worn and weary, with but a few members present, they often with an axe to grind and willing to trade, all succumb to the member from Iowa . . . from Florida . . . from Colorado [each of whom] wants a new hospital, and so on ad infinitum.

"Out from committees come resolution after resolution after resolution, calling for legislative action, many highly controversial. Resolutions killed in one committee have experienced resurrection in another and sprung to life again. After each convention, the National Legislative Committee finds itself with something over a hundred convention mandates for enactment into law. The vice-chairman of the National Legislative Committee has frequently warned that this could not go on forever.

"Some of our resolutions have displeased the drys, some have shocked sincere pacifists, some have affronted citizens desiring greater cooperation in world affairs, some have ruffled certain nationalities, some have discredited citizens of high standing, some have offended the medical profession, some have wounded large numbers of those professing Protestant faith, some have alienated high-minded service men, many have antagonized big business. The Portland Convention by an almost unanimous vote passed the bonus resolution, thereby alienating most of the editorial opinion and a great body of the non-service people and of the common, ordinary folk of the country.

"I am wholly aware that any strong organization, as any strong individual, is bound to incur opposition, no matter what it merits, no matter how just its cause. I am not seeking now to assess or to allege blame, nor to say what I should have done or refrained from doing had the power been mine to do or not do so. Rather, I am calling attention to what I believe to be an indisputable fact, that since our organization has slowly and in part inevitably developed an opposition, that there has gradually developed a suspicion of our purposes and doubt of our patriotism. One by one we have antagonized.

"The New Deal for America and the new deal for veterans present a challenge and an opportunity for the American Legion. If we are merely obstructive, if we are not actively constructive, we will have declined the challenge. If we fail intelligently to evaluate ourselves, if we fail to assert and assume our place in American life, as the great patriotic organization of all time, if we fail to sense changing conditions and changing opinion, if we fail to realize that for the American Legion, America is first, we will have missed our opportunity, and opportunity may not come again.

There is a tide in the affairs of men,
Which, taken at the flood, leads on to fortune;
Omitted, all the voyage of their life,
Is bound in shallows and in miseries.

"For the American Legion, the tide again is at the flood. Let us take it."

Harry Colmery chose a tragic figure to quote. But he apparently found that the lament of Brutus in Shakespeare's *Julius Caesar* (act IV, scene III) fit the present occasion. The lines also were imbued with motivational imperatives that Colmery knew were essential to Legionism.

The accumulation of veterans' benefits, a process that the Legion had helped further appreciably over fourteen years, had evaporated with the stroke of a presidential pen. The superstructure, though as Colmery maintained not the underpinnings, of veterans' benefits had been razed. The Legion had measured its relevancy by the job done so far. Now it seemed that much of that basic work was to be done again.

The next twelve months would be occupied in seeking to reverse the Economy Act. The plan that emerged partitioned the overall need into four requests: 1) a return to disabled veterans of all benefits granted by the World War Veterans Act that were in effect before March 20, 1933; 2) hospitalization for veterans unable to pay for those services; 3) restoration of service-connected presumption of disabilities as understood by law before the enactment of the Economy Act; and 4) protection for widows and dependent children of veterans according to the World War Veterans Act.

The "Four-Point Program" was, of course, nothing short of a call for complete dissolution of the Economy Act provisions dealing with veterans' affairs.

Oddly enough, help (though not directly) would come from the very president whose signature had created the Economy Act.

AMERICAN LEGION JUNIOR BASEBALL

Reviving the Game

In the early 1920s, on the threshold of the Golden Age of Sports, fewer boys and men were playing amateur baseball than in the pre–World War I years.

A survey for the years 1923–24 by the National Amateur Athletic Federation (of which the American Legion was a "unit member") showed that while golf, tennis, football, basketball, and track and field were more popular with amateurs of all ages, baseball showed no corresponding increase in popularity.

Some blamed the game-throwing culprits of the Chicago White (tinged "Black") Sox, who had been summarily chastised for their part in the 1919 gambling scandal. Former federal judge Kenesaw Mountain Landis, who, though not a member, became a popular speaker at Legion conventions, was the new baseball commissioner, the lord high protector of the sport determined to revive its reputation.

American Legion Americanism Commission Director Frank C. Cross called for action to fight the seamier aspects of "professionalism" in amateur sports. The Legion, he said in December 1925, was "more than a match for avaricious money changers who seek to defile the temple of sportsmanship by bartering in amateur sports."

But the first real impetus for a nationwide baseball program for boys came from a guest speaker at the South Dakota department convention meeting in Milbank in 1925. John L. Griffith, Athletic Commissioner of the Western Conference (Big Ten) colleges, recommended that the Legion take on a campaign for the physical fitness of the nation's youth. Griffith's friend, State Commander Frank G. McCormick, agreed; before the department convention was over, it had produced a resolution urging that the national organization adopt a baseball program for teenagers during summer school vacations.

At the national convention that year in Omaha, the idea met with enthusiastic approval, and National Commander James A. Drain gave it his hearty support. A new Legion program was born, one that in succeeding years would involve millions of American boys.

South Dakota continued to point the way. L. B. "Stubbs" Allison of the University of South Dakota spoke to the N.E.C. at its May 1926 meeting and explained the work of the South Dakota department in promoting baseball for boys. At that point there were over 925 teams in the state, he said.

For Stubbs and others, there were several reasons for such a program. First, Stubbs said the nation had produced a generation of "softies." He also cited the findings of World War induction centers that an alarming number of young men were not physically fit for military service. Finally, a national program such as baseball for boys under age seventeen could prove that the Legion "was for more than the bonus."

The Junior All-American Baseball League, formed with the help of the National Amateur Athletic Federation, began in the spring of 1926. Legion posts in fifteen states organized baseball teams and local competitions, which included teams sponsored by other organizations from which would emerge sectional and regional winners for play-off series leading to a junior world series for the top two teams.

One of the best reasons to expect success with the Legion's new baseball program, it was said, was its system of elimination contests, which produced two teams to play in a junior world series.

The Americanism Commission had been made responsible for Junior Baseball's sectional, regional, and national (world) series. Assistant Americanism Director Dan Sowers was placed in charge of this new community service program.

Such an ambitious program, of course, would require more funds than Legion posts and the national organization could supply. Sowers inquired of the major league club owners about help to fund the program, which would not only increase the popularity of the sport but also train a new crop of professional players.

At first, though, he found that politics within the major leagues had Baseball Commissioner Landis pitted against the club owners over the rights to money accumulated in the commission's share of recent world series purses. Landis was holding the fund as being due the players, whereas the owners contended it was theirs. From that position, Legion friend Landis could not be expected to make a contribution from the commission's fund nor to ask the owners for money to support Junior Baseball. Consequently, that avenue for funding was abandoned that year.

So with financing uncertain, Sowers juggled the duties of arranging transportation, housing, playing the games, publicity, and trophies for the national series.

With much confusion and misunderstanding about who would pay for what, the first Junior Baseball World Series occurred at the National Convention in Philadelphia on October 11–18, 1926, the fiftieth anniversary year of professional baseball. Four teams qualified, those from Yonkers, New York; Springfield, Ohio; El Dorado, Kansas; and Pocatello, Idaho.

The boys from Idaho and New York were the first-round victors. When these two teams faced each other the six runs scored by the lads who came the farthest to play paled against the twenty-three runs scored by the team from New York Post 321. Only the soul-stirring, running-and-leaping one-handed catches by Idahoan first baseman Crawford kept the score from being a worse rout.

Cornelius McGillicuddy, better known as "Connie" Mack, manager of the Philadelphia Athletics of the American League, attended the games at the stadium of the Sesquicentennial Exposition. He was impressed that at the regional playoffs "whole towns . . . close their stores and attend the games en masse." The former big league catcher, the acknowledged gentleman of major league baseball, remarked, "The national junior baseball series sponsored by the Legion this year for the first time will do more for the future of baseball in America than anything I can imagine."

There was no Junior Baseball World Series in 1927. The national convention which began with an excursion to Paris had been a grand but expensive event; therefore Junior Baseball that year was limited to contests within departments.

But the Junior Baseball World Series was back on the field the next spring. The major league clubs agreed on February 14, 1928 to fund the transportation costs for the teams to regional and sectional tournaments and to the national series that year, and to continue to contribute in that fashion. For this the club owners' association appropriated $50,000. They agreed to also pay the transportation and housing costs and provide game tickets to the majors' World Series for the winning Junior Baseball team. Each team member would also receive a solid gold, twenty-one-jewel, Elgin pocket watch specially engraved.

After the conclusion of a successful season, Sowers reported in November to Judge Landis and to the presidents of the major leagues, Ernest S. "Ban" Barnard (American) and John A. Heydler (National), on the year's activities.

More than 100,000 boys in forty-four states and the District of Columbia had played baseball in the program. A team had come from Panama to compete in the eastern sectionals. This, Sowers said, was only scratching the surface. He hoped to see a half million boys involved the next year. The San Antonio national convention in 1928 had voted unanimously to continue junior baseball as a major part of the Americanism program.

To Sowers, "Probably the most important lesson that baseball holds . . . is its lesson in democracy. The game as played under the Legion's program brings together boys from families in all positions in life . . . playing together . . . for what each was worth in himself. . . ."

"We have tried to carry on this program without annoying the people in professional baseball" with requests for money or special privileges. And while "I doubt . . . if the activity has put an extra penny in the cash box of any ball club, it has put in the record of American history an outstanding, unselfish, and generous contribution toward the building of character in those youngsters who are steadily marching on to manhood to take over the reins of the affairs of this country in the future."

To the boys who reached the national play-off berths, Sowers explained, "You have now . . . stepped into an experience that many grown persons never attain—national attention. Upon you even the honor of the American Legion rests, because the Legion will be judged according to whether its effects, as reflected by you, have been worthwhile in its endeavor to encourage fair play, an underlying principle of good citizenship which the Legion is trying to promote in this baseball activity."

In midsummer 1928, the third season for the increasingly popular American Legion Junior Baseball national program, the crack of a twelfth inning, game-winning hit in little Clinton, Indiana was heard throughout the baseball world and beyond.

In the Vermillion County championship game in late June between the Clinton Juniors and the Binford Cubs, the score was tied at seven after nine innings. Two scoreless innings later, a Cub batter connected solidly, and the ball shot over the head of the shortstop. The runner on second base came home as his fellow Cubs cheered their sudden-death victory.

The game was over. But controversy surrounding the game-winning R.B.I. had just begun when the Clinton Juniors lodged a unique protest: the dramatic hit had come off the bat of the only girl on record playing American Legion Junior Baseball.

Though it was not until the twelfth inning that the protest was made, after Margaret Gislo had collected several hits, had tagged two runners at second base, and had fielded seven chances without an error, the Clinton team had a point. As the rule book stated, "Any boy is eligible to participate or play on a team. . . ."

The matter was appealed to Legion state athletic officer Robert Bushee who, evoking the relevant wisdom of Solomon, found Margaret fully qualified to play, but with her gender having been ignored in the rule book, he suspended her for a few days. Wisdom also required that he instantly turn to Dan Sowers, national director of the Legion's baseball program. Though Sowers had not anticipated girls playing, he found, to his credit, no justification for barring them from the game.

Soon the national wire services were calling for a story. Public relations staffers at National Headquarters in Indianapolis cautioned Sowers to reserve a decision until he conferred with no less a sports *luminary than the major league commissioner himself, Judge Kenesaw Mountain Landis, whom Sowers saw in Chicago on June 30.*

Sowers's statement after meeting with the colorful commissioner resonated Legionism. "In view of the service of our women in the World War and to the American Legion and the nation through the American Legion Auxiliary, it is held that . . . a girl . . . who has fulfilled all the requirements as to team registration and age eligibility will be entitled to play on teams competing in the regional and sectional tournaments and in the Junior World Series."

Margaret Gislo and the Binford Cubs won the state championship. But the young hardball nine from the crossroads town were defeated in the regional tournament by the team sponsored by Chicago Marine Post No. 9. The next year the National Americanism Commission settled the matter by passing a rule prohibiting girls from playing American Legion Junior Baseball. Young Margaret Gislo's debut with the boys of summer had been brief but memorable. (Subsequently, in another era, the Legion would bow to the prevailing attitude, which would allow both sexes to participate in young people's sports activities.)

The Depression brought challenges to the Legion's baseball program. When many people were needing money for essentials, the purchase of baseball equipment was necessarily put aside in many households. Similarly, funds from businesses and other sources of team sponsorship shriveled.

The 1933 and 1934 seasons were bleak, but the Legion generated internally the funding necessary for a bare bones program. Judge Landis had told Sowers that there was no money to be had from the Baseball Commission or the club owners' association.

When newspaperman and Legionnaire James F. O'Neil of Manchester, New Hampshire (later national commander), learned of the dire straits of Junior Baseball, he took the concern to his boss Frank Knox (first state commander in the Granite State and later secretary of the navy in World War II). Knox counseled against seeking corporate backing. Instead, he primed the pump with a check for $5,000 and challenged other newspaper owners to contribute. The funds raised were sufficient to continue the program.

In 1935, with the first flickering of the light at the end of the tunnel of economic despair, the Major League Club Owners Association restored $20,000 of the original annual funding.

Thus was perpetuated another Legion community service program. Meanwhile, the next generation of major league ballplayers was learning the game, memorizing and practicing the "fundamentals." In little Adel, Iowa, for example, the coach (a mailman when not on the ball diamond) of the Legion team recommended that a young shortstop consider becoming a pitcher. That player strode to the mound and began building a reputation for himself as a true American champion.

Later, Bob Feller's professional baseball career repaid the confidence of his early Legion coach by exemplifying the best qualities of the sport and the Legion's sponsorship of it for boys. In 1962 the strike-out king of his day (eighteen in one game) became the first Legion alumnus to be named to the Professional Baseball Hall of Fame.

RECOVERY

THE MOVE TOWARD A BILL OF RIGHTS FOR VETERANS

1934 – 1944

I

Restoration

Legion lobbyist John Thomas Taylor had long since acquired an abiding sense of déjà vu.

The recent post-Economy Act doldrums reminded him now of the many months after World War I when veterans seeking the few benefits available to them were shunted among overworked, underfunded, or poorly administered government agencies, forcing the disabled, particularly, to go begging for proper rehabilitation.

Each day he worked the Hill, Taylor went wearily "over the top" (Great War sayings still flavored the vernacular), buttonholing, cane-thumping, planning yet more chess moves to advance the Legion's legislative program.

While understanding the complexity of the problem, Taylor often expressed a personal predilection, the uncomplicated principle that right must prevail over wrong. If the Legion was right in its advocacy for veterans, then it should proceed full-speed ahead. If Congress disagreed and balked, Congress was wrong and that was that. He had long since disabused himself of any indecision on that count. So he reasoned and so advised national officers that they not become downcast and demoralized in these times.

But Taylor knew his work was cut out for him. For as Ray Kelly of Michigan, Legislative Committee chairman, would say loftily in May 1934, there had been a "splendid structure of our patiently builded legislation, written with the loving hands of devotion in a noble cause for the protection of our war-disabled." But that structure was almost gone. Where to start to rebuild? The answer to that, of course, was to begin on the turf Taylor knew best, Capitol Hill.

He had been point man before. Now he must apply his experience and knowledge of the federal legislating process to reinstate veterans' rehabilitation on the scale from which it had been toppled. For despite Harry Colmery's perceptive and evenhanded summation of the cause and effect of the Economy Act, the harsher aspects of the law as enacted would substantially diminish the life-style of many disabled veterans. Amputees, battle casualties, tubercular and shell-shocked veterans had just had their compensation cut more than half. About 100,000 of the service-connected group had been thrown off the rolls. These were but the most obvious instances.

So while the shock waves set off by the Economy Act continued to reverberate through veterandom during the summer of 1933 and into 1934, the Legion unveiled its Four-Point Program, reminiscent of the "fourfold" program with which a similar fight had begun many years earlier (and by which adjusted compensation had been won).

The four points now included; (1) restoration of previous rates for service-connected death and disability compensation; (2) the return of nearly 30,000 "presumptive" cases once again to the rolls disallowed by the review and appeal boards; (3) regaining the general hospitalization privilege for veterans; and finally, (4) appreciable aid for the widows and orphans of World War service men.

Ed Hayes of Illinois, elected national commander at Chicago, spent much time in Washington personally conducting the legislative campaign for restoring benefits to the disabled. When he wasn't in the nation's capital, Hayes crisscrossed the nation, taking the message to the public in the exhaustive itinerary now typical for national commanders.

He and other Legion spokesmen were quick to add that at least now (by January 1934) the budget-cutting fervor in which the Economy Act had been passed was changed. Now F.D.R. was asking for billions of dollars for relief. The Legion was not out of step to ask for restoration of lost benefits for veterans. Such a Legion advocacy was actually occurring within the much larger context of the federal relief programs, such as the Public Works and Civil Works administrations, during the winter of 1933–34 and into the spring.

But National Commander Hayes and others stressed that such relief measures were not designed to meet the unique needs of disabled veterans. Disarming one-liners, though belittling the complexity of the issue, spoke the mind of many. An N.E.C. man contrasted the amount of money spent on a national reforestation program to that cut from veterans' programs. It was difficult, he said, to see "how we as a nation were going to get out of the woods by planting more trees."

Meanwhile, a hopeful Congress debated many measures aimed at recuperation from the trying times of the Depression. Even an abbre-

Franklin D'Olier (PA)
1919-20

Frederick W. Galbraith, Jr (OH)
1920-21
(died in office, June 9, 1921)
(Bretzman)

John G. Emery (MI)
1921
(finished the term of Frederick W. Galbraith who died in office)

Hanford MacNider (IA)
1921-22

Alvin M. Owsley (TX)
1922-23

John R. Quinn (CA)
1923-24
(Bretzman)

JAMES A. DRAIN (WA)
1924-25

JOHN R. MCQUIGG (OH)
1925-26

HOWARD P. SAVAGE (IL)
1926-27

EDWARD E. SPAFFORD (NY)
1927-28

PAUL V. MCNUTT (IN)
1928-29

O. L. BODENHAMER (AR)
1929-30
(Shrauer, Little Rock)

Ralph T. O'Neil (KS)
1930-31
(Harris & Ewing)

Henry L. Stevens, Jr. (NC)
1931-32

Louis A. Johnson (WV)
1932-33

Edward A. Hayes (IL)
1933-34

Frank N. Belgrano (CA)
1934-35
(Harris & Ewing)

Ray Murphy (IA)
1935-36
(Bretzman)

Harry W. Colmery (KS)
1936-37
(Bretzman)

Daniel J. Doherty (MA)
1937-38

Stephen F. Chadwick (WA)
1938-39

Raymond J. Kelly (MI)
1939-40
(Kaiden-Keystone Photos)

Milo J. Warner (OH)
1940-41

Lynn U. Stambaugh (ND)
1941-42
(Bretzman)

Roane Waring (TN)
1942-43

Warren H. Atherton (CA)
1943-44

Edward N. Schieberling (NY)
1944-45

John Stelle (IL)
1945-46

Paul H. Griffith (PA)
1946-47
(Harris & Ewing)

James F. O'Neil (NH)
1947-48
(Blackstone Studios)

S. Perry Brown (TX)
1948-49
(Bretzman)

George N. Craig (IN)
1949-50

Erle Cocke, Jr. (GA)
1950-51
(Bretzman)

Donald R. Wilson (WV)
1951-52
(Chase News Photo)

Lewis K. Gough (CA)
1952-53

Arthur J. Connell (CT)
1953-54
(Chase)

Legion National Commanders toured the nation and met the noteworthy wherever they traveled. In 1923 Alvin Owsley was photographed with Douglas Fairbanks and Mary Pickford.

In late 1946 and early 1947, Legionnaires nationwide collected 3 million toys in the "Operation Tide of Toys" for European refugee children. The toys were distributed in Europe by CARE, Inc. (U.S. Army photograph)

During the Korean War, the Legion's interest in the nation's foreign relations came of age. Here National Foreign Relations Commission Chairman Donald R. Wilson, soon to be National Commander (1951-52) testifies before the Senate Foreign Relations Committee in May 1951, urging ratification of the North Atlantic Treaty. National Legislative Director John Thomas Taylor (left) presented Wilson to the Committee.

Henry D. Lindsley (TX) presided at St. Louis Caucus and was named Past National Commander at the Minneapolis National Convention in 1919.

First staff of The American Legion National Headquarters in Indianapolis, 1919-20. L. to R.: Gerald Murphy, Publicity Director; C. F. Siegrist, Auditor; Russell Creviston, Assistant Adjutant; Percy Monson, Director of Administration; George Rennick, Director of Emblem Division; unidentified; C. F. Sheridan, Service Division head; Lemuel Bolles, National Adjutant; H. E. Ludloff, Organization Director. (Indianapolis Star)

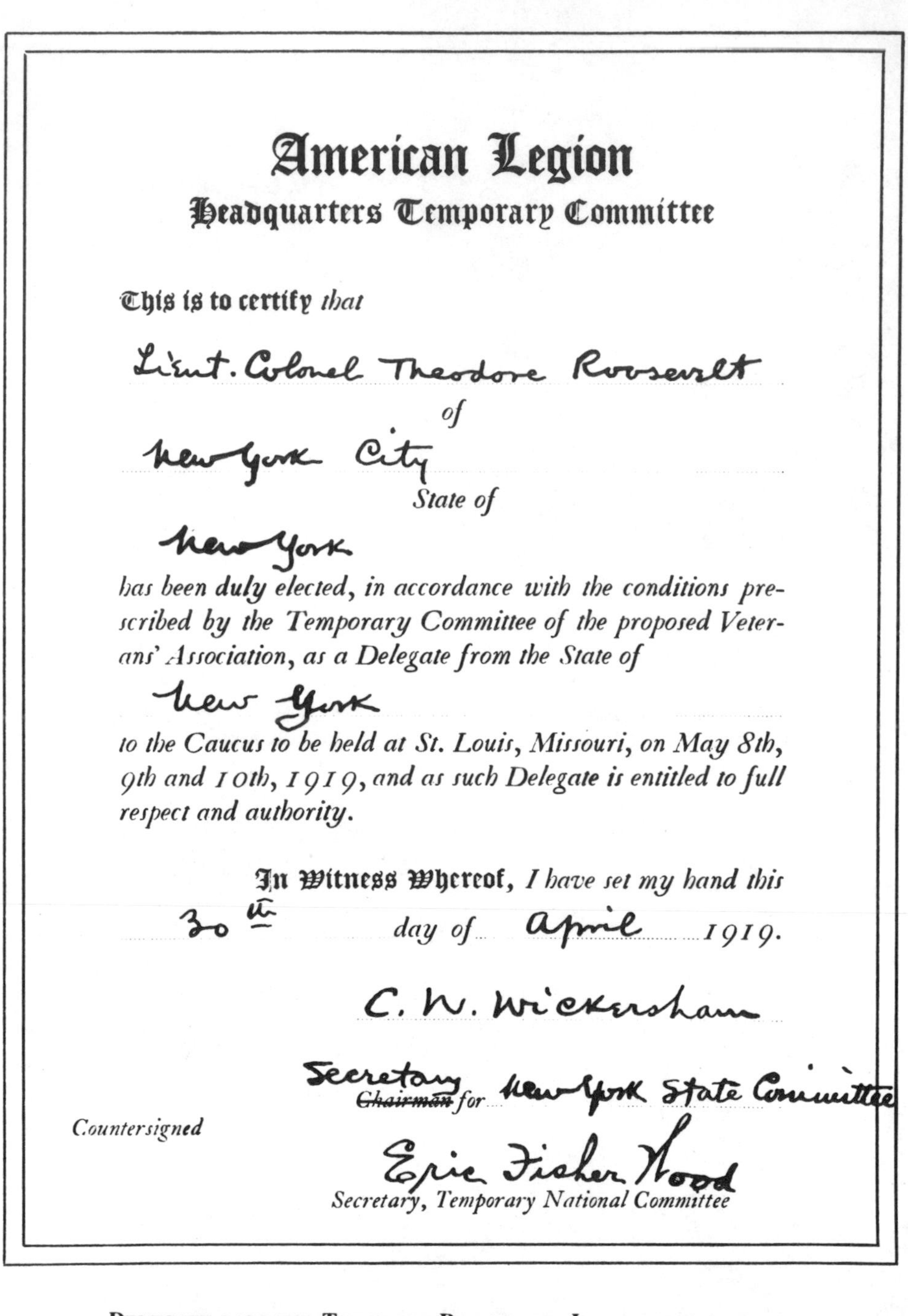

American Legion

Headquarters Temporary Committee

This is to certify *that*

Lieut. Colonel Theodore Roosevelt

of

New York City

State of

New York

has been duly elected, in accordance with the conditions prescribed by the Temporary Committee of the proposed Veterans' Association, as a Delegate from the State of

New York

to the Caucus to be held at St. Louis, Missouri, on May 8th, 9th and 10th, 1919, and as such Delegate is entitled to full respect and authority.

In Witness Whereof, *I have set my hand this*

30th *day of* April *1919.*

C. W. Wickersham

Secretary ~~Chairman~~ *for* New York State Committee

Countersigned

Eric Fisher Wood

Secretary, Temporary National Committee

Delegate card for Theodore Roosevelt, Jr. to represent the Department of New York at the St. Louis Caucus.

Lt. Colonel Theodore Roosevelt, Jr. (NY), Legion founder, named Past National Commander at 1949 National Convention at Philadelphia.

Eric Fisher Wood (PA), Legion founder, named Past National Commander at 1955 National Convention in Miami Beach, Florida.

LEGION PRESENTATION TO PRESIDENT WARREN G. HARDING AT THE WHITE HOUSE BY AMERICAN LEGIONNAIRES, JUNE 30, 1921. L. TO R.: PNC FRANKLIN D'OLIER; THOMAS W. MILLER, NATIONAL LEGISLATIVE COMMITTEE CHAIRMAN; PRESIDENT HARDING; FRENCH EMBASSY MEMBER; M. JUSSERAND, FRENCH AMBASSADOR TO THE U.S.; COL. THEODORE ROOSEVELT; NATIONAL COMMANDER JOHN EMERY; DELANCEY KOUNTZE, MEMBER OF THE PARIS CAUCUS; JOHN THOMAS TAYLOR. (Copyright Harris & Ewing)

BENNETT CHAMP CLARK (MO), LEGION FOUNDER, NAMED PAST NATIONAL COMMANDER AT 1926 NATIONAL CONVENTION IN PHILADELPHIA.

The American Legion's first membership poster, painted in 1919 by Ernst Hamlin Baker from a photo posed by three members of the temporary national headquarters staff at 19 West 44th Street, New York, N.Y.

THE CIRQUE DE PARIS, SITE OF THE PARIS CAUCUS OF THE AMERICAN LEGION, MARCH 15-17, 1919.

THOMAS W. MILLER (NV) PRESIDED AT THE PARIS CAUCUS AND WAS NAMED PAST NATIONAL COMMANDER AT THE 1968 NATIONAL CONVENTION IN NEW ORLEANS.

THE PARIS CAUCUS, MARCH 17, 1919, AT THE CIRQUE DE PARIS.

THE ST. LOUIS CAUCUS, MAY 8-10, 1919.

DELEGATES ON THE DAIS AT THE ST. LOUIS CAUCUS. THEODORE ROOSEVELT, JR. SEATED AT CENTER OF FOREGROUND.

Social gathering during first national convention, Minneapolis, November, 1919.

Parading at the first national convention of The American Legion, Minneapolis, November 1919.

Milton Foreman (IL), Legion founder, named Past National Commander at the 1921 National Convention in Kansas City, Missouri.

National Commander Hanford MacNider (IA) with Marshal Foch in the dining car of the American Legion Special train in which the French World War I leader toured the United States in 1921. (Photo copyright by Gravelle.)

President Herbert Hoover addresses the 12th National Convention of the Legion in Boston, 1930. Also shown: General John J. Pershing (seated to left of empty chair), to right: National Commander O. L. Bodenhamer, Mrs. Hoover, former President Calvin Coolidge, Mrs. Coolidge, Secretary of Navy Charles F. Adams, and Allan Hoover.

Eben Putnam (MA), 1st National Historian (1920-1933), got the Legion involved in obtaining federal funds for building the National Archives.

The Washington, D.C. Headquarters of the Legion, acquired in April, 1934, at 1608 K. Street, N.W., housed the Rehab, Employment, and Legislative Committees, and branches of the National Defense, Publicity, and other divisions.

The Chalfont Building, corner Michigan and Pennsylvania Streets, Indianapolis, housed the National Headquarters after the Legion moved from the Meridian Life Building and before the first Headquarters Building was constructed in 1925. (Indianapolis Engraving Co.)

Opening session, Fifth National Convention, San Francisco, October 16-19, 1923. Note Legion band from Department of Arizona in foreground.

NATIONAL HISTORIAN (1933-48) THOMAS M. OWEN, JR. (AL) SHOWS WINNING ENTRIES IN THE POST HISTORY CONTEST AT NATIONAL HEADQUARTERS, 1939. *(The Indianapolis Times)* OWEN WAS LATER DIRECTOR OF THE MANUSCRIPTS DIVISION OF THE NATIONAL ARCHIVES.

NATIONAL HEADQUARTERS OF THE AMERICAN LEGION, CONSTRUCTED 1925, EAST VIEW INCLUDING THE BLACK GRANITE CENOTAPH, INDIANA'S TRIBUTE TO THE WORLD WAR I DEAD.

MS. EMMA C. PUSCHNER (MO), FIRST DIRECTOR, NATIONAL CHILD WELFARE DIVISION (1927-1950).

Working for veterans. The Depression-era 1931 Legion Unemployment Conference, Mayflower Hotel, Washington, D.C., September 14, 1931.

(Acme Newspicture, Inc.)

The National Executive Committee meeting at the National Headquarters, 777 North Meridian Street, Indianapolis, early 1940s. Legion Lobbyist John Thomas Taylor second from left at front. Behind Taylor is Committeewoman Julia Wheelock of the Department of Italy. PNC James A. Drain (WA) is to Taylor's left. Behind Drain is Watson Miller, Director of Rehab. (Central Photo)

President Franklin D. Roosevelt signs the American Legion's G.I. Bill of Rights for World War II veterans, June 22, 1944. l. to r.: Senator Bennett Champ Clark (D MO), Rep. J. Hardin Peterson (D FL), Rep. A. Leonard Allen (D LA), Rep. John E. Rankin (D MS), Rep. Paul Cunningham (R IA), Rep. Edith Nourse Rogers (R MA), Frank Sullivan (Legion National Legislative Rep.), Senator Walter F. George (D GA), National Commander John Stelle (IL), Senator Robert F. Wagner (D NY). (Indianapolis Photo Co.)

Congressman John Gibson (D GA) steps down in Washington, D.C. from the plane held for him in Jacksonville, Florida, so that he could cast the decisive vote on the G.I. Bill. (Press Association, Inc.)

The American Legion's Special Committee on the G.I. Bill in a working session, Spring, 1944. from left: PNC Harry W. Colmery (KS), Ralph Mitchell (CA), Elliot Hayes (National Publicity Div.), unidentified, Dave Camellon (Hearst News Service), Jack Cejnar (acting national public relations dir.), unidentified, Frank Riley (*Boston American*), Chairman John Stelle, T. O. Kraabel (Rehab Dir.), Francis Sullivan (acting national legislative director). (Press Association, Inc).

Opening session, 22nd National Convention, Boston, September 23, 1940.

AMERICAN LEGION MEDICAL ADVISORY BOARD, FIRST MEETING, JANUARY 17, 1945, HELD AT THE SELECTIVE SERVICE HEADQUARTERS, WASHINGTON, D.C., TO ADVISE THE LEGION ON MEDICAL MATTERS RELATING TO THE REHABILITATION OF RETURNING SERVICE PERSONNEL. L. TO R.: DR. WINFRED OVERHOLSER, CAPT. WATSON MILLER, COL. ESMOND R. LONG, REAR ADMIRAL WILLIAM C. AGNEW, COL. LEONARD G. ROWNTREE (CHAIRMAN OF THE ADVISORY BOARD), LT. COL. LOUIS H. RENFROW, DR. ALBERT N. BAGGS, MAJ. GEN. GEORGE F. LULL, T. O. KRAABEL, DR. WILLIAM STROUD, CAPT. RAYMOND C. WELLS, (LT. COL. CHARLES W. MAYO WAS ABSENT WHEN THE PICTURE WAS TAKEN). (Press Association, Inc.)

GENERAL DOUGLAS MACARTHUR ADDRESSING THE 33RD NATIONAL CONVENTION IN MIAMI, OCTOBER 15, 1951.

National Commander George N. Craig presents Rep. Edith Nourse Rogers (R MA) with the American Legion Distinguished Service Medal at 1950 Legion Convention for her work in Congress for Veterans. National Chaplain Rev. Edward J. Carney looks on. (Acme Photo)

PRESIDENT HARRY S. TRUMAN SIGNS NATION'S FIRST "UNIVERSAL MILITARY TRAINING AND SERVICE ACT" INTO LAW, JUNE 19, 1951 (PUBLIC LAW 51). FRONT ROW: TRUMAN, ANNA ROSENBERG, GEORGE C. MARSHALL; SECOND ROW, L. TO R.: REP. CARL VINSON (D GA), NATIONAL COMMANDER ERLE COCKE, JR., REP. OVERTON BROOKS (D LA), SEN. HENRY STYLES BRIDGES (R NH), SEN. LYNDON JOHNSON (D TX), REP. DEWEY SHORT (R MO).

FIRST NATIONAL HEADQUARTERS BUILDING INTO WHICH THE LEGION MOVED IN 1925 (NEAR PHOTO CENTER). THE CURRENT NATIONAL HEADQUARTERS BUILDING, OCCUPIED IN 1950, IS ALSO SHOWN AT LOWER RIGHT. THE CENOTAPH AND THE FOUR BLACK GRANITE COLUMNS TOPPED BY GOLDEN ROMAN EAGLES, INDIANA'S TRIBUTE TO THE STATE'S WORLD WAR I DEAD, CAN BE SEEN BETWEEN THE TWO BUILDINGS.

THE THREE LEGIONNAIRES WHO AT THE ST. LOUIS CAUCUS DRAFTED THE PREAMBLE TO THE LEGION CONSTITUTION. HAMILTON FISH (NY, CONGRESSMAN FROM 1920-45); JUDGE GEORGE N. DAVIS (OR); JOHN C. GREENWAY (AZ) SHOWN HERE AS DEPICTED IN STATUARY HALL, WASHINGTON, D.C. THE PREAMBLE, SAID TO BE A MASTERFUL EXAMPLE OF AMERICAN IDEALISM, HAS BEEN CHANGED ONLY ONCE IN 70 YEARS. THE WORD "WAR" WAS CHANGED TO "WARS" IN 1942 WHEN WWII VETERANS WERE ADMITTED AS MEMBERS.

(Statue photo, Architect of the Capital, United States Capitol Art Collection)

THE HISTORICAL PERSPECITVE AS SEEN IN LEGION POSTER, 1952.

viated catalogue of bills under consideration gave one an indication of the business and the problems at hand: the Tariff Bargaining Bill (permitting the president to bargain for reciprocal tariff cuts with other nations); a tax bill with amendments boosting surtaxes and estate taxes and making all income tax returns public records subject to inspection; the Fletcher-Steagall Bill to extend the present temporary plan of bank deposit guarantees for another year (but putting off a permanent guarantee); the Stock Exchange Regulation Bill; and more appropriations for relief and Public Works Administration expenses.

Similarly, the Legion's Four-Point Program had been devised to address not only the Economy Act (enacted March 20, 1933) and the resulting rules and regulations promulgated thereby (on March 31), but also the Independent Offices Appropriation Act (June 16), which temporarily restored some benefits, such as those of largely presumptive mental or tubercular cases, and the Executive Orders issued in early June and late July containing modifications of the just-enacted Economy Act.

Just before Christmas 1933, Taylor and Hayes called at the White House for the now customary rite of presenting the Legion's legislative program to the president. They emphasized, of course, the Four-Point Program.

They had not long to wait for action. Congress convened a few days later (on January 3, 1934) and began immediately to consider veterans' legislation in the form of the appropriation for the Veterans Administration.

Taylor had assumed that after congressmen had returned home and had heard from their constituents, they might be more generous when returning to this session in considering veterans' legislation than they had been earlier when zealously passing the Economy Act.

By this time, also, local communities were witnessing the plight of disabled veterans and their dependents affected by the most immediate of the Economy Act's cuts. This became especially apparent when they saw the burden of veterans' needs being transferred from the federal government to local charities, and when local resources became strained, community leaders took note.

And so, it was hoped: a new year, a new attitude on the part of Congress. On January 8 the Legion bill containing the Four-Point Program was introduced by Senator David A. Reed, minority leader of the Veterans Subcommittee of the Senate Finance Committee. On January 8, Senator Walter F. George, the committee chairman, introduced a similar bill for the Legion. Taylor had achieved nonpartisan cooperation.

But four days later and just nine days from the opening of Congress, the Independent Offices Appropriation Bill, containing the funding of the Veterans Administration, was passed by the House. Taylor charged that the bill had been rushed through to stymie new veterans' legislation that would correct the Economy Act's unconscionable budget slashes in veterans' benefits.

He was thankful, however, for a "legislative rider," dealing with federal pay restoration, which was attached to the I.O.A. Bill in the form of an amendment. That amendment, in effect, would allow more legislation to be considered as an attachment to the I.O.A. Bill just passed by the House. To Taylor and other Legion legislative strategists, that was an invitation that fairly begged to be acted upon.

Taylor and the National Legislative Committee worked to convince key senators to endorse the Four-Point Program, and, more importantly, to attach that program to the I.O.A. Bill as the amendment allowed.

Alerted to the Legion's latest strategy, F.D.R. moved to offset the amending of the I.O.A. Bill by issuing four Executive Orders on January 22 amending the Economy Act regulations. These orders increased the base rate for the disabled from ninety dollars to one hundred dollars a month; liberalized the eligibility rules for treatment in hospitals of nonservice connected cases; increased the funeral allowance; and made possible the payment of full compensation to disabled veterans employed by the government who were earning specified amounts. The Legion, however, continued to push for its Four-Point Program.

Hearings were held by the Senate Appropriations Committee at which National Commander Hayes was invited to testify. The V.A. chief appeared, also, and said the cost of the Legion's program would exceed Hayes's estimates.

On the last day of January the Appropriations Subcommittee voted 5 to 4 that the Legion's amendment was not appropriate for amending the Independent Offices Appropriation Bill. But the next day the full Appropriations Committee disagreed, voting 12 to 10 that the Legion bill was indeed appropriate according to the "Economy Rider" attached to the I.O.A. Bill. Taylor and Hayes were invited to draft an amendment incorporating the Four-Point Program into the bill.

When the draft was completed, the Senate Appropriations Committee deferred to the administration, which, surprisingly, offered to provide support for the bill with its new amendment. The Senate debated the bill until February 27, then adopted three parts of the amendment, eliminating the benefits for widows and orphans of veterans.

Now the fortune of the Legion effort began to change. When the full Senate could not be convinced to adopt the current version of the amendment, that body made changes in it that in turn made the bill a sure target for veto despite the administration's support earlier. What's more, though the bill passed the Senate on February 27, its return to the House resulted in its being taken from the speaker's desk and referred back to the House Appropriations Committee, a tactic Taylor said had not been used for forty years, and which he assumed was employed so that House leaders could reorganize their efforts "to bind the majority on an administration program."

The House majority failed to coalesce, however, and the I.O.A. Bill, with the amendment attached to which the Legion objected, was considered just as it came from the Senate, in a form certain to be vetoed.

But after much debate, the House agreed to its own version of the amendment to be made to the I.O.A. Bill. At this point the Legion plan was more or less intact. When a vote was taken, that amendment was adopted by one vote.

This revised version was sent then to a House and Senate conference. After further refining and a favorable review once again by the two houses, the bill was amended, immediately "engrossed," and hurried to the White House.

The surprise factor was far from being played out, however, when the next day it was learned that the president's veto message was at that very moment on its way to the Hill. After it was read in the House, however, a vote to override was a resounding 310 to 72 victory for the Legion bill. In the Senate, heated debate over whether to sustain or override the vote continued for seven hours. But at about five o'clock in the afternoon of the February 28, Vice-President Garner left the rostrum and turned the gavel over to Senator Bennett Clark, a former parliamentarian of the House and a Legion founder.

Clark, determined to force a vote, expertly curtailed the filibuster in progress, and at seven o'clock on the evening of the same day the bill passed by a vote of 63 to 27, overriding a presidential veto in the process. The I.O.A. Bill, with three-fourths of the Legion amendment intact, was now Public Law No. 141 of the 73d Congress. In part, this enactment restored the disability compensation rates to the standards of the World War Veterans Act, the pre–Economy Act standard.

It was a memorable day in the career of John Thomas Taylor. Anyone given the credit for gaining a veto was sure to be feted by the Washington press. But the victory, coming a year and eight days after the disappointing decree for massive economizing, was more properly celebrated by all those who had had service-connected disability allowances curtailed for a while. Many presumptives could also join in the celebration.

Other, smaller scale restorations had occurred, provided by the administration, such as the president's Executive Orders referred to above (but said to be attempts to offset the momentum of veterans' organizations working for full restoration). All these had been welcomed, as had the decision not to close regional offices of the V.A., which would have forced once again the adjudication of all cases back to Washington, D.C. and away from the convenience of regional offices.

The most impressive feature of this victory was the reversal of what had been billed as the largest "savings" intended to be realized by the

Economy Act—that taken from the World War service-connected disabled. Now that intent had been reversed categorically.

Taylor, basking in the delight of victory, dared, nevertheless, to point out that not all the economizing intended by the act of that name had been curtailed. There was still about $90 million worth of payments to non-service-connected cases that would not be made. (He noted this even though the Legion had at that point never requested Congress to enact non-service-connected disability payments.) There was, in fact, still some $265 million in "savings," he said, which the remaining provisions of the Economy Act were estimated to reap in 1935.

But it was satisfying to know that Congress had agreed to three points of the four for which the Legion had fought: those for death, disability, and hospitalization benefits. It was a good year's work.

II

"The bonus—pay it in bonds or beans, but pay it!"
(an admonition heard in the N.E.C.)

All during the campaign to restore funds cut by the Economy Act, the subject of adjusted compensation continued to be debated. Of particular interest were the method and the time table for payment.

Now that the Economy Act cuts had been substantially restored, representatives on the Hill favored by a two-to-one margin the bill of Texas Representative and Legionnaire Wright Patman for immediate payment of the adjusted compensation certificates.

Adjusted compensation—the so-called "bonus"—was a subject popular now that the Depression's cold grip had all but curtailed the availability of ready cash to the average wage earner (and there were now many thousands of unemployed workers throughout the nation).

The original adjusted compensation legislation, before its passage in 1924, had bounded and rebounded between the chambers of Congress for a long time. It had been licked the first time it was presented in the House and the Senate. Then it had been put through the House but not the Senate. Following that it had survived both chambers only to be vetoed by President Hoover. The next time out it had passed the House but not the Senate. Then passage in both houses had been followed by yet another presidential veto. But that time the veto had been overridden and the measure became public law.

Following that victory, the issue of how and when the compensation should be paid had been bandied about within the Legion. Consecutive national conventions had taken the patriotic high road in seeking to preserve the intent of the Adjusted Compensation Act of 1924 for compensation in the form of twenty-year paid-up life insurance with borrowing privileges attached. The N.E.C. had reversed this once, in 1931, considering it not unpatriotic to call for immediate cash payment to relieve the plight of veterans currently in need of cash for such essentials as housing and food.

The National Convention that year, however, had corrected this break with the customary policy and resumed the stance honoring the conservative intent of the act of 1924 for sure, eventual compensation in the form of paid-up life insurance.

But the 1932 convention in Portland voted for immediate payment even as the bonus marchers, the "Bonus Expeditionary Forces," were making demands in Washington, D.C. for immediate relief in the form of a true bonus. Similarly, national conventions in 1933 and 1934 reiterated the call for immediate payment.

At the Miami Convention (1934), Harry Colmery, former National Legislative Committee chairman, was appointed to chair a committee of nine to forge the eventual legislation that would embody the convention's will that the certificates be redeemed soon and for full value. The committee included Congressman Wright Patman.

Before any resolutions were heard, Colmery asked each committee member for opinions about the matter. He listed three goals: to maintain the integrity of the Legion; to maintain the goodwill of the veterans of America; and, particularly, to honor the popular opinion among World War veterans that payment should be immediate and for full value.

When Colmery called for motions, Lyle Thorsness of Illinois reiterated the substance of bills comrade Patman had already introduced in Congress. Therein was a serious problem presented to the Legion. Though for a good cause, Patman's bill spelled out how the compensation was to be paid, a matter the Legion traditionally refused to include in its bills. Patman and two others voted for the motion, but the other six voted it down.

Other motions were offered. Colmery appointed a subcommittee to collate the two major points of view that had emerged. When that smaller group returned, they reported that full cash payment of the certificates seemed, they said, not to be an inconsiderate or opportunistic request to be made of the government, "since the government of the United States is now definitely committed to the policy of spending additional sums of money [for] hastening recovery from the present economic crisis."

Patman, of course, hoped the Legion would come around to supporting his bill (he would later complain loudly that the Legion had abandoned him). Colmery insisted that no support was intended. It was the Legion's manner, Colmery reiterated, to point out the various rehabilitation needs of veterans and to call for action, but *not* to suggest the ways and means of financing the government's obligations to veterans. Colmery invoked a sacred tenet—"policy, not politics."

Colmery and obviously many others in the organization did not oppose cash payments. Unlike the new public works programs introduced by F.D.R. that had created new debt, he reasoned that adjusted compensation was a debt already agreed to in 1924. For certain, it should be paid, and there were several ways of doing it: by tapping funds already available; by issuing ninety-day notes; by issuing bonds; or, as Patman would have it, by printing more currency. Those were the choices of Congress and not the American Legion.

This special convention committee's draft of a call for payment of the certificates went to the Convention Legislative Committee, which presented it to the convention. The convention in turn mandated cash payments and handed to the National Legislative Committee the job of seeing to it.

When the Legion policy regarding "the bonus" was announced in the national press, the differences between Patman's stance and the official Legion policy were featured prominently, making it appear as if a rift had developed in the organization. National officers were particularly perturbed when the congressman criticized the Legion's national leadership from the floor of the House of Representatives.

Colmery complained that Patman was taking unfair advantage of his position as a congressman. He lashed out at those "who don't give a damn about the Legion or the veteran [but who] if by promoting and encouraging something which will bring to them a bloc support from their own constituency, can see the open opportunity to personal preference and personal advancement."

Colmery noted that during the first round of congressional hearings on making the compensation payments sooner than originally enacted, and in cash, National Commander Frank N. Belgrano was invited to appear before the House Ways and Means Committee. At that point, the well-known Californian's occupation as an international banker was given little notice. But when the matter became the center of debate on the floor of the House and with Belgrano sitting in the gallery and unable to respond for himself, Patman coined the alliterative jibe "Belgrano bankers' bonus bill" in an unusually personal attack on Legion leadership.

(N.E.C. man and well-traveled banker Bill Stern from Fargo, North Dakota, who long supplied comic relief to the N.E.C. while exerting appreciable influence, once asked why the Legion's bill was being called a bankers' bill. Colmery answered half in jest that it was because "in the curve of things in the last few years," with banks either closing their doors or foreclosing on the debt ridden "the most unpopular being in American citizenship is a banker.")

The Legion's official opposition to Patman's funding proposal was enlarged upon when Patman and others insisted upon attaching monetary reform measures to *all* bills that called for appropriations. This stand meant that even if his own bill failed and the Legion bill survived, there was a chance that some such reform rider would be attached to the bill. Such an action would not only run counter to Legion practice, but also would certainly cause the president to axe full and immediate payment.

John Thomas Taylor sought to show that the president was set against "printing press money" by repeatedly pointing to F.D.R.'s refusal to take advantage of discretionary funds made available to him, such as the funds that accompanied the Agricultural Adjustment Act (which was later invalidated by the Supreme Court). The Legion, itself long on principle, was nonetheless determined this time to pursue legislation unencumbered by principled riders such as those emanating from Patman's crusade for monetary reform. There was sufficient principle in following the mandate of a National Convention at this point.

The first session of the 74th Congress convened on January 3, 1935. In the first four months of work, 7,774 bills in the House and 2,701 in the Senate were introduced. Many of these measures were for relief from the onslaught of the Depression, and were as creatively conceived and as wide-ranging as the problems faced. On January 14, Representative Fred M. Vinson, Legionnaire from Kentucky, introduced the Legion bill for full and immediate payment mandated most recently at the Miami Convention. Hearings were held on March 4 and 5. On March 13 the Vinson-Legion Bill, H.R. 3896, was favorably reported to the House by a vote of 23 to 1. On March 18, the Rules Committee allowed consideration of the bill, whereupon the House resolved itself into a committee of the whole to consider it.

But the rule also provided that even though the bill had had a favorable report, it would be open to amendment and that other immediate payment bills could also be considered. This unusual procedure allowed the Patman Bill, H.R. 1, to be offered as an amendment, including its call for a change in the monetary system through expansion of the currency. John Thomas Taylor complained that the bill had not even been considered by the Banking and Currency Committee.

The National Legislative Committee's worst-case scenario happened when on March 21, the Patman bill was adopted by a vote of 202 to 191 *as an amendment* to the Vinson-Legion Bill.

National Commander Frank Belgrano needed encouragement. Not only had the adjusted compensation bill developed into something the Legion could not support, but Belgrano had been badgered lately by questions raised by the press and by some organizations generally opposed to veterans' benefits about why, after having said for years that there should be no cash payments, the Legion was now calling for a cash "bonus."

On April 2, 1935, he called a special session of the N.E.C. He "thought it best to eliminate once and for all those statements made over the radio and from the platform that the national officers of this organization and the National Legislative Committee were determining these issues by themselves."

So the Executive Committeemen heard formal addresses and detailed reports followed by a prolonged exchange of views about the subject. Congressman Patman would later claim that it had been a secret meeting, but Taylor and others answered that though they had gone into executive session, anyone with a legitimate concern or contribution could have been heard.

Belgrano appointed a special subcommittee to collate the viewpoints on the subject. When the ten-member committee returned, it reported full support of what Belgrano had done to advance the Miami Convention mandate for payment of the compensation.

They resolved:

"That all World War Veterans have a right to expect that their Adjusted Service Certificates will be paid in full at this time at face value and with cancellation of interest accrued and refund of interest paid."

That the Legion "is not concerned with the merits or demerits of inflation or in any other controversial question that is not within the scope of the activities" of the organization.

And, "believing that the only bill which is reasonably assured of final passage is one which includes no other question than the immediate payment" of the certificates, Belgrano and the National Legislative Committee were directed to pursue the tactics already under way for gaining passage of a bill in the present session of Congress such as had been originally intended, without the baggage of the Patman funding plan.

At hearings on April 22–24, Belgrano and Taylor appeared before the Senate Finance Committee along with members of the Legion's Legislative Committee. The national commander spoke for more than an hour. Since the Legion bill had been effectively overshadowed by Patman's measure, the Legion actually had no bill to support. Instead, there was now but a message of need and of urgency to deliver. Nevertheless, the organization had been heard. Apparently there were those who were listening.

On April 25, the Senate committee met in executive session and Legion founder Bennett Clark maneuvered the striking of the Patman amendment, for which were substituted provisions drafted by Chairman Pat Harrison of Mississippi for the exchange of certificates for negotiable bonds. This new combination of measures—the Legion bill and a new funding concept—was once again redrafted to include the choice of a bond or cash in payment. That version was adopted by a vote of 12 to 8 and favorably reported to the full Senate.

But there continued to be a cloud over the proceedings from here on. Though the current version passed the House on March 22 (318 to 90) and the Senate on May 7 (55 to 33), it was vetoed on May 22. Though immediately passed again in the House by a vote of 322 to 98, the veto was sustained on May 23 in the Senate 54 to 40.

John Thomas Taylor called the first session of the 74th Congress (January 3 to August 26, 1935) "one of the most heated and controversial sessions in many years." There was much to wrangle about: some 10,000 bills had emerged in the House, along with 408 joint resolutions, 373 resolutions, and 40 concurrent resolutions. Similarly crowded had been the Senate docket, with 3,473 bills, 178 joint resolutions, 204 resolutions, and 24 concurrent resolutions. From this plethora, 414 public laws, 67 public resolutions, and 358 private laws had emerged.

It had been a blustery session with much bloodletting. But most of the administration's program for sweeping Depression relief and reform to forestall any such disastrous aberrations in the future had been considered and dealt with. Some of it was so progressive and otherwise controversial, however, as to be now before the Supreme Court, which was considering the constitutionality of some measures.

In September, the St. Louis National Convention reiterated the stance for immediate payment. New National Commander Ray Murphy took up the cudgel for the cause. Once again the same assignment was handed to the National Legislative Committee—to continue the campaign for immediate and full payment.

Thus among all the legislation that would be introduced in the second session was yet another Legion bill for full-value, adjusted compensation payments to be made as soon as possible. It was launched on the crest of changing opinion by many in the know that "bonus" legislation would come to fruition in the second session of the 74th Congress convening on January 3, 1936. There were now, in fact, fifteen such bills before the Senate Finance Committee and forty before the House Ways and Means Committee. Once again, the noninflationary bills were said to have the edge on surviving the expected veto.

National Commander Murphy told newspaper reporters that if the two other major veterans' organizations (the V.F.W. and the D.A.V.) would join with the Legion in pushing the Legion's bill, success was in sight. All three organizations were fundamentally in accord on the matter of the certificate payments after meeting in their most recent conventions.

This was an election year, when all the House and one-third of the Senate members were up for reelection, so the controversial political issue of the "bonus" fairly begged to be resolved. Politicians had to declare themselves on the issue to satisfy one of the most common questions put to them this time around. And with the momentum being weighted to relief measures, the bonus, misnamed or not, was a familiar refrain for its inherent hard-cash promise.

There was, also, a hope in the nation's far-flung business community, legislative strategists at Legion National Headquarters perceived, that looked to immediate payment of the certificates to stimulate the national economy. Furthermore, the feeling that something positive would be done this time around was bolstered by a poll in December 1935 by the American Institute of Public Opinion, which showed that fifty-five percent of the people, said to represent all walks of life, wanted the bonus to be paid.

The day after New Year's Day, National Commander Ray Murphy and National Legislative Committee Chairman Bob Colflesh came to Washington to meet with the committee, with the national officers of the V.F.W. and, by phone, with those of the D.A.V. They were joined by Representatives Fred Vinson and Wright Patman. At 11 P.M. on the evening of January 1 this group issued a statement signed by the three veterans' organizations announcing accord in several provisions for bonus legislation: (1) immediate and full cash payment; (2) refund of interest paid on loans on certificates; (3) cancellation of interest accrued and unpaid; (4) choice of cashing certificates or drawing interest on the maturity value of those not surrendered; and (5) issuance of special government obligations in lieu of certificates (valued currently at half a billion dollars) now held as security by the United States Life Insurance Reserve Account.

From another conference the next day came an invitation to Representative and Legionnaire John W. McCormack of Massachusetts, a member of the House Ways and Means Committee, to join in sponsoring the bill. It was decided, also, that Bennett Clark would sponsor the bill in the Senate. In addition, notice was sent to all members of Congress that the three veterans' organizations had joined together to support one plan for paying the bonus.

As soon as the House convened, Vinson introduced H.R. 9500. Later that evening, while the House was recessed to hear the message of the president, Legion Legislative committeemen called on Representative John J. O'Connor of New York, chairman of the Rules Committee, to ask for a rule for immediate consideration of the bill when it was reported out by the Ways and Means Committee that was scheduled to meet January 6. It had been decided to await action on the House bill before starting activity in the Senate.

Soon Patman agreed to cosponsor Vinson's bill rather than insist on his former amendments about how the bonus funding was to be raised. A redrafted bill, now H.R. 9870, was reintroduced by Vinson on January 7. The Rules Committee came through, making the bill part of the order for business on January 9. All efforts to amend the bill this time had been defeated, and the bill was passed by a vote of 356 to 59, and this just a week after the convening of Congress.

Attention now shifted to the Senate, where hearings were held by the Senate Finance Committee on the House bill. On the Senate floor soon thereafter, amendments were offered. On January 20 the final vote was taken—74 yeas, 16 nays. Back in the House then, the measure was voted upon yet again, with 346 for and 59 against the version coming from the Senate.

An hour after the house speaker signed the bill, Vice-President Garner signed it, and Representative Parsons of Illinois, chairman of the House Committee on Enrolled Bills, personally carried the bill to the White House. Along with the bill went some pertinent information: in each house of Congress there was an excess of support over the two-thirds majority required to override a veto.

Nevertheless, F.D.R. quickly dispatched a personally written veto message to the House on January 24, where just as quickly it was overridden. When the Senate convened three days later, after token efforts by party faithfuls to sustain the president, the Senate voted 76 to 19 to override. The Independent Offices Appropriation Bill was sure of becoming law and with it the Legion-inspired measure that stamped on the adjusted compensation certificates a cash value and a promise to pay soon.

The president had made his point with the veto message, but was apparently convinced that the bonus would not be stayed any longer. Two hours after the veto-override vote, National Commander Murphy and Administrator of Veterans Administration General Frank T. Hines called at the White House to confer with the president. On the way to the meeting at the White House, V.A. head Hines gave Murphy a supply of specimen blanks for applying for payment of adjusted compensation. By midnight the forms were being sent by airmail to Legion department headquarters for reproduction. Earlier that evening, National Commander Murphy had explained to a national radio audience about the new procedure for gaining payments.

Several weeks later, the appropriation for paying the bonus was enacted. By April 25, approximately 2,900,000 applications had been filed at the V.A. for the bonds.

The campaign since 1932 to have (what most persisted in calling) "the bonus" paid out in a depressed economic climate had been concluded successfully in 1936.

III

"Absolute Neutrality"

National Legislative Committee Chairman Bob Colflesh welcomed a new topic of discussion and voiced the opinion of many during the N.E.C. meeting in November 1936.

"I have felt for many years that the matter of the payment of the adjusted service certificates was a millstone around the neck of the American Legion, and I am glad that we got rid of that and now have cleared the decks, legislatively and otherwise, for a real altruistic service on the part of the American Legion."

The "service" to which Colflesh referred to was the need for the Legion to respond to the disturbing events in Europe, likely to be more threatening to the United States than the thorny issue of adjusted compensation had ever been.

As the international scene roiled with conflict, the Legion's National Convention in St. Louis the previous fall had marked a return to the site of the organization's American beginning sixteen years earlier. The historical perspective, therefore, undoubtedly played a part in many resolutions adopted at this homecoming.

Resolution 666 of the Foreign Relations Committee, for example, spoke to the present stark reality of the widening conflict in Europe with a remnant of the buoyant idealism of the veterans who had gathered in St. Louis in the spring of 1919 after "the war to end all wars."

"Deeply conscious as we are of the disturbing elements which say that war must come and that there is no hope for peace, we stand confident and unafraid in the American Legion in our belief that peace is possible, and we offer all our efforts to its practical accomplishment."

The resolution proceeded to call for "absolute neutrality" of the United States. It was a brave and noble intent by Legion policy makers. But as world events dictated, it was quickly becoming a doubly improbable prescription for peace.

It was not unusual for spokespersons to state their organization's stance favoring or opposing neutrality. By the year of the St. Louis Convention, Adolf Hitler had been in power for three years. Already he had caused disquieting rumblings of war. Later he would begin outright armed aggression against his neighbors. Also, the reform movement in Italy, at first looked on with favor by many in the United States, had taken objectionable twists and turns. There Benito Mussolini's Fascism proved to be but another strident variety of totalitarianism, which, along with the rise of Nazism in Germany, was chiefly responsible for a series of neutrality acts by Congress between 1935 and 1939. When in July 1936 the smoldering discontent in Spain erupted into civil war, it was thought prudent to augment America's neutrality stand by including civil wars as further conditions in which American trade was restricted. Previously, the laws had referred only to wars between nations.

Thus the neutrality acts of 1935 through 1939 were largely aimed at avoiding incidents that might draw America into the various conflicts brewing or actually being fought on European or Asian battlefields. Specifically, the laws restricting American shipping had been addressed to keeping American ships and citizens out of the way of German submarines.

What were seen by some as good-sense measures of avoidance were interpreted by others as little more than abject surrender of the rights relating to free commerce with the world, the beginning of an abandonment of the concept of neutral rights.

For its part, the Legion backed the neutrality acts, since each one in its time was a sequential reaffirmation of Legion National Convention mandates calling for "absolute neutrality," now but a dimming hope. In so doing, Legion resolutions emphasized reliance on the neutrality laws already on the books, at the same time calling for a strong national defense, a long-standing Legion advocacy.

It had been twenty years since hundreds of thousands had marched off to a grand adventure and found instead death and destruction on a scale so immense as to shell-shock a generation. Nevertheless, the war was remembered vividly by those who now raised the full spectrum of objections to even the hint of America becoming involved in another global catastrophe.

While the Legion's confidence in existing laws for maintaining neutrality showed a credible desire for peace, the vagueness of how that admirable intent could and should be implemented caused concern and complaints from many Legionnaires.

Within the Legion, as in the larger society of which the organization was representative, there was debate ensuing between two camps: those who recommended that the United States play an active role on the international scene by coming to the aid of those put upon by the dictators in Europe; and those who, their critics said, wished the nation to withdraw within its borders and wait out the current conflict in Europe.

Again at the 1936 Cleveland Convention, a resolution was passed dedicating the American Legion to a strict policy of neutrality:

"The American Legion wishes that the U.S. remain at peace with all nations of the world, and therefore resolves that we urge the U.S. government to maintain a strict policy of neutrality regarding foreign affairs and that the nation be kept from any alliance which might draw this country into war."

The N.E.C. in November 1937 appointed a special subcommittee to interpret recent mandates regarding neutrality. But after lengthy discussion, the entire motion was tabled for want of agreement on a concrete definition of the root word of this compelling issue.

Vague assertions notwithstanding, national officers were convinced, also, that public sentiment was against the nation becoming involved in yet another world war. Legionnaires who spoke to Legion audiences large and small, particularly national officers and those at Headquarters, were convinced that the prevailing sentiment of the general public was for a hands-off, noninterventionist rationale. The views of Legionnaires, it seemed, were once again consistent with popular opinion generally in the nation.

The sincerity of the Legion's call for neutrality was soon tried. On December 12, 1937 the U.S. gunboat *Panay,* while on the Yangtze River, was bombed and sunk by Japanese aircraft as it guarded American citizens and possessions during the Sino-Japanese conflict.

When news of the incident reached the States, Legion National Headquarters received many requests for statements of reaction. New National Commander Daniel J. Doherty replied that it was not proper for his organization to make statements about such matters. The Legion, he explained, viewed the situation "in a wholly neutral manner." And if that response sounded vague, it was because "the American Legion has not even attempted to define the term 'neutrality.' "

Defined or not, "Neutrality is our surest safeguard against being dragged into other nations' quarrels through the back door," Doherty assured a national radio audience soon thereafter. "If we are to stay out of these foreign conflicts on the military front, we must keep out of them on the economic front."

One sure way to become immersed, he said, was to go about blithely selling munitions to belligerent nations on credit or making loans for that purpose. The American Legion had asked the government to maintain a strict policy of neutrality regarding foreign affairs.

Such pronouncements, however, were unsatisfactory to many. Though Japan apologized and paid some indemnity, relations between the United States and Japan continued to deteriorate. A documentary film about the *Panay* incident appeared in theaters throughout the nation during the winter of 1937–38. A Legion departmental publicity chairman from Wisconsin suggested that after the showing of the film in local theaters, a talk prepared by National Headquarters be given in which the Legion would state its abhorrence of war while stressing the need for a universal military service law for the nation.

But National Adjutant Frank Samuel responded that, first, the Legion had no official statement other than its convention mandate and, second, that it seemed to him and others at National Headquarters that the *Panay* film "savors of considerable propaganda."

In this latter respect, Samuel spoke for many others who had hearkened in the days just before the United States entered World War I to similar appeals in a flurry of propaganda made by European countries and to persons at home promoting intervention. Now the sharpest critics, those most disillusioned by the political outcome of that war, questioned whether or not British democracy was actually threatened. Was it not actually British imperialism that America was being cajoled into saving?

There was, also, the assumption gaining in circulation and credence that anything such as the *Panay* incident that was a potential "war scare" would surely be used by those who sought to ease Depression woes at home by creating jobs producing armaments for the developing market overseas.

Such a method for combating the residual effects of the Depression was unwise for two reasons, noninterventionists argued. First, the economic uplift derived from armaments production would be relatively short-lived at best and otherwise artificial. But most objectionable was an inherent danger—the business of supplying arms made it difficult, likely impossible, for the seller to remain neutral. Sooner or later one of the belligerents would consider arms sales to an enemy to be an act of war.

The arguments in opposition to isolationism were equally noteworthy. If, for example, absolute neutrality were to be implemented and the nations being threatened or actually invaded were unable to buy arms from the United States, then the aggressor nations would be assured deadly success. Most attention had been placed on the course of events in Europe, where Britain and France had navies and generally ruled the sea routes to the United States, although they were plagued by German submarines. Those who were keeping a wary eye on the Japanese incursion into China, however, were quick to point out that China had no navy capable of establishing a supply line to the United States. There, Japan seemed assured of having an unimpeded advantage.

At the May 1938 meeting of the Executive Committeemen, the World Peace and Foreign Relations Committee reported, "It is now apparent that even the word 'neutrality' is a relative term." The committee had no particular recommendations to make regarding the standing neutrality mandate, generalizing, however, that "we consider a proper neutrality policy, whatever that may be, a perfectly proper part of the Legion's general peace objective."

Shortly after Legion delegates met in national convention at Los Angeles in the fall of 1938, Hitler promised Great Britain, France, and Italy at the Munich Conference that acquiring the Sudetenland was the main objective of his "new Germany." Three weeks later, however, his designs upon Czechoslovakia were made known; the Führer was not as easily appeased as British Prime Minister Neville Chamberlain had indicated hopefully in his statement, subsequently scoffed at, that there would be "peace in our time."

Legion officials, as others, were eagerly attuned to any hint by the president or the secretary of state to the direction the nation would be taken by congressional action or, F.D.R.'s detractors warned, executive fiat.

They had not long to wait. John Thomas Taylor was on hand to note the surprise effect of a March 7, 1939 press conference in which Roosevelt declared flatly that the current neutrality act had failed to contribute to world peace.

As Taylor and others sensed immediately from reading between the lines, there were actually two compelling aspects to this remark. First, the president had now publicly expressed his dissatisfaction with a law of the land (and this was a president well-known for tilting continually at the status quo). Second, by implying that the neutrality laws had been framed in whole or even in part to contribute to world peace, and not just peace for the United States, was the president now implying that the United States was poised to enter the war? That was the immediate reading by alarmists among the isolationist camp.

Roosevelt, of course, was but echoing earlier statements of Senate Majority President Alben Barkley of Kentucky, who asserted that U.S. foreign policy was designed to preserve peace in the Western Hemisphere *and* "to make some contribution to the preservation of peace in other parts of the world."

To the relief of many, the president had not called for the repeal of the neutrality acts in this news conference. He had even voiced opposition to the war referendum move then under way in the Senate.

But, as is often the case when a president hints at some course of action without actually formally recommending it, he had encouraged (or had foreknowledge of) the more direct action of others. For on the day following the press conferences, Senator J. Hamilton Lewis of Illinois introduced a bill to repeal the neutrality acts of 1935, 1936, 1937, and 1938 in favor of a doctrine of neutrality enforceable by the chief executive's own interpretation of what was happening and what should be done about it.

This, even more so than a similar but smaller-scale provision of the Embargo Act, was the red flag to the isolationists. Here was a proposal to give the president carte blanche in judging whether the United States would engage in practices on behalf of Allied nations, actions that would surely escalate, they said, leading to war.

When the Senate Committee on Foreign Relations began hearings on the bid to repeal the acts, Senators Bennett Clark and Gerald Nye, two who had sponsored the original acts, worked to see them survive.

Others similarly took a stand for neutrality. Congressman Hamilton Fish of New York, Legion founder and coauthor of the Legion "preamble," who had made a name for himself earlier by his anticommunist fervor, now went to work in characteristically resolute manner on the side of noninvolvement of the United States in the European war. In a speech broadcast over NBC radio April 21, 1939, Fish, who preferred to be called a noninterventionist rather than an isolationist, leveled a series of Emile Zola–esque "J'accuse" retorts against all those in the government who, he said, were gradually leading the country into war.

As the debate continued over defining "neutrality," and playing the "what-if" parlor game about how the enigmatic, would-be indifference termed "neutrality" should be maintained, the word itself was well on the way to becoming a cliché. As Hitler's intentions became unavoidably obvious, the obtuse and otherwise confused polemics of neutrality were largely made moot. While reiterating its stance on neutrality, the Legion increasingly emphasized national defense, citing the rationale of James Monroe's famous contribution to international relations —the Monroe Doctrine.

Believing as had Monroe (along with his contemporaries Thomas Jefferson and James Madison) that the peace in the Western Hemisphere was a rightful concern of the United States, Legion policy held, as had Monroe and his colleagues, that the nation should abstain from war action in the Old World. The Legion had recently stated its support of the Kellogg-Briand Treaty, which sought to outlaw war as an instrument of international-policy disputes by proposing a kind of international morality based on world opinion as its chief arbitrator. Even as Hitler continued to send troops ever farther across the European mainland and Mussolini pursued his own brand of aggression, Legion speechwriters admonished against becoming involved in either "the one-thousand-year-old boundary disputes of Europe" or the "underwriting by the U.S. of the status quo of Europe at any time."

National Commander Steven F. Chadwick even read from Monroe's handiwork when giving public addresses. No mere antiquated archival curiosity, the 116-year-old doctrine was as applicable in 1939, he argued, as it was when it was conceived and adopted. Chadwick told the Executive Committee of the Department of New York on April 20, 1939, "Our forefathers left the old countries to dedicate themselves to a new way of life, free and independent, and to get away from the futility of hundreds of years of quarreling and fighting in Europe." Look to the First World War, he said, and the disillusionment experienced after it was concluded. The only response should be, "We should not do it again!"

He recited the "isms" that had risen in Europe instead of democracy and which "threaten our own institutions." The prudent, necessary American solution to the widening and ever more bloody conflict in Europe (Chadwick did not mention the war in China) was, first, to reinvoke the Monroe Doctrine, and second, to implement a strong defense.

Chadwick also referred to the Legion's long-recognized status as the standard bearer of Americanism by proposing that a strong defense include a defensible system of democracy. Rather than debate the so-called distinctions between Communism, Nazism, and Fascism, national leaders should do all in their power to "eliminate their breeding place, the swamp of continued depression."

The greatest possible contribution the nation could make to eventual world peace, Chadwick suggested, was to provide a shining example of success and a stouthearted, righteous refusal to meddle in the affairs of other countries.

But the May 1939 meeting of the N.E.C. included some who voiced a quandary. "How," one wondered, "can you defend Brazil if some European country attacks it and still pursue a policy of nonintervention, of keeping our hands out of things? It seems that either the [neutrality] resolution at [the 1938] Los Angeles [National Convention] took in too much territory and contradicted itself so far as policy was concerned, or else they didn't realize what they were doing."

This Legionnaire spoke the mind of many across the nation who wanted more than academic ponderings and esoteric explications. As they became engaged in increasingly intense debate on the local level about events in Europe and Asia, particularly as they became concerned about the possibility of current neutrality laws being repealed for more permissive measures, they made their concerns known at National Headquarters and asked for clarification of the Legion's position.

Post Commander John E. Heenan of the Noble Callahan Post No. 237 in Troy, New York posed a related question to the New York department headquarters. Having heard that President Roosevelt was sure to seek revisions in the Neutrality Acts before the adjournment of Congress, Heenan had complained to New York Department Commander Frank C. Love that the likely revision—a repeal of the embargo on exporting armaments to belligerents—would give the president powers much too broad, powers possibly to engage the nation in war, powers for which even their constitutional nature was questioned.

Noting that Hitler had taken over munitions plants in Austria and Czechoslovakia, Heenan wondered if that meant the United States must match that production. "Are we to become the arsenal of the world?" he asked rhetorically. Heenan also believed that while much attention was being given to the conflagration growing in Europe, Roosevelt "has failed to find the existence of the gigantic war in China." Once that trouble spot was "found," it, too, was a likely quagmire, Heenan implied, for U.S. involvement.

As for their own post, they had few doubts about how to view the issue. Post 237's Adjutant Edward J. Jones explained that unlike national, his post had no difficulty defining neutrality as "that state of political conduct on the part of this government which will absolutely prevent any entanglement in any war or wars between any nations anywhere in the world except the two Americas."

For Post Adjutant Jones, the relative problem of the past was all too vivid. "We . . . remember only too well the tremendous amount of propaganda which was showered upon our heads before we foolishly believed that we as a nation had to go to war in Europe to save Democracy. We do not want that to happen again and we as individuals are bombarding our senators in Congress and the representatives, too, with a barrage of letters and telegrams saying so."

Jones reiterated the literalist view of the text of the Legion "preamble" about "promot[ing] peace and goodwill on earth." He complained that National Headquarters had not come forth with a specific policy that hewed to the text of that admirable credo.

When Department Commander Love explained that "the question you raise is of national scope and not a state matter," Heenan wrote to National complaining of the apparent lack of an official policy statement and advice tailored to a department the size of New York.

To the many inquiries such as that from Post 237, National Adjutant Samuel could reply only that national conventions and the N.E.C. had not put forth an official definition of neutrality nor had those governing bodies recommended a proper definition to the government.

Samuel could observe that the division of opinion was not solely that of National Headquarters.

Department conventions later that year were the scene of a similar dichotomy. The Department of Missouri, for example, meeting in convention at Joplin in late August had witnessed both extremes of opinion. In one instance, the empty right sleeve and A.E.F. "overseas cap" of the veteran who "rose" from a makeshift "tomb" in a demonstration for world peace marked him as one who had seen the worst to which American citizen soldiers would be subjected if the nation entered another world war.

Meanwhile, on a busy Joplin street corner, other Legionnaires hanged Adolf Hitler in effigy while a drum and bugle corps played "Over There." Reportedly, hundreds of spectators cheered the act and the implication of the rousing lyrics that had accompanied those who had marched off to the First World War.

The worldwide membership of the Legion provided for a view of events that now figured daily in newspaper headlines. A cablegram from National Executive Committeeman James L. McCann of the Department of France in late August 1939 gave insight from a strategic vantage: "President Roosevelt's generous appeal will probably be ineffective in preventing Hitler's brutal aggression on Poland. It is clearly our [U.S.] national duty as well as our utmost interest to assist England and France in stopping this abominable exercise of force. Right must be made master of might. Democracies must be preserved in spite of collusion of dictators. Rapidity of decision, prompt application of it, [is] essential. Public opinion should demand immediate complete intervention [in] case Hitler pursues mad determination. Please circularize."

The cablegram from Paris was late in reaching National Commander Chadwick, who was traveling in the western U.S., and he did not answer until September 4, three days after Hitler invaded Poland, as McCann had none too happily predicted. Nevertheless, Chadwick repeated the long-standing Legion position. "The American Legion can take no course at variance with the declared policy of our nation as expressed by the president."

Chadwick claimed once again to know the tenor of public opinion in America. "While the thought of our nation, if I can judge its temper, is one of entire sympathy with the position of England and France, the vast majority of sentiment in this country is that, having once taken our ideals to Europe, contributed to a victory and offered a proposal for or a means of preserving the peace, and having seen this proposal fail, there is no great disposition at the present time to again actively intervene in European affairs."

The national commander concluded, "It will be a long period before the temper of the American people will again be ready to approve the throwing of American manhood into the European conflict."

But before long, National Adjutant Frank Samuel was openly expressing the frustration he and others felt when responding officially to this issue. To another, he wrote, "The National Organization has interpreted these various actions [National Convention resolutions about neutrality] in their necessary sequence as leaving us without a definition of our own idea of proper terms of neutrality and likewise without any suggestion to the Congress as to what we think should be the Government's definition of neutrality."

Hitler's entry into Poland, preceded by a decimating Luftwaffe bombardment of Polish airfields, presaged the long war to follow. Some in America longed for action against the oppression they read about in the daily headlines. On September 2, the day after the first strike against Poland, a Legionnaire from the Kiffin Rockwell Post 2 in Asheville, North Carolina telegrammed to National Headquarters his offer to join an " 'American Legion Corps in France' " as an expert [at] mechanization and [as a] male nurse" if such a unit were to be organized.

National Commander Chadwick hurried to reply by telegram that same day, perhaps to offset any such movement by those who would use the name of the American Legion in forming corps of volunteers, that "while understanding your natural sympathy" he could only reiterate the now customary need for "the observance of a neutrality of act and deed."

"We have continuously as an organization counseled the youth of America to keep out of the military forces of other nations," Chadwick added. But he may have tipped his hand when he observed, "Volunteering for such service only reduces the manpower and strength of America at such time as our nation may be called upon to act and has proven in every instance in history a source of embarrassment to our state department. My counsel is to wait and follow the course of our American government."

Chadwick again advised against initiating direct action when the Alabama Department Commander Charles R. Wiggins submitted the text of a telegram he wished sent "through channels" to the president, telling of his department's readiness "at any turn of affairs to perform any service to insure safety and welfare of America." It was the consensus of eighty posts in that department, Wiggins said.

The national commander replied that with the National Convention scheduled to meet later that month, "communications to the president should be held to reflect full national sentiment. Meanwhile, let's sustain him in his declared neutrality policy."

But letters to National continued to bring action-oriented offers for involvement in the armed forces of other nations. A Legionnaire from a post in Columbia, South Carolina responded to a "recent newspaper appeal [by] our president asking personal effort [from] every peace officer in reporting any perverse action [by] foreign elements [i.e.] espionage or acts of sabotage" by suggesting that National Headquarters offer the services of the Legion for this work. "Poland is but a second Belgium [the first to be overrun in WWI]. We as veterans know now our work was but half done," this one said.

National Adjutant Frank Samuel replied that such a program might, indeed, be discussed at the Chicago National Convention a few days later. He pointed out, however, that the Legion's organizational documents stated that membership in the Legion "does not affect nor increase liability for military or police service." So "we would not consider constituting our membership as vigilantes nor would we have the authority to deputize our members as peace officers when it comes to detecting espionage or acts of sabotage." Instead, the organization would "work along legislative lines" to bring about similar results. He reminded the South Carolinian that concerning subversive activities, the Legion "had much influence in the creation of the Dies committee and in seeing that it should be continued." That House Committee to Investigate Un-American Activities, commonly called by the name of its chairman, Texas Representative Martin Dies, had been established in May 1938 to look into allegations arising from the activities of Nazi, Fascist, and Communist organizations in the United States.

Just before the National Convention met in Chicago in September 1939, England and France declared war on Germany. Yet the convention called for (1) the expansion of U.S. armed forces "to maintain our neutrality;" (2) the president and Congress to avoid intervention in the war; and (3) Congress to remain in session during the current circumstances.

The next month, the editorial entitled "America First" in the October 1939 issue of *The American Legion Magazine* cited the developing alignment of warring nations in Europe. The editorial remonstrated, "It is 1914 all over again. What is the duty of the United States of America in this crisis?" Remembering "those fifty thousands slain and the host who have died since 1918 as a result of war service, with the thousands of our fellows whose physical and mental sufferings due to the war will remain with them till death," the editorial writer demanded "it must not happen again." This nation "can and shall keep out of the shambles across the seas. Our duty is to America first."

By October Legionnaire Congressman Hamilton Fish had gathered forty-six present and former U.S. representatives and others into the National Committee to Keep America Out of Foreign Wars.

Fish's committee sought to counter what was said to be the efforts of the press, particularly of a few often quoted columnists, to make it appear that entry into the war was inevitable because the arms embargo was about to be repealed. Not so, Fish said. Congress was still wrangling over that issue and a conclusion was not in sight.

The vast majority of the American people, no less than ninety percent according to Fish, opposed "foreign entanglements"—this time the supplying of arms—which, he said, would inevitably lead to war. Fish pointed out that a nonpartisan majority of forty-one like-minded representatives, later joined by others to make a majority, had defeated efforts to repeal the embargo the previous June (1939). Now the repeal of the arms embargo and the Senate-proposed "Title and Carry" bill would be the first step to war, Fish and his committee warned. For that would be followed, he said, by efforts to establish credit and loans to potential arms buyers. Then, war.

Fish's National Committee to Keep America Out of Foreign Wars wasn't alone. World hero Charles Lindbergh had by now acquired a second reputation, but one around which swirled much controversy unlike reaction to his epic airplane flight of 1927. "Lucky Lindy" now spoke out against U.S. involvement in the European war. Much criticized for being hosted by officers of the German Reich on his self-appointed inspection tour of that country's air force, he insisted that the German war machine was much larger and more capable than any he saw in Europe. He advised Europeans not to oppose their German neighbors. Nor should the United States enter the fray, he said.

On the evening of October 27, 1939, after debating for nearly a month, the Senate passed a neutrality bill by a vote of 63 to 30 which, in effect, repealed the arms embargo. At the same time, the Senate also defeated Senator Robert M. Lafollette, Jr.'s war referendum by a vote of 73 to 17.

In early November, a House vote of 243 to 181 sent to the president the makings of the Neutrality Act of 1939, which repealed the arms embargo. By the president's signature at noon on Saturday, November 4, commerce with all belligerent nations was put on a "cash-and-carry" basis. Now shipments of arms, munitions, and implements of war could be shipped to warring nations. American vessels were prohibited, however, generally from carrying passengers and goods to the ports of nations at war, and citizens were not permitted to travel on ships of belligerents. Furthermore, American merchant ships could carry only those arms necessary to maintain control on board. The cash-and-carry provision referred to the condition that all title and interest in the goods in question had to be transferred before such goods left American shores. Also, there was to be no financial credit given to the belligerents. The Munitions Control Board was retained as the agency for licensing and regulating exports of arms, ammunition, and implements of war.

The special session of Congress was immediately adjourned, and the president now had discretionary authority to recognize officially a war between foreign states and to issue proclamations under which the cash-and-carry provision could go into effect.

Now the keep-America-out-of-the-war fervor that had been building had a clear focus for protest. Before, the dreaded possibility was only that. Now the president had the authority that many had feared. And The American Legion was in the forefront of the movement to keep the nation out of the war.

In the November issue of *The American Legion Magazine,* National Commander Kelly's name appeared over an article entitled "Keep Out—Keep Ready!" The nation looked to the Legion, to "the more than 1,000,000 men and women who had seen war service," for a response to the armed conflict abroad. The advice of the Legion was to stay out of the war.

The "keep ready" advice referred to national defense. "The answer to the question of providing the best neutrality insurance is to develop and to increase the armed defensive forces of this nation to a size adequate to meet any future circumstances which can conceivably endanger our national integrity." Beware "subverters and saboteurs within our own boundaries," Kelly warned, who aimed to weaken the will of the people to defend themselves. The message: remain neutral, but strong enough so as not to lose the fight if it came to the nation.

But the message was increasingly mixed. The news release from the National Publicity Division in Indianapolis in December was titled, "This is not our war." National Commander Kelly offered the customary opinion that "our nation [should] stay out of Europe's age-old conflicts." But he also recognized that "today the prospects of preventing the spread of the conflict to other nations appears dark. How soon the tempo may be increased to a point where it will threaten most seriously to embroil our own country is beyond our ability to predict." The nation must be armed sufficiently to defend its neutrality.

There was much room for caution, Kelly indicated. "Let's review history and learn from our past experiences that news from foreign countries is censored for the purpose of crystallizing the attitude of neutral nations in their favor." Work on Americanism, he advised Legionnaires, echoing the advice of his predecessor. "Sell America to Americans."

In the early months of 1940, those safely ensconced in government bureaus in Washington charted the aggression by Germany and other Axis powers. But the view from close up, where picturesque European cobblestone streets echoed the marching of invading armies, was a vantage not to be envied. The cablegram sent to National Headquarters from the Paris post on May 19, 1940 was eloquent in its brevity: "For God's sake, wake up Legion before too late. McCann"

German troops had begun an invasion of Denmark and Norway in early April. When the Anglo-French forces that had gone in support of the Norwegians fell back, Germany then entered Luxembourg, the Netherlands, and Belgium. Neville Chamberlain, who after the Munich "surrender," had resigned, was replaced by Winston Churchill as prime minister in a coalition government faced with combating the Germans driving toward the English Channel. British forces sent to aid Belgium were forced to flee the continent at Dunkirk. Within days of his latest and most anxious cablegram, N.E.C. man McCann would see the opening of the Battle of France and that country's subsequent fall in late June.

Once again, in late September 1940, the Legion came to Boston (previously in 1930) in the persons of 1,451 delegates representing a membership of 1,069,267. An estimated three million spectators watched the twelve-hour parade as 125,000 Legion men and women from across the nation and foreign departments displayed their colors and their vigor. The marathon procession marched up Beacon Hill to the statehouse to be reviewed by Legionnaire Governor Leverett Saltonstall and other notables.

On Sunday, Legionnaire ministers were invited to speak from several local pulpits. At the Cathedral of the Holy Cross, a high military mass was celebrated. William Cardinal O'Connell told the members of the Legion that "You have a right to be heard. In God's name banish war hysteria. . . ."

The previous convention—Chicago, 1939—had met just three weeks after the German invasion of Poland. Those gathered in Boston had had several months in which to hear about German aggression. At Chicago the theme song, the one most often played by the bands, was "Roll Out the Barrel." In Boston there was a different mood evident in the numerous renditions heard of "God Bless America."

When the National Defense Committee called for "all practical aid to Britain and those aligned with her in their fight for freedom," the delegates responded with hearty approval.

The National Convention Foreign Relations Committee, too, addressed the issue, working for two days to compose an opinion on U.S. aid to Britain. The committee finally brought in a report urging the government "to exercise all lawful means to prevent the shipment of war materials to the aggressor nations," and to "continue to extend to all peoples who are resisting aggression the fullest cooperation consistent with our obligations, our security, our liberties, and our peace."

That sentiment ruled the day. Aid to Great Britain was the crux of the matter for most people, because providing aid to one side would surely bring a war declaration by the other.

Toledo lawyer Milo J. Warner was elected national commander on the first ballot. He had been nominated by Lynn U. Stambaugh of North Dakota, who had come to the convention as a candidate for the office. Roane Waring of Tennessee, another aspirant, seconded the nomination.

In October 1940, Warner was saying that the nation had no business getting into the war. But by early December he was defending aid to Great Britain and China, saying that that method of helping the cause of democracy did not constitute U.S. involvement in those theaters of war.

From August 1940 to the end of the year, the monstrous Battle of Britain raged. The world was impressed by the tenacity of the British to defend their island fortress against the massive Luftwaffe air offensive against R.A.F. bases, British shipping, factories, and major cities.

How had America's British cousins defended themselves? National Commander Warner determined to find out firsthand. The suggestion, he said, came from "Legionnaires in the field" who were concerned about the defense of the United States.

Warner met with Secretary of State Cordell Hull on January 15 and the president the next day, outlining four reasons for the trip: to provide firsthand knowledge of the ways in which the British civilian population was coping; to stimulate Legion membership in support of such measures at home; to aid the Legion in crystallizing public sentiment to that end; and to supply the Legion's Foreign Relations Committee with factual, up-to-date information at a time when that resource was said to be in short supply.

Both Hull and Roosevelt had encouraged the trip, Warner said. He had canvassed the entire N.E.C. by telephone roll call while planning the trip, reminding each of the Boston Convention's mandate calling for aid to Britain. All but one of the committeemen favored the idea.

The national commander chose three other Legionnaires to accompany him: Legion elder statesman and Past National Commander Franklin D'Olier; Major General Frank Parker, U.S.A. Retired, commander of the A.E.F.'s First Division; and his aide Joseph S. Deutschle, a former Associated Press staffer for many years who had spent fourteen months in France during the World War.

This small party of Legion observers left New York at 9:00 A.M. on February 5 (from La Guardia Marine Base) by Pan American Clipper Ship, and by way of Bermuda and Horta in the Azores arrived at Lisbon Thursday evening at 5:00 P.M. (Lisbon time). From Lisbon they flew to England on February 8 and set up their headquarters at London's Claridge's Hotel.

Warner and the others visited the midlands at Coventry and Birmingham, the west coast at Bristol, and the channel coast sites of Portsmouth, Southampton, Bournemouth, Folkestone, and Dover. They visited army, navy, and R.A.F. installations, Home Guard battalions, and British Red Cross units.

They witnessed air raid precautions and visited defense factories, observation posts, communal feeding services, and London fire brigades. They viewed bomb-and fire-damaged docks while observing the wreckage of months of bombing from across the Channel. The tragic enough death figure set at 25,000 in the bombings seemed miraculously low, Warner said, considering the extent of the damage and the length of time the air raids had been occurring.

The Legionnaires met with King George VI, and with Prime Minister Winston Churchill at 10 Downing Street, who told them, "Give us the tools and we will finish the job." During the eighteen days they spent in England the four collected an impressive amount of information about the day-to-day defensive functions of a nation at war.

Though the detailed plans whereby civilians could react to devastating attack were revealing and important, the chief result of the Legion mission to England was the confirmation of the urgency of Great Britain's need for the matériel to continue their defiance of Hitler.

Warner was convinced that Great Britain needed the matériel and that it needed it now!

That spring, President Roosevelt approved the Lend-Lease Act on March 11. British financial credit was low for acquiring the war matériel needed. This measure allowed the president to recognize the need of, and to comply with, any nation whose defense was vital to the interests of the United States. The first loan amount was seven billion dollars. A few days later, Roosevelt voiced the nation's generosity and its protest of the dictators by promising to increase the aid ultimately in whatever proportions were needed for a total victory.

The N.E.C. in May adopted five policy resolutions relating to the implementation of the latest neutrality law, those for, (1) the use of the navy to insure the delivery of war materials, food, and medical supplies to Great Britain to win the Battle of the Atlantic; (2) the resignation of Secretary of Labor Frances Perkins (for appearing lax in not deporting labor agitator Harry Bridges, an Australian); (3) the issuance of a frank statement by the president regarding all the facts constituting immediate danger to the country; (4) legislation outlawing strikes and lockouts during the period of the present emergency; and (5) recommending the purchase of Defense Bonds.

When the delegates gathered for the National Convention at Milwaukee in mid-September 1941, the topics of their comradely conversations ranged from a possible shortage of antifreeze (the supply was said to be taken already for military vehicles) to the absence of several acquaintances who were now back in military service. Many Legionnaire fathers spoke of sons now in training camps, a year after the Selective Training and Service Act had been implemented.

Those who had returned or would soon return to serve with the armed services included former national level staffers and volunteers. Before long, John Thomas Taylor would report for duty with the War Department's Bureau of Public Relations as assistant to the director. Col. Theodore Roosevelt, Jr., would command his old regiment, the 26th Infantry, 1st Division. Brigadier General Eric Fisher Wood would command the 53d Brigade, 28th Division.

There was time for the customary camaraderie. Rebel yells punctuated the convention hubbub when Julius Franklin Howell, a ninety-five-year-old Virginian commander-in-chief of the United Confederate Veterans, present in full dress uniform, rose to speak. (The Seventy-fifth Encampment of the G.A.R. was being held in Columbus, Ohio.)

Though the presence of the most famous doughboy of all, Sergeant Alvin York, was announced, the view to the past was soon interrupted by the message to the convention from Great Britain's Winston Churchill bringing attention once again to the current pressing problems.

The real issue on the floor of the convention was once again isolationism versus intervention. What would emphasize those differences of opinion was the "Russian question."

In June, Germany's attack upon Russia presented the Legion with a quandary: should Legionnaires support aid to this Communist stronghold because that nation was currently fighting the Nazis?

Legion response to this issue, the conventioneers knew, would be given wide press coverage. Official opposition by the nation's largest veterans' organization, some said, would signal American sentiment in that direction. Conversely, a vote for aid would be said by some to indicate that the nation was moving closer to actual intervention with troops.

The isolationist "America First Committee" movement had staged a large meeting in the convention city, attended by Legion founder Bennett Clark and Past National Commander Hanford MacNider, a vocal supporter of the committee along with *Chicago Tribune* publisher Col. Robert R. McCormick. Their message was clarion clear: stop all endeavors that would lead inevitably to war.

The convention keynote speech was given by Legionnaire Frank Knox, Secretary of the Navy, who explained the current practice of giving navy protection to all lend-lease shipments. He further stated that the navy was ordered "to capture or destroy by every means at their disposal Axis-controlled submarines or surface raiders encountered in these waters. That is our answer to Mr. Hitler's declaration that he will try to sink every ship his vessels encounter on the routes leading from the United States to the British ports."

New York Mayor and Legionnaire Fiorello H. La Guardia, now also director of Civilian Defense in the U.S., followed Knox. "We are not neutral!" the fiery mayor shouted at the summation of his speech.

The highlight of the deliberation on the convention floor came when Past National Commander Ray Murphy rose to deliver the report of the National Foreign Relations Committee. Most major points stressed therein were agreeable to a majority of the delegates: support of the president and Congress; repeal of the existing neutrality act; and approval of the current foreign policy of the president (although Past National Commander Hanford MacNider was widely known to demand that the president spell out just what that foreign policy was. Particularly, was this our war or not?).

But when Murphy broached the subject of lend-lease aid to Russia, the hall buzzed. Immediately, Jack Abrams of Washington presented a minority report countering aid to the Communist capital of the world. For an hour the debate continued. Others of note in addition to MacNider, including Past National Commander Chadwick and Bennett Champ Clark, disapproved of helping the Russians.

Tom Connally of Texas, Legionnaire delegate and chairman of the U.S. Senate's Foreign Relations Committee, spoke in favor of the majority report. When Drury Phillips of Texas moved that the minority report be tabled, the roll call that followed (the only one at the convention other than that for the election of national commander) was an 874 to 604 mandate for the Legion to back aid to Russia. (An earlier resolution against government aid to Russia had been voted down in the Foreign Relations Committee by 34 to 16.)

The official stance, then, favored extending aid to yet another ally (the word itself rankled many), a decidedly unneutral gesture and indication, perhaps, that intervention in a more substantial way—that of American citizen-soldiers—was inevitable after all.

This was not to mean, of course, that the Legion had softened its abhorrence of Communism. A few hours later, the convention soundly reaffirmed the Legion's ingrained opposition to world domination by the proponents of Marx and Lenin. Indeed, the hated "ism" of longest standing—the ideology of the very nation the convention had just said should receive from the United States the wherewithal to combat Hitler—was ranked above the more recent Nazism and Fascism as an ideological scourge.

IV

Day of Infamy

Newscaster and Legionnaire (chaplain of the National Press Club post) H. R. Baukhage came close to missing the biggest story of his life on a Sunday in early December 1941.

While walking in Rock Creek Park along the Potomac on December 7, Baukhage stopped by his father's home, and by staying longer than he had intended was reached there by his employer at the National Broadcasting Network's Blue Network (later ABC), who told him to go to the White House immediately.

An announcement at the Redskins-Eagles football game in the national capital had ordered all military personnel to report for duty on the double. Military channels of communication had just carried word of an extraordinary event.

Arriving at the executive mansion at the same time as Baukhage was Presidential Press Secretary Stephen T. Early, Baukhage's commanding officer on the armed forces newspaper *Stars & Stripes* in Paris during World War I. Early told his former colleague about the message received shortly before by Navy Secretary Frank Knox from Adm. Husband E. Kimmel in Hawaii: "Air raid on Pearl Harbor. This is not a drill."

The newscaster, whose trademark introduction to his newscasts was "Baukhage talking . . ." asked Early for permission to set up the first-ever live spot news coverage from the White House press room. In the next few moments he announced to an aghast American public that the nation had been attacked.

The "day that will live in infamy," as President Roosevelt called it, began on Oahu, Territory of Hawaii, when Japanese planes attacked U.S. navy ships and personnel at Pearl Harbor.

For nine hours Baukhage reported information brought in by Stephen Early and others. Though lacking sufficient news copy, he did not reveal for a while that he, indeed, was broadcasting from the White House.

At first, with no other help from his studio than the hookup, he left the microphone every few minutes to hurry to the front door to see who was arriving or departing so that he could report their having conferred with the president. Later, the network sent him background material on the unfamiliar locale of Pearl Harbor and on the condition of the navy there, also about American relations with Japan and other information to fill the time between the official bulletins intermittently brought down to the press room. Soon CBS, Mutual, and local city stations arrived, and newscasters attempted to sort out the facts of this shocking turn of events.

Quite by chance, Baukhage already had some background information of his own. On Saturday, the day before his famous broadcast, he had visited the Japanese Embassy, where an envoy had talked with him briefly about Japan's current national leadership, mostly trivial material customary when governments change leadership, as had happened recently in Japan. But that information was being censored, Baukhage surmised, by the first secretary of the embassy who refused to answer any detailed questions about Japanese politics and particularly about military matters. After the conversation, Baukhage was hurried out. But in leaving, he remarked to a clerk about the unusual number of embassy staff members in attendance for a weekend; he noticed especially their rushing about bearing stacks of papers, as if some emergency required the removal or destruction of embassy records.

On Monday morning, Congress declared war on Japan, as President Roosevelt had requested. Since Japan earlier had helped form the Axis alliance with Germany and Italy, the United States was now at war with those countries that were already on the move and well prepared to continue.

National Commander Stambaugh previously had scheduled a meeting for December 9 and 10 in Washington of the chairmen of three new national committees created in November by the N.E.C., those of Naval Affairs, Merchant Marine, and Civil Defense, all of which worked under the aegis of the National Defense Committee. As they came together now, the tenor of the discussions had taken on a much more somber sense of immediacy. Before, it had been "what if?" Suddenly it was "now that . . ."

In the December issue of the Legion's newspaper format publication, *The National Legionnaire,* Stambaugh appealed to Legionnaires: "It will be part of the task of our older, more experienced men and women to give leadership and wisdom to younger Americans. Let us do it truthfully, calmly, honestly, and fearlessly."

V

A Bill of Rights for G.I.s

The entry of the United States into the war took the steam out of the dispute between the isolationists and the interventionists within the Legion. The patriotic zeal with which the larger allegiance of both groups was tempered helped direct their actions to support a nation at war.

The shift of emphasis that now occurred within the Legion looked to what lay ahead for another generation of veterans-in-the-making (and for the "retreads," those former doughboys and gobs who would see military service again). It required no great revamping; even twenty plus years after the fact, the effects of the First World War were seen daily in the lives of disabled veterans.

But an important development in the area of Rehab was about to take place. Two decades of work were about to be refocused, and the result of that exercise in long-range planning would change the nature of veterans' affairs for all time.

Following the First World War, the efforts of rehab workers had been divided between doing battle with the existing but often unresponsive government system for benefits and with causing new benefit programs to be established, which in turn had to be guarded against dismemberment through cuts in appropriations and improper management. But the years of winning and losing battles on Capitol Hill had also allowed some occasional respite for pondering blue-sky, constructive what-ifs.

One concept, in particular, innovative on a scale not dared before, was rattling around National Headquarters: What if all veterans' benefits previously established to make up for time lost during military service that otherwise would have been spent in education and establishing oneself in an occupation and as a homeowner were to be restated comprehensively and in such a way as to aid the national economy and society in general? Visionaries among the national staff and the national-level volunteers began outlining just such a concept.

It came about as an accompaniment to the daily routine of Rehab work centered in the Washington, D.C. headquarters and, particularly, in the annual Rehab conferences leading up to the Second World War.

After gaining three-fourths of the Legion's Four-Point Program of restorations after the Economy Act, the major legislative thrust of the Legion's Rehab program was to improve, correct, and maintain the restored benefits and to relate the present benefit program to the real-life situations of veterans. The major exception was the need yet for a comprehensive program of benefits for veterans' dependents—the long-slighted widows and orphans.

The Rehab conferences held in Washington, D.C. after the restoration of the Economy Act cuts, attempted to focus on the duties of the Veterans Administration—the policy procedures, personnel, extensions, and improvements of facilities, and the ever-present case adjudication.

In January 1942, T. O. Kraabel, the new Director of Rehab Division following Watson Miller, who left to accept an appointment with the federal government, addressed the Rehab conference being held in Baltimore. The rapid influx of additional workers to the nation's capital brought about by the expanded emergency and defense programs had made the move from Washington to Baltimore necessary; hotels and meeting places had already been taken for the emergency war workers.

The conferees, meeting for the first time during wartime, discussed rehab services to members of the new armed forces and their dependents, as well as the likely effects of the war economy and war effort on Rehab work.

The next year, the twentieth annual conference returned to Washington in February to discuss the tremendous changes that would follow the war when millions of service personnel would return home. Something had to be set in motion that would aid mightily in that transition.

Thus began, unobtrusively, in a matter-of-fact fashion, the move toward a comprehensive benefits program. It had its traceable beginnings in as traditional a Legion exercise as the appointment by National Commander Warren Atherton of a committee on November 30, 1943 to consider the long-range view of veterans' benefits now that American citizen-soldiers were involved in another world war.

Chaired by John Stelle of Illinois, the committee included Harry Colmery, Sam Rorex, W. Bea Waldrip, Robert McCurdy, and three ex-officio members: Maurice F. Devine, Lawrence J. Fenlon, and Robert W. Sisson.

It came about on this date because Atherton had just completed a telegraphic survey of the states, in which he inquired about the status of disabled men and women of the armed services after almost two years of war. What he found was at the least alarming and, even in the most objective light, highly unsatisfactory. Something had to be done, and as usual, national-level volunteers when thinking of corrective measures thought of federal legislation.

Within two weeks of its appointment, the committee met in Washington, D.C. on December 15. National Rehab Director T. O. Kraabel, along with National Legislative Committee Executive Director Francis M. Sullivan, and other staffers of the Washington office already had provided an analysis of the reports received from department service officers and field secretaries requested by Atherton in his survey. Kraabel and the others had compiled recommendations for the physical and economic rehabilitation of the returning new veterans.

The committee met with officials of the V.A., the Navy and War departments, and congressmen; with representatives of labor, industry, agriculture; and with educators and others. In the series of consultations and midnight recap sessions by Legion officials, an omnibus bill began to take shape.

Though the physically disabled were of first importance, all veterans could be assumed to have incurred some personal handicap, be it educational or economic. Before long it became obvious that, considering the number of persons to be involved as beneficiaries of such a large-scale program, the planners were actually addressing not only veterans, but also fundamental aspects of the nation's hope for postwar prosperity.

And there was a need to hurry! The benefits about which they were brainstorming for all those now currently fighting overseas would have to be in place before several millions of service personnel returned to civilian life.

After just five weeks of existence, the committee had compiled by January 6, 1944, the first draft of the eventual legislation. There were three fundamental facets. First, there needed to be a strong legal framework for a rehabilitation program that would facilitate the transition from armed forces personnel to workaday citizens once more. Second, all functions of such a program should be incorporated in the V.A., which, therefore, needed to be made ready to accommodate the coming work load. Third, a close corollary to the second, the creation of new federal agencies that might muddy the waters in the impending new era of veterans' affairs was to be guarded against with a constant vigilance.

The committee was pleased to find help coming from the nation's press when the information from Atherton's survey of rehab conditions was released. The Hearst organization assigned three fulltime reporters to the project. Popular support of this kind, it was hoped, would soon be visited upon representatives and senators in Washington, who in turn would be more receptive to Legion lobbying efforts in this regard.

Four days after the first draft of a Legion bill was created, a bill incorporating the facets of the omnibus measure was introduced in the House of Representatives on January 10 by John Rankin of Mississippi, chairman of the Committee on World War Veterans' Legislation. The bill H.R. 3917 was at this point called the "Servicemen's Aid Act of 1944."

The next day a companion bill was introduced in the Senate by Bennett Champ Clark, Legion founder and senator from Missouri. Ten other senators joined Clark in sponsoring S. 1617.

Back at the Legion's Washington headquarters, planning sessions went late into the night for the grand venture to enact a massive program of benefits for returning veterans. For a while the bill was referred to only as any evolving legislation had been. But the more the planners and visionaries began sensing the probable impact of the program they were outlining, a more appropriate designation seemed necessary. The suggestion that caught fire immediately upon its utterance was a unique combination of recent wartime slang— "G.I." for government issue—with the name of a respected historical document —the Bill of Rights. Hence, "The G.I. Bill of Rights." The name stuck, shortened often to the G.I. Bill. But by whatever handle it came to be known in the years to follow, the essence of the program was obvious in the customary appreciation with which the words were spoken.

Convinced that public involvement was needed for speedy congressional approval and action on the matter, National Commander Atherton designated the upcoming Legion birthday, March 15, as a "national sign-up day" on which petitions should be signed urging action in Congress. Legion posts went to work in their communities.

At this point, also, the much worked over and amended bill was thought to be in need of a complete rewrite. S. 1667 was, therefore, compiled; and again Senator Clark introduced the bill on March 13. All facets of the original measure were included except for Title II, that dealing with muster-out pay. The bill bore signatures of sponsorship of no fewer than eighty-one senators. Four days later the Senate Finance Committee approved it on March 17 and on March 24 the bill passed the full Senate, 50 to 0.

In the House, however, the bill met with lengthy debate. There was general agreement with the fundamental principles represented. Representative Rankin's large committee (twenty-five members) spent more time poring over the finer points. That debate continued through April and May.

During this time the Legion's N.E.C. met in Washington (April 26 to May 2) to add to the momentum of the measure with the help of other national committees, commissions, and boards of the Legion. After several more days of deliberations, the House reported out its version of the bill, differing mainly in administrative details from that of the Senate version.

On May 18 the House bill passed that chamber by a vote of 387 to 0. With such seeming unanimity, the bill seemed sure to become law.

But a procedural and otherwise customary stopover for final adjustments by a joint Senate-House conference committee on May 21 created the kind of legislative drama that aged Legion Legislative Committeemen prematurely and which depicted the knife's edge on which legislation occasionally balanced before enactment or condemnation to the congressional dustbin.

Late in the afternoon of June 9, after the joint committee had pondered the companion bills from the two chambers of Congress for almost a month, Congressman Bernard W. (Pat) Kearney, a New York Legionnaire, alerted members of the Legion's committee that had originated the measure that there was trouble.

Joint committee member John S. Gibson, representing the Eighth District in Georgia and known to favor quick passage of the bill, had returned home during the deliberations. But his proxy vote had just been rejected by the joint committee chairman.

Gibson's absence created a three-to-three tie, with Congressman Kearney being supported by Representatives James Hardin Peterson of Florida and A. Leonard Allen of Louisiana. Gibson's vote, acceptable now only if cast in person, was needed to break the tie, which if allowed to stand would sink the entire bill. "Find Gibson," Kearney said. If he wasn't present at 10:00 A.M. the next day to break the tie for the Legion bill, the cause was lost.

So began a spirited attempt to beat the clock and produce Gibson at the conference committee table. Representative Gibson was 900 miles away in rural south Georgia, but his actual whereabouts in that region were not known.

To solve the problem, the Legion relied on its diverse membership network and the goodwill of a few key players in the drama, nonmembers who, nevertheless, immediately complied with requests for extra effort and understanding.

First there were the telephone operators, two of them, one of whom reported a five-hour delay in telephone transmissions in that part of Georgia. She comprehended the importance of the need to locate Gibson, however, and agreed to stay on the line to his home in the town of Douglas when it was found that he was not home.

While she rang the Gibson house at fifteen minute intervals, someone at the Washington headquarters of the Legion thought to call the night city editor at the *Atlanta Constitution,* Dupont Wright, who used his paper's telephone priority to phone Gibson acquaintances to try to locate the congressman. In this way it was learned that Gibson was thought to be driving from Valdosta to his home in Douglas. More calls went out to radio stations in Valdosta and Atlanta, requesting them to run news alert spots directed to the congressman to make his location known. Georgia state policemen were also asked to look for Gibson's car.

It occurred to the group of Legionnaires at the Washington office that the army air base at Waycross, Georgia, might present a means of transportation for the congressman if clearances could be obtained for such an unusual mission. The officer in charge, Col. William Fillmore, a Legionnaire, explained that he needed clearance from his commanding officer. Failing to find him, another search was begun for no less than Assistant Secretary of War Robert Patterson, who was traveling somewhere in California.

So another call, this time to the *Los Angeles Examiner,* helped locate Patterson, to whom National Commander Warren Atherton appealed. Patterson authorized the flight.

At 11:00 P.M., six hours after the need for his presence was first made known, Gibson returned home. When he answered the phone, he reported the arrival of a car from the army air base. When he arrived at the base, however, it was learned that the plane was inoperable. So Colonel Fillmore substituted a car and two drivers for a mad dash to Jacksonville, Florida, where, it had been learned, there was a 2:20 A.M. commercial flight to Washington, D.C. Those at the Washington headquarters of the Legion convinced airline officials to authorize the delaying of that flight until Gibson could get to the Florida airport.

Congressman John Gibson arrived in Washington with just enough time to get to the conference room at 10:00 A.M. on June 10, angry that his proxy vote had not been honored, but relieved that the vote had been won for the G.I. Bill. The Senate approved the joint committee version on June 12, the House on June 13. On June 22, the president signed the bill into law, Public Law 346 of the 78th Congress. Five Legionnaires stood by for the signing of the "Servicemen's Readjustment Act of 1944:" National Adjutant Donald G. Glascoff; Past National Commander Colmery; Ralph W. Mitchell, aide to the national commander; Francis M. Sullivan, executive director of the National Legislative Committee; and G.I. Bill Committee Chairman John Stelle.

From official start to finish, the move for a G.I. Bill took just five months and produced the greatest single legislative victory for which the Legion could lay appreciable claim.

The bill provided a nearly complete package for helping service personnel to re-enter civilian ranks, offering compensation for temporary unemployment and subsidies for medical care, mortgages, and educational needs. With respect to education, the G.I. Bill would help create the greatest surge ever of college enrollment, eventually to include about eight million ex-service people.

But even at the jubilant signing ceremony, the full impact of the G.I. Bill could not be imagined. It would remain for the postwar era to produce an impressive measure of the bill's importance to the nation.

THE LEGION'S LOBBYIST
John Thomas Taylor

When in 1934 Washington, D.C., socialite Alice Roosevelt Longworth looked down her patrician nose at the recently arrived "New Dealers" led by her maverick cousin F.D.R., she saw few she would invite as luncheon guests. (She guessed them to be less stodgy, however, than their predecessors.)

Instead, for the readers of the December issue of The Ladies Home Journal, *she turned to those whom she said had been heretofore neglected by Washington hostesses—"the important and powerful lobbyists." The first of these to come to mind was the American Legion's own resident aristocrat, John Thomas Taylor, who, Longworth wrote, "has more power on 'the Hill' than anyone I can think of offhand."*

Being singled out in Longworth's chatty article, which was titled "Lion Hunting in the New Deal," would likely meet with Taylor's approval, begging being lionized as he did with unabashed aplomb.

Wavy maned, mustachioed, well fed and partial to Lobster Newburg, sporting pearl gray spats, a snap-brim hat, and a white linen handkerchief tucked in his lapel pocket and armed always with a Malacca cane, Col. John Thomas Taylor was the acknowledged dean of lobbyists. Self-confident to a fault, his perpetual expression of suppressed fury was the practiced mirror-perfect visage of a determined, no-nonsense advocate for veterans. Affectation or not, it was the countenance of one widely acknowledged to be a success at his vocation.

A "lobbyist" to many was one who plied nefarious machinations in the netherworld of back door, side room, over-the-transom politics. Taylor, however, took pride in the title and the work. Into many a cumbersome radio microphone in the mid-1920s he bellowed, "I'm a lobbyist and I'm proud of it," when introducing his role in spearheading the ambitious legislative agenda of the young veterans' organization.

Dynamic, decisive, resolute, Taylor was rarely without impressive fireworks to accompany the exhibition of his talent and ego. Like the Legion itself, he burst onto the scene of veterans' advocacy with energy, ambition, and ability. His store of righteous anger over any slight dealt out to veterans and his untiring capacity for the legwork required for successful lobbying were traits counted upon by the first American Legionnaires.

If one were to fashion credentials for the ideal lobbyist for the new veterans' organization, Taylor's own would more than suffice. Lawyer, political savant molded by Pennsylvania political machine boss Senator Boies Penrose, and later soldier of the First World War present at the birth of the American Legion in Paris, Taylor had happily realized his calling in combining these three careers into one now with the Legion.

*Taylor had obviously found the concepts propounded at the Paris Caucus to his liking. While yet in France, he offered the use of his office in Washington for the operation of the Legion's essential print organ in the early days—*The Weekly*—and as an office for the organization's joint chairmen of its National Legislative Committee, Luke Lea and Tom Miller. When he returned to the States in the fall of 1919, he took over the day-to-day work of the Legion's legislative effort while Lea and Miller assumed what would become the typical volunteer chairmen roles. Taylor eagerly assumed the role of strategist, provocateur, and, just as comfortably, that of workhorse of the Legislative Committee's exhaustive function of overseeing a mountain of legislation year after year.*

As vice-chairman of the National Legislative Committee, he worked gratis until receiving his first pay from the Legion in 1920. Thereafter for the next three decades he was personally involved in every legislative victory and every disappointment of Legion legislation.

He quickly acquired a reputation for aggressive lobbying tactics as an uncowed buttonholer but also as a master of the tedious, pedestrian, mundane detail work necessary for becoming the complete lobbyist. In the process he acquired a success rate acknowledged by both friend and foe alike.

Called "one of the most aggressive members of the craft" in the January 1930 issue of the North American Review, *Taylor at that point had been "a fixture . . . for a decade." The writer for the* Review *suspected him of getting "a good deal more fun out of his profession than the average lobbyist."*

He also became a reference librarian for federal legislative activity, an oracle to whom the politicians turned for information. In the early days before the politicians acquired large staffs and personal libraries of reference materials, Taylor's meticulous record keeping was a quick and accurate source for checking the record of any piece of legislation in which the Legion had an interest.

Taylor's notebooks bulged with the information that he had recorded faithfully on note cards as he sat in the galleries and observed the activity on the floor of the House or Senate, or, later, as he spoke on the telephone to members of Congress. And the bold flourish of his signature dominated a continuous flow of correspondence with key House and Senate members, particularly committee chairmen, whom he regarded as the key players in the legislative drama he relished.

Taylor willingly shared the requested information when asked by congressmen, all the while collecting due bills that had value for returned favors. Representing presumably a voting bloc to reckon with—the large, new, and, in the early years, politically untried veterans of the First World War—Taylor's voice for that constituency was heard and heeded. All the while, his frequent talks before state and national conferences of the Legion kept him informed and aware of the attitudes of that segment of the population.

With the engraved gold pocket watch given him by an appreciative N.E.C. after an impressive legislative triumph—the passage of the Adjusted Compensation Bill, the so-called Bonus Bill, in 1924 over President Coolidge's veto—Taylor counted many anxious moments of congressional action as in the next few years he engineered the overriding of other presidential vetos.

After ten years of his flamboyant and self-possessed style, however, Taylor had accumulated a number of foes, even within the Legion, so that in 1930 there was some rumbling of an ouster in the making. It rankled some, for example, that he often eclipsed the periodic national commanders in attracting attention to himself.

Though characteristically gracious to all, but in a manner many perceived to be theatrical and condescending, Taylor had many sharp edges exposed. He was particularly hard, it was said, on politicians who were also Legionnaires, demanding that they walk the Legion line on pending legislation. But when National Commander Ralph T. "Deke" O'Neil was pressured to appoint someone else to the position, many department commanders and adjutants responded that while they might not like the man personally, his exhaustive knowledge of the legislative give-and-take, his unflagging advocacy for veterans, especially the disabled, and most tellingly his success rate made him an essential member of the national team.

He was retained. Pocketing this new vote of confidence even if lacking the affection of many of those with whom he worked, Taylor reminded his critics that membership in the Legion tended to rise during periods of particularly hard-fought confrontations with Congress. With there being few times when a campaign for veterans' benefits was not being waged, there was also the Taylor style to enthuse N.E.C. men, and department commanders and adjutants to new heights of individual achievement for the Legion.

Taylor's stature increased, notably with the press, when he figured prominently in the reversal of that part of the Economy Act that in March 1933 had suddenly and shockingly depleted most of the previous gains achieved for veterans. F.D.R. had provided the plan and the zeal for that temporarily sweeping setback in veterans' affairs. Taylor had led the successful countercharge to restore the fourteen-year gains, scoring yet another override of a presidential veto in 1934.

Depicted in his First World War uniform complete with an impressive array of medals, Taylor peered from the January 21, 1935, cover of

TIME *as if looking askance at some unyielding member of Congress. There he was billed as the "high priest" of Legion legislation who had "put three Presidents [Coolidge, Hoover, F.D.R.] in their place."*

Renowned Legion speechifier Past National Commander (1922–23) Alvin Owsley was fond of saying, "We have linked the name of the Legion with the destiny of our country." To the extent that that was true, during the thirty-year tenure of John Thomas Taylor much congressional action that had affected the nation's destiny had on it the thumbprint of this bold lobbyist, who from 1919 to 1950 strode the halls of Congress with verve and panache. John Thomas Taylor died on May 20, 1965, at age seventy-nine.

BOYS STATE AND NATION

The Legion's "Boys State," the long-running civics lesson in life-sized simulation sponsored by the Legion since the days of the Depression, originated as have many Legion programs—in an informal gabfest of Legionnaires at an official gathering—this time at the Illinois Department Convention in 1934. There department officers were convinced that Depression-era radicalism was infecting young people who, it was said, had little enough understanding about and thus respect for the uniquely American institution of democracy. The idea for instantaneous, whole-cloth yet intensely instructive units of self-government was aired at that meeting, and plans were made for setting up a boys' civic forum the next year.

On June 23, 1935, Legion posts, 40 & 8 Voitures (posts), Auxiliary units, and civic and fraternal organizations sponsored 217 boys who met at the Illinois State Fairgrounds in Springfield to govern themselves for a week. Recently cleaned and disinfected cow barns on the fairgrounds became cities, towns, counties, or other governmental subdivisions of the premier "state" (in which, Hayes Kennedy, first president of the Boys State Corporation, remembered, there was one "shower bath" available for the delegates).

Two political parties were formed by the boys, which advisers were careful to keep from being mere replicas of existing national parties. Party caucuses were held, then candidates were selected for state governor, a legislature, and others down to minor county and municipal offices. After a round of spirited speeches and an election, the legislature met for three days to pass laws for governing the state.

Thus the first Boys State fulfilled the expectations of the founders by giving the boys a participatory view of democratic government. There was another object lesson as well: an "agitator" appeared on the scene attempting to distribute "Communistic" leaflets to the boys, but he was summarily arrested and placed in a cow shed overnight. Hustled away the next morning, he was warned not to return.

On the final day, the boys went to the tomb of Abraham Lincoln and, facing east toward George Washington's memorial, they pledged "to dedicate and consecrate a portion of all of our waking hours to acquiring a thorough flag education, and to the dissemination of this knowledge throughout our homes, our schools, our cities, counties, and state, and . . . [to] cooperate toward making flag education an essential basic element in good citizenship."

Illinois Legionnaires and their counterparts nationwide took seri-

ously the threats to customary American governance that they perceived in radicalism. Closer to home was the concern that young people were getting a skewered view of how governments could and should function, since a greatly depressed national economy prompted a spate of anomalies for which there were no quick solutions. As the life-styles of many were being changed radically, the hope for the future, especially for young people, was greatly dimmed.

Here, then, was a seedbed for radicalism ranging in sources and practice from academic ponderings to hooliganism. Many Legion posts had taken an active interest in local Civilian Conservation Corps camps and had observed radical agitation there by Communists and others. Boys State founders had discussed the Young Pioneer Camps conducted by Communists, where, it was said, high school–age boys were taught that democracy was outdated and should be replaced by Communism.

The purpose of Boys State, therefore, was more than an intensive lesson in how governments operated. The point of it all from the beginning was higher-plane thinking: why *was the traditional American way better than any of the methods being hawked lately for reordering the society? Hayes Kennedy, a law instructor at Loyola University Law School, had observed that many of the young men beginning the study of law had little background in the structure and operation of American government.*

The Legion Magazine *observed in September 1936 that "democracy is being derided abroad by both the dictatorship of the right and . . . of the left. Through Europe and in the Orient the spokesmen of the new autocracies have been shouting that the American doctrine of rule by all the people is a fallacy. We see whole nations abroad living under the bayonet rule of small groups, responsible only to themselves, which have seized power by force and have abolished most of the rights which Americans assume belong to every citizen. In our own land false prophets seize upon our own minor shortcomings to support the contentions of Europe's men on horseback that our whole system is doomed. We have our homegrown Communists and Fascists who parrot everything derogatory said about us abroad, who preach that the way out of America's economic and social ills is by destroying liberty and the rights which we have built up in more than 150 years of self-government."*

James F. Barton, national director of publications, called Boys State "an excellent and practical way of learning just what the duties and obligations of citizenship are. . . ." It helped make the point when some "states" were permitted to use the same ballot boxes that the delegates' parents used in real local and national elections.

The Inter-Department Americanism Meeting held at Cleveland's Wade Park Hotel on July 19–20, 1935 adopted the plan of the Department of Illinois for a Boys State as potentially a part of a national

Americanism program for the next year. The plan, augmented by the experience of the first Boys State held in June, was put into the proper form for the National Convention in St. Louis later that year. The convention liked the idea and designated it as an official part of a national Americanism program that already included Boy Scouts; Sons of the American Legion; Constitution Week in the schools; the municipal, town, or city survey by students; C.C.C. camps; Big Brother units; and Junior Baseball.

In 1936, the first National Boys State Conference was held in Chicago. Hayes Kennedy presided at the meeting, which was attended by Legionnaires from nine states. That year the departments of Ohio, West Virginia, and Pennsylvania joined Illinois in establishing these "schools for citizenship," as Past National Adjutant Russell G. Creviston called them. The Illinois Boys State in 1936 commemorated Legion leaders by naming county units after such Legion luminaries as the first seven past national commanders: Lindsley, D'Olier, Emery, Galbraith, MacNider, Owsley, and Quinn. Before long there were counties named for other Legionnaires of note, such as National Adjutant Frank E. Samuel. In 1938, there were eighteen Boys States. That year also, at the West Virginia State College the Department of West Virginia held what Chief Counselor Leonard Barnett believed to be the "first Negro Boys State" in the nation. There the fifty-nine delegates, Barnett wrote to National Publicity Director Ed McGrail on June 18, "conducted themselves in a manner befitting those who would have set a tradition for those who are to follow."

To the delegates of Boys States of 1938, Past National Adjutant Russell G. Creviston wrote, "Many of us who served in war so that democracy might survive are perplexed by the things that we see . . . in the world today. To act intelligently as citizens, it is necessary that you shall have practical knowledge of the manner in which your government is operated. It is necessary that you shall be given the means of determining for yourselves that our form of government made it possible to build the greatest nation in existence today.

"The American Legion [is] desirous of passing on to you a nation in which you shall have the right to work . . . unhampered by those of authority who would stamp out freedom of thought and of action."

Certain individuals, of course, have come to be associated with the beginning of Boys State. In addition to Hayes Kennedy, who was Illinois Department Americanism Chairman at the time in addition to his teaching of law, there was Harrold L. Card, a high school teacher and Illinois Department Boys Scout Chairman who had once organized a "city" among Boy Scouts in much the way Boys State would develop. Bill Mundt, Illinois Department Adjutant and an early Boys State Corporation member, was an enthusiastic early participant, as was Department Adjutant Paul G. Armstrong. Another was John Stelle, then Illinois's Lieutenant Governor and later a national commander of the

Legion, who advised Kennedy to incorporate Boys State, as Kennedy later recalled, to "keep it out of Legion politics." All these helped foster the idea and advance it appreciably.

By 1940 there were thirty-four Boys States. Such a successful array of participating departments seemed to call for another event to expand the experience to the federal level. Thus a "Boys Forum of National Government" was organized in 1946 after the lifting of some World War II–era travel restrictions. In Washington, D.C. the delegates, two each from the participating departments, held a political convention and organized a Boys Senate while meeting in a U.S. Senate caucus room.

President Harry S. Truman, life member of Post 21 in Independence, Missouri, received the boys at the White House. The promise for the future that Truman saw in this exceptional group moved him to state that the republic would be "good for a thousand years." The Boys Forum of National Government was adopted by the National Convention later that year in San Francisco. In 1949 the name was changed by the Philadelphia National Convention to "Boys Nation."

GROWTH AND REFORMATION IN THE ATOMIC AGE

THE POST-WORLD WAR II AMERICAN LEGION

1944 – 1949

I

Anticipation: Looking to the Postwar Era

With the enactment of the Veterans Omnibus Bill—the triumphant G.I. Bill of Rights—in the summer of 1944, the Legion thankfully accepted the task of helping untold thousands of veterans to apply for this new array of benefits and for monitoring the Veterans Administration's compliance with this new, magnanimous law.

Now, too, Legionnaires who had founded the organization more than twenty years earlier were once again addressing the full-scale need for veterans' rehabilitation.

As the organization's resources would allow, Legion Rehab work would reflect the newly enlarged task of the V.A. for dispensing the services and benefits of the G.I. Bill. The Legion continued to monitor the V.A., which like its predecessor the Veterans Bureau, had been an often stubborn target of Legion darts as well as the appreciative recipient of Legion backing.

There had been a recent change at the top of that agency. Brig. Gen. Frank T. Hines had been administrator at the Bureau and the V.A. for twenty-two years and was generally regarded as a friend to veterans. A veteran himself of the Spanish-American War and World War I, Hines, nevertheless, had been criticized often by many in the Legion who complained that he allowed his concern for budgetary matters to hamper the "benefit of doubt," which Legion Rehab workers often invoked when disagreeing with the way one law or another was administered by the V.A.

Hines's successor was Gen. Omar N. Bradley, appointed by President Truman to take charge of the V.A. on August 15, 1945. The popular Bradley came at a time when there was talk of moves afoot to consolidate and reorganize government bureaus and other offices. Such a development, in the view of Legion national officers, would threaten the independence of the V.A. With that agency facing a drastically increased work load—from a clientele of five million to now upward of eighteen million—it was essential, the Legion held, that the V.A. not be amalgamated, consolidated or otherwise included in any other government department or branch. It must remain responsible only to the people and overseen primarily by Congress and the president.

Title II of the G.I. Bill was already stimulating the construction of hospitals and other expansion programs at the V.A., the first of which was under way already in late 1944. In May of the next year came the welcome announcement of more new hospitals to be built and expansions to be made at several other sites.

Any mention of V.A. hospitals at this time would bring to mind the poor reputation some V.A. facilities had acquired, so much so as to trigger action by the House of Representatives after a series of articles published in early 1945 in a few popular national magazines spotlighted poor medical and hospital procedures.

An article in the March 1945 issue of *Cosmopolitan* magazine detailed objectionable practices at V.A. hospitals at Castle Point, New York and Dayton, Ohio. That article was reprinted in the widely read *Reader's Digest.* The April 1945 issue of *Harpers* magazine told of the runaround given veterans seeking benefits in the first few weeks after returning to civilian life.

In an attempt to regain public confidence, Administrator Hines, as one of his last official acts, asked the Legion, the V.F.W., and the D.A.V. to help him compose a survey form regarding V.A. facilities. The three organizations joined in preparing a questionnaire that was then distributed throughout their organizations.

After Jack Oakey, director of the Legion's National Field Service, had seen the results of the survey and had read the magazine articles, which he said had "caused a tempest at the V.A.," he reviewed the reports of his field secretaries. He found that the survey ordered by National Commander Edward Scheiberling, which included reports of the department commanders, "does not jibe with those of the field secretaries" whose "glowing reports of the good conditions at V.A. hospitals" made Oakey "a little suspicious."

"We are on the spot," Oakey wrote in a June 18, 1945, confidential memo to the field secretaries, "because people are now asking what did we do to help the situation?" He noted, however, that many of those in the field had already reported observations of some of the same problems referred to in the widely read magazines. He warned the field secretaries that there were those in the Legion who said that "perhaps [their] territories . . . should be changed periodically because they . . . get too close with the V.A. hospital people they are surveying and checking up on." But he also repeated his disagreement with a policy of such periodic reshuffling of territorial assignments, knowing that many of the rehab workers in the field had established themselves in the community in which they lived. He hoped a word of caution would suffice. On further consideration, Oakey apparently comprehended the overall picture—that V.A. hospital practices generally were less objectionable than the select instances of obvious dereliction.

The results of the survey by the veterans' organizations seemed to confirm that more positive picture. The results handed Hines showed that while there were indeed a few sites at which immediate review and changes were needed, generally, V.A. facilities ranged from comparable to very much better than similar civilian facilities, the justifiably objectionable situations at certain hospitals notwithstanding.

Affiliation

It was at this point that one of the most positive developments of the Legion-V.A. relationship would occur.

The Legion practice had been to generally eschew affiliating with any other organization, preferring, instead, to pursue its own various programs of service to veterans and the nation.

But the word "affiliation" took on new meaning, decidedly positive, when, before the end of World War II, Legion Rehab planners began looking for ways to increase the quality of medical care for veterans.

A concept considered by the 1943 National Convention in Omaha was the Department of Wisconsin's Resolution 580, which called for new V.A. facilities to be located adjacent to a qualified medical school or institution and that the V.A. "secure the assistance and cooperation of the faculty and staff of all medical schools possible." The mutually helpful aspects of such an arrangement were readily apparent: up-to-date medical care for veterans and teaching-hospital arrangements for medical education in the nation. Like other particularly noteworthy recommendations coming from the field, this one arose from a general need—more and better hospital care for veterans—and progressed to a specific plan that would revolutionize the practice of veterans' medicine. The concept would come to be called simply "affiliation."

While national Rehab planners began laying the groundwork for such a major combination of efforts in this far-reaching and inclusive venture, the Legion's Medical Advisory Board was established, giving the National Rehabilitation Committee the benefit of expert medical knowledge, just as affiliation would aid the patients of V.A. hospitals.

Shortly before the 1945 National Convention, it was announced that such a board had been organized, chaired by Col. Leonard George Rowntree, M.D., recently the chief of the Medical Division of Selective Service. The 1944 Chicago National Convention had created the post of chief medical adviser (Dr. H. Kennon Dunham, the longtime medical adviser to the Legion, had died in early 1944). Dr. Rowntree selected a group of well-known medical experts to help him advise the Rehab Division in working to meet the increased volume of medical problems forthcoming from the present and the previous World War.

In addition to his work at Selective Service, Dr. Rowntree had been chief of medicine at the famous Mayo Clinic, a professor of medicine at the University of Minnesota and Johns Hopkins, a director of the Bio-Chemical Foundation in Philadelphia, and an internationally known researcher in glandular functions.

Joining Dr. Rowntree on the advisory board was Col. Louis H. Renfrow, also formerly of Selective Service and past chairman of the Army-Navy Committee of the American Dental Association; Maj. General George F. Lull, deputy surgeon general of the army; Rear Adm. William J. G. Agnew, deputy surgeon general of the navy; Col. Esmond R. Long, chief of the TB section in the Office of the Surgeon General; Col. Charles M. Mayo, chief of a general hospital on foreign duty during the war and a member of the Mayo Clinic in Rochester, Minnesota; Dr. Winfred Overholser, an internationally known psychiatrist and currently superintendent of St. Elizabeth's Hospital in Washington, D.C.; Dr. William D. Stroud, professor of cardiology at the University of Pennsylvania; Capt. Waltman N. Walters, chief of surgery, Naval Hospital, Philadelphia Navy Yard (and standing in currently for Colonel Mayo, who at that time was out of the country); and Captain C. Raymond Walls, formerly chief of the dental section of the Selective Service. Most of these persons had served in both world wars.

Among other duties, the board worked with department medical advisers who in turn worked with "post surgeons" to complete a nationwide coverage of medical advisory services. The Board reported in 1945 for the first time at the annual National Rehab Committee meeting. Since its organization it had met monthly to "stimulate all health services" in the armed forces for veterans and their families; to advise Legionnaires working in the areas of rehabilitation and legislation; to act as a speakers bureau for Legion meetings and congressional hearings and to provide articles to medical literature; and to encourage medical research in disease (particularly the troublesome tropical diseases affecting service personnel who had served in the South Pacific and elsewhere) and other conditions affecting veterans, their families, and, thus, the general public.

Of particular interest in this area, also, was rheumatic heart disease. That disease had been called recently the "national killer of the population," a dismal designation formerly given to tuberculosis before an intensive national educational campaign greatly decreased the threat of that disease. In focusing on heart disease, the Medical Advisory Board recommended that the Legion encourage the American Heart Association with a grant of $25,000.

Soon after the appointment of General Bradley as the director of Veterans Administration, Public Law 293 of the 79th Congress established a Department of Medicine and Surgery at the V.A. This was an important development and of particular interest to the Legion because the new department was given the responsibility of establishing a residency training program.

This development helped complete, moreover, the cycle needed for "affiliation." Soon three types of residency programs at V.A. hospitals and clinics were established: affiliation with medical schools through a deans' committee to apply the "deans' committee plan"; affiliation with a group of representative doctors in a community for the training and education of residents at selected V.A. sites to apply the deans' committee plan; and establishment of an educational group composed of certain full-time personnel at selected V.A. facilities for the training and education of residents.

In the first two types, the "deans' committee plan" was employed, that for the part-time appointment of both medical consultant physicians with professorial rank who were connected with approved medical schools and attending physicians with less than professorial rank but with teaching appointments in approved medical schools. Both groups were made available to the V.A. to observe and advise on medical practices there. In this arrangement, not only was the professional staff at V.A. installations increased in number, but, also, the expertise of nationally reputed medical consultants was bound to increase the quality of medical care given to veterans.

Rehab workers heard at the National Rehab Conference in 1946 that currently there were forty-five medical schools cooperating with twenty-eight deans' committees at thirty-two general medical and tuberculosis hospitals for up-to-date diagnostic and therapeutic services as well as intensive training of residents. In addition, at thirty-seven medical schools operating with twenty-four deans' committees, arrangements had been made for full care of neuropsychiatric patients at thirty-five neuropsychiatric hospitals and mental hygiene clinics. As of August 1, 1946, some 650 resident physicians were on duty in the V.A. under the various programs of affiliation. In each case their presence meant state-of-the-art expertise. From this point forward, the National Rehab Division and Committee (later Commission) maintained a keen interest in the affiliation program, the deans' committee plan, and the locating of new VA facilities near medical education centers.

In 1945, for the first time in several years, there was no Rehab conference in the spring because of the government's request that preference in travel and hotel accommodations go to returning military personnel. Instead, Rehab field secretaries and area chairmen met with the executive group of the National Rehab Committee in early February to discuss several topics of importance, including insurance, claims and ratings, Board of Veterans Appeals, vocational training and education, medical and hospital service, expansion of the V.A., V.A. personnel, employment activities and programs, readjustment allowance, loan guaranties, discharge, and disability boards of review.

The Legion's National Rehab Division had already begun to work with department and state service officers and national field secretaries to establish an adequate information coordinating service so that all who qualified for the benefits would know about them.

Rehab's Field Service was recently expanded to twenty-seven, including the director and overseas secretaries. As an experiment, one field secretary was assigned to an army hospital and one to a navy hospital with a 1,500-bed capacity. It was thought appropriate that several World War II veterans be employed and assigned to the Field Service and that an apprentice-training program be initiated. Rehab Director Kraabel asked, also, that several new positions be filled in the areas of medical consulting, contact, vocational training, claims, and the inevitable clerking help necessary to process the increasing number of inquiries and claims.

Even though employees of the Rehab Division reflected proudly on the attributes of the G.I. Bill, the reverence in which they held the general concept of that landmark law did not extend blindly to its every subsection and paragraph. Amid all the activity of preparing for the implementation of the act, Rehab workers were also recommending changes.

In July 1945 they were calling for refinements and upgrading changes to be made, as in the payments of tuition and other fees to ex-service persons who were now attending colleges; enlargement of advisement and counseling services to students; the redefining of the term "reasonable normal value" as used in the loan guaranty title; the waiting period for the determination of eligibility for loans; the expansion of business loan guarantees; and the educating of officials at lending agencies, especially those in small communities, to the various programs of the G.I. Bill.

National Convention Resolution 665 of 1944 had called for a comprehensive program for informing World War II veterans of their rights under Title II of the G.I. Bill, and of the provisions of Public Law 16 of the 78th Congress, commonly known as the Vocational Rehabilitation and Training Act. Soon after V-E Day, May 8, 1945, approximately one million veterans availed themselves immediately of the educational and training programs administered by the federal government just as soon as they were discharged from the armed forces. Many more were expected to do the same after V-J Day.

Alerting veterans to the new benefits created more work for the Legion claims and appeals staff. The resident savant in that area, Charles Stevens, and his small staff were soon deluged with inquiries and requests involving veterans' and dependents' claims, insurance, appeals, and boards of review matters. Stevens had already begun working with V.A. personnel to implement a system of mutual helpfulness for the disposition of cases referred to his office. He was proud of the work the Legion's rating schedule committee had done in studying and analyzing the 1933 schedule for rating disabilities. That work, he reported, had been reflected noticeably in the 1945 schedule recently approved and announced by the V.A.

Perhaps the most memorable event, certainly the most publicized, relating to Rehab in 1946 was the furor caused by the way in which National Commander John Stelle caused public attention to be riveted for a time on the V.A.'s problems in providing the new services and benefits to the large number of ex-service persons returning to civilian life.

Stelle, a former governor of Illinois, had chaired the special committee that had drafted the G.I. Bill of Rights. His chairmanship had helped him launch a successful campaign for the office of national commander the next year after the enactment of this famous bill. Though he had participated in the Legion's most shining legislative accomplishment so far, Stelle's year as national commander was one of much controversy inside and outside the Legion, particularly that generated by his charge of the V.A.'s "unbalanced diet of promises."

In mid-January 1946, Stelle complained in writing to V.A. Administrator Bradley, reminding the general that Resolution 528 of the Legion National Convention in Milwaukee in 1941 had made specific recommendations, and this before the war, for "revamping and elevating" the medical and hospital services of the V.A. Had those recommendations been implemented, the V.A. could have better weathered the war and now the postwar situation, Stelle wrote.

The national commander complained about the seeming slowness in the hospital construction program and particularly of V.A. publicity given recently to the practice of contracting out medical care to private hospitals. Was that a tactic for temporarily helping to meet the need or was it an indication of a definite trend for the future? If the latter, such a move, Stelle wrote, would surely diminish the medical professionalism of the V.A., hindering the special medical and neuropsychological needs of veterans.

There was, also, the customary catalog of complaints about the whole gamut of V.A. hospital operation practices. From August to December 1945, T. O. Kraabel had received no fewer than 235 individual recommendations on thirty-two different V.A. hospitals from Legion service officers, department adjutants, and field secretaries. He delivered the recommendations in person, by letter, or by phone, depending on the urgency involved, to General Bradley. While on many of the recommendations Kraabel received some acknowledgment, he reported receiving no report of action taken by the V.A. In addition, Legion Rehab workers had questioned several V.A. policy matters in the area of medical and hospital care: availability of army or navy medical records on new claims, space for Legion representatives at V.A. stations, lagging construction of hospitals, and personnel and space difficulties in field offices.

Failing to receive an answer from Bradley to his letter or any report of action at the V.A. that satisfied him, Stelle stepped up his protest by circulating a letter to all senators and congressmen, in which he reported on a survey taken by Legion service officers and other Rehab workers that told of the backlog of thousands upon thousands of veteran applications for benefits and services. Thousands of applications had not even been acknowledged, the survey showed. It seemed apparent that too little effort had been taken to deal with the immense workload the V.A. was sure to have visited upon itself at the end of the war. The letter ended with a call for a congressional investigation of the V.A.

In a press conference in Washington held simultaneously with the distribution of his letter, Stelle read a 1,200-word statement that included a detailed "Ten Point Objective:" 1. Direct action by the V.A. to get complete records and adequate examinations at time of discharge from the War and Navy departments to reduce the tremendous number of veterans who were required to appear for reexams. 2. Immediate procurement from any source of hospital beds so that the 7,000 applicants already processed and waiting could be immediately hospitalized and so that in the future there would be no such waiting list. 3. Reduction of the 102,830 unprocessed applications for education and training under the G.I. Bill. 4. Reduction of the 20,411 pending claims for waiver of insurance premiums. 5. Quick elimination of the 18,847 undisposed of death claims. 6. Immediate reduction of the 287,000 unanswered letters to a current basis by the employment of the many applicants for the V.A. jobs. 7. Expansion of temporary hospital facilities by taking over army and navy establishments while other facilities were being constructed. 8. Ruthless dealing with any government agency that was delaying proper housing for the veteran thereby preventing the pursuit of his educational career or the reunity of his family (this, admittedly, was not a V.A. responsibility; but the V.A., the national commander said, could help by focusing on and pointing up the problem). 9. Hastening of further decentralization of the V.A. to the field whereby veterans and their representatives could have direct contact with V.A. officials and not be forced into correspondence that languished in the immense backlog at Washington. 10. The promotion of the first nine points by (a) the V.A. using its legal authority to requisition building materials, supplies, and equipment for hospitals; (b) using the still-existing Selective Service to obtain needed hospital personnel; (c) bringing in nationally known and experienced insurance men to set up an insurance system; and (d) taking over emergency office space for regional and local offices.

In the discussion that followed the news conference, Stelle reviewed the ten objectives and in commenting about the need for an experienced insurance consultant to reorganize and update the V.A.'s insurance system, he was moved to add, "What we need in charge of the V.A. is a seasoned businessman, not a soldier, however good a soldier he may be." Those few words sparked a controversy that burdened the relationship of the Legion and the V.A. for several months.

Hardly had Stelle uttered that remark than it was recast in the press as a demand for Bradley's ouster. Soon it was assumed by many, including Legionnaires, that the national commander had stepped over the line of legitimate criticism of the V.A. to launch a personal attack on the popular, much honored Omar Bradley. Stelle and the Legion Headquarters denied any such intent. But the headlines persisted for several weeks in reporting a Stelle versus Bradley imbroglio, a development that distracted attention from the Legion's long list of justified complaints about problems at the V.A. and that caused divisiveness within the Legion itself.

The lines of conflict had been drawn. Bradley, too, made available to congressmen a letter "prepared as a result of the criticism of the national commander" in which the V.A. head sought to counter the criticism point by point. Neither man was disposed to back down, especially in view of the wide coverage in the press of their tiff.

Some remembered Stelle's previously vehement disagreement with the V.A. over the location of a medical facility in his home state of Illinois. He had preferred one site and the V.A. had chosen another. Was the national commander merely enlarging on a personal gripe? Though staffers at National Headquarters introduced into the fray documents reportedly proving that Stelle's much publicized news conference preceded the V.A. decision on locating the Illinois facility in question, the suggestion of vindictiveness stoked the embers of controversy.

Many Legionnaires believed that a statement such as Stelle had made and the statements attributed to him were sure to reflect on General Bradley personally.

Though some faulted their national commander, others focused, instead, on firsthand knowledge of frustrating inadequacies in V.A. services. Walter Naughton, department historian of California, informed National Public Relations Director Ray Fields in February that while 150 beds had been made available in his state for the treatment of ex-service personnel, one million or more veterans were soon to be discharged there. Also, 500 World War II mental cases, "many of them slight ones . . . easily corrected and rehabilitated," according to Naughton, had been placed in the state's mental institutions because the V.A. couldn't take care of them. "Here we have kids . . . thrown in with murderers, [the] criminally insane, sadists, hopheads, sex perverts, etc. How does Bradley and his VA answer some of these things in California alone?"

With the indictment by the Legion of unsatisfactory, even alarming, V.A. practices and then the furor over Stelle's supposed insult to Bradley to consider, the N.E.C. met in mid-February, several weeks earlier than usual, to hear not only about the problems at the V.A., but about what was now a problem of public relations. It was only the fifth time in the twenty-seven-year history of the Legion that such a special session had been called.

National Commander Stelle wired an invitation to General Bradley to attend the N.E.C. meeting for a "firsthand discussion" of the problems at the V.A. But Bradley objected strongly to the wording of the invitation announcing as it did a "most respectful hearing." To him that word implied a cross-examination or some other objectionable review of his administration. The teletype message from the Washington Legion headquarters to National Headquarters in Indianapolis told the story succinctly: "Bradley rejects invitation."

The administrator had sent a telegram to the national commander on the afternoon of February 7 saying, "Nothing helpful to V.A. would result in a meeting between you and me at this time." He did offer to meet with Stelle and a group of N.E.C. men at the V.A.'s central office in Washington. T. O. Kraabel later attempted to convince Bradley to attend the N.E.C. meeting, but to no avail. Kraabel's teletype message to National on February 14, three days before the N.E.C. meeting, contained his regrets about "the failure of my mission" even though he felt he "did my level best" to convince the general to attend the meeting. Bradley's aide, Colonel Chester B. Hanson, was believed to have implied that if the general were given another invitation, more judiciously worded, he might attend. But, soon thereafter, Bradley himself called the Legion's Washington office to say that because of the publicity surrounding the affair, he was definitely against attending, even though, he had reportedly told Kraabel, he recognized that the N.E.C. "is composed of outstanding business and professional men" with whom he "would have liked to discuss veterans' matters."

Perhaps to get the jump on the publicity to be generated by the N.E.C. meeting, Bradley called a press conference the day before and announced several policy updates and changes in practices that Legion criticism had been focused on of late.

The N.E.C. met on Sunday, February 17, in Indianapolis for a ten-hour session in which the subject of Stelle versus Bradley was given exhaustive review. The meeting was kept open to the fifteen newspapers represented and to radio reporters. The Executive Committeemen heard and generally accepted Stelle's explanation of his conversations and supposed confrontation with Bradley about the Decatur, Illinois site that he favored for the locating of a women veterans' hospital.

The N.E.C. returned a supportive finding after hearing other national officers support Stelle's version of several disagreements he had had with General Bradley. After appointing a seven-man group of N.E.C. men, including Past National Commanders Harry Colmery and Warren Atherton, to accompany Stelle to Bradley's office in answer to the general's invitation for a conference, the N.E.C. signaled the spirited and determined continuation of the Legion's long-running watchdog role that it played in its relationship with the V.A. Stelle earlier had invoked the privilege of his office to assign the more than two million members of the Legion as "watchdogs for the rights of veterans and their efficient treatment under existing federal law." Now the N.E.C. directed the preparation of a monthly "progress report" on the status of V.A. services "based on grassroots information to be supplied by the 13,400 posts."

The April issue of *The American Legion Magazine* included the article "Stelle Was Right!" showing the committee named to confer with Bradley. In the article, Boyd B. Stutler, the magazine's managing editor, beat the drum for Stelle's having called attention to nothing short of a "tragic breakdown" of the V.A.'s delivery of benefits and services. Stutler decried the fact that some news writers and radio commentators had twisted Stelle's statements as a personal attack on General Bradley, "himself a Legionnaire."

Criticism continued throughout the summer of 1946, with salvos being launched by both the V.A. and the Legion.

At the national convention in San Francisco later that year, General Bradley got his chance to vent his frustration with the criticism leveled by Stelle. On Monday, the opening day of the convention, though never faulting the American Legion in his speech (though obviously the general was chastening the Legion for allowing Stelle to speak for it in the manner to which Bradley strenuously objected), Bradley listed his objections to the recent criticism of himself. Specifically he directed each of his retorts to, "My host, your national commander." Repeating that tactic more than a dozen times throughout his relatively short speech, the V.A. administrator drew attention in a manner rarely if ever done before to the actions of a Legion national commander in a way that heaped on that officer the full responsibility for the current confrontation between the Legion and the V.A. That point he sought to make clearly near the end of his speech by saying, "What we have been able to accomplish during this year in the Veterans Administration has been achieved not because of, but in spite of, your national commander."

After the election at the National Convention of another national commander, Paul H. Griffith of Pennsylvania, the steam of controversy appreciably dissipated. At least it was no longer daily headline fodder. The Legion could assume a more conciliatory and less strident voice when dealing with the V.A. Both the Legion and Bradley were relieved.

Once again, National Headquarters continued with more traditional tactics as an advocate for veterans, concerned at this point about a V.A. overwhelmed by the millions of returning ex-service personnel applying for and requiring benefits and services.

The educational provisions in particular of the G.I. Bill had generated an enormous amount of interest and involvement by returning veterans. One million veterans were expected to take advantage of educational provisions of the bill in 1946.

During the summer of 1946, the Legion's Special National G.I. Bill Legislative Committee considered the nation's difficulties in dealing with the greatly increased demands for higher education from returning veterans. The committee did not have to rely on secondhand information; in addition to pursuing higher education, veterans had formed American Legion posts on college campuses and, in the process, had begun an active, vocal interaction with the national organization.

The committee discussed several problems caused by the great number of persons returning to civilian life and the consequent strains being placed on teaching facilities, on-the-job training, and housing generally. It suggested that the list of the benefits (such as tuition and books) distributed by several departments should include, also, the names of small colleges so that not all the former G.I.s would rush to the larger, "name" institutions.

The committee studied each benefit allowed in the G.I. Bill, as well as the experiences, results, breakdowns, problem areas, deficiencies, outright failures, and suggestions heard so far about what should be done legislatively or administratively to improve and strengthen the act.

They knew that before the war, colleges and universities, professional and technological schools, teachers' colleges, and normal schools (junior colleges) had been full. The newest schools of higher education had been established many decades before, and there were few new schools opening. Now it was likely that the potential enrollment increase would double or triple. Many looked to the example of New York State for the new practice there of establishing emergency "college centers," specially chartered institutions where a few thousand more students could take classes from teachers drawn from area schools to teach part-time and where the curriculum had been tailored to veterans seeking semiprofessional and technical education. These new college centers, also, had housing facilities provided by the state.

As resolved at the 1944 National Convention, the Legion began its own American Legion College at National Headquarters in July 1946, consisting of three "terms" of two weeks each year to be attended by one hundred students (at least one from each department, the others to be apportioned from departments of larger memberships) to study the Legion's various programs for veterans and how these should be promoted on the local level. Here the students, all World War II veterans, were taught by fellow World War II veterans, recently hired Headquarters staff members who had been assigned the job of equipping the students to disseminate authoritative information about Legion programs to yet more World War II veterans nationwide.

After a few months of closely observing the situation nationally, the committee reported just before the San Francisco National Convention of 1946 that the G.I. Bill provisions for education and training needed further remedial legislation. At this point, about sixty-five percent of those seeking education went to college and thirty-five percent for job training. The peak in this process was expected by the V.A. to come in the spring of 1947. Individual committee members had observed in their home regions how this immense experiment in the formal education of untold thousands was unfolding. Several ponderables were being clarified: the number of veterans who would go to college or to job training, the way in which college facilities might accommodate the sudden phenomenal growth with additional classroom space and teachers, the availability of housing, the much questioned adequacy of the subsistence pay allowed veterans going to school, and, finally, the number of personnel that would be required at the V.A. to process all the education applications and follow-up work.

Once again Legion spokesmen pointed to a lack of foresight apparent on the part of the federal government. While the government was now heavily involved in distributing college tuition and subsistence pay to veterans, it had not provided for new school facilities or housing for the new students. At least for the veterans needing medical care, the government had already built several hospitals. But for those who sought higher education, no comparable program of expansion and accommodation was in sight.

The education of veterans also created another problem given wide coverage in the press. It was becoming apparent that there were many instances of fraud arising in the misuse of payments to veterans and by those who misrepresented educational and training services to veterans in order to receive the veterans' educational benefit payments.

A large program such as this of benefits funded from the public coffers certainly stood to lose much from bad publicity, even that caused by relatively few persons who misused what was an essential advancement for many. General Bradley, particularly, was angered by the revelations of fraud. He warned that continuation of this problem would endanger the programs. Some in Congress were quick to take action to cut funding. An amendment to the G.I. Bill passed in the closing moments of the 79th Congress for which no hearings had been held and with little or no debate or publicity, cut some educational benefits by fifty percent. Deserving veterans were being hurt as a result of the dishonesty of a few.

In early 1947, the Legion's Vocational Training Advisory Board adopted a sixteen-point plan to maintain the integrity and the usefulness of the job training aspects of the G.I. Bill, which among other purposes sought to use existing public school facilities for veterans' vocational education when otherwise not being used.

National officers were not the only ones who dealt with the growth problem in higher education. In early 1946, a special conference of college Legion posts submitted a resolution calling for the employment of five Legion collegiate national field representatives specifically to aid them in the establishment of more college posts. National judged it to be a good idea. One collegiate field representative was assigned to each of the areas overseen by the five national vice-commanders.

The conference of collegiate posts also called for emergency housing to be built to help ease the critical housing shortage facing veterans attending college. They likened the problem to the housing shortages that occurred around defense plants during the war. The government had acted then to house defense workers; the same kind of help was needed now, they said. Since all troops, except those on occupational duty, would be discharged by March 1, 1946, the problem was bound to become larger.

While higher education and job training were popular G.I. Bill benefits, neither fully encompassed nor addressed the needs of those who wished to enter or return to agriculture, a general employment classification which before the war had included more workers than any other occupation: fifty-five percent of the current citizen-soldiers of World War II had agricultural background and about two million of them reportedly would be returning to that occupation.

The Legion's new Special G.I. Committee on Farms began work in 1946 to formulate three aspects of a program for aiding veterans with on-the-job training; farm financing; and, particularly in the West, the availability of public land on which veterans had preferential filing rights.

The first difficulty veterans had in this area was that of securing operational loans for farming. Officials at the Farm Security Administration (F.S.A.) were heard to complain that their agency had not been given a budget in accordance with its large number of applicants, thus a nettlesome backlog of several thousand loan applications. Legion Rehab Committee Chairman Robert M. McCurdy arranged a conference of personnel from the F.S.A., the Reconstruction Finance Corporation (R.F.C.), and Legionnaires on the National Farm and Rehab committees to discuss possible solutions to this problem. The meeting resulted in the R.F.C. loaning its fellow agency the money to cover the 25,000 applicants for farm loans until the time when a new budget for the F.S.A. could be devised.

Another such meeting with a commissioner of the Bureau of Reclamation was arranged to plan a land settlement program that would allow veterans to establish farming and ranching operations. It continued, however, to be slow going in the placement of veterans on their own farms and ranches. The bureau was already six months behind its own schedule for authorizing projects on which for the next five years veterans had preferential filing rights. Legion committee members charged that the bureau was bogged down in politics as well as being stymied by an unproductive planning process said to continue interminably and without useful results.

They charged also that project sites in California, Washington, Oregon, Idaho, and Arizona were standing idle awaiting the selection of farmers to occupy available farms. Agriculture Committee Chairman Max R. Brents of California had visited all these sites on his way to and from the National Convention in 1946. He judged the potential for success on the various-sized farm units to be excellent if only eagerly waiting veterans were finally to be placed there. In California's Imperial Valley alone, 250,000 acres had been set aside for farms for veterans. Similarly, the Klamath project near the California-Oregon state line contained eighty-six farm units (for which there were 2,024 applicants). The work of preparing reclamation projects, also, had and would continue to provide employment for veterans, if only the government's inertia on the matter could be counteracted.

To new National Agriculture Committee Chairman Charles L. Brown of Missouri, the Legion's "product is service," not nearly enough of which had been given to agriculture. There was even a legitimate tie-in, he said, with one of the Legion's honored "basics:" "Agriculture is the soundest basis of an unquestioned Americanism, and the ownership of a 40-, 80-, or 160-acre farm is the surest antidote to un-Americanism thinking and subversive activity" that one could find. And while "a hungry stomach can always be filled from the products of a farm," conversely "a hungry stomach is the best place to sow seeds to wreck the American plan."

The Legion needed to pursue agricultural legislation, Brown said, as surely as it needed continual vigilance and initiative for other types of legislation. The special focus of the committee must be on the "family-type" farms in contrast to the "industrial farm operators" who had less difficulty getting farm loans. Congressional appropriations must be made, and the weight of the Legion was needed to make that happen. Brown asked, also, that John Thomas Taylor be directed to bring his considerable lobbying skills to bear in testifying against the repeal of the 160-acre limitation in the reclamation laws. The repeal, Brown said, was backed by "absentee landowners and big operators in the West." If that provision was abolished, "it will constitute the greatest single disservice to veterans wanting small farms in the Western states."

All who set out to solve postwar problems wrestled with the immense need for housing.

The San Francisco National Convention in 1946 had authorized a Special Veterans' Housing Committee (also called the Special G.I. Committee on Housing) that surveyed the conditions aggravating this problem. Before long, the committee announced that nothing short of a state of emergency existed. "In every section of the country, in almost every town and city, and in many rural areas, veterans are unable to find adequate living quarters for themselves and their families. A degeneration in the American way of life is immediately apparent and will have lasting effects unless corrected."

The housing shortage actually had begun even before the war. The depressed economy of the 1930s had hamstrung the housing industry from keeping pace with the population increases for two decades. Now another six years had followed with little permanent residential construction occurring. Now the many millions of people who had been gone from traditional town and city life, whether in the armed forces or having relocated for defense production work, were wishing to relocate.

The problem of inadequate housing, in fact, was now threatening to surpass unemployment as the most critical problem facing the nation. The government's Veterans' Emergency Program was finally operative by mid-1946, but the few building "starts" in the program were almost exclusively single dwelling units, while veterans needed affordable rentals and low-cost "starts."

In another housing-related matter, the plans that had been made for the dispersal of surplus government property in the form of surplus building materials and equipment had floundered. According to the Legion Housing Committee, the War Assets Administration had been disastrously slow in the disposal of such items. Not only that, but the hoarding of building materials by federal agencies, including the armed forces, was said to have occurred on a large scale. If such materials had been released, the welcome supply reportedly would serve as a buffer in a critically short market. But some agencies still refused to produce inventory figures of what supplies they controlled. (In addition, much of the building materials that were made available were kept from the market by the shortage of suitable transportation, giving rise to black markets in some places.)

Similarly, the Federal Public Housing Authority (F.P.H.A.) had also come in for much criticism for slowness in its relocation of temporary dwellings on college campuses and in municipalities. The F.P.H.A.'s supervision of existing permanent public housing was faulted for accommodating tenants who had incomes that exceeded that of the average house-hunting veteran. The F.P.H.A. was also said to be disposing of permanent war housing at current market prices to present occupants who, again, could more afford to purchase the homes they had been living in than could veterans. Legion spokesmen charged "business as usual" in these instances even though there were now many thousands of veterans struggling to make do.

The new National Housing Agency, also, came in for criticism. Though it had been established to find housing for veterans, it was said to be spending an inordinate amount of time perpetuating itself instead of attacking the problem of housing shortages.

The Legion Legislative Division had worked to achieve remedial legislation in late 1945, particularly to raise appraisal standards to current-day prices. A bill aimed at that need was passed, but the new appraisal system thereby created for G.I. loans while being more realistic was, nevertheless, said to be inequitable and generally unfair to the veteran.

When the president lifted the ceiling prices on building materials (but retained for the time being the wartime rent controls) those who needed housing looked anxiously to what would develop, as the principle of free enterprise was once again invoked for evening out the surfeits of a wartime market.

Owners of rental properties at this point were preferring to sell under the present conditions of inflated prices rather than continue to rent their properties while government rent controls were still in effect.

There was, also, the problem of the lack of a labor force for building housing for veterans and their families. Labor representatives said the labor supply was adequate. But Legion workers in the field of employment pointed instead to a misleading national average. In some regions labor was scarce for building the type of homes average veterans could afford. Particularly was there a scarcity (perhaps union induced, it was implied) of skilled journeymen and apprentices. Labor costs had risen greatly; the average construction employee's pay per hour was now twice what it had been before the war. Labor unions were said to be extending the period of apprenticeship much longer than necessary and failing to settle strikes in the industry. Such practices greatly retarded building programs, it was charged. The recent removal of wage stabilization controls, however, was seen as, perhaps, aiding a needed distribution of the labor supply now that more straightforward wage adjustments could be made.

Special Housing Committee members visited most states and observed the problems firsthand. Then they drafted a comprehensive plan for consideration by Congress. Specifically, they called for the president to create an emergency housing board comprised of World War II veterans representing the various veterans' organizations "to coordinate and pursue to a speedy conclusion the lagging and now demoralized veterans' housing program."

In this plan, a national "coordinator" would perform that much needed function among the Federal Housing Authority, the Civilian Production Administration, the mortgage arm of the Reconstruction Finance Corporation, the nation's home loan bank system, the War Assets Administration, the Department of Justice, the V.A., the Federal Works Administration, and the Federal Public Housing Authority.

The Legion committee also called for the F.H.A. to be strengthened and more adequately funded, and that it be given the responsibility for updating wartime rent controls (to cease altogether when four million new housing units had been built after the official date of V-J Day, September 2, 1945) and building codes that would reflect new thinking about the current problem. On the local level, Legion posts were asked to report any unauthorized nonresidential construction that most likely was diverting scarce materials from the critical need for new homes.

Still paralleling the critical shortage in housing was the persistent unemployment problems of veterans. By mid-1946 Rehab workers were finding much fault with the implementation, actually the lack of it, they said, of G.I. Bill Title IV provisions pertaining to employment.

It was charged also that inadequate job counseling, unproductive employment placement, and the failure of many employers to honor veterans' preference were all contributing to unemployment among veterans. When in November 1946 the public employment offices were returned to individual state control, Legion posts were asked to monitor the competency of the job counseling and placement services offered there.

When Congress set out to answer widespread criticism of the on-the-job training program arising from the G.I. Bill because of abuses by unscrupulous employers and "goldbricking" veterans, the Legion's Employment Committee acknowledged that there was obviously a need for better policing of benefits, but objected to what it saw as much unfair criticism. If funding for the program was cut, many more honest veterans would be affected unfavorably, they said, than the few who did commit fraud.

On the brighter side was the proclamation by the president for a week in October to be designated as "National Employ the Physically Handicapped Week." Such a time of public recognition could go far in helping the cause of physically handicapped veterans seeking employment.

It was back on the defensive, however, when federal funding to the Veterans' Employment Service (V.E.S.) was slashed. The National Employment Committee raised the cry that this agency was "a child of the American Legion . . . under the Wagner-Peyser Act of 1933," and for eleven years had been shunted from agency to agency. Yet, despite these difficulties, the V.E.S. had not only survived but had also done a credible job of securing gainful employment for veterans.

Similarly, when the G.I. Bill was enacted, the Veterans' Placement Board was created under Title IV, and for the next two years that agency had operated acceptably under the U.S. Employment Service. When in mid-November 1946 the public employment offices were returned to the states, the V.E.S. remained housed with the Department of Labor, and Congress cut its funding to the point of nearly eliminating it as a national bureau. Once again, then, the Employment Committee, with the help of the Legislative Division, was able to get most of that funding restored.

In early 1947, Employment Committee Chairman Lawrence J. Fenlon spoke of a "calm before the storm" that was indicated, he said, by recent developments at some federal agencies relating to the rights of veterans returning to jobs, specifically regarding the threat to veterans' reemployment seniority rights, which now were said to be subject to collective bargaining that had occurred during World War II when veterans were absent from their jobs. There were, also, ceilings on the wages earned by those in on-the-job training, something else which certainly had not been included in the draft of the G.I. Bill which Legionnaire Harry Colmery had composed at his Mayflower Hotel suite in Washington, D.C. and which had been introduced in Congress soon thereafter and would become the "Servicemen's Readjustment Act of 1944."

Not all attention was given to the national scene. The Employment Committee knew that the employment problems were actually community problems, hearkening back to the Depression, and much had to be done to solve them on that level. Therefore the committee recommended the establishment of veterans' employment committees in every community as well as community postwar employment committees, such as those outlined in the national committee's manual, "The American Legion Program for Maximum Employment." That program had begun in 1943. Since then, some useful experiences had been recorded for replication by communities.

As Rehab Committee Chairman Bob McCurdy noted, it had been a "hectic period." He tried to describe the period of transition from war to peace during the preceding twenty months. It was a time that "has quite naturally been marked with the ups and downs of misunderstanding, inefficient performances in some fields, and disturbed viewpoints on what should or should not be done to the greatest advantage or interest of veterans. Patience and tolerance have been exhausted in many instances, and many who are engaged daily in the rehabilitation program proceeded with frayed nerves and probably with some irritability." There had been many phone calls and other communications "received from time to time urging a belligerent attitude and a fighting attack upon the whole problem." That, McCurdy explained, would have been counterproductive.

II

"LeGIon"

Bob McCurdy and the others could not forget, of course, that many of the logistical and other problems that had been heaped on the Rehab Committee and other national program functions were due to the current record-setting proportions of veterans to the general population, which also meant hundreds of thousands of new Legionnaires.

While many national-level volunteers focused on the problems of returning ex-service personnel to find jobs and homes, others looked with pleasure and hopeful anticipation on the rush of veterans in 1946 to join the Legion.

The Chicago National Convention of 1945 ordered that the name of the World War II Liaison Committee be renamed, appropriately, the Expansion and Stabilization Committee, the purpose of which was to coordinate and otherwise aid the expansion and stabilization of the Legion membership. At their office at National Headquarters, Committee members developed activities that could be undertaken at the community level for increasing membership and keeping members active in new and old programs for public service in their communities.

In November 1946, the committee was given the more straightforward title of Membership and Post Activities Committee. But the work was the same, as was the purpose: to address the impressive increase in membership.

That there should and would be an organization of World War II veterans was one certainty amid an era of wartime uncertainty. As early as October 1940, when sixteen million men were required to register with the Selective Service, the call for a "Legion of Conscripts" arose spontaneously from many quarters, espousing the creation of an organization to inform draftees of their rights.

The Legion's Milwaukee National Convention in 1941 entertained a resolution from the Department of California for an "organization of men now called into service." A similar resolution came from the Henry H. Graves Post No. 1 of Jackson, Mississippi. Both resolutions were referred to the N.E.C.

Some said that an organization of that nature could also enlighten citizen-soldiers to their responsibilities to guard against "fifth columnists." But National Adjutant Frank E. Samuel wrote the adjutant of the California Department on November 24 that there did "not now appear to be sufficient reason why the American Legion should attempt to organize or supervise the organization of men who have completed their selective service." Less than two weeks later, the nation was at war, reeling from the attack on December 7 by Japan on the American fleet of military ships lined obligingly side by side at Pearl Harbor.

In the month following the declaration of war on Japan, national officers began hearing about the intentions of some posts to open their membership rolls to all who were now serving and would honorably serve in the armed forces. This "jumping of the gun," as Assistant National Adjutant Donald G. Glascoff called it, posed serious problems. The necessary membership eligibility dates for military service had not been set yet, for example. An even more basic consideration than that was the issue of whether or not the Legion should remain an organization of World War I veterans exclusively.

One longtime N.E.C. man from New England spoke for many in

telling National Commander Lynn U. Stambaugh that he was "definitely opposed to absorbing the men engaged in the present war" into the membership. First, "these men are considerably younger than we are." Second, the younger men, he felt, would be "ambitious" for leadership roles which, while "a perfectly natural tendency," would likely be "a source of controversy between the men who have built up the . . . posts . . . and the younger men. . . ." Third, he believed that the younger men would differ with their elders in the organization about social functions and community projects. Since effective programming depended on there being agreement and good feelings about these two standard post activities, the two groups were said to be incompatible on this count, also.

The N.E.C. man stressed that the Legion should welcome the new veterans back into the community and assist them when problems arose and should continue to serve as a legislative advocate for the new veterans. And when "the time comes for these boys to form their own organization," the Legion should help in any way possible. Legion posts should be open to them until they should form their own organization, at which time they should be welcomed into the ranks of veterans organizations.

But the American Legion was not the place for them, this one said. "For the next generation [i.e., in time] the American Legion will have its own problems affecting its million or more members [and so] there is a wide enough field for us to function to our own advantage and to the advantage to the nation."

Others contemplating that the veterans of Château-Thierry and Belleau Wood would be merged with those of Bataan, Corregidor, and other locales to enter the war lexicon recently asked if there were to be two N.E.C. men from each state, one each to represent the World War I and the World War II members. Particularly regarding the finances of a two-war Legion, there was at this point a very distinct "us and them" attitude about the money collected from each group and about how, and for whom, it was to be spent.

The lingering and nearly fatal financial woes of the early years of the Legion were not easily forgotten by those who had been there to agonize over the matter. Would a doubling or tripling of the membership bring in enough money to finance properly and effectively the operation of the Legion with its much larger membership? Or would the soon-to-be majority constitute in fact a new American Legion increasingly attuned to the needs of World War II veterans to the near exclusion, or at least a deemphasising of, the lingering needs of the founding generation?

Some national-level volunteers and staff members identified no less than sixteen points to consider in the matter of whether or not their organization should embrace a two-war membership. Dated March 13, 1942, the list of ponderables was made available to N.E.C. men, department commanders, and adjutants for discussion at the May N.E.C. meeting. Arranged in two columns of pros and cons, the list had been composed of remarks received in correspondence at national headquarters.

For example, some had said that the Second World War was but a continuation of the first and that it was entirely natural for the younger veterans to belong to the same organization as those of the earlier war. Others, however, countered by pointing out that the average age at that point of World War I veterans was 49, while their counterparts of the current war were 28–29, with little if any comparable interests and, of more probability, with conflicting objectives. While the pros reported hearing new veterans anticipate their eligibility as Legionnaires, the cons recalled that in 1917 they had not wanted to join the then-existing veterans' organizations, preferring to begin their own. To which, the first replied that many new members would want to join the organization to which their fathers and mothers belonged. But, they were told, the majority of new veterans would not have those ties, anyway.

Would World War I members resent paying their post dues while possibly losing their voice as to how each post's income should be spent, what with their dues being overshadowed by the much larger funds accruing from an influx of World War II members? And what about the basic definition of eligibility: this was total war and many in the civilian defense forces would desire membership depending on how the eligibility clause was rewritten. There were even those anxious over the possibility of subversiveness coming with thousands of new members. Should the new, younger veterans be welcomed in and educated in the Legion principles or kept out? Surely, some said, a "purist" attitude must be maintained; objectionable "isms" and other ideologies were sure to spring up in the wake of several tumultuous years during which governments had been toppled, and the map of Europe had been redrawn.

Regarding the soul-searching about whether to extend membership to World War II veterans, it would be wrong to judge those World War I members who did not favor the expansion in membership as being stubbornly resistant or insisting on exclusivity. Theirs was instead a genuine, if provincial, adherence to the goals of the organization's founders—to take care of their own generation. Most of these fully expected the World War II veterans to form their own organization and were prepared to welcome it into the brotherhood of veterans.

Ultimately, of course, it was the very concept of rehabilitation that convinced the majority of Legionnaires that the nature of the need for rehab, the overriding commonality of it all, knew no partisanship relating to one war or generation.

One of the most honored concepts on which the Legion had been founded and which continued to motivate it was the need for rehabilitation. Only as a secondary purpose had the Legion been established to preserve the memory of the founders' service and sacrifice during World War I.

Particularly convincing as a reason for a two-war organization was the belief that the hard-won success of World War I veterans in forming an effective and lifesaving rehab advocacy demanded that their World War II counterparts not be required to reinvent the wheel of veterans' rehabilitation.

Damon Runyon wrote in his syndicated column in early April 1942 that many World War I veterans considered World War II as "a continuation of their old World War." To this way of thinking, all these veterans were united in the struggle against tyranny and oppression. Furthermore, it had occurred to Runyon, too, that many of the younger veterans were, indeed, the sons of Legionnaires, and it would be good for fathers and sons to be members of the same post where possible and where the younger men could build on foundations already established. Runyon, also, with the speculative penchant of journalists, was impressed with the social and political influence he assumed would result from a two-war Legion likely to become "the most powerful organization for any purpose in the history of any country."

Indeed, the majority of Legionnaires, at the many posts that took informal votes on the subject, agreed that those who were being called to serve in this war should be taken in as members. Many posts adopted resolutions proposing that the Legion amend its constitution to take in these new citizen-soldiers. The Legion should not allow itself to become a to-the-last-man club of World War I members only, these advocates said.

The momentum for taking in the newer veterans began in earnest with the N.E.C.'s action in May 1942 in submitting the matter to the entire membership for discussion and decision. The Constitution and By-laws Committee had already made a detailed study of the proposal for expanding the Legion's membership. Committee Chairman Harry Benoit led the study on the amending of the Legion constitution and its charter to change the eligibility requirements. His committee had first inquired of the departments about the sentiment in the field. There was a consensus: open the membership to World War II veterans.

Congress would have to amend Public Law 47, "An Act to Incorporate the American Legion." The decision to proceed to that step would have to be made by a National Convention, Benoit's committee concluded. For that to happen, it was recommended that the N.E.C. resolve the Legion petition and request Congress for that purpose.

At the National Convention that year in Kansas City, Legion founder Thomas W. Miller, chairman of the Committee on Constitutional Amendments, reported that his committee recommended a constitutional amendment—Convention Resolution 192—that had been introduced by the Department of Indiana, which would make "veterans of the present war eligible to membership in the American Legion." Indiana's resolution was similar, Miller reported, to resolutions from thirty-eight other departments. Resolution 192 was adopted.

Even as an action of the convention, some aspects of the move were not completely understood. Soon after the convention, National Commander Roane Waring posed the primary question about eligibility to several past national commanders and a few leaders in the N.E.C. Specifically, "What is the intention of the Kansas City Convention—to seek congressional action that would permit the immediate membership of the soldiers of the present war, or, to permit their membership after they had completed their service and received an honorable discharge?"

Among the many who pondered the ramifications of a two-war Legion, Legion publicist and historian Richard Seelye Jones focused on the trade-off of anticipated positive publicity about the Legion's growing in this manner as against the just as certain hoopla over which post took in the first World War II veteran in each town, city, state, and the nation. The event would certainly cause a rash of claims and counterclaims, no doubt leading to ill will that would linger long after the intended good-natured competition had been concluded officially.

Jones advised, however, that the departments and posts might as well be allowed to progress at their own enthusiastic pace on the matter, and that national publicity work be put off awhile so that National would not be perceived as trying to dampen the spontaneity of the posts vying for "firsts." In this manner, he said, national could step in at the proper time and still hope to visit some order on the process of taking in veterans of World War II.

What evolved in this regard proved to be similar to Jones' advice.

In October 1942, National Commander Roane Waring, National Judge Advocate Ralph B. Gregg, and the chairman of the National Legislative Committee, Maurice F. Devine of New Hampshire, conferred in Washington on the nature of the legislation needed for a change in the Legion's founding documents. The opinion that prevailed was that the Kansas City Convention's resolution meant veterans were eligible for membership only after having completed their military service.

Representative Raymond S. Springer of Indiana introduced H.R. 7675 on October 8. Two companion bills were also introduced: H.R. 7677 by Nevada Representative James G. Scrugham, and S. 2837 by Missouri Senator Bennett C. Clark. Though many national legislators had asked for the privilege of sponsoring the amendatory change in the Legion's constitution, these three were accorded the privilege because of their ties to the birth of the Legion. Springer and Scrugham were both incorporators of the Legion's Act of Incorporation of September 16, 1919, and Clark had participated in the Paris Caucus.

Hearings on H.R. 7675 were held before the House Judiciary Subcommittee on October 12 and the bill was favorably reported to the entire committee, which favorably reported it to the House on October 13. It was passed the next day.

On the Senate side, a lack of quorum in the Senate Judiciary Committee stopped action on Monday, October 12. But on October 19 the committee unanimously reported it, and the bill passed the Senate on October 22. Because of a three-day recess, the bill reached the president on October 29, and he signed it immediately.

The eventual Public Law 767 of the 77th Congress, approved on October 29, 1942, changed Article IV regarding eligibility, from the original 1919 text to read, "Any person shall be eligible for membership . . . who was regularly enlisted, drafted, inducted or commissioned and who was accepted for and assigned to active duty in the Army, Navy, Marine Corps, or Coast Guard of the United States at some time during the period between . . . December 7, 1941 and the date of cessation of hostilities. . . ." (Later, Public Law 495, by act of the 79th Congress, approved July 9, 1946, added the date of September 2, 1945 as that for the cessation of hostilities.)

There was still the question of the eligibility of those currently in the armed forces. In his numerous visits to military camps, stations, installations, and expeditionary forces, National Commander Warren Atherton was convinced that military personnel wanted immediate membership in the Legion rather than having to wait for discharge and return to civilian status. He recommended that they be given that privilege. Atherton spoke later in the summer to department commanders and adjutants, providing them with suggested drafts of enabling resolutions and constitutional amendments to that end. But the national convention determined that service personnel had one job to do at that point—win the war. The other job, that of being Legionnaires, could wait until their discharge.

The World War I members who expressed particular misgivings about the joining together of the two groups of veterans were right at least about that most obvious of differences, the disparity in age.

When the physically fit younger veterans began joining Legion posts, they were possessed of a particular passion for basketball, then the most popular team sport for amateurs (swimming, too, had been greatly popularized by the introduction of that activity to many in basic training). Basketball quickly became a signature activity of Legion posts, much as Junior Baseball had been for many of these very members shortly before the war.

Membership was, indeed, increasing with enthusiasm that mirrored the spirited action on hardwood basketball courts across the nation. The million member mark was passed on January 27, 1944, the earliest in any year for that number to be recorded on the large wall chart at National Headquarters.

The day after the war in Europe came to an end on V-E Day, May 8, 1945, National Headquarters, in a Western Union "day letter," urged department commanders to "intensify World War Two liaison activities" to enroll veterans already honorably discharged and those soon to be involved in the imminent massive demobilization of the armed forces. Such persons in the posts could become "a growing nucleus around which further membership efforts can be built." Plan homecoming parties for them, whether they be on leave, furlough, or discharge. Post officers were encouraged to "Tell the Legion story."

By the middle of 1946, the U.S. armed forces, having numbered about thirteen million during the war, was smaller by about half, and by the end of the year numbered about two million. The Legion, meanwhile, was experiencing its peak year of growth. Those enrolled as of August 28 numbered 3,292,264, of which sixty-nine percent were veterans of World War II, a gain of 1,651,322 that helped swell the size of posts nationwide and begin 3,000 new posts (many composed entirely of World War II veterans and many womens' posts). All this occurred within twelve months. A number of posts that had surrendered their charters became active again. Departmental news services reported weekly increase figures rather than merely the traditional annual figures. With the expansion came new Auxiliary units, too, greater in both number and size. *The National Legionnaire,* which had originated in 1935 as a monthly national newspaper to keep Legionnaires informed of activities on the national level, began appearing at two week intervals for a few months. The newspaper was forced to return to a monthly schedule in November, however, and was thereafter limited to eight pages because of a still short supply of newsprint.

At state conventions in 1946, the departments of Arkansas, Georgia, Idaho, Minnesota, and Nebraska elected World War II Legionnaires as state commanders. New National Commander John Stelle made a point of appointing at least two or three World War II members to every national commission, committee, and board.

The title of a booklet distributed to all posts indicated the attitude at National: "Git 'Em and Hold 'Em."

III

"Keep the Air Full of the Legion"

After the first surge of World War II veterans had joined in 1945, the national public relations effort was revamped. A few weeks before V-E Day, the National Public Relations Division was revitalized to increase the output of news releases and other materials. Branch offices were established in New York, dealing principally with radio programming, and in Los Angeles for the filming of Legion events and educational and promotional programs. In the first four formative months, P.R. Division staffers had also helped forty-six departments establish public relations offices of their own, as well as serving as conduits for the production of national-level public relations.

The New York radio branch soon developed a weekly program schedule for the next year. By early December 1945, sixty percent of the radio stations in the nation (more than 500) had agreed to include Legion broadcasts in their programming formats. Other radio stations were requesting the large "platters" used to audition Legion radio scripts.

The P.R. Division also initiated a weekly American Legion National News Service (A.L.N.S.) clip sheet and for that purpose greatly enlarged the small, 2,000 name "hit or miss" mailing list ("pitiful . . . for so big an organization," Director Ray Fields said), into a list of 19,800 names, including every daily and weekly newspaper, every college and labor publication, all radio station owners, managers, and commentators.

While the clip sheet was important for disseminating information other than the hard-and-fast news of Legion events and position statements, the *News Service* also included a weekly editorial series. For those publications that had a firm policy of writing all their own editorials, some would take the facts contained in the A.L.N.S. releases and incorporate them into their own editorials. Fields soon reported, "Our correspondence is the heaviest of any division now and is growing by leaps and bounds!"

Director Fields and his staff had targeted the National Convention in Chicago for a publicity coup to reflect the sky's-the-limit sense of anticipation now as the Legion stood on the threshold of record-breaking membership enrollment. He assigned five staff members to cover all committee meetings, arrange press conferences, and issue releases. They were told also to remain continually at the service of personnel from press, radio, magazine, photo-service, and newsreel companies. In this way they assisted reporters from 103 newspapers (this was the first time, Fields said, that newspapers outside the convention city had attended a National Convention in as large a number), twenty-three radio organizations, as well as newsreel personnel from News of the Day, Universal Pictures, Paramount, Pathé, Fox Movietone, and All-American News.

Special emphasis was placed on producing a high volume of "trunk line words" to be carried by the wire services. Fields became the kind of statistician only another P.R. director could appreciate; he reported 49,500 trunk-line words sent out from the convention, not counting the additional transmission by regional wire services (International News Service, 15,000; Associated Press, 10,000; Transradio, 18,000, and United Press, 6,500).

Fields also counted the photos taken of convention happenings and made available for national distribution: fifteen wire photos by Acme Newspictures, fifteen by International News, seventeen by Associated Press; these in addition to another eighty-nine sent out via the regular picture service by these companies. Professional zealot Fields continued to count. Having estimated that still photographers had used 10,000 flashbulbs, he asked how his own official photographer had done. That staffer, he found, had used 207 flashbulbs and had captured convention imagery on 187 negatives. The P.R. Division director was particularly pleased to see that the television division of Columbia Broadcasting Company had devoted about three hours total to convention coverage.

To gauge the national coverage of the convention, Fields looked to other news events of the week, which included the GM strike at Detroit, Gen. George Marshall's testimony before the Senate Military Affairs Committee, and the arrival of Prime Minister Clement Attlee for "atomic discussions." Yet fully twenty-five percent of the news photos distributed from collection points in New York City by the film companies, he found, had been of Legion convention activities. Convention planners, of course, contributed to such wide coverage; they had arranged for a group of must-cover convention speakers, including Admirals Ernest King and Chester Nimitz and Generals James "Jimmy" Doolittle, Dwight Eisenhower, Leslie Groves, and Alexander Vandergrift.

After the convention, and near the end of the year, Fields reviewed the first few months of the P.R. Division, particularly the cost to the Legion for salaries, traveling expenses, convention expense, telephone and telegraph, stationery and postage, and radio production, and including all publicity for the divisions and office expenses for the four offices (Indianapolis, Washington, New York, and Los Angeles). It had all been done for about half of what had been budgeted, or about $8,200 per month. Fields advised that annually this estimated $100,000 "investment" should grow to "around $300,000" (as it would in 1947) so that he could "keep the air full of the Legion."

In December 1945, Fields observed, "The boys are being discharged in huge groups, the memberships are pouring in (fifty-two per cent ahead in advance memberships [at this point] as compared with a year ago). The prospect is for three million, and we had better hit while the iron is hot."

The American Legion Press Association (A.L.P.A.) of editors of Legion national and department publications and writers of columns for other newspapers became more active. Though independent of the National Public Relations Division, the A.L.P.A. worked closely with that division in a revitalized fashion. Actually organized by the national convention of 1924, it had been dormant for a few years before being reactivated in 1942. Since then it had increased in size and activity. In June 1947, the A.L.P.A. included 268 members, representing 199 Legion publications.

The P.R. Division office in Washington, with its staff of four in addition to one secretary, focused on press coverage in the nation's capital. The work assignments increased when National Commander Paul Griffith during the Legion year 1946–47 used the Washington headquarters as a base of operations more extensively than previous commanders and with the production of a weekly legislative newsletter for Legion departmental and other publications. The newsletter was patterned after the popular *Kiplinger* newsletter. In addition, the P.R. office informed hometown newspapers of every instance in which local Legionnaires (usually national officers) came to Washington for Legion work. The national "slick" magazines were also targeted for Legion news and pictures, those such as *Pic, Salute, McCall's,* and *Colliers.*

The New York P.R. office's focus on radio programming generated national radio broadcasts of Legion news and views every week. A typical week of radio fare could include the national commander talking on housing problems and Legion solutions, universal military training, and other topics on ABC's "Headline Edition;" John Thomas Taylor on CBS's "In My Opinion" holding forth on affirmative lobbying; and Veterans Preference Chairman Herbert Jacobi on CBS's "Opinion Please" speaking about the mission of his committee. Vocational Rehab Chief Cecil Munson was heard to speak many times on veterans' problems. National committee and commission chairmen and members helped to spread the Legion message by appearing on national, regional, and local broadcasts speaking on various Legion advocacies. The chief public relations assignment, of course, was to see how many times the national commander could be scheduled on national and regional radio, from newsmaker debates and remarks at congressional dinners to the "Eddie Cantor Show" and the "National Barn Dance."

Legion movies were also produced, such as that showing the highlights of a dinner given by the national commander for members of Congress who were veterans. There National Commander Griffith had appeared with movie actor Robert Montgomery and playwright Robert Sherwood, both recent Oscar winners for their work in *The Best Years of Our Lives.* Another film featured the 1947 national high school oratorical contest finals in Charleston, West Virginia, at which a $4,000 college scholarship was awarded to the winning orator. A Technicolor movie of the 1946 National Convention in San Francisco was also produced, as were newsreels of Armistice Day and Washington's Birthday activities at Arlington Cemetery and at Mount Vernon respectively. The efforts for universal military training were focused on in a film produced for that ongoing campaign.

That the Legion had an impressive variety of programs and activities in which returning citizen-soldiers could opt to serve their communities was evident in the list of the 615 scripts the national P.R. Division created for the radio series "This Is Our Duty." Episodes in that series included Legion messages about Child Welfare Month, Flag Day, Boys State, forest conservation, driving safety, immigration education, rheumatic fever, Return to Religion, voting, disaster relief, and subversive activity, to name but a few. Radio "platters" had also been distributed containing dramatic presentations for Memorial Day, Lincoln's Birthday, Victory Day, Armistice Day, Washington's Birthday, Navy Day, Pearl Harbor Day, as well as on universal military training, and speeches, editorials, and spot announcements about the full gamut of Legion activities.

The Legion had distributed over thirteen million pieces of literature listing veterans' rights and benefits in 1942 when World War II veterans' eligibility for membership had been authorized. Now as the P.R. Division worked to blanket the nation in print and on the radio with Legion news, the organization's built-in audience of World War II members who now outnumbered World War I members five to two was a fertile field for enlightenment in Legionism. Few, indeed, were the conversations at National Headquarters during 1946 that were not sprinkled liberally with growth statistics. Not even the enrollment figure in January 1947—3,279,000 members in 15,021 posts—told the real story. Another set of figures came closer: within the previous twelve months the gain actually had been more than 1,640,000 new members and 2,600 new posts.

A longtime Legionnaire, President Harry Truman led the list of the famous to wear the Legion cap, followed, in that realm, by 5 members of his cabinet, 3 Supreme Court justices, 28 senators, 154 representatives, and 26 governors. But the other members of the president's home post, Tiery J. Ford Post No. 21 at Independence, Missouri, were much more typical of the Legionnaires now joining in large numbers across the nation.

With posts either already established or springing up in every city, town, village, and whistle-stop in the country, no veteran was far from a Legion service officer, some 30,000 in number; service officers' efforts were bolstered by more than 650 full-time, Legion-paid state, district, county, and local rehab officials who in turn could look to twenty-seven national field secretaries for guidance in medical, legal, claims, and employment specialties.

If some still agonized over the reformation to come in which World War II veterans would eventually take over the Legion's programs and responsibilities, others touted it as "the greatest partnership team ever seen in this country." These enthusiasts depicted the two generations as working shoulder to shoulder, as indeed was true, in thousands of American Legion posts—the first community centers in many locales.

The sixty-three students of the first American Legion College, all World War II veterans, heard Legion founder John Thomas Taylor expound on legislative achievements following the enactment of the G.I. Bill (and liberalizing amendments in 1945): the passage with 218 congressional signatures of a terminal leave-pay bill for enlisted men and women, which had been banished to a congressional committee pigeonhole, then rescued by a Legion-instigated discharge petition; changes in the surplus property act to allow World War II veterans a share in such goods; the Wyatt Housing Bill for housing veterans at educational institutions; liberalization of government life insurance, putting veterans' policies on a par in privileges with those issued by private companies; an overdue twenty percent cost-of-living increase in compensation for some disabled veterans; and the enactment of legislation for expanding, modernizing, and otherwise improving V.A. hospitals.

There was another side to the boom year in membership. The complaint was heard occasionally that no more than ten percent of Legionnaires, presumably those most involved in national, regional, and state activities, could state with understanding what the Legion's constructive actions had been regarding veterans' housing, unification of the armed forces, and adequate national defense, to name but three important topics set forth repeatedly in the *National Legionnaire* and treated with less immediacy in *The American Legion Magazine.*

It was even supposed that most Legionnaires could not state specifically how democratic was the process by which the national organization arrived at positions on these and other important national issues. It was not unusual, for example, for the national commander and national adjutant to receive numerous letters requesting, and often demanding, that the entire membership be polled after some policy statement had been publicized in Legion or other publications. In each case, the national adjutant or another to whom he assigned the inquiry dutifully reiterated the essential answer that there was no constitutional authority for such a practice.

Was this an acceptable standard, the best to be expected? The national adjutant and others were often heard to say that after National Headquarters had participated in district and department conferences and at national meetings, it was then the responsibility of the departments and posts, particularly the latter, to stimulate and maintain interest in national programs. The American Legion College was an attempt toward that end by an organization that professed to generate knowledgeable local leadership. At National Headquarters, maintaining the integrity of the now well-known Legion emblem was metaphorically akin to the nurturing of high-quality leadership from national to post level.

One of the aspects of Legionism that American Legion College graduates were expected to absorb and explain was how, indeed, the organization was democratic. The college's lessons on that subject pointed out that rather than having national-level decisions based on the latest polling of the membership, it had been the Legion's practice from the beginning to rely on representation that had been duly arrived at —National Convention delegates each representing 1,000 members, and, for the N.E.C., one committeeman for each state. The 3,700 accredited delegates to the 1946 national convention had been largely elected at district meetings by post delegates (themselves chosen at post meetings) and confirmed by department conventions. They were then, theoretically, representative of the whole.

It was a practical method, of course; otherwise, the organization faced logistical problems in governance: no meeting hall in the nation could accommodate even the number of delegates and alternates necessary to represent directly each of the now 16,000 posts.

Even if it were true that there was a large disparity between the relatively few who comprehended the issues and all those remaining who didn't trouble themselves to think through the official policies and positions of the Legion, what the successive ranks of national officers had proposed was generally found to be agreeable to the membership. In National Adjutant Glascoff's view, "Through the years little if any of the basic Legion policy has been adopted that did not pretty well have the preponderant support of our membership." He had arrived at this opinion, he said, from several years of scanning post resolutions, letters to National Headquarters, and the other direct and indirect means of gauging sentiment in the field.

IV

U.M.T.

One issue in particular that was likely to engage the attention of every Legionnaire was the rapid and, many feared, debilitating effect on the armed forces by the demobilization after V-J Day. That, many said, was reason enough for a resurgence of interest in the Legion's long-standing call for universal military training (U.M.T.) to be made a fundamental aspect of the nation's preparedness.

The first Legionnaires had proclaimed at the first National Convention in 1919 that it was essential to keep the peace by letting the nation's preparation for war not be a secret. Captured German documents assembled at the Nuremberg trials pointed up the low regard in which Adolf Hitler had held the military preparedness and even the basic resiliency of the United States and other nations he assumed would oppose, but not militarily, his plan for world domination. Even if viewed as the rantings of a madman, Hitler had managed to cause a world conflagration during which America had begun to prepare for war in earnest only after the German regime already had begun to grind its closest neighbors under a massive, fully developed war machine.

Thus the Legion's call for national military preparedness—to be achieved appreciably through the concept of universal military training—was given new emphasis after World War II. Supporters of U.M.T. pointed to the enactment of Selective Service in 1940 as perhaps the most significant factor in the nation's being able to respond in any serious way immediately after the attack on Pearl Harbor, at which point nearly one million men had partially or wholly completed basic training. Repeatedly, it was said that the approximately 80,000 officers who came from the Reserves and the occasionally maligned R.O.T.C. program in the prewar years had been the saving of the nation's bacon when in 1940 and 1941 the nation began to prepare for war.

Within a year after the attack on Pearl Harbor, the United States landed combat forces on the scenes of subsequent battles. But earlier, U.S. protests against Japanese encroachment on Manchuria in 1931 and the Italian invasion of Ethiopia in 1935, to name only two such episodes, had been invalidated, many charged, by the common knowledge that the United States was not prepared militarily to back up its protests. Meanwhile, the Führer set about building his sinister thousand-year Reich, reportedly even moving up his timetable a few years in derision of largely unarmed neutrals such as the United States. That such an attitude could be held, U.M.T. advocates said, and, indeed, the chance even of another world war, was due in unfortunate measure to the unpreparedness of the United States.

Those who went to Minneapolis in late 1919 to help form the Legion carried with them, and expressed in no uncertain terms, their determination that never again should American citizen-soldiers be thrust into warfare without appreciable basic training. That insistence had found expression over the next twenty-five years and now following World War II in the many bills taken to Congress for enacting U.M.T. At the same time, however, there evolved the many prewar treaties that U.M.T. advocates considered a collective siren song of appeasement hardly more effective, ultimately, than the often derided assumptions of British and French diplomats which Adolf Hitler summarily had disregarded.

The heroism of the British and Russians in defending their nations, and the rapid (and, hence, more expensive) mobilization by the Americans were not anticipated by the Nazis. But that reaction by the Allies had also been costly in other ways. The most devastating costs had been in the lives of the defenders of freedom, the European Allies particularly, but also the United States.

The Legion's most recent and intense efforts so far for U.M.T. began with the election of Warren H. Atherton of California as national commander at the national convention at Omaha in 1943. Atherton, chairman of the National Defense Committee for several years (1938–43), had become a student of U.M.T. as well as an advocate for it. As national commander, he appointed a subcommittee of the National Defense Committee to draft a plan whereby the nation could have the advantage of U.M.T. and at the same time have the least interference possible in the educational and economic lives of the young men of the nation.

To chair the committee Atherton chose S. Perry Brown of Texas, a former doughboy who often complained that his own unpreparedness for warfare had been no less dangerous than were the artillery fragments crashing around his World War I foxhole. Brown and the others conferred with university and land-grant college associations, agricultural groups, religious groups, patriotic organizations, the armed services, the National Guard Association, and others on the issue.

Brown's committee concluded it was high time that the armed services provide the nation with a program of U.M.T. and that it be enacted into law by Congress. When the National Guard Association opposed this action, the Legion reiterated its support of U.M.T. but revised its role by drafting its own plan, which would be referred to the armed services for review. The plan was presented to the 26th National Convention at Chicago in 1944. This time the National Guard Association, the Reserve Officers Association, and educators generally spoke favorably of the principles involved, but the armed forces objected to it. Convention action produced a resolution requesting Congress to enact immediate legislation embodying the principle of U.M.T. as expressed in a general plan detailing length of service, ages of participants, and other provisions.

Congress did not move on the matter as the Legion had hoped. The House had already formed its Select Committee on Postwar Military Policy, which did agree to hold hearings and make other investigations into the need for U.M.T. That, Legion legislative planners knew, was at least a start.

The N.E.C. instructed the National Defense Committee to continue its study of an implementation of U.M.T. that the Legion could support. The committee was also authorized to begin an educational campaign to persuade the public that such a program for preparedness was needed, that it was not the steely tip of a wedge of militarism aimed at the foundation of the Republic, and that ultimately it would prove far less costly than the traditional method of an under-the-gun mobilization for war.

One of the chief methods of collecting information and at the same time promoting the concept of U.M.T. was the hosting of conferences and meetings in which those representing constituencies having an interest in the subject could meet to discuss the numerous aspects of such program for the involvement of millions of persons.

The first concerted legislative action in this stage of the long campaign for U.M.T. came in the 79th Congress with the Gurney-May Bill (H.R. 515, S. 188). In late February 1945, a committee representing the armed services released a plan to counteract that of the Legion.

The House (Woodrum) Committee did hold hearings on the subject in June 1945 and reported favorably to Congress on the principle of U.M.T. On August 25, 1944, War Department Circular No. 347 had been issued and, presumably on the advice of Chief of Staff General George C. Marshall, had outlined a postwar military establishment in which to build a national defense.

Later in 1945, President Truman delivered on October 23 a special message to Congress on the subject of legislation to establish military training. Emphasizing preparedness and recommending "comparatively small professional armed forces." The president observed, "The backbone of our military force should be the trained citizen who is first and foremost a civilian, and who becomes a soldier or a sailor only in time of danger." Listeners among the Legion were pleased to hear him say that "universal training is the only means by which we can be prepared right at the start to throw our great energy and our tremendous force into the battle." These same listeners were especially encouraged when the president listed as an element of a postwar military organization "a general reserve," which would be possible only if Congress followed his recommendation for "the adoption of a plan for universal military training."

At the Legion's Washington headquarters, members of the National Defense Committee and the National Legislative Committee compared the president's plan with the one that they had developed. They found few differences. Subsequently, the National Convention mandated the next step: the presenting to Congress of a collection of documents making their point: a bill incorporating the mandates of the 1st, 2d, 26th and 27th national conventions; General Marshall's Circular No. 347; the principles set forth in the National Defense Act of 1916 as amended; the broad principles contained in the Gurney-May Bill; the report of the House Select Committee on Postwar Military Policy; and, finally, the capstone of the effort so far, the recommendations of Legionnaire President Truman. In addition, the Legion offered a detailed plan for putting a U.M.T. program into action immediately.

"The American Legion Plan for Universal Training for National Security" was released by the National Defense Division in December 1945. From 1919 to 1940, the Legion had been content to express favor for U.M.T. but to leave it to the War Department and Congress to follow through on the matter. Then came World War II, and the matter was largely left to rest for the duration of the war. But now it was time, national officers believed, to continue the campaign for U.M.T. with vigor and determination. Now they had a definite, detailed program to offer.

In December, also, the national commander appointed a National Security Committee to carry out the mandate of the past national convention and the N.E.C.'s December meeting—to advocate a specific plan of military training before Congress. Since in the last war (and the one before that) the army and navy were ninety-eight percent civilian, any move by the government to strengthen national defense would logically call for training to be given those who were going to do the defending. But when trying to impress such a thing upon Congress, members of the National Security Committee quickly found themselves in competition with other matters of importance, such as the railroad strike, the labor actions led by John L. Lewis, and the Fair Employment Practices Act, as well as the creation of United Nations, the British loan, and the extension of the draft.

They did get a hearing before the House Military Affairs Committee on December 14. That, however, was the extent of the attention received on the Hill at this time. Legion National's next move was to send field secretaries into the districts of the congressmen on the Military Affairs Committee to build support for a U.M.T. bill. In the meantime, representatives from the Legion met with the V.F.W., the D.A.V., the Reserve Officers Association, and the National Guard Association to draft a U.M.T. bill acceptable to the five organizations. The final version was taken to Congressman Andrew J. May, chairman of the Military Affairs Committee, who introduced the bill as H.R. 6544. Senator John C. Gurney also introduced the bill as S. 2303.

U.M.T. spoke to national preparedness through manpower. But preparedness, particularly preventative measures, now involved a new and frightful aspect also. It was not an idle query when an editor at *Look* magazine wired National Commander John Stelle on April 15, 1946 for the Legion's answer to the current *Look* Forum Question: "Should control of the atomic bomb, its raw materials and manufacturing process, be turned over to the U.N.?" The subject was one which, perhaps more than any other, symbolized the new era into which the nation had entered.

Stelle reiterated the 1945 National Convention resolution recommending that "all secrets of manufacture of the atomic bomb be maintained exclusively by the U.S., Canada, and Great Britain for the safeguard of mankind." Such a position opposed the advice given by Legion supporter Bernard M. Baruch who, as chairman of a government study commission, had recommended sharing such information through the U.N. Stelle, however, speaking for the Legion, stated that other nations "should not be jealous of our guardianship [of] an instrument developed mostly through our enterprise, at our cost, and at great and unknown hazard to thousands of our fellow citizens."

The atomic force that had devastated two Japanese cities in 1945 had been defined in voluminous detail by the United States Strategic Bombing Survey chaired by Past National Commander Franklin D'Olier. That group, established by the secretary of war on November 3, 1944 to study the effects of Allied aerial attacks on Germany, was asked by President Truman on August 15, 1945, to conduct similar studies on the effects of the bombing of the two Japanese cities, specifically regarding casualties, civilian defense, morale, community life, utilities and transportation, various industries, and the general economic and political repercussions. The survey included the observations of engineers, architects, fire experts, economists, and doctors. The overall picture derived from their observations and conclusions showed destruction previously unimaginable.

The American Legion had stated its own opinion about the control of atomic energy soon after the horrific detonations of atomic bombs in Japan in August 1945. One of the first publications produced by the Legion following those blasts was a pamphlet entitled "The Atomic Bomb and Universal Military Training: Can Science Stop War?" distributed the same month as the devastation of Hiroshima and Nagasaki. (The point of the pamphlet was that nations would still need trained ground forces.)

The Legion's Special Committee on Use and Control of Atomic Energy, composed of the chairmen of the National Legislative, Security, Defense, Aeronautics, Military Affairs, Naval Affairs, Civil Defense, and Merchant Marine committees and four selected World War II veterans, which first reported to the N.E.C. in June 1946, turned its attention to recommending vigorous support of legislation relating to the domestic use of atomic energy. The committee's resolution called for (1) a full-time civilian commission to be appointed by the president, "with the advice and consent of the Senate," to have complete supervision over the entire field of atomic energy; (2) the widest possible freedom for scientific and technical research and development, limited only by interests of national security; (3) the control by the government of all fissionable material; and (4) the establishment of a military liaison committee to work with the civilian commission.

"Principles and Policies Regarding the Use and Control of Atomic

Energy," released with the Special Committee's first report, set out the points above and sought to encourage discussion of the topic. "All sorts of prophecies are being made about atomic power. Some say it will be the agenda to end civilization. Others say power from atomic energy will revolutionize all world aspects. The wide variance in predictions comes about largely from the fact that most of the prophets have little more than a crystal ball to guide them."

The federal commission for which the report and the pamphlet called was, in effect, "a monopoly and a public agency beyond American thought and tradition," for "to this agency [must be] given powers beyond those given to any previous agency. But we are dealing with a power never before known, and much greater than we have ever imagined, and we must take steps accordingly. Tradition must be set aside, previous ideas and ideals must be changed, national security must be the first thought."

The 28th National Convention in 1946 reaffirmed the long-running call for U.M.T. The next spring Perry Brown reminded the N.E.C. that the wartime armed forces of fifteen million had been reduced now to less than two million troops still in uniform, and that U.M.T. should still be a priority along with the current considerations about unification of the armed forces. What better time to push for U.M.T. than now during the restructuring of the nation's defense manpower?

In the fall of 1947, Past National Commander Warren Atherton reminded the N.E.C., "Some people think that another fight in the world is brewing, and what we do about U.M.T. may prevent it." Atherton was referring, perhaps, to the actions of Russia in dealing with those countries around which it had dropped "the Iron Curtain," a term attributed to Winston Churchill but that had been used before by others in Europe to whom the despised barrier was even closer at hand. In March, President Truman had enunciated his concept of "containment" of Soviet expansion. The Truman Doctrine was first applied when the president approved an appropriation in May of $400 million to strengthen the defenses of Greece and Turkey. He promised the same help for those in Europe seeking to resist Russian encroachment. Such actions, of course, would require military manpower.

Atherton pointed to the success of the National Legislative Committee in getting the current U.M.T. bill out of congressional committee the day before Congress adjourned. That bill, therefore, would be on the calendar in the next session. The Bill, H.R. 4278, was a training measure that would give training without conscription into the armed services in a program to be administered and controlled by a civilian commission responsible only to the president.

The latest campaign for the cause was to begin on Armistice Day, November 11, and to continue with petitions being distributed nationwide for signatures in such abundance as to impress federal legislators, home for the holidays, with the need for U.M.T. The Legion planned large-scale demonstrations during its own proclamation of the week of January 6–12, 1948 as "National U.M.T. Week," just as Congress was reconvening.

Later that year, the new "Security Commission" (a product of the "commission plan" of reorganization) met and rewrote for the 81st Congress the Legion's bill for "National Security Training" (N.S.T.), a new appellation chosen to offset often heard complaints about the so-called militarist tone of universal *military* training. The commission also determined that reemployment benefits should be written into the plan. After more review by other national officers, the bill was handed to the National Legislative Committee's director for introduction in Congress. In addition to the usual production and distribution of promotional literature, the Security Commission also called for a letter-writing campaign to impress upon legislators that the revamped N.S.T. bill, soon to emerge as S. 66 and H.R. 1305, was one of great importance.

There was now, in fact, a National Security Training Committee, headed by Granville Ridley who, along with John Thomas Taylor and National Security Commission Chairman Erle Cocke, Jr. of Georgia, appeared before the Senate Armed Services Committee on March 3 to testify for the N.S.T. bill. Little more could be done in the thirty minutes allotted to the testimony than ask that more time be given later for full testimony.

Although the repeat appearance was long in coming, in the meantime, a letter writing campaign was undertaken to continue to sound the trumpet for N.S.T.-U.M.T. As the date of the termination of the Selective Service Act approached (in 1950), National Security Commission Chairman Erle Cocke, Jr. reiterated a familiar caution: "In world-power politics, military strength is paramount."

It was, Cocke reminded the N.E.C. in November 1949, a time that fairly begged for the show of a strong national defense. "Events of the past few weeks have made it mandatory that we reevaluate our overall national security program. Our monopoly on the atomic bomb no longer exists. We know definitely that Russia has brought about a controlled atomic explosion and our only hope for security is through self-protection. This means an adequate and immediate civil defense structure that will enable our communities and their people to minimize the initial attack of any aggressor nation."

Noting the threat of "total warfare," Cocke spoke within the current context of fear created by the already proven destructiveness of atomic power. "Our generation has witnessed [that] the tiniest particle in the universe—the atom—has become the biggest thing on earth." He confessed to a "grave and sober spirit" regarding national security.

The amazing mushroom cloud that had formed over Bikini Atoll three years earlier in the experimental blasts of atomic bombs was now the symbol of an uneasy outlook on what lay ahead. Was it a specter presaging darkened horizons of inevitable "atomic" warfare or was it the motif for technological advances and a motivation for world-community cooperation? Potentially it was both a paradox to be puzzled over even as the nation that had created *The Bomb* was now made uneasy by the accomplishment.

In late 1949, Legionnaires once again mirrored the general population as they pondered world events and their nation's security.

ON THE ATTACK AGAINST A NATIONAL KILLER

The American Legion took on a national killer—rheumatic heart disease—in 1945.

The Legion's Medical Advisory Board, appointed in 1944 and composed of several nationally known doctors, reported the next year on what steps the Legion, and the nation, should take to improve the health of veterans, their dependents, and the general public. The board's first report included the recommendation that a grant be given to promote the fight against heart disease. The nation's long-running campaign against tuberculosis had been a success. Now rheumatic heart disease—a killer of children—had become "public health enemy number one."

The disease was said to kill twice as many a year as cancer, seven times as many as TB, ten times as many as diabetes, and nearly four hundred times as many as infantile paralysis. There were an estimated four million cases of heart disease then in the United States (1946), accounting for one in every four deaths in the nation, or 400,000 deaths a year.

Obviously there was a need for research into the cause of and cure for rheumatic heart disease. Therefore, the board chose to draw the Legion's attention to the American Heart Association, an organization which had focused specifically on cardiovascular diseases, but which had "struggled along for years with little or no financial support," according to a board memo to the National Rehab Committee in May 1945. The memo included the recommendation that the Legion grant $25,000 to the association "to inaugurate a nationwide program in the study, prevention, and treatment of rheumatic heart disease."

The next month the Rehab Committee adopted the recommendation as a worthwhile expenditure from the Rehab Committee's contingency fund of $50,000. The matter was then handed to the national commander, national adjutant, and the chairman of the national finance committee for their approval and action. National Rehab Chairman Robert McCurdy recognized that this gesture "may be without precedent," but he believed it would "stimulate a factor of public relationship of untold value."

Such a move was indeed unprecedented. A contingency fund recently had been set up to fund veteran rehab programs. Some of those ap-

proached for advice remarked that they knew little of the American Heart Association; but even if they did, they were still of the opinion that the fund should not be disturbed in such a manner.

At this point the A.H.A. was not well-known outside the medical profession, though it had emerged as the only national organization in this particular field of health, after having been incorporated in New York in 1924 as a nonprofit public health and educational organization to increase the knowledge of and stimulate interest in diseases of the heart. The A.H.A.'s board of directors consisted of eminent heart specialists and teachers from all parts of the United States and Canada. Through the publication of literature in this field, other publicity, scientific meetings, and exhibits, the A.H.A. sought to inform medical professionals of current research and treatment of heart disease. The monthly American Heart Journal, *the world's leading serial publication in the field, was under the editorial direction of the association and was a respected source of information for the A.H.A.'s 2,500 members in 1944 when the chief interest of the organization was rheumatic fever.*

In January 1944, the A.H.A. had sponsored a conference on rheumatic fever to focus on the public's needs and the action that could be taken. A result was the formation of the Council on Rheumatic Fever, which was composed of representatives from several organizations in the fields of medicine, public health, nursing, and social services.

Knowing that rheumatic fever and the consequent heart disease it caused constituted one of the most serious health problems in the armed services, that it was the leading cause of death of Americans between the ages of five and eighteen, that its cause was still unknown, and that few doctors and nurses had been trained to recognize and treat the disease, it was not surprising that the Legion's Medical Advisory Board should target the disease as the one most in need of research and cure. Since initial funding was needed for the A.H.A. to begin work, the board recommended that the Legion provide that funding.

As much of a precedent that it was for the Legion to grant money to another organization, the matter was soon taken before the Chicago National Convention of 1945, where Resolution 319 was passed. Recognizing a chance for the Legion to take the lead in vitally important work for public health, the convention directed the National Rehab Committee to expend the amount of $25,000 toward that end, to be conducted through and under the auspices of the Medical Advisory Board.

Soon the American Legion Auxiliary took part in raising an amount of money equal to the Legion appropriation. On May 29, 1946 Dr. Leonard Rowntree, chairman of the Legion's Medical Advisory Committee, presented a check for $50,000 to Dr. Roy W. Scott, president of the A.H.A. The ceremony announced the working relationship of the Legion and the Association; increments of the total amount would be *dispensed periodically according to a plan in which a medical researcher would be hired.*

Specifically, half of the donation was directed to (1) a comprehensive program to render the rheumatic diseases reportable, and stimulating and implementing a case-finding program among school children and on the community level and (2) the initiating of a guidance program for the prevention of the disease and for the care of the victims, to include adequate treatment, convalescent care, vocational rehabilitation and training, and suitable placement in jobs. The remaining half of the grant would be used to research the relationship of bacteria to the incidence of primary and repeated attacks of the disease.

Legion-sponsored research began soon. In September the American Council on Rheumatic Fever announced that a one-year Legion fellowship had been given to N.Y.U. College of Medicine for work by Dr. Samuel T. Schlamowitz for a biochemical study that focused particularly on the metabolism of patients with rheumatic fever. A second fellowship went to the House of the Good Samaritan in Boston, where Dr. Joseph Warren was researching the changing physiology of hormones in adolescents.

A nationwide educational campaign conducted in 1947 aided the identification and treatment of rheumatic heart disease. Legion posts and Auxiliary units distributed pamphlets and other materials giving factual information. Valentine's Day in February was a rallying point for the most intense publicity. Executive officers of the A.H.A. readily acknowledged that the Legion deserved full credit for creating a national consciousness of the crippling and deadly effects of the disease.

For some Legion departments this initial encouragement by the national organization was just the beginning for their own impressive campaigns to raise money for the cause. In Minnesota, for example, a fund-raising drive to raise a half million dollars was begun to establish an ongoing research fellowship at the University of Minnesota and the Mayo Clinic. Post No. 41 in Syracuse, New York began underwriting the total cost of a community-wide rheumatic fever program in cooperation with local cardiologists and the public schools. This post also established a convalescent home for children suffering from the disease. Post No. 34 in Lancaster, Pennsylvania sold "heart seals" and prompted the establishment of the Lancaster Heart Association.

Similarly, other posts, knowing that over fifty percent of the children in the nation were now children of veterans, established community programs of their own, many of which looked to the Social Security Act in which the Crippled Children's Services provision offered a state grant-in-aid program, implemented by the Childrens' Bureau, for combatting heart disease in children.

The stimulus provided by the Legion and the Auxiliary was apparent, also, in the observance of the first National Heart Week during February 1947. Next year came the enactment of the National Heart

Act, Public Law 655, 80th Congress. Signed by President Truman on June 16, 1948, the act created a National Advisory Heart Council and added the National Heart Institute as one of the National Institutes of Health in the Public Health Service. In addition to stimulating research on heart diseases, the Institute's Heart Information Center at Bethesda, Maryland began disseminating its "Circular" in August 1949 to health departments, medical groups, voluntary health agencies, welfare and other organizations, and lay and professional health workers all over the nation.

The Legion Rehabilitation Division's "Memorandum," circular number 15 of June 15, 1949 announced the final accounting by the American Council on Rheumatic Fever of the original Legion-Auxiliary $50,000 contribution: "No one will ever be able to gauge the real benefit that will flow from the great work that was stimulated and is now being carried on in behalf of veterans, children, and the public generally. Truly it is a humanitarian program which merits continued backing in our several communities and states."

Thus did the Legion and the Auxiliary invest in health research—"the small gift that saved thousands of lives."

THE KOREAN WAR ERA

1949 – 1955

I

"Six Survival Secrets for Atomic Attacks"
The American Legion Magazine, February 1951

No nation ever exhibited its military resources and resolve and its patriotic fervor more jubilantly.

Annually, Legion parades in National Convention cities, like the one in August 1949 in Philadelphia, provided entertainment for untold thousands of spectators and served as the nation's most ambitious animated tableau of patriotism.

Another Legion tradition, the gala Homecomings for new national commanders, which had been held for the past thirty years, had generally been in places like the county seat town of Brazil, Indiana, where on November 3, 1949, a six-mile-long American Legion parade dazzled new National Commander George N. Craig's hometown (population 9,000 "when everyone was home," Craig quipped).

The first national commander whose military service had been wholly in World War II stood with honored guests at the reviewing stand on the courthouse square while for two hours the parade units proudly passed by. Indiana Governor Henry F. Schricker had called for statewide observance of "George N. Craig Day," an event billed as "the most elaborate celebration in the state's history."

During the festivities, four "jet propelled" fighter planes of the type that a year before had made a record-breaking transatlantic flight flew from the 56th Fighter Group Air Force base at Selfridge, Michigan, and rendezvoused at 1450 hours (CST) over a radio station antenna in Terre Haute before making an impressively thunderous pass, at 1,000 feet, over the town. A second "fly-over" included three World War II B-29 bombers from a base in Texas.

Earthbound and cold, the crowd of 30,000 ("We expected about 10,000," Craig recalls) consumed the "tons" of sandwiches prepared by local church, fraternal, and civic groups. That evening the popular tenor Morton Downey, radio personality and perennial "featured soloist" at Legion national events, was master of ceremonies for the program in the local high school building. Craig, who like many before him had emphasized that the American Legion was basically a community organization, spoke to a nationwide radio audience that evening from microphones arranged on the basketball court of his hometown gym. In his speech he promoted a community self-help program, the Legion's "Build America Plan."

True to the intent of the founders, the Legion in the 1950s was community-based but national and international in its interests and impact. As spokesman for the nation's veterans, Craig was assured the attention of the press and the public. This Homecoming night he called for "the free exchange and coordinated effort of a defensive force," meaning the unification of the nation's armed forces. He pledged energetic support by the Legion for the four-year-old United Nations organization that now worried over the encroachment of Communist Russia into Eastern Europe.

In his radio broadcast, Craig read a resolution from the 1919 convention regarding the threat of world Communism. "We are passing through a period of jitters," he said, referring to reports in late September that Russia had tested its first atomic bomb. The Legion's longstanding concerns for national defense and internal security, he said, were appropriate for the present, as well.

In his campaign for the office of national commander, Craig had traveled 108,000 miles across the country and had seen "the ravages being done to old-fashioned American character by new philosophies of life imported from abroad." He spoke of the increasing number of government subsidies that to him and many others warned of "creeping socialism," which, he feared, would erode the pride and, ultimately, the effectiveness of many traditional endeavors.

The national commander accepted the validity of patriotic idealism. He and the others who had risked their lives for the ideal would not be timid about defining it. And they had little doubt about how to perpetuate "100% Americanism." Almost all the reasons that one found in the Legion "preamble" for "associat[ing] ourselves together" helped sustain and preserve that standard of perfect-score patriotism.

The Legion's Americanism Commission in particular was charged with ensuring that, as stated in a period *Americanism Manual,* the nation's flag remained "floating from the lofty pinnacle of American idealism. . . ."

The Legion's Americanism program in the post–World War II era included a wide variety of programs: flag etiquette; authoritative canons on the observance of patriotic holidays; youth activities, such as the vigorous Junior Baseball program and the more cerebral and unique large-scale civic education program—Boys State; sponsorship of the irreproachable Boy Scouts; cooperative ventures with the National Education Association; a seemingly protectionist stance on immigration (but including educational assistance for naturalization) that was more sociopolitical determinism than stiff-necked isolationism or ethnic bias; and, finally, active opposition to Communism.

Some program areas underwent developments of note in the immediate postwar era. For example, during the war, many home front activities were hampered or even curtailed. After the war, as industries retooled for consumer goods, popular entertainments such as sports were resumed. American Legion Junior Baseball was one of the earliest and easiest post programs to be restored. The facilities remained and the equipment was easily obtained, funded often by businesses like the local Ford dealership or Coca Cola bottler. So "Play ball!" was heard again at post hardball diamonds. Junior Baseball was one of the most popular activities in thousands of American communities.

In the field of education, following close on the heels of the monumental 1944 G.I. Bill of Rights, Resolution 728 at the 1946 National Convention supported a point President Truman had made in his State of the Union message earlier that year, in which he had urged the passage of federal legislation to aid education. Thereafter, the Legion gave "active, wholehearted support" to S. 246 during the 81st Congress. The measure passed. Congress then began a series of aid programs including school lunches; funds to improve the teaching of mathematics, science, and foreign languages; money to colleges to build dormitories; and aid to those school districts where large, tax-free government property holdings would otherwise diminish the financial base for schools.

At the same time, the Americanism and Child Welfare commissions worked together to help alleviate the overcrowding of the nation's schools. This involved local initiatives, of course, since the federal government, while passing substantial legislation for aiding education, consistently took a hands-off approach to subsidizing the building and operating of elementary and secondary schools.

With the enactment eventually, however, of wider ranging legislation for federal aid to education, the federal government became substantially more involved in the lives of schoolchildren, a role that historically had been a local one.

The Legion National Convention at Los Angeles in 1950 again had endorsed federal aid to education. But in the fall of 1952, the N.E.C. voiced a complaint about the encroachment of the federal government into local common schoolhouses, objecting to "the tendency to centralize power over education of our youth in the federal government." This the N.E.C. stated "in principle [because of its opposition] to the appropriation of federal funds for the provision of grants or assistance to the secondary school system of the respective states." The Legislative Division was directed to present that position to Congress on all future legislation.

The Legion long had had an interest also in legislation regarding immigration, another subject of interest to the Americanism Commission (though not on an individual immigrant level regarding admissions, appeals, or deportations). Similarly, from the beginning of the Legion in 1919, posts sponsored naturalization schools for the foreign-born, an activity performed in consultation and cooperation with the federal courts.

The Legion had long opposed any great influx of immigrants, stating that immigration should be "moderate" and regulated so that immigrants could be readily absorbed into the general population; it also upheld the idea that at no time should immigrants displace veterans in employment or housing, a major concern following World War II.

The Legislative Division continued to monitor immigration legislation closely and to aid the Immigration and Naturalization Service in gaining adequate operational funding for enforcing the laws. The Americanism Commission, meanwhile, aided in the naturalization process by continuing to suggest educational curricula for citizenship courses in the naturalization process.

The Legion's 28th National Convention, which heard J. Edgar Hoover's rousing attack on Communism in the United States, appropriated $250,000 for expansion and further development of the Americanism program. This dramatically increased funding, Americanism workers said, testified to an acute awareness of the increasing importance of the program and the need for a greatly strengthened fight against Communism.

The Americanism Commission began reviewing and updating long-running policy statements regarding the Legion's stance against subversiveness. The N.E.C. in May 1949 changed the Legion *Manual of Ceremonies* to include a stand against Communism suitable for the cold war age.

Americanism workers, enthused by a transfusion of funds while being compelled to action by current events, were depicted by a National Executive Committeeman in May as "the people who on the local and departmental level are the watch-horses that chase the Reds." When the N.E.C. reconvened in November, that same fervor was apparent in the resolution offered to commend Judge Harold R. Medina and the jurors who earlier that year (1949) had tried eleven accused Communists in New York. The trial had large implications, one committeeman said. "It was our judicial system that was on trial along with the Communists." (In the N.E.C. meeting in May 1951, a committeeman reminded his cohorts, however, that the convictions in the New York court were for perjury, contempt, passport fraud, et cetera, and not specifically for being Communists or for subversive activity.)

It appeared now that much was happening to threaten the peace of the world; much of the agitation was laid at the door of the Soviet Union. Parents worried about the effect on their children of the threat of "the bomb." Kindergarten children drew mushroom clouds hovering over prostrated stick figures. Adults themselves, amid doomsday brooding, spent an inordinate amount of time considering bomb shelters. Concern continued to mount about the U.S.S.R.'s boldness in pursuing Lenin's vision of world domination.

In this atmosphere, events close to home shook the confidence of the nation in its ability to protect itself from espionage. Several sensational cases of spying were played out in lurid detail in the newspapers in a seemingly unending tableau of national embarrassments. It seemed that every month of 1950, for example, brought some new, proven, or alleged case of damaging espionage.

The world situation seemed to many to be waiting for a kind of chemical equilibrium: the international scene roiled with ideological and, in Korea, bloody conflict that it was widely assumed would surely lead to the emergence of an all-dominant element. Would it be the United States or the U.S.S.R.?

The widespread concern was real. President Harry Truman was certainly not alone in referring to the "Cold War" as World War III. According to leading public opinion polls, a majority of Americans wanted action against subversives.

Though there was recent military victory over the oppressive regimes of the vanquished Axis powers, the present onslaught of aggressive world Communism was spread as successfully by agitation as by armed conflict. Indeed, the Cold War was not to be waged as simply as former conflicts. Formerly, presidents waged war; now they must wage war *and* fight Communism.

President Truman had declared international Communism an enemy of the United States. Earlier that same year, the president had issued his Executive Order 9835 on March 21, 1947, "Prescribing Procedures for the Administration of an Employee's Loyalty Program in the Executive Branch of the Government."

Even before the blatant Communist aggression in Korea, National Commander George Craig had invited other organizations to join the Legion in combating Communism. His All-American Conference met first at New York's Hotel Astor on January 28–29, 1950. As Craig explained, he had called the meeting to form a united front against Communism, to devise methods for strengthening governmental agencies so that they could restrain, even abolish, Communist activities, and to try to coordinate activities of the groups present. Of the eighty organizations invited, sixty-six responded, sending 150 delegates representing major patriotic, religious, civic, fraternal, labor, business, professional, philanthropic, and social organizations with a total membership said to be sixty to eighty million.

The conferees heard former ambassador to the U.S.S.R. Lt. Gen. Walter Bedell Smith, current commander of the First Army, who charged that Moscow had established a fifth column in the United

States. Senator Karl Mundt, a Republican from South Dakota, spoke about the nuclear bomb threat posed by the U.S.S.R. Columnist and Legion favorite George Sokolsky drove home the point that Communism was neither a political nor an economic system but a tyrannical philosophy bent on world domination.

Officials of the A.F.L. and the C.I.O. told of their efforts to rid their organizations of Communists. Msgr. Fulton J. Sheen and Rev. Daniel A. Poling, editor of the *Christian Herald* (and the father of one of the four military chaplains who died after giving their life jackets to others on their torpedoed ship), stressed faith in God as the real means for victory over Communism.

Later that month, on the floor of the U.S. Senate, Senator Mundt praised the conference, saying, "It appears that at long last this country is to have an all-America [and] pro-America organization solidly enough supported so that an effective program can be devised and promoted at the grassroots level to defeat the pagan poisons of the Godless Communist conspiracy."

Press references to National Commander Craig noted that his military service was in World War II, a proclamation of sorts that a new generation of veterans was on the rise in the Legion. The election of a World War II veteran, not to be belabored or passed over lightly, was inevitable if the organization was to survive, to acclimate itself to a new era.

While the Legion increasingly came to be an organization of second-generation citizen-soldiers, it began also to look to the future; the average World War II veteran had much of his or her life yet ahead. But the two most demanding challenges during George Craig's year in the top office were ones that returned from out of the past: the economizing move precipitated by "the Hoover Report," and Universal Military Training (U.M.T.), a long-standing goal of the Legion.

The first of these two challenges chronologically to present itself was that laid down by what had come to be known as the "Hoover Commission" (the Commission on the Organization of the Executive Branch of Government). The Legion was particularly concerned about the portions of the Hoover Report that provided a blueprint for radically revamping the Veterans Administration, the agency for which the Legion was both an avid critic and advocate.

Craig's stature as a candidate for Legion national office was built in large measure by his efforts as a state-level officer in the field of veterans' benefits and rehabilitation. As a post commander, southern vice-commander of the Department of Indiana, and as that department's National Executive Committeeman, he had led efforts for passage of housing and hospital programs for veterans. He had attracted nationwide attention in 1947 and 1948 when he successfully battled discrimination against veterans at the Knox, Indiana, Federal Housing Project. In that tussle, after presenting a resolution (subsequently adopted) to the N.E.C. that pointed up abuses of power by the Public Housing Authority, he had testified before congressional committees and in federal court. Subsequently, the alleged abuses at the Indiana site ceased. Now as national commander he was soon to be embroiled in a rehabilitation-related battle on a much larger scale.

The Legion had succeeded, generally, in maintaining a high-road response when reacting to public policy emanating from the federal government. But its unyielding stance on veterans' benefits pitted it against a venerable political institution in the person of Herbert Hoover.

Though the former president had been beleaguered while in office by the catastrophic economic malaise that seared the word "Depression" on the consciousness of a generation of Americans, he had acquired a reputation as a world-recognized humanitarian for the hunger relief work he had organized with impressive precision during and after both world wars. His very name had become a synonym for integrity in government. When the Hoover Commission was created by unanimous vote in July 1947, he was given another chance to campaign for government economizing, which was his trademark but had been sidetracked during his troubled administration.

The Hoover Commission had been the quintessential blue ribbon panel. Among its members were Dean Acheson, soon to be secretary of state; Arthur Fleming, former Civil Service commissioner; James Forrestal, former secretary of defense; Senator George D. Aiken of Vermont; Senator John McClellan of Arkansas; and former ambassador to Great Britain Joseph P. Kennedy.

Near the end of the commission's existence, Hoover, writing in *Fortune* (May 1949), appealed for a close reading of the many and detailed parts of the commission's report. "The burden now shifts from the shoulders of the commission to the citizens themselves who must undertake a real and continuing responsibility" for economy and efficiency in government. Six presidents along with several congressional committees had tried to reorganize the executive branch. All had met a stone wall of resistance erected by the numerous bureaus and departments, each wanting to be exempted from reform. The bureaus usually had some group that went to bat for them, such as associations of contractors, conservationists, farmers, labor, or banking interests. Hoover called on the general public to read the report and to apply pressure on their elected representatives in the federal government to bring about the reforms the commission had outlined.

After the Hoover Commission published its report (actually several reports), it passed into bureaucratic Valhalla as of June 12, 1949. Congress passed and the president approved on June 20, 1949, the Reorganization Act of 1949 as the mechanism available for eventually implementing recommendations of the Hoover Commission on which both chambers of Congress might agree. The act included that "no provision contained in a reorganization plan shall take effect unless the plan is transmitted to the Congress before April 1, 1953."

Consequently, the timetable of the act would create a busy and often frustrating three and a half years for the American Legion as it opposed the Hoover Report on several matters: (1) a proposed "United Medical Administration" (said to contain "the germs of socialism"); (2) a government veterans' insurance corporation; (3) the curtailment of hospital construction; and (4) changes in home loan policy and veterans' preference.

The May 1949 meeting of the N.E.C. had resolved "unalterable" opposition to several specific recommendations of the report. Many veterans, when hearing the word "economy" applied to veterans' benefits, thought immediately of the Economy Act of 1933. N.E.C. men voiced emotions redolent with the fervor of the founding caucuses: in 1919 they had been disgusted by the inability of the government to meet their needs for rehabilitation; now thirty years later they were being aroused by a new threat to established benefits.

The 31st National Convention in Philadelphia concurred. Throughout the months ahead, Legion speakers would reiterate what to them was "readily discernible": that the Hoover Commission's recommendations had been "honestly made" but by those "who had no experience in dealing with . . . veterans' affairs." Legion spokesmen were particularly agitated by those who urged the adoption of the recommendations in toto, even sight unseen—the "pig in a poke" often referred to by George Craig and others.

National Commander Craig told the 300 Legion service workers at the twenty-seventh annual Rehab conference in February 1950 that the Hoover Commission had not sought to learn from the Legion's considerable knowledge of veterans' affairs. Craig flatly labeled the recommendations for the split-up of the V.A. as an attempt to create more political patronage by creating more government jobs at new bureaus, which the report proposed for taking over some V.A. functions. "The last thing the nation needs now," he said, was "more porkbarreling."

To the Legion's inveterate and bombastic lobbyist John Thomas Taylor, still a force in the lobbying trade and still described as being "oldtime, well-informed, well-connected," the Hoover Report was but another volley in the twenty-year campaign conducted by many to interfere in veterans' affairs. Taylor was the Legion oracle in matters relating to things congressional, dating back to the era when his law office served as a makeshift Legion Rehab headquarters. The cane-waving, spats-sporting, loquacious provocateur for veterans' rights pointed out that all program areas of the Legion would be affected by the Hoover Commission's recommendations. But those that affected veterans' benefits directly, he said, should be specially targeted for defeat.

The Legion was not alone in its criticism of some portions of the Hoover Report. House majority leader John W. McCormack of Massachusetts had issued a press statement on January 26, 1949, stating that "the Hoover Commission failed to recognize that the V.A. was already set up on the one basis on which veterans' affairs could be handled with the greatest dispatch and the least cost." There should be no division of authority, he said, in the vast operation of administering the affairs of veterans. The Veterans Administration figured prominently in the Hoover Report, and the Legion, from the first days of the V.A., had monitored that agency closely.

Commander Craig agreed with McCormack's assessment. The commission's plan on this matter was "a foolhardy backward step," he said, that would return veterans "to the days of 1920–21 when [they] got a real runaround on a well-greased shuttle from bureaucratic door to door with half a dozen federal agencies going through the motions of trying to serve them. . . ."

The V.A. had actually been formed during the presidency of Herbert Hoover himself and with his blessing. This the Legion was fond of repeating in print and elsewhere.

For thirty-one years, the Legion had been convinced that a single agency was the best conceivable method of administering all types of benefits to veterans. Now, the Hoover Report was recommending that a few functions of the V.A. be taken outside that agency, most notably the medical and insurance functions, the first to be combined with the military and public health hospitals to form the proposed United Medical Administration, the second to be replaced by a government corporation to handle veterans' insurance. The Legion strongly opposed both of these recommendations.

Granted, the V.A. had a "checkered past," as the saying goes, and the Legion many times had voiced sharp criticism of the agency. In one sad era before World War II, the V.A. had acquired a reputation as a warehouse for suffering veterans, complete with medical incompetence like something out of a Dickens tale of woe. But the V.A. had made some progressive and impressive changes, a most notable one being the "affiliation" of V.A. hospitals with leading medical colleges, a development for which the Legion had been an active advocate.

Anyone who set about examining the V.A. was immediately struck by its size. As of November 1949, the agency administered some 300 laws potentially providing benefits for the nearly nineteen million living veterans as well as dependents of deceased veterans. (Living veterans, together with their dependents, comprised about forty percent of the nation's population.) These benefits included disability compensation; pensions; vocational rehabilitation and education; the guaranty of loans for the purchase or construction of homes or farms, or for businesses; readjustment allowances for unemployed veterans; National Service and U.S. Government Life Insurance; death and burial benefits; adjusted compensation; emergency officers' retirement pay; hospital and outpatient treatment; and domiciliary care.

In addition to this, the V.A. also administered the insurance article of the Soldiers' and Sailors' Civil Relief Act of 1940 for persons active in the military service.

There were 133 hospitals and domiciliary centers and 12,000 beds under contract in non-V.A. hospitals. The agency provided medical care for a daily average of 107,000 veteran-patients, outpatient medical and dental care for more than 2.5 million veterans annually, and conducted about 7.4 million physical and dental examinations each year. If the sixty-seven new hospital facilities now in the planning stage for the agency were to be built, the V.A. capacity would be approximately 131,000 permanent beds.

The V.A.'s accounting duties were immense. Compensation and pension payments were made to 2.3 million persons yearly and to the dependents of 645,000 deceased veterans. Over $2 billion annually went out for education and subsistence allowances to 2.5 million veterans. The 7.5 million life insurance policies in force had a face value of $42 billion. Approximately 1.8 million home, farm, and business loans had been guaranteed by the V.A. It received 170 million pieces of mail annually (more than that received by all the residents of Kansas City, Missouri, in 1949). The V.A. had a working force of 185,000 full-time and enough part-time employees to be equal to 51,000 full-time positions. Of this total, 116,000 were engaged in providing medical, hospital, and domiciliary care for veterans.

Large as it was, the V.A. was but one of many agencies and bureaus the Hoover Commission had examined. Certainly it was widely agreed that the executive branch needed review.

But there were several recommendations that caused serious concern for the Legion. Some caused outright alarm. Before long the Hoover Report was seen as a strong weapon that could be used to force budget cuts, particularly in federal expenditures for veterans' hospitals.

Truman himself had given Rehab officials pause when in his national budget messages he indicated his hope that none but service-connected illnesses would be treated at government expense. He had also expressed his wish to see some segments of the V.A. transferred to a newly proposed agency of cabinet-level status. In fact, the entire aura surrounding the president's "Reorganization Plan Number 27" was troubling to the Legion. This particular plan submitted by the president to the House Committee on Expenditures would transfer veterans' benefit programs to a proposed cabinet-level agency to be called the Department of Health, Education, and Security (the forerunner of the Department of Health, Education, and Welfare). Such a move, critics said, likely would cause veterans' affairs to be de-emphasized, leading to the eventual loss of veterans' benefits one by one.

The Hoover Commission had recommended that its brainchild—the United Medical Administration (variously called United Medical Services)—should be placed in the new agency. If that happened, the Legion feared that the educational benefits program for veterans would also become a candidate for transfer to the new agency. That, it was charged, would cause the ultimate fracturing of the V.A.

In addition to these bothersome anticipations, there were more concrete happenings that concerned National Rehab officials. In March 1950, V.A. head General Carl Raymond Gray, Jr., had ordered a reduction of 7,800 personnel. "This reduction," he said, "will not completely offset the shortage of funds for the current fiscal year" but would "place us in a position to enter the next fiscal year with employment at a level which is within the funds we have requested of the Congress." One of the reasons for the shortage of funds for the year, he said, was the pay increase granted to federal employees by Congress, which, in the V.A., amounted to about $21 million. As yet, no appropriation to offset this amount had been received. "The estimated shortage for this fiscal year will be from 29 to 39 million dollars," Gray said.

What would be the effect on the local scene? The reduction in staff at the Reno, Nevada, hospital, for example, as reported by Legion National Field Representative James P. Mulcare, would mean eighteen fewer staff people out of a total of 274, with the cuts being fairly representative of the entire staff.

Another service officer farther east, however, reported a different side of the issue, pointing up the individuality of each site. At the Wood, Wisconsin, center, there was a waiting list of 792 would-be patients (not unusual at V.A. facilities). In the hospital proper, 422 were on the list for treatment (93 medical, 128 surgical, 64 TB, and 137 neuropsychiatric). The domiciliary had a waiting list of 370.

Yet the planned cut in personnel at Wood threatened to eliminate the educational and manual arts therapy divisions of the physical medicine rehabilitation program. And that was not all. Of the total of 197 employees to be cut, 125 had recently been hired so that a building known as Annex 2 could be opened—a 226-bed facility for acute and intensive treatments and upon which approximately $400,000 had been spent to equip it as an intensive treatment building for neuropsychiatric patients.

In these instances and many others, cuts in the V.A. budget would create hardships among veterans needing specialized care. This came at a time, Legion field staff persons knew, when the patient load was increasing rather than declining as government crystal ball gazers had said earlier.

While cuts within the V.A. were objectionable, the U.M.A.—United

Medical Administration—that the Hoover Commission had recommended in its call for V.A. hospitals and those of the military services to be merged with public health service facilities into one government agency was no less disapproved of by the Legion. Not surprisingly, V.A. head Carl Gray was mounting his own campaign of opposition as well.

The Legion was quick to use the term "dismember" to describe what U.M.A. would mean to veterans' medicine, warning that such a reorganization of medical facilities would threaten a very special facet of the V.A. They referred to the more compassionate and understanding dispensation of medical services to veterans given at the V.A. during its better moments. This was something, it was said, that could not be legislated or ordered into being at a hospital where veterans were not the primary patients. That particular sensitivity, this argument went, was particularly endangered by "dismemberment."

Mississippi's National Executive Committeeman Ralph Godwin explained to the Louis M. Jigitts Post No. 110 the Legion's opposition to U.M.A. that "the major benefit programs for veterans are so dependent upon and integrated with the medical, hospital, and domiciliary care programs as to preclude their separation from the V.A. without disastrous effects on the efficient administration of veterans' benefits."

Godwin touched upon another and far more controversial issue—nonservice-connected illnesses, for the Legion a principle inextricably intertwined with the concept of veterans being a special class of citizens. The study of veterans' legislation could be divided into two principles: first, that the government had a big obligation to veterans with service-connected disabilities; and, second, that military service itself in time of war conferred on the veteran special governmental benefits. The first principle was generally accepted, if sometimes begrudged in some quarters. The second, however, especially when applied to the government paying for the treatment of nonservice-connected illnesses, often provoked bitter debate.

Those who insisted on the special-class status of veterans pointed out that the term "nonservice-connected illnesses" did not particularly mean trivial afflictions. Godwin pointed out that in 1949, fifty-six percent of those cases were TB (3,804), mental illnesses (18,689), and "General Medicine and Surgery" (14,009). "We feel," he said, speaking as a national officer, "that a veteran, even with a nonservice-connected disability, is entitled to a little extra treatment from the government he fought to uphold, provided he needs such treatment."

Godwin was one of the lucky ones, he said, who survived service in World War II without any service-connected disability, and he did not feel that he was entitled to free hospitalization at the expense of the government.

"But who can say what scars wartime service left upon any man? Maybe he was not wounded; maybe he was not sick; but he served. He left his home; he left his family; he jeopardized his job opportunities. The younger men left a few of their most precious years of life behind, never to be regained, regardless of any benefits under the G.I. Bill of Rights or any other benefits."

At this point, when Godwin and others explained the Legion's opposition to select portions of the Hoover Report, they were responding not only to the now-defunct Hoover Commission, but also to a compelling public initiative called the "Citizens Committee for the Adoption of the Hoover Report." The Citizens Committee was a national organization representing a popular movement for economy in government, itself a proper subject for study. It had come into being exactly as President Hoover had envisioned, to do what he had explained in *Fortune* should be done.

As rousing in rhetoric as it was noble in purpose, an early Citizens Committee national newsletter proclaimed, "The Hoover Report is a great and precious document [that] has been given into our hands . . . for action—NOW!"

Chaired by Dr. Ralph Johnson, president of Temple University, the Citizens Committee's purpose was to transform Hoover Report recommendations into public policy. As favored by Illinois Governor Adlai Stevenson, the committee also spawned state level and even city committees ("little Hoover Commissions") to give administrative government on every level a good going over.

With its "Waste Not, Want Not" letterhead logo, the Citizens Committee was admirably successful in its efforts to publicize its intentions. It had little difficulty finding headline fodder in the many instances of excess, duplication, and outright chicanery in government spending, all of which was sure to catch the attention of increasingly economy-minded taxpayers. That part was easy.

The hard part would be transporting the effervescent commodity of public sentiment through the give-and-take of Congress and emerging with public laws reminiscent of what the Hoover Commission had recommended.

The Citizens Committee had inherited an ambitious lobbying agenda; the Hoover Commission had made 277 recommendations. Out of those recommendations, administrative action was required for 114; substantial legislation or added appropriations (judiciously scrutinized, of course) was needed for another 124. Those remaining required general reorganizational legislation.

To its credit, the committee worked diligently. In October 1949, Senate Report 1158 listed ninety-three plans, Senate bills, and resolutions introduced by the committee for considerable government reform. A comparable number of plans and bills had appeared in the House.

Legion staff members at the Washington office became better acquainted with the personnel of the Citizens Committee office there than they had with the members of the Hoover Commission. The

Washington staff of the Legion had complained that though the office of the commission at 1626 K Street had been but four doors away from the Legion's building at 1608, Hoover Commission members neither invited aid in compiling their reports on veterans' programs nor readily accepted offers from the Legion for informational exchanges. (In this connection, the Citizens Committee claimed that the Hoover Commission had been a management study group that had held no hearings except for those held by its task forces. The committee, also, was in the habit of implying that the presence of Past National Commander Franklin D'Olier as chairman of the Task Force on Veterans Affairs for the Hoover Commission represented Legion participation. The Legion emphatically disagreed.)

Acquaintance, however, did not indicate agreement on the many issues relating to veterans' affairs on which the Legion and the Citizens Committee differed. There was fundamental disagreement, for example, on the vital special-class contention of the Legion for veterans when considering benefits. Opposition to this concept was viewed as an attempt, real or otherwise, to destroy the identity of veterans and to denigrate them as merely persons receiving a questionable federal bounty. As T. O. Kraabel, director of the Legion's Rehabilitation Division, repeatedly pointed out, "It is our belief that the government created a special class when it selected millions of young Americans for [military] service."

Legionnaires also bristled when medical care of veterans was likened to a "special interest," a label generally uttered with an air of condemnation. Instead of "special interest," the Legion preferred the term "special social need." (The side of the fence on which one came down on these two terms generally meant one had made a choice between viewing the Legion as basically a pressure group for veterans' benefits or as a service group advocating veterans' medical care.)

All the while, critics continued to claim that the only special-class distinction was that created when hospitalization and other medical care for nonservice-connected ailments were granted to veterans. That, they said, was "socialized medicine for a favored group."

There was little doubt about the popularity of governmental economizing or the shoring up of the structure of government so that people-serving efficiency could shine forth from behind the alabaster edifice of federalism. A Gallup poll in mid-March 1950 showed that the Hoover Report was backed by a ratio of twenty-five to two by voters familiar with it. Though sixty-nine percent of those polled said they were uninformed on the report, they overwhelmingly favored the goal of the Hoover Commission—to pare away all the waste, graft, and inefficiency in the process of economizing the federal government.

Senator Karl Mundt, a Legion friend on many fronts, including that relating to the perceived threat to the V.A. by the Hoover Report's U.M.A. proposal, told George Craig in late February 1950 that his like-minded colleagues in the Senate had been "bombarded by a great wave of letters protesting our position." The letters came from "high-minded citizens with noble purpose," he said, who insisted that the entire report be adopted but appeared ignorant of the large job to be placed before Congress in implementing the many and various recommendations contained in the report.

No less a Legion luminary than Harry Colmery himself was a member of the National Citizens Committee. But Colmery had become involved, he told George Craig, to gain a firsthand, front-row view of the movement. He "reserved the right to disagree with the program wherever I see fit, and with specific reference to veterans and things which affected the interest of veterans."

It was Colmery's considered opinion and, therefore, one honored in the upper echelon of the Legion, that the Legion should "beat the programs and policies advanced by the Hoover Commission . . . by facts and logic, primarily." It is well, he said, to know that for twenty years Herbert Hoover had been an outspoken advocate for economizing on veterans' benefits. But he cautioned Legion leaders not to rely on that point alone. "Beat the thing by positive means and methods. And don't attack Mr. Hoover; that is not popular and is not convincing enough."

In New York, the statewide Citizens Committee boasted the membership of William J. "Wild Bill" Donovan, a Legion founder. But Edward F. McGinnis, the Legion's national public relations director, found Legionnaire Donovan eager to consider the Legion's contentions that the Hoover Commission had not considered the veterans' programs conscientiously enough. McGinnis reportedly found the general "anxious to have the facts because he will not only withdraw his support but will be willing to get into the fight on our side if the facts warrant it."

Legionnaire Sam W. Reynolds of the Reynolds-Updike Coal Company in Omaha was, also, a member of the local Citizens Committee. Reynolds stated, reasonably enough, to Craig, "I am an American first, a Legionnaire second." But he was also keeping an open mind on the subject of the Hoover Commission's report. He stressed that economizing simply as a disciplinary measure, since in general it seemed necessary, would not do if veterans, especially the most needy among them, were to be hurt.

Reynolds said that the Legion should concede that waste and inefficiency did indeed exist in the V.A. and that some economizing should be done. By this forthright admission and observation, the Legion could retain the respect of people and Congress, he said.

Perhaps the Legionnaire most often referred to in Citizens Committee literature was the Legion's first national commander, Franklin D'Olier, who served as chairman of the Hoover Commission's Task Force on Veterans Affairs.

References in Citizens Committee publicity materials to D'Olier's work with the Hoover Commission haunted the Legion for some time. First, there was the stature of the man as first national commander, not a role to be played down by the Legion. Second was the man's current position as president of Prudential Life Insurance, with its distinctive Rock-of-Gibraltar corporate logo, one of the nation's best known. The third and perhaps most aggravating matter was the numerous editorials printed about the Hoover Commission while it was newsworthy, publicity that perpetuated the incorrect information that D'Olier had recommended the establishment of a veterans' insurance corporation separate from the V.A.

Though D'Olier attempted eventually to explain his own views in these matters, his comments were not widely publicized. As George Craig lamented, getting D'Olier's disclaimers into the record could have "pulled a lot of fangs."

D'Olier was not the only past national commander to become associated with local Citizens Committee initiatives. Alvin Mansfield Owsley (Past National Commander, 1922–23), known for his spellbinding oratory, was chairman of the Department of Texas's Hoover Report Committee. National Adjutant Hank Dudley wrote to Owsley, explaining that "fifteen or sixteen staffers in Indianapolis and Washington have done nothing else but study the Hoover Report and its effect on veterans" and that their findings were that some of the recommendations made in the report should be opposed and legislation proposed for enacting these measures must be thwarted by right-thinking Legionnaires.

Owsley was advised that other Legionnaires who had occupied national offices, such as Ed Hayes (Past National Commander, 1933–34) and Pat Cliff, chairman of the Rehabilitation Commission, had worked long and hard against the veterans' affairs portions of the report.

The prevailing opinion at some Legion posts, however, was that the Hoover Report should be adopted in its entirety. These posts broke with National by publicizing their supportive views. They were likely to be reminded, however, by the Department Policy Committee that while they had the right to criticize the Legion's position, they should review the resolution adopted by the 20th National Convention concerning official Legion policy, which stated that "any department or departmental organization which is in disagreement with any portion of the program of the American Legion so adopted, [should] transmit its objections without publicity through channels to the National Organization for consideration." There were posts, however, that both visibly and vocally continued to promote the Hoover Report, reflecting a popular attitude in their locality. In this manner, these posts showed again that the American Legion was representative of the nation, even if it meant opposing the official stance of National Headquarters.

National was not alone, of course, in opposing select portions of the

Hoover Report. Some instances of criticism even defied political partisanship, ignoring Herbert Hoover's stature as Republican elder statesman. For example, an Oklahoma Legionnaire informed George Craig that the Republican State Convention in Oklahoma City went on record asking that the Hoover Commission position on the disintegration of the V.A. be reexamined. Also, Republican congressmen from Illinois signed a statement supporting some of the Hoover Commission's recommendations but not those relating to veterans' affairs.

Though a popular and active force on the national scene, the Citizens Committee was not the only organization that became active in the wake of the Hoover Commission. In early October 1949, at the original National Headquarters building in Indianapolis at the southeast corner of Meridian and St. Clair streets, National Adjutant Henry H. "Hank" Dudley met George Craig at the door one morning with a UPI story about the activities of another group, the solidly named and austere sounding "Tax Foundation, Inc." Among other things, the Tax Foundation recommended that the V.A. be authorized to investigate the ability of patients to pay for nonservice-connected hospitalization and to require payment on the part of those vets found able to pay. Hearing that yet another group was organizing for action alongside the Citizens Committee, Craig vowed to beat them all at their own public appeal game.

To Jack Little, chief of the Legion's press section and formerly of the Hearst-run *Chicago Herald-American,* the Tax Foundation was "another hideous example of the insidious antiveteran propaganda of which the Legion has warned." In an interoffice memo, Little asked Legion National Publicity Director Jack Cejnar, "What is back of this self-styled 'research organization'?" John Thomas Taylor, Little said, had assured him that the foundation was "definitely big, big business." Cejnar replied that the foundation's board of directors "reads like a 'Who's Who' in the National Association of Manufacturers." It reminded Little and the others of "Old Nell," the National Economy League of the early 1930s, which had launched an unabashed frontal attack on veterans' benefits that had been instigated by the Economy Act of 1933. The Tax Foundation, it seemed, had adopted an oblique approach to achieving the same ends.

Craig asked T. O. Kraabel to gather facts and figures about the issues raised by the Citizens Committee, the Tax Foundation, and other such groups. By mid-November, Craig could tell those who were in the field making speeches about the Hoover Commission that "our boys in Washington are working day and night to get the information assembled" for speeches to be used at department and post meetings. "We are moving heaven and earth to get this thing in shape as quickly as possible. Frankly we were caught short and are now working overtime to make up the difference."

Remember, Craig and others cautioned, the Legion was not defending the V.A. as such, but rather the principle of a one-stop, service agency being made available to veterans. Newspapers, they said, had not printed the real story. Constructive changes made in the V.A. in the two years since the Hoover Report were not being reported. Instead, Craig and the others complained, run-of-the-mill editorials tediously contained stale figures and misleading generalities. Carl Gray of the V.A. also had ordered new public relations efforts to publicize current statistics substantiating select V.A. efficiencies.

The job of gathering information sometimes was rewarded with a select and prestigious audience. On January 25, 1950, President Truman asked George Craig to compile relevant statistics from the Legion's viewpoint relating to a proposed 16,000-bed cutback in V.A. hospital construction, a move that the Legion vigorously opposed. In his report, which was marked "confidential at the president's request," Craig reviewed the V.A. hospital situation from the vantage of construction, staffing, and location. He listed fourteen sites on the construction program that had been affected by midstream reductions of beds.

All of these hospitals were located in metropolitan areas with medical schools and could be well supplied with specialists in all required categories. He listed six sites that recently had been scrubbed from the construction program, all of which the V.A. "could very readily staff." To these Craig added nine more proposed sites that the V.A. said would be difficult to staff, but that could be staffed properly "based upon our own studies."

Craig's report to the president reflected much time already spent in collecting information and in formulating defensible positions on the main areas of disagreement between the Legion and the Hoover Report relating to hospitalization of veterans, insurance, hospital construction, home loans, and preference in government employment.

Often during this period, though, national officers would complain that while collecting, corroborating, and analyzing that information was an enormous task, an even greater problem was getting it publicized. Though the Washington staff had been told by knowledgeable sources that the Legion position on these subjects was generally supported in Congress, nevertheless, Jack Cejnar admitted to the New Jersey Department director of public relations that "we are definitely losing the fight in the press." Newspaper editorial writers "are not informed, but accept the arguments of our opposition as gospel. Arrayed against the American Legion is BIG money, which is making available to our opponents plenty of capable manpower and good publicists and a press that knows on which side its bread is buttered. The American Legion has to operate with a limited budget and certainly an inadequate publicity staff."

The Legion itself stirred up the ire of the Citizens Committee with a cartoon distributed by the American Legion News Service (A.L.N.S.)

that depicted Mr. Hoover saying, "They all look alike in pajamas." That particular generic quip, not actually attributable to the former president, had already come to encompass the thought that veterans should not be considered any differently than others for medical care. Citizens Committee Chairman Ralph Johnson considered the cartoon "scurrilous" and "a savage caricature" of Mr. Hoover. Legion friend Senator Karl Mundt, referring to the "hornets' nest" controversy surrounding the cartoon, recommended that National Commander Craig "avoid . . . pillorying former President Hoover since Americans . . . have come to have a high respect for him as an elder statesman and a great American."

National officers were particularly perturbed when post commanders received a letter in March from Herman W. Steinkraus, president of the U.S. Chamber of Commerce, appealing to them as fellow veterans to support the Citizens Committee's point of view. Such direct contact, it was thought, was unsporting. About the opposing viewpoints, Steinkraus engaged in a bit of understatement. "We seem to be in disagreement," he wrote.

In mid-December 1949, the Citizens Committee sponsored a National Reorganization Conference in Washington, D.C., during which the Legion asked to meet with Hoover himself. At the arranged meeting, the Legion was represented by National Commander Craig and Past National Commanders Louis Johnson, Franklin D'Olier, Ed Hayes, and John Quinn. Craig recalls the meeting as being less than friendly, not even cordial. Hoover "talked down to us for about an hour. He was rude, profane; I would even say vicious. When he was finished, he dismissed us without allowing us the courtesy of making our formal presentation."

At a conference on January 7, 1950, at National Headquarters, where officials had been gathered to be apprised of the Hoover Commission fight, John Thomas Taylor strode "like a caged lion" up and down the aisles of the N.E.C. room ("They loved it," Americanism staffer James R. Wilson recalls), challenging his fellow Legionnaires to become a committee of the whole for the battle ahead. He repeated a traditional Legion maxim: "The cold, inanimate tools of war are always paid for in cash on the barrelhead. But the human costs of the war, the cost paid by our fighting men and women in lost arms and legs and sight and health, are always charged." This new economy purge in the form of the Hoover Report, he said, would trim the rights of veterans, but not the cost. Make Legion opposition unmistakably clear to Congress, he urged. The effort must continue until the Legion's point of view prevailed.

The chairman of the Legion's Rehabilitation Commission was equally animated. "The American Legion is the greatest name in rehabilitation!" Robert McCurdy said. An infantry captain in World War I with four battle bars on his Victory Ribbon, McCurdy had also spent thirty-five months of continuous hospitalization before being discharged from the army. This former amateur prizefighter and current city manager of Pasadena, California, (and chairman of the Rose Bowl Parade) was afflicted by crippling arthritis. Now with his spine parallel to the ground, speaking from a specially designed step constructed for his use, "Chairman Bob" was himself an inspiring example of positive attitude and untiring, effective volunteerism in spite of physical difficulties.

Always an effective speaker for the Legion's Rehab advocacy, McCurdy proclaimed, "We are the experts." Those who formulated the Hoover Commission's recommendations on veteran medical care should acknowledge the Legion's thirty-one years of experience in that field and listen to expert advice, he advised.

In February 1950, the Citizens Committee produced its "White Paper Number One" subtitled "Facts Regarding the Hoover Commission's Recommendations Relating to Veterans' Affairs." It was billed by the committee as "a refutation of certain public statements currently being made about the effect of the Hoover Report and veterans' activities." The white paper quoted many Legionnaires, from post commanders to national officers, stating various criticisms of the report that Citizens Committee text then attempted to refute.

The Legion's official print response came in the May 1950 issue of *The American Legion Magazine* in a sixteen-page article answering the committee's white paper point by point. In preparing the article, magazine editor Robert Pitkin met with T. O. Kraabel, Bob McCurdy, and Charles Stevens. Playing devil's advocate, Pitkin said, "I'm going to prove to you that the Hoover Commission is right, and you guys knock me down." As Pitkin recalls, the "knockdown" was impressive; the amount of background information these Rehab savants commanded astounded him. "Charlie Stevens knew everything that had happened legislatively in veterans' affairs since day one." As Pitkin listened to Kraabel, McCurdy, and Stevens expound on the complexities of the subject (and with some expert copy from Ed McGrail) the magazine article took shape. Upon publication it became the authoritative, definitive statement of the Legion's stance on the many issues involved. The Legion also produced a pamphlet, titled "Again the Target of Economy," to treat select sections of the Hoover Report and to answer negative criticism of the Legion viewpoint.

The Citizens Committee continued to work toward its goal of shepherding the Hoover Commission recommendations through Congress. By the end of the year, twenty percent of the recommendations made a year before had been accepted either through issuance of Executive Orders, as was the case more often, or by the enactment of enabling legislation.

Meanwhile, National Commander Craig was supplied with a stock speech that listed nine ways for the V.A. to live within its present means: (1) limit hospital construction to locations where they could be properly staffed; (2) use available Defense Department hospital beds (in sponsoring the G.I. Bill of Rights, the Legion had recommended that the V.A. take over, whenever and wherever feasible, some of the hospitals of permanent construction built by the armed forces); (3) reactivate the Federal Board of Hospitalization (which had been in operation from 1921 to June 30, 1948) as the authority to consider government hospital matters involving interagency dealings; (4) modernize the V.A. insurance operation (specifically the clerical operation); (5) decentralize V.A. district office activities; (6) reduce special services activities and personnel; (7) reevaluate physical medicine rehabilitation activities; (8) combine regional offices with other V.A. facilities; and (9) simplify and reduce the plethora of forms, instructions, regulations, and other agency paperwork.

The Legion itself was no stranger to the need to economize. National Commander Craig had reminded the N.E.C. in November 1949 that the organization had had to borrow money each year for the last three to meet its budget. He, for one, was determined that the organization would live within its means in the present year. Though the annual per capita national dues at this time was raised to $1.25 from the longtime rate of $1, that increase was promised for rehabilitation work. The heady expectations based on the phenomenal peak in membership in 1946 had proven to be excessive. Membership was declining. National Headquarters was faced with a fundamental predicament for any national organization—self-doubt during a disappointing membership downturn.

During this time also, the importance of effective communication within a large national organization came in for review and some criticism. In particular, the national network for disseminating information and official communiqués was found to be less than dependable. Washington staff members who went to regional conferences got the impression that brochures and the many clip sheets and other materials that had kept mimeograph machines humming at National Headquarters for weeks beforehand had not reached "down to the 'grassroot' member," but instead had "more or less stopped at the department level."

The word went out from National: field representatives were to devote much more time to placing Legion literature about the Hoover Report. Visit local newspaper editors, they were told, and seek out Legionnaires who were members of a local Citizens Committee or a Junior Chamber of Commerce.

In Washington, Legion spokesmen—paid staff members and high ranking volunteers alike—made many trips along Pennsylvania Avenue to Capitol Hill in the following weeks to appear before congressional committees and reiterate the Legion's stance on the various legislative measures stemming from the Hoover Report. A select few received special attention.

For example, Legion witnesses appeared in hearings on H.R. 5182, which called for merging certain medical services of the V.A. with the armed forces and those of the Public Health Service. This was the dreaded U.M.A. measure against which the Legion railed loud and long. It called, the Legion said, for an unworkable mixing of medical treatment: veteran (civilian), military (highly specialized), and public health (preventative and research). Under this yoke, it was said, the veteran not only would lose his right to exclusive hospitalization but his identity as a veteran, also, disassociating him from his service to his country, for which he deserved medical benefits.

Another development witnessed by Miles Kennedy, director of the Legislative Division and successor to John Thomas Taylor, began to take shape. He observed now that there existed a peculiar hint of and, in some cases, more obvious antagonism to Legion testimony on the proposed U.M.A. bills. "At our hearing before the House Committee on Expenditures in the Executive Departments (on H.R. 5182) on March 29, a lot of time was taken by certain members of the committee in cross-examining the national commander." George Craig testified, along with Dr. Charles W. Mayo and Dr. Leonard G. Rowntree. A Legion staff member noted the manner in which Craig had been questioned by a few congressmen: "bitterly" by Richard W. Hoffman (R., IL), "critically" by Chet D. Holifield (D., CA). One representative warned against "brass knuckles" letters by Legionnaires to congressmen.

In April, Legion testimony on the Senate's U.M.A. bill, S. 2008, was given in a similarly "pretty unfriendly" atmosphere, Kennedy reported. Some congressmen did support the Legion position, however. Republican Congressman Harold C. Hagen of Minnesota had testified earlier that "veterans are happy and pleased with the present setup" of the V.A. medical services. Congressman Carl Hinshaw of California, later in the hearing, condemned the "bastard" bill at length.

Washington-based staff members kept tabs on the Hoover Report–related legislation. By May, two of the reorganization plans inspired by the report had been defeated: those for the National Labor Relations Board and the Treasury. Eight more were introduced midmonth, some to be aired in the Senate, others in the House, depending on the nature of the reform proposed. Of these, plans for revamping the Interstate Commerce Commission and the departments of Agriculture and Commerce were said to be bound for defeat.

Soon, however, other events would produce headlines larger even than those detailing government economizing.

Late the next month, on Sunday, June 25, at 0400 Korean time, the North Korean army crossed the 38th parallel into the Republic of Korea. This well-armed, Communist juggernaut pushed aside the inadequately prepared and equipped R.O.K. forces.

Within days, American troops, under the blue and white flag of the United Nations, were again in combat.

II

"And who stands safest? Tell me, is it he
That spreads and sells in puff'd prosperity
Or blessed with little, whose preventing care,
In peace provides fit arms against a war?"
ALEXANDER POPE

"An Ostrich, or an Eagle?"
AMERICAN LEGION U.M.T. BROCHURE TITLE

The past national commanders and National Executive Committeemen who attended the conference that Commander Craig called for Saturday and Sunday, July 15 and 16, 1950, to discuss the Korean situation reaffirmed the need for universal military training. During the meeting a telegram arrived from Bernard Baruch. "Go to it for U.M.T.!"

When Watson B. Miller of the Rehab Division returned to Washington on Monday, he attempted during his appointment with Maj. Gen. Harry Vaughan, Truman's army buddy, longtime friend, and now aide, to have a reference to U.M.T. written into a speech the president was soon to deliver to Congress. Miller was unable to get in to see the president, but on Tuesday Vaughan had relayed a message from Truman: "Tell Watson to tell the Legion that I have always been and am now 102 percent for U.M.T. If we had had it in 1947 we wouldn't be in the fix we are now."

Miller proudly telephoned the message to Indianapolis and asked that the teletype operator there transcribe the message and send it back to Washington to become part of the official files of that office. When Miller, back on the phone with General Vaughan, reviewed the text of the message with him, Vaughan acknowledged its correctness but asked that it not be published verbatim.

U.M.T. as a most important factor in a national defense structure had first been promoted by World War I veterans. The goal was always U.M.T. and not "U.M.S."—universal military *service,* which was said by the Legion to be old-world conscription in peacetime.

These former doughboys had vivid memories of what a lack of military training meant. Some recalled how they had reached front-line trenches before being taught how to load their rifles, close the bolts, and attach bayonets.

National Executive Committeeman Tom Miller, who as a young congressman had helped found the Plattsburg Training Camp Program before World War I, expressed the ongoing perplexity. "Less than five years ago our splendid armed services on land and sea were brought home and demobilized without any regard to what we were facing on the international firing line. The thought of future wars is abhorrent to those nineteen million American men and women who sacrificed the best years of their lives in two world wars . . . I hope the country will wake up to the true situation before it is too late."

National training programs, though not universal or military, were not unheard of. There was noteworthy precedence. For example, the popular Civilian Conservation Corps (C.C.C.) between 1933 and 1942 housed, fed, and clothed over three million jobless young men. The C.C.C. had also strengthened them physically, made many visible improvements on the land, and served to occupy many men during the Depression. Though not military in purpose, the large-scale nature of the experiences gained in organizing the C.C.C. provided important lessons to those charged later with mobilizing manpower for World War II.

Similarly, the Citizens Military Training Camps program (C.M.T.C.), authorized by the National Defense Act of 1920, involved up to 30,000 young men annually at fifty camps (from 1926 to 1940 at Regular Army posts) where they spent thirty days each summer ostensibly being prepared for appointments as Army Reserves and noncommissioned officers. Supported and promoted by the Legion's Americanism Commission (which stated that "there is no militarism about the camps"), C.M.T.C. applications (a key word in the comparison/contrast with U.M.T.) were handled by a national civilian group—the Military Training Camps Association—represented in each county and school district. After 1928, units of the Organized Reserves administered the program. Another stated purpose of the C.M.T.C. was "to develop closer national and social unity by bringing together young men of all types, to teach the privileges, duties and responsibilities of American citizenship, to stimulate the interest of the young of this country in the importance of military training, and [to be] an asset vital in the problem of national defense."

A week after the mid-July conference in Indianapolis, another meeting there, this time of department commanders, heard Past National Commander Paul H. Griffith, now Assistant Secretary of Defense, say on Sunday, July 23, that orders had been given in the Pentagon for the immediate drafting of a military training bill.

That afternoon, also, National Commander Craig delivered his "Decision Now" talk over CBS. The tone was one of immediacy, of impending danger: "There no longer can be any doubt of the gravity of the crisis facing America and the world today. We are balancing on the perilous brink of World War III." He reiterated Truman's warning that "armed aggression may take place in other areas . . . Greece, Turkey, Iran, Indochina, Formosa, or the Philippines."

The Legion had declared its own state of emergency. Craig introduced the Legion's "patriotic example": "The American Legion as of now throws overboard for the duration of the present crisis its advocacy of any new veterans' pension legislation. We shall support no bonus bills. We shall ask [for] no additional benefits or extensions of time under the G.I. Bill of Rights except to make them applicable to those now fighting your war in Korea. It is a case today of powder or pensions—bullets or bonuses."

The national commander repeated the Legion's abhorrence of war profiteering. He noted the invasion of South Korea as being but a checkmark on the timetable of world Communism. He complained of inadequate training and insufficient weapons and supplies for those American soldiers dying in Korea even as he spoke.

Craig credited George Washington with a quote on military preparedness: "Had we had a trained army in the beginning, we never should have had to retreat." With similar admonishments from the Preamble of the U.S. Constitution, and from the Gospel of St. Luke ("When a strong man armed keepeth his palace, his goods are in peace. . . ." 11:21), Craig interjected a plug for U.M.T. into the national broadcast. The lack of preliminary military training was "inexcusably cruel," he said. "No segment of the American people could be more fervent in their desire for peace than those who have felt the hardships and pain of actual conflict, and these veterans of the American Legion have never retreated in this peace objective."

Craig appealed "to the mothers and fathers of our American youths" as he explained that "U.M.T. is not regimentation. It does not mean the immediate drafting of your son into the armed forces." Rather, it was a training program "to discourage international bandits from perpetrating acts of violence that make necessary the drafts of your sons into the fighting forces." U.M.T. was "security insurance" for the nation and "survival insurance" for eventual soldiers.

"Three million men who have been through it are trying to give you the benefit of their painful experience so that you and your sons will not have to go through it again. The forensic vapors of rhetoric will not run the engines of war. Nor will they train our boys." The nation needed U.M.T.; the concept "has gathered dust in congressional pigeonholes too long." Action was required; write your senators and representatives, he urged. "It is your decision now!"

On July 24, the N.E.C. gave Craig authority, by telephone vote, to go forward in an all-out effort to obtain legislation on U.M.T.

Less than a month after the outbreak of hostilities in Korea, National Legislative Director Miles Kennedy assessed the mood of Congress in mid-July regarding current U.M.T. bills (S. 66 and H.R. 1305). Kennedy and Past National Commander Warren Atherton (1943–44) visited or telephoned several key congressmen and found that the consensus was for U.M.T. (Prime Minister Robert G. Menzies of Australia had recently addressed the House and received hearty applause when he said his country was building up its fighting strength by training young men under a national service system.)

But, as Kennedy told Granville Ridley, chairman of the Legion's National Security Training Committee (a holdover term synonymous with U.M.T.), many of the congressmen recommended delay. Most "would be guided entirely by what the president and/or the Department of Defense wants done in the matter," even though Kennedy found that most of those interviewed said, as had the president earlier, that had U.M.T. been in effect "two or three years ago, we would not be in the 'mess' we are today" in Korea.

Kennedy noted, of course, that the terms of all 435 representatives, and 35 of the 96 senators, would expire on December 31. Some of those with whom he spoke had requested that he not use their names in reporting his survey of opinion; primary dates were, in fact, quickly approaching (August 3 in Tennessee, with others following closely behind).

The Legion was not alone in favoring U.M.T. The *New York Journal-American*'s issue of July 28 included a full page editorial cartoon depicting the Communist threat being held back by a well-prepared G.I. The stark and brooding illustration was reprinted by the American Legion News Service. The Hearst chain of newspapers, particularly keen on the Legion's one hundred percent Americanism program, featured editorial cartoons, stentorian in tone, in favor of U.M.T. On August 1, thirteen Hearst papers in major cities around the country backed the Legion's call for U.M.T. The emphasis in editorials, and a point stressed by the Legion, was on manpower preparedness rather than reliance on vast buildups of armaments alone. For as Legion National Security Commission news releases had stated earlier, bombers and armaments alone had not stopped the enemy advance in Korea, but armed and trained soldiers had.

To call U.M.T. a controversial issue was to understate the situation. The issue was quickly and thoroughly politicized, of course, since it was sure to generate much attention on the local level. Though many agreed the concept was good for the nation's defense, the measure could be political suicide. Voting in Congress for a measure to require every mother's son barely out of high school to receive military training was seen as a poor way to get to Washington or to stay there in office. As the adage went, this would not play well in Peoria, even though, as the Legion believed, Peorians would be better trained by U.M.T. for military combat and, therefore, would help discourage attacks upon the United States by those who sought to take advantage of nations which trained soldiers only after having been attacked.

Indeed, on this issue particularly the reactionary side of Congress was apparent and not its foresightedness, it was often said. Political expediency often won out over more objective thinking. Political careers, it was assumed, were automatically held in the balance with this issue.

At that point, there appeared, also, to be conflicting signals about presidential interest in U.M.T. In a meeting with Mr. Truman on July 26, National Commander Craig, accompanied by Past National Commanders John Stelle and Louis Johnson, were led to believe that the president still favored U.M.T. But the Legion's Legislative Division staffers knew that the mood on Capitol Hill was such that only if Truman gave some unmistakable sign that he was willing to see it become the law of the land would Congress act favorably on the subject.

Ninety minutes after speaking with the president, Craig and the others conferred with Senator Millard N. Tydings of Maryland, chairman of the Senate Armed Services Committee. Tydings favored legislation for U.M.T. But rhetorically he asked, "Can you produce in writing a commitment from Truman for U.M.T.?"

Hardly, Craig had to admit. One didn't do business that way in these circles. Support, favor, and productive like-mindedness found outlets in legislative action, but rarely in anything as compromising as a note from the president.

When Craig left Senator Tydings's office, he learned that the news services at that moment were carrying a report that Truman appeared disinclined toward U.M.T., and specifically that he would not ask for a U.M.T. program during this session of Congress. In the hours that followed, the president did not challenge the widely publicized news brief. (According to many who have charted and gauged the progression of activity on the subject, U.M.T. was thus dealt a staggering blow. Regardless of limited and temporary successes in the future, Truman's hesitation at this particular point, they say, sounded the death knell for U.M.T. Craig was unequivocal. "He killed it," he says in retrospect.)

At the time, Craig continued to urge U.M.T., saying only, "For some reason or reasons, more or less unknown to us, we have not received the administration's support for our proposed U.M.T. bill that we had been led to believe we would get." On August 4, 62,000 enlisted reservists were called up for twenty-one months of active duty. The draft again would become the nation's chief means of manpower procurement.

Efforts for U.M.T. continued despite Truman's disappointing refusal of support. On the afternoon of August 17, Senator Tydings introduced S. 4062, the Legion's U.M.T. bill. Once again Legion staffers began distributing materials promoting the concept.

On August 22, the full committee agreed to report out the bill, leading Past Department Commander William G. Burns of Illinois to state in a letter to Senate Majority Leader Scott W. Lucas, in an attempt to sway Lucas to support U.M.T., that such an action was "a clear indication that there is nothing political in the issue." In hearings on that day and the next, Gen. Omar Bradley, chairman of the Joint Chiefs of Staff, testified, as did Past National Commander Louis Johnson, now Secretary of Defense. National Commander Craig, also, appeared, along with Mrs. Marie L. Sheehe, national president of the American Legion Auxiliary, and Mrs. Laura Goode, its Past National President. Karl T. Compton of M.I.T. and Col. Blake R. Van Leer, president of Georgia Institute of Technology, also spoke for U.M.T.

In subsequent hearings of the Senate Armed Services Committee, California Department Commander Lewis K. Gough painted a grim picture for those assembled. "At present, we find ourselves as a nation facing one of two eventualities—either total war or a long period of tension and watchful waiting while we build and maintain our country's military strength. In either case, we must have an uncommitted military force as a strategic reserve to balance uncommitted Soviet power and to deter further Communist aggression. This means Selective Service for immediate needs and National Security Training for the long range pull as a coordinated and companion program."

He also repeated a long-standing Legion belief: "Our nation cannot afford to maintain a large standing military force for a long period of time. The only way we can maintain security with economy is through National Security Training." Such a conclusion, Gough said, was the recommendation of the president's Advisory Commission on National Security Training in 1947. "The Korean conflict might never have developed had we taken definite steps during the last three years to demonstrate our ability to back the United Nations in checking Communist imperialism. If the world knew we had a body of trained men to implement a resolute policy for peace, it would have served as a powerful deterrent to aggressive action anywhere in the world. It took us one year in World War I and two years in World War II to bring our military force to the degree of readiness to take the offensive."

Time was "the most fragile of strategic weapons," Gough said. It would not be possible in the future, with the ascendancy of air power, including guided missiles and monumentally increased bombing capabilities, to arm this country quickly enough. Specialized training was becoming ever more necessary in the armed forces. The luxury of time for training, particularly in the case of surprise aggression, would no longer be available.

In time of war, Gough pointed out, "Ninety percent of our trained manpower must come from the civilian component," but since the end of WWII, "less than five percent of our military budget has gone to training of civilians for security and for war if it comes." National security training is "security insurance," Gough said, for the nation and for the young men who would be called to serve. Gough also stressed the economy of such training.

The call to action went out along the Legion's national lines of communication. George Craig implored every post "to be a U.M.T. microphone." A Legion staffer suggested that pro-U.M.T. newspaper editors, who often engaged in molding public opinion on a variety of subjects, should write letters and send telegrams to their congressmen favoring U.M.T. (Eugene Pullium, of the *Indianapolis News,* when approached, replied that molding public opinion was one thing, but sending telegrams was quite another. He wouldn't "get into the lobbying business.")

The Legion's National Security Commission Chairman Erle Cocke, Jr., stated on August 3 that though "there is an undercurrent of opposition, as indicated by the press," "eight out of ten" persons polled still favored U.M.T. (A new Gallup poll reported that seventy-eight percent of those polled favored U.M.T.)

Cocke believed S. 4062 could "be passed in this session of Congress" if Legionnaires acted promptly in letting the entire Congress know of their support for it.

On Monday, August 28, Past National Commander Perry Brown sat in with the Senate Armed Services Committee, which was in executive session, and helped revise S. 4062 in a manner acceptable to the Legion. Erle Cocke and Granville Ridley, too, met with the Senate committee the next day in time to see several Legion suggestions accepted. On Wednesday, the discussion and drafting session continued, along with two hours spent discussing whether to push for a bill during the current session or to appoint a subcommittee to work longer on a bill for the next session in January (as the president preferred).

A letter received from the president requested that delay. It would be impossible, Truman said, to put U.M.T. into effect at present because officers necessary for training could not be spared from the war in Korea. (The Department of Defense insisted that it would take a year or two before such a program would cease to interfere with the present draft.) Senator Tydings agreed "reluctantly," it was said, to postpone action on a U.M.T. bill until the January session. On the afternoon of August 30, the Senate Armed Services Committee voted 8 to 3 to put off action on a U.M.T. bill until January.

That day in the Legion's National Headquarters in Indianapolis, there were in the mailroom 17,433 copies of the Legion's *News Service* Bulletin 187, addressed and awaiting pickup; they were stored temporarily as waste paper. The bulletin's appeal for a barrage of pro-U.M.T. letters was suddenly made useless by the delaying action on U.M.T. by the Senate. Legion Archivist Verna Grimm (widow of Warren Grimm, who had been killed in the 1919 "Centralia Massacre") asked Jack Little for the U.M.T. files for the Legion Archives "now that U.M.T. is finished."

Senator Tydings did appoint a subcommittee to draft a comprehensive U.M.T. measure for the new Congress. Lyndon Johnson was made chairman of the "Preparedness Subcommittee" and was joined by senators Virgil Chapman (D., KY); Estes Kefaver (D., TN); Lester C. Hunt (D., WY); Styles Bridges (R., NH); Leverett Saltonstall (R., MA); and Wayne Morse (R., OR). Jack Cejnar assumed that all but Saltonstall were "U.M.T. friends." (Saltonstall would later prove to be less the enemy of U.M.T. than first thought.)

But the subcommittee put off work on a U.M.T. bill in favor of more pressing business. As Lyndon Johnson stated late in the year to new National Commander Erle Cocke, Jr., "The present exigencies of the Korean situation have necessitated considerable rearrangement of legislative plans," so much so he could not say "when we will proceed" with the U.M.T. matter. (On November 6, General MacArthur had reported what the West had feared most: Communist Chinese were now fighting U.N. troops in Korea.)

Johnson stated support, however. "I quite agree with you that the long range concept for maintaining our military posture should be geared to a system of universal training rather than a complete revision of our traditional plan of maintaining no larger an active duty force than is necessary."

Carl Vinson, who chaired the House Armed Services Committee, explained in more substance to Cocke that "under present world conditions, imposing a requirement for a standing military force far in excess of anything we have ever attempted before, I hardly see where we have the manpower to undertake any training program at this time, other than active duty training." He did look for the day, however, when "we can actually implement a sound universal military training program."

At the time, the "present world conditions" to which Congressman Vinson had alluded were pressing down on Washington, where the mood was gloomier now than it had been in June when the first news of the Korean invasion broke. The disheartening estimates of combat losses in late November helped impress on the public the harsh reality of the Communist Chinese intervention in the war.

In mid-December, Erle Cocke, Jr., Miles Kennedy, Granville Ridley, and Leonce Legendre met with defense department personnel who were drafting a Department of Defense manpower bill that, the Legionnaires were told, would be a combination of Universal Military Service (the draft portion of the U.M.T. bill for those nineteen to twenty-six) and training (for eighteen-year-olds).

The Legion, also, had been at work writing a bill. In late December, when Senator Richard Russell (D., GA), chairman of the Senate Armed Services Committee, agreed to introduce a training bill for the Legion, Erle Cocke, Jr., and Miles Kennedy immediately went to work to obtain the prestigious designation "S. 1," a public relations gambit aimed at emphasizing the importance of U.M.T. Anna Rosenberg, Truman's manpower expert at the Department of Defense, was "very much opposed to our introducing the Legion's legislation as S. 1," Miles Kennedy informed the others. Lyndon Johnson was also opposed, Kennedy said, but he was not as vocal as the others. Kennedy assumed that the senator from Texas would side with the Department of Defense on matters of difference between that bill and the Legion's bill. When it was found that the Department of Defense bill would not be ready until after the convening of the Senate on January 3, the S. 1 designation seemed assured for the Legion's bill. Miles Kennedy planned to sit in Senator Russell's office all day if necessary on that date to see that it did happen.

In addition to its legislative efforts, the Legion continued to publicize U.M.T. Those who had conferred with higher educational institutions about U.M.T. had complained of "fuzzy thinking" among educators about the subject. It was, therefore, assumed that educators generally did not understand that there was, first, an immediate emergency and, second, a need for a long-range program for a reservoir of trained manpower. A Legion-sponsored conference drew 900 persons (including representatives of 400 colleges) to a discussion of military preparedness or, as was the present object lesson, the lack of it.

At the conference, proponents of U.M.T. posed many leading statements: "Korea is Bataan and Guadalcanal all over again." "We have allowed our foreign policy to outrun our ability to enforce it." "The first American troops to Korea went, among other purposes, to buy time for yet another American buildup." "Who in the past has defended this country during times of catastrophe? It has been the citizen-soldier, from Main Street, U.S.A. Professional soldiers never have been more than a minute part of our defensive forces in any war." "U.M.T. is a peacetime program of survival training." "Do we want old-world conscription, or democratic U.M.T.? U.M.T. is not conscription, it is a program of instruction under civilian control and administered by a civilian commission."

At this meeting and elsewhere, Legionnaires were also careful to differentiate between U.M.T. and U.M.S. At the N.E.C. meeting in November, committeemen branded U.M.S. in peacetime to be "conscription," just as Legionnaires had done since 1919, calling the draft compulsory peacetime military service.

On January 8, 1951, the opening day of the second session of the 82d Congress, the National Security Training Act of 1951, S. 1, was introduced by Senator Russell. While the Legion had established precedence over the Department of Defense for introducing a U.M.T. bill, there was much discussion yet to come with the Department of Defense in the hope that a composite bill could be drafted for consideration by the Senate.

At a meeting in Mrs. Rosenberg's office on February 5, Granville Ridley asked that four provisions be included in the Department of Defense bill still in the drafting stage. Together these four points helped spell out the Legion's concept of U.M.T.

First, upon the elimination of compulsory service (the "draft" part of the bill) U.M.T. would be made mandatory. Second, the real power to supervise and control the program would rest with a civilian commission. Third, a National Security Training Corps would be created into which youth would be inducted instead of directly into the armed forces (as in the Department of Defense bill). Finally, the civilian commission would receive its funding directly from the Treasury Department instead of having it channeled through the Department of Defense.

The Department of Defense agreed to these provisions. At the end of the meeting, Ridley asked the drafting committee of the Department of Defense to "effectuate our agreement instead of drafting it all out the window." He was assured, he reported, by Mrs. Rosenberg that his wishes would be honored.

Some believed at the time that were it not for the Korean War, U.M.T. might not have been given the attention it was in the early 1950s. Granville Ridley said that U.M.T. could not be passed in peacetime. "Unfortunately, the threat of war is essential to awaken the people to the necessity of such legislation."

Yet the war also caused the subject of U.M.T. to be fractured by considerations of "now" and "later," since it was generally conceded that present needs usually superseded long-range planning.

There was, also, tradition to consider, as reiterated by Gen. J. Lawton Collins, army chief of staff, testifying before the House Armed Services Committee on February 28. General Collins was careful to describe his testimony as being supportive of "the bill proposed by the Department of Defense" for universal military service and training. "The traditional military policy of this country," he stated, "has always been to maintain an active army of sufficient size to withstand only the initial shock of war until we could mobilize our National Guard and Reserve Corps and as much of the rest of our resources as were required. That should continue to be the policy." But, the general added, "If we are to continue our traditional military policy of placing a large measure of dependence for preparedness for defense upon our National Guard and our Organized Reserve Corps, then we must make it possible for them to achieve the degree of preparedness that modern war requires. I am convinced that they cannot do this without some sound system of universal military service and training."

Time was a prime factor, the general said, echoing Lewis Gough's point at an earlier hearing. In World War I and World War II, while the Allies bore the brunt of the fight, the United States had some time to bring military units to full strength before placing them in action (insufficiently trained as they were all too often). Not so in Korea.

General Collins described the initial U.S. operations in Korea as one grand display of unpreparedness. The Regular forces had not been kept at full authorized strength. Just before June 1950, "the Regular Army was 38,000 men under the strength of 630,000 originally authorized by Congress for the fiscal year 1951. We had been struggling for months trying to reach and maintain that strength through volunteer recruiting alone, since we had promised Congress that we would not use the Selective Service Act except as necessary to fill that gap between authorized strength and the number of men we could obtain through recruiting alone. But despite the fact that we were required by law to accept enlistments for such short terms as one year—a terribly costly and inefficient way of doing business—we were unable to get sufficient volunteers, and our strength had dropped gradually to 592,000."

Using the army's Table of Organization system for determining the strength of army units based on combat experience, MacArthur's Eighth Army was short 32,000 men. The American 24th and 25th infantry divisions and the 1st Cavalry Division of MacArthur's Eighth Army (occupational troops in Japan) were rushed into Korea with two-battalion regiments rather than the authorized three, and with all units much under strength.

Efforts to strengthen the Eighth Army included pulling trained men, those immediately available, from under-strength Regular units. "We pulled nine battalions of infantry, armor, and artillery from these units, and selected individuals from every organization in the army to obtain trained cadres for six additional battalions. The 2nd Infantry Division was brought up to strength by stripping our remaining units still further and was then dispatched to Korea. The 3rd Infantry Division was similarly strengthened, though we simply could not get it to full strength before it had to sail. We had to take a regiment from Puerto Rico for the third regiment in this division. The 11th Airborne Division was decimated in order to provide General

MacArthur a full-strength Airborne Regimental Combat Team, the 187th Airborne Infantry."

What remained of the Regular Army in the United States was but one division, the 82d Airborne. And this with the Eighth Army still short of units to recompose its original strength, not to mention the missing support units for rounding out an army for field operations. When "the overall strength of the army fell, two corps headquarters in Japan were eliminated," which included "essential signal and engineer troops." These, and other support units—antiaircraft, field artillery battalions, ordnance, transportation corps, and quartermaster units—had to be brought from the United States. At this point, National Guard and Organized Reserve Corps company-sized units were ordered into active service, many of which were themselves as much as fifty to seventy-five percent under strength. But these units, smaller than required, had to be supplemented by Selective Service and another toss of the net into the Reserve and the Guard. The Reserve, particularly those men not in units, provided another 128,000 by the end of November 1950, proving "one of the primary purposes of the Organized Reserve Corp . . . in times of emergency." These individuals reported for active duty in units in Korea, in units destined for Korea, and as trainers for new recruits.

In this hurried process, there was not time to give proper consideration to variations in individual circumstances regarding numbers of dependents or length or nature of service among the reservists. For example, by using the standard "Military Occupational Specialties" system for calling up reservists (the method MacArthur used "properly"), a World War II vet with the desired military occupational classification was called up, though he may have acquired a family since his last service; but another reservist, living across the street and who had never been overseas and had no children, was not called if his "Military Occupational Specialty" was not required. In fact, the bulk of reservists called up initially were veterans, many married and fathers. They, however, represented the necessary pool of trained men so essential, especially in the initial phases of war. Had a U.M.S. and U.M.T. program been in operation, General Collins said, this first call-up could have been manned largely from "trained young men who had not already served their country in action and who had not yet acquired large numbers of dependents."

It was also necessary, General Collins said, to "start the activation of two new Regular Army divisions and six National Guard divisions and three Regimental Combat Teams into active military service." Selective Service, out of operation since January 1949, had required two or three months to begin full operation. Fourteen weeks more were needed for the most rudimentary basic training for "selectees" (and some more time for unit training once such an entity was fully put together) before they were "reasonably competent to fill the ranks of a combat unit." Many from Selective Service first went to Guard units for training by "the fine cadres of officers and noncommissioned officers who had experience during the last war."

Remember, also, the general said in closing, that the army of today depended more on ever increasingly sophisticated weaponry and on the surge in air power. That, too, must be considered when a reservoir of trained citizen-soldiers was contemplated.

In early March, a series of actions was taken on the Legion's U.M.T. bill, S. 1. At 11:20 P.M. on March 8, Miles Kennedy reported to National Adjutant Hank Dudley in Indianapolis by wire, "Of all the tough luck that could happen to us, it has happened. Senator [Virgil] Chapman [D., KY] who was going to lead the fight against the Johnson [of Colorado] Amendment [the Johnson-Bricker Amendment] on the floor this afternoon, was critically injured in an automobile accident this morning. We lose that vote which brings the calculations down to 'even steven' and anything can happen." Before his teletype message was sent, Kennedy added that he had just been informed that Senator Chapman had died, and that, upon hearing the news, the Senate had adjourned immediately.

At 2:25 P.M. on March 9, Clarence H. "Cap" Olson, assistant director of the Legislative Division, informed Dudley that the Johnson-Bricker Amendment, which had been put together by Edwin C. Johnson (D., CO) and John W. Bricker (R., OH) to segregate U.M.T. from the Draft Bill—that is, to split S. 1 into two parts and simply extend the draft but defer all action on U.M.T.—was defeated 68 to 20. "This is much better than we expected and seems to be the last big hurdle in the Senate."

At 4:18 P.M., Olson reported that the "[Robert A.] Taft [R., OH] Amendment to limit S. 1 to four years [was] voted down by a score of 58 to 30. Little is left in the Senate now but the shouting." The "shout" was a vote of 79 for, 5 against, and 11 not voting. Of the fifty-six senators who were veterans, only four voted against the bill.

S.1, the Universal Training and Service Act, had passed the Senate, calling for U.M.T. on a "standby basis" with a lowered draft age (to eighteen) and the period of service increased from twenty-one to twenty-four months. It was the first time in thirty-two years of trying that the Legion had convinced either house of Congress to approve U.M.T.

From the Senate, the action moved to the House in mid-March, where, on March 12, the House Armed Services Committee had voted 17 to 14 to keep U.M.T. under consideration. "It is a case of now or never!" stated the March 13 "special issue" of the Legion's *Legislative Bulletin,* noting the close vote in the House committee. "Don't let the wide margin in the Senate give false confidence," the bulletin warned. "There was a great deal of maneuvering there and several amendments intended to kill off U.M.T. were voted down. The same will be tried in the House, so wire your representative."

The *Bulletin* charged politics plain and simple: "The opposition is trying to befog the issue by throwing in all sorts of controversial and confusing words." Of the plethora of amendments offered, "few, if any, have anything to do with U.M.T. They want to attach a ceiling on military manpower to U.M.T. They want to attach restrictions on troops to General Eisenhower's North Atlantic army to U.M.T. A lot of this can be definitely charged to politics and politicians. We are not crying 'Wolf' just to be writing!"

Legionnaires across the nation stumped for the cause. Past National Commander George Craig and others from Indiana let their eleven congressmen and senators know their wishes. Craig, who had joined the U.M.T. campaign workers in Washington who met daily at this point, sent an urgent message to the Indiana Department officers on March 6 to explain the situation. "It is tough here and pretty sticky. If you knew what a hell of a time we are having you would drop everything else and get this job done."

Other Legion communiqués sought to make the point. The two-inch-high block letters in the Legion Public Relations Division's *News Service Bulletin* number 201 shouted "THIS IS *IT!* U.M.T. Faces Crisis In House! Do YOUR Part NOW! Legion Chief's Plea." Legion staffers who composed the *News Service Bulletin* requested a new photo of National Commander Cocke. Before, in Legion publications, the young national commander had been shown with a characteristic smile. Now those working on *Bulletin* layout wanted a portrait showing him "in serious fighting mood."

Meanwhile, the "Chief," in the midst of his world tour through the Philippines, Korea, and, eventually, Europe, cabled National Headquarters. "We have a man on third base, let's bring him home." The vivid story of Cocke's survival during World War II was again featured in the *Bulletin* with special emphasis on how military training had helped save his life after a Nazi execution attempt. "My Military Training Taught Me To Survive," the headline stated. Cocke was asked, also, to send a "radiogram," dateline Korea, to House majority and minority leaders stating that U.M.T. would have prevented untold casualties among the soldiers already killed as the war raged there.

Soon Cocke was asked to return stateside and lead the campaign for U.M.T. in the House. He returned on April 11, whereupon a remark he made at a New York airport press conference about the conduct of the war set off a tiff with Truman. In response to a reporter's question about the effectiveness of MacArthur's military strategy, Cocke remarked, "He's fighting with one hand tied behind his back," referring to the "limited war" imposed on U.N. forces, which kept them close to the 38th Parallel.

Just hours earlier, Truman had relieved MacArthur of his Far Eastern command. Given the stature of the two principal players in this drama and occurring amid a time of national emergency, the Truman-MacArthur confrontation was bold headline copy by anyone's reckoning.

To Truman's mind, it was not a time to take MacArthur's side, as Cocke had seemed to have done even as the crescendo of criticism was about to build over the general's "firing." Before Cocke could get to the White House for his scheduled debriefing by Truman, he was informed by Presidential Press Secretary Steven Early that his appointment at the White House had been cancelled. Newspaper headlines chimed, "Truman Rebuffs Legion Chief, Cancels Interview" and "Truman Snubs Legion Chief on Mac Issue."

There was, also, confusion at this point about how U.M.T. was doing in Congress. With the U.S. armed forces now numbering three million, would a program such as U.M.T.—a long-view measure—receive serious consideration? Was S. 1 getting attention only because of the provision to extend the draft to July 1, 1955?

Legion spokesmen feared losing the apparent momentum of the last few days. On April 10, Ed McGinnis, while in Washington, informed the Indianapolis Headquarters, "for the love of Mike please get any idea of obituaries or black borders out of your mind. Apparently our people believe the headlines and radio reports which were completely misleading to the effect that U.M.T. is dead. It is not dead!"

As in Edgar Allan Poe's "The Raven," events "followed fast and followed faster." To National staff members in Washington, that was how it seemed, at times even down to the poem's doleful mood. On April 12, Jim Murphy answered Jack Cejnar's request for a lead story on U.M.T. ("that might hold up for a week or so") with the explanation that it was impossible "in light of the last twelve hours, to furnish a story that would stand up tomorrow, let alone next week."

The vote came on April 13. The House U.M.T. bill passed 372 to 44, whereupon conference committee reconciliation began, continuing through May.

Then, on June 7, "Cap" Olson wired the news that the House had "just adopted the conference report on S. 1 by a vote of 339 to 41. The bill will now go to the president for signature." On June 19, at a ceremony that included a beaming National Commander Cocke, President Truman signed Public Law 51, the combined draft and U.M.T. measure.

The nation's first-ever "Universal Military Training and Service Act" was on the books. Implementation, however, was another matter. "We've won an important skirmish, but the big battle is yet to come," Cocke said.

By July 10, the first Korean truce negotiations began. Though an extremely fortunate event for the immediate conflict, talk of truce may have caused a lessening of interest in long-range preparedness by such means as U.M.T. George Kelly recommended to Jack Little that Legion publicity about the signing of Public Law 51 should not be treated as the culmination of the often mentioned thirty-plus-year fight for U.M.T. Such references would tend to give the impression that all the Legion wished regarding U.M.T. had been accomplished, he warned.

(Miles Kennedy spoke for many when he discussed what he felt was a major blow to U.M.T. publicity. In mid-May, Kennedy wrote, "It looks as though General MacArthur in his testimony [before Congress in early May] has killed U.M.T." When pointedly asked about the value of U.M.T., the general had expressed little enthusiasm. Later, in a January 1952 article in *The American Legion Magazine,* MacArthur held forth on the historical and present value of the nation's tradition of "citizen-soldiers." But while the article was a matter of record, the general's remarks to Congress were more a matter of public memory.)

After the signing of Public Law 51, the president, answering to a provision of the law, appointed members to the National Security Training Commission (N.S.T.C.). He chose as chairman former senator James W. Wadsworth, a well-known and long-standing advocate of military preparedness. Wadsworth had been cosponsor of the Burke-Wadsworth Bill in 1940, which became the Selective Training and Service Act. Years earlier, he had been influential in the development of the National Defense Act of 1916 from which had come the National Guard.

Other commission members brought with them impressive credentials and interests. Dr. Karl T. Compton, scientist, engineer, and former president of M.I.T., had been chairman of the earlier Advisory Commission on Universal Training in 1947. William L. Clayton had been assistant secretary of state for economic affairs (1944–46) and under secretary in the same area (1946–47), and as such worked closely with the designers of the Marshall Plan. Earlier, he had been assistant secretary of commerce (1942–44). Admiral Thomas C. Kinkaid had commanded the Seventh Fleet during World War II. Lt. Gen. Raymond S. McLain, comptroller of the army, had been the only National Guard officer to command a corps (the XIX) in World War II. The executive director of the commission was Townsend Hoopes, a former secretary of the Armed Forces Policy Council and an assistant to Secretary of Defense James Forrestal.

The primary task of the commission was to compile for Congress by October 29 a report about the implementation of U.M.T. On July 31, National Commander Cocke met with this U.M.T. commission at its office in the Pentagon to begin discussions on the Legion's suggestions for that eventuality. As Cocke had said, there was more to do to realize fully a Legion goal. At the Legion National Convention in Miami in mid-October 1951, the Legion's ultimate governing body resolved, "Whereas, the American Legion has carried the torch for U.M.T. over the past thirty-two years, the organization should redouble efforts for securing legislation to make U.M.T. a reality." (The published convention proceedings was dedicated "to our heroic dead in Korea. . . .")

The N.S.T.C. worked for four months devising a program for U.M.T. When it appeared in late October, the N.S.T.C.'s report, "Universal Military Training, Foundation of Enduring National Strength," contained legislative recommendations that included a broad outline for a military training program; measures for the trainees' health, safety, welfare, and morale; a code of conduct; disability and death benefits; measures to implement the commission's policies and standards; and a compilation of trainees' obligations, duties, liabilities, and other responsibilities.

While Public Law 51 called for the establishment of the N.S.T.C., additional congressional action was needed to implement the actual training program that the N.S.T.C. was to design and then present to Congress as a bill.

The N.S.T.C. continued to permit the Legion to sit in on sessions for drafting legislation and listened to the principles that the Legion had long envisioned. But since the evolving bill was not available for the 1951 National Convention to consider, new National Commander Donald R. Wilson appointed an executive group to study the work of the N.S.T.C. For this job, Granville Ridley was joined by Past National Commanders Perry Brown, Warren Atherton, and Paul Griffith and legislative staffer Miles Kennedy, along with Martin Buckner, George Kelley, and Bruce Henderson.

In mid-December, Ridley and the others set out a plan for National Commander Don Wilson's consideration, which called for the Legion to draft its own U.M.T. bill. Later that month, Miles Kennedy drafted the Legion's bill, and Don Wilson intensified the Legion's insistence on civilian control of U.M.T.

Wilson emphasized the inspection corps in his appearance before the House Armed Services Committee on January 28, and the Senate Armed Services Committee on February 14. Such a group, he said, must be "of high caliber and thoroughly trained," Wadsworth's own words almost exactly.

In early January, 1952, the Legion's U.M.T. committee and the N.S.T.C. agreed that each would present its own bills in order to enter into public debate all the considerations each group felt strongly about but upon which there was not complete agreement. The Legion differed from the N.S.T.C. on four items, three of which, according to the Legion, the N.S.T.C. had given over to the Department of Defense. The Legion insisted that the bill (1) leave the National Security Training Corps strictly a civilian training corps, (2) retain control by the commission of budget estimates, (3) give the N.S.T.C. access to Department of Defense records for estimating costs and other purposes, and (4) allow U.M.T. graduates to discharge their Reserve obligations sooner than the eight years stated in the N.S.T.C. bill.

Actually, the Legion produced two bills, introduced on January 8 as H.R. 5903 by Representative James Van Zandt of Pennsylvania on the Republican side of the aisle, and on January 15 by Democrat Overton Brooks of Louisiana as H.R. 6032. The N.S.T.C.'s bill, H.R. 5904, was reported out February 7 by a vote of 27 to 7. In the Senate, Richard B. Russell introduced S. 2441 for the Legion on January 16, 1952. He was joined by Senators Byrd, Bridges, Moss, Knowland, Cain, Johnson, Hunt, Stennis, and Kefauver.

The two-bill tactic in the House was an attempt by the Legion to retain its political evenhandedness while acknowledging the very political tradition of involving both major parties. Two bills were necessary because of a House rule preventing more than one name on a bill. In the Senate, however, as many names as desired could go on the bill.

Past National Commander Warren Atherton met informally with James Wadsworth on January 25. Wadsworth, who expressed himself freely, Atherton said, was "against the voluntary plan of the Armed Services." Earlier, Congressman Vinson had sent up trial balloons for a volunteer system that were summarily shot down by his own House Armed Services Committee.

Wadsworth wanted an immediate pilot program for U.M.T. He also called for a "Corps of Inspectors . . . the heart of civilian control" whereby U.M.T. could be guided and supervised. Though he did not want them to be included in Civil Service, he assumed that would be the case.

While identical in many respects to the proposal of the president's N.S.T.C., the Legion-backed bill differed sharply in insisting that the budgetary and administrative authority be lodged with the civilian-controlled N.S.T.C. The N.S.T.C. Bill (S.1 5904) called for the secretary of defense merely to consult with the commission on annual budget estimates for the National Security Training Corps. Under the Legion bill, the defense chief would be required to submit such estimates to the commission for approval. In addition, the commission would determine and submit directly to the president its own cost estimates for its administration. "Whoever controls the appropriation for the Corps will control the Corps," the Legion contended. Such was "the very cornerstone" for guaranteeing the power and effectiveness of the N.S.T.C.

Also, the new Legion bill called for those graduates of the initial six months of training who volunteered for and completed three years of service in the National Guard or Active Reserve to be relieved of further obligation for Reserve duty. Public Law 51, which had been enacted the previous year, required U.M.T. grads to put in seven and a half years in any branch of the Reserve.

As National Commander Wilson explained, the Legion's U.M.T. program gave the N.S.T.C. power to gain three objectives vital to any U.M.T. program: (1) control of the cost; (2) control of the proportion of administrative personnel and trainers to trainees; and (3) the induction of U.M.T. graduates to enlist in the National Guard or Active Reserve units. So that the N.S.T.C. could be economical, other advantages included throwing away the tables of organization followed by the professional services; preventing U.M.T. from being used as an excuse for creating more high-ranking officers; and insuring that U.M.T. would serve to build up and maintain the strength of National Guard and Active Reserve units.

By early February, Miles Kennedy considered the Department of Defense bill, H.R. 5904, to have been amended to meet Legion requirements and to be, therefore, worthy of Legion support, a move calculated, also, to show Legion willingness to support the bill even though it had originated at the D.O.D.

Kennedy also complained that "our opponents are putting out false information over the air, in the press, and by word of mouth to the effect that the Legion has given up on U.M.T., and that U.M.T. does not have a ghost of a chance—the same line of bunk and false propaganda that was handed out last spring at the time U.M.T. was under debate."

It seemed, also, that the tide of opinion, significantly that expressed by members of Congress, was going against U.M.T. "Every senator and congressman we talk to has the same complaint: they are being swamped with opposition mail and most of them have not received one single letter in support of U.M.T. . . ." Kennedy urged a promotional blitz of pro-U.M.T. messages from Legionnaires and others ("especially those who have young sons"). The American Legion Auxiliary had come through as usual, handily outdistancing Legionnaires in letter writing.

When action on the Legion's bill, H.R. 5904, heated up, Miles Kennedy teletyped Indianapolis on February 26 with the news that "things are getting worse by the minute." Later that day, Kennedy again reported, saying, "Washington newspapers give U.M.T. 50/50 chance at best. It is hard to believe that there has been such a tremendous about-face by so many members of Congress but the cold hard facts are there."

National Commander Wilson, noting that the vote would likely be a voice vote that would evaporate within the sanctity of the congressional chamber, with only the totals being reported to the public, threatened at a February 28 dinner for congressmen that he would publicize their votes on U.M.T. Wilson's action brought several heated complaints of Legion "bullying."

On March 4, an opening move to kill the entire bill was defeated. A vote of 196 to 176 showed the close margin. The move pitted a two-year representative, young William H. Bates (R., MA), a WW II veteran who was popular with younger members of Congress, against House Speaker Sam Rayburn, who had been in Congress thirty-seven years before Bates had arrived. When Bates moved to strike out the bill's enacting clause, an act by which he announced, also, his intentions of following up with a motion to send the measure back to the House Armed Services Committee "for study, which is so desperately needed," Rayburn took the floor "as a very old friend" and immediately drew a standing ovation. Pleading for an orderly manner of procedure, Rayburn asked, "Recommit this bill for further study? How many years of study have we had on this subject? Do we not have the moral fortitude and the courage to meet this issue? If we are not ready today, when will we be ready?" The House, therefore, rejected this first veiled attempt to kill the bill.

Committee Chairman Vinson attempted a compromise by proposing a ban on the start of inductions under U.M.T. while the draft was in effect. Vinson's measure, also carrying a termination date of July 1, 1958, for U.M.T. (U.M.T. backers said it must be permanent to be effective), was accepted on a standing vote of 126 to 19. This was followed by an amendment by James C. Davis (D., GA) to prevent the draft from being reinstituted after U.M.T. started, a measure approved 104 to 61.

In midafternoon, Kennedy teletyped a message to Indianapolis that for the first time used the term "recommit" to indicate a possibility of the bill's fate.

"Is that right: 'Recommit'?" Indianapolis asked.

"Recommit," Kennedy confirmed.

According to Kansas Congressman Edward H. Rees, responding to constituent F. E. Kummer, adjutant of Hillsboro Post Number 366, who had inquired about what had happened on the floor, the fate of the bill was propelled by a substitute amendment offered by Indiana Republican Congressman Charles B. Brownson to put U.M.T. in the high schools. With several congressmen away from the debate at that point, the Brownson Amendment was temporarily approved but was defeated in a roll call. When some of the absentees returned, the House went into plenary session, whereupon a ruling from the chair wiped out all the preceding amendments. A vote on the original bill, without any amendments, was thereby forced.

Moments later came the bad news. H.R. 5904, indeed, had been recommitted by a vote of 236 to 162 to the House Armed Services Committee, ostensibly for further study. Nine of the twelve members of the committee voted to return it. For all practical purposes, however, it was killed. (S. 2441, though voted out of committee, was never considered by the Senate.) This late in the session, there was little chance of the House bill appearing again. This bit of legislative legerdemain would go down in Legion annals as little more than political expediency. Parliamentary gamesmanship or not, the effect and the motivation angered the Legion.

Virginia Congressman Porter Hardy, Jr., acknowledged to George E. Heller, national field representative of the American Legion, that there was "confusion" on the floor of the House over the maneuverings on H.R. 5904. Congressman Hardy favored the bill but insisted that Congress retain the power to repeal it, without presidential veto, if the program didn't work. However, he added that while teaching citizenship to U.M.T. trainees was a good idea, "if under the guise of teaching citizenship there are classes in public housing and public power and civil rights, I believe Congress should have the power to terminate the program quickly."

The next day, Robert Pitkin in *The American Legion Magazine* office in New York checked his copy for a story with Martin Buckner, director of the National Security Division: "On Tuesday, March 4, the House of Representatives buried the enactment of U.M.T. again, sending it back to committee without facing the issue, as National Commander Wilson had warned. When the parliamentary maneuvering was over, election year do-nothingness had had its way on a grave matter of national safety, and most voters were none the wiser as to where their representatives stood. The most openly destructive and evasive trick was a counterproposal to put U.M.T. into high schools, an implausible mixture of national defense with state and local institutions. After suggesting several amendments, opponents sent the bill back to committee as an unwise measure. There was no roll call, so there was no official record of these ringleaders of legislative evasiveness." Buckner attested to the accuracy of the news brief and did not object to the string of acerbic adjectives.

Don Wilson drew more fire with his comment at a speaking engagement that there was probably "rejoicing in Moscow" over what the House had done to the U.M.T. bill.

Thus, though briefly advanced further than ever before, U.M.T. was rendered all but academic. In criticizing the Legion's efforts, Martin Buckner complained to Lewis Gough that the Legion too often overlooked the time lag in motivating and educating its own membership to support issues such as U.M.T. The Legion's "last-minute calls for congressional letters have been ineffective, many times to the extent of creating an attitude of futility at the department level." Hence, "we have lost the initiative in the U.M.T. campaign." Timing, Buckner said, was extremely important when legislation was pending in Congress.

N.S.T.C. member Gen. Ray McLain took the Legion to task for not having done more to get U.M.T. passed. McLain told James R. Wilson of the National Security Division, "This is the critical year for U.M.T.

If we cannot put it through at this time there is no use monkeying with it anymore.

"Personally," McLain continued, "I believe U.M.T. spells the answer to the question as to whether or not we are going to have this caste system by legislation [Selective Service] and reserve acts which enchain a part of our young men to military responsibilities for eight years and let the rest of them go. Unless this is corrected, we are certain to have a morale situation that will shake this nation and shake it to its very foundation."

The N.S.T.C., for its part, immediately went to work on a new U.M.T. plan. Representative Carl Vinson urged the House to defeat a proposed cut of N.S.T.C. operating funds. Instead, all funds for the commission were soon cut (though a subsequent appropriation of $37,500 was granted to the commission). Proffered such a pittance, the N.S.T.C. scaled down its operation drastically.

The Legion, too, reevaluated its U.M.T. strategy. Some looked to the coming presidential elections for hope. Dwight D. Eisenhower had opened his presidential campaign as a Republican candidate recently in Abilene, Kansas, on June 2, 1952; he was nominated by the G.O.P. in mid-July 1952. Perhaps the Legion's long struggle to have U.M.T. adopted as a basic method of military preparedness would receive some appreciable support from the former general of the U.S. Army who had often complained of unpreparedness and of inequities in the draft. When campaigning for the presidency, Eisenhower had stated that U.M.T. and Selective Service could not work concurrently.

With the shadow of Korea thrown across the daily news copy, U.M.T. proponents still asked if the nation was now ready for the kind of preparedness program that Past National Commander Perry Brown, "Mr. U.M.T.," had sorely needed in his World War I foxhole and for which he had campaigned since doffing his doughboy uniform.

At least there was now a public law in hand, though that measure apparently entailed little but lip service to a universal training program. Odds takers favored the draft. It was at least a known quantity in spite of all its inconsistencies. U.M.T. stalwarts continued to forge ahead, saying that the very newness and largeness of their concept were its main selling points.

III

"Come out swinging!"

ROBERT MCCURDY, "Mr. Rehabilitation" and former boxer,
at the 26th National Rehab Conference

Training was one thing; the casualties of war was quite another. While newspaper headlines told of the fighting in Korea and formerly obscure Korean place names became household words in America, the Legion's advocacy for veterans' benefits continued, with an immediacy borne out by the headlines.

Two weeks after the U.N. Security Council formulated on June 25 and 27, 1950, its famous resolutions to send U.N. forces to Asia to repel the invasion by Communist North Korea into South Korea, National Commander Craig wrote to key congressmen asking them to consider amendatory legislation to provide equal entitlement to benefits for members of the U.S. armed forces fighting in Korea.

On July 23, 1950, department commanders and others at National Headquarters resolved to "petition Congress to enact such legislation as may be required to extend by law to the members of the armed forces now in the field, or who may hereafter be ordered into the services under the present emergent circumstances, the status of veterans for the purpose of assuring them and their dependents the [disability, death] benefits now applicable to veterans of the great wars."

Several other bills related to veterans' affairs had been tossed into the congressional hopper following the outbreak of the conflict in Korea. As the bills seemed to multiply, top-ranking Legionnaires doubted that a viable rehabilitation program could arise from such a scattergun approach. They feared that an uncoordinated effort would eventually produce a bill and ultimately a law that would fail to meet the needs of these future veterans.

By mid-August 1950, the Legion's National Legislative and National Rehabilitation Commissions were engaged in preparing an omnibus bill to meet the need that had been already expressed.

On September 13, late though it was in the congressional session, the Legion's bill H.R. 9644 was introduced. Two weeks later, the N.E.C., in preconvention session at Los Angeles in early October, reaffirmed the policy set forth in H.R. 9644. Within days the National Convention's Resolution 342 added its confirmation of the effort.

One of the major differences between the Legion's bill and those being introduced by individual congressmen was the determination of just who would benefit most from the proposed legislation: those in overseas service alone, or, as the Legion intended, those in either foreign or stateside service.

In the time remaining in the congressional session, no hearings were held on the bill. There was one particularly notable measure that was enacted, however: Public Law 895 (December 28, 1950), which extended eligibility for membership in the American Legion to Korean war veterans. In less than a decade, the Legion had opened its ranks to veterans of two more wars.

H.R. 9644 succumbed to the congressional timetable; when the 81st Congress adjourned, the bill was dropped. But another effort had already begun following the Los Angeles Convention. With Convention

Resolution 342 in hand, the National Rehabilitation Commission prepared a new bill that was introduced on January 9, 1951, as H.R. 1217. A similar bill, S. 714, was introduced on January 29. Hearings, however, were hard to come by. Legion representatives were not invited to appear for hearings on H.R. 1217 until mid-April. The Senate held no hearings on the bill languishing there.

If action lagged on Capitol Hill, events elsewhere, specifically at the registration desks of several V.A. hospitals, were soon to put a spotlight on an embarrassing slight directed at veterans returning from Korea. For during the last months of 1950 and the first months of 1951, many instances came to light in which Korean War veterans were refused hospital treatment at many V.A. facilities for ailments that the veterans said were service-related but which had not yet been adjudicated as such by the V.A. A *casus conscientae* was all that was needed for news of the general situation to be catapulted to front-page notoriety.

On May 9, 1951, the components of such an explosive story came together. A twenty-one-year-old Korean combat veteran attempted to enter a Tucson V.A. hospital for treatment. He was denied admission, and local Legionnaires took up the cause. The incident at the V.A. facility was widely reported in newspapers and radio broadcasts. The plight of this veteran was suddenly cast as an all too poignant example of many similar situations.

The director of the V.A. hospital in Tucson, in refusing treatment to the young veteran, cited a congressional law that categorized the hapless applicant as a peacetime soldier (there being as yet no formal declaration of war) and, therefore, ineligible for admission. As the director explained, "Under the present setup, no returned veteran from Korea is eligible for hospital benefits unless he had been discharged from the service because of a duty disability." Himself painfully aware of the apparent contradiction, the director pointed to the tragically inadequate catchphrase "police action" in Korea. "If it isn't war, I'd like to know what the hell it is!"

The next morning, May 10, National Commander Erle Cocke sent telegrams to key members of Congress urging action on Legion bills H.R. 1217 and S. 714.

Cocke also protested to Carl Gray at the V.A. He urged the administrator to look again at the authority he had under Regulation 6035 to care for the sick and disabled veterans of Korea. "I have just returned from that area and I can attest to the grueling ordeal these youngsters are going through. They are certainly conducting a fighting and shooting war."

On Thursday, the president sent a letter to the Senate soon after it convened, suggesting that Korean veterans be provided the benefits of medical and hospital care, compensation, and pensions similar to those received by World War II veterans.

Congress showed admirable alacrity; by joint resolutions, just such a measure was rushed through both houses. Public Law 28 was signed by the president on May 11. Honorably discharged veterans of the fighting in Korea were now entitled to hospitalization, medical care, domiciliary care, and burial benefits.

"The Congress has finally gotten around to recognizing the 'police action' in Korea as a full-fledged war," just as the Legion had called it the previous July, the American Legion News Service reported. "It took the full force of public opinion to rouse the Congress to action," the report continued, referring to the Tucson incident and the subsequent burst of congressional energy from which emerged Public Law 28.

With this law in place, the Legion looked to other immediate needs, such as the shortage of hospital beds and the need for more doctors in V.A. hospitals. In N.E.C. meetings of the period, methods were discussed for further augmenting medical education. Earlier, the successful "affiliation" of V.A. hospitals with leading medical colleges had established a mutually beneficial program of education and expert care.

There was a long-range objective, also. A month after the president signed Public Law 28, the Legion, appreciating the momentum created by its passage, urged the extension of the G.I. Bill of Rights to all honorably discharged veterans of the Korean War. A special appeal was made on June 22, 1951, the seventh anniversary of the signing of the original G.I. Bill by President Roosevelt. Since the signing of that landmark measure, ten million World War II veterans had benefited by the act's provisions for education, training, and loans. The social and economic impact of the original G.I. Bill made a current edition of it popular, practical, and expected, the Legion said.

On July 16, the president signed Public Law 550, already dubbed the Korean War G.I. Bill of Rights. Five basic benefit areas were included: education or training; guaranteed or insured loans for homes, farms, and businesses; unemployment compensation; mustering-out pay; and employment help.

To the Legion's Public Relations staff, the timing was, at least, fortuitous. The next day was the Legion's press conference about the upcoming National Convention in New York, a perfect time to announce what the late-edition newspapers of the previous day had first revealed: The Korean War G.I. Bill of Rights was a reality.

Even as the Korean War G.I. Bill came into being, the threat of budget cuts at the V.A. continued.

National Commander Cocke had met with Gen. Carl R. Gray in the V.A. administrator's office on December 1, 1950, to reacquaint Gray with the thinking of the Legion on current matters. Cocke inquired about the situation at the V.A. relating to incoming veterans of the fighting in Korea, especially now that the fighting seemed to be expanding. The general complained that the agency had lost 4,000 employees to the armed forces, including 250 doctors. He had protested to the war-manpower officials, telling them, "If I can't perform correct medicine, I'll close beds."

Gray also complained about Department of Defense, Selective Service, and other manpower officials who were delegating to local medical advisory councils the selection of doctors and reservists with any appreciable medical training to serve in Korea. More often than not, the local officials recommended that V.A. doctors be tapped since, they argued, the community did not need them so much as it needed the doctors in private practice.

T. O. Kraabel, who also attended the meeting, noted that Gray was of the opinion that he administered the agency at the behest of Congress and that veterans' programs and the planning of veterans' affairs should come from the initiative of the veterans' organizations and thus should be ordered by Congress. From that point on, his jurisdiction began. Cocke, however, urged Gray to extend his activity into planning. What, for example, Cocke asked, was the V.A. planning for the handling of the Legion's omnibus program for Korean War veterans? Gray replied that he was anticipating that eventuality and would be ready for it.

Ten days after the Legionnaires met with Gray, Dr. Leonard Rowntree, chief medical adviser to the Legion's Rehabilitation Commission, called the Washington office from Miami on December 11 with information he had just learned from Dr. Paul B. Magnuson, the V.A.'s chief medical director. Magnuson, while fishing in Florida, had received a radio message from his assistant back at V.A. Central Office who relayed the startling news that the Bureau of the Budget had ordered a 1,800 personnel cut in the V.A., to be followed soon by the release of another 4,000 employees. Dr. Magnuson, who had snubbed Legion Rehabilitation Conferences and whose barbed jibes at the Legion's rehabilitation work had caused many ruffled feathers and produced Legion resolutions calling for his dismissal, had now turned to Dr. Rowntree for help by requesting that the Legion vigorously protest this threat to veterans' medical services.

Dr. Rowntree suggested that Legion Department personnel quiz the directors of several V.A. hospitals for the truth about what the cuts would mean to service at those facilities. When T. O. Kraabel and Legion medical adviser Dr. H. D. Shapiro did so, they found that the situation was fully as threatening as Dr. Magnuson had indicated. The intrusion, according to the Legion, of the Bureau of the Budget into the matter of veterans' benefits was yet another issue raised in the current V.A. cutbacks controversy.

There was continued work also by those still seeking to see enactment of the many economizing measures recommended by the now defunct Hoover Commission.

Congress, in passing the General Appropriations Act of 1951, had given the Bureau of the Budget additional powers for controlling the allocation of funds to certain federal agencies from quarter to quarter. The act further stipulated that the bureau find a way to trim the national budget by $550 million. The bureau already had an operational section given entirely to V.A. matters; and of the $550 million sum, $5 million was to be taken from the V.A. But the bureau itself subtracted another $5 million, a cut that would affect the areas of claims, medical care, insurance, and contact. The Legion protested immediately that because of the existing backlog of applications for outpatient services, the cuts actually involved many more persons than those currently estimated.

By mid-March, several bills inspired by the Hoover Commission were introduced in the Senate. Staff members of the Legislative Division waited anxiously for the bills to be printed and distributed. For several months thereafter the tug-of-war continued between the V.A. and those who doled out appropriations. The Legion watched, and occasionally entered the fray to lobby for or against some matter of concern.

In March 1952, the Legion launched its "Operation Victory," a public relations campaign that, it was hoped, would encourage its members and others to renew their opposition to the barrage of legislation inspired by the Hoover Report. John Thomas Taylor was put in charge of this project, adding his flamboyant touch to promoting the idea that the "victory" to which the gambit referred was an essential goal, not as yet a reality. Taylor asked all Legionnaires and members of the Auxiliary and their friends to take an active part.

Taylor hit hard at the provisions of S. 1140 to create a new executive department to be known as the Department of Health, with a cabinet-rank secretary, into which it was proposed would then be consolidated the Public Health Service, the Department of Medicine and Surgery of the V.A. (and all V.A. hospitals and outpatient services for service-connected cases only), and all general hospitals of the army, navy, air force, and some civilian hospitals in the United States and the Canal Zone.

"Telegraph or write your senators immediately," Taylor advised. S. 1140 was "the kingpin of all the antiveteran legislation now before Congress!" "Remember," he was fond of saying, "no legislation is dead until the Congress closes its big brass doors and the sergeant at arms goes home with the key."

The war of words escalated. In early April, the talk of further cuts in the V.A. budget evoked more colorful prose from Legion publicists. News releases charged "stunning slashes . . . by hasty and penny-pinching concepts of economy" for "lopping" hundreds of millions of dollars in a single stroke from the V.A. budget. The "senseless cuts . . . would disastrously cripple V.A. service and would add a tremendous load upon American Legion workers . . . [and] . . . would cause much injustice to hospitalized veterans." A House measure was called the "Cruelest Stab . . . a merciless blow . . . disabled veterans will be ousted . . . employees to be fired. . . ."

"Stop the axe!" one communiqué exclaimed.

The mood to slash budgets elsewhere, too, was loose on the land, and more organizations emerged, following the pattern of the Citizens Committee. The Committee on Federal Tax Policy, for example, chaired by former Under Secretary of the Treasury Roswell Magill, produced a pamphlet in February explaining a view of the national tax structure and budget expenditures in which the federal budget could be trimmed by ten billion dollars. The Legion noted that out of that figure was one-half to one billion dollars that would come from programs of benefits and services for veterans.

Earlier, Senator Harry F. Byrd of Virginia had gathered similar-minded budget critics (the unofficial but influential "Byrd Committee") to review periodically the federal budget. The committee, it was learned, was of a similar opinion as the subsequently formed Committee on Federal Tax Policy.

Over and above these ad hoc citizens' action groups, there was, also, the Joint Committee on the Economic Report, which had official status, having been created by the Employment Act of 1946. Composed of fourteen members, seven each from the House and Senate, this group provided analyses of the president's annual economic report and, in general, advised the president and Congress on the country's economic condition.

The stature of the Joint Committee made its report a primary reference document for the final Appropriations Act for 1952. When the act appeared, it justified the Legion's anxiety, for it recommended larger reductions in appropriations for veterans' programs than any since the Economy Act of 1933.

All these deliberations over V.A. cutbacks, and in general over tax revenues and the spending of tax money, were due in large measure to the accelerated outlay of funds for conducting the war in Korea. As Senator Joseph C. O'Mahoney of Wyoming stated, there should be "increased taxation, rigid governmental economy, and a pay-as-we-go policy, to carry on the Korean War."

Though a few well-organized citizens' watch-dog groups were aligned against the Legion regarding economic matters impinging on veterans' programs, the most compelling action, of course, took place in Congress. There, in its ideological labyrinth, high-stakes political checkmating and contests of wills and clashes of personality animated the Hill. Legion staff members and volunteers often marveled at the way things turned out. From gambit to stalemate, what occurred in the Senate and the House was sometimes disappointing, often amazing, and occasionally encouraging.

In early June, Ed McGrail informed National Commander Cocke that a recent newsletter from the Citizens Committee to its adherents stated, "The measures to effect a Veterans Administration reorganization were virtually vetoed by Representative John E. Rankin (D., MI) last week." It was Rankin, the Citizens Committee observed, who could kill any bill he chose by refusing to give it a hearing in the Veterans Affairs Committee that he chaired.

Rankin had already informed the Citizens Committee in early May 1951 that it was his committee's policy to restrict testimony to that of officials of government agencies, members of Congress, and the four veterans' organizations chartered by acts of Congress. With the exception of some congressmen who might be called to testify, all the above were opposed to Hoover Commission–instigated changes in the V.A. Things were looking down for the Citizens Committee regarding veterans' affairs and looking brighter for the Legion.

The same Citizens Committee newsletter contained a dirgelike recitation of bills assumed lost to their cause: H.R. 3317 and 3677 (for creating an insurance corporation within the V.A.), H.R. 3686 and 3316 (for reorganization of the V.A.). All these had been referred to the House Veterans Affairs Committee, where Representative Rankin had effectively doused the last remaining spark from the tinder of economizing zeal related to veterans' affairs. Earlier, the practice of the Citizens Committee to get some of the less controversial bills passed and onto their scoreboard had been a successful tactic. Now these major bills were floundering.

The Citizens Committee communiqué, also, acknowledged another phenomenon: the first session of the 82d Congress, as of June 20, had passed fewer than half the bills of either session of the preceding Congress in the same span of time. (This was the Congress, however, that passed Public Law 51, the Universal Military Training and Service Act.)

To this seemingly insouciant legislative body, the Citizens Committee had submitted nineteen bills, fourteen of which were deferred, to be sent unceremoniously into political cold storage. Furthermore, the all-important nod of favor from the Bureau of the Budget had been withheld from an additional twelve of the measures that required judgments regarding appropriations. Finally, of the fifty-one plans submitted by the Citizens Committee to the president, not one, as of yet, had been forwarded to Congress for consideration.

In the meantime, the cutbacks already made in V.A. programs continued to cause concern to the Legion. One of the more disheartening aspects of the cutbacks was the effect on the V.A.'s contact offices, the initial point where a veteran personally could discuss his relationship with the V.A., his eligibility for benefits and entitlements, and his need for authentic V.A. information. Veterans of the Korean War, especially, would be hit hard by curtailment of this service. Two hundred of these offices were now being considered for closing.

News reports in the press about each legislative attempt to have Hoover Report thinking adopted into law included quotes from the many supporters. T. O. Kraabel found it "particularly alarming" when he heard veterans' benefits called "welfare programs." But he heard it more and more. He could but echo the long-standing sentiments of the Legion: "The cost of caring for the disabled veteran is as much a part of the cost of war as are the cash moneys paid for the ships and guns and tanks and planes." He and others were particularly fond of a line dropped into many of National Commander Don Wilson's speeches: "May I remind you that you are dealing with human suffering and misery and not just dollars."

Critics of the intervention of the Bureau of the Budget into VA-hospital fiscal matters coined a new term—"slide rule hospital care"—referring to the operation of hospitals by bottom-line considerations only, with seemingly little appreciation that patient care and the long waiting lists involved not merely facts and figures but also disabled veterans. Most recently, the bureau had imposed a virtual freeze on hiring and on new hospital construction.

At its "Second Reorganization Meeting" on February 18, 1952, the Citizens Committee announced that it would disband on May 31 to avoid becoming embroiled in partisan politics in the current presidential campaign. Committee head Dr. Ralph Johnson announced, however, that five special subcommittees dealing with the departments of the Post Office, Agriculture, Interior, Civil Service, and the V.A. (specifically relating to "unification of medical services") would continue to work "on their own a little longer on an informal basis." Herbert Hoover immediately advocated the forming of a new organization to replace the committee.

In early June 1952, the Senate restored the bulk of the V.A.'s 1953 operating funds, which had been previously cut by the House. The Senate's Independent Offices Appropriation Subcommittee restored $68 million of the House's $86 million cut for the vital categories of administration, medical, hospital, and domiciliary services. (A $12 million "carryover" from the previous year was also authorized.)

The impending large-scale reduction of V.A. medical and hospital personnel had been averted. It also meant that twenty-one nearly completed hospitals could open rather than being delayed indefinitely or even abandoned. Many personnel cuts were still in the offing, however.

National Commander Don Wilson and National Rehab Chairman E. C. "Pat" Cliff had pleaded for just such a restoration of funds in a two-hour appearance before the subcommittee on May 8.

In April 1953, longtime N.E.C. leader William G. McKinley began a series of discussions with National Commander Lewis Gough about the present direction of the Rehabilitation program of the Legion. He shared observations he had made about what appeared to him to be the current trend of thinking in Congress and at the V.A.

McKinley's thoughtful observations and knowledgeable advice was a combination of historical perspective and present-day Legionism. The New Jersey committeeman was "concerned with improvement of Legion management in [rehabilitation]." He did not want to make "any public blast. I'm not out for any scalps. I've no pride of authorship and don't give a damn for any personal publicity or fame. I just want to stir up interest in overhauling our most important activity.

"It is the function of management to constantly seek improvement and efficiency in our business. We are playing with over a half million dollars of the comrades' dough and we should try to get the highest return on that money. That is my purpose of criticism and my method is just within the family—let's wash our linen in our own laundry."

To McKinley, a change clearly was called for. "If we can do as I suggest—improve our Rehab setup—we will go a long way to restoring our prestige in this field. Right now we are on the defensive. Let's get back the initiative."

To do that, he strongly suggested that a research analytical section be added to the National Field Service and that that new resource be "tied in with the department service organization."

The Legion needed "much more painstaking analysis" to "stand up to the coming investigations and criticism of others." For example, the Rehab Commission must state its studied judgment on (1) "the liberality of the law regarding nonservice cases of illness," and (2) "the appraisal of bed requirements" at V.A. hospitals.

"Pensions are the next thing to come in for review," McKinley warned. "What other eventualities will [we] be facing soon? Anticipate them. We must meet this situation on solid ground. We must talk the same language—dollars and cents. Let's not kid ourselves that the compassionate side of the issue is the only one to present."

The Legion had been "up to now, too complacent," had not gathered all the information needed, had not been insistent enough on being told the truth. "We've been told some untruths and have stuck out our necks with Congress. Previously we have taken the V.A. dope and trotted on up to the Hill. Don't let the V.A. play us for a patsy!" "Don't go on conviction only," the veteran committeeman and Rehab volunteer advised. "Go also on knowledge."

"You may be certain that the Legion will be faced with serious and complex problems in Rehab from now on out. I firmly believe we shall have to consider all federal programs on the basis of cost and tax dollars to an extent we have never before experienced. It is senseless to ignore the obvious. I am convinced that the various congressional committees are doing extensive research . . . with an eye to costs and appropriations. We had better do likewise."

Times were changing. "We are no longer faced with a battle with the Hoover Commission or the [U.S.] Chamber of Commerce or any other organization. We must now face up to Congress itself. I am greatly concerned and regard the future as a direct challenge of Legion capability."

National Commander Gough met with President Eisenhower at 12:30 P.M. on May 25, 1953, and delivered a personal plea for adequate appropriations for the V.A. for 1954. At the same time, V.A. officials were appearing in closed session before a House appropriations subcommittee on the Hill. The Bureau of the Budget had cut $279,168,000 from the V.A.'s total appropriation request, which had been approved by the previous administration. At the White House, Gough was telling Eisenhower, "It is just incredible that anybody would suggest breaking faith with the nation's disabled defenders at a time when battle casualties are still mounting.

"But," Gough continued, "that is exactly what Congress is being asked to do. Casualties in Korea are continuing. The Korean veteran will consider these reductions in benefits and services a blow below the belt."

On June 18, 1953, the House reversed itself by a vote of 394 to 2 in passing up to the Senate a money bill allowing enough funds in 1954 to operate all beds and services in V.A. hospitals and homes that could be staffed and used, some 114,315 beds altogether.

The reorganization plan on which Carl Gray at the V.A. had worked was also about to be acted upon. The plan, which Gray had kept close to the vest for many months, had been eagerly awaited. On July 2, Acting Administrator H. V. Stirling informed National Commander Gough by letter that the plan, first announced on November 26, 1952, and again in "amplified" form on January 12, 1953, had been approved and that directions had been issued to commence the reorganization within the V.A. immediately.

After a quick reading, Gough agreed, in general, with the changes calling for streamlining the administration of the agency, with clear separation of staff and operating functions. There were to be three main operating divisions: the Department of Medicine and Surgery and the Departments of Insurance and Veterans' Benefits.

This reorganization of the V.A. was to become effective on September 7. Admiral Joel T. Boone, former physician to three presidents, was to continue as chief medical director responsible for the Department of Medicine and Surgery. The Department of Veterans' Benefits was to take responsibility for all benefit programs including compensation and pension, vocational rehabilitation and education, loan guaranty, guardianship, and contact.

So a generally progressive and Legion-approved reorganization at the V.A. was under way. But soon the attention of National Legislative Division personnel was caught by something that appeared in the recently signed Public Law 108, passed on July 10, which had to do with the use and interagency trading of government buildings. Previously, staff members had passed over this bill, now law, with little concern, pressed as they were with the review of and reaction to numerous other measures arising out of Hoover Report recommendations.

Now, however, it was pointed out that paragraph four of the first section included curious phrasing about "economizing to be done by abolishing services, functions and activities not necessary to the efficient conduct of government." Furthermore, there was a provision for a new commission to study the executive branch of the federal government and to make recommendations to Congress for any changes that would create economy, efficiency, et cetera.

Gough had been informed recently that the president's Advisory Commission on Governmental Operations, chaired by Nelson Rockefeller and which included Milton Eisenhower and Arthur Flemming, did not intend to ask for changes by legislation in the V.A. organization.

This new opening, then, for yet another look at the executive branch was one waiting to be utilized by some other group. Legion workers recalled the final appeal of the Citizens Committee for, and Herbert Hoover's expressed willingness to chair, yet another budget-minding commission.

Looking again at the Declaration of Policy section of Public Law 108, the possibilities for an attempt to consolidate services now performed by the V.A. with similar services and functions of other agencies seemed real enough for the Legion to investigate. Meanwhile, Miles Kennedy had learned from Jack Young, the executive officer of the president's Advisory Commission on Government Operations, that regarding such an eventuality as another economizing commission, "We should assume a watchful, waiting stance, and [Young] is pretty close to the throne, and we have found him to have sharp judgment on these matters."

On July 22, 1953, Harvey V. Higley was sworn in as administrator of the V.A. Higley was known to be in favor of the preservation of the V.A. in much the same form as recommended by the Legion. T. O.

Kraabel called a few of the "older division heads in the V.A." to ask about their impressions of what the future held for the agency. He was pleased to report that "they think that the V.A. will be left alone for some time." Many there believed that veterans' programs had been assailed often and long enough already and the best thing now was to permit them to be stabilized under the new reorganization and the new administrator.

(There were many at the V.A. for whom a call from the Legion was a fraternal matter, too. In June 1952, T. O. Kraabel noted the retirement of Deputy Administrator O. W. Clark, known as "the last of the 'Palace Guard' or 'Four Horsemen,' " who ran the V.A. during the two decades prior to the close of World War II. Clark had participated in the Legion's 1919 Paris Caucus.)

As if to prove the wisdom of King Solomon's weary observation that there was nothing new under the sun, national officers had scarcely begun to feel some relief that the V.A. budget battle had not left more casualties than it had before Washington-based national staffers began hearing more concrete references to the formulation of a second Hoover Commission. The tireless Mr. Hoover, for whom the Hoover Dam had been named, had been asked by President Eisenhower to cast his keen eye on the nation's flood control, navigation and irrigation systems, and its electrical power.

However, with some encouragement from the president (at least at the start) Hoover had planned a much more ambitious agenda based on Public Law 108. Though he remarked that at his age he should be fishing instead of reorganizing governments, he heaved to with impressive energy. Looking back at the many failed proposals of the first Hoover Commission, the dauntless campaigner for economic accountability in government was determined to build on his previous spade work, his own version of a dam, one restraining the massive flow of public money said to be misspent.

For the Legion, the advent of yet another Hoover Commission, likely to scrutinize veterans' affairs again, meant much work ahead. The "watchful, waiting stance" for which Miles Kennedy had been advised became the order of the day once again.

IV

"Goodwill through worthwhile services."
(National Executive Committeeman William G. McKinley)

The Legion's functional entity "Membership and Post Activities" was appropriately named, as two Legion truisms attested: "Membership is the life's blood of the organization; it provides the manpower for the programs and the finances," and "Membership is a post operation."

As C. W. "Pat" Geile recalls, "The Legion was swamped with members at the close of World War II. Practically everyone in the service had heard of the American Legion. They came in faster than the organization could absorb them. [Membership] established them as veterans. If you wear a Legion pin, you're proving that you were a veteran."

Later, however, when the next dues period began, World War II veterans had started their education under the G.I. Bill of Rights, had gotten married, or were actively pursuing job opportunities. Consequently they didn't have the time to devote to the posts.

Membership rolls in 1947 through 1950 had decreased following the all-time peak year of 1946 when World War II veterans, with free time on their hands, joined Legion posts in record numbers.

The National Membership and Post Activities Committee reported in 1948 to the National Convention "a slow-up year" for a number of reasons. "We found that many new posts chartered since the close of World War II are made up of and officered by young veterans who don't have a full knowledge of the American Legion's programs and activities and therefore have had a hard time developing interesting post programs which help build for membership renewals each year.

"We also find that many of the oldtime members, in turning over the leadership of the posts to the younger members, have failed to follow through and remain active and give to the young leadership the vitally important advice and guidance based upon their experience."

On September 1, 1949, the Philadelphia National Convention adopted a resolution for a twenty-five-cent increase in the annual dues, which had been one dollar for many years. The increase was used primarily to aid rehab and child welfare work. Though there was a rush of membership renewals when a time was set for rejoining under the old dues rate, the following months showed little encouragement for breaking the pattern of decline.

As representative of the nation as a whole, the American Legion was susceptible to many factors at work in the larger populace, all of which affected membership each year as posts engaged in the latest membership drive.

Membership Director Charles M. "Chuck" Wilson connected the sharp rise in unemployment to the fall in Legion membership. While he didn't spare Legionnaires for "the inertia of many district, county, and post officials," he believed that membership numbers reflected, also, "the adverse publicity and public opinion about the Legion's fight against the Hoover Commission recommendations" for cutting veterans' benefits.

When during the next spring he conferred with the Michigan Department Commander Addington Wagner (later to become national commander), Wilson learned that Legion opposition to parts of the Hoover Report had definitely hurt the Legion membership drive in that state. There, too, the Junior Chamber of Commerce had begun to confront Legionnaires who opposed the JayCee's blanket acceptance of the Hoover Report.

What was to some adverse publicity, however, as Wilson reasoned, may actually have helped to gain members among those who were favorably impressed with an organization that would fight for veterans during a time when it was much more popular to take the opposite side.

National Commander Craig suggested in June 1950 that his successor "make an intensive grassroots membership tour" immediately after the 1950 National Convention. On September 28, 1950, at the Los Angeles Convention, Craig's charge to those newly elected as department commanders and district, county, and post officers was that "the first responsibility is to build for a greater membership during the coming year."

Erle Cocke, Jr., elected at the Los Angeles National Convention, endorsed the membership tour. Cocke, at twenty-nine, was the youngest national commander and was an exuberant, gregarious survivor of a harrowing World War II capture and subsequently a patient in a lengthy and tortuous rehabilitation. Setting out immediately after the convention, Cocke visited posts in some forty states in the next several weeks.

When *Time* magazine called in late 1951 for membership statistics, Ed McGinnis, making a judgment about the tone of the article to come, was "cagey but accurate." When a squib in the November 12 issue reported "the decline of membership in veterans' organizations," Jack Cejnar replied to the magazine that the current trend was typical of that of a five-year period after World War II. "We have about reached the end of the five-year dropoff since 1946, which was a natural result following the first enthusiastic rush of joining," Cejnar explained hopefully. He pointed out also that younger veterans had other primary interests, such as going to school, getting married, and becoming established in occupations. But the Legion "was having its best membership start since 1946." As of November 2, all but four of the fifty-eight departments were ahead in their advance enrollments from a year ago, the best showing that early in the last five years.

At the Miami Beach, Florida National Convention in 1951, Erle Cocke praised post officers for stopping the five-year annual membership decline.

With all the attention in speeches and in Legion printed materials to strengthening the organization through increased membership rolls, many examples were given of successful efforts by posts and departments.

Many Legionnaires had been concerned that veterans returning to civilian life after serving in Korea had received little recognition. Legionnaires knew that readjustment to civilian life after a tour of duty in a combat zone was a disillusioning and often heartbreaking experience. Morale could be low, too, for the Korean veteran, who found apathy at home about the war in which he had been involved only days before.

In mid-February 1952, the annual membership campaign was 100,000 members ahead of the previous year's campaign on the same date, and promotional materials reflected the hopes for a record membership year. Many favored the shorter membership campaign period —Armistice Day (November 11) to Thanksgiving—for concentrated membership efforts. There was, also, the hope that a good membership year could show that the American Legion, indeed, could attract and keep members even while lobbying selectively against the popular Hoover Commission's report.

The Legion, however, could not take for granted the population that it claimed to represent. C. M. Wilson reported, "The Citizens Committee [the advocate for the Hoover Report] now has a new satellite operating under the name of the Independent Veterans Committee, which claims to represent all veterans who do not belong to recognized veterans' organizations." The claim "is just so much poppycock," Wilson added.

In the late fall of 1952, a survey by the Bureau of the Budget found that the average age of Korean War veterans was twenty-two, an observation that related to the potential of that group for membership in the Legion. For example, of the 30,777 current loan applications to the V.A., only 1,787 were by Korean War veterans, more of whom were searching for jobs or were involved in education and training, thus engaged in less establishment-oriented pursuits. (The survey also showed that those who fought in both World War II and Korea had an average age of thirty years.)

By the national convention in St. Louis in 1953, there was an increase of 14,364 members over the figure for the previous year. But at the N.E.C. meeting in October, William G. McKinley pointed out that the Legion still was trying to reach twenty million potential members with the same number of "salesmen" as it did when there were only four million veterans from whom to gain members. Now, he said, there were 3.5 million World War I vets; fifteen million from World War II, and 1.5 million from the Korean War. More membership volunteers were needed, he and others advised. So the "Knock On Every Door In '54" slogan emphasized a campaign of larger proportions than some in past years.

The annual membership roll call by telegraph on Tuesday, October 13, was encouraging as department commanders and adjutants met in Indianapolis to present their membership goals for the coming year.

Subsequently, the total for 1954 membership pledges to reach National Headquarters by the first of the year was 1,661,605, a figure 50,000 above the pledges of the previous year.

Yet many observed and complained meanwhile that although they held vast potential for membership growth, the recently returned Korean War veterans, even considering their average age and the fact that their life-styles often did not mesh well with the older members of the Legion, were not at all well represented in the American Legion. Granted, the Legion had worked admirably and would succeed in the pursuit of a Korean War G.I. Bill of Rights. But appreciative though Korean veterans might have been, that impressive advocacy on their behalf alone would not cause them to become active Legionnaires. What else could be done? Reaching these newly eligible potential members would continue to be a subject of concern for National officers through the 1950s.

V

The American Legion Magazine during the early 1950s sought to encourage membership campaigns by reporting the success, and the occasional antics, of Legionnaires who had signed up large numbers of new members. The implication was ever-present that a larger Legion could advance more effectively the goals of the organization's basic programs. Many issues of this publication also carried news about an often assailed though traditional benefit for citizen-soldiers—veterans' preference in federal employment.

If the National Economics Commission had a patron saint for its veterans' preference advocacy it was Rudyard Kipling's "Tommy Atkins," the hapless soldier given preferential treatment "when the guns begin to shoot" but for whom later "it's 'chuck him out, the brute.' "

When during World War II the Veterans Preference Act of 1944 (the same year as the emergence of the G.I. Bill) had been passed, it may have seemed to the commission that Kipling's "Oh, there'll surely come a day when they'll grant you all your pay" had been realized.

Though there had been earlier enactments of such legislation, the history of veterans' preference was rife with charges and countercharges. In 1928, after numerous complaints about disabled veterans not receiving a sufficient number of appointments, President Coolidge created a special committee to study the situation. Chaired by Legion founder Hamilton Fish, and with Legion lobbyist John Thomas Taylor a member, along with Veterans Bureau Director Frank S. Hines and others, the committee made recommendations that improved the employment status of disabled veterans and their wives or widows who were seeking jobs with the federal government.

Another committee, created by President Hoover in 1931, investigated charges of misuse of the preference system by veterans. John Thomas Taylor was a member of this committee, also. The Economy Act of 1933 had set out provisions for reduction of employment in government jobs and recommended dismissal of one member of a married couple employed through veterans' preference as the second priority (of four) for reducing the government work force.

In 1943 the American Legion, D.A.V., V.F.W., and the Civil Service Commission came to substantial agreement about which bills to support from among the several then in Congress attempting to address the matter.

The Legion had long called for the existing patchwork affair of administrative and executive orders that had developed over the years to be made national policy by Congress, whereby there would be established an all-important protective sanction of legislative approval. President Roosevelt agreed, particularly with two bills then in Congress, and approved the resulting legislation on June 27, 1944. In January 1948, the law was amended to add a new group entitled to preference: the widowed, divorced, or legally separated mothers of veterans. The Veterans Preference Act of 1944 had become the basic legal framework for the preservation of an American citizen-soldier tradition—attainable employment in the federal government for those who had served in the armed forces. (This preference added additional points to the veteran's score on civil service exams.)

As in the past, however, veterans' preference continued to be assailed. In 1950 and 1951, more bills were introduced in Congress that, the Legion charged, would diminish the basic benefit of veterans' preference.

There was a victory for preference advocates when in 1952 the final service date for eligibility for World War II vets to gain preference points, formerly set for April 28, 1952, was extended by Congress to July 1, 1955, thereby honoring the service of Korean War veterans, also.

In 1953, however, the five- and ten-point boost in veterans' civil service exam scores, which constituted the heart of "preference" and which could boost a score to the eligibility list for available jobs, was largely eliminated. Previously, a score less than passing could be enhanced by the five or ten preference points applied to the test score. Now a passing score was required before preference points were added.

With the enactment of Public Law 83-271, the provision for veterans who had been granted the ten-point preference to be placed automatically at the top of the eligible list evaporated. Subsequently, a ten percent or higher disability rating was required for automatic placement at the top of the list. All others rose on the eligible list according to their scores, some of which had been increased by the preference points added upon the applicant having achieved a passing score.

For several years to come, the mention of veterans' preference in National Economics Commission reports triggered a conditioned response: what new danger to the concept has been devised by its foes?

A Legion Initiative and the Mental Health Movement

Rehabilitation for many war veterans involved a long and tortuous journey back to mental health.

The treatment of mental illness in the postwar era had advanced from the insulin and metrazol "shock therapy" of the 1930s and the electroshock of the mid-1940s to the use of psychosomatic medicine. But it was also an era of "lunacy tests," and of mentally ill persons often being confined in local jail cells while awaiting the all too frequent one-way trip to the state "insane asylum."

Resolutions urging the adoption of a national mental health program had been presented to Legion national conventions after World War II. On April 29, 1950, Dr. Leonard G. Rowntree, formerly the chief medical examiner for Selective Service before becoming medical adviser to the Legion, convened a group to consider a nationwide mental health program for the Legion to sponsor. Key Legion advisers and volunteers were present. Dr. Charles W. Mayo, Legionnaire and son of Mayo Clinic cofounder Dr. Charles H. Mayo and a well-respected surgeon in his own right, joined Dr. Rowntree in representing the Legion's Medical Advisory Board. The National Rehab Commission Chairman Robert M. McCurdy, Director T. O. Kraabel, and Senior Medical Consultant Dr. Hyman D. Shapiro were present. The Child Welfare Commission was represented by its former national director, Emma C. Puschner, the present director, Randel Shake, National Vice-Chairman David V. Addy, and Charles W. "Pat" Geile, Associate National Director. The Auxiliary's Child Welfare chairman, Mrs. Hope Reed, was present, also.

Dr. Rowntree began with a troubling frame of reference: of the eighteen million men examined by draft boards in the war years, six million were permanently disqualified "on military standards," and, of that number, two million were judged to be unfit on "psychiatric grounds." (George Craig would later exclaim, "Why, there were enough draftees in the last war rejected on mental grounds to whip the Germans.")

The Legion had realized a "100 to 1" benefit, Rowntree said, by its gift of $50,000 in 1946 to the American Heart Association; the 1949 fund drive for the association had raised nearly six million dollars.

Now there was the need to wage a fight against another widespread and debilitating malady—mental illness.

The spontaneous discussion that followed reflected the mental health care situation in the nation.

Emma Puschner reminded the group that the Child Welfare Commission had established its credibility in this field through its "whole child" concept. Mental hygiene had long been a traditional part of the regional child welfare conferences. She informed the others that at the upcoming White House Conference on Children and Youth in December, which was held every ten years and attended by the Legion, the subject of mental health was to be one of the main topics. The Child Welfare Commission was eager, Ms. Puschner said, to join with the National Rehabilitation Commission in formulating a plan for wider-ranging Legion sponsorship.

The nation's mental health program, Dr. Rowntree said, "is at the lowest ebb of any of the medical programs. Many doctors have considered psychiatrists only as good custodians." But "the good work done by psychiatrists during World War II" had helped some doctors to view the work more favorably. He spoke of the formulation of a "foundation" which would have two primary objectives: (1) the prevention of mental illness through a program of education, and (2) worthwhile improvement in the humane care and scientific treatment of the mentally ill.

Dr. Shapiro estimated that about fifty percent of the doctors now practicing had witnessed at least some facet of mental illness during their wartime experiences. He believed that sixty percent or more of the mentally ill could be returned to productive lives if given proper care during their first year of treatment. Currently, only about eight to ten percent of such patients were helped substantially.

T. O. Kraabel mentioned that there had been some talk about a merger of three existing mental health organizations (the National Committee for Mental Hygiene, the American Psychiatric Association, and the National Foundation for Mental Hygiene) to form a national organization with lay leadership and medical direction.

Perhaps this timely opportunity of the proposed merger was just the means to which the Legion looked for help in establishing a nationwide mental health organization, a move possibly to be patterned after the boost that the Legion had given to the American Heart Association earlier with its grant to get that organization started to national prominence.

Dr. Rowntree believed that the time was right for a major effort by the Legion. "The origin, the numbers, the objectives, and the position of the American Legion in this country" made it the logical source to provide the leadership in dealing with "this most difficult medical problem we face today."

National Commander Craig, an early and strong supporter of a mental health program, joined the meeting in progress. "We don't care who does it so long as it is done expertly," he said. "All we need to do is to initiate and support this [new] organization." Such a vital matter of public service, he said, "is why we are in business." While the thrust was national in scope, many veterans would benefit. Bob McCurdy added that many families of veterans would also benefit from a Legion-backed mental health program.

In May, Craig spoke before the N.E.C. about the proposal. Never one to mince words, Craig charged, "The American people have piddled around all of these years without any concentrated, concrete, forward-looking program. Now, the American Legion has an opportunity to be the catalytic agent to bring together all of these forces with a view of getting doctors for our veterans' hospitals. There are more veterans per capita who suffer mental disability than any other group of our people. I'm tired of picking up my evening paper and seeing where 'Vet slits wife's throat with German bayonet.'

"The malicious fiction that persons with disturbed minds are somehow culpable for their afflictions and therefore to be kept in the shadows of society represents a major impediment to medical science. To dispel the phony fears and pride on which this phobia rests is a job in which lay people have a special responsibility—and one which American Legion members will be asked to meet in a special way. We must face the facts. The fundamental fact in this instance is that the diseased mind is as much a pathological condition as the diseased heart or lungs, and is equally responsive to treatment."

The N.E.C., in its closing session late on May 4, 1950, voted to contribute $25,000 to "the appropriate national agency for mental hygiene for the purpose of initiating and starting a national program for the mentally ill."

T. O. Kraabel and Hank Dudley began meeting with officials of the three mental health organizations that intended to merge. They spoke principally with Dr. George Stevenson, medical director of the National Committee for Mental Hygiene, the largest and oldest (since 1909) of the three and the organization that had done much to bring about (with Legion support) the National Mental Health Act of 1946, which expended up to ten million dollars annually for training, research, and grants to states for mental clinics.

On September 13, 1950, the merger was made official, and the National Association for Mental Health (N.A.M.H.) came into being with 200 potential members (50 from each of the predecessor organizations and room for another 50).

The $25,000 Legion grant allowed the new organization to mount an information campaign and recruit additional financial support much as had the American Heart Association.

Legion volunteerism for the program was channeled through the N.A.M.H.'s Division on Community Clinics, which helped communities establish psychiatric clinics and, for existing clinics, helped the board, staff, and community get better service. Paid staff were also involved. Legion field staff, for example, were instructed to check the extent to which existing community clinics were using federal vocational rehab funds in the field of mental rehab.

The process of gathering information continued. The news was often discouraging. It was unhappily noted, for example, that psychiatrists, taken for military service to perform routine medical examinations, left many communities without any psychiatric help, often just as local clinics were being set up.

There were many bright spots, however. Several new clinics had been opened and the evolving network of information and individuals had done much to match specialists with local situations ranging from Fort Wayne, Indiana, to Madison, Wisconsin, and to El Paso and Austin, Texas. Truly, the work and its appeal were nationwide. (In Scranton, Pennsylvania, the new clinic owed its existence to a Legion post there.)

By late 1951, the members of the American Association of Psychiatric Clinics for Children had aided N.A.M.H.'s Division on Community Clinics in conducting a nationwide survey of clinics. These professionals had also served to guide communities in developing clinics and in investigating existing clinics and training centers.

The N.A.M.H. worked in a number of ways at publicity. Regional conferences were organized for doctors, nurses, ministers, teachers, and others; booths were taken at the conferences of related organizations (Randel Shake manned a booth at the National Conference of Social Work in Atlantic City); a national directory of psychiatric clinics was begun; brochures and a guide to be used by communities in establishing clinics were published. N.A.M.H. staffers in the field, in turn, visited Legion posts looking for volunteers to serve in state hospitals. A "national demonstration" rural health program intended as a prototype for possible replication nationwide was established in Hunterdon County, New Jersey, involving general practitioners, nurses, teachers, ministers, and county extension service agents.

In April 1952, the American Legion Auxiliary, acting on a resolution adopted at its convention in Miami in 1951, added its welcome support to the new mental health program by adopting it as a special project for its Child Welfare Program. In this way the Auxiliary continued to work with the Legion as it had in aiding the American Heart Association, the March of Dimes, and the Foundation for the Study of Prevention and Cure of Cancer. Mental health, then, had become yet another of the Legion's interests, and for which the organization would work to dispell the erroneous presumptions about causes and curability.

BETWEEN THE CEASE-FIRE AND THE FIRESTORM

1955 – 1965

I

U.M.T., the Last Hurrah?

In late 1954, the N.E.C.'s subcommittee on legislation for the coming year designated U.M.T. as the priority item on the Legion's legislative agenda. The National Convention meeting a few weeks earlier in Washington, D.C., had produced resolutions 68 and 220, which mandated that U.M.T. be so emphasized.

The fragile cease-fire in Korea was still in place, but the volatility of the situation there was sure to keep the matter of military manpower, including training, a chief concern of military and political officials.

Universal Military Training—U.M.T.—was a thirty-six-year byword of the organization. But U.M.T. was a long way from becoming the basis upon which the nation's defenses depended in the essential way that the Legion had long emphasized.

There were many reasons for this, of course, but a typical prepared speech for Legion spokesmen of the period reiterated what were felt to be two recurring reasons: "A group of congressional leaders, heeding the loud cries of vocal minorities, have consistently blocked the passage of real U.M.T. legislation. Secondly, and equally important, the military services themselves have never given all-out support to the idea."

The campaign continued, however. The three-man committee appointed by National Commander Seaborn Collins, which included

Past National Commander Erle Cocke, Past National Commander Perry Brown, and Granville Ridley, met with representatives of labor unions, church groups, other veterans' organizations, educational associations, the Selective Service, the president's National Security Training Commission (a product of the misnamed Universal Training and Service Act of 1951), and the Department of Defense to acquaint these groups with the Legion's motives and arguments for N.S.T. (another name for U.M.T., and also called C.M.T.—Compulsive Military Training). It seemed apparent that some measure for strengthening the nation's reserve forces would be forthcoming.

This newly reformed Legion National Security Training Committee, chaired by Granville Ridley, first met in Washington early in the fall of 1954. By December, it had completed the draft of a bill. On January 6, 1955, the bill was introduced in the 84th Congress as S. 2 by Senators Russell, Kefauver, Stennis, Symington, Jackson, Bridges, and Saltonstall. The same day a House version was introduced by Carl Vinson as H.R. 1630 and on January 17 as H.R. 2377 by Overton Brooks (D., LA).

The Democratic party majority resulting from the 1954 congressional elections was seen as an advantage to those pushing U.M.T. With Republicans in the White House and Democrats controlling both houses of Congress, the Legion would promote its own bipartisan stature. Called a "great pulse-taking group in this nation" by Past National Commander Erle Cocke, the organization would ask leaders of both parties to consider the need and the equality of a universal, compulsory system for military training.

In the House, a subcommittee of the House Armed Services Committee, chaired by Overton Brooks, conducted hearings on the subjects of U.M.T. and the Reserve. In that process, bills by the Legion and the Department of Defense were considered. That subcommittee presented its report, and a compromise bill, H.R. 5297, which included several points contained in the Legion bill but was primarily a Department of Defense bill supported by the president.

H.R. 5297 included a series of sanctions and inducements aimed at (1) attracting younger men into service than were presently enrolled in reserve units; (2) requiring reservists to complete their training period (many previously had dropped out); (3) gaining authority for ordering six-month volunteers back to active duty when necessary.

Farm, labor, and other groups complained that this opened the door to U.M.T. When the bill was taken to the full House in mid-May, the adoption of an antisegregation amendment put forth by Representative Adam Clayton Powell, Jr. (D., NY) embroiled the matter in that additional issue and effectively stymied further action.

The next month, during a three-day civil defense drill, President Eisenhower spoke to the nation on June 17 from underground at the

Pentagon and put forth another argument for a reserve plan. In a national disaster, such as a nuclear attack, he said, "One trained reserve battalion in the proper place would be worth five divisions located 1,000 miles away." This was not a time to "attach social, political, or any other kind of legislation" to much needed reserve legislation, he said.

A few days later, the House Armed Services Committee drafted a new bill, H.R. 7000, lacking the antisegregation provision as well as some other facets that the president, the Department of Defense, and the Legion had wanted. The Senate version was somewhat more acceptable to the navy, marine, and air force leaders in helping to refocus the bill on enlarging the reserves rather than competing with volunteer enlistment in those branches. H.R. 7000 passed the House on July 25 and the Senate the next day.

President Eisenhower, when signing the bill into law on August 10, expressed disappointment in it. The measure, however, would strengthen the Reserve structure, he said, and would allow the president to order up one million Ready Reservists in an emergency proclaimed by him.

For several years now, from the attack on Pearl Harbor through the Korean War, while campaigning for U.M.T., the Legion was obliged to support the military draft, and, currently, Reserve legislation and laws so as not to appear unpatriotic in times of national emergencies.

Now the 84th Congress's H.R. 7000, with presidential signature becoming Public Law 305—the Reserve Forces Act of 1955—was yet another case in point of the now customary practice of going along with prevailing methods of dealing with the training of manpower for national defense.

National Commander Collins called this eleventh-hour congressional approval of compromise legislation, which in its final form featured a voluntary six-month training program and compulsory Reserve duty, "a promising step toward a strong Reserve," as represented by the seven reserve components: National Guard, Army Reserve, Navy Reserve, Marine Corps Reserve, Air National Guard, Air Force Reserve, and Coast Guard Reserve.

While a step in the right direction, it was neither compulsory nor universal. Congressman Overton Brooks, long aware of the Legion's timeworn efforts, put it succinctly to Granville Ridley. "This is not U.M.T.!"

As finally approved, the Reserve Forces Act brought about a modified version of U.M.T. Though the act did not guarantee as strong a civilian Reserve force as the Legion believed necessary, it did remove "major inequities of the present system," Collins said (seeking to find the positive side to yet another disappointment regarding U.M.T.), "while inaugurating a plan of basic training designed solely to strengthen the Reserve and providing reasonable means of enforcing

Reserve obligations." A few weeks later, Legion National Convention delegates called for the "speediest possible implementation of training and service."

Three months after the act had been signed, the Pentagon acknowledged a slow start with far fewer volunteers than it would take to meet the Department of Defense's expectation of 5,000 by the end of the year. In that light, the expectation of 100,000 volunteers in 1956 or more than 8,000 a month seemed unlikely. Defense officials, in public statements, remained optimistic, however, relying presumably on certain provisions in the new plan that they hoped would prove attractive to draft-eligible young men and which, it was said, had not been effectively advertised as yet.

Now that something had been done to bolster the nation's Reserve component, the Legion's National Security Training Committee sought ways to encourage the success of this plan, flawed though it was judged to be. The committee visited every army installation where the volunteer program was conducted and reported finding good quality training and leadership.

So Legion National Headquarters called on Legionnaires to continue to promote enlistments in the six-month program for seventeen- and eighteen-year-old youths by stressing the benefits of the program to parents, eligible youths, and high school faculties in their towns and cities. It was the best plan, they were asked to point out, for young men to discharge their military duties with the least interruption in their education and way of life.

Legion staff members, not wishing to have disappointment construed as outright rejection of the act, prepared communiqués for the membership that referred to the act positively yet reminded readers that it did not do all that it should. A special issue, dated August 10, 1955, of the *Security Newsletter* from the National Security Training Committee, published one day after the president signed H.R. 7000, called enactment of the law "a measure of success greater than ever before realized" in the thirty-seven-year "quest for a youth training program. It is a beginning, a base upon which an effective U.M.T. program can be built." Though not as strong and all-inclusive as the Legion had hoped for, it was "the first time this nation has had the means of training large numbers of young men for effective Reserve service," National Commander Collins stated.

It was explained that the principal objective of the act was the establishment of a Ready Reserve of nearly three million men and a Standby Reserve of another two million, all of whom were to support active forces of nearly 2.9 million personnel. Collins called this "unprecedented recognition" by Congress of the essential role of a trained civilian reserve as the bulwark of peacetime defense.

The act, while operating concurrently with Selective Service, was designed to produce the necessary trained manpower for a strengthened Reserve by a modified U.M.T. program, direct enlistments into the Ready Reserve and National Guard, one-year enlistments in the Ready Reserve, and shortened terms of service for enlistees and draftees willing to serve in the Ready Reserve.

The program would permit some 250,000 youths seventeen to eighteen and a half years old to volunteer for six months of active duty training, following which they were to agree to serve in the Ready Reserve for seven and a half years. Trainees were to be given fifty dollars a month along with transportation and subsistence, and their period of training to be deferred until after graduation from high school or upon turning twenty. Once in the program, they were to be provided with protection of health, safety, and welfare in a manner to be submitted to Congress as the Civilian National Security Training Corps. Thus in these last two respects, the program was faintly reminiscent of the Legion's earlier recommendations for a U.M.T. program. (But the fifty-dollar-monthly pay immediately was contrasted to the seventy-eight dollars already being paid members of the National Guard. The Legion quickly set about pushing for equity in pay between the two organizations.)

The National Convention that year acknowledged the usefulness of the recent Reserve Forces Act, but reiterated the long-standing call for U.M.T. and particularly that the training be compulsory and universal.

At the convention a subcommittee of the Legion's Military Affairs Committee outlined changes it felt should be made in the Reserve Forces Act, which was now only a few weeks old. Most objectionable was the fact that while 100,000 young Americans were becoming age eighteen each month, only about 20,000 were being drafted into the armed forces. Such figures, it was assumed, would discourage many from volunteering for the new opportunities in the Reserve or the National Guard. There was also the need, it was said, to solve the inequality in pay between the National Guardsman and the Reserve volunteer.

Though some speculated about how much the act would help the nation's lagging reserve forces, most agreed that a trial run of a few months was required before any serious judgment could be made. Nevertheless, as a matter of habit it would appear, the National Convention of 1955 produced resolutions calling for supportive legislative amendments to make the training program compulsory.

National Commander J. Addington Wagner, elected at Miami, advised against an unduly hasty call for changes in the new law. He assigned to the National Security Division the responsibility for helping posts and departments to understand the provisions of the Reserve Forces Act so they in turn could inform young men and encourage them to volunteer for the armed forces. Ed Shelton, executive director of the president's National Security Training Commission, sent James

Wilson, director of the Legion's National Security Division, copies of the commission's report, which was required by law, on the health, safety, and welfare of the trainees. This information was passed along to chairmen of the committees of the National Security Training Commission and the special U.M.T. chairmen.

Even though the volunteer training program enacted was far from what the Legion had hoped for, the N.E.C. at its May 1955 meeting noted that at least unlike the immediate post–World War I and –World War II period, it was not being seriously suggested in Congress that the armed forces be drastically reduced.

It was pointed out that the Communist military buildup and consequently the increased pressures exerted in Korea, Indochina, and Formosa called for realism to supplement idealism in stopping the Communist conspiracy for world domination. The National Security Training Commission coined the slogan "Strength Welded to Economy" to take advantage of the recent passage of the Reserve Forces Act while acknowledging the need for fiscal responsibility.

Though there was yet one remaining vestige of U.M.T. conceptual purity—the National Security Training Commission—its reports and very reason for being were largely ignored by the executive branch and Congress. In February 1956, Granville Ridley told a House appropriations subcommittee that was considering the next year's operating funds for the National Security Training Commission (headed by Gen. David Sarnoff and including Past National Commander Warren Atherton), "Provision of this commission is vital to the success of the six-months training provision of the Reserve Forces Act." Ridley and others had noted a disconcerting if inevitable development: commission members were themselves becoming ever more discouraged with having to go hat in hand to a generally unreceptive Congress each year for operating funds.

Established originally to plan for the welfare, morale, health, and personal safety of trainees should an U.M.T. program ever be established, the commission had been asked to perform the same duty relating to the voluntary trainees to whom Ridley now referred.

Ridley urged the granting of the modest $75,000 annual budget for the commission, which was slated to go out of existence on June 30 if its budget was not renewed. Ridley also appeared before the Senate Appropriations Subcommittee to urge restoration of the commission's budget.

To U.M.T. proponents, the Reserve Forces Act of 1955 was a stopgap measure that would serve for the next ten years as the system that national level volunteers and staff would seek to amend and bring more in line with Legion thinking.

When Legion Military Affairs Committee Chairman William C. Doyle appeared before the House Armed Services Committee on April 20 to keep the Legion's view before that group, he remarked that since the Department of Defense was placing more emphasis than ever on reserves in its long-range plan for national defense, it was highly advisable that the pay inducements for the "civilian soldiers" of all the reserves be made equal to that of the National Guard. The Legion had already formed a Reserve Equalization Committee within the National Security Training Commission and worked with Senator John J. Sparkman (D., AL) to secure parity of treatment of regular Reservists with National Guard officers in respect to pay and retirement benefits.

Granville Ridley conferred with Selective Service head Gen. Lewis B. Hershey and the general's legislative expert, Colonel Franck, about how suggested amendments to the act would affect the operation of Selective Service.

Conferences with officials at the Department of Labor, in view of the act's creation of a continuous shifting of Reservists, selectees, and enlistees between the labor force and the armed forces, brought about the 1956 National Convention's Resolution 533, which called for an aggressive program of job restoration for Reservists.

Meanwhile Granville Ridley noted "some friendly division of opinion among those who have worked so long on our U.M.T. program," especially on the matter of whether to acquiesce to manpower bills being drafted by others, particularly the Department of Defense and the National Guard, regarding the Army Reserve–National Guard controversy over the extent of active duty training that should be required of National Guard enlistees.

Work though they did to keep the concept of U.M.T. alive in the minds of congressmen and others, Ridley told Erle Cocke, Jr., in June 1957, "There has been a good deal of sentiment expressed for a restudy of our program" regarding U.M.T. What evolved, of course, in light of the difficulty experienced over the years in getting U.M.T. enacted, was the practice of assigning the matter to special-project status while attempting to deal with (1) the reality of entrenched thinking by Congress and the general public about the obligation of military service, and (2) the changes that might be effected in the existing law governing military service of citizen-soldiers.

Though in no way indicating a lessening of the importance of U.M.T. as far as the Legion was concerned, the matter was not stressed during the Legion's lobbying for various defense-related measures. However, the subject was addressed whenever possible. For example, while William C. Doyle was testifying in Congress in January 1959 for extension of the current draft law to July 1, 1963, he heard some complain of the failure of the Reserve Forces Act to attract the number of volunteers the Department of Defense had said was minimally required to defend the nation in time of war. Doyle referred to U.M.T. as a solution. The volunteer enlistment program set forth in Public Law 305 was said to be decidedly less than an outstanding success when after one year there were 40,000 volunteers instead of the 100,000 for which the military services had hoped.

Though the Legion continued to draft new U.M.T. bills that were periodically introduced in Congress, the continuation of the cold war, as marked by events that haunted the daily newspaper headlines from the mid-1950s on, caused Legion observers, and, hence, their counterparts charged with lobbying for successive legislative agendas, to focus on a wide range of mandates that at times overshadowed the long campaign for U.M.T.

National Security Training Commission Vice-Chairman W. C. "Dan" Daniel reminded the N.E.C. meeting in May 1956 that the world mission of Communism had not changed. "Neither the death of Stalin, nor the rise and fall of Malenkov, nor the promotion of Khruschev or Bulganin, nor the dissolvement of the Comintern, would bring about a change in policy." The goal of world domination was made more threatening by the elimination of any doubt, according to Daniel, of Russia's ability to attack the United States with nuclear weapons. "Every day is D-day for America," he said.

Daniel cited the large outlay by the federal government for national defense as an enormous expenditure to deter aggression. Now Russia had recently displayed new supersonic fighters, new all-weather fighters, new turbo-prop and long-range bomber jets, all in impressive numbers. In particular, Russia's T-37 "Bison" bomber reportedly had been developed in two years, one-third the time it took the United States to develop its B-52. Also, the Russian submarine fleet was growing, as well as the total number of surface ships like destroyers and cruisers, Daniel pointed out.

Indeed, alarming changes were occurring in world affairs. In particular the subject of atomic weapons, formerly touted for shortening the war with Japan, continued to be a matter of great concern.

So it was that the West was primed for a shock when the 23-inch-diameter, 84-pound Sputnik I was sent aloft on October 4, 1957, by the United States' archrival and chief nemesis, the Soviet Union. Previous indications that Russia had the capability of launching such a satellite had been dismissed as propaganda. Now the proof was orbiting the earth every ninety-six minutes.

This dramatic and threatening opening of the "space race" caused much concern among Legion national officers who oversaw policy issues ranging from federal aid to education (to boost science and technology instruction) to the gamut of national security and foreign relations issues.

What's more, that first metal sphere launched from Communist Russia (there would be two more in quick succession and of greatly increased size) also heralded the beginning of what would become a continual sense of panic over "elapsed time," the period of time between a bomb's launch and its detonation. So with the continuation of cold war–era missile research and buildup, the time factor—the short time it would take to reap the devastating consequences of firing nuclear weapons—was much the worrisome topic among defense planners.

Such a state of emergency, the Legion had learned before World War II and again with the Korean War, was not one in which long-range, preparatory measures such as U.M.T. were likely to be considered in a manner that would lead to actual implementation.

Instead, Legion publicists and Legionnaires from the many posts around the nation continued to educate eligible trainees, their parents, their instructors, and their prospective employers to the advantages of the six-month-long program for military training implemented by the Reserve Forces Act. One method for achieving this end was for posts to send representatives to local high schools to speak with graduating seniors about military service.

II

Battling Phoenix

The Legion's viewpoint about military manpower was never allowed to supersede the preeminent and "basic" reason for the organization's existence—veterans' rehabilitation. Relating to that sphere of advocacy currently was the initiation of yet another move for reorganization of the executive branch of the U.S. government. This, of course, would likely mean another assault on the V.A.

There had already been two attempts in quick succession at reorganization: the Hoover Commission and then the popular movement led most notably by the Citizens Committee.

The need for reform had often been voiced by occupants of the White House and by congressmen and senators, along with the general public in the post–World War II years who agreed that the federal government needed trimming, having grown as it had during the Depression and World War II in the number of agencies and the number of ways it touched the lives of individuals and institutions.

Now, early in the Eisenhower administration, Public Law 108, passed during the 83rd Congress and approved on July 10, 1953, created the Commission on Governmental Operations, which like its predecessor would be headed by Herbert Hoover. The membership of the group included the attorney general; the director of the Office of Defense Mobilization; two university deans, one a Republican, the other a Democrat; as well as two U.S. senators and four U.S. representatives, all similarly chosen for their political affiliations.

Hoover set out to display his trademark forte—efficiency engineering in cutting governmental redundancies and inefficiencies. But the authorization this time included that of looking into substantive matters of policy. Particularly targeted were those aspects of government that competed with private enterprise. Editorial writers called it a move to "get government out of business."

From 1949 through the summer of 1952, the Legion had monitored the first Hoover Commission closely and later sought to counter the much publicized campaign of the national Citizens Committee for lobbying Congress with bills growing out of commission recommendations regarding some veterans-related matters.

The Reorganization Act of 1949, which had been preceded by a similar law in 1945 and by the Administrative Procedure Act of 1946, invited the president to submit a series of reorganization plans during a seven-year period (to 1957).

These reform measures were scheduled to take effect within sixty days unless disapproved by a simple majority of the members of Congress. The holdover Hoover Commission recommendations were prime fodder, of course, for this process.

Reform was not easily accomplished, however, regardless of how much agreement there was for its need. Congress had rejected eleven of President Truman's forty-one reorganization plans. Even his request for emergency reorganization power after the outbreak of hostilities in Korea was rejected by Congress.

It was now President Eisenhower's turn to recommend some reforms. Since it was usually suspected by Congress that presidentially proffered reforms were thinly veiled attempts at transferring power from the legislative branch to the executive branch, Congress was characteristically jealous. Not surprisingly, debate again was spirited. Even for the popular Eisenhower, the success rate of reforms emanating from the White House would continue to fall shy of the perfect mark.

Nevertheless, Legion national officers viewed the advent of the second Hoover Commission and the reports that were released in January 1955 as warily as they had before.

One such report advocated a major overhaul of the health and medical services provided by the federal government and which were depicted as being part of a "cumbersome system," to the tune of cutting some $250 million, much of that reflected in particularly sharp cutbacks on services to veterans. The commission charged that there was "goldbricking" by some veterans and called once again for veterans to pay for their own nonservice-connected ailments if they were financially able.

The commission also recommended that twenty veterans' hospitals be closed, for a savings, it was said, of five million dollars each year. Similarly, the commission recommended that no new V.A. hospitals be built, except for those now in construction.

Just hours after the release of this commission's first report relating to veterans' affairs, the Legion public relations office in Washington released a bristling statement that called the commission both misinformed and uninformed.

Expressing shock and disappointment at the "purely dollars-and-cents basis" on which Hoover's Commission on Governmental Operations would put services to disabled veterans, the Legion communiqué questioned the contention that no new V.A. hospitals were needed and that some could even be closed. "The existing number of V.A. hospital beds is short of the total authorized by Congress," the release stated.

Furthermore, the statement charged that the commission "apparently wants to make ability to earn the single criterion for determining [a] veteran's entitlement to disability compensation." That, the statement continued, "would be totally unrealistic and a reversal of the present fair standard arrived at after many years of trial and error."

National Commander Seaborn Collins wrote President Eisenhower on March 1, 1955, reminding him that the Legion itself had supported efforts to reduce the cost of government, even the costs involved in veterans' benefits where more efficiency could save the taxpayers money. But, he complained, Hoover's zeal in cost-cutting failed to recognize the "special consideration" that veterans had earned through wartime service. Collins called on the president to carefully review the commission's recommendations for veterans' medicine and disability compensation.

The National Rehab Commission's resolution adopted at its March 1955 conference in Washington contained vitriolic condemnation of the recommendations for cuts in medical services to veterans. The cuts were "vicious, unwarranted and unjustified, unfounded, uneconomic, and heartless."

Troubling to Legion national officers, also, was the commission's recommendation to transfer the authority to evaluate the extent of a veteran's disability to the V.A.'s Department of Medicine and Surgery. Currently, they pointed out, the complicated laws, rules, and regulations governing rating were a joint legal, occupational, and medical matter exercised by the V.A.'s Department of Veterans Benefits where the matter should remain.

While battling the new crop of recommendations of this second Hoover Commission, national officers soon found themselves in yet another confrontation with Gen. Omar Bradley. This time the topic was one that the first generation of Legionnaires had debated among themselves—pensions.

This new review of veterans' pensions had its origin in a news release read by Presidential Press Secretary James G. Hagerty while the President was at the Lowry Air Force Base in Denver on August 28, 1954. There was both good and bad news.

On the positive side, it was encouraging to hear that the president had just signed H.R. 9020 and H.R. 9962 for increasing payments to veterans for service-connected disabilities (or death compensation to their dependents) and to those receiving nonservice-connected disability pensions.

Then the president spoke of austerity in veterans' affairs. "We must recognize the fact that, because of the inauguration and growth of closely related—and uncorrelated—federal programs designed to provide assurances against want to all our citizens, there are today many instances of uneven and inequitable benefits. Under the present system, for example, there are no means of taking into account the degree of a veteran's need—no relation between payments received under the veterans' pension laws and payments received, for example, under our Old Age and Survivors Insurance System."

Therefore, he continued, "It is essential that steps be taken to examine the entire structure, scope and philosophy of our veterans' benefit laws in relation to each other and to other government programs. I am ordering such a study."

On January 14, 1955, Executive Order 10588 established the president's Commission on Veterans' Pensions. A few weeks later, on March 5, Eisenhower appointed his friend Omar Bradley to chair this commission for clarifying the relationship of veterans' pensions to Social Security and other family-protection plans. Bradley, a self-described "dedicated fiscal conservative," would now tackle one of the most historic and hallowed of veterans' benefits—pensions. He was already assumed to be of the opinion that the great social advances of the previous twenty years had reduced the need for soldiers' pensions. There was now Social Security, old-age pensions, state unemployment insurance, industrial retirement plans. Did veterans covered by Civil Service pensions, for example, need another source of government support? Before these programs had been established, there were four million veterans; now there were twenty-one million, with hundreds of thousands being added each year. Those were the figures and the pension philosophy that impressed General Bradley. (Past National Commander Don Wilson would soon remark that it seemed to him that the Bradley Commission had conceived its function to be that of discrediting the veterans' pension program.)

Legion National Convention mandates over the years regarding the liberalization of disability pensions generally sought (1) the reduction of disability and/or unemployability requirements because of attained age; (2) higher annual income limitations or permission to exclude certain additional types of income from the computation; and (3) increased monthly rates of pension.

Uniformly rejected at national conventions was the "general service" type of pension, that paid on the basis of attained age alone without any disability or income requirements. One lone convention, that in Miami in 1948, overrode the tradition and voted approval of general service pensions. With that as a legislative mandate, a compromise plan that emerged as a call for such a pension was presented as a Legion bill to Congress, where it passed the House after a bitter struggle but died in the Senate. The next year, the consensus of Legionnaires was again back on track—upholding the usual convention Rehabilitation Committee's rejection of general service pension resolutions in favor of more moderate ones that sought various liberalizations in the existing program's disability requirements, income requirements, and rates of pension.

As in the past, any discussion of veterans' pensions evoked a basic tenet of Legionism: that veterans were a special class of citizens. In the current context, any attempt to compare veterans' pensions with Social Security benefits ignored that basic principle. It was but a compounding of the offense, furthermore, to assume that Social Security should replace the pensions to which veterans were entitled as a partial monetary recompense for an employment handicap acquired in service to their country.

It was the Legion's belief that veterans' pension programs had been founded upon a concept completely dissimilar to that underlying Social Security. Veterans' pensions related to a select group of persons who had defended their country in times of emergency, which was seen as being the highest form of patriotism. Social Security, on the other hand, was an insurance program into which both employees and employers contributed and from which employees would be compensated eventually.

National Commander Addington Wagner appointed three Legionnaires from the national-level volunteer ranks—Past National Commander Don Wilson, who was the chairman, Dr. Carl J. Rees of Delaware, and Dr. Deward H. Reed of New Mexico—to monitor the work of the Bradley Commission and to respond as the official Legion task force on pensions.

In mid-May, National Judge Advocate Bertram G. Davis and national staffers Robert B. Pitkin, John J. Corcoran, and Edward M. McGrail called on the executive director of the Bradley Commission, Gen. Ernest M. Brannon, at the commission's new quarters (which Davis called "extensive"). The party from Legion Washington headquarters asked that informal talks be held occasionally as likely being more productive than formal, structured talks. Brannon agreed.

In mid-August the two groups met again. The Bradley Commission members asked for information accumulated by the Legion about veterans' pensions. Wilson informed them that although, in most cases, historical and academic background studies such as they requested had not been done, the information that they requested was available in other forms and would be readily shared. Wilson explained the inner workings of the Legion and how its operational functions and its specialists and other Rehab workers could contribute to the commission's study.

The subject of the V.A.'s schedule for rating disabilities, of course, occupied an important part of the review of the pension system by the Bradley Commission.

In this area as in others, part of the problem of relating Legion policies and positions was the difficulty of transferring whole-cloth Legionism to the understanding of a wider audience, even assuming that audience had no preconceived notions about what veterans deserved in the way of benefits.

Magazine editor Robert Pitkin (son of professor and author Walter B. Pitkin, whose 1934 book *Life Begins at Forty* had become a popular slogan) was often called on to contribute observations and opinions about the abstract nature of Legionism. Pitkin knew the task of expressing Legion concepts and attitudes was difficult even when attempted in the organization's own official magazine. He related to Past National Commander Wilson in late October 1955, "There is no practical basis for arriving at a compensation rating schedule whose validity would be entirely demonstrable in a scientific way." Furthermore, he added, "When it comes to the actual construction of a rating schedule, experience, and the shared opinion of persons with experience, has provided, and is likely to provide, the only practical method of devising a schedule. Several kinds of experience are needed, including political, economic, medical, and humanitarian."

Therefore, he concluded, "We cannot apply an objective yardstick to any rating schedule and thereby demonstrate that it is a proper schedule, although rehabilitation folks can criticize any schedule on the basis of their experience with veterans, and such criticism may be valid."

The 3,165 delegates to the National Convention in Miami in 1955 favorably considered three resolutions in particular that spoke to the disability pension issue: Resolution 40 from the Department of California, 70 from Massachusetts, and 528 from Rhode Island.

In a final roll-call vote, 2,110 of the delegates rejected the proposal that the Legion seek to obtain legislation to provide for the payment of a pension of one hundred dollars a month to all honorably discharged veterans of World War I who were sixty years of age, regardless of need. In effect they reaffirmed the present system that provided cash awards to veterans of both World Wars and the Korean War, veterans of all ages, who were permanently and totally disabled and who had proved their need for assistance.

After the convention, National Field Service Director Nicholas Lynch, Jr., complained about the misleading press stories about both the Legion's current and its historical view on veterans' pensions. He was particularly angered by the references "in blazing headlines," often on the front page, to the convention's having rejected a proposal for an unrestricted pension for World War I veterans. It was not that simple or new a matter, Lynch said. He reiterated the complaint that rarely did the newspapers explain in any helpful detail that for many years there had been a pension for World War I veterans based on disability, unemployability, and need. Nor was it explained that for that period of time, also, the Legion had sought to have those three requirements liberalized.

Long-standing Legion opposition to a "general pension" notwithstanding, the legislation prompted by the 1955 National Convention's resolutions did evolve as an attempt to placate those who repeatedly raised a clamor for a general pension law. The Rehab and the Legislative Commissions had had to consider two aspects, particularly, of the pension issue: the practical aspect of acquiescence to the will of the membership as discerned by the action of their delegates to the National Convention, and the academic aspect, the knowledge gained through experience and study that indicated that the Legion had traditionally opposed that type of pension because the existing-needs clause could always be used to answer charges of raiding the treasury.

The N.E.C., at its November 1955 meeting in Indianapolis, set out a program of increased allowances for aged veterans based on the factors of unemployability and economic need. It was to be the legislative priority for the Legion in 1956. Relying not only on the Legislative Division, National Commander Wagner appointed a special committee to steer the program through the second session of the 84th Congress.

The Legion's bill had three objectives: to increase the current non-service-connected compensation rates, to raise the annual income limitations, and to gain automatic qualification for any veteran reaching the age of sixty-five as being eligible for a government allowance if his or her income was within the prescribed limits.

"Our purpose," National Commander Wagner said, "is to take care of the aged veteran who is in economic distress due to unemployability and [who] has a low income or no income at all."

World War II veteran and Legionnaire Representative William Jennings Bryan Dorn (D., SC) presented the Legion bill incorporating this latest effort toward a pension bill to the House Committee on Veterans Affairs on January 12. H.R. 7886 was "a Bill to amend part III of Veterans Regulation Numbered 1 (a) to liberalize the basis for, and increase the monthly rates of, disability pension awards."

Announcements of the bill, dubbed "the War Veterans Security

Bill," sent to the press depicted an organization of three million members gearing up on all levels, in 58 departments, 435 congressional districts, 3,070 counties, to press for additional pension monies for veterans "who face their declining days across a dreary prospect of old age disabilities, unemployability, and inadequate income."

Soon, also, National Commander Wagner announced new personnel for his special committee to spearhead the drive for the enactment of the pension measure. Past National Commander John Stelle and National Legislative Commission Chairman Herman F. Luhrs would cochair the group, which included two past national commanders, Governor George N. Craig and Erle Cocke, Jr., who were joined by Michael M. Markowitz and Maurice Stember.

Though the Bradley Commission paid a courtesy call on the president during the last week of March 1956, during which General Bradley was photographed turning over the commission's report to the president, the report had not actually been printed yet. When the report was finished and made public, the seventy recommendations it contained were scrutinized at Legion National Headquarters. As expected, many essential elements of Legion philosophy were not upheld, including the special-class distinction for veterans, nonservice-connected medical benefits, the inappropriateness of substituting Social Security benefits for veterans' pensions, presumption of service connection for a wide range of diseases, and the right of dependents to veterans' death benefits.

Complain, argue, and debate as the Legion would, the Bradley Commission recommendations carried weight with the president and with many in Congress and the public sector who had been critical of veterans' pensions for many years. Legion communiqués accused the Bradley Commission of having created "an unfavorable climate of opinion concerning pensions, which has served in large part to nullify our efforts to secure further liberalizations."

In those circumstances, the Legion's bill, H.R. 7886, did not succeed. Though passed by the House, it died in the Senate Finance Committee. Nor did subsequent attempts at accomplishing the same kind of measure meet with any more favor than had H.R. 7886. Many critics were saying that the Legion should not seek modification of disability pensions, but work to enhance a compensation program for the service-connected disabled. One consolation for those lobbying for the Legion was that the greater the spread created between the two distinct categories of disabled, the greater the chance that pension awards would be increased.

At this time, also, there appeared a move by some World War I veterans to break away from the Legion and other veterans' organizations to form their own group, primarily to push for a one-war general pension. The Veterans of World War I in the U.S.A., Inc., was chartered by Congress on July 18, 1958, only the fourteenth such charter granted since the Civil War. Olin Teague, House Veterans Affairs Committee chairman, had dissented, saying that the only reason the "Wonnies," the moniker summarily given the group by the press, had organized was to badger Congress for a pension.

The Legion National Convention at Chicago in late 1958 adopted four resolutions relating to the pension issue. Four bills, moreover, were drafted in December for the January opening of the 86th Congress. The bills were designed to (1) increase rates of death compensation and of disability and death pension payable by the V.A.; (2) increase the annual income limitations governing the payment for disability or death; (3) provide further basis for determination with respect to disability for pension purposes; and (4) provide pension for widows and children of veterans of World War I and the Korean War on the same basis as that for World War I veterans.

These bills constituted the Legion's new "Three-Point Pension Program," a simplified version of the desired effect of the four bills above. The Three-Point Pension Program called for (1) an increase in the pensions paid to veterans and their widows; (2) an increase in the amount veterans and their widows could earn before losing their pensions because of that income; and (3) an end to restrictions denying pensions to (a) veterans hospitalized for TB, (b) widows and orphans of World War I and Korean War veterans, and (c) veterans aged sixty-five or older who were not totally disabled or on limited income.

The administration had a pension program to offer Congress, too. That program, based in appreciable measure on the Bradley Commission report, was contained in H.R. 7650, passed on June 15, and a similar but diminished version passed by the Senate on August 13. The House agreed to the Senate version on August 14, but dropped the provision reopening the National Service Life Insurance (N.S.L.I.) program to World War II veterans, a program the Legion had worked to restore. When the Senate, too, agreed to keep the N.S.L.I. portion from reappearing in the bill, that version was sent to the president for his signature.

The signing of the much-traveled H.R. 7650 occurred in a setting that brought back memories of service and sacrifice. During his European tour, while visiting the country home of Britain's Prime Minister Harold MacMillan, President Eisenhower signed the bill, and the Veterans Pension Act of 1959 became Public Law 86-211.

Anyone who had ever worked on federal legislation knew that there had never been, nor was there likely to be, a perfect bill or subsequent enactment of law. The bill or law had not yet been written, or contemplated, about which someone or some group was not moved to make improvements according to their point of view.

Certainly the 1960 National Convention at Miami agreed, for it considered fifty-five resolutions on the pension issue. The Convention Committee on Rehabilitation pondered these many views and produced Resolution 320, which it put forward to amend the new pension law (86-211) with several changes. Upon adoption, the mandate by the convention included a liberalization of the rates and income limits of veterans, a repeal of the requirements that certain veterans had to count part of their wives' incomes as their own, and a repeal of the restriction on the amount of pension that could be paid to a veteran during periods of hospitalization or domiciliary care by the V.A. Basically, the resolution called for a pension of one hundred dollars a month plus allowances for dependents of veterans with the greatest need.

Proudly, then, Resolution 320 upheld the traditional Legion notion that an honorable pension was one made available for all war veterans in need. At the Legion's request, Olin Teague introduced H.R. 886 on January 3, a bill based on Resolution 320. National Headquarters asked post commanders to help generate a letter-writing campaign to support the bill.

Post commanders were also asked to remind the membership that a lack of Legion solidarity threatened the impact of a unified veterans' organization. They were reminded that largely because of the work of the Legion about one-third of all World War I veterans were now receiving a pension, that about one-half of all veterans over the age of sixty-five were on the pension rolls, and that an average of almost 400 more were being enrolled at the V.A. for pensions *daily.*

Knowing of the Legion's intent to continue to reformulate the pension laws to its view of what they should be, Olin Teague handed Clarence H. "Cap" Olson and John Corcoran a bill of his own in March 1962 and told them bluntly that it alone would be reported out of his House committee in about ten days. He insisted on receiving a statement from Legion National Commander Charles Bacon right away about the Legion's reaction to it.

As Bacon read the bill his displeasure mounted. In the confines of National Headquarters he described the bill to National Legislative Commission Chairman Jerome F. Duggan of Missouri as "a pitiful demonstration of throwing 'sop.'" Yet he did not want the Legion to be on record as refusing to support a raise in the rate of compensation for service-connected disabilities, which the bill did offer, inadequate "sop" that it might be. He and his advisers labored over a letter to Teague that would make that point without either supporting or rejecting the bill.

Teague introduced the measure, H.R. 10743, on March 14, and it was reported out by his committee after an executive session on March 19. There had been no hearings. Before the introduction of the bill, National Commander Bacon had testified before the committee on February 27, explaining that ten years earlier, in 1952, the Legion had taken issue when Congress created an imbalance in the compensation structure by an act granting greater compensation increases to those with service-connected disabilities evaluated at 50 percent or more. This imbalance, Bacon said, had been compounded by subsequent acts of Congress so that currently a veteran with a 90 percent disability received only 79.5 percent of the payment received by a veteran with 100 percent disability. Now he saw that that imbalance, reflected throughout the gradations of the current disability ratings, had been retained in H.R. 10743.

The Legion, however, sought a true balance of payment based upon percentage of disability. Such "percentage ratings" were based upon the theory of the average impairment of an individual's earning capacity. If this impairment did not reflect a true percentage of the payment for the total disability, then it was obvious that the rating schedules should be amended accordingly. Also, the Legion wanted all the disabled to receive compensation for the care of their dependents, not just those with a 50 percent or higher rated disability.

Furthermore, the cost-of-living increase given in 1957 had been the most recent one in the service-connected disability compensation rates. Surely, Bacon and the others argued, the nation could correct at least one of these injustices at this time.

But Teague's bill had been publicized widely, and a reminder from National Headquarters that the Legion had a long-standing policy of not signing petitions of other organizations fell short of convincing many members about why the national commander had not joined the leaders of the eight other veterans' organizations in signing a petition approving H.R. 10743.

Did the Legion intend for veterans to become indigent or destitute before they could expect help? Not so, national officers responded. They pointed instead to H.R. 886 and H.R. 2237, both Legion bills that would liberalize the existing disability pension law by increasing the amount of pension payments and giving special attention to veterans aged sixty-five or over. These bills, it was pointed out, had not been allowed to emerge from Teague's House committee.

Regardless of the national commander's explanation, the defection continued by many World War I members who were disappointed that the Legion, which had begun as their organization, had not taken a more active role in pushing for a World War I general pension.

In early July 1962, Virginia Department Acting Adjutant Wilbur Walker alerted National Headquarters that his department had lost "about 1,000" of its World War I members to the Veterans of World War I of the U.S.A., Inc., which with much press coverage was sponsoring its own bill, H.R. 3745.

To those such as the Virginia department adjutant who wrote to inform National of opinions strongly expressed in their departments or who themselves complained that the Legion did not seem concerned enough about World War I veterans, National Commander Bacon and others sought to reiterate the lesson learned from experience, that nonservice-connected pensions for veterans and their dependents and survivors should be based on a reasonable display of personal need. Why? Because granting aid only to the needy had always been the most effective argument before Congress and the public.

Nevertheless, H.R. 3745 continued to attract much attention on Capitol Hill. Perhaps it was the fact that congressmen were being lobbied by a new group, the World War I veterans organization, which was being both feted and roasted in the national press for its insistence on a World War I general pension.

Those at Legion National Headquarters who were experienced in legislative odds-taking gave the Veterans of World War I in the U.S.A., Inc., little chance of obtaining passage of a new pension measure. As "Cap" Olson explained to someone in the field in mid-July 1962, "Even our own H.R. 886 faces a fiscal struggle [with the Bureau of the Budget] and yet would cost scarcely more than one-third of the proposal contained in H.R. 3745." Even if the bill were to emerge from the House committee and be passed on the floor of the House and the Senate the president would certainly stop it in its tracks.

When National's refusal to join the band wagon for H.R. 3745 continued to raise complaints from World War I Legionnaires, National Commander Bacon issued a news release in late July in which he reminded all that a resolution proposing support for that very bill had failed to win the approval of the previous National Convention. The last time a separate World War I pension proposal had gained even enough support to secure a roll-call vote in a National Convention was in 1958, when the motion was rejected 2,597 to 414.

The National Convention a few weeks later in Las Vegas discussed the subject, then came to the same conclusion, even though some departments made it known that for one reason or another they had rarely if ever supported the Legion's stance on pensions. A motion to substitute a formal statement of support for H.R. 3745 instead of convention Resolution 317, which contained the revisions that many thought should be made in the existing pension law, brought yet another round of spirited debate on the subject. One delegate reminded the convention that the average age of World War I veterans was sixty-nine and that "we can no longer delay the movement of any legislation to bring them justification."

But in the end, after Robert McCurdy had reminded the assembly that the seventy-eight members of the Convention Rehab Commission, representing all of the states, had adopted Resolution 317 unanimously, the vote was taken and the resolution was adopted.

In due course, Resolution 317 became H.R. 1927 and was introduced on January 17, 1963, by Representative Roland Libonati (D., IL), a member of the House Veterans Affairs Committee. The March issue of

The American Legion Magazine carried a detailed account, including charts and other figures, for the bill's provisions, and addressed the "shortcomings and related problems" of Public Law 86-221, which had gone into effect in July 1960. The article ended with the story of one disabled veteran in Vermont whose pension benefits had been curtailed after the V.A. had ruled that insurance money he received upon the death of his wife could be considered under Public Law 86-211 as income (even though the veteran stated that burial and other expenses far exceeded the insurance settlement). With this closing image, chosen, of course, to show someone oppressed by the legislation, the present law could only be said to be "harsh," even "cruel."

In early May, Cap Olson was assigned the task of developing "a plateau of opinion favorable to veterans' legislation," and, of course, to H.R. 1927 in particular after it was apparent that there had not been much progress made on the Legion's major legislative program. Subcommittees of the National Legislative and Rehab commissions met for frank discussions.

On the evening of the adjournment of the May N.E.C. meeting in Indianapolis, in one of the traditional late-night confabs in Bob McCurdy's room at the Indianapolis Athletic Club, McCurdy and his guests developed a basic proposal for gaining favorable public opinion for the revisions of the current pension law.

It was agreed that there was a need to bring that message to the greatest number of members of Congress and veterans alike. One said that there were several departments that had not been particularly agreeable to National's views on the pension issue and that still supported either a separate World War I pension or a "general pension" not based on need, or both. In some of those departments there had been little assurance that previous information about National's stance on pensions had been distributed to the posts, so much in disagreement had been the department officialdom. McCurdy and his cohorts determined that fact sheets developed about the inequities in the pension law and the need to reopen the N.S.L.I. program would be distributed to a much larger audience than before.

Someone recommended that those who persisted in calling for a more generous one-war pension award be told that many thousands of World War II veterans were already beyond sixty-five years of age and that before long hundreds of thousands of them would be in the same category as their counterparts from the earlier war. Would the nation stand for another massive appeal for yet another one-war pension? Not likely. Work with and on the existing pension structure, he advised. Amending existing laws was the name of the game on Capitol Hill. Creating entirely new statutory systems was much more difficult, even for seasoned congressmen.

The estimation of the poor chances of the Veterans of World War I of the U.S.A., Inc., for gaining the enactment of their bill, H.R. 3745, were close to being correct.

In the process, the proposed World War I pension program was not spared attack by the press, similar to those attacks leveled numerous times at Legion efforts for raising the public consciousness of veterans' rehabilitative and economic needs. Not all such editorials and articles were as acerbic as that which appeared in the Springfield, Missouri, *Daily News* (November 12, 1963), in depicting "These blowsy old freebooters [who] have stood paunch-deep in the public trough ever since 1918. . . ." But the reaction by many in the press, even if not expressed so bluntly and demeaningly, was, nevertheless, antipension.

In April, Cap Olson and others met with Congressman Libonati to inquire about the chances of H.R. 1927. They were told that the bill would probably be voted out of the committee but would likely be modified to comply with the administration's desire for a lower overall dollar figure to cost between $100 and $200 million. In such form it would bring about modest increases in the current payment and income limit structure and it would add about 250,000 persons to the pension rolls. That, reportedly, was about all the congressman could see Congress doing at this time.

So what chance did the Legion's bill have? "Get to the president," Libonati was said to have advised, for President Johnson presumably was already gauging the political value of pension legislation.

The congressman's assessment was proved correct; the bill was brought out on August 5 to the all but unanimous approval of the House.

Cap Olson observed that "no legislative endeavor of the American Legion in recent years has received more attention from the national commanders and the staff than proposals to improve the present pension law."

In August, John J. Corcoran, National Rehabilitation Commission director, told the Senate Finance Committee that the Veterans Pension Act of 1959 had not lived up to its promise, that aged and disabled veterans desperately needed what was provided in H.R. 1927, and that for over a hundred thousand veterans the bill was needed to counter a proposed increase in Social Security being counted as income by the V.A. for pension entitlement purposes. Corcoran observed that it was curious that when veterans' legislation was proposed, there were always those who worried aloud that it was beyond the economic capabilities of the nation. Yet that concern was not as often applied to legislation that would improve the salaries of government or military personnel or that provided monies for foreign aid.

H.R. 1927, however, was slated for a happier fate. One of the pleasant duties early in the tenure of new National Commander Donald E. Johnson was to issue telegrams of thanks to Congressman Olin E. Teague and Senator Russell Long on October 5 for their help in the passage of the bill in the House on August 11 and finally the Senate on September 28. Indeed, the help of these influential members of Congress had been essential, especially when, as Cap Olson complained in early June, the time was "long past when we can browbeat Congress into submission" over legislation.

"Veterans' legislation is not an easy task," Olson said, particularly now that the Bureau of the Budget, the president's office, and many others entered into the process in determining the fate of legislation that would cost great sums of money. (Many at National Headquarters had been disappointed with the lack of enthusiasm among members in helping to publicize the need for legislation.)

President Johnson signed the bill on October 13, which as Public Law 88-664, scheduled to go into effect on January 1, 1965, also allowed for service- and nonservice-disabled veterans who were being turned down for life insurance to purchase National Service Life Insurance for a limited amount of time, beginning in May 1965. It was estimated that 1.4 million veterans would benefit from the liberalization of the pension law, and that 3.3 million veterans qualified for the new offering of N.S.L.I. coverage.

Once again the often frustrating but equally exhilarating (when it succeeded) cycle—the resolution-to-law process, a Legion tradition for forty-five years—had been completed. So, too, had a familiar consequence been observed: new federal laws relating to veterans' affairs often needed amending to restore certain provisions for which the Legion had lobbied originally but which had been struck from the legislation before its passage and delivery to the president for his signature.

Occasionally some other variant within that cycle could be observed, as in late March 1965 when the former commander of Post 747 in tiny Senecaville, Ohio, stood on the floor of the U.S. House of Representatives and introduced three bills to liberalize and amend the new pension bill on which the printer's ink was barely dry.

Democratic Representative Robert T. Secrest rose to sponsor H.R. 6409, the result of a recent Legion National Convention mandate for liberalizing the reasons for permanent and total disability determinations on a V.A. rating action; H.R. 6408 for yet another increase in income permitted and in the disability and death pension; and H.R. 6410, to exclude certain incomes from determining annual income for pension purposes. All three bills were summarily referred to the House Veterans Affairs Committee for consideration.

III

Dateline: Cuba, Laos, Vietnam . . .

As important as the "pension wars" had been for some national officers and staff members, the work assignments for others required that they scan the horizon of foreign affairs and national defense. What they were seeing was alarming.

Developments in Cuba, nearly within sight of the U.S. border, caused much concern. In January 1959, Fidel Castro had engineered the overthrow of the Batista government and a few weeks later visited the United States, vowing that there were no Communists in his coterie of revolutionaries. That proved not to be the case, and by January 1961 the United States had broken off relations with the nearby island nation, now a fountainhead of Communist agitation in Central and South America. The debacle that met U.S.-supported anti-Castro forces attempting to invade the island at the Bay of Pigs in April further cemented the stance of the two governments. The United States did manage to have Cuba expelled from the Organization of American States early the next year.

That year, also, President Kennedy had demanded the removal of Soviet missiles from Cuba and had backed up the announcement by blacklisting ships trading with the Castro regime. The action also included a naval quarantine of offensive weaponry. The "Cuban Missile Crisis" lasted officially from October 22, 1962, to January 7, 1963. But U.S.-instigated ostracism of Cuba continued. In all, it was assumed that about sixty percent of the ocean traffic to Cuba was cut in 1963 as well as an appreciable amount of air traffic. The Legion recorded many resolutions supporting various U.S. actions in this regard.

Meanwhile, the United States was about to become much more involved in yet another world hot spot. The failure of the French in Indochina to resist the onslaught of Communist aggression on their long-held colonial possessions, particularly in the already divided country of Vietnam, had gained the attention of the U.S. government, which had sent economic aid to South Vietnam when the French left. Before long, military advisers were sent to help the South Vietnamese combat Communist troops from North Vietnam. In 1961, two American helicopter units were dispatched to the area.

Though Vice-President Lyndon Johnson had visited South Vietnam in May 1961 to show U.S. support for President Ngo Dinh Diem, U.S.

disenchantment with the Diem government caused a cooling of relations in 1963; but the United States was quick to support the provisional government that followed Diem's overthrow later that year. From that point, U.S. aid continued to increase, as did U.S. military manpower in embattled South Vietnam.

The resolution considered by the N.E.C. at its May 1962 meeting characterized the concern, and the confusion, of many about what was transpiring in Southeast Asia. The discussions that ensued characterized the evolving awareness of those who were pondering the escalation of U.S. involvement in that part of the world.

In opposition to Communist domination there, the Legion Foreign Relations Commission had resolved, in keeping with the often discussed "domino theory," that "the preservation of a free government in South Vietnam is essential to the welfare of the freedom-loving nations." Noting the "affirmative and cooperative action" taken by the United States in that area, the commission desired that "our government take whatever additional positive action as is necessary . . . to maintain a strong position and preserve Southeast Asia against further encroachment of Communist domination."

But the national committeeman from Virginia, L. Eldon James, asked what was the "affirmative and cooperative action" that had been taken so far?

Commission Chairman Emilio S. Iglesias explained that the term "affirmative action" referred to U.S. support for the formation of a coalition government in Laos in compliance with the negotiated armistice of 1954 which sought to end the fighting in that region.

"A coalition government with Communists?" James asked.

Iglesias acknowledged that the matter was not only confusing, but also that apparently the intent of the Geneva Accord had been stalemated regarding Laos. He reviewed the arrangement negotiated by Averell E. Harriman in 1961 regarding a cease-fire in war-torn Vietnam and the neutrality of Laos to be maintained by a three-way coalition of Communists, pro-Western elements, and neutral parties.

So how then, James continued, could one call for "further positive action" when, first, the coalition envisioned was to include Communists and, second, no "positive" action was occurring currently?

One must use generalities, Iglesias replied, when composing resolutions aimed at supporting U.S. involvement in world affairs.

Not so, others said. One interjected that if the words "Laos and" were stricken from the resolution, then it would focus on Vietnam, where, presumably, a more acceptable government had been or could be formed.

But Past National Commander Art Connell asked if omitting Laos from this resolution meant that the United States should not continue to assist the process of stabilizing that government or to prevent the expansion of Communism there?

That, National Commander Bacon said, was another matter altogether and required yet another resolution by the Foreign Relations Commission. So the revised resolution regarding support to Vietnam was carried.

But the next morning, in considering more foreign relations resolutions, some committeemen objected to the use of the term "neutral police force" in describing the action that the United States, or even the U.N., should take in various areas of conflict and Communist aggression. Chairman Iglesias acknowledged that, indeed, it "appeared to be an inconsistency" to use the word "neutral" when actually meaning action friendly to the West.

Committeeman Peter B. Wilson of Idaho agreed. "I think a neutral police force is just fine as long as it is neutral my way."

But neutrality in Vietnam, Laos, or any of the other trouble spots around the world was a commodity in short supply. The Foreign Relations Commission's report to the N.E.C. the next spring sought to clarify its position on the situation in Southeast Asia.

"The American Legion has never considered the Laotian problem to be distinguishable from the overall major problem of Southeast Asia, namely, the threat of Communist domination of the entire region. We believe that the United States—together with the other interested free nations—should provide the nations of the region with whatever military and economic assistance is necessary to enable them to rid themselves of internal Communist influence, to resist external Communist pressure, and to pursue their respective destinies as free and independent states."

Obviously, the report continued, the present form of coalition, "nonaligned" government in Laos, had been doomed from the start. That was apparent now especially with the recent activity of the Communist Pathet Lao forces. The "affirmative action" the United States was taking in Vietnam was endorsed, as was the stationing of U.S. troops in Thailand.

Two years later, another spring N.E.C. gathering in 1965 heard the Foreign Relations Commission resolve that it "fully supports U.S. assistance to Vietnam" and urge "increased commitment of American forces to that area." The commission also called for "employment of such military measures as would ensure the destruction of the forces of aggression—at both the places of their attacks and at the source of their power, as military judgment decides."

The United States in recent weeks had increased the number of forces it had in South Vietnam and had mounted retaliatory air strikes against North Vietnam. What about the numerous proposals from domestic and foreign sources that the United States seek a negotiated settlement of the Vietnamese conflict?

"The American Legion insists that there be no agreement . . . to enter into discussions with . . . Hanoi, Peking, or Moscow until and unless North Vietnam halts its aggression against South Vietnam in keeping with the two previous negotiated settlements of the Vietnamese conflict," the national commander replied.

The United States was becoming embroiled in a land war in Asia.

POINT AND COUNTERPOINT

THE VIETNAM ERA

1966–1976

In the late 1960s and early to mid-1970s, protesters and naysayers, the respectable and riotous alike, exhibited their exasperation about the nation's floundering in the exotic quagmire of Vietnam and about a host of other real and alleged ills affecting the body politic and Western society in general. All the while, the American Legion maintained itself as the ready, shining patriotic bulwark mentioned in the revered "preamble" to the Legion constitution.

Particularly it was the work, as if in unison, of three national commissions—Americanism, National Security, and Foreign Relations (the latter two would be joined at the division level in 1969)—which helped form the Legion's public image during this time. The interrelated interests and concerns of these three commissions, rooted in Legion "basics," related directly to a dilemma facing the nation—an increasingly unpopular war and the reaction of the American public to matters of national defense, foreign relations, and citizenship in general.

To be sure, throughout the period the spectral influence of the founders of the Legion in 1919 was apparent. The resolutions adopted in this ten-year span promoted World War I–era Americanism along with a foreign policy and a national security stance tailored now to a troubled nuclear age.

While some opinion leaders adopted vaporous "situational ethics," the Legion worked to maintain the luster of a patriotic touchstone and to ensure national security. Thus would its chronicles for the 1960s be closed and those for the 1970s begun.

To insiders, there was no remarkable difference in the way the three commissions operated. The tradition of resolving problems and conflicts was staunchly upheld, was still the chief expression of Legionism. Still heard was the essential question, "Is it germane?" Seasoned Legion volunteers continued to ponder the language and derivation of proposed resolutions and the effects they would have on the membership, the Congress, and the public.

Each group continued to work separately on its own agenda. As before, the scope of collective interest for the three commissions continued to constitute an impressive array of public services and concerns.

It seemed at times, however, that many resolutions considered by the commissions were interchangeable. Occasionally a resolution tumbled from the always bountiful hopper with the appearance of having been a joint effort of all three commissions. On one occasion National Judge Advocate Bertram Davis was called upon to consider a resolution presented to the N.E.C. in May 1967, in which he found an unworkable mix of "whereas" and "resolve" clauses, one or more attributable to each of the three commissions.

When it was recommended that this resolution be dismantled and, thereby, scuttled in its current form, Henry Clay, the committeeman from Louisiana, suggested a compromise befitting his namesake. "The American Legion for the last number of years has procedured itself to death just in this same method. We have passed resolutions which have been couched in such language as to mean almost nothing. The impact of the Legion as a result of this type of activity for the last ten or fifteen years has gone down and down." Members were being lost, according to Clay, to smaller veterans' organizations "who are taking stronger stands."

"The American Legion became great," Clay continued, "not because of this type of activity, but because it was willing to stand up and be counted when the chips were down."

Judge Davis consulted the Reorganization Plan of October–November 1947, particularly the outline of authorization contained in the section entitled "Membership and Purpose of Commissions and Committees":

Americanism in Legion parlance included the promotion of obligatory patriotic observances that have accrued from living in a democratic nation, along with the combating of subversive activity and the promotion of citizenship-minded programs for young people.

National Security meant absolute, honorable national-scale safety (preferably through far-from-being-enacted Universal Military Training) from aggression by powers bent on world domination and which, many believed, were at that moment stalking the United States across the landscapes of already subjugated nations.

Foreign Relations involved the ever-widening involvement, influence, and reciprocity required of a world power and a member of the U.N., such as the United States.

High sounding pedigrees. And each program area mirrored much public concern. One in particular—Americanism—involved volunteerism on a scale that compared favorably with that of any national organization, leading many in the number of volunteer hours spent in positive-minded, constructive programs unique to the American Legion, such as Boys State and Boys Nation (with similar activities for girls sponsored by the Auxiliary) and the Oratorical Contest, all for the enlightenment of American youth about the privileges of citizenship.

There was another side to the definition and promotion of Americanism: the Legion was often accused of overstating the case. If there was one complaint voiced as often as that old saw about the Legion supposedly being a treasury raider for veterans' rehab, it was that allegedly the Legion's standards for patriotism were too rigid.

The Legion, however, would reply that it was only upholding the symbols of that uniquely successful protest 200 years earlier—the American Revolution. One symbol in particular—the American flag—which in abundance adorned every Legion celebration of patriotic holidays, was now the subject of controversy for the way it was often displayed, or ridiculed, by those protesting the war in Vietnam.

As for countersubversiveness, it seemed to the collective Legion mind that the free society for which its members had fought in wartime seemingly had allowed an ideological Trojan horse to be taken in, from which had emerged harmful "isms" threatening to infect the nation's unions, educational institutions, entertainment industry, and mass media.

The rhetoric of radical political change reverberated across the land, accompanied often by obstreperous affronts to order and authority, to much, in fact, for which the Legion stood.

So in the 1960s, as the antiwar protesters commandeered a large share of dinner-time network news minutes, stalwarts in Legion caps were made out to depict dispassionate conservatism and status quo obstinacy. This characterization, which provided convenient news "color" for those editing current events for public consumption, was undeserved, largely untrue, and historically inaccurate.

The chief concern of the National Security Commission at this time was the threat to the United States caused by the modernization of weaponry, particularly that of missiles. The rocketry that Germany had launched against Great Britain during World War II had undergone advancement at an astounding pace as all major nations sought to further develop it as a modern instrument of war. Now there were missile delivery systems which, launched from Europe, could reach the heartland of the United States. That threat occupied much of the time of the nation's defense planners.

The nation's foreign relations were inextricably linked with national security. Any remaining hint of isolationism had most likely not survived the Korean War. The American Legion, at least since then, was certainly in the forefront of organizations keenly aware of "the big picture" of world events.

Within the Legion, the study of specific aspects of national defense and foreign relations had long been assigned to a roster of committees, the recitation of which sounded like a combined version of the Defense and State departments.

The complaint was heard occasionally that the American Legion was but parroting the policies of these two cabinet-level departments. The national commissions on national security and foreign relations did support federal government actions many times. But as was often explained to critics, the Legion had often gone its own way and, in so doing, cut new paths regarding these matters.

The matter of the Vietnam War, of course, occupied most of the time and attention of the two commissions. The Legion, too, eventually would come to complain about the manner in which yet another "limited" war was being waged.

But for the first stages of the conflict, the Legion, as the preeminent patriotic organization, supported the government. Successive foreign relations commissions had been well acquainted with the ways in which the United States had become involved.

Several years before U.S. troops were engaged in fighting in Vietnam, the U.S. government had contributed military equipment and economic aid to the French in their losing struggle to retain control of Indochina. In 1954, a conference in Geneva negotiated an armistice; thereafter, the efforts of Cambodia, Laos, and Vietnam for self-government became an ongoing interest of the United States.

When the United States became part of the Southeast Asia Treaty Organization (SEATO), it pledged help in case of "armed attack" within the region. In particular, the United States helped bolster a series of governments in Saigon that were beset by Communist-led guerrilla forces from North Vietnam and by similar forces operating in South Vietnam as well.

With aggression from North Vietnam a continuing activity, President Eisenhower in February 1955 sent the first U.S. military advisers to train the army of South Vietnam. In May 1961, after Viet Cong activity had increased markedly for more than a year, President Kennedy sent one hundred U.S. jungle specialists to South Vietnam. By the end of that year, thirty-three U.S. army helicopters and four hundred air and ground crewmen had been added. Thereafter the number of personnel was increased substantially. By the end of 1963, 16,300 U.S. troops had been sent. By the end of 1964, the number was 23,300.

On August 2, 1964, U.S. destroyers *Maddox* and *C. Turner Joy,* cruising the international waters of the Gulf of Tonkin off North Vietnam, were attacked by North Vietnamese torpedo boats. Two days later, more attacks brought an announcement from President Johnson that retaliatory air strikes would be made on sites in the north. The president's recommendation for such action was overwhelmingly adopted by Congress with the Tonkin Resolution.

The Legion's 1964 National Convention in Dallas adopted a resolution calling for the destruction of the forces of aggression in Southeast Asia at both the places of their attacks and at the sources of their power. National Commander Don Johnson later declared Legion support of the president's actions in his Veterans Day address in Long Beach, California. "There is but one answer for Americans in that ugly little war in Vietnam and that is victory, a victory which will stem the tide of Red aggression not only in Vietnam but in all of Southeast Asia." So "the American Legion can see no justification for the government of the United States . . . indulging in wishful thinking that there may be a softening of Communist policy or any deviation from the oft-pronounced objective of world dominance."

In February 1965, following a Viet Cong attack on U.S. advisers at Pleiku during which 8 Americans were killed and 109 wounded and an attack on U.S. army barracks at Qui Nhon in which 23 Americans were killed and 21 wounded, the national commander sent a telegram to President Johnson supporting "the retaliatory action which you have ordered to be taken against the Hanoi regime." The N.E.C. adopted Resolution 5, which had been put forth by the Foreign Relations Commission at its March 15 meeting, a resolution that insisted that there be no agreement by the United States to enter into discussions with North Vietnam, China, or the Soviet Union until and unless North Vietnam halted its aggression against the south.

In April, National Commander Johnson warned against "another Korean-style stalemate." The war in Vietnam must be won, he said. There should be no cease-fire or recess until the North Vietnamese halted their aggression.

If in hindsight the national commander's statements would seem mocked by the actual results in that conflict, it is important to note that one thing the Legion's official stance in the early months of the war accomplished, if temporarily, was to maintain a sense of purpose for the war.

Legion spokesmen occasionally told of having seen war first-hand. A hell on earth though it was, it was the tragic alternative to cruel subjugation under a "people's republic" form of government currently being thrust upon many smaller nations around the world.

Thus the American Legion provided an example of support for the government to which had been delegated the means and the authority to wage war.

"There has been much confusion—created in part by Communist propaganda machinery," National Commander Johnson said. "The American Legion has, by its own convention mandate, placed itself on record as supporting fully the firm stand taken by President Johnson to defend Vietnam and to bring a true and just peace to that harassed area of Asia."

The national commander recognized that this was an increasingly unpopular stance. Nevertheless, he said, "For college students and even top-ranking members of the Senate to propose a 'bombing recess' or a 'cease-fire' by our military commands in that area approaches the realm of hysteria. Nothing would be accomplished except to aid the Viet Cong in the realignment and strengthening of their military positions.

"A true peace for millions of lives, our own included, is actually the reason the United States went to the defense of Vietnam. For this nation, we must first stem the Communist invasion—and then talk of peace."

The next month, National Commander Johnson, Foreign Relations Director Warren MacDonald, and speech writer Rod Anderson were in Vietnam from May 14 to May 17. They met with U.S. Ambassador Maxwell Taylor, Gen. William Westmoreland, commander of the U.S. Military Assistance Command, and South Vietnamese Prime Minister Dr. Phan Huy Quat. They also saw that this was a new kind of war. "Every village is a front line," the national commander said. The war "is being waged in the villages, on the military, economic, and social front."

After leaving Saigon, Johnson spoke by telephone from Singapore to radio station KCRG in Cedar Rapids (which served his home area in Iowa) and complimented American troops for the job they were doing. From an outpost in the Mekong River delta area he had looked into Viet Cong–held territory. A veteran of the European theater in World War II, he once again sensed the closeness of war. The helicopter in which he was traveling was forced to take evasive action to avoid enemy fire. While in the air he had seen the effects of enemy mortar rounds exploding among munitions at Bien Hoa air base when the Viet Cong began their summer offensive. The result, he said, resembled "a small atom bomb cloud."

Johnson reiterated the contention that this was not a civil war and instead was "a war of infiltration, subversion, terrorism and invasion." He was particularly eager to point out that the Vietnamese themselves were heavily engaged in fighting the war alongside the Americans. The "noise" he now heard in the United States decrying the war was at the very least a "disservice to [American] servicemen."

The national commander was convinced that the air strikes that President Johnson had announced two months earlier in February on staging areas in North Vietnam had been effective. (Just days after the national commander's visit, however, the bombing was stopped for a few days in an attempt to encourage peace feelers from the North.)

Until now it had been an air war for the United States, one of supporting South Vietnamese ground forces. But in early June 1965 came a fateful decision. The State Department announced that U.S. commanders in Vietnam had been authorized to commit their ground troops to combat if it appeared that the South Vietnamese needed their help.

The next month, at a press conference in Honolulu during the Hawaii department convention, the national commander called for the bombing of all enemy military targets in North Vietnam, not just supply lines but particularly troop and missile bases. Though acknowledging the possibility of reprisals by the Red Chinese, "The Legion feels action must be taken because of the strategic importance of Southeast Asia and our moral involvements due to commitments to it."

The national commander cited the "strategic importance" of Vietnam among the nations of Indochina, referring perhaps to the idea of the "domino theory," which in the early years of the war depicted the chain reaction that, many said, would occur should South Vietnam fall to the Communists.

A most memorable aspect of the war, of course, was the spate of antiwar protests growing to fever pitch in the United States. National Americanism Commission Resolution 19 coming out of the N.E.C. meeting in May 1965 reflected the times.

Bristling with righteous anger at Communism's stealth and now its armed aggression, Resolution 19 argued that the "firm stand taken by President Johnson to defend Vietnam and to bring a true and just peace to that harassed area of Asia" had been clouded "during the past several weeks" by "confusion created in the minds of the American public as to our aims and policies due largely to Communist and pacifist propaganda," a charge, it was said, supported by "documentary evidence."

Crediting the president with "honest efforts to resolve the situation by offering peaceful discussions, peaceful economic assistance," the N.E.C. men resolved, hereby, that the Legion reaffirm its support for the president's "strong and militant stand in the face of continued and mounting aggression." The resolution also "condemns those individuals and organizations who under the guise of peace would have the president seek 'peace at any price.' "

Resolving aside, the Legion was dependent in large measure as always on post-level activities to relate its views to the membership and to the general public. New York Department Adjutant Maurice

Stember, an influential, long-time Legionnaire, outlined methods in October 1965 by which posts could support the war. "I strongly urge that at your November meetings a period of time be devoted to a civic action program in support of our military." Stember advised "concentrating on obtaining community expressions of support . . . and encouraging our servicemen in South Vietnam with letters and gifts of a practical nature to demonstrate that the overwhelming number of Americans wholeheartedly support" them in contrast to the recent demonstrations and draft card burnings.

On October 21, 1965, the new national commander, L. Eldon James of Virginia, returned from his own trip to South Vietnam after having visited seven of its forty-three provinces and having met many South Vietnamese citizens, including province and hamlet chiefs and schoolteachers, as well as U.S. military personnel. "The Communist threat," he reported, "preying upon innocent and oppressed people is highly organized and is vicious beyond description." He had seen, he believed, "the distant but no less important threat to all freedom-loving people everywhere."

To the president, James promised that the Legion would remain "a vanguard of loyal Americans who will offer public evidence of our support of your vigorous, forthright, and intelligent policy in South Vietnam."

Legion national officers held that the advice of the senior officers of the government should be heeded, that there was an urgent and obligatory need to halt the advancement of Communism into South Vietnam.

Second-guessing the government's policy was not condoned. As Warren MacDonald, director of research at Washington headquarters, phrased it, "The subject is far too complex and the picture is an ever-changing one." MacDonald's two trips to Vietnam in 1965 had convinced him that "from all I have seen and heard, our leaders, while not military men themselves, are making the great majority of their hard decisions on the basis of the best available military judgment."

The Legion's position on the matter was "that the aggressor should be hit and hit hard both at the places of his attacks and at the sources of his power—but only as military judgment decides." That was the way the war was being conducted so far, MacDonald believed. Action in Vietnam had been "based on military considerations [and] not political considerations," except for the bombing pause.

There was, however, a widespread public debate. As a national organization that included members from a variety of political parties, major religions, and economic strata, the Legion similarly encompassed many views on the war regardless of what public opinion groupings one chose to use.

Two elder statesmen, contemporaries of Legion founders, voiced their individual opinions to National Commander L. Eldon James in

January 1966, during thc month when President Johnson announced the resumption of bombing after a thirty-seven-day pause and following Ho Chi Minh's demands that the United States accept Hanoi's peace plan. Esteemed G.I. Bill guiding light and Legion elder statesman Harry Colmery explained his own discontent with the way things were going in Vietnam.

"Although I approve the position which my country has taken, and where it stands, with respect to Vietnam, I do not approve what is being done and how it's being done." President Johnson, Colmery said, took the title of commander in chief too seriously. To the well-known Kansan, neither President Johnson "nor [Dean] Rusk nor [Robert] McNamara know anything about fighting a war.

"Lyndon Johnson is a compromiser. That trait, along with his use of force based upon authority that he has, accounted for his success as a legislative leader. That prescription will not cure the situation in Vietnam, and unfortunately the parrying and delay which goes with it mounts up to additional sufferings and hardships and death."

Furthermore, Colmery continued, "In my humble opinion, Mr. Johnson does not understand the people of the Far East. . . . In politics, in business and in social affairs, the people of that area" did not react as might Anglo-Saxons to the president's offering of "a 'symbol of peace.' "

What bothered Colmery most, was that while the chess game of negotiation continued at its frustratingly slow pace, "our American men are being killed every day, and sorrow and suffering follows in the wake."

If one was concerned about the threat of Communism to free civilization, "We have no alternative," Colmery said in conclusion, but to wage war against its most violent, aggressive manifestation, such as that exhibited by the Vietnamese Communists.

Another Legionnaire, the well-known World War I aviator, early promoter of aviation, and current chairman of the Legion's National Aeronautics and Space Committee, Roscoe Turner, held forth on another aspect of the war: stateside draft card burnings and other campus disruptions.

Turner's own flair for publicity was legendary, ranging from his self-styled uniforms and his cockpit companion—a real live lion named Gilmore—to his impressive list of air-racing records and later his aviation business successes, which had made him a popular spokesman for military and civilian aviation. Now this man to whom flamboyance was a conservative notion spoke out about the current spate of antiwar protests.

Concerning "these birds" who used their college status to evade their military obligations and, further, to agitate for a "subversive influence in the country," Turner said, "I am for changing their rating and [for] pick[ing] them up."

Turner believed that "anytime anyone speaks or acts contrary to the best interests of this country he comes under the classification of either subversionist, seditionist, or traitor." And, he added, if the existing laws against this are not strong enough, "I am in favor of making them stronger." He had made that point to all the members of the House and the Senate Armed Services Committee. (Commander James subsequently informed Turner that he did not believe the Selective Service Act "was intended to classify persons for induction in the service based on their political views.")

Turner also held to the view that "Mr. McNamara is definitely disarming this country." Belittling a cadre of "dreamers and theorists" in the State Department, the Americanism of some of whom he questioned, Turner similarly objected colorfully, referring presumably to Secretary of Defense McNamara, that in his view the nation had ignored its finest military leaders, instead "substituting a theorist and his mechanical boxes to whittle away at our security."

Turner was proud to be "from the Billy Mitchell school of thought, having served under him in France during World War I"; therefore, he believed wholeheartedly that "our security is in the ability of our air power to keep the air and space clear of the enemy so that our surface operations can be efficiently carried out.

"We have passed the political stage," he reportedly told L. Mendell Rivers of the House Armed Services Committee. "Our survival is at stake!"

When President Johnson ordered the latest resumption of the on-again, off-again bombing of North Vietnam, National Commander James telegrammed a Legion message of support. "In view of Hanoi's total disregard of American peace overtures and the prolonged period of the cessation of bombing of North Vietnam . . . the decision to again strike at targets above the 17th Parallel . . . has the unqualified support of the American Legion." The bombing, James continued, "was necessary to limit the cost in casualties to the defenders of South Vietnam" beset by "Communist aggression."

James, too, had often reiterated the view that a false war of unchecked "liberation" would spread rapidly throughout Southeast Asia. He believed that "those who contend that our national security is not at stake are shortsighted indeed."

To a Lincoln High School student in Wisconsin Rapids, Wisconsin, who had inquired how the war might be stopped, National Commander James replied that it could be stopped very simply if the Communists "operating from China and North Vietnam will discontinue their efforts to impose their form of government by force upon the people of South Vietnam." The United States, conversely, was not forcing its assistance on the South Vietnamese but was giving it "in response to a plea for help."

Furthermore, "When you go to the aid of a friend who is in trouble, you do not desert him until the trouble is ended," James wrote. Noting that "no one who has fought in war approves of war," that experience, nevertheless, "serves to establish clearly in your mind the fact that values worth having are worth fighting for." He likened the South Vietnamese, fighting for self-determination in the governing of their unfortunate half of Vietnam, to the "patriots" of the American colonies in 1776. Similarly, a loss in Vietnam would mean a fight closer to home eventually "to preserve our own freedom."

But it was becoming clearer that a growing and increasingly vocal segment of Americans did not see things that way regarding the war.

In early March, by conference-call hookup, the national commander spoke to forty-four department commanders, urging them to begin a letter-writing campaign with messages to Senator William Fulbright, whose televised hearings on the conduct of the war had large audiences, and to President Johnson. "We've been talking patriotism; here's an opportunity to act." He then sent to departmental officers copies of a weighty State Department document on the legality of U.S. involvement in the defense of South Vietnam.

In what was billed as a major speech before the Conference of National Organizations at Williamsburg, Virginia, on April 28, 1966, National Commander James took the occasion to respond to certain statements of Senator Fulbright made in the senator's far-reaching inquiry into the means, methods, and legality of the war in Vietnam.

James expressed "complete harmony" between the Legion and the administration's "understanding of the nature of the Vietnamese conflict." He particularly disagreed with anyone who persisted in calling that conflict a civil war rather than a clear case of Communist aggression. Since the Geneva Accord of 1954 had divided the country in two, one Communist and one non-Communist, civil war, at least technically, was not the proper term to be used, James believed. To him the current red-flag term "escalate" should be used, instead, to define the furthering of freedom. Once again he voiced the belief that "the fighting in Vietnam can only be described as a major part of the total Communist conspiracy to control the world." As supportive evidence, James attributed to North Vietnam's defense minister General Giap the statement, "South Vietnam is the model of the national liberation movement of our time. If the special warfare that the United States imperialists are testing in South Vietnam is overcome, then it can be defeated anywhere in the world."

James cited the tremendous buildup begun the previous May by U.S. combat forces in South Vietnam as being the result, not the cause, of increasing Communist aggression. James questioned Senator Fulbright's understanding of Communism. He urged the senator to visit South Vietnam and meet those for whom American forces were fighting.

Yet there was a change brewing regarding even the Legion's support for the war effort. There was, for example, a new emphasis developing regarding the well-being and rehabilitative considerations involved in the eventual return of armed forces personnel to civilian life.

Also, not long after the first major escalation of U.S. involvement in the war, at least by early 1966, there was evidence of growing dissatisfaction within the organization regarding the conduct of the war.

True, National Convention mandates still called for strong support of U.S. war aims, even urging more vigorous steps such as renewed bombing to stop the flow of Communist forces and supplies to the Viet Cong. And national officers still maintained that helping the South Vietnamese defend themselves against Communist aggression was of critical importance to U.S. national security.

Legion National Headquarters continued to distribute news releases and bulletins decrying North Vietnam's blockage of U.S. peace initiatives and the continuation of troop infiltration in the South. The 1965 Portland (Oregon) National Convention's position of strong support for U.S. objectives and policy in Vietnam was repeated the next spring along with the call for increased efforts to stem the killing and wounding of American combat troops. National Commander James wondered aloud for "thinking Americans . . . why don't we get on with the job?" of winning the war.

But it fell to the same N.E.C. at its spring meeting in 1966 to adopt a call for a reevaluation of the conduct of the conflict in Vietnam "as to strategy, tactics, and logistical support, and that the leadership and concepts of our military people, trained in the art of war for the security of this country, be given primary consideration in the planning, execution, and conclusion of this conflict."

In the "whereas" clauses of another resolution it was recalled that in early 1962, spokesmen for the Department of Defense had said that the war was going so well that 1,000 personnel could be removed in a month and those remaining would be ordered home by 1965. But now, with over 250,000 American armed services personnel in Vietnam, there were no withdrawals in sight. Noting the Legion's support of military systems for national defense, such as the B-70 supersonic bomber, "the Dynasoar," the antimissile programs and others, "all of which have been written down or canceled by the Department of Defense," the Legion now called for some accountability relating to the war effort.

News of the two resolutions in particular traveled fast. Immediately after the adjournment of the N.E.C., National Commander James appeared on local Indianapolis station WISH-TV, where he was asked if the Legion had just jumped ship regarding its former unfailing support for the war.

"Commander, I understand the American Legion has come out with a strong condemnation of our government's position and conduct of the war in Vietnam," the newsman said. James later admitted to "shock," thankful at least that the effect had been blunted somewhat by his having quickly reviewed the two resolutions side by side, one emanating from the National Security Commission and the other from the Foreign Relations Commission, just before he appeared at the television studio. The "resolve" clauses of the two resolutions when thus collated did appear to send differing messages about what course the Legion wished the government to pursue regarding the war. James could see how in these times a newsman might jump at the chance to report "strong condemnation" by an organization such as the American Legion.

The national commander, however, preferred to think of the N.E.C.'s actions (wishing all the while, however, that there had been better coordination) as being a review of the circumstances that had caused changes in the way the government had conducted the war and the resolutions, specifically, as having stated that change, without implying that the Department of Defense or the secretary of defense deserved censure. He was particularly concerned that the resolve clause of one of the resolutions—that asking that the government "use every military effort to successfully conclude the war"—not be interpreted by alarmists as meaning that the Legion now advised that the military "Drop the Bomb!"

James determined to "highlight and spotlight the tone" of the resolutions, which reemphasized the Legion's strong support for U.S. objectives and policy in Vietnam "and our deep concern that further and more effective steps should be taken to halt Communist aggression [there] and reduce our casualties." When pressed for specifics, he referred to the need for "greater emphasis on military considerations, both in the planning and in the execution of the 'further steps' necessary."

The day after his appearance on TV in Indianapolis, the national commander wrote to Secretary of Defense Robert McNamara and to Secretary of State Dean Rusk, informing them of the continued support of the Legion for the government's objectives and policy in Vietnam. Explaining again that the Legion was not attempting "to play the role of military or diplomatic authorities," the N.E.C., however, had taken the position "that in the face of mounting casualties and the failure so far to find a way to obtain a negotiated peaceful settlement, a reevaluation of strategy, tactics, and logistical support may well be in order." Finally, James suggested that the opinions of the military leadership should be given more credence in adopting "more vigorous measures," such as the interdiction of the Ho Chi Minh Trail, the destruction of enemy fuel supplies, and the closing of Haiphong port and other supply facilities used by the enemy. This, the national commander acknowledged, constituted a "more forceful position" than had been taken previously by the Legion.

Thus a questioning mood had developed within the Legion national leadership just as it had among the general public. In this environment, resolutions offering various, even opposing, views about the conduct of the war likely would be aired at national conventions and at meetings of the National Executive Committee. Robert Lyngh, assistant national adjutant, acknowledged in early June 1966 to a Legion staffer in the field that the Legion's foreign policy "does have certain inconsistencies." One thing for certain, he said, was that the Legion had "consistently supported the policy of the president with reference to American participation in the conflict in South Vietnam." Why? Because "the legally constituted government of South Vietnam requested help in repelling aggression sponsored by North Vietnam."

National Commander James also addressed the widespread concern of many about being kept ignorant of important information about how the war was progressing.

A resolution adopted at the spring 1962 N.E.C. session had called for the government to inform the public better about the war. Foreign Relations Commission Resolution 41 was actually based on a suggestion Dean Rusk had made to the National Foreign Relations Commission the previous March. The national commander informed Secretary Rusk that he was calling on the more than 16,000 Legion posts across the country to take the lead in organizing and implementing a nationwide information program aimed at building support for U.S. involvement in Vietnam based on a fuller understanding of the true nature of the conflict there and the connection of events there to U.S. national security "and the survival of freedom everywhere." Posts were invited to conduct "Vietnam forums" not for debate but for the presentation of factual data about the reasons for U.S. forces being in Southeast Asia as well as to distribute literature detailing the government/Legion stance.

Often the Americanism, National Security, and Foreign Relations Commissions met jointly at national conventions or at other times to hear speakers from the inner sanctums of the State or Defense departments. The Foreign Relations Commission meeting at the sixth annual Washington National Conference in March 1966 heard top-level State Department officials deliver briefings at the department. There, also, Secretary Rusk spoke to the group informally about the key issues of the war. That evening the commission was feted in the Diplomatic Suite of the State Department Building by the Department of State American Legion Post No. 68.

Public statements of government intentions to the contrary, a major escalation in the war was announced on June 29 with the bombing of the immediate areas around Hanoi and Haiphong.

Meanwhile, Henry Cabot Lodge, ambassador to South Vietnam, began secret meetings with Polish and Italian envoys in Saigon in an attempt to find ways to begin negotiations with North Vietnam. Publicly, President Johnson called for unconditional peace talks.

In July the Department of Defense predicted U.S. strength to be 375,000 troops by year's end, with a total of 475,000 possible for the spring of 1967. The Joint Chiefs of Staff had approved General William Westmoreland's request for a total of over half a million personnel by the end of 1967.

But in September, study groups reported to Secretary Rusk that Operation "Rolling Thunder," the code name for the bombing operations, had little or no measurable effect on North Vietnam's ability to conduct military operations in the South. Pacification, too, it was said, had taken steps backward. The next month the Secretary of Defense authorized that fewer troops be engaged than the Joint Chiefs had recommended.

Meanwhile, the extending of Legion membership to those fighting in Vietnam and others in the armed forces at the time was being pondered. As before, the subject revolved around the need to establish an official date for the beginning of the shooting war.

Legion National Membership Director C. W. "Pat" Geile had responded to a Vietnam veteran who in June 1964 had inquired for membership that "letters such as yours are among the most difficult . . . to answer."

A dozen or more resolutions for adjusting the cutoff date for membership eligibility (July 27, 1953, the date of the truce in the Korean War) had come before the Dallas National Convention in 1964 by way of the Convention Committee on Constitutional Amendments. The standing Committee on Membership recommended that the national commander appoint a special committee to study the whole matter and report its findings to the May 1965 N.E.C. meeting, where the report could be distributed to department conventions during the summer in preparation for a discussion and possible action at the following National Convention to be held in Portland, Oregon. The Dallas Convention's Resolution 504 mandated that approach.

As a reference service to the committees above, Thomas V. Hull, Legion Indianapolis Headquarters Librarian and Archivist, counted nearly 300 resolutions that from the founding of the Legion to January 1965 had been acted upon by national conventions regarding proposed changes in Article IV of the constitution.

Historically, eligibility "cutoff" dates had been an arduously debated matter from the founding of the Legion. National officers in 1919 had pondered the eligibility of those who had been involved in actions like the 1918 expedition to Siberia after the Armistice of November 11 that year and of those who had been inducted after the Armistice. Similar debates had occurred after World War II and the Korean War.

As to the Legion's avowed rehab advocacy, Assistant National Membership Director J. Lloyd Wignal explained to the commander of Selma, Alabama, Post No. 20 that "at the present time those who are wounded and sustain a service-connected disability are covered by practically all of the V.A. benefits for hospitalization and compensation that are available to veterans of the three major wars." Also, a "little G.I. Bill" was being considered by Congress to provide educational benefits as well, an action the Legion supported, for this group of "Cold War veterans" as they were becoming known in discussions about whether or not to change the Legion's membership eligibility requirements.

Edward T. Hoak, department adjutant of Pennsylvania, reminded National Headquarters in April 1965 that since July 1, 1958, there had been several campaigns in which American troops had been engaged that could rightfully be termed "hostile" (in Lebanon, Vietnam, Quemoy and Matsu, Congo, Berlin, Laos, Cuba). Hoak enclosed a copy of a letter President Kennedy had written on December 4, 1961, which in establishing the Armed Forces Expeditionary Medal given to those who served after July 1, 1958, referred to the military action for which they may qualify for the medal as being "hostile action."

Before the Portland National Convention in 1965, National Headquarters public relations staffers pondered the effect of a no-change vote regarding the current eligibility cutoff date. If the required majority was not mustered and a resolution for change was rejected, how were they to explain that action in light of the Legion's consistent support of the government's war efforts?

During the convention, the announcement on August 26 about convention action that day began with a masterstroke lead paragraph by the American Legion News Service bulletin:

"The mammoth American Legion, which only twice in its forty-six-year history found it necessary to change its eligibility regulations, has set the machinery in motion that is expected to admit thousands of new veterans by next year."

Had Vietnam veterans been taken into the Legion? Not yet. Instead, the ameliorating reference to work in progress was offered. The "machinery in motion" was actually the appointment of yet another special committee that was to submit a resolution by March 1, 1966, for the consideration of departments at their various conventions and for final action at the 1966 National Convention in Washington, D.C.

Thirty-one departments had already submitted resolutions for change to the Portland Convention. Some departments had selected January 1, 1958, as a new qualifying date for membership. Others chose August 5, 1964, the day of the first U.S. retaliatory action in Vietnam.

The resolution drafted by the special eligibility committee headed by Past National Commander J. Addington Wagner was distributed on May 10 with a cover letter by National Commander L. Eldon James, who was "hopeful your department will join in accomplishing the adoption of the enclosed resolution at the forthcoming National Convention," thus declaring Vietnam veterans eligible for membership in the American Legion if their military service had begun on August 5, 1964, or later.

In anticipation of the change, the national commander's "V-Team" of key Legionnaires at all levels readied themselves for a welcome; the Legion publication *Advance* was tapped to carry suggested local activities slanted toward Vietnam veterans; and National Membership and Post Activities staffers began developing training programs such as those to build new posts, perhaps to be made up entirely of Vietnam veterans.

The first resolution, number 433, brought before the Washington, D.C., National Convention on Tuesday, August 30, 1966, petitioned Congress to amend the Legion's federal charter for the admission of Vietnam veterans. The resolution was shouted to approval by the nearly 3,000 delegates. On Wednesday, Congressman Emanuel Celler, chairman of the House Committee on the Judiciary, called up H.R. 17419 for unanimous passage at about 12:05 P.M. A copy of the bill was rushed to the Senate chamber where Senator James Eastland, chairman of the Senate Judiciary Committee, called it up for similar passage at about 12:35 P.M. Returned to the House, the bill was engrossed, enrolled, and signed by the speaker, then returned to the Senate for the signature of the vice-president before being returned once again to the House, from where it was to be transmitted to the White House. Legion Legislative Director Stringer and staff members John Mears, Charles Mattingly, and former staff member Sam Murphy accompanied the bill on its circuitous rounds.

At 11:05 A.M. on September 1, the last day of the convention, National Commander James announced, "We have been summoned to the White House to witness the signing of the bill bringing Vietnam veterans into membership eligibility." He asked for a suspension of the rules so the election of a new national commander could be moved up a half hour to accommodate the event. Legion founder Tom Miller moved the suspension of the rules. The motion was seconded and handily approved. The quick action was due in no small measure to the efforts of the National Legislative Commission and its director, who since May had been working for the passage of such legislation. Preconvention surveys of the delegates indicated overwhelming if not unanimous support for welcoming Vietnam veterans as members.

New National Commander John E. Davis accompanied James, other Legionnaires, and friends to the Cabinet Room at the White House, where at 1:20 P.M. President Johnson transformed H.R. 17419 to Public Law 89-550. The president noted that there was occurring in Vietnam "the same battle for which the Legionnaires have fought three times before in this century. So I think it is quite appropriate that they should open their rolls to those who carry our flag today."

(On December 21, 1980, the cutoff date for membership eligibility was set at May 7, 1975, and the beginning date set back to December 22, 1961, a change requested by Legion National Convention Resolution 387 in Houston that year.)

In the late fall of 1966, new National Commander John E. Davis, the former two-term governor of North Dakota, took up the customarily demanding itinerary of the office, determined to wage a campaign for the winning of the war in Vietnam, the government's will to achieve that end now being openly questioned. As the national commander traveled the width and breadth of the nation, the National Public Relations Division generated a barrage of news releases quoting him and bearing the datelines of the Legion's small-town, grassroots presence. From Sanford, Maine; Laurel, Mississippi; Worcester, Massachusetts; Barre and Montpelier, Vermont; and Tempe, Arizona, came the Legion message of "peace through strength," the need to halt the flow of Communist troops into South Vietnam, complaints that Laos and Cambodia were allowing their countries to be used as infiltration routes, warnings against even the thought of abandonment of commitments to South Vietnam, and in general the urging of "firmness" in conducting the war.

In December, Davis, too, visited South Vietnam. He came away with four suggestions for concluding the war: stop the enemy from fleeing into and deploying from Laos and Cambodia; give U.S. military commanders in the field the prerogative of selecting military targets in North Vietnam; deny the use of the port of Haiphong to military traffic; and close the routes of infiltration and supply from north to south.

National Security Commission Chairman Emmett G. Lenihan concurred, citing also the "common sense" of the "overwhelming majority" of the commission in recommending nonnuclear solutions to the fighting.

While the national commander addressed the war issue, others looked closer to home for concerns that the Legion should address. William C. Doyle reported for the National Security Commission to the N.E.C. in October 1966 that "of immediate concern," and sharing equal billing with the war, was "lawlessness in our land." Another cited a "growing hostility toward law and order."

Doyle quoted retired associate justice of the U.S. Supreme Court Charles E. Whittaker, who had written in an article in the September issue of *FBI Law Enforcement Bulletin* that there were "ancient and universal lessons" to be learned from the fall of societies that "became lawless," the first evidences of which "appeared in the toleration of disobedience of its laws and the judgments of its courts." And now "in recent times all of us have daily seen and heard an ever-increasing number of accounts that show, with unmistakable clarity, the rapid spread of a planned course of lawlessness in our land that threatens seriously to get out of hand. . . ."

Americanism resolutions of late had depicted the Legion as being in the forefront of organizations that could help in restoring respect for law and order. The resolutions promoted obedience to laws, cooperation with and the aiding of law officers in distress, promotion of law-abiding ideals through the membership of many Legionnaires in other organizations, and the commendation of citizens who performed outstanding deeds in support of law and order. Along the same line, the Legion asked members of the clergy of all faiths to learn more about the problems of law enforcement and how their own religious service might better bridge the gap between peacekeepers and those engaging in violent protest. A related program was proposed by the Conference of Department Chaplains, which called for post chaplains near Job Corps Centers to plan religious programs for corps personnel.

One tactic at antiwar protests that the Legion found particularly obnoxious was the desecration of the American flag. The Americanism Commission pushed for a flag-preservation law that would make it a crime to desecrate "our National Colors"; many incidents had received wide national publicity for those demonstrating against U.S. foreign policy and the war in Vietnam.

The Americanism Commission succeeded in gaining the "emphatic and unanimous" adoption by the N.E.C. of resolutions calling for flag-protection laws. One such resolution called for "the American Legion [to] rededicate itself . . . by flying the greatest symbol of this democracy of ours . . . daily . . . until peace is restored in Vietnam." The National Legislative Division was unsuccessful in having the resolutions turned into law, however.

Another pertinent resolution called for legislation to amend the Immigration and Naturalization Act to make provisions for control of travel by U.S. residents outside the country. The resolution was aimed at, among others, those who appeared to be volunteering themselves for the propaganda mills of North Vietnam by visiting that country even as Vietnamese Communist troops were killing American service personnel.

In mid-March 1967, National Commander Davis stated his agreement with the president's escalation of the bombing of North Vietnam. He agreed with Congressman Gerald Ford, who had asked recently, "Why are we pulling our best punches in Vietnam?"

At the N.E.C. meeting in October 1967, the National Security Commission expressed support for two government actions that had taken place recently. One was the bombing of targets in North Vietnam in and around Haiphong, which had been off-limits to American planes until now. While called "commendable," however, the bombing action was said to be "insufficient."

The second event was the announcement by Secretary McNamara that a "thin" antiballistic missile system would soon be deployed in the United States. For ten years the Legion had been calling for just such a move. Especially in light of the Soviet Union's initiation of its own extensive ABM system and assumptions about Red China's growing nuclear and missile capability, the secretary's announcement, though belated in the estimation of the Legion, was welcomed.

Down from the missile-threatened skies to the streets once more, the National Security Commission reiterated its complaint about "the breakdown of law and order in our land." Recalling recent organized riots and disorders that had "rendered helpless" several large cities, the chairman of the National Security Commission, Emmett G. Lenihan, continued his predecessor's emphasis on "the rekindling of national respect for law and order" by promoting the slogan "Freedom Is Not Free." Many Legion posts, meanwhile, adopted programs for honoring law enforcement officers as a way to show respect for law and order.

The forty-ninth National Convention in Boston in late August 1967 adopted a ten-point declaration of policy about the war. The declaration had been composed by a joint committee of members of the Foreign Relations and National Security committees at the convention.

Reiterating the Legion's strong support for assisting the people of South Vietnam, whose defense was still said to be in the vital interest of the United States, the resolution commended U.S. troops, expressed deep concern about increasing casualties, and insisted on the removal of political limitations placed on military leaders who, it was resolved, should be given whatever was required to win the war, including permission to "terminate" enemy sanctuaries in Cambodia, Laos, and the DMZ. The Legion also called for an immediate lifting of restrictions placed on the nature and scope of bombing targets in North Vietnam and strongly recommended the closing of the port of Haiphong "by whatever military means are considered most feasible and effective."

There was, also, a reiteration of the belief that the right to dissent should be honored, but that any violation of law in doing so should be prosecuted to the fullest extent.

Convention delegates at Boston elected William B. Galbraith of Beemer, Nebraska, as national commander. Visiting Vietnam shortly thereafter, he called for a resumption of the bombing. Each bombing pause previously had been used by the North Vietnamese to resupply and re-equip their regular units as well as units of the Viet Cong. The Communists' ability to sustain their forces in the south had consistently frustrated U.S. attempts at overall victory. The basic principle of "interdiction," or denying to the enemy at the battlefront the use of munitions, supplies, and manpower reserves, should be applied, Galbraith said.

In early December 1967, National Commander Galbraith issued a letter to all post commanders in which he urged attention to an attached letter from Congressman Olin E. Teague, chairman of the House Committee on Veterans Affairs, who had asked assistance in countering the growing influence of the anti–Vietnam War demonstrations.

In Vietnam, Galbraith had found armed forces personnel aware of the growing dissent at home. That dissent, he said, had "recently reached new heights of irresponsibility in Washington when an unruly and disrespectful mob attempted to disrupt the vital work of the Department of Defense at the Pentagon."

Teague, who had visited Vietnam three times, opened his letter by citing "a horrible and dirty war in Vietnam" in which the American men fighting there were not getting the full support of the American people. The government's decision to enter the war there, right or wrong, should be supported, especially in ways that upheld the fighting personnel, he wrote.

"The veterans of other wars are the natural leaders in building the needed support," Teague continued. "Every honest dissenter, dishonest dissenter, draftcard burner, peacenik and draft-dodger is prolonging the war; and these efforts are organized," encouraging the North Vietnamese to continue to kill more Americans. The Texas congressman recommended that local forums be organized and that wires and letters be forwarded to elected representatives and the president supporting the U.S. armed forces in Vietnam.

The two letters reached most posts on or before the anniversary of the bombing of Pearl Harbor on December 7.

The Tet Offensive, beginning in late January 1968, brought attacks by Communist troops on almost every one of the forty-five province capitals. During this time also came the beginning of negotiations for a cease-fire.

To a Masonic luncheon group in Wilmington, Delaware, in March 1968, National Commander Galbraith spoke about the public perception of the Legion's stance on the war. The Legion, he said, "always has based its major policy decisions on what we believe to be the best interests of America." That was what had influenced the backing of what was often said to be the Legion's "hard-line policy" regarding Vietnam.

As for the negotiations that were beginning tentatively and secretively, that aspect of the war, Galbraith often said, was no game for amateurs. Furthermore, "Our freedoms at home imperil our negotiators' chances of success. Here [in the United States] any amateur may broadcast his own cure-alls whether he understands the pitfalls or not, whether he has any responsibility or not, whether or not he cares if our interests are served or not.

"Judging from experience, the wilder the amateurish criticism, the more our news media will feature it. And if it is political as well, so much the more." That, he held, was a "terrible threat to a negotiated peace." He credited George Washington with the observation that negotiating to end the Revolutionary War was a "game more dangerous than use of arms" because it had preyed on the war-weariness of the people to surrender at the peace table what his troops had won in battle. Galbraith noted that in this election year 1968, the "recklessness" of mass media opinion-forming was worse than ever. And it all worked, he said, to prolong the war.

Certainly the matter should be discussed openly. But "we should have an end to people without responsibility trying to spell out the details of what should be done while ignoring the principles." That, he said, was what he heard on television almost every day.

On March 31, 1968, the bombing was halted over about three-quarters of North Vietnam. The first meeting between U.S. and North Vietnamese diplomats occurred on May 13 in Paris.

The National Convention in New Orleans in early September, the fiftieth anniversary of the convening of the Legion's supreme governing body, produced Resolution 441, another product of a joint National Security–Foreign Relations Committee, which proclaimed the support the Legion was prepared to give the government in principle. Now included was the statement that the Legion "deplores the continued and increasing loss of men and the impossibility of total victory because of political limitations." Resolution 441 also repeated the call for government reliance on military judgment in the field, insisting on the removal of limitations on military targets.

The Legion's concern about law and order was particularly acute at the National Convention of 1968, meeting as it did shortly after the national convention of the Democratic Party in Chicago, where demonstrations in the streets and the confrontations inside the hall where the Democrats met provided several days of riveting television coverage.

The report of the National Security Commission to the N.E.C. meeting in October 1968 reiterated the Legion's concern, even alarm:

"Law and order must be maintained to protect the rights of all. Only through the orderly processes of government and law can social justice and equality of opportunity for all be secured.

"To permit an individual to determine which laws are 'good' and which are 'bad' would disrupt the foundation of judicial processes. Law must be the supreme factor in the orderly working of society, and order, without which there would be no civil rights, can be maintained only by adherence to the laws of our land."

Try as the Legion might to impress upon the government that the war must be fought on wider fronts and with a more militarily successful resolve, November 1 marked the beginning of a complete halt of the bombing. By mid-December, new National Commander William C. Doyle was urging the organization to be continuously sensitive to the delicate current negotiations about the war and, therefore, not to make any statements in the name of the Legion that would encourage North Vietnamese leaders to continue to delay peace negotiations in the hope that America would concede more the longer the negotiations were drawn out.

From January 18, 1969, the peace talks continued, now expanded to include South Vietnam and the Viet Cong (National Liberation Front). Near the end of the month, President Richard Nixon spoke about the possibility of withdrawal of both U.S. and North Vietnamese troops from the south.

For five years the Legion had supported the government's conduct of the war. As to the public response to the war, National Membership Director J. Lloyd Wignall observed that a major difficulty with a limited war was that "it is hard to become concerned with something that does not vitally affect our daily life, and the Vietnam War has been that kind of war. With the minor exception of additional taxes, many of our citizens and many of our Legionnaires are not personally affected. We do not have the rationing and total commitment that we had during World War II." Such an attitude "is an injustice to our young men," Wignall continued, "but it is the way we have elected to fight this war." Wignall advised posts to use Vietnam veterans as speakers for post activities. "They are received . . . with some degree of fellowship," he said, "and it is not necessary to overcome the suspicion which greets some of us of a previous generation."

Wignall also recommended a way to combat the stigma being attached to those who had participated in the war by the use of college veterans' clubs, which, he observed, "provide a voice of moderation and reason that is needed on our college campuses today," especially if these veterans would form themselves into "recognized clubs on campus so that they could provide an effective voice in student affairs."

In early 1969, the Paris peace talks had come close to being stymied by procedural matters involving such ignoble arguments as how the conference table should be shaped and who was to sit where. Yet, two months later, on June 8, President Nixon, while at a conference with South Vietnam's Nguyen Van Thieu on Midway Island, announced his plan for the first withdrawal of U.S. troops.

The delegates to the national convention in Atlanta in 1969 complained about foot-dragging in the peace negotiations and reiterated the view of past conventions that the United States should pursue negotiations but not abandon South Vietnam. On the floor, a call for an immediate all-out offensive by the United States if the north did not agree to a cease-fire immediately was voted down.

Spirited floor debate on three resolutions hearkened to earlier, more formative days when the Legion was hammering out its identity and sense of purpose.

On these three issues delegates lined up behind fellow Legionnaires who employed their oratorical skills to call to question, or to support, convention-committee recommendations. Two Legionnaires, former congressmen O. K. Armstrong and Roland Libonati, took opposite views of a joint Foreign Relations–National Security resolution regarding Vietnam. Armstrong favored a get-tougher approach; Libonati warned that the war was bankrupting the nation in lives and dollars spent. The original resolution calling for the more moderate stance was sustained, but it took a roll call vote to do it.

Similar debates rolled across the floor, on the subjects of increasing the membership eligibility to those whose service had occurred after the "shooting dates" in World War II and Korea (to comply more with the dates recognized by the V.A. for war service), and on allowing post and county level officers of the Legion to serve while also holding remunerative public offices. Again both these resolutions were defeated by roll call, the latter even after having been brought in by the Convention Committee on Constitutional Amendments. Those favoring the public officeholders argued that, especially on the local level, the Legion needed the leadership talents of those members whose popularity had gained them public office. In this matter, however, the traditional apprehension about partisan politics disrupting the Legion won out. Once again Legion tradition had been preserved.

The delegates heard but were not particularly convinced, it appeared, by keynote speaker Defense Secretary Melvin Laird, who delivered a detailed proposition for cutting the defense budget. Closer to home, however, where it appeared most of the attention was, the delegates expressed dissatisfaction with the "meagerness" of the educational benefits then being offered Vietnam veterans. They also asked for more governmental protection against pollution.

Just before the opening ceremonies of the convention, the N.E.C. had pondered the often studied subject of military manpower. This, too, was a subject of much concern outside the Legion as well. On March 27, President Nixon had moved toward all-volunteer armed forces when he assigned former Secretary of Defense Thomas S. Gates to chair a committee to develop a comprehensive plan for eliminating conscription. At the same time, a Department of Defense committee was preparing recommendations to improve the attractiveness of service under that department's "Project Volunteer."

The Legion, however, as keeper of the flame for U.M.T., was quick to state its opposition to reliance chiefly on voluntary forces. The preconvention N.E.C. pondered an American time line of defense needs, concluding that from the first recorded instances of the need for armed forces, the colonies, the states, and the nation had not been able to rely on consistent and timely voluntary defense forces.

As one committeeman pointed out, in 1775 a draft had to be initiated to supplement the forces of Gen. George Washington. Again in 1786, the Continental Congress had failed to raise the forces it had authorized. In 1812, when the country was once again at war with Great Britain, Congress repeatedly authorized increased military strength with little success and was finally forced to rely on state drafts to meet quotas. Years later came the presidential draft of 1862 when the first rush of volunteers had dissolved during the long and bloody battles of the Civil War.

Committeemen reflected on the Selective Service law, enacted May 18, 1917, which for the first time set forth the personal military obligations of citizenship. The American Legion had come on the scene two years later and, based on the harrowing wartime experiences of its members, never ceased to call for universal military training.

The Selective Service Act, which was passed on September 16, 1940, was a peacetime measure, but it was designed to meet the emergency of war, also. When war came, the system furnished both the number and the type of individuals deemed acceptable for military service, but only after the first inductees were rushed to the war with inadequate training, many believed. Approximately sixty-six percent of those who served during World War II, it was said here, were drafted by the Selective Service, and among those who enlisted, a large number were thought to have been induced to join because of the existence of the draft.

With the 1940 Draft Act due to expire in March 1947, President Truman had decided that the armed forces of the United States should be placed on a completely volunteer basis. A year later, however, he asked Congress to reinstate Selective Service so that the armed forces could be built up to authorized peacetime strength for the preventative defense of the nation and to meet foreign commitments in "this unsettled time."

The draft initiated the next year selected men between the ages of nineteen and twenty-five for twenty-one months of service. Even with that, the army, upon the outbreak of hostilities in Korea in late June 1950, found itself with undermanned divisions ill-equipped for combat. Many regiments were comprised of a couple of undermanned battalions, each of which included undermanned companies. The Selective Service Act was extended in 1950 for one year.

A year later came the Universal Military Training and Service Act, which, regardless of its name, was a draft with little resemblance to the Legion's concept of U.M.T. Reserve veterans of World War II had already been called up to serve again since there was not time to train new troops for the full-blown war that had exploded in Korea and in which the first combat actions had resulted in the U.N. (chiefly U.S.) forces being driven back to a perimeter around the port of entry.

Since then, the draft had provided service personnel during the Berlin buildup, the Cuban missile crisis, and now Vietnam. Since 1967, the strength of the armed forces had been maintained at approximately three and a half million.

Now the president seemed to be moving toward all-volunteer armed forces. The Legion official view was one of skepticism. (A presidential commission would soon recommend that means of eliminating the draft before the law expired in June 1971. But the president, though he had advocated the all-volunteer concept when campaigning for office, soon backed major reforms in draft legislation, instead.)

The Legion celebrated its fiftieth anniversary in 1969. To commemorate the sites of the Legion's American birth, the N.E.C. met in St. Louis in May and in Minneapolis in November instead of the traditional site of National Headquarters in Indianapolis.

The collection of Legion memorabilia produced that year included, most prominently and with no small effort by Director of Research Warren McDonald, a fiftieth anniversary commemorative six-cent stamp (a major undertaking in itself) first issued on March 15 in

Washington, D.C. There was also a medallion; the march composition "The American Legion, Fifty Years of Service" by Meredith Wilson of *Music Man* fame; and many other items of interest, including the "Flame of Freedom" gas torches presented by posts to their communities to be lit at public ceremonies on March 15; and a commemorative bottle and other items available from the Emblem Sales Division.

Others helped the Legion celebrate. The Anheuser-Busch corporation sponsored a film entitled *The Golden Mirror,* in which Past National Commanders Don Johnson, John Quinn, and James Powers recalled the history of the Legion. Pan-American Airways sponsored a film, *Gift to the Nation,* featuring President Nixon, Postmaster General Winton M. Blount, and National Commander William C. Doyle at the annual Washington Conference of the Legion in March 1969.

The "service" about which composer Wilson wrote was exemplified by the special project of the Legion and the Auxiliary to provide permanent lighting for the Tomb of the Unknown Soldier and the temple facade of Memorial Amphitheater at Arlington National Cemetery.

In 1926 the Legion had called on the government to guard the Tomb of the Unknown Soldier from vandals. In 1937 the sunrise-to-sunset guard duty was expanded to a twenty-four-hour guard system to stop the persistent souvenir hunters and others from chipping away at the tomb. On Veterans Day in 1969, the Legion was host for the ceremonies at the cemetery and at the Army and Navy Club for a luncheon honoring representatives of fifteen of America's wartime allies.

Other occurrences helped popularize the Legion's longevity. The S.S. *American Legion,* a 700-foot cargo carrier, was launched on February 27 from Chester, Pennsylvania. But one event, in particular, small in comparison to many others, was likely to evoke appropriate emotions. Many are the N.E.C. men and others who recall the overwhelmed feeling they received when they first entered the N.E.C. room on the top floor of National Headquarters in Indianapolis and viewed the larger-than-life oil painting at the head of the center aisle, which depicted the pathos of the French and American alliance of World War I.

When the Legion's golden anniversary observance officially began, Leon Reni-Mel, official artist for the French Ministry of War and creator of the now famous painting "America" that dominates the podium of the N.E.C. room, visited his creation once more. Reni-Mel's inspiration for the painting grew from the pen-and-ink sketch he had made during the war of an American doughboy aiding a fallen French soldier. He subsequently decided to transfer the image and the concept to a painting of heroic proportions. Starting on Armistice Day, November 11, 1918, he worked for a year on the painting. Though President Woodrow Wilson acknowledged the offer of the painting, it remained unclaimed in France until 1922, when an American Legionnaire asked if it might be presented to the Legion. With the help of the

French government, the transfer was made in Paris on May 6, 1922, in a public ceremony.

Now, in 1969, fifty years after the first rush of artistic inspiration, the artist, like many World War I Legionnaires, recalled images of a country rescued by American citizen-soldiers from foreign domination. In a quiet moment in the N.E.C. room, as he stood quietly beside his impressive painting, Reni-Mel personified the span of years that the Legion now celebrated.

It was at the largely celebratory N.E.C. meeting held at Minneapolis in November, the site of the Legion's first National Convention fifty years before, that the organization adopted a new position regarding the Vietnam War.

Until then, although the Legion had constantly advocated a military victory in South Vietnam, the N.E.C.'s Resolution 2 in November 1969 supported President Nixon's plan for the gradual withdrawal of American troops as being perhaps the only solution short of resuming all-out war. Both the president and the Legion insisted that such action occur alongside "Vietnamization," the strengthening of the South Vietnamese to protect themselves, to hold free elections, to work for economic progress, and to be free from fear of aggression through the backing of the United States.

That resolution was echoed by Resolution 26 at the N.E.C. meeting in May 1970, shortly after President Nixon had announced U.S. action in Cambodia to destroy Communist sanctuaries on that country's border with South Vietnam. A few weeks later, in a joint statement with his V.F.W. counterpart, National Commander Milton Patrick urged a letter-writing campaign against the Senate's Church-Cooper Amendment, which was a legislative attempt at limiting the president's authority to conduct military operations such as he had just revealed, actions, Patrick said, "solely to protect the lives of American servicemen and to insure that we will be able to continue the orderly withdrawal of our troops."

There was substantial opposition both in Congress and among the American public to either a renewed U.S. military effort or an indefinite commitment of troops to the war. As one Legion bulletin stated, since President Nixon had "ruled out a military victory in Vietnam," the Legion supported "any means necessary to insure a just peace and a solution to the conflict—whether political or military—that will give the South Vietnamese people the right to self-determination." Washington headquarters staffers worked to keep that view before the White House, the Congress, and the State and Defense Departments. They also worked to encourage constructive efforts to locate and return POWs and MIAs.

The 1970 National Convention in Portland, Oregon, adopted convention resolution 46 reiterating the stance taken at the previous convention regarding the United States' extricating itself from the war.

The new national commander voted in at the Portland National Convention in 1970 was Alfred P. Chamie of California, who took the now customary trip to Vietnam. In a civic luncheon speech in Los Angeles in mid-January 1971, Chamie saw "hopes for peace . . . brighter than in the recent past." He had observed that the pace of battle for U.S. troops and the number of casualties had markedly diminished.

The enemy was relying on hit-and-run terrorist raids typical of the early stages of the war now that they were "seriously weakened," Chamie said.

The national commander also spoke favorably of the progress of Vietnamization, saying the South Vietnamese were "more than holding their own." He reported visiting "quiet, fully pacified" areas that just two years earlier had been the scene of heavy Viet Cong attacks.

In March, Chamie told Maryland Legionnaires in Baltimore, "An indiscriminate withdrawal of all American forces from South Vietnam at this time would be unrealistic. A planned and orderly withdrawal of the type that is now taking place is both feasible and practical." He spoke of the president's having increased the number of U.S. troops to be returned from the war as being a sign of U.S. sincerity regarding peace.

That additional reduction, Chamie said, undoubtedly had been served well by U.S. military actions in Cambodia, which he had been told in Vietnam had destroyed large caches of arms and supplies of food for the enemy as well as having cut their communications and supply lines. In early February there began forty-four days of bombing action on the Ho Chi Minh Trail in Laos in an effort to hamper further the enemy forces' method of matériel resupply and manpower.

Chamie reiterated the current chief concern of the Legion, that prisoners of war and those missing in action be accounted for and returned to the United States as soon as possible.

Though National Commander Chamie, as chief spokesman for the Legion, talked glowingly of American troop morale, other National Headquarters staff members responded to correspondence in which members and nonmembers alike expressed their frustrations with the war in Vietnam.

National Security–Foreign Relations Division Director James "Jimmy" Wilson answered a letter in mid-March 1971 from Commander C. T. Johnson of Post No. 76 in Austin, Texas, who described the incredulity of many of his friends and acquaintances, both members and nonmembers of the Legion alike, over "the pussyfooting of our politicians in making promises and promises" about the way the war was going. The commander of Post No. 76 reiterated the mournful litany of statistics of American combat deaths, casualties, POWs and MIAs. In his own community he had visited with families that had been touched tragically by the war.

Wilson replied that the incursions into Cambodia and Laos, which many said would surely drag out the war and impede the removal of American combat troops, were actually necessary to the Vietnamization program. He reminded the former post commander in Texas that the withdrawal schedule set by the president had been upheld.

Assistant Director John M. Kane similarly responded to a letter in which a Catholic priest in Rapid City, South Dakota, a "former member of the Legion," resigned from the Legion in part because the organization had "seriously abdicated [its] role in directing the course of action this nation must follow in this and all future wars." The priest cited a recent Harris poll that reportedly found that sixty-one percent of Americans concurred that all troops should be out of Vietnam by the end of the year. He also depicted a yawning credibility gap created by the State Department that had disenchanted a majority of Americans. Furthermore, he said, the public was disgusted by a war that had produced such lurid news as a My Lai massacre.

Kane replied that the Legion routinely and by actions of its two chief representative governing bodies expressed suggestions, recommendations, and calls for action regarding foreign policy. But in the end, it was the elected officials of the federal government who made the decisions about the policies of which this man complained. As for "parroting" the State Department line, as the priest had charged, Kane recommended he review the foreign relations resolutions adopted by the Legion since 1945, a list that certainly did not constitute complete agreement with State Department actions during the same period.

Kane wrote that "the best way to end the conflict in Vietnam is through negotiations, but not through dictation of the terms of settlement by North Vietnam." So the Legion supported Vietnamization, the gradual withdrawal of American forces on a rational and gradual basis, the military measures necessary to guarantee the success of both policies, and, finally, a complete withdrawal of U.S. troops only after the POWs were returned.

Such inquiries, complaints, and other expressions of discontent were, of course, widespread. One recent and significant expression of which was the Mansfield Amendment to H.R. 8687, the Military Procurement Authorization Bill, which would establish a final date for the cessation of hostilities in Indochina. Fifty-seven senators voted for a total withdrawal of U.S. troops from Indochina in six months; thirty-eight voted against the amendment.

In a news release in October 1971, National Commander John H.

Geiger voiced the Legion's opposition to the amendment. "Any limitation on the ability of the president as commander in chief to conduct military operations in Southeast Asia would endanger the lives of our fighting men and make more difficult the achievement of a just peace."

In March 1972 there occurred an indefinite suspension of the Paris peace talks. In mid-April, the president ordered the bombing of Hanoi and Haiphong. The Legion pledged its support, emphasizing that these new actions should not detract attention and resources from successful Vietnamization. Near the end of the month the peace talks resumed, only to be suspended again in early May.

The mining of ports in the north, the interdiction of land and sea routes used by the north, and resumed bombing of the north followed the escalation of efforts by the enemy particularly in actions across the DMZ.

Meanwhile, in this a presidential election year, National Commander Geiger referred to statements by candidates for that office who objected to the president's war policies. Such statements were "divisive and defeatist," and likely to encourage Hanoi in its demands, he said.

When informed in June of North Vietnamese complaints that U.S. bombing was destroying the crucial dike system in the north, Geiger quipped, "Their soldiers might perform a better service at home repairing the dikes rather than inflicting misery, suffering, and death on others through their aggressive ventures into foreign territory." The reports of damages to the dikes had been attributed often to "a well-known [American] actress" who had gained much attention "with her concern for a nation that has killed 50,000 American men." Geiger, as a war veteran and engineer, questioned the unnamed actress's "competency to evaluate the military tactics of our men or the damage effects on the enemy's canals and dikes." He recommended that U.N. Secretary General Kurt Waldheim organize a professional team of expert hydraulic engineers and military observers to inspect the alleged damage. That, he said, "would do much to separate propaganda from fact."

On August 12, 1972, the last U.S. combat troops left South Vietnam, though there remained 30,000 or more advisers, technicians, and helicopter crews. New National Commander Joe L. Matthews of Texas reaffirmed the Legion position in favor of Vietnamization and of the resumption of the bombing of North Vietnam to support the South Vietnamese forces who had been under increased attacks from the North.

National Commander Matthews also spoke of another subject of much public concern in stating the Legion's opposition "to any amnesty for draft dodgers or deserters until after the fighting has ended, after our POWs and missing in action have been repatriated and accounted for." Only then and "by a review of each individual case under existing procedures available to the courts and the president" should a program of amnesty proceed. As for the Legion's own acceptance of Vietnam veterans, Matthews reported that they now made up the second largest membership group, giving "a younger profile" to the organization.

In October, the bombing north of the twentieth parallel ceased. Early the next month presidential adviser Henry Kissinger outlined at a news conference the prospects for an agreement to bring the war to an end. National Commander Matthews hailed the news. The Legion, Matthews said, "will seek to serve those who lost loved ones in this terrible conflict as we have served others from previous periods of conflict."

In mid-December, amid claims of infiltration by the north, and though peace talks were continuing, President Nixon's "Linebacker II" move resumed bombing above the twentieth parallel. The actions were halted on December 30, 1972. At this point even the Soviet news agency Tass called for "immediate stoppage of the actions and speedy signing of an agreement on ending the war."

Though much attention was still being paid to events in Vietnam, another matter of foreign relations concerned national officers in 1972.

The Legion had supported the establishment of the U.N. in 1945 as the best hope for world peace and international cooperation. Since the Korean War, any mention of U.S. military manpower had a U.N.-related side to it, just as any mention of trouble spots in the world likely to need U.N. military assistance meant the potential involvement of U.S. military personnel.

Now, after many years of observation, the Legion regularly criticized the U.N. as being shot through with loopholes by which the Soviet Union, as the chief U.S. adversary, could stymie by veto and other machinations what the United States viewed as constructive action.

After twenty-seven years of existence, the U.N., according to a Legion Foreign Relations Commission resolution, was in need of basic changes in its voting, fiscal, and administrative procedures, indeed in its very structure, if it was to function as "more than an international debating society." While lauding U.N. peacekeeping forces and subsidiary technical agencies, the Foreign Relations Commission now cited the specific provision in the U.N. Charter that called for a complete review this year of the U.N. Charter, (which, it was now charged, the

U.N.'s General Assembly had failed to do) an action that possibly could lead to charter revisions that the Legion advocated.

The Legion supported a continuation of U.S. membership in the U.N. but called for the review to be initiated soon and requested that several basic changes be made:

Reduce the U.S. share of the U.N. budget from the present 31.52 percent by 5 percent a year over three years to 15 percent; eliminate the estimated U.N. debt of some $200 million by a onetime equal-share assessment of all 132 members; require all members to pay their annual assessments on time; make voting power proportionate to budgetary assessment, gross national product, and population, and, in the process, eliminate the two votes that the Soviet Union dictated to the Ukraine and Byelorussia; eliminate the single-nation veto power in the Security Council for a majority of the permanent and present members; strengthen the quality of Americans with professional positions on the secretariat staff; require the decentralizing of some U.N. functions to other world cities instead of expanding the U.N. headquarters in New York; and, finally, recommend presidential appointment of a small, nonpartisan advisory council composed of private citizens to assist the Bureau of Internal Organization Affairs of the State Department and the U.S. delegation to the U.N. on aspects of U.S. policy and participation in the U.N.

If these reforms were not achieved by the close of the Twenty-Seventh General Assembly of the U.N. later that year, the Legion urged the United States to withdraw its membership.

The Paris peace talks resumed on January 8, 1973; a week later all bombing, mining, shelling, and other offensive actions directed at North Vietnam ceased. A week and a half later, a cease-fire was signed in Paris on January 27. The agreement included the release of all American POWs. The nation at last had some respite from its longest war.

In addition to a contingent of Legion national officers who continued to work with the League of Families of Prisoners of War and Missing in Action, others soon gave serious attention to the subject of a postwar relationship with the North Vietnamese regime. Of particular concern was the matter of an American tradition—aid for rebuilding war-torn countries, whether allies or adversaries.

National leaders were not alone in pondering this thought. To Post No. 36 in Gering, Nebraska, the emotion-laden matter of giving aid to a Communist nation and especially to North Vietnam should be to foreign relations what the nearby 700-foot-plus promontory Scotts Bluff was to the undulating sand hills surrounding the post—it fairly begged for attention.

In his letter to National Headquarters in March 1973, Post Commander Jim Shiers wrote that, first, there was the matter of some one thousand MIA personnel unaccounted for; second was the "flagrant" violations of the cease-fire agreement by forces from North Vietnam and the Viet Cong. Could the United States really consider aiding a Communist government that had cost the nation "ten years of lives and dollars?" Shiers asked.

The Nebraskan was told that the National Foreign Relations Commission had considered the subject during the Washington Conference in February and that all action on it was put aside until "all our POWs are repatriated." At present, the Atlanta National Convention's Resolution 428, which had been adopted in 1969, was the ruling policy: opposition to all aid to Communist nations.

Longtime Legionnaire and experienced U.M.T. advocate Granville Ridley of Tennessee pondered the same issue. Did the president have discretionary funds at his disposal which could be used as aid to North Vietnam, thus avoiding a congressional appropriation specifically for such aid?

If so, there was an urgent need for legislation positively forbidding such aid. But National Commander Matthews counseled a wait-and-see approach, saying also that Secretary of State Rogers in late February had promised the Senate Foreign Relations Committee that no funds would be appropriated for aid to North Vietnam without the express support of Congress. That stance had been reaffirmed subsequently by the president in a March 1 press conference. Any letter-writing campaign by Ridley or others, he added, should wait until all the POWs had been returned and a satisfactory accounting had been made of the MIAs.

When the war did end for the United States, the National Security Commission asked the question, Was it not a valid defense doctrine that significant reductions in active forces must be offset by strengthening and improving the nation's Reserve forces? The commission pointed out that the Department of Defense in 1970 had declared that in the future the Reserves and National Guard would be the initial and primary augmentation forces for the active forces and also that Congress in 1973 had declared its intention that the Reserves would be used to meet additional manpower needs of the active forces before any inductions would be made. The Department of Defense had even developed the "Total Force Policy" to obtain the most defense for the least cost and with the least delay.

Since at this point the National Guard and the Reserves comprised more than thirty percent of the force-in-being that would have to respond immediately to any future military emergency, the Legion went on record as supporting the Total Force Policy and urged Congress, the Department of Defense, and the military services themselves to provide adequate funding and sufficient training and equipment to ensure the immediate availability and combat readiness of the Reserves and National Guard.

Though the war was ended, Legion commissions had not forgotten war-era happenings to which they had objected.

The Americanism Commission in the spring of 1975 could only lament that as yet there had been no congressional approval of the U.S. Flag Code jointly sponsored currently by the diverse duo of Senators Strom Thurmond of South Carolina and Birch Bayh of Indiana. A House bill of the same nature was under consideration as well.

Similarly, the commission regretted the loss of the House Committee on Internal Security, the death knell of which was to be sounded at midnight on April 30. The disbanding of that group, the commission said, meant that except for the Senate Subcommittee on Internal Security of the Committee on the Judiciary, there was no legislative oversight of internal subversion.

The mood of the National Security Commission was also downcast in some respects. At the May N.E.C. meeting, Chairman Emmett G. Lenihan expressed the sadness felt by many upon seeing television news coverage of the last helicopters to leave Saigon. South Vietnam's "fate [is] apparently sealed," Lenihan lamented. On April 20, the remaining U.S. armed forces, marine, ground, and helicopter units, and air force transport crews had begun the withdrawal of American military and civilian personnel and some Vietnamese. A few days later, a Communist government was established in Saigon.

President Gerald Ford proclaimed May 7, 1975, as the termination of the "Vietnam Era" for purposes of veterans' affairs as conducted by the V.A.

A few days earlier, National Commander James M. Wagonseller issued a statement about "the twin tragedies of South Vietnam and Cambodia," which were tragedies for the United States, too, he said. But "there is a lesson to be learned from recent events. If we as a nation have discovered that we should never again become involved in the so-called political wars, the wars we have no intention of winning, then some ultimate good may yet come from these catastrophes."

A Ten-Year Rehab Retrospect 1966–76

The National Rehab Commission had not been idle during the period. The phrase "sponsor and support legislation amending" often prefaced statements of the legislative goals of that commission.

For though there was, indeed, much veterans' legislation already in place, the commission did more than maintain status quo during this period and faced more than the small-scale problems that arose from the natural course of bureaucracy.

Longtime Rehab Commission Chairman Bob McCurdy explained the most pressing concern at the National Convention in 1966 in Washington, D.C. "We see a growing threat to the status of veterans through various programs, starting with Medicare and the 'Great Society' programs that are now being installed. This is a genuine threat."

The loss of veterans' identity by their being absorbed into new government programs was not a new threat. But this time it involved what were generally hailed of late as being great boons to social welfare and stability. Yet the Legion and other veterans' organizations complained that those programs for the betterment of many classes of individuals did not fully recognize the special-class distinction of veterans. If veterans' benefits were not allowed to exist separately from these new programs, it was said, ultimately the distinction of military service would be short-lived with veterans being required, along with nonveterans, to enroll in one or more of the "Great Society" programs dispensing benefits in common to all.

So during this period the Rehab Commission pursued a course of watchful waiting for signs of absorption of V.A. programs into Medicare and the Department of Health, Education, and Welfare. At the same time the commission marked progress with a series of accomplishments. Described in periodic reports to the N.E.C. and to national conventions were Legion legislative efforts said to have "corrected," usually by liberalizing, some of the perceived shortcomings of preexisting laws.

In so doing, as those drafting the resolutions for such actions were advised by one commission member, "We ought to follow the old military rule that the language should be restrained, but the meaning should be unmistakably clear."

It should come as no surprise, of course, that the Legion also would concern itself with the natural enough but problematic phenomenon of the aging of its members. Years earlier, when the Legion approached its tenth year of existence, National Commander Edward E. Spafford (1927–28) had declared, "Our organization will exist only a very few years, and if when our existence or our span of life is finished, we are able to contribute something which will leave a desire in the minds of other people that unselfish service only cries its word of praise, which is so worthwhile, then the existence of the Legion will have been justified."

But the organization had not died out for want of new members as

Past National Commander Spafford had expected, and many of his cohorts of the World War I era now needed help. So part of that "unselfish service," of course, was necessarily directed to aged and aging Legionnaires. With census records showing five million veterans over the age of sixty-five, and with many World War II veterans approaching retirement age, there was much concern now that because of the drastic rise lately in the cost of living, many aged veterans and their dependents were living near or below the poverty level. The problem was made greater when periodic increases in veterans' pension payments for these same people automatically triggered reductions in Social Security payments.

That situation was discussed at a symposium at the 1966 National Convention by the Joint Rehab and Economic Subcommittee on Problems of the Aged and Aging along with another problem affecting the aged veteran—hospitalization and sickness insurance for the veteran reaching age sixty-five and for his immediate family.

Fortunately, during the latter 1960s, Congress looked kindly, in general, toward veterans, even if some presidential administrations did not. With the military buildup for the Vietnam War that began in 1965, attention naturally had been drawn to that segment of the population, especially when by 1968 several hundred thousand service personnel were returning to civilian life each year.

These numbers, however, did not compare with the onrush of those who had returned from World War II nearly all at once. So the returning Vietnam veterans, like those from the Korean War, did not constitute, as a group, a particular single point of view as had their predecessors.

The war in Vietnam did cause Congress to bestow benefits much like those that were enacted for veterans of the two previous wars. And the G.I. Bill of Rights for post–Korean War veterans (those who served after January 31, 1955) was the Veterans Readjustment Act of 1966, which President Johnson signed on March 3 of that year (Public Law 89-38).

Perhaps the most important provision of that act was the college-level educational benefits offered to Vietnam veterans. Payments for attending vocational and farm training were soon added, but the latter benefit drew few takers in this age of beleaguered farmers losing their equipment and sometimes even their farms. In fact, the small number of those accepting the various benefits was disappointing to many of the act's sponsors.

Rehab Commission members had listened intently to President Johnson's message to Congress on January 31, 1967, regarding service personnel and veterans. The speech pleased John Corcoran, Rehab Division Director, who observed that this was the first time a president had sent a message to Congress recommending such broad beneficial legislation for veterans. Though it had been the practice of previous presidents to urge veterans to look to welfare programs to meet needs not directly related to military service, President Johnson had said that "although many of these [Great Society] proposals will have an important relationship to programs for veterans and their survivors, it is important that we do more. We must be certain that they do not adversely affect the pensions paid to those veterans who are eligible for both benefits." (This president, however, would attempt to hold the line on veterans' benefits, in the process closing a few V.A. hospitals, too.)

Later that year, at the 1967 National Convention in Boston, there was created the Vietnam Veterans Advisory Committee to develop a frame of reference for rehab advocacy involving veterans of that conflict, a growing number of whom were attempting to settle back into civilian life at this point.

Having learned that the quick rotation of these servicemen often caused a lack of complete medical surveys and good dental care, one of the first measures that the Rehab Commission previously had considered on behalf of this new group was for dental benefits.

But these veterans, like their predecessors, also needed rehabilitation in the form of disability compensation and pensions, medical care, survivors' assistance, and home purchase and career aid.

Those with service-connected disabilities, too, received cost-of-living increases in compensation payments beginning in 1965 and again in 1968 when H.R. 16027 passed and was enacted. The resultant Public Law 90-493 had developed out of a recommendation by the president's Veterans Advisory Commission, which was chaired by former Rehab Commission Chairman Robert McCurdy. This act increased by one hundred dollars the monthly disability compensation paid to the totally disabled and provided an eight percent increase for those partially disabled, payable January 1, 1969. Similar increases were achieved in 1972, 1974, 1975, and 1976.

For a while in 1965, the Legion had looked on incredulously in a period of V.A. cutbacks and closings even as disabled veterans of the war in Vietnam were expected to come home in ever larger numbers.

The traditional bed-count game also continued. When changes were made in any hospital, whether by funding cuts, V.A. reclassification of beds by use, or when a facility was renovated or enlarged, Rehab Commission members looked to the proportion of beds assigned for specific types of medical care to make sure that the kind of medical care veterans needed in that area was being performed.

While Rehab workers monitored the bed counts, the Rehab Commission reiterated its stance that the beds be used or kept available for deserving veterans and not their widows or children. At the same time the Legion waged a different kind of benefits campaign, seeking medical treatment for these dependents on a contract basis with their local hospitals.

The bed-count issue was further aggravated occasionally when it was recommended that the few remaining Public Health Service hospitals be closed and that the patients, most often former members of the Merchant Marines, be sent to V.A. hospitals. To this the Legion continued to object.

The other chief concern regarding V.A. hospitals was the annual appropriation granted to them by Congress. The Legion consistently lobbied for larger yearly appropriations. Like the ongoing bed count, cuts in funding for hospitals required continual what-if projections outlining the effects each spate of proposed cuts would have on specific hospitals. Of particular interest in this regard was the effects funding cuts would have on the *type* of professional expertise to be eliminated.

Sometimes the problem of V.A. funding was writ large, as when the National Convention in 1970 pondered President Nixon's veto of a recent Independent Offices Appropriation bill for fiscal 1971 because it contained non-V.A. related provisions to which he objected. At times like this, especially, Rehab Commission members called for a separate appropriation for the V.A. As large and important as the work of the V.A. was, it should enjoy its own place in the president's cabinet, they said, an idea that at times seemed to be gaining momentum on the Hill.

National Rehab officers believed that every time the matter of an annual appropriation for the V.A. was wrangled over in Congress, the V.A. was that much more susceptible to the machinations of those determined to see its services transferred to other government agencies. Rehab reports of the period contain many references to the dreaded threat of "dismemberment."

At one point there was even a recommendation by the American Medical Association (A.M.A.) for converting V.A. hospitals into community hospitals staffed by private physicians. National officers had met with the A.M.A. to air the Legion's concern in this matter.

In May 1971, National Commander John T. Geiger reported feeling "assured that for the first time in many years, the American Legion has predicted where we are going to face the battle. We have drawn the line over which we hope the politicians will fear to tread. This is the first time we are ready in advance, rather than trying to catch up to legislation which is adverse to the service you want [for veterans]."

The "ready in advance" philosophy was augmented when the National Convention in 1971 established the Veterans Medical Care Committee as, as one member described it, "a watchdog committee to see what Congress will do regarding the [proposed] national health insurance program [i.e. current legislation] in regards to our V.A. medical care." The committee was also primed to look for moves for an H.E.W. takeover of V.A. hospitals.

The committee, composed of members of the newly renamed Veterans Affairs and Rehabilitation Commission along with department service officers, was mandated to investigate (1) the adequacy of the V.A. medical care program; (2) the potential impact on that program of a national health insurance program (there were currently at least five bills in Congress on this matter); (3) the reasons for the continuing necessity of an independent medical care program within the V.A.; and (4) "any other matters of medical care of veterans not otherwise covered in the previous points."

The Veterans Medical Care Committee made its interim report in March 1972. In the intervening months the group had met with many government officials and private practitioners in the medical care field. The report was a detailed defense of the present V.A. medical care program, written as an argument against any national health plan or any other plan or program which would be used to replace or greatly change the V.A. program.

By late fall 1972, however, the special committee was busy planning lobbying tactics for the 93rd Congress and seeking to have protective wording safeguarding the integrity of the V.A. medical care program included in national health insurance legislation that was sure to be considered by Congress. The committee also determined to let it be known, especially to Legionnaires, that they were on the scene and on the Legion's side on the subject of national health insurance. In May 1973, the committee considered the latest development: a proposal by the V.A. for legislation that would require private insurance carriers to reimburse the V.A. for the cost of medical care for nonservice-connected cases among their policy holders. For its part, the committee continued to work for the exclusion of the V.A. medical care program from any national health insurance legislation.

The committee reported to the N.E.C. in October 1973, "We don't always agree with PNC [Don] Johnson [now V.A. head]." But when Johnson spoke to the N.E.C. in August 1973, his audience roundly cheered their comrade when he spoke about the coming reorganization of the V.A.'s Department of Medicine and Surgery, due for October 1, and about the need, the "main mission," to preserve the V.A. as an agency for the independent administration of veterans' programs, including particularly the preservation of the integrity of the V.A. hospital and medical care program from any plan or organization for the delivery of national health services.

New National Commander Robert E. L. Eaton, elected at the Honolulu National Convention in 1973, appointed an ad hoc committee in January 1974 to study and evaluate the administration's national health program, particularly in how it related to the Legion's own objectives regarding veterans.

After working through this new assignment, the committee reiterated the observation of the earlier committee whose "investigation clearly established that the enactment of national health insurance will have a traumatic diverse effect on the V.A. medical care program." The committee identified two "clear and specific dangers." The first was the gradual or precipitate conversion of the V.A. system into a public instead of a veterans' agency. The second was a vast reduction in the number of veterans who would be eligible for V.A. care, since existing law required many to certify their inability to pay for their own care in order to receive V.A. care.

The ad hoc committee recommended continued Legion opposition to all national health plans, even a conservative one, which did not contain specific guarantees for continuing the V.A. medical care program. That line of reasoning and lobbying would continue for sometime afterward whenever the subject of national health insurance was considered in Congress.

During this time there was also the ever-present subject of considering a bonus for World War II and Korean War veterans that persisted in a constant flow of resolutions to National Headquarters. When the subject surfaced at the National Convention in 1967, new Rehab Commission Chairman William F. Lenker moved for rejection, reminding the delegates that many times in the past national conventions had taken the position that the G.I. Bill was adequate. (As after World War I, many World War II veterans had received state bonuses.) The year 1967 also had brought the Veterans' Pension and Adjustment Assistance Act (S. 16; Public Law 90-77), which increased pensions and authorized a cost-of-living increase averaging 5.4 percent in the nonservice-connected pensions.

Though refusing to lend its influence to the creation of new pensions, the commission did push for cost-of-living adjustments and rate protections. Periodic increases followed. Pension safeguards were added when H.R. 12555 was enacted (Public Law 90-275) in 1968, providing that increased Social Security benefits would not lower veterans' pensions. In 1970, a system went into effect that adjusted pensions and Social Security payments so that changes in the latter did not decrease the former. Also in 1970, the income-ceiling limitations and the nonservice-connected payments were raised, including those for dependents and survivors. Two years later, pensions and the attendant income limitations were raised an average of eight percent, and in 1973 came a cost-of-living increase of ten percent. In 1974 an increase of twelve percent was made. Another adjustment was made in 1975 to counteract for one million veterans or their survivors a Social Security increase that would have decreased these pensions.

Coming with the original G.I. Bill in 1944, the term "readjustment" when applied to returning veterans had become a fixture in the congressional glossary. In 1974, the Senate's overriding of the first presidential veto of a veterans' education bill (H.R. 12628) brought about the Vietnam-era Veterans Readjustment Assistance Act of that year (Public Law 93-508). Both houses had dumped the veto with resounding majority votes.

The act increased educational benefits by 22.7 percent for post-Korea and Vietnam-era veterans. Funds were also increased for on-the-job training and for the disabled needing vocational aid. The impressively increased benefits had been a congressional measure all along the path to enactment, involving joint efforts of the two houses for an entire year to agree on the various provisions. After several changes, at times decreasing then increasing benefits, or vice versa, the veto override came in early December 1974.

In the spring, H.R. 6574, containing improvements in the life insurance programs of members of the military reserves and veterans of Korea and Vietnam, became law (Public Law 93-289) on May 24. The Veterans Omnibus Health Care Act of 1976 (Public Law 94-581) gave veterans with service-connected medical problems preference in outpatient care over those with nonservice-connected problems.

The Rehab Commission continued to work for a veterans' general health insurance program.

In the year of the nation's bicentennial birthday, a Senate study committee looked to the organizational structure of the Senate. The work of that body had increased in size many times since the first federal legislators met to debate the future of the young republic.

The study group, a bipartisan effort headed by Adlai Stevenson (D., IL) and William Brock (R., TN), recommended a sweeping reorganization of the structure of Senate committees, calling for the elimination of many committees, including those on Veterans, Space, Small Business, District of Columbia, Nutrition, Post Office, Ethics, Joint Atomic Energy, and Joint Economic. The functions of these groups tagged for the cutting block would be redistributed to the fifteen committees suggested to remain.

Specifically, the Stevenson-Brock group recommended that the function of the Veterans Committee should fall to two committees: housing to the Committee on Banking, Housing, and Urban Affairs, and all other veterans' programs to one called Human Resources, which included control of labor, public welfare, and health. The Legion, of course, objected strongly. The Veterans Affairs and Rehab Commission's Resolution 20 to that effect was presented to the N.E.C. in October 1976.

The resolution insisted that veterans' committees in both houses of Congress were needed. The almost thirty million veterans of all wars, with their dependents and survivors numbering more than another fifty million persons, made up one-third of the U.S. population and their benefit and other programs totaled about twenty billion dollars of the nation's budget.

It had only been since the Legislative Reorganization Act of 1970 that the Senate had had a standing Veterans Affairs Committee. A comparable committee of the same name had been established in the House in 1924 (and had been called at that time the Committee on World War Veterans Legislation). Before 1970, the variety of veterans' affairs had been assigned to Senate committees on Finance, Labor, and Public Welfare. (It was the Senate Finance Committee that had debated the original G.I. Bill of Rights.)

Past National Commander Don Johnson provided some perspective for the N.E.C. in October. "It seems that every decade or so, there is some kind of assault upon the V.A. and the veterans' rights and the veterans' benefits of this country. Sometimes it comes in a frontal attack such as we experienced in 1965 with the ordered closings of V.A. installations.

"But this is an insidious attempt, in my opinion, to reduce the rights of all veterans. The expertise that has been built up over the years, and the staffs of the respected houses of Congress, will be lost. We will be put in together with all the other welfare income maintenance and life payments.

"This is the most important resolution that has faced this committee [the N.E.C.] at this particular session."

Johnson urged committeemen to sound the alarm when they returned home.

Gauche or not, during the nation's bicentennial birthday in 1976, it might well have been said that the nation entertained a year-long American Legion parade.

One of the most impressive parades of all that year had actually started from Wilmington, Delaware, on April 1, 1975, and would travel over 24,000 miles and touch each and every state in the bunting-bedecked Union at least once in its twenty-one-month march.

The Freedom Train stopped in 138 cities across the land and invited observers to tour the nation's democratic heritage and greatness as the train's moving walkway conducted them past the exhibits in the twenty-six red, white, and blue cars.

Two steam locomotives had been rejuvenated to pull the train in a fashion sure to inspire enthusiasm (assisted a few times by diesel power). The former Reading Railroad T-1 No. 2101 had been rescued from a Baltimore scrap yard; Southern Pacific's retired No. 4449 had been revived from repose in a Portland, Oregon, city park. The T-1 would pull the train in the Northeast, where track clearance limitations required the slightly smaller engine. On the western route, the 425-ton SP "Daylight" GS-4 powerhouse with eighty-inch high, 2,352-pound drive wheels would pull the train from near Crystal Lake, Illinois, in late July 1975, to Sacramento, California, and eventually on around to Birmingham, Alabama, for a Memorial Day arrival in 1976. (Texas provided its own locomotion—former Texas and Pacific Railroad steam engine No. 610—for the pull across the Lone Star State.)

From the head of the train to the rear were exhibits entitled "Beginnings," "Exploration and Expansion," "Growth of the Nation," "Origins," "Innovations," "Human Resources," "Sports," "Performing Arts," "Fine Arts," and "Conflict and Resolution." Two "Showcase Cars" brought up the rear. Lighted for nighttime viewing, the first showcase car included historic means of transportation. The second glass-enclosed car contained the Freedom Bell, twice the size of the Liberty Bell in Independence Hall in Philadelphia on which it was modeled and dedicated to America's children by the American Legion and the Auxiliary.

The seven-and-one-half-foot tall, eight-and-one-half-ton bell had been cast at the 300-year-old N. V. Petit & Fritsen Bell Foundry of Aarle-Rixtel in Holland. Composed of copper (eighty percent) and tin (twenty percent), the bell weighed eight tons, including a 600-pound, eighty-inch hand-forged steel clapper with a bronze ball, and was tuned an octave lower (and in the key of F, for "Freedom") than the Liberty Bell, which had sounded for the last time in 1846 on George Washington's birthday. The bell would later be placed at Union Station in Washington, D.C., a gift to the nation from the American Legion.

THE NATIONAL EXECUTIVE COMMITTEE
The Volunteers Debate

When in 1969 the N.E.C.'s process of considering resolutions was changed so that debate would occur in committee meetings rather than on the floor of the N.E.C., some reminisced about the powers of persuasion, logic, and eloquence of well-respected committeemen of ages past. Others, however, remembered the harangues, tirades, and other time-wasting usurpations by those who commandeered a convenient audience for a moment, or many insufferable moments, in the limelight.

The new process was designed to encourage a more democratic consideration of resolutions. Similarly, the process for producing resolutions was revamped to increase the germane quality and overall effectiveness of these basic tools for governance and official expression. The upgrading process overall also emphasized layers of liaison for a smoother flow-through of the time-honored practice of arriving at resolutions. Insiders would refer to the changes, and the Legion betterment that was intended and resulting, as characterizing the "Stone Era," referring to the long service of E. Roy Stone Jr. (SC) as committeeman and chairman of the influential Resolutions Subcommittee, which epitomized the value of the N.E.C. to the organization.

It was a change for the better, of course, but a change that by its very purpose recognized the value of the N.E.C. to the governing of the organization. And the N.E.C. had long been the scene of Legion debate.

"Occasionally here we work according to the Marquess of Queensberry Rules," a N.E.C. man stated at the May 1949 meeting, referring to the famous mid–nineteenth century rules for prizefighting. It was not a completely facetious observation. Anyone who heard the robust reciting of the Pledge of Allegiance at the opening of N.E.C. meetings could not doubt the stamina of those assembled to exercise vigorously the democratic process, whether on the N.E.C. floor as in times past or in a commission forum.

Actually, it was a combination of the fourteen succinct rules for the operation of the N.E.C., contributed by elder statesman and quintessential volunteer Bill McKinley (NJ), coupled with provisions in the Legion constitution that were used by this interim governing body and debating society known as the N.E.C.

In the post–World War II era, the N.E.C. continued to embody the executive and legislative continuity within the American Legion between national conventions. Furthermore, it was in the N.E.C. where much of the leadership capability of the Legion was discovered, forged, exhibited, and proven.

Committeemen, leaders in their departments, spoke for the blue-cap, grass-roots viewpoint. They were the audience before which each new program initiative (or review of continuing programs) had to play. The N.E.C. could give rousing support or be a hard ticket. "We must do the executive thing and not only the human thing," one member said.

The composition of the N.E.C. was beginning to change, if ever so gradually, during this period, as World War II veterans came into important positions at the local posts and began occupying the series of "chairs" that led to national office. It has been generally agreed that there occurred a relatively smooth transition from a World War I membership that had framed the organization's constitution (a document that did not foresee another generation of veterans) to a membership which in 1946 was, numerically, at least, predominantly made up of World War II veterans. Both groups can be credited—the former for resiliency, the latter for the will to perpetuate "the basics" of the Legion. Continuity of action was the key, of course. There was no abrupt, foundation-shaking change to threaten the continuation and impact of vital programs. Gradual as it was, and complained of as it may have been by some, the changing of the guard evolved in a manner that allowed for survival.

But it didn't happen overnight. The N.E.C. would be dominated by World War I members through much of the 1950s. In early 1949, one member, no doubt speaking for many, complained that not enough progress had been made in "turning over the reins" to the World War II vets. He spoke specifically of the few committee assignments given to the younger members. But Past National Commander James O'Neil quickly pointed out that World War II vets had been brought to the N.E.C. as consultants and that already some World War II vets were serving as post and department commanders as well as delegates to national conventions. That, O'Neil said, was the proper way to go. There was "no more democratic organization in all the world than the American Legion."

O'Neil had identified an important facet in the continuity of the American Legion. The World War I veterans, with an average age of fifty-seven in 1949, were, for purposes of volunteerism, in the prime of their lives professionally and economically. Yet they presided over the transformation of the organization in a fashion that allowed it to survive. (Some World War II veterans had formed smaller organizations rather than join the Legion.)

But the American Legion story includes this vital development of self-perpetuation at this particular time: the veterans of World War I determined that their American Legion would not fade out as a last-man club.

The World War I committeemen and others were not totally unselfish in taking in World War II veterans. Having become accustomed to being part of a national organization that in the 1920s and 1930s had made congressmen listen, had eased the plight of disabled comrades and of thousands of dependent children, had served as a fire bell for national security, and had seen the emblem of the American Legion become one of the most recognized and respected motifs on the American scene, they were not likely to relegate themselves to mere vague imaginings or reminiscences about things past.

In no way did the transformation come as a complete surprise, of course. The seed was in the G.I. Bill of Rights. It was World War I veterans, after all, who had forged the bill and fought for enactment, the beneficiaries of which were predominantly World War II veterans.

The debate by Legionnaires about subjects of interest to veterans, National Commander (and later governor of Indiana) George Craig said, was "the most profound I have ever dealt with."

The N.E.C., Craig said, was a reflection of the positive side of volunteerism. "They are there because they are interested in it." Also, the N.E.C. was "absolutely unfettered . . . the most consummate legislative group I have ever dealt with, and that includes Congress and the Indiana Senate and General Assembly." While "the Congress and the state legislatures are pockmarked by special interests," the Legion wasn't. "They have no constituency for which they must do a special favor. They do what they think is good for the country." There was appreciable openness. Except for the infrequent executive session (usually for selecting the Legion's prestigious Distinguished Service Award) the press was allowed to attend the meetings.

Issues discussed were national in nature. Debate, therefore, could focus on large-scale issues and initiatives. One had only to monitor the N.E.C. to learn not only what was of interest to all veterans, but also what were the major issues of the day.

Procedural matters fairly teemed with parliamentary nomenclature; newcomers needed a crash course in the committee's technical terminology. Sometimes the fate of a resolution rested on a procedural move within the larger debate. One had to pay attention.

Debate was frank and free. The atmosphere much of the time was, indeed, that of a serious deliberative body. Oratory was respected; long-windedness was not. One committeeman, echoing a famous statesman, put it succinctly: "Speeches can be immortal without being eternal." And immortality was reserved for a select few. As a committeeman said at the May 1949 meeting, "All the best brains of the American Legion are not in this room now."

Debate occasionally crackled with controversy and confrontation. Past National Commander John Quinn once charged that the suspen-

sion of the rules at one point was little more than procedural maneuvering to defeat a measure he favored. The tactic was potentially destructive: "If you want to split the Legion wide open, that is just the way to do it!"

Another time, angered by recent actions by the Soviet Union, the N.E.C. considered a resolution to call for all Russian diplomats to be thrown out of the country. But National Commander Don Wilson, himself an outspoken critic of the Soviet Union, cautioned those assembled not to vote in a state of vexation. The white heat of the moment subsided somewhat and the resolution was reconsidered. The "executive thing" was being done.

One particular standard for judging the merits of resolutions to be considered by the N.E.C. was often voiced: "Is it germane to the basics of the Legion?" Resolutions found wanting were summarily rejected (McKinley Rule 9 d 1).

"Nongermane" resolutions were inappropriate either on a small or a large scale—the first benefited too few and the second attempted too much. Those who sought to correct some injustice done to an individual or to commend someone on a local level failed from nearsightedness.

Others failed to fly if they were too ambitious. One member said in October 1952, in the spirited debate over national foreign policy and shocking international events, "The commissions are not just doing their business but [are] trying to take over the government." Past National Commander John Quinn once asked, "Aren't we leaving the basic principles of the veterans' problem . . . [and] trying to build up the country on the basis of the American Legion and not letting somebody else have their share [of responsibility and initiative]?" The N.E.C., he said, should "direct our attention to our own affairs . . . and not take in a reformation of the world."

Legion lobbyist John Thomas Taylor warned that other organizations and interests were eager to have the Legion do their lobbying for them on a myriad of measures that were in no way "germane." One committeeman complained during this time that "this continual resoluting" should be limited to "the good of our veterans, our members, our communities, states, and the nation." Others, never at a loss for reasons why each proposal very much related to the "veterans' problems," argued eloquently for more wide-ranging involvement.

Just what, indeed, brought about "the good of our veterans" was far-reaching and complex, and the "germane" standard itself continued to be debated. Yet the "basics" of rehab, national security, child welfare, and Americanism more often than not were held to by the N.E.C. in judging what was properly "germane."

The work of the N.E.C. was yet another opportunity for the American Legion to show that the importance of "the basics" should rise above partisan politics. The natural wariness of those of opposing po-

litical persuasions was eased considerably when working on rehab, child welfare, or any other of the Legion's many service programs. The N.E.C. chamber was comparatively safe ground; camaraderie was based on veterandom and not, necessarily, on political affiliation.

N.E.C. meeting dates were on the calendars of many in the federal government and elsewhere. Experts in various fields appeared before the Legion's national commissions and committees and before the entire N.E.C. There was, therefore, an enlightening exchange: committeemen heard authoritative, even privileged, information from speakers who, in turn, had access to an audience of persons influential on the local level.

Television cameras were brought into the N.E.C. room for the first time on May 3, 1951, during the first meeting at the new National Headquarters building in Indianapolis. As the local WFBM-TV cameraman panned the chamber, the announcer intoned, "This group is composed of men as representative of the nation as democracy can make it." Television viewers heard Legionnaires speak knowledgeably and with conviction about foreign relations, national security, the value of one hundred percent Americanism, and other topics.

The television audience, also, heard many regional accents; committeemen did represent a certain cross section of America. Having served in their particular wars, they had taken places in government, public or private management, labor, or some other pursuit affecting, and affected by, all the economic and political phenomena that touched upon the lives of everyone else. When public education was the topic, it was not unusual for a Legionnaire who was an educator or a school board member to rise and make his contribution to the discussion. Similarly, others in myriad occupations brought their views as well as that of their departments to the N.E.C. debates.

Though disagreements and occasionally rancorous exchanges occurred, there was a genuine attempt to maintain fraternity. Few could remain unmoved by the half-minute-long memorial observances that began: "It has pleased Almighty God, the great commander, to summon to his immortal Legion our beloved comrade. . . ."

Before being dispersed to the four corners of the nation (and to foreign departments), committeemen were reminded by National Commander Art Connell in his closing remarks in October 1953, "Anything that has transpired here is water over the dam as far as any personalities are concerned."

Those who did not heed his admonition were doing only "the human thing" and not the "executive thing." And the "executive thing" would remain the same whether practiced in the 1940s, 1950s, or the 1980s and 1990s and on the N.E.C. floor or in national commission meetings.

MOMENT OF PAUSE; MOMENT OF REFLECTION

PARDON, PANAMA, PREFERENCE, AND THE COLOR ORANGE

1977 – 1984

I

Just before the presidential inauguration of early 1977, *The American Legion Magazine* depicted the foreign policy challenges facing the president-elect in an article titled "The Worlds of Jimmy Carter." The bicentennial year presidential campaign had focused on domestic problems. Many questions about how the nation should and would pursue its world leadership role had been left unanswered.

There was, the article stated, a fortunate if fragile "moment of pause" in world conflict. But "the patterns set by World War II are beginning to change." In Africa and the Middle East, "the pause is ominous." Meanwhile, détente, for all its promise of easing the perpetual alert on the part of major opposing world powers occasioned by the cold war, had but "blurred" those still unresolved conflicts, particularly in the Far East and Europe.

In Latin America, too, there was impending change where with promptings from the ideological left and right the drama was being played out on several stages against a backdrop of anti-American propaganda. Regarding the continued U.S. operation of the Panama Canal, there would likely be made some "concessions" (a term that, according to the Legion's view, soon would prove to be a gross understatement).

It was now Jimmy Carter's turn to deal with the international problems that inevitably "fell at Washington's doorstep." The magazine wished the new president "Godspeed."

Soon the Legion's good wishes were overshadowed. Though the Washington headquarters was located only three blocks and around the corner on K Street NW from the Oval Office, the Legion would find itself far removed from the new president's views on several matters of foreign and domestic policy.

This was particularly so when after less than twenty-four hours in office, a presidential proclamation on January 21—Carter's Executive Order No. 1—granted "full, complete, and unconditional pardon" to all those who had violated the Selective Service Act between 1964 and 1973: approximately 9,000 convicted draft evaders; 4,522 unconvicted draft evaders; and an unknown number of persons who had failed to register for the draft. (Excluded from the pardon were employees of the Selective Service and those whose violations involved force or violence. Though the pardon did not include military deserters, the president called for an expedited case-by-case review of all deserters and those who received less than honorable discharges during that time.)

A Senate resolution protesting the pardon was defeated by a slim, telling two-vote margin, and a House move endorsed by the Senate for withholding an appropriation for administering the pardon was largely ineffective because the pardon program required little funding.

From the first time during the Vietnam War when the pardon—then referred to as an amnesty—for draft evaders was being mentioned, the flash point of opinion on the subject was quickly reached. The Legion response was immediate and disapproving.

As early as March 1972, National Commander John H. Geiger had appeared before a Senate subcommittee to present Resolution 207 of the 1971 National Convention opposing a blanket amnesty. Geiger pointed out that the review board established in 1946 had looked at all 15,805 cases of draft evasion following World War II. That board had included the Legion's James F. O'Neil, a special assistant to the secretary of the navy during the war, later a national commander of the Legion and the publisher of the magazine.

The May 1972 issue of the magazine had asked what was to the Legion the key question: "The Amnesty Question for Draft Evaders: Are They All the Same?" That rhetorical inquiry introduced the argument that each case of draft evasion and desertion from military service should be judged individually. Certainly not all draft evaders, this argument went, had acted on high principles. There were even criminals, at one extreme, who avoided the draft to keep from getting arrested for their crimes. But a blanket amnesty, pardon, or whatever one chose to call it, was said to operate on the assumption that only one group or class of draft evaders existed. That, the Legion said, was patently not so, even though numerous newspaper headlines insisted otherwise.

When in mid-February 1973 some of the POWs returned, National Commander Joe L. Matthews reiterated the Legion stance that amnesty for deserters and draft dodgers was "a matter for a duly constituted court of law" to determine. Yet "to endorse blanket amnesty for those who chose to run away to exile rather than serve our country would dishonor these fine men, and all those who gave their lives and indeed all who served in these trying times."

The subject continued to be as controversial as the unpopular war from which it sprung. The March 12, 1973, issue of *U.S. News & World Report* reported that according to one national survey, amnesty "ranks second after school busing as the most delicate political issue in the nation today," stirring up deep feelings as shown in the barrage of letters received by newspaper publishers and by members of Congress.

The Legion National Convention that year in Hawaii passed Resolution 41 from the National Security Commission, which spoke of "responsibility" and "obligation" for serving in the military when called on to do so and opposed any amnesty or freedom from prosecution for those who illegally avoided the draft or deserted from the armed forces. Instead, it emphasized, "Each case should be reviewed under existing procedures available to the courts and the president."

The next year a policy statement on the subject acknowledged an "emotional problem with overtones of justice tempered with mercy and understanding" that had been made worse since the Vietnam conflict was indeed "a bitterly divisive one." But the statement stressed that the charges about the immorality of this particular war were misplaced; the real immorality, it was said, was the refusal of draft evaders and deserters to comply with the government's order for their military service. Furthermore, the complaint was often heard among veterans that the unlawful acts committed by draft evaders and deserters were reported in the press as protest while the genocide committed by the Viet Cong was largely unmentioned.

Legionnaire O'Neil, the only surviving member of Truman's Amnesty Board, pointed out that no amnesty had been given following the Korean War, proof, he said, that the matter was not to be taken lightly and certainly should not be automatic.

Following President Ford's announcement of a plan for amnesty, National Adjutant William F. Hauck issued a statement on September 16, 1974, stating that the president's proclamation of that date "violates the principles for which millions served their country honorably, thousands died in combat, thousands more were wounded, many are hospitalized, while others remain missing in action." Again it was said that civilian and military courts should be allowed to try the cases of those accountable to them. A few weeks later, a National Security/Foreign Relations Bulletin (October 18, 1974) drew attention to those who had refused the presidential amnesty program, the "many [who] are vociferously opposed to doing penance for what they felt was 'a just cause' by entering the restitution program."

Two years later, in late 1976, the Legion was still issuing statements opposing both a pardon and an amnesty. In December of that year, after the presidential election, National Adjutant Hauck and others at the Washington headquarters of the Legion met with a member of President-elect Carter's transition staff to repeat the strong opposition to the granting of general amnesty. A few days earlier, 101 congressmen and 5 congressmen-elect, in a move headed by Mississippi Democratic Representative G. V. "Sonny" Montgomery, had made the same point to the incoming administration.

But on January 12, 1977, Carter's choice for attorney general, Griffin Bell, revealed the first details for the plan for pardoning Vietnam draft resisters and evaders at his confirmation hearings. Bell explained that convicted draft evaders would be pardoned, charges of draft evasion would be dropped against those not yet convicted, immigration procedures would be formulated to allow those who fled the country to return, and a review would be organized for those who had received a less than honorable discharge for opposing the war while members of the military forces.

National Commander William J. Rogers (1976–77) had spoken out against the pardon on every occasion open to him between the election and the inauguration. But he advised against a suggestion by a post adjutant in Philadelphia that the Legion's color guard boycott the inauguration ceremonies. "Such an action would not be an affront to one man, nor would it be an effective argument that might dissuade Mr. Carter from his declared amnesty plan. It would be an affront to the office of the president and to our Constitution. And I believe it would lower the traditionally high standards of conduct that the American Legion represents," Rogers answered.

Before the inauguration, however, Rogers's news release of January 19 criticized President Ford for awarding honorable discharges for certain categories of about 700 deserters as being "untimely and unwise." Though Rogers did not quarrel with the president's rationale,

"We believe that in the eyes of the general public the distinctions between President Ford's actions and President-elect Carter's proposals will most certainly be lost, and are bound to have a softening effect on future White House pardon actions." It was hoped that Carter would take note of the case-by-case review of his predecessor's Clemency Board and incorporate the same in his own plan rather than proceeding with a blanket pardon.

As a sidelight to the actions of the Legion regarding the presidential pardon, Past National Commander J. Addington Wagner (1955–56) had suggested that National Commander Rogers check the constitutionality of the president's action. If there was "a feasible chance" that the pardon was unconstitutional, Wagner "would strongly recommend" that the Legion file an action in that regard, preferably "in conjunction with the other veterans' organizations . . . to avoid his venting any vindictiveness toward" the Legion. Earlier, Wagner had suggested, also, that National Adjutant Hauck check into the possibility of a violation of the Selective Service Act by the issuance of Executive Order No. 1.

That query, too, went the way of National Judge Advocate B. G. Davis's opinion, reached after reviewing in early February the pleas drafted by the Foundation of Law and Society challenging the president's right to grant an unconditional pardon, that Article 2, paragraph 2 of the U.S. Constitution contained what he assumed to be grounds for dismissal. "There is no question in my mind that the presidential power of pardon is absolute and is not subject in any way to legislative control," he explained to Past National Commander Martin B. McKneally (1959–60) who, also, had inquired about the matter.

In a Legion magazine editorial message in the March 1977 issue, National Commander Rogers acknowledged "the shocked, sickening sensation" that followed the granting of the pardon. Earlier, when candidate Carter had outlined the pardon at the Legion National Convention in Seattle in the fall of 1976, the mood on the convention floor was unmistakably and vocally against it.

But though, as Rogers stated, "the pardon hits at the base of our beliefs" as Legionnaires, the deed was done. Given the comprehensiveness of the pardon, the national commander posed two questions: How about granting "blanket" benefits for those who served in all wars and were now beset with inflation? How about a "blanket" rewriting of Selective Service laws to effect universality of service?

So the matter was decided contrary to Legion wishes, indeed principles. But throughout, though the mention of amnesty, pardon, "forgiveness," or whatever the subject was called rankled most Legionnaires, the president's action was considered a combination of an affront to honorably discharged veterans and a threat to national security. What would happen should the nation face another emergency requiring armed forces and the compliance of thousands of persons with draft laws? As Internal Affairs Director J. Lloyd Wignall stated to a Legionnaire who cancelled his membership and complained about those on the floor of the Seattle National Convention who booed when presidential candidate Carter stated his intentions for granting a pardon, "deep down . . . Legionnaires are more fearful of what this will do in the event the United States faces other emergencies in the future, and I am sure we will."

Wignall and others at National Headquarters received numerous letters from members and others decrying the pardon, letters replete with uniquely American exuberant dissent ranging from lawyerly logic to patriotic homilies.

There was at least one sigh of relief by National Headquarters staff and officers during the spring of 1977. The permanence of the Senate Veterans Affairs Committee, which the Senate Reorganization Committee headed by Senator Adlai E. Stevenson, Jr. (D., IL) said should become a subcommittee of the Human Resources Committee, was retained by a voice vote requested by Senator James B. Allen (D., AL) while in committee. Senators considering the recommendations of the Stevenson committee reportedly were impressed by the response received from Legionnaires across the nation in favor of keeping the committee as it was.

Heartened by the survival of the Veterans Affairs Committee, National Commander Rogers appointed a special ad hoc committee chaired by William F. Lenker, chairman of the Legion's own Veterans Affairs and Rehabilitation Commission, to take a close look at several areas of concern, of which there were many.

For example, the controversial National Academy of Science's "Study of Health Care for American Veterans" was deemed "hostile to the maintenance and continued improvement" of the V.A. medical care program. Other developments this ad hoc committee focused its attention on included the proposed V.A. reduction of 5,000 beds; the Senate's containment bill, S. 1391, on hospital costs; the likely effect of the general mood for welfare reform, particularly that which might affect veterans' compensation; veterans' pension legislation; the president's discharge review program; another Senate bill, S. 457, which suggested changes in the delimiting date for education and training programs; the fight for veterans' preference against judicial review; and President Carter's special military discharge review program.

Thus continued the traditional efforts to relieve in some fashion the burden of physical and other disabilities of veterans. For if the Legion had not single-handedly invented the wheel of veterans' rehab, it could take much of the credit for the design, the continual refining of the mechanism, and the paving of the road for its use.

All involved legislation, and Legion spokesmen had presented sixty-one statements to a total of forty-three congressional committees on a variety of issues, many of which were resolved ultimately by presidential signature. By year's end, of the more than 200 bills that had become public law during the first session of the 95th Congress, fifty-two of them satisfied American Legion resolutions wholly or in part.

A few days before the adjourning of the first session of the 95th Congress on December 15, 1977, Veterans Affairs and Rehab Commission members could point with pride to six new laws in particular, representing a cross section of the efforts and interests of Rehab workers: a 6.6 percent hike in service-connected compensation and dependency and indemnity benefits for veterans and their survivors; $15 million for fiscal 1978 and 1979 for improvements at state veterans' homes; auto assistance allowances for disabled veterans of World War I; some improvements in the pay of V.A. doctors and dentists; a 6.6 percent increase in G.I. education and training allowances and other liberalizations in that area; and a new law denying some benefits to certain persons with upgraded discharges that had not been okayed by a discharge review board's separate determination.

The bulk of that work had been channeled through an essential function—the National Legislative Division—whose few National Headquarters staffers, often aided by national officers and other volunteers, went to Capitol Hill in good times and bad, when in favor and out of favor.

The practice of lobbying had changed from the days when the bumptious John Thomas Taylor's clout included large measures of clatter. Ed Lord, assistant legislative director, acknowledged, "We do not slam fists on desks to get our point across; ours is a businesslike approach." That was much more effective, Lord explained, in working, as was required now, with legislative staff members who surrounded congressmen.

Three registered Legion lobbyists, Ed Lord, Mylio Kraja, director of the Legislative Division, and Phil Riggin, had the job of letting Congress know the Legion's opinion on legislation or subsequent congressional action relevant to veterans. Registered to testify themselves, the three were also permitted to present expert witnesses such as the national commander or directors of Legion divisions, among others.

The time clock answered slavishly to the dictates of the work; timetable anomalies were rather to be expected. At 2:30 A.M. on the morning after the 95th Congress was to have been adjourned (the clock had been stopped at 11 P.M.), Mylio Kraja was still on the Hill honoring a Legion mandate for an eight percent increase in G.I. Bill benefits. That bill, the next-to-last one dealt with by Congress before its closing, became law. Earlier, in April, the Legislative Division team made twenty-four presentations before congressional committees in four weeks as they pursued increased compensation, pension, and education benefits for veterans.

II

Less than a year after President Carter's draft pardon had proved so irksome to the Legion national leadership, yet another move caused a similar outcry as another affront to Legion principles.

Carter and Panama's Gen. Omar Torrijos Herrera had signed two agreements on September 7, 1977, one giving the Central American country control of the Panama Canal in the year 2000 and another allowing the United States to retain the right to enforce the neutrality of the canal zone.

In March 1978, the Senate voted to ratify the first of the two treaties, that for the United States to maintain the neutrality of the canal. Consequently, National Commander Robert Charles Smith increased his efforts to publicize the Legion's opposition to the second treaty for transferring control of the canal to the Republic of Panama. Moments after the 68 to 32 vote adopting the resolution of ratification of the neutrality treaty, Smith had remarked at a news conference that "the vote was a misrepresentation of the majority will of America." What modifications had been adopted along the way, Smith contended, had come about merely as cosmetic "window dressing" so that some senators could support the president and yet sidestep heavy opposition from their constituencies.

The national commander had recently completed a five-day briefing in Panama and the canal zone. There he had met with representatives of the 1,600 resident Legionnaires and with U.S. Ambassador William J. Jorden; the president of the Republic of Panama, Demetrio B. Lakas; officers of the U.S. Southern Command; and the governor of the canal zone, Harold R. Parfitt. Smith came away still convinced of the original Legion view that the United States should not relinquish sovereignty and control of the canal because the nation's economic health and security interests were closely tied to what happened there. Giving up sovereignty, it was said, would make it possible, even likely, that Panama would take any action it wanted, and legally so.

National Commander Smith held out hope for defeating the second treaty. To national officers, he reported having "watched in the Senate gallery [on March 16] as thirty-two senators registered their objection to the Neutrality Treaty so that only significant concessions by the White House assured its passage. Statements made during the debate strongly suggest that a number of senators who supported the first treaty are deeply troubled over provisions contained in the second."

The Legion's opposition to the second treaty included three major points. First, it was argued that because of the current "financial stress" in the United States it was not the opportune time to take on the financial burden that would surely come from increased tolls and from the "millions" of dollars reportedly due to the Panamanians with the enactment of the treaty for transferring ownership.

Second, it was said that existing threats to U.S. security would intensify with the loss of control of the canal since Russia's navy was becoming larger and more powerful. Doubters were told to remember the outcome of the revolution in Cuba. Those who said that U.S. carriers were too wide to use the canal were reminded that there was other canal activity to recognize—a critical amount of U.S. trade goods went through the canal, too.

Third, it was thought by some that the U.N. Charter could indeed preclude the United States from assuring the neutrality of the canal zone once sovereignty, jurisdiction, and control had been relinquished.

That, in essence, was the opinion, the strong sentiment, of the Legion against the canal "giveaway." But it failed to carry the day.

It was some small consolation, perhaps, that for a president whose initiatives in foreign relations would be pointed to as the most far-reaching and successful of the actions taken during his tenure in office, the Panama Canal treaties were widely and loudly criticized and their ratification came about on April 18 only after lengthy and heated congressional debate.

Canal-related actions by the Legion thereafter were largely principled parting shots. Resolution 398 adopted at the New Orleans National Convention in 1978 prompted the Legion to support Congressman George Hansen's (R., ID) amendments to a few funding bills then being considered that would preclude the spending of funds in the canal zone for its eventual transfer to Panama. Hansen had objected to reports from the canal zone that the United States was already giving up property there while refurbishing some sites to accommodate the consolidation of armed-services personnel.

III

Controversies such as those surrounding amnesty and pardon for draft evaders and the Panama Canal were cresting waves on a sea of current events now made particularly treacherous by an undertow of economic malaise.

In the long run, though many Legionnaires and others would recall the pardon and the canal issues with distaste, the most memorable recollection of the latter 1970s for many would be the shock of dollar-a-gallon gasoline. Suddenly it appeared that America's house was sitting on shifting sands beneath which was critical Arab oil.

In this troubling, anxious context, the Legion's National Economic Commission continued to call for government accountability for policies and practices that directly affected the economic well-being of veterans. The commission had four major goals for the immediate future: curtailing the continuing problem of unemployment among Vietnam-era veterans; preserving veterans' preference in federal employment; encouraging agricultural growth; and battling the nation's energy problem.

The first goal particularly, that for combating the large-scale problem of unemployment among the most recent veterans, required much background work—usually involving largely unsung journeymen's lobbying efforts to see that the essential appropriations were made to employment programs within the Department of Labor that targeted Vietnam-era veterans. (At the same time, commission members were told not to forget the disabled and the older veterans who sought employment.)

As for the nation's energy problem, the Legion had advocated a "Federal Office of Energy Science and Technology" even before President Carter's Energy Secretary had been established as the newest addition to the cabinet in August 1977.

From its membership the Legion could convene specialized knowledge. One example was the conference presided over by Commission Vice-Chairman Joe Holzka of New York in early 1977, when Legionnaires from Maryland, Virginia, Delaware, Pennsylvania, New York, Massachusetts, and the District of Columbia gathered in Annapolis to discuss economics-related legislative measures for satisfying recent mandates. The conferees looked especially hard at complaints that the Small Business Administration was failing to comply with Public Law 93-237 for giving veterans special consideration in small business loans.

Though energy production in 1977 rose slightly, the increase in consumption far outstripped production gains. Imported fuels, of course, were used to offset the gap, a measure thereby defining periodically the extent of the "energy crisis." Though the president eventually got an energy conservation bill passed, national consumption of energy, particularly of oil, continued to rise. The gap filled by imported oil was kept below that of 1977 primarily because that was the first full year of a supply coming through the pipeline from Alaska's North Slope.

It was inevitable that the public service orientation of the Legion should be geared to the popular concern about the nation's energy supplies and consumption during this period. That concern was heightened, of course, by the national security implications regarding an energy supply open to threat.

In early September 1978, new National Commander John M. "Jack" Carey said the Legion's ability to publicize the need for energy conservation because of its national presence was "crucial to our country's future." Speaking to a conference of Legion department energy chairmen in Indianapolis, he pointed out that Saudi Arabia, supplying about half the U.S. national consumption of oil, was located in a region around which the Soviet Union "is closing a ring . . ." Loss of

Seaborn P. Collins (NM)
1954-55
(Chase)

J. Addington Wagner (MI)
1955-56
(Bretzman)

W.C. (Dan) Daniel (VA)
1956-57
(Chase)

John S. Gleason, Jr. (IL)
1957-58
(Chase)

Preston J. Moore (OK)
1958-59
(Chase)

Martin B. McKneally (NY)
1959-60
(Chase)

William R. Burke (CA)
1960-61
(Chase)

Charles L. Bacon (MO)
1961-62
(Chase)

James E. Powers (GA)
1962-63
(Chase)

Daniel F. Foley (MN)
1963-64
(Chase)

Donald E. Johnson (IA)
1964-65
(Chase)

L. Eldon James (VA)
1965-66
(Chase)

John E. Davis (ND)
1966-67

William E. Galbraith (NE)
1967-68
(Chase)

William C. Doyle (NJ)
1968-69
(Chase)

J. Milton Patrick (OK)
1969-70
(Chase)

Alfred P. Chamie (CA)
1970-71

John H. Geiger (IL)
1971-72
(Chase)

JOE L. MATTHEWS (TX)
1972-73
(Chase)

ROBERT E. L. EATON (MD)
1973-74
(Chase)

JAMES M. WAGONSELLER (OH)
1974-75
(Chase)

HARRY G. WILES (KS)
1975-76
(Chase)

WILLIAM J. ROGERS (ME)
1976-77
(Chase)

ROBERT CHARLES SMITH (LA)
1977-78
(Chase)

John M. Carey (MI)
1978-79
(Chase)

Frank I. Hamilton (IN)
1979-80
(Chase)

Michael J. Kogutek (NY)
1980-81
(Chase)

Jack W. Flynt (TX)
1981-82
(Chase)

Al Keller, Jr. (IL)
1982-83
(Chase)

Keith Kreul (WI)
1983-84
(Chase)

Clarence M. Bacon (MD)
1984-85
(Chase)

Dale L. Renaud (IA)
1985-86
(Chase)

James P. Dean (MS)
1986-87
(Chase)

John P. Comer (MA)
1987-88
(Chase)

H.F. "Sparky" Gierke (ND)
1988-89
(Chase)

Miles S. Epling (WV)
1989-90
(Chase)

MAURICE STEMBER (NY), NAMED PAST NATIONAL COMMANDER AT THE 1975 NATIONAL CONVENTION IN MINNEAPOLIS.

NBC RECORDED THE COMMONWEALTH EDISON DRUM AND BUGLE CORPS AT THE 1937 NATIONAL CONVENTION IN NEW YORK. (NBC Photo)

Dr. T. Victor Keene

Walter Myers

Robert L. Moorhead

Three Indiana delegates to the 1919 Minneapolis Convention who succeeded in having the National Headquarters of The American Legion moved to Indianapolis. The three were special guests of the Legion at the 1950 dedication of the present headquarters building.

The Hawthorne Caballeros of Hawthorne (NJ) Post No. 199 display one of their 13 winning flags at Legion "Nationals."

The inspection line, a requirement for many years during national contest time.

THE "INDIAN" CORPS OF ST. PAUL POST NO. 6 AT 1938 NATIONAL CONVENTION IN LOS ANGELES. (ACME)

At National Convention 1978, National Commander Robert Charles Smith and National Adjutant Frank Momsen congratulate The Westshoremen of Post No. 272 (Linglestown, PA) as American Legion Senior Drum and Bugle Corps National Champions.

A proud moment when passing the reviewing stand.

The Garfield Cadets (formerly the Holy Name Cadets of Garfield, NJ, later renamed the Cadets of Bergen County) are shown with ten American Legion national title flags, more than any other Junior Drum Corps. (Maurice D. Knox Jr.)

The National Executive Committee governs the Legion between national conventions. National Commander Preston J. Moore presides at a meeting in 1959 in the NEC Room of National Headquarters. James V. Demarest (NY), Chairman, National Public Relations Commission, reports to the Committee.

After the peak membership year of 1946, the 1950s and 1960s saw many spirited, but occasionally disappointing, membership campaigns as the Legion appealed to veterans to join and increase the organization's capacity for community service and its clout in Washington.

Professional baseball and the American Legion Baseball program enjoy a close relationship. The starting lineup of any major league team includes a majority of graduates of ALB. Here, with Maryland Department Commander Stanley King, National Commander John E. Davis presents alumnus Frank Robinson, Baltimore Oriole outfielder, with the ALB Graduate of the Year Award in August 1967. Robinson played for the Captain Bill Erwin Post 337, Oakland CA.

ROBERT M. MCCURDY (CA), CHAIRMAN, NATIONAL REHABILITATION COMMISSION, 1952-67.
(Consolidated News Pictures)

VIETNAM VETERANS JOIN THE AMERICAN LEGION, MARCH 3, 1967, AT WICHITA, KANSAS, IN AN INITIATION CONDUCTED BY DEPARTMENT REHABILITATION STAFF MEMBERS.

Legion relief funds have been applied to a variety of needs over the years, most notably to child welfare, disaster relief, and the conquering of disease, among other uses. The American Legion Vietnam Relief Fund provided gifts including sewing machines and sewing supplies distributed by the 1st Infantry Division and Vietnamese social workers to this refugee village near Saigon.

In its 50th Anniversary year, the "Gift to the Nation" from the Legion and the Auxiliary was permanent lighting for the Tomb of the Unknown Soldier at Arlington National Cemetery. National Commander William E. Galbraith hands Secretary of the Army Stanley R. Resor, a "kick-off" check for $50,000.

The Legion's long-standing advocacy for a strong national merchant marine was symbolized in the February 27, 1968 launching of the 700-foot, 32,000-ton full container ship "S.S. American Legion" at number one shipway of Sun Shipbuilding and Dry Dock Co., Chester, PA, for service between the U.S. and Europe. In a subsequent Maritime Day dinner speech, National Commander William E. Galbraith (MO) called the nation's maritime policy "a watered down proposal that is truly a betrayal of the American Merchant Marine and all it stands for in the building of this nation."

With the nation's capitol in the background, longtime Boys State Chairman (NJ) Harold A. Eaton, also Dean of Counselors for Boys Nation, meets with Nation delegates in the mid 1950s.

The Legion Preamble phrase "We associate ourselves together . . ." includes the practice of presenting public figures with awards in numerous fields of endeavor aligned with Legion principles. National Commander John H. Geiger (IL) Presents newsman Lowell Thomas with the Legion's Public Relations Award on March 1, 1972, at the Washington Conference.

The Legion's large-scale civics lesson, Boys Nation, annually introduces outstanding young men to the practice of self governance (as the Auxiliary's Girls Nation does for young women). Here participants in the Nation meet President John F. Kennedy.
(Consolidated News Pictures)

During the Legion's 50th Anniversary in 1969, French artist M. Reni-Mel reviewed his World War I-Era painting "America" which hangs in the Legion's National Executive Committee Room at National Headquarters in Indianapolis. Madame Reni-Mel accompanied the artist.

The Legion's National Foreign Relations Commission ponders the issues of the day facing the nation as world leader. Here Commission Chairman Dr. Robert P. Foster (MO) greets Sayed Ahmad Galaui, an Afghan freedom fighter, during the 1981 Washington Conference.

Legion testimony before congressional committees is both commonplace and a fundamental part of the organization's operation. Here National Commander Alfred P. Chamie, accompanied by Legion founder Tom Miller and other Legionnaires, and many more in the audience, testifies in February 1971 before the House Veterans Affairs Committee in the Caucus Room, Old House Office Building, during the Legion's annual Washington Conference. (Consolidated News Pictures)

THE AMERICAN LEGION AUXILIARY HAS WORKED CLOSELY WITH THE LEGION FOR DECADES CONTRIBUTING FUNDS FOR PROGRAMS SUCH AS CHILD WELFARE. HERE NATIONAL PRESIDENT OF THE AUXILIARY (1962-63) MRS. OLLIE L. KOGER (MARY) ADDS SILVER DOLLARS TO A SCALE BALANCED BY THE CHILD ON THE SWING TO RAISE MONEY FOR BUILDING ANOTHER SCHOOL IN THE DOMINICAN REPUBLIC, THE AUXILIARY PROJECT FOR 1963. LEGION NATIONAL CHILD WELFARE DIVISION DIRECTOR RANDELL SHAKE INCREASES THE WEIGHT BY POURING MILK INTO A SNIFTER.

(Reni Photos)

THE LEGION'S 50TH ANNIVERSARY YEAR INCLUDED THE ISSUANCE OF A COMMEMORATIVE 6¢ STAMP. NATIONAL COMMANDER WILLIAM C. DOYLE (NJ, 1968-69), ALONG WITH POSTMASTER GENERAL WINTON BLOUNT, SHOWS AN ENLARGED VERSION OF THE STAMP DESIGNED BY ARTIST ROBERT HALLOCK WHO DEPICTED THE "CITIZEN" HALF OF THE AMERICAN EAGLE WITH TALON HOLDING THE OLIVE BRANCH OF PEACE SYMBOLIZING THE CITIZEN-SOLDIER ROLE OF VETERANS.

National Commander Al Keller (IL, 1982-83) presents a check to Jan Scruggs, originator of the Vietnam Veterans Memorial in Washington, D.C. The Legion raised over $1.2 million from its members to apply to construction costs, the largest single donation to the Memorial.

Gen. Robert C. Kingston USA (Ret.) describes the role of Honduras in Central America for members of the Legion's Policy Coordinating and Action Group (PCAG), who in three teams lead by National Commander James P. Dean, conducted an extensive study mission to Guatemala and Honduras in the summer of 1987.

LEGION POSTS SERVE IN MANY WAYS, SUCH AS PROVIDING CUB SCOUTS WITH LESSONS IN FLAG ETIQUETTE.

THE LEGION'S VETERANS PLANNING AND COORDINATING COMMITTEE MEETS WITH ADMINISTRATOR OF VETERANS ADMINISTRATION HARRY N. WALTERS AT THE LEGION WASHINGTON, D.C. HEADQUARTERS IN LATE DECEMBER 1985 TO DISCUSS THE EFFECT OF FEDERAL BUDGET-BALANCING LEGISLATION ON VETERANS' BENEFITS. FACING, L. TO R., ARE VINCENT BLACK, DR. N.L. GAULT, JR., MYLIO KRAJA, ROBERT W. SPANOGLE, WALTERS, NATIONAL COMMANDER DALE RENAUD. TO RENAUD'S LEFT ARE PNC E. ROY STONE, JR., PNC JAMES P. DEAN. ALSO SHOWN (FOREGROUND), WILLIAM M. DETWEILER, HUGH DAGLEY, BRUCE THIESEN.

TV ACTOR AND LEGIONNAIRE LARRY WILCOX OF "CHIPS" AND JOHN SWIFT OF WEST ROXBURY (MA) WERE AMONG THE THOUSANDS AT THE 1989 NATIONAL CONVENTION IN BALTIMORE TO CALL THEIR CONGRESSMEN AND SENATORS TO REGISTER THEIR SUPPORT FOR A FLAG AMENDMENT.

National Commander H. F. Gierke and Auxiliary President Alice Galka delivered petitions to Capitol Hill bearing one million signatures calling for a constitutional amendment to protect the flag. Senators John Warner (VA) and Robert Dole (KS) attended the Legion's news conference just before National Convention in Baltimore.

At the 1989 National Convention in Baltimore, all living Legion founders were inducted into ANAVICUS (Army, Navy, and Air Force Veterans in Canada, United States Unit). Seated, l. to r., Vahan Dukmejian, 97; George Bentley, 91 (standing); and PNC Hamilton Fish, 100. Standing l. to r. George T Campbell, Dominion President army, Navy and Air Force Veterans in Canada; PNC Erle Cocke Jr., honorary founder; Bentley; PNC Judge Daniel Foley, ANAVICUS president.

The American Legion Baseball patch has been worn by thousands of teams over the years and is displayed in action here at the 1989 ALB World Series played at Millington (TN) between teams from Puerto Rico and Woodland Hills, California.

E. Roy Stone, JR. (SC) named Past National Commander at the 1987 National Convention in San Antonio. (Chase)

WASHINGTON, D.C. HEADQUARTERS OF THE LEGION, DEDICATED AUGUST 14, 1951 BY PRESIDENT HARRY S TRUMAN. THE BUILDING, RENOVATED IN 1989, CONTAINS THE NATIONAL REHABILITATION, LEGISLATIVE, NATIONAL SECURITY AND FOREIGN RELATIONS DIVISIONS.

Lemuel Bolles (WA)
1919-24
(Bretzman)

Russell G. Creviston (IN)
1924-25

James F. Barton (IA)
1925-32

Frank Edward Samuel (KS)
1932-43

Donald G. Glascoff (MI)
1943-48

Henry H. Dudley (NE)
1948-56
(Bretzman)

Emil A. Blackmore (WY)
1956-67

Ernest N. Schmit (ND)
1967

William F. Hauck (IN)
1967-78
(Chase)

Frank C. Momsen (MN)
1978-81

Robert W. Spanogle (MI)
1981-
(McGuire Studio, Inc.)

that oil would not only cause "at least forty percent of the work force of this nation to become unemployed," but would greatly threaten the nation's ability to defend itself.

The move was welcomed by conferee Robert I. Hanfling, executive assistant to the deputy secretary of the Department of Energy, who promoted the president's energy program, the subject of debate in Congress for a year over proposals for coal conversion, utility rate reform, and natural gas deregulation. Hanfling welcomed National Commander Carey's recommendation that Legion department energy chairmen provide forums of public discussion to aid the public's understanding of the problem by bringing together environmentalists and oil producers to discuss the issues.

The conferees heard also from Dr. E. Linn Draper, Jr., director of the Nuclear Reactor Laboratory at the University of Texas, who spoke for nuclear energy. Dr. Draper complained that a web of regulatory delays and protests by antinuclear groups had stymied widespread use of nuclear power in the United States. He criticized President Carter for not voicing favor of nuclear power "out loud."

The conferees heard about futuristic means for attaining some measure of energy self-sufficiency with wind, solar, and geothermic power, as well as the nuclear fusion about which Dr. Draper spoke. Back home once again, the Legionnaires hadn't heard the last of rising energy prices; gas pumps reflected a jump in the world price of oil from $16 to $30 a barrel, a major factor in the 13.3 percent increase in consumer prices during the year 1979. Throughout the late 1970s, the energy issue continued to draw the serious attention of Legion national officers.

If the energy crisis seemed to defy solution, Legion national officers and staff could look to legislative victories to gauge the effectiveness of their work in more traditional areas. Of most consequence in this regard was the number of new laws that, as recurring legislative reports invariably stated, "satisfied, in part or whole," Legion mandates. At the close of the 95th Congress in mid-October 1978, the count was 125 out of 633 laws enacted.

The Legion was particularly proud of having helped to reform the veterans' pension program so that future cost-of-living increases (C.O.L.A.s) would be tied to the Consumer Price Index. Also, pensioners remaining under the current program would be protected, and all pensioners were assured an income standard above the national poverty level, with $800 being added to the yearly rates for needy World War I veterans. Similarly, veterans disability compensation had been increased by 7.3 percent.

Veterans looking to buy homes were heartened to learn that the V.A. home loan guarantees had been increased from $17,500 to

$25,000 and specially adapted housing grants for severely disabled veterans had been raised $5,000 over the former figure of $25,000.

Another long-standing Legion interest was answered by Public Law 95-429, a new law of note that provided $96.5 million for the Defense Civil Preparedness Agency for fiscal 1979, a welcome figure though a small part of the $117.3 billion granted to the Department of Defense.

The Foreign Relations Commission could point to a new law funding internal security advances for foreign nations, which included the lifting of a three-year partial arms embargo against Turkey and the resumption of the recently curtailed U.S. intelligence facilities there.

Other Legion interests had been favored. The Congress had passed new eligibility dates (in Public Law 95-346) for Legion membership to include those who had served in the latter part of the Vietnam conflict. Children and Youth workers were pleased that almost $570 million had been appropriated for programs that they had backed, including $1.29 million for school nutrition programs for the next year. Also, the Child Abuse Prevention Act had been extended to include a national program to help child adoption and the placement of foster children who had special needs.

Rehab workers, however, were wise to take only the quickest of glances back over their shoulder at recent accomplishments. The educated guess of the members of the Veterans Affairs and Rehab Commission and the National Legislative Commission was that the potential problem to be anticipated when lobbying the 96th Congress would be that of budget restrictions that would affect the Veterans Administration.

Already, the V.A. itself was reducing the number of beds available, eliminating many staff positions, and cutting funds at every medical center and clinic nationwide. Robert E. Lyngh, director of the Legion's Veterans Affairs and Rehab Division, testified before Senator Edmund S. Muskie's (D., ME) Senate Budget Committee on March 14, 1979, and urged the committee to order the V.A. to stop the reductions. "The current and projected reductions have already begun to curtail health care services to veterans," Lyngh said.

Lyngh laid the blame at the door of the Carter administration's Office of Management and Budget for the V.A.'s current cutting of funds for hospital beds and staff positions, funds being used instead to increase chronically low V.A. staff salaries. The Legion's Veterans Affairs and Rehab director flatly refused to accept the view of the V.A. head and that of the agency's chief medical director that increased efficiencies in administration and the use of available resources could combine substantially to insure against real loss of health care service to V.A. patients. "We say that is not true, and we have the evidence to prove it," Lyngh said. He produced reports by some of the V.A.'s own field officers along with similar testimony from Legion service officers who all told of inadequate health care at V.A. facilities directly connected to the reductions in beds, staff positions, and other losses caused by the withholding of funds already allocated.

Particularly at such times, Lyngh said, veterans in the nonservice-connected category had become even more vulnerable than usual when cutbacks occurred. He was careful to observe for the record that the cuts had not been ordered by Congress, but instead by the V.A. after pressure from the Office of Management and Budget. He asked Congress to issue a legislative directive to the V.A. to resume use of the funds in question.

At the same time, the reform-minded Carter administration was hoping to make changes in the civil service. That, in veterandom, translated into eliminating veterans' preference. Indeed, it was charged that veterans' preference was the likely "whipping boy" in the current administration's efforts at civil service reform.

The National Legislative Division's fact sheet on veterans' preference, distributed in July 1978, noted that testimony given by the General Accounting Office in October 1977 before the House Subcommittee on Civil Service included information from a study by that agency that found no conclusive evidence that veterans' preference had had a negative effect on the hiring of nonveteran minorities into the civil service. Nor, it was found, would the elimination of veterans' preference likely help more women to be hired into the civil service.

Two months later, on September 11, 1978, the House voted 281 to 88 for a measure that, unlike one submitted by the administration, made only minor changes in the hiring procedures for federal employment.

It seemed, therefore, that the tradition of post–World War I veterans' preference would remain intact now for the Vietnam-era veteran. Some said it had thus survived the most serious threat since the despised Economy Act of 1933. Once again, Legionnaires and especially Auxiliary members had flooded congressmen and senators with correspondence urging the Legion's view on the matter.

Before long, the 95th Congress would bring about the most substantial changes, it was said, in the civil service system in almost a century. Not only were the administration's recommendations for weakening veterans' preference disregarded, but also the preference point system was actually improved by the Civil Service Reform Act of 1978.

The Civil Service Commission had been replaced by two new agencies: the Office of Personnel Management and the Merit Systems Protection Board (a new board of appeals to hear employee grievances). A third agency was added to the scene: the Federal Labor Relations Authority, which would act after the manner of the private sector's National Labor Relations Board, for hearing complaints arising in federal employment.

The president had been successful in bringing about a system for merit pay in the civil service and the adoption of more leeway for federal managers to weed out incompetent employees.

On October 18, 1978, Past National Commander Robert Charles Smith and National Commander John Carey attended White House ceremonies for the signing of two major pieces of veterans' legislation: the Veterans Disability Compensation and Survivors' Benefits Act (H.R. 11886) and the Veterans Housing Benefits Act (H.R. 12028), both the product of strenuous Legion lobbying. The first provided for a 7.3 percent increase in the disability compensation for veterans against increased inflation of the previous year.

The next summer brought more good news about veterans' preference in federal employment. The U.S. Supreme Court in early June 1979 voted 7 to 2 to uphold the constitutionality of veterans' preference laws in federal, state, and municipal civil service employment.

The suit had originated in Massachusetts, where it was charged that the practice of preference discriminated against women. The Bay State's veterans' preference law was an obvious choice for such a test because it gave *absolute* preference to qualified veterans over all others who applied for state civil service jobs.

Justice Potter Stewart, writing the majority view, stated that no violation of the Constitution had been proven. "Nothing in the record demonstrates that this preference for veterans was originally devised" to keep women "in a stereotypic or predefined place" in the state's civil service.

The Legion hailed the decision as a reaffirmation of the concept that a grateful government, from the national to the local level, should, as now confirmed, reward ex-servicemen with jobs in preference to other applicants.

During the course of the action on civil service reform, one development, unexpected but encouraging, was prompted by Congressman James Leach (R., LA) who, although he had authored a bill used by the administration to justify cuts in the V.A., now asked to be heard before the House Veterans Affairs Committee to clarify the intent of his amendment in the Civil Service Reform Act passed a year before.

What his amendment set out to do, Leach explained, was to lower the total federal employment level to that of September 30, 1977, "on a government-wide basis and not on an agency-by-agency basis," and to permit the increase each year of the total number of employees hired by the percentage increase in the population. The V.A. should not be singled out for staff cuts in the manner that had occurred, the congressman said. To that end he had informed the Director of the Office of Management and Budget, he said. Leach had also referred to Legionnaire Lyngh's testimony and stated agreement with the view that the V.A. should be excluded from the general employment cut for which his original amendment called.

IV

The Supreme Court's propreference decision was appreciated, also, for what it was hoped that finding would do to dislodge the stigma attached to the service of Vietnam-era veterans.

The National Commander's Public Relations Award for 1979 was given at the Washington conference to James H. Webb, Jr., a much decorated marine Vietnam veteran who had subsequently served for two years as assistant minority counsel for the House Veterans Affairs Committee before returning to teach at his alma mater, the U.S. Naval Academy. In accepting the award Webb said that the Vietnam veteran had been made to lack "the dignity of his service."

National officers were particularly attuned to Webb's comments. The dignity and, especially, the necessity of that service was, of course, an essential principle of the American Legion.

Therefore, in the late 1970s, when new veterans' organizations were being established to address single-issue agendas, and with the news magazines calling the Legion "traditional," supposedly attuned mainly to veterans of World War I, World War II, and Korea, it is important to note that the staff working to implement mandates in the area of national security and foreign relations, and who kept national commanders informed on the variety of speech topics in that field, was composed chiefly of Vietnam veterans.

It was essential that each national commander should have behind him the Legion's paid staff members to collect, analyze, interpret, and report information used in the innumerable speeches to be delivered at a wide range of settings, from out-of-the-way posts to large conventions of other national organizations.

G. Michael Schlee headed the National Security and Foreign Relations Division based at Washington headquarters, assisted by Frank Manson, James Hubbard, and Spence Leopard. Together, these four Legionnaires and Emmett G. Lenihan, who chaired the National Security Commission, and Dr. Robert P. Foster, chairman of the National Foreign Relations Commission, worked to make the mandates of the Legion known to Congress. (As if a hedge against ever having a free minute, National Security/Foreign Relations Division staffers had also been handed the duty of administering a diverse group of programs including law and order and crime resistance, Reserve Officers Training Corps awards, aerospace education, and the Legion blood program.)

The "pause" in threatening world events, which the editorial staff writer of the Legion magazine had noted in the January 1977 issue, depicting the foreign relations challenges facing the new administration, had proved temporary. And all the while the National Security/ Foreign Relations Division staffers had been busy charting national and international events that called for Legion position statements.

There was, of course, the necessary response to make to the current administration's policies and moves. The Carter defense policy had three basic fronts: (1) applying brakes to the nuclear arms race with the Soviet Union; (2) strengthening the nation's conventional forces stationed in Europe; and (3) cutting the Pentagon budget for manpower costs and closing some military bases.

This president, like those before him, never lacked for those of differing views. Those on the right found insurmountable fault with the evolving versions of strategic arms agreements with the Russians; those on the left opposed giving more aid to NATO. Within this philosophical and political tug-of-war, the American Legion worked to relate its traditional views to current events.

A vital element in the Legion's interest in national security was an insistence upon a military manpower continuum: the past, the present, and the future were of necessity interlocked in the need for a strong ready reserve (manned someday, it was hoped, by universal military training).

Though national officers could speak knowledgeably about the various aspects of the nation's security and foreign policy that captured headlines and animated White House news briefings, the one topic in particular with which they all had had personal involvement was military service. Of particular concern was the ongoing debate about the pros and the cons of an all-volunteer military force.

The statutory authority of the draft ended in 1973, six months after the last draft call had been issued by the Selective Service. For almost thirty years previously there had been compulsory military service. Since 1973 the military forces had been made up of volunteers.

About the same time in January 1979 that National Commander John M. "Jack" Carey was being presented with an award by Robert E. Shuck, acting director of the Selective Service, for the Legion's support over the years, the Department of Defense released a study, called for by the Senate Armed Services Committee in its military authorization report for fiscal 1979, of the effectiveness of the all-volunteer military force concept. The report stated that an allied success, should a major confrontation occur in Europe, was not assured; more strategic planning was needed, it was stated, before European-based U.S. troops could hope to checkmate their opposite numbers.

Specifically, according to the Department of Defense report, the nation's ability to defend Europe in a conventional conflict was "well below" what the Department of Defense considered necessary. There was the likelihood that American forces could not be mobilized quickly enough for an effective defense.

Furthermore, it was recommended that there be established some form of mandatory registration and training (but not a full-scale conscription) so that reserve shortages could be met. Some improvement and limited reactivation of the Selective Service system should be instituted, the report concluded.

According to the report, the all-volunteer experiment had maintained a manning level within 1.5 percent of congressionally authorized levels. But some problems, too, were acknowledged: a decline in recruit test score averages in the army; increasing navy discipline cases; growing enlistment attrition rates as high as fifty percent more than during the draft years; a tightening of the recruit market; and a reported scarcity of enlistment officers who themselves had the technical training promised in the enlistment posters that decorated their offices.

Legion national officers had taken note of the reference in the secretary of defense's annual report to Congress concerning fiscal year 1980. The secretary expressed concern about the Soviet military buildup. Not only in numbers and weight of armaments was that continuing development a threat, but perhaps more importantly, the Soviet Union was assumed to depend on military forces rather than more peaceful means such as trade (where they had serious difficulties) for exerting power over smaller countries. In the past, military invasion, intimidation, arms sales, or the control of Soviet-backed leaders within those nations had been the pattern of the Soviets.

Soon after reading the secretary's report, James Hubbard testified before the Subcommittee on Military Personnel of the House Armed Services Committee in March 1979 and cited what the Legion held were deficiencies in the all-volunteer force concept.

He predicted that the current trimmed-down Selective Service system would find it difficult to provide the necessary manpower to the armed forces should a national emergency occur. The Department of Defense had recently called for 100,000 inductees to be in training 60 days after an emergency call and another 650,000 within 180 days. That, according to Hubbard, was little more than wishful thinking given the current capabilities of Selective Service, which, he also pointed out, had not had a permanent director for the past two years.

As to the suggestion by some that the system be consolidated under the Department of Defense, Hubbard disagreed. "The system provides the president and Congress with an instrument by which contact can be maintained with the citizenry at the grassroots level through the governors and local board members."

In testifying before the Senate Appropriations Committee, Hubbard called the administration's proposed defense budget "not realistic in terms of inflation and price increases." Such a budget was a dangerous signal to send other nations, Hubbard said, and should be made to include funding for a Nimitz-class aircraft carrier, the immediate development of a multiple-aim, point-basing system for America's ICBMs, and the accelerated development of the MX missile system and all modes of the cruise missile. There should, also, be a draft for the Individual Ready Reserve and a serious investigation of proposals to cut funds to some of the military "people" programs, such as commissary funding and exchange subsidies overseas. Moreover, educational incentives and other programs should be developed to aid and ease personnel problems.

The site of the Legion's 61st annual National Convention in 1979—Houston, Texas—helped focus the attention of Legionnaires on the can-do aspect of American know-how and initiative. Dubbed variously "Bagdad on the Bayou," "Space City, U.S.A.," or "Oil Boomtown," this small town grown large had benefited in large measure from the fifty-mile-long, deep-water ship channel that led to the third largest seaport in the nation, and that also boasted an international space center and was a petrochemical nerve center of a nation in the middle of an energy crunch.

Whether the mandates coming from the Houston National Convention were any more perceptive and discerning than those produced previously would depend on a quantifier's scale of ultimate effectiveness.

What was apparent was that there was much worry within the Legion over the belief that the nation's primary rival, the Soviet Union, had made major improvements in its military strength over the past decade and that the United States had not followed suit.

One speaker at the convention, Adm. Thomas Moorer, USN (Ret), former chairman of the Joint Chiefs of Staff, said that regarding U.S. retrenchment in national defense since World War II, the comic strip character "Pogo" had it right: "We have met the enemy and they is us."

Not long after the convention, however, it was said among national defense planners that the public sentiment against military buildups and other defense measures following the Vietnam War had largely subsided. Before, most such measures had been defeated hands down, particularly if there were any hint of committing American troops to trouble spots around the globe.

Now, it was claimed, there were several indications that things were changing, such as there having occurred the smallest cut in the Pentagon-requested military budget in several years, and reversals, with congressional approval, of President Carter's intended reductions in defense spending and the number of troops providing Korea and the Indian Ocean area with a U.S. military presence. Finally, the administration similarly had decided to retain the missile systems that earlier had been slated for removal in President Carter's SALT II plans.

Those favoring a new U.S. military assertiveness did not lack for reasons that supported their views. The Soviet Union's backing of Arab forces against Israel in the fall of 1973 and Cuban troops being sent to Angola were just two cases in point indicating, they said, that the Soviets were stepping up their efforts for world domination.

But, especially when Iranian factions took American hostages in November 1979 in a manner that defied basic principles of international diplomacy, the reticence toward military solutions that followed the U.S. pullout from Vietnam was largely being overcome. Finally, it was more generally agreed that with the Soviet invasion of Afghanistan, the efficacy of détente was largely depleted.

In mid-March 1980, James Hubbard and E. Philip Riggin, the deputy director of the National Legislative Commission, told the House Appropriations Subcommittee on HUD—Independent Agencies that it was essential that the Selective Service system be given the funds to extricate itself from the "deep standby status" to which it had been relegated. Only then could it provide even the minimum manpower needs for the armed forces, the Legion lobbyists said. They also expressed again the belief that the system should remain in the hands of the local boards.

The call for a revitalized Selective Service system, along with the similar opinion of the Department of Defense and others, was met with congressional approval on June 25, 1980, and hence legislation requiring the registration of nineteen- and twenty-year-old men for a draft not yet established. A five-year hiatus of draft registration, begun by President Ford in April 1975, was ended. Two days later President Carter signed Public Law 96-282, which granted $13.3 million to upgrade the system's computer capability and to register four million men. The president had called for this in his State of the Union message on January 23 in response to the Soviet invasion of Afghanistan the month before. (He had asked that women be registered, too, but Congress disagreed.)

The next summer, on June 26, 1981, one of Jim Hubbard's many trips to the Hill was to urge a pay boost for military personnel, stating that it appeared that the armed forces were becoming "the employer of last resort" for many poor recruits.

About the same time, and without much fanfare, the Selective Service system in the summer of 1981 began a nationwide search to select those who wished to serve on local "standby" draft boards should a return to conscription be ordered by the president and Congress.

The presidential campaign of the previous year had been enlivened occasionally by debate about a revival of the draft. President Carter had favored the draft for national emergencies; presidential candidate Ronald Reagan had professed that it was not needed.

During his last year as president, Carter had reactivated the Selective Service system; by executive order he had required young men to register at age eighteen. The U.S. Supreme Court in March 1981 had heard a suit that charged that requiring men only and not women to register was unconstitutional. But the court had ruled that male-only registration did not defy the Constitution.

On June 1, 1980, Selective Service Director Bernard Rostker informed the Legion and other organizations including the League of Women Voters, the Urban League, and the NAACP, along with church groups, that the system needed 10,000 citizen volunteers for some 2,000 local draft boards. Mindful of criticism during the Vietnam War that the poor and minority youths made up most of the drafted personnel, Rostker had outlined a method for appointing local board members who as nearly as possible represented the racial composition of the communities served by the county-level boards. It was intended that a lottery would single out those young men to be called, with twenty-year-olds going first. There were to be no education deferments.

By early September 1980, Selective Service Director Rostker reported a ninety-three percent registration rate.

(Past National Commander Don Johnson [1964–65], who had also been director of the V.A. from 1969 to 1974, sought to correct two negative labels often attached to Vietnam veterans. These new veterans, he said, were, as a group, not the least educated of all ex-servicemen and their rate of less than honorable discharges was not higher than among those who served in World War II and the Korean War.)

After the National Convention in the fall of 1981, National Commander Jack W. Flynt urged the president to honor the executive order requiring eighteen-year-old males to register for the draft. "It is past time that the youth of our country become reimbued with that sense of duty," he said. New Selective Service head Thomas Turnage had announced that compliance with the registration program during 1981 had fallen to seventy-seven percent, a fact attributable, it was assumed, to the uncertainty about whether the new administration would continue the program.

In what the American Legion News Service called "a smart 'about-face,' " Ronald Reagan dismissed his earlier campaign rhetoric and on January 7, 1982, ordered an open-ended extension of mandatory registration of eighteen-year-old males with the Selective Service.

One of the Legion's largest national security and foreign relations concerns during Ronald Reagan's first four years in office was U.S. support of the government of El Salvador against local Communist guerrilla forces. The Legion's long-standing opposition to Communist expansion came to focus on that trouble spot for its proximity to the United States and its potential as an object lesson for surrounding countries.

In late April 1981, National Commander Flynt placed a wreath at Mexico's National Monument, attended a ceremony honoring American war dead buried in Mexico City's American Cemetery, and visited the American Legion School at Magdalena Petlacalco. At a news conference in Monterrey, he stated the Legion's opposition to direct military intervention in the Central American nation of El Salvador.

But when in March 1983 the president seemed poised to send more U.S. military advisers to El Salvador if an increase of $110 million in military aid was not approved by Congress, Legion spokesmen pointed to a 1982 National Convention resolution that agreed with such action.

Soon thereafter, National Commander Al Keller, Jr., (1982–83) applauded the president's four-point plan for action in Central America, which had been announced to a joint session of Congress on April 27, 1983, for democratic reform, economic development aid, security assistance, and support for flexible negotiations with which the United States could agree.

Keller informed the president of the Legion's own Western Hemisphere Task Force report given to the N.E.C. at its May 1983 meeting, which went a step further than the president had, calling instead for a "Marshall-type Plan" for the "economic-political malady" of that region.

Such an economic support program, Keller wrote, would foster significant funding, regional cooperation, and a long-term commitment by the United States and the resident nations so that democracies could shine forth from a dismal historical perspective scarred by banana-republic turmoil and corruption. Furthermore (and related more directly to U.S. security), failure to institute such a plan as the Legion was now proposing could eventually bring about a "creeping Pearl Harbor" to strike much closer to home.

Keller called for a bipartisan effort in the legislative branch similar to that exercised after World War II, when "enlightened statesmanship" produced such successful innovations as the O.A.S., N.A.T.O., and the World Bank. That bipartisan, long-range thinking was needed now, Keller wrote. It had been in that spirit, the national commander implied, that the Legion's Western Hemisphere Task Force had been formed in the spring of 1980 to alert America to its vital role in the Caribbean basin and Central America.

It had been the same task force that had recommended a "Marshall-type Plan," reminiscent of the original, post–World War II plan, which the originator himself had called "a cure rather than a palliative," to address the economic and political ills of the region that made the countries there susceptible to Communist overtures no less so than a war-torn Europe after World War II had been beset by Communism.

The chairmen of the National Security and Foreign Relations commissions, Roger A. Munson and Dr. Robert P. Foster, had visited Guatemala in late June 1983 and talked with President Rios Montt, Guatemalan military officers, a former insurgent, and others in official capacities as well as civilians in the field.

Members of the two commissions at the Seattle National Convention in late August 1983 heard Deputy Assistant Secretary of Defense for Inter-American Affairs Nestor Sanchez explain that U.S. policy for Central America emphasized economic aid and the training of local military forces but did not include the use of U.S. combat troops.

"Our friends in Central America do not need U.S. combat troops," Sanchez stated. "They do need our material resources and our help in training their armed forces." He cited the help that the Sandinistas in Nicaragua had received from the Soviet Union and from Cuba, both of which, he said, were determined to force El Salvador, Guatemala, Honduras, and, no doubt, Costa Rica to accept Communist regimes.

Another assistant secretary of state for Inter-American Affairs, Langhorne A. Motley, told of the administration's determination to send economic aid and advisers for training local military personnel. Motley spoke of the "four Ds"—democracy, development, dialogue, and defense—as essential elements in a U.S. program to rescue and stabilize Central American nations.

After the Seattle Convention, new National Commander Keith Kreul continued the promotional effort for a Marshall-type Plan for Central America. He recounted its merits in a postconvention appearance before the National Bipartisan Commission on Central America, which had been formed in July and was chaired by former Secretary of State Henry Kissinger. Kreul recounted the comprehensive attributes of the Legion proposal, which considered economic, social, political, and security needs, which was multilateral and long-term, and which was said to be understandable to the American public as well as morale-building for U.S. allies to the south.

Kreul pointedly remarked that if the long string of U.S. "failures" in Vietnam, Cambodia, Laos, Angola, Iran, and Afghanistan were continued in El Salvador, it would likely mean the psychological breaking point for those yet retaining some modicum of trust in the reliability of the United States as an ally.

Back at his Washington headquarters office, Kreul stressed the need for the Legion to inform the public about events in the countries connecting the continents of the Western Hemisphere.

V

One particular challenge regarding informing the public in the post-Vietnam years was that related to the annual membership campaign: the job of attracting and holding Vietnam veterans to the Legion.

J. Lloyd Wignall, now national membership director, knew that the Legion had much competition for the time, money, and interests of potential members. While in January 1976 there were 600,000 Vietnam veteran members, that figure placed against the figure of persons whose service qualified them for membership still left much to be desired.

The 1970s saw efforts given to the goal of establishing a post in every community. That way, every veteran could belong and, therefore, receive the service to veterans that the Legion could give, and veterans could be of service themselves to their communities.

During Past National Commander James Wagonseller's year (1974–75), the Legion began a new post campaign. One year later the results were pleasing; the number of new posts chartered was larger than the number of posts cancelled. That hadn't happened since 1954. A two-decade trend had been reversed.

Legionnaire C. M. Courtney of Mound, Minnesota, a member since the founding of the Legion and a department commander in 1924, had some perspective from which to volunteer a few observations about membership in the Legion. In December 1975, he shared a conviction that "men need to have their higher impulses appealed to. They need the emotional massage that comes from an unselfish devotion to cause." Courtney stressed the importance of "indoctrination" of new members in the meaning of the precepts contained in the Legion "preamble."

For the 1977 "Dare to Care" membership campaign National Membership Director Robert W. Spanogle had stressed that those at local posts who had accepted the responsibility for gaining new members and keeping old ones would exercise by their labors an appreciable amount of control over the fate of the world's largest veterans' organization. Start early and keep going all year, Spanogle recommended.

That year Spanogle emphasized the service-to-community aspects of Legion membership. The next year, with the concern mounting that the Legion was not attracting Vietnam veterans in the numbers many believed possible, in fact essential, Spanogle set out to answer the inevitable question, "What is the American Legion doing to recruit the Vietnam-era veterans?"

First, he pointed to the Legion's Outreach Program in which Vietnam veteran-students at 2,100 colleges in the United States were alerted by post service officers and college counselors to their benefits and rights as veterans. (That program had been discontinued in January 1975 when the volunteer army concept became effective and program services were no longer cost effective.) Subsequently, the ongoing campaign to keep the G.I. Bill current with cost-of-living increases was publicized as yet another Legion mandate that had yielded positive results on several occasions and that was a sign that the Legion deserved the support of new members.

The Legion was the organization said to be most ably equipped to lobby for veterans' preference; and since Vietnam veterans were among the most chronically unemployed, that effort on their behalf for employment was also advertised as a reason for joining. Similarly, the Legion was working to gain increased loan guarantees under the V.A. home-loan program for the new veterans. The Legion claimed credit for a recent law offering veteran loan guarantees for the purchase of mobile homes.

The Legion was also in the process of having Congress change the eligibility dates for membership from a cutoff date of August 15, 1973, to May 7, 1975.

Finally, it was pointed out that Vietnam-era veterans now comprised the second largest group within the membership of the Legion, a group that included the national membership director himself. The next year, National Adjutant Frank C. Momsen could list nearly fifty percent of all management personnel at National Headquarters as Vietnam-era veterans, including one executive director, one assistant executive director, two directors, two deputy directors, seven assistant directors, and five field representatives. He also knew of three department chief administrators who were Vietnam-era veterans. "In the relatively near future," Momsen stated to someone in New Hampshire who wrote to complain about the supposed lack of representation on the national level of these new veterans, "the entire success and future of the American Legion will rest in their hands."

In 1978, new National Membership Director Thomas J. Haynes addressed the same question posed the year before by his predecessor, but from a different angle. There was, he explained to a district commander in California in December 1978, "no single method which has been successful in every case when attempts are made to recruit Vietnam veterans." They "must be approached on an individual basis," Haynes added.

But, he added, "Because of the difference, not only in the Vietnam War, but in the times when Vietnam veterans were being raised, their experiences and occasionally their actions appear different than those from World War II or Korea." Though Haynes believed that their ideals and dedication to the principles of democracy were the same as those of other veterans, "It is the difference in the ways in which they express themselves which quite often leads to a misunderstanding of their purpose." For example, the characterization that they were impatient and expected immediate action on matters of change or innovation could well have been caused by having been reared in an age when "immediate results were the rule," as in fast food, instantaneous entertainment waiting at the television set, and jet travel that defied time and distance. "The average Vietnam veteran has never known the meaning of the phrase, 'All good things come in time.' "

However, most of them were "beginning to mellow considerably" and have "begun to raise families and . . . to experience the frustrations and challenges of raising America's next generation." They were ready for membership in an organization such as the Legion, Haynes said.

Robert Spanogle, now director of internal affairs at the Indianapolis National Headquarters, represented the Legion at the Center for Policy Research's meeting in mid-December 1978 to discuss the preliminary data summary from the Vietnam Era Research Project of the V.A., which related to the current psychosocial functioning of these veterans. The Research Project was a congressionally mandated study of the readjustment patterns of Vietnam veterans in employment, achievement, life satisfaction, family, and other personal relationships.

Spanogle objected to the sampling of the veterans represented in the study. First, most had been selected from metropolitan areas; second, the total sample was not large enough, he believed, to provide a true picture of the national scene. Though the study indicated that Vietnam veterans appeared less likely to join veterans' organizations or, indeed, organizations in general, that assumption, Spanogle argued, could have been prejudiced by the sampling. "No organized group, whether it be religious, veteran, union, or community, does well in highly industrialized areas," he reported to National Commander John M. Carey. "I believe the disintegration of neighborhoods, the flight to the suburbs and general unrest of highly industrialized areas have not been conducive to membership in organizations." Instead, he looked to the compilation of more data, especially that gathered from smaller towns and rural areas.

The director of internal affairs acknowledged surprise at one particular finding in the study. "I think it is rather startling . . . that the Vietnam veterans' peers [nonveterans interviewed] generally agree that the government's treatment of the Vietnam-era veteran was generally bad. That is certainly a change in the attitude of six or seven years ago."

All the information Legion staffers could gather on scientific studies of Vietnam veterans helped in formulating tactics to increase their numbers on the membership rolls. But it was necessary, also, to look within, to examine past campaigns and present attitudes about membership in general. As Tom Haynes explained in January 1979 to Professor Dr. Charles R. Figley of Purdue University, who was planning a study of Vietnam veterans, "the majority . . . are now over the age of 30." It was certainly important to recognize that the mean age of Vietnam veterans in January 1979 was 31.9 years. (He added that there were over 178,000 female Vietnam veterans to be represented in any such study.)

That, of course, would make a difference in the way the Legion approached potential members. Previously, "Our membership promotions are slanted toward a general audience figured at an average age of 50 years old."

In August 1979, National Field Representative James L. Buntin advised Hillsdale, Michigan, Post No. 53 Commander Gloria Johnson that in his travels he observed that the posts were signing up Korean and Vietnam veterans "at a much faster rate than just a few years ago." And, "I find that the posts signing up and keeping the younger veterans are the ones which change their programs and social activities calendar to meet the needs of the younger veteran" with such activities as basketball, baseball, bowling, and golf tournaments. He also recommended that "as much of your activities as possible be family oriented. With inflation like it is today, many younger veterans, just like the rest of us, are looking for organizations which offer us something which our family can be a part of" without inhibitive costs. (In early 1979 it was reported that more than 1,794,000 Vietnam era veterans had applied for home loans, evidence that the demographics of this group were changing rapidly.)

When several complaints were received at National Headquarters or were referred or reported to national officers from the field that Vietnam veterans were seeing many posts as caring for little more than "booze, broads, and bingo," membership campaigners responded. As National Field Representative Robert S. Bishop explained in July 1980 to the Vietnam Veterans Membership Committee chairman of Post No. 62 in Salina, Kansas, the Membership and Post Activities section of the National Internal Affairs Division was putting together a package "that we can use all over the country in workshops and meetings to sensitize the older veterans . . . to the unique problems faced by Vietnam veterans" and particularly "to erode the barriers that many Vietnam veterans perceive when they look into or join the Legion." (Earlier, reports had come from Arizona, Colorado, and elsewhere about the disbanding of new posts composed entirely of Vietnam veterans because those members had become dissatisfied with the seeming slowness with which the national organization responded to their resolutions for select changes in veterans' affairs.)

Tom Haynes, director of internal affairs at National Headquarters in 1980, also believed that year was an important point in the effort to attract Vietnam veterans. "We find that people tend to join in greater numbers after they have been out of the service for seven years," he told a reporter from the New York newspaper *Newsday*. Furthermore, membership had also received a boost from "times of great national stress similar to what we have experienced this year," referring to the nation's economic malaise and the holding of American hostages in Iran.

A *Newsday* photo used to illustrate the article, entitled "Legion Recruiting a New Image," showed older veterans in Legion caps representing a marked contrast to the younger veterans, many of whom complained of posts with a staid membership relentlessly guarding the status quo.

To National Commander Michael J. Kogutek in August 1980, the Legion was "a sleeping giant." Choosing to see "tremendous growth potential" yet "the millions of veterans who are eligible but who haven't been asked," Kogutek encouraged department commanders, adjutants, N.E.C. men, and membership chairmen to "get the principles of the American Legion the widest possible public exposure" so that this organization that "is powerful enough to make some changes in the local community and the halls of Congress" could continue to address "the pressures of inflation, lack of faith in the government, mistrust of big business, foreign aggression, terrorism, energy, and the erosion of veterans' benefits."

To make his point about solidarity of interests and the importance of numbers, he cited the Legion's recent successful efforts to override a presidential veto, only the second time in thirty years when a Democratic Congress overrode a president of the same party, for the passage of the Veterans Administration Health Care Amendment Act of 1980. He also cited a recent Harris poll commissioned by the Legion that showed that the most often quoted reason for joining the Legion was that it fought for veterans' rights and benefits. The second most frequent reason for joining was because a friend had asked the new member to join.

The simple act of asking a friend, acquaintance, or stranger, particularly if he or she were a Vietnam veteran, continued to be an often cited aid to increased membership. Another Harris poll the next year, 1981, showed that sixty-one percent of the Vietnam veterans surveyed said they would join the Legion if asked, but only one in ten had been asked by a Legionnaire to join. In February of that year, Wayne L. Godwin, national program coordinator for new posts, told Commander Wallace F. Thrall of Post No. 461 in Pembine, Wisconsin, that "obviously, our membership is not aggressively extending a sincere invitation to join our organization."

National Commander Jack W. Flynt, elected at the Honolulu National Convention in 1981, laid out the facts of the matter. The Legion lost some 260,000 members each year through attrition and needed to replace that number just to break even on its membership tally. Flynt told the fall conference of department commanders and adjutants that membership would receive high priority during his year, specifically that he would aim for an increase of 70,000 members over the 1981 final total. He called for the establishing of 174 new posts over and above the number expected to be cancelled during the coming year. And the focus of new member campaigns should be directed at Vietnam veterans. Remember, Flynt said, the Legion founders had understood the importance of a large membership base. It was no less important now.

There was, however, a discouraging decrease in the final tally of 1982. In October 1982, National Commander Al Keller, Jr., presented to the department commanders and adjutants conference his objectives for the coming membership year. In early December, in letters to department commanders who had failed to reach their second membership target, he admitted to be "less than enthused at the progress we have made thus far." He admonished the commanders for apparently not accepting the objectives "with the total seriousness in which they were presented." Or, perhaps, they had failed to follow through on the commitments they had made at the conference when they returned home to the hard work of signing up new members. Keller refused to accept the excuse "that our membership deficit is caused by a per capita dues increase that became effective in January." Rather, the loss in numbers "is realistically being caused by pessimistic attitudes, an expectation of a loss." The national commander assured department commanders that membership reports would receive his closest scrutiny.

Though the downward trend continued through 1984, response to the Membership Action Plan adopted in early 1983 was encouraging to National Membership Director Jim Adcox. Individual membership workers understood "the need of extraordinary effort," he stated in an American Legion News Service bulletin in early April. The "Welcome Back" program would continue to the end of that month, and Adcox believed, "We can now at least see the light at the end of the tunnel." At that point, 175,000 more members were needed for 1983 to show an increase. But the light of which he spoke—an increase in membership over the previous year—was another year away. The trend would bottom out after membership year 1984.

VI

The concern about attracting Vietnam veterans as members required that some national officers and staff members become well versed in the psychology of that segment of veterandom. Pondering national security and foreign relations kept some other national staff members and volunteers keenly attuned to current events. But the contemplation of Rehab during the late 1970s and early 1980s, particularly that regarding Vietnam-era veterans, was equal parts hindsight and anticipation.

The article "The Legacy of Vietnam" in the September 1978 issue of *The American Legion Magazine* was reminiscent of the first few issues of *The American Legion Weekly,* which soon after World War I had described a strange and troubling debilitation, the affliction called "shell shock," that was affecting the former members of the A.E.F.

"Shell shock" was now an antiquated term, but one of the darker aspects of the legacy of these newest veterans was a new, more clinically sophisticated but no less chilling glossary of symptoms and maladies, including such terms as "delayed stress syndrome." The article was by then Purdue University professor Dr. Charles Figley, who had worked with Legion National Headquarters Internal Affairs head Robert Spanogle in investigating the readjustment problems of Vietnam veterans who, as a group, appeared to have more difficulty with postwar personal relationships, keeping jobs, and other reentry situations than had their counterparts of previous wars.

(It wasn't until early in 1980 that some psychological symptoms were designated "post-traumatic stress disorder," in what the field of psychiatry called its Bible, "DSM III," the diagnostic and statistical manual of psychiatric disorders, and therefore were recognized officially by the American Psychiatric Association and subsequently by the V.A.)

The effect of one wartime experience in particular, even three years after the official close of the Vietnam era, was, however, of much causal uncertainty. The magazine article did not even mention the various maladies soon to be blamed on exposure to the toxic herbicides used in Vietnam.

But before long, the Legion set about pursuing one of the most important and dramatic quests taken on by the organization in this era. It was to be a mission that would range from the jungles of Vietnam to the examining rooms of V.A. hospitals, and along the way would course through the offices of chemical manufacturers and university scientists, as well.

For the shattering effect of mustard gas in the Great War was no more insidious than the symptoms soon to be blamed on the bane of these younger veterans—the defoliants used in Vietnam to make the enemy more visible but that, it was increasingly suspected, continued to attack the health of all those who had been exposed to them.

This secondary weapon of war had been used because the physical environment of Southeast Asia played such a decisive role in the waging of the Vietnam War. So in armed-forces lingo, an "area-denial technique" had been employed. The air force's "Operation Ranch Hand" was begun in 1962 for defoliating, eventually, approximately fifteen percent of South Vietnam and parts of Laos, principally to deny the Viet Cong the sheltering triple-canopy jungle foliage that masked their travel but also to a lesser degree to destroy rice paddies on which they depended for food.

Continuing until 1971, "Operation Ranch Hand" spread some nineteen million gallons of herbicides from planes like the C-123 "Provider" and from helicopters, jeeps, armored personnel carriers, trucks, and even backpack apparatus. The defoliants, called "agents," were identified by colored stripes—green, pink, purple, orange, white, blue —on fifty-five-gallon drums and were sprayed in sweeping operations over the canopy of jungle and mangrove forests; applied in abundance on the perimeters of base camps and along waterways, communications lines, and roadsides; and around cache sites. Of the drums that for nine years were a common sight at camps and supply dumps and that, emptied, were sometimes used as makeshift washing machines, the predominant color from 1962 to 1971 when the practice was discontinued was orange.

In many places the defoliants were effective, giving the appearance of having been the scene of a massive fire. But to the dismay now of many who were on the scene when "Agent Orange" was applied, the herbicides apparently had not only polluted the countryside of Vietnam but had continued, it was increasingly claimed, to exact a tortuous price from ex-service personnel who had been exposed to the highly toxic chemical compounds.

Legion rehab workers in the field and those at National Headquarters became aware in the 1970s of the growing suspicion that there was a link between the defoliants and a series of health problems experienced later by Vietnam veterans, which included skin rashes, cancer, and even birth defects in veterans' children.

In April 1978, the V.A. had begun looking for scientific evidence that dioxin, one of the most toxic substances known to man and an ingredient in Agent Orange, could be stored for long periods of time in human body fat. That action by the V.A. had been prompted in part by the stories in the news media about more and more Vietnam veterans who were blaming illnesses on the herbicides. By mid-February 1979, the V.A. reportedly had received about 500 applications for compensation from veterans claiming to have suffered some effects from exposure to dioxin. By now, also, the V.A. had adopted a policy of examining those who made such claims.

The V.A. also began a detailed search for scientific evidence that would help in the formulation of a policy for honoring claims based on the suspicion of exposure to Agent Orange.

The Legion's first official act recognizing the threat that Agent Orange posed to the health of Vietnam veterans was a resolution that came out of the N.E.C.'s October 1978 meeting. Resolution No. 6 called for support and publicity for the V.A.'s attempt to locate veterans who were exposed to the herbicides. National Headquarters urged posts to help publicize the current V.A. policy. National Adjutant Frank C. Momsen informed all department adjutants about the urgency of the matter, trying at the same time to keep the message from being unnecessarily alarming.

"While there is no positive evidence of the noxious effects on the health of individuals exposed to these herbicides which is of a permanent nature, it is widely agreed that it is necessary to provide such individuals with meticulous medical follow-up for prolonged periods of time in order to obtain answers about the health-related effects of herbicides." The V.A. was promising a "thorough" exam to all those who claimed toxic effects from that source.

Meanwhile, the Legion was gathering information about the possible effects of Agent Orange. As a new subject of study, information came from whatever sources could be found. For example, some Swedish studies were referred to that indicated that forestry workers who had been exposed to dioxin were found to have a startlingly high incidence of soft tissue sarcomas, not unlike the Vietnam veterans who were complaining of herbicide exposure. From that point forward, the issue "was on the front burner," as one Rehab Division staffer put it.

In 1979, the national convention in Houston approved Resolution 158, which urged the V.A. to move ahead without delay to determine the range of effects of Agent Orange and to adopt a more objective attitude in adjudicating claims relating to that cause.

A few weeks later, in a report dated November 16, 1979, the General Accounting Office acknowledged that "between 1966 and 1969 a large number of U.S. ground troops in Vietnam were in areas sprayed with herbicide orange both during and shortly after spraying. The Department of Defense took few precautions to prevent exposure because at that time it did not consider the herbicide to be toxic or dangerous to humans."

Furthermore, "Marines assigned to units in sprayed areas can be identified, but army personnel cannot because army records are incomplete. Troops' actual exposure or the degree of exposure to the herbicide cannot be documented from available records. Also, the long-term effects of exposure remain largely unknown."

By this time about 4,800 Vietnam veterans had approached the V.A. for treatment of illnesses they assumed were caused by working near, handling, or being sprayed by Agent Orange.

In December 1979, following the release of the Government Accounting Office report, Congress passed the Veterans Health Programs Extension and Improvement Act of 1979 (Public Law 96-151), which directed the V.A. to prepare a plan for the study of Vietnam veterans experiencing health problems thought to have resulted from exposure to Agent Orange. The act also directed the Office of Technology Assessment to view the study plan within 180 days of the passage of the act, which was signed on December 20 by the president.

Not until the next spring, in mid-April 1980, did the V.A. host a conference of those interested in bidding on the work of conducting the study. The next month the National Veterans Law Center began legal action protesting the procedures used by the V.A. in soliciting bids.

In the meantime, during the tenure of V.A. head Max Clelend, President Carter's appointee, a triple amputee veteran of Vietnam who himself had been exposed to the herbicides, the V.A.'s official view was that it was "unclear" whether exposure to the chemicals caused any long-term effects on human health. However, Cleland told a House Veterans Affairs subcommittee in late February 1980, "We shall continue to provide every eligible veteran in need of treatment appropriate medical care regardless of causation. We owe them no less." So far, Clelend reported, 1,233 disability claims based on exposure to Agent Orange had been decided by V.A. regional offices, of which twenty-one were found to be service-connected though in none of them was it necessary to prove Agent Orange as a causative factor.

That subject—causation—was one of much contention, as it would continue to be. But in this respect the Legion, meanwhile, had had noteworthy success. After six years of representing a Legionnaire in Iowa who had filed a claim for disability compensation based on his exposure to ionizing radiation during twenty atomic tests in the 1950s on Eniwetok atoll in the Marshall Islands, he was compensated. Though V.A. rules and regulations did not often allow one such case to set a policy-altering precedent, the Legion's Director of Veterans Affairs and Rehab, Robert Lyngh, called the decision to compensate that veteran truly a landmark. Legion bulletins urged veterans who had participated in atmospheric tests conducted from 1945 to 1962 in Nevada and at Bikini and Eniwetok atolls in the Pacific to contact the Defense Nuclear Agency. The victorious veteran, Orville E. Kelly of Post No. 52 in Burlington, Iowa, was founder of the Association of Atomic Veterans. In the book that he wrote about his experiences as a cancer patient, he estimated that perhaps 250,000 men had been exposed to the A-bomb tests.

With that encouraging victory, Veterans Affairs and Rehab staffers looked more confidently now to the apparent need for action on behalf of the growing number of ex-service personnel who were attributing a series of debilitating illnesses to Agent Orange. (Several of the subsequent Legion-inspired congressional bills aimed at the Agent Orange problem also included provisions for those who had suffered from radiation exposure.)

In May 1980, Legion Chief of Claims Services John F. Sommer, Jr., who had been exposed to Agent Orange himself as a medic in Vietnam, pointed out to the Senate Veterans Affairs Committee that though the Environmental Protection Agency (E.P.A.) had declared dioxin a health hazard, the V.A. still hadn't come to that conclusion and so far, he said, had turned down all claims for benefits based on exposure to dioxin.

In June 1980, the Legion queried its service officers at V.A. medical facilities about the handling of those veterans who were claiming health problems from exposure to Agent Orange, asking them "to determine if there are any V.A. facilities where Agent Orange examinations are not being conducted in a thorough and compassionate manner."

Later that year, the National Convention at Boston in August adopted Resolution 110, which mandated the Legion to sponsor and support legislation to assign the congressionally ordered Agent Orange study to an independent agency.

Though one of the Legion's many functions over the years had been as a publishing house for information about a wide variety of concerns and services to veterans and the general public, it had not as yet produced a pamphlet on Agent Orange, waiting, as was the V.A., upon findings of studies on the subject. In the meantime, department service officers had been alerted to search for Vietnam veterans who might have been exposed to the toxic chemicals.

But if the organization was not publishing information, it could collect data from its members. So the Veterans Affairs and Rehab Commission began distributing memos on Agent Orange to department service officers and rehab directors, at the same time enclosing printed questionnaires asking for information from members and others about physical exams they may have had at V.A. facilities. In particular, had their fears of dioxin poisoning been taken seriously? The information gathered in this manner was made available to congressional committees and federal agencies investigating the Agent Orange screening being done by the V.A.

Legion field survey volunteers and field staff persons insisted on one procedural matter in particular when the government began funding and establishing the veterans' center program aimed particularly at those persons alienated from all or most vestiges of officialdom regarding veterans' affairs—the use of patient military histories by examining doctors. Such records, it was stressed, were essential in the diagnostic procedure prompted by claims of post-traumatic stress disorders and other health problems.

Soon there was legislation in the works to expand the study sponsored by the V.A. and to provide priority medical care to those whose illnesses were being blamed on Agent Orange. Congressman and Vietnam veteran Thomas Daschle's (R., SD) H.R. 2953, for example, would provide government-paid health care if a V.A. or a private practice doctor accepted even the probability that the illness diagnosed was associated with exposure to dioxin.

The Legion's 1980 Boston National Convention Resolution 110 had mandated the drafting of legislation, which, in turn, was introduced in

January 1981 by G. V. "Sonny" Montgomery as H.R. 1173 "to amend section 307 of Public Law 96-151, by assigning the responsibility of designing a protocol for, and conducting an epidemiological study of, veterans who were exposed to Agent Orange, to an independent scientific agency."

By mid-November 1980, the V.A. reported that approximately 30,000 veterans had presented themselves for examinations for the ill effects of Agent Orange. But the Legion continued to solicit the responses of those examined.

It was not until early February 1981 that the review by the General Accounting Office (which had been ordered by a district federal court) of issues arising from the bid protest was resolved in favor of the V.A. for the continuation of the bid-to-contract process. Three months later, on May 1, the V.A. chose the School of Public Health at the University of California at Los Angeles to design the study plan.

It was decided, also, that the team's work would be further evaluated by members of the National Academy of Sciences–National Research Council, the Congressional Office of Technological Assessment, the Interagency Work Group to Study the Possible Long-Term Health Effects of Phenoxy Herbicides and Contaminants, and the V.A.'s own Advisory Committee on Health-Related Effects of Herbicides.

In June 1981, the Senate followed the example of the House, voting 98 to 0 on June 16 that the V.A. should provide health care to Vietnam veterans exposed to Agent Orange. The measure also provided health care to veterans who had been exposed to atomic radiation in weapons tests as well as other toxic substances.

With the all-important presidential signature affixed, the bill became Public Law 97-72 in early November 1981 and allowed the V.A. to expand the Agent Orange study to include other health problems, whether due to chemicals or general environmental conditions, which might at some time be considered health-threatening.

In late 1981, the Legion and others complained about the methods used by the U.C.L.A. group relating to research data of the Agent Orange study. Legion spokesmen said that the study was so cloaked in secrecy that even the symptoms for which the study would look had not been made known. It was charged, also, that there were a number of other flaws in the U.C.L.A.-designed protocol.

In March 1982, John Sommer remarked, "Veterans should consider the source," when it was suggested by the Dow Chemical Company, a major producer of Agent Orange and the target of many lawsuits by Vietnam veterans, that some of the health problems blamed on their dioxin-laced defoliant could actually be melioidosis, a bacterial disease unique to Southeast Asia. The Legion's medical consultant, Dr. Thomas FitzGerald, countered that the army was certainly aware of the presence of melioidosis, having "diagnosed and treated 342 cases, in which there were 36 deaths." So, confusing the effects of Agent

Orange with melioidosis was not something military physicians were likely to do, Dr. FitzGerald said. (Dow also distributed clinical reports linking dapsone, a malaria prevention drug, to illnesses that Vietnam veterans had blamed on Agent Orange.)

In early October 1982, the Legion was still asking Congress to prod the V.A. to follow through with the Agent Orange study three years now after the study originally had been ordered. John Sommer complimented the V.A. on the amount and quality of research done on the subject so far, yet the long-term study was still not yet under way.

Though the agreement with the U.C.L.A. School of Public Health had been signed in May 1981, it had floundered when drafts of the research procedure were met with objections by three government advisory panels on Agent Orange. There had been much discussion and disagreement, for example, about the composition of the groups of veterans to be studied. One group was to be presumed to have been exposed, another was to be believed not exposed. Some recommended a third group—Vietnam-era veterans who did not serve in Vietnam. Such an expansion of the study had been made possible when Congress allowed the V.A. to look into other hazards facing those who served in Vietnam.

The Legion welcomed expansion of the study, but only as long as Agent Orange remained the main emphasis. Time was also of vital importance. The clock continued to run on physical deteriorations now blamed on Agent Orange.

The coordinating of efforts and findings, meanwhile, continued. The Congress-mandated V.A. study included a search through 1,200 scientific publications for medical and scientific articles on dioxin from which was formed a two-volume reference source for health care professionals. Also, a report on "Operation Ranch Hand," the study of air force personnel involved with the dangerous contaminants, was slated for publication in late 1983.

There were, meanwhile, at least another ten Agent Orange research projects of note under way by V.A. medical investigators, some using animal and some human tissue-culture experiments for studying reactions to dioxin.

In addition to these, a V.A. mortality study was scheduled for completion in mid-1984 that would compare the death rate and causes of death of veterans who did and did not serve in Vietnam. At the V.A.'s St. Louis Medical Center, a study was under way involving pairs of identical twins, one of whom served in Vietnam while the other did not. Also, a study begun in 1979 was under way among the 45,000 Australians who served in Vietnam.

Finally, since 1978, the Armed Forces Institute of Pathology had been collecting tissue samples from Vietnam veterans, samples that had been obtained in surgery or from autopsies. The Legion called for that study to be enlarged to include samples from Vietnam-era veterans who did not serve in Vietnam.

For its part, the Legion published an extended article in the January 1982 issue of *The American Legion Magazine* that would serve as its official presentation for Legionnaires and others about what was known and being done currently about the scourge of Agent Orange. By that time, more than 67,000 Vietnam veterans had gone to V.A. hospitals to take the Agent Orange physical exams. And to that point some 11,000 had claims in progress for illnesses that they attributed to wartime herbicide exposure. None of the claims so far had been allowed by the V.A. for Agent Orange complaints, for as the magazine article stated, "Proof is what everyone demands—and no one has."

National Convention 1982 in Chicago adopted Resolution 410, which called for an independent scientific study of Agent Orange, as well as the presumption of service connection by the V.A. regardless of when the disability became evident. Resolution 410 would also require the payment of compensation when the children of Vietnam veterans were born with health-related defects blamed on Agent Orange.

In January 1983, Legion spokesmen lauded the decision that the Centers for Disease Control (C.D.C.) in Atlanta would take over the V.A.'s Agent Orange study, but criticized the projection that conclusions would not be available for five years. As National Commander Al Keller said, "The American Legion is not going to put this issue in the closet until 1987. We will urge the timely release of all relevant findings as they become available" to the C.D.C. so that victims could receive immediate care.

By mid-March, there was generally convincing scientific evidence that three medical disorders were most likely attributable to Agent Orange: some soft-tissue sarcomas (cancers); porphyria cutanea tarda (P.C.T., which affected the liver, blood, and skin); and the skin lesions of chloracne. (For sixteen months previously veterans had the benefit of priority medical treatment at V.A. facilities for suspected Agent Orange effects, despite the lack of positive proof.)

Soon thereafter, Representative Thomas Daschle introduced his bill, H.R. 1961, which sought to establish presumption of service connection allowing compensation for these three medical disorders.

Daschle's bill was criticized, however, by Harry Walters, V.A. administrator, in testimony before the House Veterans Affairs Subcommittee on Compensation in late April 1983. Walters said that there was still not sufficient evidence for presumptive compensation, and he complained that the bill would severely threaten the basic premise and jeopardize the very viability of the agency's compensation program.

Walters was ready to agree that there was a causal relationship between dioxin and the three disorders detailed above; but, he said, the matter of the time factor between exposure and the initial occurrence of the disabilities had not been dealt with conclusively.

(Earlier, Legion rehab spokesmen had reminded the congressional subcommittee that previously some disabilities had been given presumptive status on less evidence than what was now emerging regarding Agent Orange. Two examples were cardiovascular disease among veterans with above-the-knee amputations and multiple sclerosis occurring up to seven years after service: both had been judged presumptive after just one scientific study each.)

Legion Chief of Claims John Sommer, Jr., again cited that traditional government malaise—"bureaucratic inertia"—and worse, for the V.A.'s stubbornness on this subject. Sommer told the Senate Veterans Affairs Committee in May 1983 that the study should be conducted instead by an agency such as the National Academy of Sciences rather than the V.A. or the air force.

Already there was distrust, Sommer said. "Veterans' apprehensions are aggravated, hospital and clinic staffs are not properly oriented to handle cases, and the feeling is increasing that the V.A. doesn't care."

Calling the V.A.'s attitude "inflexible" about the presumptive nature of the health consequences of Agent Orange, the Legion called on Congress in June to force the decision about which diseases now blamed on the defoliant should be presumed to be service-connected.

For this purpose the Legion supported Senator Larry Pressler's (R., SD) S. 786, which mirrored the Daschle bill in calling for presumptive status for the three diseases of chloracne, porphyria cutanea tarda, and soft-tissue sarcomas.

By summer 1983, the Legion was looking to federal legislators to be prepared to consider the scientific evidence and to decide what diseases afflicting veterans were caused by Agent Orange.

All the while, the Legion continued to call for the disclosure of periodic results of the C.D.C. study rather than waiting until 1987, the projected date for the final report. But getting few results, the Legion in late 1983 joined with two scientists to conduct an independent study that would involve a sample of 15,000 Vietnam veterans living in six states in a search for the health effects of those veterans' military service, their adjustment to family life and employment, and their attitude toward the V.A.'s health care and other benefits.

National Commander Al Keller announced the joint effort at a news conference in Washington, D.C. Titled "The American Legion and Columbia University Study of Vietnam Era Veterans," the study would be developed and conducted by a husband and wife team, both epidemiologists experienced in health studies: Dr. Jeanne Stellman, associate professor of public health, and Dr. Steven Stellman, assistant vice-president for epidemiology for the American Cancer Society.

The study, based on a model used by the American Cancer Society, would use trained volunteers to collect the data from a select sample of several thousand Vietnam veteran Legionnaires. Other Legionnaires would constitute a control group of Vietnam-era veterans who had not been in Vietnam.

Those who volunteered to help conduct the study trained in October and November 1983 and then administered detailed questionnaires in the first two months of 1984. The data was computerized and analyzed during the spring so that preliminary reports and reviews could be published during the summer months. The final report was planned for later that fall, after a scientific advisory panel had periodically monitored and reviewed the study procedure, data, and results.

In the meantime, the Legion's traditional lobbying efforts on the Hill continued. A Senate bill, S. 1388, was approved unanimously on November 18, 1983, just two hours before adjournment of the first session of the 98th Congress. The bill gave a cost-of-living adjustment in veterans' disability compensation, but passage had been delayed by a week-long debate about whether an Agent Orange amendment could be attached.

Senator Alan K. Simpson (R., WY) had sought to bring the bill to the floor under a unanimous-consent agreement prohibiting debate or amendments. Senators Alan Cranston (D., CA) and Arlen Specter (R., PA), who sponsored another bill, S. 1651, had agreed to this move.

Next, it was hoped that H.R. 1961, when it came to the Senate, would pass, also. (Each of these bills also contained presumptive language pertaining to ionizing radiation exposure residuals.) E. Philip Riggin, now Director of the National Legislative Commission, cautioned insiders that the bills still faced resistance or even outright opposition from the majority leadership of the Veterans Affairs Committees in both chambers. Similarly, "lukewarm" support, at best, was expected from the two other largest veterans' organizations, the V.F.W. and D.A.V.; nevertheless, "We view the actions of November 18 as a decided victory," Riggin said. For one thing, the measure had become, with the parliamentary maneuvering of Senator Cranston, the pending business of the Senate, so the entire Senate would have an opportunity to vote on the issue rather than having it bottled up in committee.

It fell to National Commander Keith Kreul to laud the House for passing Representative Daschle's bill in February 1984. The Senate passed its version of an Agent Orange bill on May 22 with a 95 to 0 vote; but the measure still carried the number of the House bill—H.R. 1961—the original enactment language had been replaced with an amendment by Senators Simpson, the committee chairman, and Cranston, the committee's ranking minority member. This made it almost identical to S. 1651, about which the Legion had had some objections.

Legion bulletins included the cautious announcement that the

House had "taken a limited step" toward compensation for those exposed to Agent Orange and radioactivity from open-air atomic testing. In addition to the three disabilities recognized as being traceable to Agent Orange, the measure would allow benefits to those with thyroid cancer, leukemia, or bone-marrow disease (polycythemia vera) who had been exposed to atomic testing.

As a compromise, the bill would grant compensation until the federal Centers for Disease Control completed another study on Agent Orange, the results of which were expected in 1987 (a date that the Legion had already complained about as being too late for its research and conclusions to join with the Columbia University study).

Meanwhile, the Legion continued to support the conducting of a study by the V.A. into the post-traumatic stress disorder and other readjustment problems of Vietnam veterans, a study that had been ordered by Congress in November 1983 (Public Law 98-160).

John Sommer, now Veterans Affairs and Rehab deputy director, assured all that the V.A.'s nationwide study would not conflict with the Columbia University and Legion effort, even though the study of Legionnaires was wholly of servicemen, whereas the V.A.'s groups would include ex-service personnel and nonservice personnel. "No one study can answer all of the questions," he said. "The results of our study will be shared with the V.A., as well as the scientific community and Congress, when our final report is issued later this year."

By May 1984, more than 770 Legionnaires had worked as register volunteers in the Legion/Columbia University Study under sixty-one "study captains." Each department had a "study chairman." The volunteers personally contacted all Vietnam veterans participating. In the six departments chosen for the study—Colorado, Minnesota, Maryland, Indiana, Pennsylvania, and Ohio—80,391 names had been randomly selected, of which there were found to be 9,500 Vietnam-era veterans representing 2,863 posts in these departments. It had been decided that going directly to the Legionnaires rather than through the nearly 3,000 post adjutants would save time. (A pretest of the questionnaire was conducted in South Dakota.)

In October 1984, National Commander Clarence M. Bacon stated the Legion's qualified support for the enactment of H.R. 1961 on October 4. Once again an important "first step" fell short of Legion expectations for Agent Orange and radiation-related compensation. Specifically, the V.A. had been told to establish guidelines for compensation to Vietnam veterans who were found to be suffering from illnesses possibly associated with herbicide exposure. The new law, Public Law 98-542, did not recognize the service connection of soft tissue tumors. The temporary nature of the compensation now granted, for claims between October 1, 1984, and September 30, 1986, was disappointing. Bacon pointed out that the government's own studies conducted by the Centers for Disease Control would not even be reported on until after the cutoff date in 1986.

But this was a beginning. Neither the topic of Agent Orange nor the halting "first-step" actions seen so far, at least, would be denied discussion.

VII

Agent Orange occupied much time and attracted much attention. All the while, the Rehab Commission and Division staff continued to pursue the traditional agenda. Sometimes an event provided a moment of reflection.

At Arlington National Cemetery on June 29, 1981, National Commander Michael J. Kogutek, implementing Resolution 177 of the 1980 National Convention, placed a bronze plaque on the temporary resting place of Ignace Jan Paderewski, who had died in 1941, an exile from his Nazi-held homeland. Paderewski had been interred at the base of the mast of the battleship *Maine* by special order of President Franklin Roosevelt, to remain there until a free Poland had been restored. Now, on the fortieth anniversary of Paderewski's death, in a ceremony taped by Radio Free Europe for broadcast to Poland, the composer's own "Minuet in G" was played, and color guard units from Gen. Joseph Haller American Legion Post No. 95 in Baltimore participated in a wreath-laying ceremony.

But Polish-American and bilingual National Commander Kogutek shared more than ethnic heritage with Poland's first twentieth-century prime minister. There was an American Legion connection, as well. The world renowned composer, piano virtuoso, and statesman had been so impressed by the Rehab endowment that the Legion began in 1925 that he became the largest single contributor to it in later years. The Legion previously had presented him with its highest award—the Distinguished Service Medal—in 1926.

National Commander Kogutek recently had made President Reagan aware of the Legion's displeasure at hearing the rumblings of an $800 million cutback in veterans' assistance programs. Veterans Affairs and Rehab Director Robert Lyngh added, "How the government treats today's veterans will affect the response of tomorrow's soldiers." Lyngh was particularly critical of the Reagan administration's attempt "to deprive the generation of Vietnam veterans of the single program enacted to assist those of their number who have had the most difficulty in readjusting from the military experience": the Vietnam Veterans Outreach Program (V.V.O.P.). A cutback in that program would be particularly injurious especially now that the Legion was calling for alcoholism to be recognized as a disease rather than "willful misconduct."

That a V.A. director had not been appointed yet by the Reagan Administration was another matter of criticism, an appointment that apparently "has had a very low priority at the White House." The chief concern was that Budget Director David Stockman's stated intentions to implement a more "efficient system" of veterans' health services probably meant that he had already taken aim at those programs.

National Commander Kogutek's telegram to the president complained about "signals . . . from your administration . . . causing much concern and confusion." He referred here to action against the V.V.O.P.; proposals to eliminate over 5,000 V.A. employees, sixty hospital wards, and purchases of new equipment; the stopping of replacement hospital construction at two sites; and decreasing veterans' employment services. Kogutek asked for clarification of the president's views.

In April the Legion went to the Hill to support a peacetime G.I. education bill by Representative G. V. "Sonny" Montgomery, but insisted that it be used as a recruitment and retention measure funded by the Department of Defense rather than being applied as a rehab benefit of the V.A. Again showing the interlocking nature of Legion basics as a system of relevant advocacies, the Legion staffer who presented that view to the House Veterans Affairs Committee was G. Michael Schlee, director of the National Security and Foreign Relations Division.

Schlee questioned a provision of the bill that would declare the education benefit transferable to ex-service personnel's dependents. For not only would that increase the cost of the program, but it also seemed unfair to older veterans whose benefits were not thus transferable. Especially, it would likely diminish the incentive of dependents themselves to enlist at some later time, Schlee said. Even at that, the Legion supported most of the bill's provisions, particularly the recognition by implication of the importance of the Reserve components in the "Total Force Concept."

That month, also, the Legion responded to the March 10 announcement by the administration of federal budget cuts that were in conflict with at least a dozen recent Legion National Convention mandates. In addition to cuts threatened in the V.A. budget, calculated customarily in the millions, this administration had also targeted child nutrition and equipment assistance programs to total cuts of almost $2 billion. The Legion, having supported the school lunch program since 1941, was alarmed. Similarly there was concern about proposed cuts in the unemployment compensation of those completing their military service, and the proposed transfer of programs within the Office of Juvenile Justice and Delinquency to the states, where in some states the programs would survive while in others they would diminish.

Also, if, as proposed, Small Business Administration loans to the handicapped were to be eliminated, disabled veterans would be affected. There were also major cuts proposed for the Federal Emergency Management Agency and the Disaster Relief and Flood Insurance area by an administration that had believed the federal government should provide fewer services than it was currently offering.

The matter of Department of Defense and the V.A. sharing medical facilities was considered yet again in July. Veterans Affairs and Rehab Director Robert Lyngh testified on S. 266, a bill that would set up an interagency of medical resources for the two agencies. Such an arrangement was acceptable, Lyngh said, but only if the separate and distinct work performed by each was not impeded. Nor should Merchant Marines or other non-service personnel be admitted to these facilities.

Having been put on the defensive by statements and signals emerging from the office of Budget Director Stockman, Legion hackles were raised yet again by a published memo from that quarter stating that many tasks by government agencies could be performed less expensively by private contractors. That was a bad idea, Legion spokesmen said, not only because of the graft, fraud, and worse that was often found in the contracting procedure, but because the message translated immediately into one more attempt to harm veterans' preference. In scanning the work categories that Stockman listed, James G. Bourie, Legion director of the economics division, calculated that about 92,000 jobs were threatened, forty-four percent of which were likely held by veterans. In testimony before the House Veterans Affairs Subcommittee on Oversight, Bourie reiterated recent national convention and N.E.C. resolutions opposing contracting policies that eliminated federal jobs.

Though not directly connected, the matter of job losses at the V.A. did relate at least philosophically with another matter of concern. S. 349 contained the latest attempt to establish judicial review for veterans' claims, a development against which the Legion had fought for many years. Instead, said Robert Lyngh to the Senate Veterans Affairs Committee, the V.A. should hire more personnel for its Board of Veterans Appeals (B.V.A.) to expedite both the number of appeals heard and the granting of subsequent benefits. The Legion itself had ten staff members working with B.V.A. cases in Washington. During the last year these ten had represented veterans in 6,424 appeals previously turned down by the V.A. These persons, especially, from daily experience, believed that not only should the government not put itself in the position of being an adversary of veterans by adopting judicial review in federal courts (which, also, Legion claims officers believed, would make for less generous claims adjustments), but also, that the productivity of the present appeals system should be enlarged by the addition of more B.V.A. personnel.

In 1981, it fell to National Commander Jack Flynt in September to object to a lagging V.A. construction program. One replacement hospital in particular that had been slated for Camden, New Jersey, had been planned as a prototype facility for geriatric medicine. When construction there had been stopped, the medical needs of aging veterans were dealt a serious blow, Flynt said. He projected the specter of "human warehousing" that had been charged before World War II.

Elsewhere, Legionnaires surveying forty-two V.A. medical centers had reported staff shortages and "marginal delivery of care," Flynt reported. Equipped before the House Veterans Affairs Committee on September 22 with field survey statistics, Flynt told of learning from the V.A. director of nursing services that 1,148 beds had been closed down on July 27 because of a nurse shortage, a serious problem that could be solved only by the immediate hiring of 625 nurses.

The next month Flynt informed the president that the $451 million proposed to be chopped from the 1982 V.A. budget was well beyond the $110 million that the Legion itself had said could be cut by a judiciously selective process without diminishing patient care. Flynt reminded Reagan that while a White House news release of September 24 had stated that "direct V.A. hospital care" would be exempt from across-the-board cuts, it now appeared that two-thirds of the cuts proposed for the V.A. would have to come from the medical care areas. Robert Lyngh, looking for figures to help visualize the effects of the cuts, calculated that the cuts would mean about 5,000 fewer medical personnel and a total turnaway rate of perhaps 3,000 patients a day from the V.A.'s 172 medical centers and 226 outpatient clinics. Flynt, Lyngh, and other Legion spokesmen sought to impress upon the president that cuts of such proportions were contradictory to his earlier promises to preserve the quality of veterans' health care and were even well in excess of cuts listed in the First Concurrent Budget Resolution and the Omnibus Reconciliation Act.

National Rehab officers and staff were, no doubt, reminded of the Legion's reputation for persistence in its system of advocacies for veterans when Legion founder and coauthor of the preamble, Hamilton Fish, laid the wreath at the Tomb of the Unknown Soldier in Arlington National Cemetery on Veterans Day, November 11, 1981, sixty years after he had been responsible appreciably for Congress's authorizing the construction of that monument. He had laid the first wreath there in 1921.

What could be taken as proof of the rewards of persistence could be found in the enactment of Public Law 97-101 two days before Christmas 1981, which set a V.A. budget of $24.1 billion, money promised for an entire year of operation rather than the uncertain amounts dealt out on three-month continuing resolutions under which the agency had been made to operate recently.

A few days later, the V.A. officialdom itself set off the alarm bells when V.A. Administrator Robert P. Nimmo announced a reassessment of a medical care construction program already approved by congressional committees and federal review boards. Nimmo's February 19 statement questioned the advisability of facets of a construction program that totaled no less than $5 billion for the expansion and modernization of existing V.A. medical centers. In near exasperation, National Commander Flynt pointed to many facilities built before World War II that were in obvious need of repair and to a World War II veteran population of 12.5 million, the average age of which was sixty-two, a point in life after which more and more health care would be required.

Nimmo's answer, in speaking before the Veterans Affairs and Rehab Commission at its February 1982 annual conference, was that "the aging but declining veteran population" must put the interest of the general public ahead of nonservice-connected benefits for themselves. While such a reassessment "will be painful," the process was "unavoidable." For "social and economic conditions in which we find ourselves are going to bring changes whether we want them to or not," Nimmo said.

The national commander and others sought to counteract similar fiscal philosophy expounded by groups such as the National Conservative Political Action Committee and the Conservative Caucus. In April 1982 a conservative coalition proposed an alternative federal budget, a plan to slash the V.A. budget by a third with repercussions in the hospital system, service-connected disability benefits, and service injury pensions, Flynt responded, "We believe several recommendations simply ignore the federal government's moral obligation to its citizenry." (The Legion, also, opposed coalition proposals for economizing in school nutrition and energy conservation research.)

From the Conservative Caucus the Legion turned to oppose the conservative administration's H.R. 5709 that month also, a measure that targeted for change a regulation established in 1932 (and traceable to the 1924 World War Veterans Act) for granting total disability payments to unemployed veterans rated sixty percent disabled. The same "extraschedular benefit," John Sommer told the House Veterans Affairs Subcommittee on Compensation, Pension, and Insurance, had been deemed important and had been retained in the 1940s as well, after having been closely reviewed by Congress and presidential commissions.

That same concept of accommodating veterans who had apparent need was painted with broader strokes when, in May, Veterans Affairs and Rehab Director Lyngh conferred with the Senate Appropriations

Subcommittee on H.U.D. and Independent Agencies. "We are very much aware that the federal government funds a plethora of programs, each of which has its advocates who present to Congress . . . compelling reasons" for maintaining those programs. "We submit, however, that none of the special interest advocates can put forward reasons as compelling as those of the veteran," a status now held by twenty-five million men and women. Asking the committee to "pardon our bluntness," Lyngh added the argument that was now advanced more often after four wars in one century: turn your back on those who served, and the next call for service could be disastrous.

Those among the Rehab Commission and Division who directed their attention to the economic well-being of veterans rejoiced in October 1982 when on the day following the expiration of the Comprehensive Employment and Training Act of 1973 (C.E.T.A.), Congress passed the Job Training and Partnership Act, of which a portion of the appropriation was directed to veterans. Specifically, $13 million of the $3.8 billion appropriation was set aside for grants to train Vietnam-era veterans, service-connected disabled veterans, and those recently completing their military service. Particularly encouraging was the provision that nonprofit organizations could apply for funding from the set-aside funds, an attractive feature to Legion departments that wanted to continue programs previously funded by C.E.T.A. or to begin new programs.

The employment situation of Vietnam veterans, in particular, was slow to find a solution. In the middle of winter 1983, unemployment among Vietnam veterans continued to rise; and the percentage, as compared against nonveteran males of comparable age groups, continued to be significantly higher. In searching for answers as well as solutions, it was noted that while veterans of previous wars usually did better in the job market than nonveterans, it being accepted that they had gained maturity and discipline while in service to their country, the Vietnam-era veteran had not fared as well. There was, of course, an important difference in that Vietnam veterans returned to a nation wracked by recession while their earlier counterparts had had little of that with which to contend. Though the degree of agreement varied, it was assumed now that the stigma of service in an unpopular war had prejudiced employers.

Thus was dealt Rehab workers another matter causing concern—the subjective nature of military service in a prejudicial environment troubled by economic conditions that had already made the route to employment rocky. Furthermore, "The pattern appears to be reinforcing itself," one American Legion News Service bulletin observed.

(There was another instance of events having come full circle: earlier in the summer, an American Legion News Service bulletin, published on July 2, informed Legionnaires that the National Public Relations Office in Washington was looking for World War I veterans who had participated in the veterans bonus marches on Washington, D.C., in 1932. On July 28 would occur the half-century anniversary of the march of the "Bonus Expeditionary Force." In a time when Vietnam veterans were experiencing an unemployment rate much higher than their nonservice counterparts, Legion public relations staffers sought references and telling imagery in the plight of doughboys and gobs similarly frustrated by unemployment fifty years before.)

The Legion reaction to the V.A. budget proposed for fiscal 1984 was more positive than in the immediate past. Veterans Affairs and Rehab head Lyngh cautiously called the proposed $1.1 billion increase in that agency's budget for the next year "reasonable." Looking closer at the direct benefit programs—sixty percent of the V.A. budget—Lyngh again pronounced Legion approval, though it was in no way exultation. He did observe that there were several areas in which budget lines did not hint of the demonstrable effects of inflation. There was even the projection of fewer employees at the V.A.'s fifty-eight regional offices, sure to delay delivery of benefits and services to the service disabled, pensioners, and survivors.

In all the consideration of the multiple millions of dollars appropriated to the V.A., the inadequate fee allowable by law for claims representation was still a matter of contention. There had always been Legionnaires who disagreed, favoring opening the process to federal courts. Lyngh again took the traditional Legion view to the Senate Veterans Affairs Committee in March 1983, opposing yet another attempt for recourse to the courts (what had been dubbed "an attorney's relief act") for claims denied by the V.A. Lyngh did inform the senators that the Legion opposed turning the B.V.A. into an independent agency of a group of administrative law judges who would continue to employ the review practice and methods as before.

Should the appeals system resort instead to a court of law, Lyngh argued, that surely would result in a *res adjudicata* environment ("the matter has been decided") in which "by the book" decisions would be more costly for all. Also, the tradition of compassion and reason in claims appeals often held out to poor and even indigent veterans would be lost forever in the creation of automatic adversarial roles into which all players would be cast.

On another matter, when those in the administration controlling the nation's purse strings sought to control federal nonmilitary spending by delaying the adjustment of C.O.L.A.s relating to veterans' benefits, Legion spokesmen again objected, principally in testimony before the congressional committees that would ponder and then act upon administration bills or those of individual congressmen or senators.

National officers and staff members were on the receiving end of some praise from the government when at the 65th National Convention at Seattle, Assistant Secretary of Labor for Veterans Employment William C. Plowden told Economic Commission members that his having all programs regarding veterans under his supervision was the result of Legion lobbying to that effect. Other government officials, speakers from the Small Business Administration and the Office of Personnel Management, attempted to look into the future and predict the economic scene, such as that for employment, all of which contemplation bore directly on the Legion's system of advocacy for veterans. They, also, heard from Legionnaires who had tried employment programs (generally on the department level) and who had observations of merit. The grand national gathering of heart and mind once again concentrated for a few hours on what veterans could do to help veterans and what their government, too, should do about matters of relative interest.

VIII

For many of those gathered at national conventions in the late 1970s and early 1980s, the most relevant concern was a far more natural phenomenon than Agent Orange, the various threatening world events, or many other Legion interests. That topic, instead, was aging.

The Legion had considered the topic before. Now there was growing interest in the subject by the general population. In late October 1980, representatives of the Legion joined others from the National Retired Teachers Association, the American Association of Retired Persons, and the White House Conference on Aging in a meeting at St. Petersburg, Florida, to discuss "Energy, Equity, and the Elderly." Florida Senator Lawton Chiles hosted a Senate Special Committee on Aging during the conference.

The next month in Boston, Maine's Senator William S. Cohen conducted a similar conference. Maryland Legion Department Adjutant Daniel H. Burkhardt attended and reported to the American Legion News Service that what the whole conference boiled down to was that "elderly people . . . are often forced to choose between food and fuel. Too often they opt for fuel, resulting in malnutrition, poor health, and further lowering of body temperature" among persons who, though they generally needed more heat, now found it to be a major burden on their pensions.

One fact hit home at both meetings: by 1981, about half of the country's male population would be veterans over sixty-five. For the remainder of the century, the majority of older American men would be veterans.

In mid-summer 1981, by congressional mandate, the V.A. formed its twelve-member committee of physicians, scientists, and educators to evaluate and make future plans for the care of America's aging veterans. One of the first tasks assigned to this V.A. Geriatrics and Gerontology Advisory Committee was to evaluate the V.A.'s eight geriatric research, education, and clinical centers, specialized units designed to attract and develop superior geriatrics staff members. The committee also helped plan V.A. research relating to the aging, sought participation from other federal agencies in related health fields, and compiled recommendations for new programs of comprehensive health care services for elderly veterans. The Legion's representative on the committee was Robert Lyngh, director of the Veterans Affairs and Rehab Division. Chaired by Ewald W. Busse, M.D., associate provost of the Duke University School of Medicine, the committee's report was due in Congress by April 1, 1983.

Lyngh testified before the Senate Veterans Affairs Committee on June 30, 1982, reminding the senators that federal law entitled veterans sixty-five and older to V.A. health care if they needed it. The V.A. could accommodate them, Lyngh said, even though "some leaders in this government, both in the executive and legislative branches, have been making statements that the government cannot, in fact, provide care for all the veterans who are now reaching and passing the age of sixty-five." More than half of all veterans never apply for V.A. medical care, Lyngh noted. He pointed to a 1977 study by the National Academy of Sciences that found that the V.A.'s active clientele was about three million out of a veterans' population of thirty million. By far the majority of those who applied were single, elderly, and poor, he said.

Lyngh reiterated a standard Legion tenet—that the V.A. medical care program be maintained first for the service disabled and then for those needy ones who subsequently applied for care. That, Lyngh said, was no more than what had been promised by another Congress in 1924 with the World War Veterans Act. What had by now been expanded and improved in many ways to become a fine comprehensive medical care program must be preserved. More and more aged veterans would need it in the future.

National Commander Al Keller also urged the Veterans Affairs committees of both houses of Congress to organize a study of new ways to provide for the medical needs of the elderly, especially in noninstitutional settings. Keller noted that many developments had occurred in this field. Each of the 172 V.A. medical centers should be surveyed to see if the redefining of individual, site-specific missions might be in order. Veterans' organizations, he said, were ready to offer a consumers' perspective.

Another aspect of aging was darkening the horizon: increasingly, the attention given to the subject and the all-important funding necessary for treating the needs associated with aging would have to compete with other federal programs in a climate of budget reduction. That, indeed, was developing as one of the major considerations with which veterans' advocates would have to struggle in the future.

An event in early 1983 hearkened back to the Legion's origins as an organization which insisted upon recognition by the government of the special status of veterans among other citizens.

The event, which would prove to be an important milestone in Legion history, was precipitated when the Supreme Court heard the case brought by a group which lobbied in Washington, D. C. on the tax laws. The group had been refused tax-exempt status on the grounds that its reason for being was to lobby. In its appeal to the high court, the group cited the tax-exempt status of veterans' organizations, chief among which was the American Legion with its active lobbying function.

National Judge Advocate Bertram Davis, in addition to preparing the Legion's amicus curiae brief, worked closely with the defendant in the case, supplying the U.S. Solicitor General with information about relevant Legion activity.

The majority opinion of six of the justices and the concurring opinions of the other three (which also joined the majority opinion—making the court unanimous) denied the tax lobby group tax-exempt status, further demonstrating without a doubt that veterans occupied a unique place in the nation.

While the decision was primarily an analysis of the activity of lobbying as it related to taxation and representation, the reasons given for allowing veterans' organizations to lobby while remaining tax-free bolstered an age-old tenet of the Legion.

As Justice William H. Rehnquist wrote in the May 23, 1983, opinion, "It is . . . not irrational for Congress to decide that even though it will not subsidize the substantial lobbying by charities generally, it will subsidize lobbying by veterans' organizations. Veterans have been obliged to drop their affairs and take up the burdens of the nation, subjecting themselves to the mental and physical hazards as well as the economic and family detriments which are peculiar to military service and which do not exist in normal civil life. Our country has a longstanding policy of compensating veterans for their past contributions by providing them with numerous advantages. The policy has always been deemed to be legitimate.

Veterans' organizations could lobby and remain tax exempt. Once again (and by a cut-in-granite unanimous decision) the all-important special status of veterans had been affirmed.

The Court decision permitted the continuation of the Legion's ambitious, active, and essential traditional function which did not rely on outside contributions, but which was funded as part of a non-secretive annual budget assigned primarily to a few salaries and to the issuance of bulletins and other communiques.

National Judge Advocate Davis, whose service in that position spanned the time of the Bradley Commission's onslaught on veterans' benefits decades earlier, likened the Supreme Court decision to the victory over the Commission's intent in that field. "It saved the bacon," Davis said. "It was a significant affirmation of the special place veterans' organizations enjoy within the non-profit tax structure of the U.S., a particular niche in the legislative tax history of this country." As such, the decision would join the most revered legal precedent of the land.

IX

A Moment of Reflection

Three events in Washington, D.C., in the summer of 1984 marked important developments in veterandom. Two were anniversaries; one was a memorial. Two spoke of life revived and sustained; one echoed "Taps." All symbolized principles of Legionism.

That year was the fortieth anniversary of the G.I. Bill of Rights which had been enacted on June 22, 1944. Past National Commander Harry Colmery's handwritten pages outlining the bill on Mayflower Hotel letterhead paper (there was a brass plaque on the door of his former suite in the Washington, D.C., hotel noting the event) were returned to the Capitol from the Legion archives in Indianapolis to be displayed in the rotunda of the Russell Senate Office Building.

Along with Colmery's rough-copy treatise on how a democratic government should help citizen-soldiers return to civilian life, which in turn had become the monumental Servicemen's Readjustment Act of 1944, was an effusion of letters from statesmen and others praising the Legion's foresight and its faith in veterans and the nation. Secretary of Education Terrell Bell wrote, "Thank heavens for the G.I. Bill! The educational benefits made it possible for me and millions of other veterans to receive further training as we readjusted to civilian life." It had been estimated that eighteen million veterans had received some form of education or training, and eleven million had been helped to buy homes. From those developments the nation had grown and been strengthened exponentially.

The second anniversary event was held, appropriately, at the U.S. Office of Personnel Management, where on June 25, National Commander Keith Kreul marked the fortieth anniversary of the Veterans Preference Act. Kreul referred to the act as having formalized laws dating to the Civil War for the hiring of veterans for federal employment. Aiding veterans in that manner, Kreul said, was proper since "veterans are the only class of citizens created by the government."

A month earlier the body of an unknown American soldier from the Vietnam War had lain in state in the Capitol rotunda for three days. On May 28 a quarter-million people had stood on Constitution Avenue in silence as the coffin had been carried the six miles to Arlington National Cemetery. The Legion national commander and an honor contingent of ten Vietnam veterans had accompanied the caisson bearing the flag-covered coffin on its two-hour journey to the Tomb of the Unknown Soldier, stopping at the Vietnam Veterans Memorial, where in a replenishing spring rain those attending had paused to acknowledge the 58,000 names that appeared on the black granite wall.

At the tomb, a twenty-one-gun salute had resounded and "Taps" had rung briefly in the respectful silence. Later, at sunset, the coffin had been lowered into the ground, joining those from previous wars in eternal anonymity though occupying a hallowed spot known to millions. As with the others, some measure of the dignity of service by this unknown soldier had been restored.

THE VIETNAM VETERANS MEMORIAL

Seldom, if ever, in the nation's history had any effort to memorialize American citizen-soldiers caused such fervor, and such furor, as that surrounding the design and construction of "The Wall"—the gleaming black granite memorial built to honor American armed forces personnel killed and missing in action in the Vietnam War.

Inscribed with the names of 57,692 who died, the Vietnam Veterans Memorial is a moving, even stunning, sight, the symbol of a nation's grieved conscience and desire for reconciliation residing in the contour of a section of the landscape between the Washington Monument and the Lincoln Memorial.

The concept for such a site was the inspired brainchild of Vietnam veteran Jan C. Scruggs of Washington, D.C., an employment specialist for the U.S. Department of Labor. Half of Scruggs's platoon had been either killed or wounded. In early 1979, Scruggs wrote to the Legion's Washington headquarters soliciting support for his idea of "a memorial not to honor the war but rather to honor the sacrifice of Vietnam veterans."

Robert Spanogle, executive director of the Washington headquarters of the Legion, was impressed by Scruggs's dedication to the concept as well as his bold if seemingly improbable expectation of a dedication ceremony on Veterans Day in 1982 (other Washington monuments had taken years, decades even, to build). Spanogle relayed that impression to National Adjutant Frank Momsen in Indianapolis. Before long, the Legion was involved in the work necessary to see the dream become a reality.

Simultaneously there began a fund-raising effort in the year of National Commander Michael Kogutek, along with a move to pave the way for the acquisition of a site, and, in general, the gaining of the complexity-ridden approval needed from various agencies for building a memorial in the nation's capital.

On July 1, 1980, Congress authorized the Vietnam Veterans Memorial Fund, which had been incorporated the year before, to use two acres of national park property in Constitution Garden 600 feet from the Lincoln Memorial. The tree-rimmed meadow at the northwestern corner of the Mall where the memorial would be built was bordered by Constitution Avenue on the north, Henry Bacon Drive on the west, with a seven and a half acre lake on the east and the Mall's reflecting pool on the south.

On May 6, 1981, the winner of a design competition open to all was announced, a competition that had attracted over 1,400 entries (perhaps the largest such competition in the nation's history). The striking and nontraditional design by Yale architecture student Maya Ying Lin was chosen twice, each time independently, by two separate panels of judges representing Vietnam veterans and design professionals.

The design, however, was met by vocal negative and increasingly influential opposition, so much so that it appeared that the project might be stymied or scuttled altogether. The complaints, and the initial refusal by the Interior Department to allow construction of the memorial to proceed, contributed to a critical delay during the latter half of 1981.

All the while, the Legion sought to encourage the Memorial Fund board of directors to stand their ground and remain a viable entity on matters relating to the design competition and the scheduling of events leading to a dedication ceremony. Current national staff members and prominent Legionnaires volunteered their services to the Fund. For example, James P. Dean (MS), later national commander (1986–87) served on the Fund's budget audit committee.

When matters became stalemated, the Legion precipitated a meeting hosted by Senator John Warner on January 27, 1982, in a Senate meeting room where from 6:00 P.M. *until nearly midnight a heated exchange of views ensued. Notwithstanding a hand-shake agreement at the conclusion of the meeting, impediments dogged hopes for a dedication date set for November 13, 1982. Principally, there was the refusal by the Secretary of the Interior to grant a building permit for the memorial.*

On the day following the meeting on the Hill, National Commander Jack Flynt interrupted an official Legion visit to Puerto Rico to meet, along with National Adjutant Robert Spanogle and Director of Internal Affairs (and Legion Memorial project coordinator) Thomas J. Haynes, with Secretary of the Interior James Watt to urge the granting of the necessary building permit for the memorial.

Soon thereafter the Legion mailed some 100,000 letters to Legionnaires asking that they in turn send telegrams to the president requesting his personal intervention in the matter, an appeal made in person also by the national commander when he visited the president during this time.

As for the building permit, if the department of the Interior would not grant it to the Memorial Board, the Legion itself, it was decided, would request it. Would the Secretary refuse the Legion? The NEC authorized such a move and that Legion follow-through was rewarded by the granting of the permit to the Vietnam Veterans Memorial Fund Board.

A ground-breaking ceremony occurred a few weeks later on March 26. The Legion had stood firm in its belief in the fair and equitable process leading to the construction of the memorial. Those closely involved in the project would recognize the Legion as the catalyst which made the dream of Jan Scruggs and others a reality by breaking the logjam of opposition to the design and to the building of the memorial.

At the ground-breaking, Past National Commander Michael J. Kogutek, in whose year the Legion's involvement with the Memorial project began, joined National Commander Flynt, a contingent of twenty Vietnam veterans and the many politicians positioned on a line 500 feet along the eventual V *shape of the monument. On cue the first spades of earth were turned as the U.S. Marine Band played "God Bless America." In his speech, National Commander Jack W. Flynt observed that "the suffering and the loneliness [the veterans] bore when they returned home . . . are finally at an end."*

At this point, the memorial concept had grown to include a plan to add a flag pole (donated with a flag by the American Legion, in addition to its $1 million donation) and a sculpture depicting three military personnel in combat dress.

The money raised was then paid to the Vietnam Veterans Memorial Fund based on construction receipts for work done on the memorial. By late April 1982, over $5 million had been raised by contributions from veterans' organizations, community groups, corporations, foundations, individuals, radiothons, unions, and special events planned for that purpose. Ultimately, over $8 million would be raised.

On August 26 the Legion National Convention in Chicago presented the Vietnam Veterans Memorial Fund with a check for $1 million (the Legion would become the largest single contributor to the project). The fund had been solicited purposefully from individual Legionnaires. By far, most donations from individual Legionnaires amounted to less than ten dollars. This method was preferred from the outset as being more meaningful and appropriate than an organizational contribution or corporate underwriting. Headquarters staff members volunteered overtime work to process the impressive flow of donations. Fund-raising within the Legion had been aided in part by the publication of a moving letter from a woman whose husband had been killed in Vietnam and who praised the Legion's efforts to help build a memorial so that her son could see his father's name on it.

In July, the first of the 140 ten-foot-tall polished black granite slabs inscribed with the names of American dead and missing in action arrived at the memorial site accompanied by the American Legion Cheverly Post No. 108, Department of Maryland color guard made up of eight persons, seven of whom had served in Vietnam, including an army nurse. This first panel listed those killed or missing in action from June 2 to July 8, 1970, and was placed on the left concrete arm of the receding V*-shaped wall about a half dozen panels from the apex.*

(From 1968 to 1981 the Washington Headquarters had housed gratis the National League of Families, an organization which, along with the Legion, continually reviewed the status of efforts by the government regarding POWs and MIAs.)

On September 20 occurred the unveiling of a presentation model of the sculpture of three young American infantrymen by Washington, D.C., sculptor Frederick Hart, to be placed at the memorial site later.

Though the product of much frenzied and anxious work, the four-day "National Salute to Vietnam Veterans" sponsored by the Legion November 11–14, 1982, helped give expression to the spirit of the thousands who had come to Washington, D.C., to be a part of the event. Those present spoke often about, and would long remember, the spontaneity readily apparent.

National Commander Al Keller, keynote speaker at the dedication of the Vietnam Veterans Memorial on November 13, spoke of honor, reconciliation, reflection, and consecration. He cited "the lonely battle" fought by Vietnam veterans. He also sought to answer the criticism of the event and the memorial itself. "There is no shame in serving with honor and courage in difficult times. And there is no shame in enshrining the names of fallen comrades in immutable stone for generations to recall."

In this statement of belief and purpose, Keller echoed the countless statements of other commemorative events that had occurred since the founding of the Legion. Few, however, had echoed more clearly and against such impressive surroundings.

On July 1, 1983, a fifty-five-foot-tall bronze flag pole was installed at the entrance plaza of the memorial, bearing a twelve-by-eighteen-foot American flag. The sculpture of the servicemen was installed on Veterans Day, 1984. National Vice-Commander Robert Turner placed a wreath near the apex of the memorial. In his speech he referred also to the almost 2,500 Americans still missing or unaccounted for in Southeast Asia.

MAINTAINING A "PRESENCE"
Lobbying in the 1970s and '80s

National Legislative Division staff members in the 1970s and '80s sought to convince the membership that the Legion had to work continually to maintain a "presence" in Washington, D.C., that is, a positive image. That could be helped along, they said, if congressmen and senators were reminded that Legion departments, posts, and Auxiliary units back home contributed to their communities with effective service programs. Such good news had a direct effect on the way in which the lobbyists were accepted into the offices of those whom they approached on the Legion's behalf. Information about Legion good works also aided the organization's credibility when Congress periodically reviewed the tax-free status of organizations such as the Legion.

Sometimes, however, the nature of Legion volunteerism worked against this. By the very definition of volunteerism, those who performed the public service not only refused pay but often the credit as well. But the Legislative Division urged members to "Take credit" in ways that would promote the organization's image regarding public service. The Legislative Division asked that brief descriptions of public service programs at the post or Auxiliary unit level be sent to Washington headquarters for possible entry into the Congressional Record.

The point, of course, was to help in this way to maintain the Legion's long-standing practice of lobbying Congress. The first organizing caucuses and the first National Convention of the American Legion in 1919 recognized that the rehabilitative needs of veterans would have to be addressed by new federal legislation.

No sooner had it been founded than the Legion began lobbying to project its noble purposes. The staff at the Washington, D.C., headquarters of the Legion, housed in a former residence on K Street NW, included full-time lobbyist John Thomas Taylor, who presented the Legion's viewpoint in a way that both utilized and built the Legion's image and credibility. In the summer days in 1919 the Legion first lobbied for its federal incorporation, the National Soldier Settlement Act, and matters relating to the resolutions made at the St. Louis Cau-

cus. Taylor, henceforth, made Legion and lobbying history during an aggressive and successful tenure.

With the large influx of World War II veterans as members, the K Street house was replaced by a new building that was dedicated by Legionnaire President Harry S. Truman in 1951. Several years earlier, in a memorable lobbying achievement, the Legion had participated in the creation of the G.I. Bill of Rights, the landmark socioeconomic legislation.

Twenty years later, however, the Legion was sometimes likened by insiders to a battleship for being so hard to turn. Some closest to the scene of its lobbying efforts believed that function needed a boost in credibility that could be gained by better quality position papers and a change in the selection of who to lobby on Capitol Hill. So during the Vietnam War, the lobbying efforts of the Legion were revamped to work in a more activist political climate and among larger and younger congressional staffs.

New, younger Legislative Division staffers were hired and put to work with daily contact with congressional staff persons and in requesting appointments with congressmen and senators, all in a move to upgrade the professionalism and credibility of the division.

Meanwhile, the division also worked to upgrade the quality, depth, and background of its testimony before congressional committees. Position papers that were handed to congressmen and senators had to present, succinctly, the Legion's arguments for or against a piece of legislation and create a readily recognizable point of view. No longer could veterans' advocates rely only on the emotional appeal that veterans deserved benefits because of the sacrifices they all made and the physical impairments that some received during military service.

Legislative Division staffers concentrated on the chairmen of veterans' affairs committees in both houses to display their enhanced professionalism in lobbying. After becoming known personally to key congressmen and senators, division staff members presented themselves and the Legion's views to others on Capitol Hill through papers and personal calls, all the while showing respect for the constraints of time on those they approached.

Back at the headquarters building on K Street, they reviewed with the staffs of other divisions the numerous mandates annually produced by national conventions. The resulting legislative agenda honored the wishes of the conventions while acknowledging the prevailing mood of Congress concerning legislation likely to be passed.

The Legislative Division sought congressmen and senators to introduce Legion-drafted legislation. They preferred members of the committees that would hear the bills; getting the all-important hearing, of course, was crucial to the advancement of legislation.

Sometimes the division worked with the V.A. in drafting a bill for which both agreed there was a need. Similarly, if a congressional armed services committee was preparing a bill that spoke to a concern of the Legion's National Security Commission, Legislative Division staff members worked with the congressional committee staffers to produce legislation that could win approval. In either instance, the Legion might be asked to give expert testimony and to give the issue involved more visibility and credibility.

Sometimes when a mandate required legislation for which little or no interest could be found on the Hill, the Legislative Division would approach a long-standing congressional friend of the Legion to introduce the bill. If the one introducing the bill was not a member of the relevant House or Senate committee, the measure usually suffered an early demise. Fortunately, such instances were not common; national convention mandates tended to be relevant to current events, needs, and to the interests of those on the Hill.

National Convention mandates, an essential method whereby the membership spoke, were transformed to legislative bills for the journey through the congressional maze and were the origins of many Legion-backed laws.

What made a good bill, one which had promise of passage and enactment? First it had to originate in a mandate that recognized a need to serve some segment, or, indeed, all segments, of the population in solving a problem.

It was also necessary that the mandate reach a resolution without being so specific that the lobbyists were locked in to an intractable position without leniency for compromise, adjustment, and refinement. A bill written properly in this fashion allowed the Legislative staff to advance it along the path to passage and eventual enactment. If, for example, the progress of a bill involved an alteration or variance from the original intent, then Legislative Division staffers requested a technical reading from the commission on what lenience was permitted. There were also consultations with other division personnel, the national adjutant, and commission chairmen to ask, "How far can we go in accepting the alternatives offered us?"

Flexibility was generally allowed as long as the original intent of the bill was not compromised or jeopardized. Often, however, a result was accepted that did not fully meet the original objective but which, nevertheless, was a step in the right direction.

If in proposing a change in public policy the Legislative Division gained Congress's acceptance of a measure that even partially satisfied a Legion objective, that was a relative giant step because Congress had thus spoken its philosophical support of the concept. Next year the original objective could be pursued through the amending process as, indeed, it often was successfully.

In this regard, it was comforting to know that Congress rarely reversed itself completely on anything in the near term. Second, once a measure became ensconced in the law books, there was an immediate constituency, a clientele, a group of people being served by the measure. The threat of public discomfort sure to be caused by removing that benefit or solution generally safeguarded the new law from repeal or reversal.

Legislative Commission members and division personnel knew that the lobbying craft relied on at least four tools for success, the first three of which were prohibited to the Legion by its federal charter: funding political campaigns; endorsing candidates; and providing an organized structure of workers for political campaigns.

The fourth—grassroots lobbying conducted en masse by the membership—was the chief lobbying tool that the Legion could employ. Consequently, lobbying by the membership had to be conducted in the most effective way possible.

To do this, the Legislative Division paid particular attention to the paramount issues before the organization, the greatest concerns at any given time (such as the Agent Orange issue or, later, the call for a constitutional amendment prohibiting desecration of the American flag), and concentrated much time and effort in advancing legislation to those ends. They knew, though, that the effect of legislative "alerts" asking for immediate grassroots lobbying by letters, telegrams, phone calls and visits of Legionnaire constituents to the Hill would wither from overuse. "There's only so many times you can go to the well," a division director observed.

The Legion's paid lobbyists, always small in number for the amount of work required of them, established a daily routine that produced the most results. Mornings began with brief reviews of the previous day's action on the Hill that were of interest to the Legion. Then there were trips to the Hill to monitor committee and subcommittee hearings or to present testimony an average of fifty times a year, most often between April and June when more hearings were held.

Mornings for the division director also included many phone calls to set up meetings, discuss refinements of legislation already under consideration, or in meetings with congressional staff persons. There was also the writing of letters to persons on the Hill and to others.

During afternoons, when most of the legislative action occurred on the floor of the House and Senate, division personnel monitored the proceedings through contacts on congressional staffs, tapes of the proceedings available at the House or Senate cloak room, and, of course, live cable TV coverage. If something broke loose on the Hill and the Legion needed to react, division staffers were better off using the phones or a fax machine rather than traipsing from office to office at the Capitol. Usually the division knew ahead of time what was likely to transpire; surprises could imply a lack of communication, something the division strove to avoid.

Afternoons also included the preparing of reports to the membership on congressional and division actions, reports that appeared regularly in monthly bulletins, The American Legion Magazine, *other communiqués, or to individuals seeking specific information about current legislation.*

Occasional evening receptions on the Hill to which Legion representatives had been invited offered some brief, to-the-point buttonholing. There were also Legion-sponsored dinners and receptions for congressmen, senators, and others who were reminded or informed of the host's policies and legislative initiatives.

What remained a constant during a period of revamping and beyond was an appreciation for the changing leadership roles in Congress of late. The 1988 elections, for example, included several key retirements that brought changes in key chairmanships. For example, both House and Senate Budget Committees and the Senate Appropriations Committee had new chairmen. A new Speaker of the House and majority leader of the Senate took their places as did several subcommittee chairmen of appropriations committees in both houses. To these changes Legion lobbyists had to adjust.

In the late 1980s, the Legion's Legislative Division set about pursuing a "macro" approach—assessing the big picture and taking action when it seemed the right time to affect or refocus national policies regarding health care, education, housing, and job training, as well as emerging national problems such as AIDS, *drug abuse, and homelessness. In all these areas, the special focus, of course, was on the veteran.*

It was vital, of course, to recognize that the organization was in competition with others for federal dollars and therefore would have to be well prepared for congressional testimony and be more forceful in presenting its positions—in effect, to compete "smarter." Legion bills would have to project good public policy and sound budgetary policy. Such is the challenge and the prescription for success in the 1990s.

In the seventieth year of its existence, the Legion could look to a tradition of aggressive and successful lobbying in Washington, D.C. Along the way, others of the lobbying craft had observed Legion tactics and successes for many years.

For example, the Legion had sought to have Veterans Day returned to the original calendar date of November 11 rather than having it occur on any convenient Monday, which was favored by the leisure-time industry and labor unions in order to make for a long weekend. In the early 1970s, Legion lobbyists and Auxiliary officers worked through state legislatures to obtain enough resolutions—eventually from forty-eight of the fifty states over a three-year period—calling for a change in the date of observance. (One Auxiliary member was particularly effective—her husband was house speaker at the statehouse.) Before long, Congress was alerted to the sentiment of state legislatures. The Legion immediately began charting the course of the resulting federal legislation.

Legislative Director Mylio Kraja (later executive director of Washington Headquarters) sent a telegram to each member of the congressional committee meeting to amend the legislation for the date change for Veterans Day, telling them that the Legion would be monitoring their meeting and their votes.

After a unanimous vote for the date change, Kraja encountered a fellow lobbyist who congratulated him on the Legion's legislative strategy. "I'm a Legionnaire," the other man said proudly. But his parting "Thanks" had a double meaning. He now would have to explain to the union for which he lobbied that the perpetual three-day weekend was no more now that the World War I–era observance date for Veterans Day had been restored.

The Legion's presence on Capitol Hill was a tradition. Remaining effective, however, was a task of the moment.

STANDING GUARD

RECKONING WITH "THE DEFICIT"

1985 – 1989

I

The fortieth anniversary of V-E Day coincided with the opening session of the spring N.E.C. meeting, May 8, 1985. National Chaplain Rev. Charles G. Rice, Jr., led the N.E.C. in prayer, asking that "the task we performed there [in Europe] be considered part of our ongoing task of holding the beacon of freedom high for all the world to see and aspire to." A guest soloist sang "Onward, Christian Soldiers," then was joined by the committeemen in singing "My Buddy," and "My Country 'Tis of Thee." The committeemen stood for a moment of reflective silence dedicated to "our departed comrades." Then, saluting the colors, they listened to the familiar "Taps."

Legionism was often punctuated by anniversaries, memorials, and public displays of thankfulness for liberty. There was also the occasional tinge of private sorrow that lay slumbering in the minds of many citizen-soldiers.

The World War I consequence that was Legionism had been imbued also from the start with a vigorous call to active civilian service to fellow veterans and to the nation. And effective service, of course, depended in large measure on the success of the organization's annual membership drives to provide renewed, vigorous volunteers for continuing the familiar basic programs.

Appropriately, then, the committeemen at the May 1985 meeting next honored the departments that had exceeded their goals for membership at that point. National Commander Clarence M. Bacon called on the national vice-commanders to recognize the twenty-four departments that had surpassed their goals for membership and that now received a "Bacon Beacon" award. He complimented the enthusiasm with which matters of membership had been undertaken recently. On this V-E Day there were 2,556,000 members, an increase of 20,000 over the year before. (The year would end with 2,641,159 members, a forty-year high that marked the end of decreasing rolls and the beginning of a steady climb.)

The year 1985 would long be remembered for congressional debate on the plan popularly named after Senate deficit clinicians Gramm, Rudman, and Hollings. The resultant Balanced Budget and Emergency Deficit Control Act (Public Law 99-177), signed by the president on December 12, 1985, established a timetable for specific actions in a gargantuan task—cutting $36 billion each year until 1991 from the federal budget.

The act was inevitable and overly long in coming. But the American Legion, dedicated to the assurance that there would be a national conscience regarding veterans' rehabilitative benefits that were paid from the public treasury, out of necessity played an adversarial role regarding benefits endangered by the act.

Proposals for such cuts were not new. Since mid-March 1985, Congress had been looking ahead, as was traditional, to the budgets for fiscal years 1986, 1987, and 1988. For at least a year and a half now the most adamant cost-cutters in Congress had been questioning specific veterans' benefits. Twenty senators had been singled out for special lobbying efforts by the Legion on these rehab matters.

It was quite clear that Congress favored "fiscal restraint." Though it had always been a sensible enough admonition in its own right, there was now a majority on Capitol Hill determined to eradicate red ink from the federal ledgers. As proof, there were a notable number who now recommended significant cuts in programs that before they had not only supported but, had actively protected as well.

National Legislative Commission Chairman Gary Sammons described the scene to the N.E.C. in May 1985. "This year's consideration of budget priorities has developed into an intense struggle in the Senate, where a budget compromise has been worked out between Senate leaders and the White House. The compromise is being bitterly opposed by those who feel that it includes too many domestic program cuts. Among the items scheduled for major changes are V.A. medical care, the Veterans Home Loan Program, small business loans for veterans, and the nonprofit postal subsidy." The House, Sammons said, was awaiting guidelines on these matters from the Senate. But Democrats on the House Budget Committee were meeting to formulate their own version of a budget.

To the Legion, the budget-balancing momentum included two specific matters of concern: the "means test" and "third party reimbursement."

The first, a test of the earnings of veterans to judge whether medical care would be given free or by cost-sharing, had been proposed several times by the Reagan administration during the early and mid-1980s.

Not only the Legion but many in the House and Senate agreed that the standards relating to salary levels or net worth of the veteran were too high. It was not uncommon, in fact, to hear the standards described as being "onerous."

A beginning point of sorts could be traced to the veterans affairs committees of both the House and Senate having been assigned the task of identifying federal budget cuts in veterans' affairs as their part in the mandated budget deficit reduction program. In the discussions that followed, a means test and a system for third party reimbursement (by private insurance companies for veterans' health claims to the V.A.) were offered as ways to cut funding in the first instance and to produce additional revenue in the second.

Throughout the summer of 1985, the means test and third party reimbursement suggestions were debated. The Legion was particularly perturbed when several other veterans' organizations that originally had opposed the idea reversed their positions on the matter of a means test. The Legion, however, remained adamantly opposed, making that position known to the chairmen of both the House and the Senate Veterans Affairs committees in July.

The controversial Budget Reconciliation Bill continued to be debated during the fall of 1985. So difficult was it for agreement to be reached on the large-scale budget savings contained in the bill, which had some 200 provisions for cuts in programs, that Congress was unable to finish work on it before the end of the 1985 session. (The bill also included changes in the Employee Retirement Income Security Act, the federal regulation of private retirement programs which affected most employers across the nation, including the American Legion.) So the bill was carried over into the 1986 session. The Legion meanwhile maintained that if the means test itself could be dealt with as a separate item in a clean up-or-down vote, it was sure to be thrown out. Such was the reading of Congress by Legion lobbyists.

When means tests were proposed, the Legion's initial response, and one it held to, was to ask the members of congressional veterans affairs committees to delay considering this any further as one of their assigned budget-cutting tactics until the V.A. provided a current demographical profile of its patients. Such a profile, it was felt, would show that by far the largest number of V.A. patients were the elderly and the poor, ones who would have been cared for by Medicare or Medicaid or some other tax-supported agency. The Legion argued also that the means test for screening claimants would cost more to administer than the V.A. would gain.

A means test (again decidedly less stringent than the Reagan administration desired) that was gaining the favor of the Veterans Affairs committees on the Hill would establish categories of veterans based on annual earnings. Thus, category "A" would include those with service-connected illnesses or incomes below $15,000 (single; $18,000 if married), for whom the V.A. would provide free care. (Also included in "A" were former POWs, those exposed to Agent Orange or ionizing radiation, those receiving V.A. pensions, World War I veterans or anyone older, and those eligible for Medicaid.) Category "B" was to be the nonservice-connected disabled with an income above $15/$18,000 but below $20/$25,000 for whom the V.A. would provide care if space was available. Finally, those filing nonservice-connected claims and who had incomes between $20,000 and $25,000, comprising category "C," would be required to pay a deductible equal to Medicare (currently $492) for care if space was available.

The other budget-balancing related bugaboo for the Legion was the concept of "third-party reimbursement" proposed by the administration in the spring of 1985 whereby the government hoped to recoup health care costs from private insurance companies that insured V.A. health care claimants. Though to many the plan seemed to be practical, even reasonable, the Legion heartily opposed it both on philosophical grounds and as a matter of practicality.

First, it was said that such a plan would change the basic nature of V.A. health care from a program of benefits already granted by a government bound by law to care for those who had sacrificed their time and health in military service, to one of "cost-sharing," with the veteran contributing to the cost of his or her own medical care through insurance premiums. Would not such a method for reimbursement merely convert the V.A. into an agency such as Medicare? What then would become of the V.A.?

Second, the plan was not practical, Legion spokespersons said, as they pointed to recent statistics indicating that only 30.8 percent of those filing service-connected claims of disability had health insurance. (Of those filing nonservice-connected claims, 38.2 percent had health insurance.) Was it to be that only insured veterans would be treated? If so, then between sixty and seventy percent of those likely to apply for medical care would be turned away for lack of insurance from which to receive reimbursement for medical care. Such a frightening (and not unnoticeably emotion-packed) development was imminent; the Legion and the V.A. nevertheless traded counterclaims about the intent and the inevitability of it all.

At the October 1985 N.E.C. meeting, the "cost-sharing" plan was further assailed as being likely to lead to "mainstreaming" of veteran patients—steering them to private sector hospitals by the V.A. as was being done with Medicare and Medicaid patients. The result, it was claimed, and in this instance more believably, would be a further deemphasizing and decline of veterans' medicine.

At the New Orleans National Convention in 1985, Representative G. V. "Sonny" Montgomery, chairman of the House Veterans Affairs Committee, cited the consensus in Congress for balancing the budget. All agencies of the federal government were being scrutinized. Even though Montgomery himself "would still prefer to leave things alone," the V.A. in particular, to no one's surprise, had been targeted for close examination.

The Legionnaires gathered as the annual preeminent governing body of the Legion heard Representative Montgomery speak for a modified version of the administration's plan for regaining the cost of veterans' medical claims by passing them along to the private insurance companies that insured the claimants. The congressman told also of the support given to his views by ranking House Committee minority member John Paul Hammerschmidt.

Montgomery's position on the matter, he said, was "a compromise." As he saw it, the inevitable choice was between substantial cuts in existing veterans' programs, and legislation which would end the long-running exclusionary contracts of insurance companies with veterans.

Regarding a means test, Representative Montgomery did not favor the version proposed by the administration, which, he said, would "promote poverty by requiring nonservice-connected disabled veterans making more than $15,000 [a year] to spend down to that level" before becoming eligible for V.A. health programs. The Legion could agree at least with Congressman Montgomery's wish for matters regarding the V.A. to be "left alone." At the same time the Legion's ongoing monitoring of V.A. services of late countered V.A. assertions that there was not room for all veterans who applied for care. Veterans Affairs and Rehab Commission Chairman W. F. Lenker told the October 1985 N.E.C. meeting that "it is presently estimated that as many as 20,000 nonservice-connected veterans are being turned away from V.A. hospitals each month, for a yearly total of approximately 240,000." He added that "of the eligible veterans, only ten percent use the V.A. facilities, because of choice, insurance, convenience, location, and so forth."

Lenker and others continued to emphasize the multibillion dollar capital investment of the government in the V.A. for fulfilling a fundamental obligation to service-connected disabled veterans, for supporting the Department of Defense in time of war or national emergency, and for training doctors, nurses, and others in medical research and practice.

The point, of course, was that this complex structure of veterans' health care should be protected by increased funding, not endangered by allowing it to decline because of cuts in funding. (The fiscal year 1986 budget called for a decrease of $154.9 million in V.A. construction alone from fiscal 1985.)

Furthermore, as National Commander Clarence Bacon stated in a letter sent to all senators on April 2, "If all federal spending could be maintained at the pace of V.A. spending over the past ten years, the government would now be operated with an annual budget of $554 billion and with a surplus approaching $200 million." The V.A., it was said, though a very large agency, "has played no major contributing role in creating the current federal budget dilemma."

II

The legion's legislative laundry list in the mid-1980s included the typically wide-ranging interests. Particularly at this time, however, did the means test and third party reimbursement issues stand out. These topics serve to point up the importance of lobbying Congress as begun by Legion founders Tom Miller, Luke Lea, John Thomas Taylor, and their successors, staff members and volunteers alike.

To one national officer, South Carolina Department's perennial N.E.C. man E. Roy Stone, Jr., chairman of the N.E.C. Resolutions Subcommittee, it seemed that the Legislative Council had not functioned as it should. That group had been established in May 1975 for one-on-one lobbying by Legionnaires who were on a first-name basis with their congressmen or senators. It was a lobbying technique to which Stone was particularly partial.

Following the report of the National Legislative Commission at the October 1985 N.E.C. meeting, Stone rose to challenge those of the council. Evoking the memory of Tom Miller, who often had stood in the N.E.C. following the legislative report to expound, challenge, or chide regarding the lobbying craft, Stone called out to a few council members who had been absent when their help was needed in Washington a few days previously. "If we were going to have a football game, by golly, we would have one helluva time getting eleven men on the field."

Called a necessary "tongue-lashing" by Committeeman William E. Christofferson, the spirited reminder of the importance of the Legislative Council had been delivered by a respected Legionnaire (two years later in 1987 Stone would be honored with the title Past National Commander at the San Antonio National Convention) who had intimate knowledge of the importance of the resolution-to-mandate-to-public-law process. To wit: a resolution in hand went no further until firmly placed in the hands of Congress. There were currently many pressing matters relating to Legion "basics" that had been addressed in that process.

For example, of particular interest to those on the Americanism Commission (and with obvious foreign relations implications) was the comprehensive immigration bill under consideration by the Senate Judiciary Subcommittee on Immigration and Refugee Policy. The Americanism Commission had always overseen the Legion's stand on immigration, and that position had long been adamantly against illegial immigration. Though the Legion had also supported government quotas in years past, the emphasis of its immigration policy until the late 1970s had been strong border enforcement.

Then in 1979 and 1980, the Legislative Commission had suggested to the Americanism Commission that a few changes should be made in the Legion's immigration policy. First, seasonal agricultural workers should be allowed into the United States to work in the Western and Southwestern states. But there should be sanctions against employers who knowingly hired illegal immigrants. Those sanctions should include fines, imprisonment, and confiscation of equipment and vehicles involved in illegal immigration.

In addition to testifying before congressional committees on the issue of immigration, Legion lobbyists took the extra step to appear before a special commission chaired by Notre Dame University President Father Theodore M. Hesburg, which had been established during the Carter administration to study immigration reform. When the commission met in Phoenix, Los Angeles, and other places, the Legion was there to be heard.

In this manner the Legion insisted that illegal immigration from Mexico and the Central American nations was bound to cause economic and political problems for the United States, the same kinds of problems, if allowed to mount unchecked, that the immigrants sought to escape in their home countries.

Furthermore, it was not solely a matter of immigration, the Legion said. Not only did illegal immigrants compete with Americans for unskilled and semiskilled jobs, but the root problems—economic malaise, political chaos, and, clearly, persecution in some countries—demanded action by U.S. foreign relations officials in dealing with Central American leaders.

The recession of 1979 and 1980, and its continuation for two more years, was another factor in the Legion's broader consideration of the nation's immigration policy. Congressional hearings revealed that illegal immigrants were working in great numbers not only in the West and Southwest, but also in cities farther to the north, in Chicago, New York, Washington, D.C., and elsewhere.

As for immigration quotas, the Legion recommended that the occasional need for certain skills on the American labor scene be considered. When those with particular skills were in short supply, quotas should be adjusted to allow immigrants with those skills to emigrate to the United States. Inasmuch as the often mentioned "baby bust" in America would result in fewer workers, the eventual shortage might have to be filled by immigrants to keep the economy vibrant.

There were other ramifications of immigration, also, that the Legion addressed, as in opposing bilingual education of immigrant children. Stressing that the historic strength of the nation came from its assimilation of many cultures—the melting pot concept—the Legion saw threats to national will and resolve when bicultural enclaves were allowed to set political agendas for their locales. Did the United States want similar trouble as that seen in eastern Canada with English- and French-speaking Canadians opposing each other? What surprises would the 1990 federal census contain regarding congressional reapportionment for 1992? The Legion found that to be of particular concern, as well as the increased expenses for schools that would be required to teach numerous languages.

The Americanism Commission was also interested in House Joint Resolution 211 regarding recognition of the pause for the Pledge of Allegiance as part of national Flag Day activities. National Children and Youth Commission members and division staffers celebrated the passage of two bills reflected in Legion resolutions, those for special designation weeks for both Reye's syndrome and for the family. A recent bill seeking to alleviate illiteracy in the nation had been welcomed, as had action by the House Elementary, Secondary, and Vocational Education Subcommittee in approving an increase of $100 million for child nutrition programs for fiscal year 1986.

There was no shortage of other issues in which Legion national commissions continued to take interest in the 1980s. The Legion's Economic Commission supported the retention of the Small Business Administration, which had been targeted for elimination in the budget-balancing maneuvers. This commission also opposed an increase in the user fee charged to those in the V.A. home loan guaranty program.

Foreign Relations Commission members decried the failure of the aid package for the Nicaraguan contra forces, while those of the Internal Affairs Commission continued to work to see the stabilization of the postage rate for nonprofit public service organizations.

The National Security/Foreign Relations Commission was observing developments relating to the president's Strategic Defense Initiative (S.D.I.), the status of the MX missile program, and the military retirement program. Such matters would be affected by the mood in Congress for cutting defense spending.

The Veterans Affairs and Rehabilitation Commission continued to protest against "ill-advised" legislation for setting up the means test and the third party reimbursement for veterans' claims. While the agenda for cost cutting went forward, there were some bright spots in the area of rehab. Some "refinements" of the nation's health care system for veterans were being considered in Congress, such as hospice care for terminally ill veterans, and an expansion of the Geriatric Research, Education, and Clinical Centers for treatment and research in the field of diseases of older veterans.

A Senate bill, S. 6, promised the continuation of a program begun in 1979 for veterans with alcohol and drug dependence and drug abuse problems, as well as assuring that money earned by veterans in work therapy programs would not be counted against annual income figures that determined pension payments.

Another Senate bill, S. 876, would set up a five-year pilot program for noninstitutional, community based medical, rehab, and social services for veterans as an alternative to nursing home care. A related bill, S. 875, outlined a pilot program to enhance the Vietnam Veterans Resource Centers by aiding in the coordination of these services with some new ones.

Finally, the House Appropriations Subcommittee on H.U.D.-Independent Agencies was considering supplemental appropriations for the V.A.'s current fiscal year. One sum of eighty million dollars, which had been approved by the subcommittee, was of particular interest to the Veterans Affairs and Rehab Commission because it was earmarked for the medical care account that was in need of funding to continue the level of employment in V.A. health care equal to the current year. The supplemental funding was due to be considered by the full House Appropriations Committee in May 1985.

Such were the hopes kept alive so far in legislation under consideration on the Hill. But by early November, Congress's aim on deficits appeared also to endanger some traditional veterans' benefits. V.A. director Harry N. Walters estimated that in fiscal year 1987 Gramm-Rudman-Hollings could cost veterans $464 million in benefits.

The year ended with encouraging developments, however. Even with the Gramm-Rudman-Hollings amendment attached, the debt ceiling bill signed into law on December 12 contained provisions exempting veterans' compensation and pension C.O.L.A.s, the two entitlements recently thought to be endangered. (The same consideration was also given to Social Security recipients.) Though cuts in the V.A. were allowed in the deficit reduction plan, the limit was one percent in the current fiscal year, beginning October 1, and two percent thereafter.

In addition to the Legion-backed provisions kept alive in the new Balanced Budget Act of 1985 regarding compensation and pension C.O.L.A.s, the Veterans Administration Health Care Amendments that were signed in December satisfied several Legion hopes. Principally in that regard, the V.A.'s existing alcohol and drug treatment rehab programs that had been operating as halfway houses and community centers were extended for three years. The same legislation gave three more years of life to the V.A.'s authority for treating veterans who had been exposed to dioxin and other herbicides in Vietnam and for those suffering radiation effects stemming from atomic tests.

The V.A. was now required to establish (actually refurbish) ten Vietnam Veterans Resource Centers that offered counseling and assistance in obtaining V.A. benefits, employment and job training, and information about chemical dependency rehab and services offered by other federal agencies.

The V.A. Health Care Amendments also included an increase in the maximum amount of coverage in the Servicemen's Group Life Insurance/Veterans Group Life Insurance programs, which was also made available to the Individual Ready Reserve and the Inactive National Guard beginning on January 1, 1986.

The year 1985 had been the sixty-sixth anniversary of the Legion's existence. That number for many now stood as the mandatory retirement year plus one and thus a reminder that World War II veteran members, the largest bloc in the organization, were concerned with matters of aging. The year was also the fiftieth anniversary of Social Security, the bulwark of economic well-being for millions of persons, but the financial integrity of which was now being questioned.

Therefore it was comforting also to know that the V.A. Amendments had authorized an increase from fifteen to twenty-five of the V.A.'s Geriatric Research, Education, and Clinical Centers.

III

The new Balanced Budget Act of late 1985 called for a series of events to take place annually from 1987 through 1991. Each year there was to be: congressional approval of a budget meeting the new deficit ceiling; legislation for new spending limits or tax increases; presidential announcement of automatic cuts from agency budgets should Congress fail in the previous goals; and finally, implementation of the presidential plan if Congress did not act or if its action was vetoed.

The Balanced Budget Act contained some protections for veterans' benefits. Nevertheless, as seen, threats were perceived continually by veterans' advocates in the ensuing rush to clarify the respective roles of Congress and the president in implementing the grand plan for reducing the deficit. (There was also the fundamental question pressed by some: Was Gramm-Rudman-Hollings itself constitutional?)

It wasn't only the congressional move to balance the federal budget that was worrisome for the Legion. It was determined also that the fine print of the Reagan fiscal year 1987 budget threatened V.A. medical care, V.A. guaranteed home loans, and other veterans' entitlements.

Those benefits, it seemed, would be radically changed despite congressional intentions to the contrary. For example, the benefits for veterans and their dependents who were enrolled in education and training programs were reduced nearly nine percent; and there was a thirteen percent cut in subsistence payments to those in vocational rehab programs. Even the handicapped were not exempt—grants to veterans who required special equipment for homes or autos were diminished, also.

Medical care for veterans was in store for a one percent reduction under the Balanced Budget Act. But the Reagan budget called for reductions in medical personnel at V.A. hospitals that, it was charged, would have an even larger effect on that care. The V.A. itself estimated that the more than 8,000 jobs slated to be cut meant that 57,000 fewer patients could be treated. National Commander Dale Renaud charged that the V.A. system was at present turning away 37,000 veterans each month. As had others before him, he, too, pointed to nonservice-connected patients of the V.A. as including "our poorest, oldest, and sickest veterans" who were the real losers amid all the budgetary belt-tightening.

Renaud and other Legion spokesmen warned also that provisions in the fiscal year 1987 budget would harmfully alter the veterans' home loan program. For example, the proposed limiting of V.A.-approved home loans, Renaud said, to $90,000 was in effect "redlining" entire sections of urban America as being unavailable to many veterans hoping to buy homes there. And prohibitions of late, such as the refusal to refinance existing V.A. loans, were bound to work hardship on many veterans.

Legion spokesmen warned that interfering with the veterans' home loan program would impede the pattern of great financial impetus to the nation brought about by the estimated twelve million veterans who, since the inception of the first G.I. Bill in 1944, had bought their own homes.

Fittingly, in the midwinter doldrums of January 1986 the V.A. posted the dollar-figure cuts for fiscal year 1986. But it was the Omnibus Reconciliation Bill for the 1986 federal budget that cleared Congress on March 20 and was signed into law (Public Law 99-272) on April 7 that brought the first means test for V.A. medical treatment of nonservice-connected disabilities and allowed the V.A. to charge the private insurance plans of veterans earning more than $20,000 annually.

Although substantially less restrictive than the administration's proposals, the means test now on the books was no less objectionable to the Legion for its having been but one facet of the massive Omnibus Reconciliation Bill.

Thus the Legion's two strongest specific objections to developments in veterans' affairs of late came to be overruled. National Commander Renaud complained of the "disenfranchising" of veterans and doubted that these objectionable parts of the new law would actually help cut the deficit.

After a few months of seeing the implementation of those two measures settle in, the Legion's Veterans Planning and Coordinating Committee (V.P.C.C.), chaired by the national commander and established to provide research and assistance to the national commissions, met on June 10 and 11 to discuss ways to increase the efficiency of the V.A. and the funding of the State Veterans Home program. Of particular interest, of course, were the ramifications of the new means test, which the Legion charged was unnecessary, even insulting. The V.P.C.C. called on the Veterans Affairs and Rehab Commission to assign field representatives to observe the way in which the means test was being applied at a few V.A. medical centers.

The V.P.C.C. also asked that the Rehab function generate a strategy for increasing the funding for the State Veterans Home Construction Program, which had been set up to give financial aid for the building of extended health care facilities for veterans, another program cut nearly in half by the Balanced Budget Act.

As for the matter of V.A. efficiency, the V.P.C.C. reviewed the V.A.'s automated data processing and called for it to be upgraded, the same recommendation that had been made by the present administrator and his three predecessors.

On the plus side, the roller coaster existence of veterans' preference had come now to include a recent 6-to-3 Supreme Court ruling in June that required states to extend that benefit to resident veterans who were not residents of the state when they enlisted or were drafted for military service. The ruling overturned a New York state law and would likely affect similar laws in as many as fifteen states. Justice William J. Brennan's written majority opinion echoed the traditional Legion tenet about "compensating veterans for their past sacrifices."

There also would be no enactment of judicial review of veterans' claims during the remainder of the congressional year. The Legion had long opposed any attempt to establish a review of individual cases and claims in the federal courts. In June 1986, national staff members from Washington headquarters testified against litigation for veterans' claims. Instead of taking possibly thousands of cases, the Legion said, into the already jammed federal court system, where it was doubted that many cases would be reversed anyway, the existing Board of Veterans Appeals should be required to evaluate more thoroughly the cases sent to it from the V.A. regional offices.

Legion lobbyists did not oppose raising the ten-dollar minimum fee, a holdover from the nineteenth century, that a veteran could pay to an attorney to represent him before the appeals board. But they insisted on safeguards being included to protect veterans from "unreasonable" attorney fees. On July 16, the House Veterans Affairs Committee voted 20 to 12 against taking the matter to the floor of that chamber. Meanwhile, the Legion itself was reevaluating its long-standing position on judicial review, seeking a workable solution to the periodic but persistent call of some to have judicial review enacted. Could the Board of Veterans Appeals somehow really be made more responsive to veterans? Perhaps some review body independent of the V.A. was the answer, some said. That was at least a point to ponder.

Late in 1986, the ramifications of Gramm-Rudman-Hollings were being felt in veterandom. In this climate of induced fiscal austerity, new National Commander James P. "Jimmy" Dean reiterated the traditional Legion belief that "all Americans benefit, if only indirectly, from the affiliations, the discoveries, and the progress being made by the V.A. in the course of caring for veterans." Conversely, "all Americans stand to lose if the system is further eroded." That was a point Dean emphasized when on September 23 he testified before the House and Senate Veterans Affairs committees. "What [in the past has] happened to veterans happens to all Americans—only sooner," he reminded them.

Dean specified one particular complaint: a full decade after the official close of the Vietnam era (as it related to military service and hence V.A. benefits), "Vietnam veterans who show symptoms of post-traumatic stress disorder have problems with physicians who fail to diagnose the condition, and adjudicators who fail to authorize appropriate compensation."

The national commander promised that the Legion would closely monitor the health care changes that Congress had passed and which the V.A. was implementing, particularly the means test. The national commander also repeated a challenge that had animated the Legion for nearly seventy years: "We will continue to seek clarification of the law's intent—an accurate picture of its human effects—and sufficient funding to assure that when available care depends on available space, the space is there."

Turning to the subject of economics, Dean addressed the administration's proposal for increasing the user's fee charged to veterans who were buying homes through the V.A. home loan program. Dean cited the "awesome economic activity" generated by the original G.I. Bill and successive legislative acts. The continuation of an important aspect of that activity was threatened now by an increased user's fee.

The 99th Congress adjourned on October 18, 1986, and National Headquarters evaluated the performance of the Legion's lobbying efforts. The wrap-up view was not as dark as it might have been. One Legion news service bulletin acknowledged that legislative victories for veterans "were not insignificant, especially considering the budgetary constraints mandated by the Gramm-Rudman-Hollings deficit reduction package."

For example, in March and again in May the president signed legislation expanding the V.A.'s lending authority. In a related matter, the Small Business Administration, threatened with closure since 1985, had been removed from the endangered list in mid-1986. Also, the laws relating to the job retention and hiring of National Guardsmen and Reservists was passed, which promised more job security for those citizen-soldiers.

Another survivor was H.R. 5299, which had contained a miscellany of veterans' matters, including several extensions, increases, and protective considerations for which the Legion had lobbied. The resulting Public Law 99-576 chiefly brought about a 1.5 percent C.O.L.A. for veterans' disability compensation effective December 1, 1986. Additionally, health care was extended to former prisoners of war; chronically ill veterans would be provided with more respite care; and a national registry of those exposed to ionizing radiation would be established. Finally, several veterans' entitlements were exempted from Gramm-Rudman-Hollings budget cuts, and women veterans would be pleased to learn that "gender-based" terminology was to be eliminated from the laws of veterans' affairs.

That was the good news. But by the end of the first calendar year of National Commander Dean's watch, the Legion was still rankled by the implementation of the means test and the third party reimbursement provision of the current budget law. Dean's "Project Concern" began gathering information about how these two new practices were being implemented. He asked department commanders and N.E.C. men to lead teams to all V.A. facilities nationwide to see first-hand just what medical care was being given, what was missing, and how attributable were the deficiencies to federal budget cuts. The teams were asked to report the number of veterans who were denied medical care because of a lack of space for them or because the V.A. refused to contract with private hospitals for their care.

During the latter half of November 1986, teams of five members each visited V.A. facilities and reported through N.E.C. men to a team in Washington, D.C., that collected the information for analysis.

"Project Concern" produced a collection of case histories to be used in the Legion's presentation to Congress about current veterans' medical care. Already suspecting that what would be found was "misinterpretation, misunderstanding, and misguided policy," Dean compared the situation to the inadequacies in the same field at the close of World War II. He geared up for another showdown with Congress on behalf of many of those same World War II veterans who as aging veterans were said to be lacking proper care. It was the greatest challenge the Legion faced at that point, Dean said.

The national commander even raised the possibility of the Legion's taking legal action against the V.A. to publicize, but more importantly to assure, that veterans would get the medical care called for in existing statutes. Subsequently, the N.E.C. at its prenational convention meeting in September adopted a resolution from the Veterans Planning and Coordinating Committee through the National Finance Commission, which authorized "litigation to challenge and clarify V.A. policies on Public Law 99-272."

IV

Having embraced the laudable maxim "policies, not politics" at the exuberant founding caucuses in 1919, the Legion from that time forward had not hesitated to push those policies, the high-minded and the down-to-earth alike, in the often rough-and-tumble world of the politicians. The arrival of the 100th Congress in January 1987 presented yet another opportunity and challenge, particularly in the Senate, where important committee chairmanships had changed hands when the Republican Senate majority of 53 to 47 was reversed to a 55 to 45 Democratic majority, an advantage Democrats had lost in 1980 after twenty years of control. In the House, the previous Democratic majority had been upped slightly.

Most recently, the year 1987 would be remembered by veterans' advocates as the year the nation's first permanent G.I. Bill was enacted. The magnanimous G.I. Bill of 1944 had been a temporary method for easing the reentry into civilian life of millions of ex-service personnel of the World War II. Similarly, three more acts of Congress were distinguished by the popular moniker "G.I. Bill," all seeking to treat successive veterans in a similar manner.

But when H.R. 1085 and the comparable S. 12 of the first session of the 100th Congress became Public Law 100-48, it was the first G.I. Bill that not only granted educational benefits for veterans, but also extended similar benefits to those who volunteered for military service—an avowed intent of the measure.

Specifically, the incentive to military service was a maximum of $10,800 in monthly payments of $300 for educational purposes for those who completed three years of active service followed by an honorable discharge. Others could serve two years in active service and then another four in the Reserve and earn $250 a month in benefits for a total of $9,000.

The "New G.I. Bill" was passed overwhelmingly by a vote of 401 to 2 in the House in March 1987. The Senate's version, S. 12, was substituted in that chamber for the House bill, passed by a vote of 89 to 0, and accepted by the House, which designated it the "Montgomery G.I. Bill" after the Democratic representative from Mississippi, G. V. "Sonny" Montgomery, who had worked for its passage. After one more favorable pass through the Senate on May 13, the measure entered the law books on June 1 with the signature of the president.

Recruitment needs notwithstanding, the president in a White House rose garden ceremony credited the Legion and other veterans' organizations with supplying essential support that helped bring the measure to his desk for signing.

Congressional action on this measure had focused attention on eligible recruits, the dwindling number of whom, it was said, would drop by nearly two million in the next decade. The armed forces acknowledged the importance of the bill for their recruitment efforts. By early May 1987, the bill's popularity in Congress was credited with having attracted 265,000 active duty recruits, chiefly because of the educational benefits contained in a bill still in the legislative process.

National Commander Dean praised the new G.I. Bill as combining aspects of two Legion basics, "a restatement of the nation's commitment to veterans, and a strong national defense." It was no less than the delegates to the 1986 National Convention had mandated (and that more than thirty years after the Legion's push for U.M.T. had received the best, and last, presidential help).

The "permanent" G.I. Bill came about with a minimum of difficulty. But it was a rockier road for the V.A. mortgage program. The Legion had long stressed the connection between the V.A. home loan program and the economic well-being of the nation. After the post–World War II building boom it was possible in many cities across the nation to point to entire neighborhoods that had sprung up in the late 1940s and early 1950s, including almost exclusively homes made possible by G.I. Bill home loans. With the coming of the G.I. Bill in the mid-1940s, the Legion, too, embarked on a new plane of economic advocacy pursued by a national commission bearing that name.

But the V.A. had divested itself of its loan portfolio as required in the Budget Reconciliation Act of 1983. That 1983 act also had brought the "loan-origination fee," more often referred to as the "user's fee," first of .5 percent in 1983, then 1 percent the next year for V.A. home loans to nondisabled veterans. Each year thereafter the administration proposed increasing the fee. (The current fee rate of 1 percent would be extended by Congress late in 1987 to remain effective until September 30, 1989.)

The administration was actively discouraging veterans from getting V.A. home loans so that the government could get out of the credit market, Legion spokesmen said. If the user's fee was increased even more, the chief advantage of the V.A. home mortgage program—the granting of loans that required no down payment—would be negated entirely.

In testimony before a congressional subcommittee in June 1987, National Economic Division staffer Emil Naschinski called the user's fee "a form of taxation . . . on an earned entitlement."

The legislation that had established the user's fee was due to expire on September 30. The Legion set about lobbying against its reinstatement and was supported in its efforts by Representative John Paul Hammerschmidt (R., AR) to whom an increased user's fee would be but another "attempt to fold veterans' programs into the morass of federal social welfare programs." The congressman drew attention to "the other end of this Mall where there are over 55,000 names etched in 100 yards of marble [on the Vietnam Veterans Memorial] . . . a stark reminder of the difference between veterans' programs [and social welfare programs]."

"That difference," Hammerschmidt continued, "we must never forget."

Another matter of concern was the outdated maximum loan guaranteed by the V.A. on homes, an inflation-ignoring $27,000. In July, the Legion testified before the veterans affairs committees of the House and Senate in support of pending legislation that would increase the maximum to $36,000. But even that figure, it was pointed out, was still far below the national average home cost of $74,324. Any increase, however, would allow lenders to raise the maximum loan amount accordingly and thus open the door for first-time home buying by many veterans.

Legion lobbying efforts would see this matter resolved when H.R. 2672 became Public Law 100-198, by which the user's fee of 1 percent, objectionable though it was, would remain the same for another two years. By this law also, the limit on home loans was reorganized as a two-tier arrangement whereby the V.A. would guarantee loans of $45,000 or less for fifty percent of the loan and loans above that figure were guaranteed for forty percent of the loan amount (or $36,000, whichever was lower).

The user's fee was but one aspect of a once successful veterans' home loan program that the Legion believed had lost much of its original luster and was now at least as accommodating to mortgage bankers, the real estate community, and others as it was to veterans, if not more so. Therefore, the Legion legislative agenda came to include initiatives designed to return the home loan program to its original purpose—to help veterans acquire homes and thereby enter the mainstream of the economy—and to make that program more financially stable than it had become.

The Legion pursued other economic concerns in addition to the famous veterans' home loan program. In fact, a "package" of veterans' economic benefits, including job training, job placement, housing, and aid to the homeless, had been put together during the recession of the early 1980s and made a part of the long-range legislative agenda. One of the first of these items was a program eventually called the Emergency Veterans Jobs Training Act, which was devised to encourage employer interest in job training for veterans but without the complicated rigmarole of previous programs of which employers had complained.

In addition to this program designed specifically for veterans, the "package" for which the Legion worked included two backup programs. In the first, veterans were included in the Jobs Training Partnership Act, originally for disadvantaged youth and minorities. In this connection, the Legion sought assurances that the private industry councils established under this act represented the needs of veterans in communities aided by the act.

The second ancillary program involved a venture into federal tax policies as Legion lobbyists succeeded in having veterans, particularly Vietnam veterans, included in the Targeted Jobs Tax Credit program for employers.

In addition to these three programs, a move was begun also to see that the State Directors of Veterans Employment were held more accountable for veterans job placement than before.

In this manner, the Legion became involved in a coordinating role regarding employment and job training programs, some of which had been effective earlier but that, the Legion believed, needed to be reviewed, with attention given to (1) the cost effectiveness (a criticism of the old C.E.T.A. program); (2) the meeting of a wider array of veterans' needs; and (3) more assurance of longevity for the programs.

Finally, there was the matter of veterans among the homeless to consider. The Legion economic package included an effort to change federal law to allow organizations, the Legion included, to repair houses repossessed by the V.A. (usually sites in such disrepair that resale was unlikely) and make them available for homeless veterans. A prototype project adopted by the Legion Department of Pennsylvania rehabilitated a former V.A. property in the Philadelphia area and provided housing for several veterans.

By midsummer 1987, the implementation of the third party reimbursement policy was said to have brought the very results that the Legion had predicted.

Reportedly, the V.A. had billed insurance companies for the first half of fiscal year 1987 for more than $27 million worth of medical treatment, of which $3.8 million had been reimbursed. Legion spokesmen questioned whether that recovery figure justified the 500 employees said to have been hired by the V.A. to process the third-party reimbursement paperwork. (The Legion would also seldom miss a chance to complain that funds from the reimbursement program went to the treasury and not to the V.A. directly.)

The Legion had surveyed 8,000 V.A. patients during the fall of 1986 and found that twenty-seven percent had basic health insurance, and seventeen percent had major medical coverage. The Legion survey also showed that ninety percent of the patients surveyed (some 7,200) lived within one hundred miles of the hospital, making them ineligible for the travel allowance offered to those who lived farther away.

At the same time that Congress was considering workaday matters such as veterans' home loans and other aspects of the mid–World War II largess for veterans known as the G.I. Bill of Rights, both the House and Senate were acting on a matter that had been introduced into thirteen previous Congresses—the elevation of the V.A. to cabinet-level status. Such a move, of course, had been favored by the Legion and other veterans' organizations as well as by a number of members of Congress who had worked closely on veterans' affairs. The V.A. and ultimately the veterans for whom it was established could gain much, it was said, by having the president's ear as a member agency of his cabinet. With 240,000 employees, the V.A. was second only to the Department of Defense in size. But vital operational matters such as funding had been channeled through the Office of Management and Budget.

The move for a cabinet-level Department of Veterans Affairs gained momentum in late 1987, especially in the House, where a major campaign for co-sponsorship had gone on in the summer and fall. Though many congressmen were involved, most prominently Representative G. V. "Sonny" Montgomery, the Legion looked particularly to New York Representative Gerald "Jerry" Solomon (R., NY) for his work in focusing attention on the matter. In August and again in October, the Legion asked Legionnaires nationwide to urge members of Congress to support cosponsorship.

Director of Veterans Affairs and Rehabilitation Robert E. Lyngh delivered the mandate of the previous year's National Convention for the V.A. to be made an executive department when he testified before the House committee considering H.R. 3471. A newspaper editorial signed by National Commander John P. "Jake" Comer was distributed soon after several major newspapers came out against the move. "What segment of society more deserves to be represented in the highest councils of government?" the editorial asked. America's veterans, it was pointed out, had responded to the call of the elected government when "diplomacy failed." But now they "face . . . the very real possibility that public policy may transform their sons and daughters into the next generation of veterans."

Former President Jimmy Carter had created two new cabinet agencies, those of Education and Energy. His successor had complained about the expansion of government, but in November 1987, Ronald Reagan nevertheless spoke favorably of the idea of a Department of Veterans Affairs. Cosponsored in the House by about 200 members, the bill quickly was cleared by the House Government Operations Committee and then by the full House in December by a vote of 399 to 17.

Throughout the remainder of the year, and for much of the next, the V.A.-to-cabinet move continued to be debated in Congress and the press.

V

Volunteerism, the energy source that long had powered Legion programs, was the focus of attention at the Washington Conference from February 28 to March 2, 1988. In an era when an administration insisted on less responsibility by the federal government for many human service programs, Commission Chairman W. F. Lenker spoke of "the values of mutual helpfulness that were rallying points when the organization was in its infancy." The chairman's observation could have been lifted from nearly any of the presentations delivered by his predecessors over the past several decades.

"Faced with ever increasing attacks and attempts to whittle away at the benefits and programs established to aid this nation's veterans, it is now more important than ever to remain vigilant." Specifically, Lenker pointed to a proposed cut in medical personnel at the V.A., and to the nursing shortage nationwide that also affected the medical care of veterans.

The Veterans Planning and Coordinating Committee, too, would issue more recommendations in 1988 for action regarding the threats to the V.A. loan program. The committee called on the National Economic Commission to draft suggestions on how the V.A. should deal with the matter. Stressing the timeliness of the issue, the committee pointed to S. 2049, which sought to establish a nine-member commission to look at the financial problems of the Loan Guarantee Revolving Fund. The administration, also, as part of the planned 1989 budget, had proposed a review and reevaluation of the loan program.

The Winter Conference also contributed to the V.A.-to-cabinet agency scenario when the more than 1,000 persons attending were urged to meet with their senators to ask for passage of S. 533 to advance the V.A. to cabinet-level status.

Hearings by the Senate committee on the bill began later in March. A Legion initiative at that point convinced national officers that the Legion advanced the V.A.-to-cabinet agency cause significantly. On March 28 there was a move to kill a measure for creating a Department of Veterans Affairs by attaching a judicial review amendment to it. In response, National Commander John "Jake" Comer attended a hearing on the matter accompanied by one hundred Legionnaires to register Legion opposition to the spoiler amendment. As in the past, the Legion presence impressed the politicians with yet another show of solidarity among voters from the home states of the members of the Senate Government Affairs Committee. A Legion "legislative alert" had been declared, and Comer had orchestrated the large group appearance of Legionnaires from the thirteen-state constituency of Committee members.

At least two Legionnaires recognizable to each of the senators involved attended the hearings, along with fifty or more from departments surrounding the nation's capital who came to swell the group to an impressive presence. The senators indeed noticed. An aide to Committee Chairman John Glenn (D., OH) acknowledged that, indeed, the Legion made its point.

That month, National Commander Comer had met with Senator Glenn, chairman of the Senate Governmental Affairs Committee, and publicly promised the committee chairman that the Legion would reevaluate its position on judicial review (the matter that had been attached to the V.A. bill and to which amendment the Legion objected).

The Legion preferred a revamping of the V.A.'s Board of Veterans Appeals. But those who still insisted on "pure" judicial review had sought consistently to have the matter attached to surefire legislation for elevating the V.A. to a cabinet department.

As National Commander Comer had promised Senator Glenn, the Legion pondered its long-standing opposition to judicial review. (The decision that would soon come out of the May 1988 N.E.C. meeting was to support an independent board of appeals; furthermore, if there was to be federal court review, it should be of V.A. regulations, not of individual veteran cases.)

Two bills were before the Senate committee currently. While one bill addressed the matter of the fee, another sought to establish a new board of veterans appeals that would function outside and be independent from the V.A., a concept that the Legion could support wholeheartedly. The same bill included a provision for judicial review of claims rules and regulations of the V.A., another Legion desire.

Those such as Senator Alan Simpson (R., WY), who supported judicial review, continued to complain that the "professional veterans" often made presumptions about representing all veterans in such matters and had even "cozied up" to the V.A. to "preserve an old system" threatened by straightforward judicial review.

Legion lobbyists, however, urged that for the present the Senate committee should encourage increased funding for the V.A.'s claims procedure, particularly for the hiring of more qualified hearing officers to meet the growing demand for their services.

An April ruling by the Supreme Court had invited even more debate on the matter of judicial review. By a 4 to 3 decision (with two justices not taking part), the court ruled that the V.A. could consider alcoholism as "willful misconduct" and therefore withhold certain benefits from some veterans for whom that problem, it was said, was not caused by a psychiatric disorder. (V.A. hospital treatment of alcoholics was not affected, however, by the high court's ruling. A case before the court involved a veteran who had asked for an extension of V.A. educational benefits that he had not used within the ten-year period because of alcoholism.)

The Legion disagreed with the ruling, believing first that the V.A. should not withhold benefits from veterans who had not met time schedules because of some disability, whatever the disability, and second, that alcoholism should not invariably be ruled "willful misconduct."

Spokesmen for doctors and other medical professionals echoed the Legion's contention, similarly complaining that though Justice Harry A. Blackmun, in writing the minority opinion, had assumed that the ruling with which he disagreed did not put the court on record as deciding whether alcoholism was a disease, the view of the majority of justices nevertheless would likely influence the issue in the future.

The 69th National Convention meeting in San Antonio the previous fall had resolved that V.A. head Thomas Turnage remove the label "willful misconduct" from claims involving alcoholism. Failing that, legislation should be passed to effect the same result, the convention had said.

The promise that the Legion would give judicial review its full attention, and the argument that judicial review deserved consideration as a separate issue rather than being tacked on to the V.A.-cabinet bill, was honored by Senator Glenn, who convened a committee session on April 14 to mark up the bill. The Senate bill, which had sixty-five cosponsors representing bipartisan support, and now with the "killer" amendment quashed, was approved by the Senate committee for action on the Senate floor.

Convinced that their lobbying and media blitz had worked, Legion national officers watched as S. 533 went to the full Senate, where those who had attempted earlier to attach judicial review to the bill were determined to continue to do so especially now that the bill seemed sure of being passed.

The debate continued, but in June the Senate agreed to treat the V.A. bill and judicial review separately. S. 533 was brought before the full Senate in July. Still wary that a judicial review amendment might be added during the floor debate, National Commander Comer kept alive the "alert" status on this subject.

During the summer the House and Senate worked out differences in the respective versions of the legislation. On July 12 the Senate passed its version of the bill, which had been approved by the House eight months earlier. To those who continued to voice opposition to the elevation of the V.A., National Commander Comer offered an alliterative retort: Congress had "ignored the bankrupt bleatings of a few who would deny veterans their earned place in the executive branch."

Success, it seemed, was in sight.

While legislation for creating a Department of Veterans Affairs in the cabinet continued to be debated, the national commander in June 1988 joined his counterparts in the Disabled American Veterans and the Veterans of Foreign Wars to express "increasing frustration" with the V.A. chief for not remedying management and funding problems in the agency's Department of Medicine and Surgery and poor service delivery by the regional offices (the V.A.R.O.s).

The joint letter of protest referred to V.A. head Turnage's "continuous accolades" about an "all's well" condition, calling such statements merely "an extension of O.M.B. [Office of Management and Budget] rhetoric." The recurring disagreement over statistics regarding the availability of patient beds was included again as well, not only out of long-standing contention, but this time because it was charged by the chiefs of the veterans' organizations that Turnage's fiscal year 1989 budget called for 3,000 fewer beds than the congressionally mandated minimum number.

In the continuing move to cut costs, Turnage unrealistically was expecting V.A. facilities to do more with less, it was said. For example, it was charged that at the regional offices the work loads were increasing even while staffs had been cut a total of thirty-eight percent already in the ten years since 1978. National Commander Comer and the others called on Turnage to honor the provisions of the omnibus bill that had included many Legion objectives (and which had become Public Law 100-322 when enacted on May 20, 1988) for such things as facilitating travel and other amenities for veterans who sought medical care at V.A. facilities.

The large-scale view of the V.A. shifted quickly to that of a specific V.A. facility when on an official visit to a hospital in Des Moines National Commander Comer met head-on with an admissions policy allowing treatment only for service-connected disabilities.

Comer immediately protested to V.A. head Turnage, who ordered the end of the restriction at this facility and at the few other V.A. medical centers then operating under the same policy. Legion publicity staffers were quick to seize upon the commander's action, the stuff of which depictions of Legion clout were made.

While displeased to find the restriction in place apparently at "the whim of a hospital administrator," the national commander acknowledged that such a development may have resulted from orders from the V.A. born of budget woes. But the way to deal with that, Comer reiterated, was for the V.A. to submit budgets that did not require cutbacks of service.

Budgetary inadequacies impinged upon another Legion interest, the Veterans Job Training Act. National Economic Commission Chairman Bruce Thiesen called the congressional legerdemain of passing the act and then neglecting to fund it "outrageous." On the positive side, the National Veterans Training Institute had been funded as had the Local Veterans Employment Representative program; and some relief had been granted to state employment services. All these were priority items on the Economic Commission agenda.

A poignant consideration for the Rehab Commission and division in the late 1980s was ongoing controversy surrounding Agent Orange. Rehab volunteers and staffers worked on two fronts: the regulatory process along with the review conducted by an advisory committee on environmental hazards that had been set up by Congress in 1984, and, of course, the legislative process.

First came attempts to liberalize the regulations and rules used by the V.A. to determine what conditions might be caused by Agent Orange exposure and how such claims should be handled. For example, was the traditional doctrine of reasonable doubt being applied to these claims? Subsequent "improved" regulations did little to favorably impress Legion Rehab workers even after the May 1989 decision by Secretary of Veterans Affairs Edward Derwinski not to appeal a federal district court ruling in California that former regulations were too strict.

Second, Rehab workers sought to gain an audience with the congressionally established committee on environmental hazards, which in turn had been given the responsibility by the V.A. for reviewing and then establishing the proposed Agent Orange regulations. Rehab volunteers and staff questioned whether claimants had an understanding and receptive audience in the committee.

The very mention of an agenda for each of the national commissions signalled that the organization was doing something for veterans. That fact was an important one to project to keep members interested, confident, and actively involved. It was also essential for attracting new members.

After the steady increase of several thousand more members each year beginning in 1985, workers in the annual membership drives could more easily believe in a goal that soon came to be held up as a motif of the apparent trend: the number 3,000,000.

At the National Membership Workshop held in the summer of 1988, the "traditional membership recruiting goal," that composed of the expectations of posts across the land, an impressive but less poetic 2,771,469 members, was projected. Soon the three-million mark gained in believability, a round number that also lent itself more noticeably to banners and buttons.

The Direct Membership Solicitation (D.M.S.) program, initiated four years earlier (but based on tests as early as 1982) and credited at this point with bringing in 600,000 new members, was expected to bring in another quarter of a million members. Thus, "the three million membership goal is a realistic one," National Commander Comer told the 350 department, district, and post officers gathered to plan the 1989 membership campaign.

Membership workers were urged to employ both the "traditional" method—long relied upon personal contact—and D.M.S. in their pursuit of members. They were also reminded that members coming in through D.M.S. needed to be brought along from the paper "holding" posts, to which they had been assigned upon joining, to actual posts where they could join their counterparts in Legion activities.

To help new members understand and appreciate Legion activities, membership campaigners could point to the encouraging view to be found in the 1988 Consolidated Post Reports. Those posts reporting had raised collectively a total of more than $41 million for community projects of their own, and had contributed more than $7.1 million during the 1987–88 membership year in helping other charity organizations to raise money.

Here then was proof that there were thousands of active posts (if only a tally of some fifty-three percent of those in existence) engaged in projects for their communities, a traditional activity. It was also proof that was most noticeable to the largest number of people and that therefore could appreciably determine its influence when it came to taking a stand on other important issues of the day. Here, too, was a membership drive appeal: join an organization that had clout in the nation's capital and at statehouses.

Another post activity of long duration, and closest to the heart of the organization, was that of the service officer. Seldom before had the services offered by service officers from the post to department level been needed more than when in late August 1988 it was noted that there was an alarming increase in "remanded" veteran disability claims, those sent back by the V.A. in Washington to the regional office of origin because of insufficient information or incomplete preparation.

Those active in this work observed that the "class of '46," the V.A. regional office workers who first came to work after World War II, were now largely retired or winding up their careers, and newer staff persons, it was said, who were now joining the relatively smaller staffs resulting from budget cuts were not functioning with the same competence as had their predecessors.

American Legion service officers were the first to observe the complaint recurring nationwide. Their observations became the substance of documented evidence for testimony before the House Veterans Affairs Committee in late summer 1988.

The national convention in Louisville, Kentucky, in 1988 elected its first "V-Vet" national commander, a justice of the North Dakota Supreme Court, H. F. "Sparky" Gierke, III.

"The torch of leadership has been placed in the hands of a new generation of veterans," the new national commander told the delegates. "There's a new respect today in our nation for the men and women who served in Vietnam [who can now] stand tall and proud."

As a "first" among his peers, Gierke would be closely observed for signs of bias toward his generation of citizen-soldiers. The organization for which he would serve as most visible spokesman for a year still had a vigorous majority of World War II Legionnaires. That point was made when the customary convention blood drive went over the top for the Louisville Regional Blood Center, with 163 pints of blood (the goal had been 150 pints) in two days after an upper age limit had been eliminated. The blood drive coordinator had found that potential donors in their late sixties were in good health and eager to participate (vigor for which the estimated 500 eventual blood recipients also would be thankful).

A few weeks later, National Commander Gierke made his first appearance before Congress and presented the archetypical Legion viewpoint concerning veterans' rehab matters. His testimony included instances of travail of two veterans, one from World War II and one from the Vietnam War, both in desperate need of V.A. help that had been diminished, he charged, by recent directives decreasing the number of hospital beds in use and the number of medical staff persons.

The National Commander emphasized a few areas of most concern: improvements needed in the process of V.A. claims and appeals; the need for more AIDS research money; the understaffing of the V.A. Department of Veterans Benefits; and the problems of aging veterans.

Senate committee member Alan Simpson (R., WY) called the national commander's presentation too dramatic and an overstatement of the problems at the V.A. But Senator Dennis DeConcini (D., AZ) complimented Gierke's "powerful, strong statement" about the unmet needs of veterans.

The spotlight of Legion attention was again focused on the Hill when after delaying the adjournment of the 100th Congress for more than a week, there was a flourish of passed bills, three of which were Legion-backed measures now being sent to the president for his signature. Specifically, in one day, October 18, the Senate advanced bills to make the V.A. a cabinet department, to reform the veterans' appeals process, and to grant a C.O.L.A. increase for V.A. compensation and pension recipients. With Veterans Day intervening, all three measures were signed by the president before Thanksgiving Day.

Also, the new Department of Veterans Affairs was launched when a presidential signature created Public Law 100-527 on October 25, 1988. The new department was slated to begin operation on January 1, 1989.

Similarly, the Judicial Review Act of 1988, which had been drafted by the American Legion, created a new process for appealing decisions by the V.A.'s Board of Veteran Appeals. The act contained the Legion's concept of such a procedure, specifically, the creation of an independent specialty court, the Court of Veterans Appeals, which would review the judgments of the V.A.'s Board of Veteran Appeals when that procedure was challenged by individual veterans. And the act contained another point of law that the Legion had stressed—that the federal court system did have jurisdiction over V.A. regulations.

Finally, the Veterans' Benefits Improvement Act of 1988 (actually combined with the Judicial Review Act) added a 4.1 percent C.O.L.A. to the compensation of some 2.2 million service-connected disabled veterans.

VI

The seventieth year of the Legion in 1989 would also mark a forty-two-year membership enrollment record.

The membership drive was a major emphasis of National Commander "Sparky" Gierke's year. A series of awards and pins identified the recipients as being go-getters among membership recruiters.

Those attending the Washington Conference in February were handed pennants bearing "3,000,000" and were feted to a Big Ten–like pep rally led by the George Washington University pep band. University cheerleaders urged them to new efforts in reaching the goal of three million members.

The conferees also heard the first-ever Secretary-designate of Veterans Affairs, Edward J. Derwinski, speak of the "hard choices" facing him in a era of budgetary constraints. Speaking frankly, the new secretary (he would be confirmed as such on March 3) indicated that veterans would not be a "priority group" when the new cabinet department competed with other agencies for funding. Derwinski, a former long-time congressman and a life member of the Legion, welcomed the Legion's efforts for veterans, but was judged as being "pessimistic" by many who heard him speak about the potential for supplemental funding for the agency he had been nominated to head.

While the spirited activity of the membership drive was under way, the proposed V.A. budget for fiscal year 1990 brought some of the sharpest criticism in many years from the Legion. Enormous sum that it was, the $30 billion requested for medical care, compensation, and other V.A. programs was not enough, Legion spokesmen said. Even though the budget included $112 million for building a new medical center, the first such planned in a decade, there were impending employment cuts at the V.A., a likely 5,000 in number, it was said, and shortfalls likely to occur in the current fiscal year. Even the increase of $185.8 million for medical care paled beside the funding deficiencies of which the Legion complained.

There was also the matter of indexing cost-of-living adjustments for veterans' disability compensation to the Consumer Price Index in such a way as to make the increases automatic rather than be passed by Congress each year.

Legion lobbyists in their testimony tied compensation C.O.L.A.s to the Consumer Price Index or to Social Security to achieve comparable increases for veterans. But they had been instructed to resist the creation of any automatic mechanism to bring that about, because periodic legislation that contained C.O.L.A.s for disability compensation sometimes presented opportunities for additional provisions that the Legion wanted but that otherwise might not find favor at the White House.

Attached to the cost of living adjustment bill, which the president was unlikely to veto, such provisions stood a better chance of survival. C.O.L.A.s made to occur automatically, however, meant lost lobbying opportunities for the Legion.

The user's fee for V.A.-guaranteed home loans was also still a sore point. The 1990 budget not only proposed retaining the fee but increasing it to 3.8 percent, a particularly objectionable move to those who already saw the fee as a case of the worst sort of double-dipping into the pockets of veterans.

Finally, among the chief complaints was still the means test, and, not far behind, the per diem rate in the proposed budget that would be required for nonservice-connected medical treatment. Category B and C veterans were already being required to pay for treatment based on the means test, it was charged, in such numbers as to greatly restrict their rightful medical benefits, some totally. A survey conducted for the Legion by an outside firm concluded that such was the case in numerous V.A. facilities.

What it came down to, Veterans Affairs and Rehab Director John F. Sommer told the House Veterans Affairs Committee in early February, was faulty anticipation by the V.A. about the services that would be required in the next year. The greatest concern was that decreased funding prescribed by Gramm-Rudman-Hollings was affecting the quality of medical care.

A few weeks later it was National Legislative Director E. Philip Riggin's turn to reiterate the growing, unabated concern of veterans' advocates over the funding problems of the V.A. There were reports now that even some nonservice-connected claimants in Category A were being turned away from V.A. health care. Riggin appealed for supplemental funds for the current year, an urgency that came ahead even of calls for greatly increased funds for 1990. Armed with figures for the relative increase of Medicare as being twice that expended for veterans' health care, Riggin pointed again to an ongoing Legion contention that funding for veterans' health care had not kept pace with federal spending generally for some time now. (Legion spokesmen were quick, however, to point out that in spite of constraints put on the V.A. since 1979, advances in efficiency had been made.)

Legion spokesmen and others from the medical education field spoke also of another problem related to the V.A.'s lack of funds. V.A. hospitals were sites where over half of the doctors trained in the United States each year spent part of their time earning their credentials. Medical school deans particularly expressed concern that V.A. hospitals that couldn't provide up-to-date equipment would greatly endanger the forty-year affiliation of the V.A. and medical schools, which had helped both veterans' medicine and medical education during that long period.

The findings of a survey by Legion field service representatives accompanying local service officers were handed to the House Veterans Affairs Committee in April, showing that in the opinion of 159 V.A. medical directors themselves, critical reductions would be made in both inpatient and outpatient treatment because of inadequate budgets. The deficiencies ran the gamut of medical care: delays in clinical appointments, less contract nursing home care, delays in surgery, reduction in pharmacy services, bed closures, and less money for equipment, supplies, and upkeep.

There was a move among governmental officials now, the Legion acknowledged, to appropriate stopgap funding. The administration was recommending $303 million to supplement the current budget; Secretary Derwinski had requested that the fiscal year 1990 budget be amended for $512 million more and had asked that the medical staff be increased by 5,093 personnel. The secretary also hoped that $85 million could be found to put into medical construction projects.

The Legion's Veterans Planning and Coordinating Committee (V.P.C.C.) met in mid-April at Washington, D.C., headquarters to hear the observations of several persons with first-hand knowledge of circumstances in V.A. facilities as well as from several decision makers in the upper echelons of the V.A. Thus from a state director of veterans affairs, a newly appointed chief judge of the new Court of Veterans Appeals, the deputy secretary of Veterans Affairs, and two who served as counsel to the House and Senate Veterans Affairs committees, the Legion's V.P.C.C. heard a discouraging forecast of developments to come regarding V.A. services falling shy of adequate funding.

While hearing a continual litany of problems created by the lack of funds at the V.A., Legion rehab workers continued to be concerned about the aging veteran population. With nine and a half million World War II veterans comprising thirty-six percent of veterans nationwide, 5.8 million of these were over age sixty-five, a number that would grow to nine million by the year 2000. With additional statistics at hand projecting large numbers of aging veterans who would suffer from one or more chronic diseases, the burden on the V.A. in the future was readily apparent.

More V.A. nursing home facilities were needed, rehab workers said, and more provisions for research and treatment of Alzheimer's disease patients. A Geriatric Research, Education, and Clinical Center should be established at each of the V.A.'s ten medical centers. (Another fifteen centers had been authorized but not funded.)

The Veterans Affairs and Rehab Commission called for the V.A. to develop a long-term plan for medical care of an aging veteran population. It was particularly important to acknowledge that older persons typically suffered from multiple types of illnesses rather than just one malady, often a combination of acute conditions occurring even while chronic conditions were being treated. There was not sufficient indication, the Legion said, that the V.A. system at present anticipated the increased personnel, patient treatment time, and inpatient treatment availability required by older veterans afflicted with the problems just described.

In this regard, the categorization of veterans by the means test, and the subsequent turning away of Category B and C veterans and even some A's, further concerned rehab workers. How would such refusals of medical care affect the health of veterans, and what alternative care would they be able to acquire? These and other questions were to be addressed by the Legion's Veterans Medical Care Task Force, a special committee appointed by National Commander "Sparky" Gierke to study the long-term impact of veterans being turned away from V.A. medical care.

When the N.E.C. met in May 1989, the subject of the sharing agreements that had been in operation for some time between V.A. and Department of Defense medical facilities came in for question when it appeared that actual mergers might be in the works as yet another means for reducing the cost of veterans' medicine.

The N.E.C. also heard Dr. Harry N. Beaty, M.D., professor of medicine and dean of the Northwestern University Medical School, tell what budget problems meant for the forty-year-old affiliation of 103 of the 172 V.A. hospitals with medical schools, a system in which this well-known specialist in internal medicine and infectious diseases had served as a trainee during his own medical education. In particular, Dr. Beaty called the status of the V.A. health care system no less than "a crisis situation" that, having developed over a long period of time, was not likely to be solved quickly.

Dr. Beaty had served as spokesman for the Association of American Medical School Deans before congressional hearings after a highly unfavorable report in early 1988 by the House Oversight Committee, which charged V.A. inaccuracy in reporting health care needs in the system. While appearing before a Senate committee the previous September, Dr. Beaty had heard several V.A. hospital personnel tell of the extent of operating deficits at their facilities. This testimony by others confirmed that Dr. Beaty's observations were not unique to the V.A. hospital with which he was most familiar. He was, he said, only repeating what these V.A. personnel themselves had testified to a situation of crisis.

Dr. Beaty listed several facets of the crisis: inadequate funding for, among other things, high-quality diagnostic equipment; the "woeful" shortage of "major ambulatory care centers"; the age of many facilities; the shortage of nurses; and the problem of attracting "high-quality physicians" because of lower wages at the V.A.

Dr. Beaty recommended that "something be done to test the hypothesis that the V.A. is too large in inpatient capacity and too small in outpatient capacity." This, of course, indicated a major restructuring of the V.A. system. But for the moment, "I hear more [medical school] deans saying . . . they are worried about their ability to continue to educate the future health care physicians and also the allied health providers in this country in some of the V.A. hospitals."

This particular medical school dean was making his point, of course, before the organization that had done much in 1946 to see that the affiliation of medical schools and V.A. hospitals came about. Now it was apparent that that arrangement for tying medical education to veterans' medicine was being hampered as well in the "crisis" situation at the V.A.

The first action in response to Dr. Beaty's first-hand view was for Rehab staffers to develop a liaison with the Association of American Medical Colleges, located in Washington, D.C., to seek specific improvements that should be made in the V.A. medical care program relating particularly to this time-tested, essential "affiliation."

Though discouraging chords like the observations about the budget shortfalls at the V.A. and the ramifications on veterans' rehab would be sounded in 1989, there were interludes of encouragement about the Legion's own vitality.

By March 9, thirty-three departments had exceeded the ninety percent mark of their negotiated membership goals for the year. As the campaign continued, National Headquarters' membership marketing personnel visited several departments to exchange ideas about recruiting. In July a special D.M.S. letter brought in another 70,000 new members. The "Gold Brigade," those who had signed up fifty or more new members, numbered 256 in late July. The latest D.M.S. appeal was accompanied by a request to sign the Legion's petition drive for a constitutional amendment banning flag desecration, an appeal that was proving to be popular across the nation.

The magic number 3,000,000 was reached just days before the delegates to the 71st National Convention were to convene in Baltimore in early September. In an atmosphere sure to spawn confidence, National Commander Gierke spoke of what larger membership rolls meant to the services the organization could offer to veterans and the nation. "Through our programs of service to God and country, the American Legion will reach out to more of our fellow citizens than ever before."

It was more than a good intention, Gierke promised. "It is no mere coincidence that the American Legion has a pattern of growth in its various program areas in the same period that its membership has climbed to 3,000,000."

Legionnaires looked to the national convention in Baltimore to provide some indication of the place a growing Legion would have in the 1990s.

EPILOGUE

WALKING THE POINT

Citizens-soldiers of WWI had been thrust from dank trenches and into combat by the soul-piercing command to "go over the top." After the war they were bid by the same words to come to the aid of less fortunate veterans and their dependents, and to fight radicalism, by joining the new American Legion.

Delegates to the 71st National Convention of The American Legion in early September 1989 elected as National Commander Vietnam veteran Miles S. Epling. Standing at the podium in the Baltimore Convention Center, Epling knew the effort and the hazards of acting on a command similar to the one which during WWI had animated the founders of the organization he now headed. This Marine Corps infantryman who was now chief spokesman for the world's largest veterans' organization was familiar with a different command to action: he invited the Legion to "walk the point."

With the thousands around him, Epling had witnessed earlier the impressive opening ceremony of the 71st National Convention celebrating the reaching, and passing by more than 10,000, of the three million member goal, the largest enrollment since 1948. Outgoing National Commander Gierke had led Department and District Commanders and other membership recruiters into the main convention hall amidst flags, 10,000 balloons, and the rousing cheers of Legionnaires.

The National Convention had convened not far from historic Ft. McHenry where in September 1814, Francis Scott Key was moved to write "The Star Spangled Banner" upon seeing a tattered American flag still waving after British ships had bombarded the fort. The traditional Legion parade which drew an estimated 250,000 onlookers, said to be the largest number to attend such an event in the city's history, was replete with the familiar red, white, and blue banner of the United States of America.

For many years the Legion's Americanism program had served as a clearinghouse for Federal Flag Code-based etiquette regarding the display and care of the Stars and Stripes. National Americanism Commission publications on the subject had been distributed widely and were relied upon as authoritative at schools and other public institutions and by private citizens. When on June 21 the Supreme Court reversed a Texas court conviction of one who burned a flag at the 1984 Republican National Convention, The American Legion was poised to react. Within days of the high court's ruling, the Legion had called for an amendment to the Constitution banning flag desecration. Anything less, it was believed, would soon be ruled unconstitutional based on the wide ranging nature of the Supreme Court decision.

Readily recognizing political expression as a form of protected speech, the Legion emphasized an essential difference between public speaking and the flag burning action which sparked the controversy surrounding the recent Supreme Court ruling. The Legion pointed out that First Amendment rights certainly were not unlimited. For example, there were long-standing laws prohibiting the destruction of public property and mailboxes, and those prohibiting child pornography, libel, and the inciting of riots.

Hours before the opening of the convention, National Commander Gierke had handed Congressional leaders petitions bearing more than a million signatures supporting a Constitutional amendment banning flag desecration. Soon after the June 21 Supreme Court ruling the Legion commissioned a Gallup poll the findings of which were announced at a news conference on August 31. More than seventy percent of those polled favored a Constitutional amendment. The thirty-two Legion departments which had held state conventions after the Supreme Court ruling adopted resolutions for amending the Constitution. National Americanism Resolution 355 when brought before the national convention received a unanimous "aye" vote mandating an amendment for protecting the flag, the symbol of all the freedoms the nation enjoyed. More than 8,000 phone calls making the same point (and reportedly closing down the Congressional switchboard twice) were placed in two days from a phone bank at the Convention Center to congressmen and senators. Before President Bush, who favored a Constitutional amendment, appeared on the stage of the convention he was presented with the Legion's petition and the results of the Gallup poll in a private meeting with the national commander.

Though effective in attracting attention to the flag issue, the Legion's imaginative campaign as reported in the print and electronic media was often played against an amorphous opposition from which, unlike the Legion, there came no recommendations for specific action to be taken by the federal government.

Congress did appear to favor going on record to protect the flag but chose instead to pursue a statute, unwilling, it was said, to oppose the prevailing media blitz even though some of the statute's most ardent supporters were heard to question its constitutionality. The Legion agreed that a statute, in the certainty of its being tested, was sure to follow the fate of the Texas court ruling.

In countering the argument of some congressmen who had supported the new federal statute (which had come into being without the President's signature) based on the Supreme Court ruling and who said that the amending process would take too long, Legion spokesmen predicted that within a year such a measure likely could be ratified by the requisite number of states. Since forty-eight states had specifically proscribed flag desecration, which in those domains formerly would have brought statutory penalties, the Supreme Court decision of June 21 and the resulting statute had made an almost nationwide review of such laws a certainty.

To those in Congress and elsewhere who said the Constitution was too sacred to be tampered with, the Legion pointed out that it had been amended twenty-six times. Furthermore, with four other amendments currently pending in Congress, the serious attempts to amend the honored document were not as uncommon as some would have it appear.

Looking first to the involvement of every Legion Division and Commission for a massive grassroots lobbying effort, the Legion would then look to state legislatures to encourage Congress to reconsider its position and to see to a Constitutional amendment. That was not an unlikely expectation; the Legion had accomplished much from grassroot lobbying. With 16,000 Legion posts around the nation and with membership gains being made, Legionnaires could be expected to lobby statehouses which in turn would send a message to the nation's Capitol calling for an amendment.

A pre-Convention Open Forum on Vietnam Veterans Health Issues had aired the views of a panel of health experts about exposure to Agent Orange and about Post-traumatic Stress Disorder. At the VA&R Commission-sponsored event, Drs. Jeanne and Steven Stellman, the health scientists who headed the combined American Legion/Columbia University study of Vietnam veterans, reiterated their view that the study was scientifically sound in spite of criticism from the Centers for Disease Control.

The Rehab Commission and Division had worked with Representative Lane Evans (IL), Co-chairman of the Vietnam Veterans in Congress Caucus, who with Representative Martin Lancaster (NC) introduced on July 25 a bill (H.R. 30004) to greatly clarify the matter of exposure to Agent Orange and the rehab benefits to be received.

The flight of H.R. 30004 was short-lived, however. Not long after a Legion news conference when the bill was introduced at which Admiral Elmo Zumwalt (later named as a V.A. senior advisor on the matter of Agent Orange exposure) and others who supported the bill appeared along side National Commander Gierke, Representative G. V. "Sonny" Montgomery, Chairman of the House Veterans Affairs Committee, issued a "dear colleague" letter calling the bill premature and otherwise unsatisfactory.

The day after the close of the Baltimore National Convention, Rehab Division personnel, along with legal counsel and a leading toxicologist, Dr. Ellen Silverguild, met with an advisory committee on environmental hazards which had been established by Congress in 1984 to review scientific studies to determine for the V.A. what conditions had been caused by Agent Orange. Disappointed that there was not more official recognition of the problems involved in Agent Orange exposure, the Legionnaires also stated the Legion's objections to the current rules and regulations of the V.A. relating to Agent Orange claims.

The VA&R Commission and Division would continue to work to resolve the various differences of opinion about Agent Orange exposure. When the V.A. announced it was awaiting yet another study, due out in March 1990, National Commander Epling objected. "Sufficient studies have already been conducted. It's time for action," he said. Some of that action came soon with the call by the Human Resources and Inter-governmental Relations subcommittee of the House Government Operations Committee for full disclosure of the records of a White House working group's review of Agent Orange effects on veterans. VA&R spokesmen hailed the move by the House subcommittee.

When the National Executive Committee convened at its fall meeting in October, the membership rolls contained a record 3,011,754. With an increase of 172,112 over the previous year's membership, 1989 was the fifth year in a row of growth. The Direct Membership Solicitation program had brought in 266,513 new Legionnaires during the 1989 membership year. Begun in 1982 and called the most cost effective way of attracting new members other than the traditional and more personal means, D.M.S. was being credited with over 900,000 new members since then. Already in mid-October the new membership year had achieved a count of 1,655,854 which was 233,021 more than the count during the same month the year before. Two DMS "mail drops" during the summer had brought in over 170,000 new members. The DMS goal for 1990 of 210,000 new members was expected to be achieved by March 1, 1990.

At the October 1989 N.E.C. meeting, the Committeemen met once again to review the wide-ranging interests and concerns of The American Legion. The National Economic Commission pondered the subject of employment for older workers, particularly the financial strictions placed on those sixty-five years and older who returned to the workplace, as well as the over 1,700 cases reported by Service Officers around the country of veterans who had sold homes which they bought through the V.A. Home Loan Guaranty program only to find later that they had not been released from liability on the loans. Commission testimony on that matter had been presented to the House Sub-committee on Housing and Memorial Affairs in late September.

In October, the National Veterans Affairs and Rehabilitation Commission considered developments relating to the means test being applied to veterans requesting V.A. medical care. At the time of its enactment, Commission reports referred to the test as boding the end of veteran medical care as it had been known previously. They objected particularly to the categorization of veterans which was the basis for the application of the "test." Now it was charged that the deductible which category C veterans paid to get medical care did not cover the cost to apply the means test, categorize the claimants, and do the billing.

The Task Force on Veterans' Medical Care gave its final report to the Committeemen on "the health status and the demographic and economic characteristics of veterans turned away from V.A. health care, and [on] the alternate sources of health care used by these veterans." While it was acknowledged in the report that longer-term studies of larger groups should be done, the point was made, however, that many veterans "are undergoing minor to significant financial and emotional burdens due to being cut off from V.A. medical care."

That conclusion had been based on a sample of 101 voluntary veteran responses from thirteen departments during July to September (sixty-four discharged from V.A. outpatient rolls; thirty-seven first visit denials). Some were seen to be eligible for medicare but were without the means to get supplemental insurance coverage. Similarly, few who had lost or been denied V.A. care were successful in receiving private sector health care. It was also found that there were still some veterans who had never bothered to establish a V.A. disability claim, even though the evidence indicated that they were eligible, because they assumed that they could always use V.A. medical facilities when needed. That, it was said, had been a safe enough assumption for many only *before* the means test had been instituted. Now medical care was not so assured.

The VA&R report also included an update on the status of the new Court of Veterans Appeals which had come about with the new judicial review law and for which the chief judge and two associate judges had been nominated by the President and confirmed by the Senate. The Legion had decided not to represent veterans before the Court, disagreeing with, among other things, the Court's self-imposed limitation of what kinds of claims to consider.

Committeemen hearing the report of the National Magazine Commission might have recalled that even before the first National Convention in November 1919, the Legion had braved the publishing challenge of producing a weekly magazine to popularize the Legion as an organization with a distinct way of thinking about veterans rehabilitation. Now seventy years later, *The American Legion Magazine*, successor to that bold, earlier (and at times financially broke) publishing venture, was still the Legion's major print means to present the Legion point of view in articles about significant events affecting the nation's defenses and other matters, and in editorials and depictions of Legionism in action as in the "Veterans Update" page.

For the Magazine Commission, the goal was the same as when *The American Legion Weekly* had been introduced seven decades earlier. Now, however, the organization had a median membership age of 60.1 years (and with 41.4 percent of the membership employed full-time) but had nearly a million Vietnam veterans and apparently many more willing to join. *Magazine* editors worked to make the Legion's chief print voice relevant to this diverse audience.

During this Fall 1989 gathering of the National Executive Committee, members of the Foreign Relations and the National Security Commissions viewed a Department of Defense video presentation on Soviet military power. They heard again the message of caution, such as that heard at the recent National Convention by Admiral William J. Crowe, Chairman of the Joint Chiefs of Staff, concerning what interpretations to apply to recent apparent changes in the Russian military posture. The National Security Commission issued its own warning: "We are on the verge of unilaterally reacting to rhetoric and promises which have yet to be enacted." Even as Russia orchestrated the appearance of retreating to a strictly defensive posture, the situation, nevertheless, required close observation, it was said.

The Commission was particularly concerned that congressional action to resolve the differences in the House and the Senate versions of the 1990 D.O.D. appropriations bill then being considered by "an unpredictable" congressional conference committee might reduce strategic programs involving the B-2 Stealth Bomber, the Mobile Missile

Systems, and the Strategic Defense Initiative. "Now is not the time to let our guard down," the Commission admonished.

The time-honored and hearty recitation of the Legion "Preamble" at the N.E.C. meeting in October 1989 proved the durability of the founders' determination. Seventy years earlier, a concept had been introduced to the Paris Caucus and immediately accepted. It had been affirmed and then defined more clearly at the St. Louis Caucus. Refined at a cold winter convention in Minneapolis, the concept emerged as high-minded, trend-setting volunteerism thereafter impressively productive on behalf of the welfare of veterans, their dependents, and the nation in general.

Now, in the fall of 1989, as the founders' successors met once again as the essential National Executive Committee, it appeared certain that the "basics" would continue to be pursued in these surroundings and with resources only at best imagined by the young men who first met in Minneapolis.

In the final days of the seventh decade after its founding and encouraged by forty-year record membership rolls, the Legion was addressing issues to which Legionism was compelled to speak. Not the least of these was the spate of astonishing events in Eastern Europe where communist governments were being swept away in waves of protest, the first acts of self-determination in decades for the oppressed who now demanded freedoms which Americans had enjoyed for two hundred years.

Soon also, from the Soviet Union, wracked by ethnic protest, economic woes, and a dispirited political scene, would come proposals by President Mikhail Gorbachev for the drastic reordering of a political system which had terrorized a nation for decades and which had dictated a costly defense posture of the United States for nearly that long. In truly a new era of international relations, the Legion "basic" of strong national defense would be pondered by the increasing number of Legionnaires who recalled the Vietnam era along with those who had seen service in the last world war and in Korea. Together they would seek some meaning, and focus their sense of responsibility while observing yet another of the all's-quiet phenomena that historically accompanied the easing of tensions among opposing forces.

With the coming of the new year 1990, the Legion would look to a national convention in Indianapolis, the first ever in the Headquarters city, to continue to demonstrate a continuation of Legionism bolstered now with an encouraging membership upswing.

Several of the program tools with which the Legion now worked to meet present challenges in veterans rehabilitation and, in general, the public enlightenment regarding Legion ideals, were founded not only in the revered "basics" but were made possible by fiscal sagacity.

In particular, the Finance Commission, the only constitutional commission (all others had been created by the N.E.C.), had succeeded most notably in the previous dozen or more years in performing perhaps the toughest of all jobs in the organization—maintaining an essential resource and, in a fast-changing environment, allocating it for the furtherance of Legion goals. Led by immediate past chairmen Churchill T. Williams and Walton Griffin and current Chairman George W. Boucek, the Commission had been bold and brave enough to back several innovations.

Thus the success of the Direct Mail Solicitation program could be credited to an outlay of funds, as could a new educational loan program, and even the popular Convention Festival event, to name but three of recent origin, which owed their existence to Finance Commissions in which was combined an appreciation of the historical perspective along with foresight to concur in program-investments for the Legion's future. Insiders would also point to the work of two groups of recent origin which had done much to help bring the collective resources of the Legion to bear on matters of concern.

The Veterans Planning and Coordinating Committee, chaired by the national commander, for example, had convened expertise and influence essential to decisively and effectively move Legion initiatives and programs forward in the areas of aging veterans, the judicial review, alternative health care, educational scholarships, and the doctor and nurse shortage at V.A. medical centers, to name but a few.

Composed of the chairmen of national commissions (VA&R, Economics, Legislative, Public Relations) along with one National Executive Committeeman and a member of the Department Adjutants' Group, the V.P.C.C. also profited, on behalf of the Legion as a whole, by the aid of three advisory committees for medical, legal, and economic matters. Each of these committees included persons chosen for their present and active vantage in the area of essential expertise.

Similarly, the Policy Coordination and Action Group, formed by the N.E.C. during the tenure of PNC James Dean and which includes the commission chairmen of National Security, Foreign Relations, Americanism, and Public Relations along with other National Executive Committeemen, Past National Commanders and representatives of the Adjutants' Group, had been established to review Legion policies regarding national security, foreign relations, and immigration. Organized during the period of growing concern about events in Central America and bolstered, like the V.P.C.C., by star-studded advisory groups, P.C.A.G. had recommended policies to the various commissions, in general seeking to focus the Legion's advocacy for a strong, secure America along the lines of the historic Monroe Doctrine.

To gather the needed first-hand information for such an advocacy, P.C.A.G. at one point had been divided into three teams and sent to three areas of Central America on fact finding missions. What was learned in this manner was shared in a debriefing with U.S. State Department officials and soon also by Legion position papers presented in various forums and formats, and presented in person to President Reagan. In the process, Legion policy recommendations regarding Central America were formulated and publicized in a manner which the Legion hoped would engender serious consideration by government officials and the general voting population as well.

That tendency to coordinate activities, to strengthen the communication among national commissions in particular, was said now to be best exemplified by these two coordinating groups. The founders had not only practiced such openness but had organized the Legion to thrive on it. But there had been periods in the history of the organization when the pursuit of programs were channeled along lines of bailiwicks instead of those of clear and complete communication. That had to be changed. The era of the 1990s, with lightning-speed electronic communications, not only invited such a move but unreservedly required it.

So, efforts were going forth to make the basic machinery of the Legion work smoothly. The increase in membership did much to enthuse the paid staff and to revitalize the long-standing volunteers as well as convince others of more recent association that Legion programs were worth maintaining and were worth all the volunteer time required.

When looking for the health signs of their organization, some sought indications beyond the encouraging membership numbers, such as what some called the "pointers": the numbers of young people participating in Legion posts-sponsored Boy Scout troops, American Legion Junior Baseball, the Oratorical Contest, the Legion's scholarships, and the other activities that animate the consolidated post reports with vital signs of life and spontaneity.

To the traditional "pointers" soon would be added another public-service initiative: an impressive expansion on the Americanism, Children and Youth Division's long-running "Need-A-Lift" directory respected and used by school counselors across the nation for locating scholarships and educational loans, was expanded dramatically.

A new, cooperative program was announced in late February 1990 whereby the Legion joined the nationally known United Student Aid Funds, Inc., underwriters of student loans, and the Indianapolis-based INB banking institution for the start-up phase of the Legion's Education Assistance Program to be introduced in five states with a $5 million initial fund for educational loans. Thus the Legion's 40th annual edition of "Need-A-Lift," and USA Funds' "Options Four" assistance program (private signature, fourth option, loans after the traditional sources of parents, schools, and government loans), would be combined in a "total information" package and backed by funds of INB for those who needed financial assistance for higher education. Before, the

"Need-A-Lift" directory had been a handbook for educational assistance. The new combined, cooperative program would back that wealth of information with actual loans.

Earlier, relief grant applications were solicited by The American Legion National Emergency Fund for "Legion family" victims of Hurricane Hugo and the California earthquake to whom insurance and local emergency relief funds were no longer available. "All the pointers are up," one said. "We are back to our precepts. And as long as our focus is external and not merely internal, we will thrive."

There was a new luster, it appeared, to being an American Legionnaire; a renewed resolve for what first had been recited seventy years earlier: "For God and Country, we associate ourselves together. . . ."

A Note On Bibliographical Sources

The American Legion Library and Archives is an important special-collections repository with source materials relating to the history of the Legion and consequently to a wide range of topics in twentieth century American history. The service of three librarians (Verna B. Grimm, Thomas V. Hull, Joseph Hovish) has encompassed the seventy-year existence of the Legion Archives/Library. The centralized subject-category filing system established by Verna Grimm in the 1920's and which relates directly to the program areas, the "basics," of Legion activity, remains the method for filing materials in this repository.

In addition to correspondence and other ephemera, the Archives/Library contains collections of verbatim minutes of meetings and a wide range of Legion publications, from official proceedings to pamphlets and brochures. The Library also includes a select collection of post and department histories, a collection of books about WWI published soon after the war and many other titles of more recent publication, and works of general reference use.

In lieu of footnotes, the preceding text is keyed to record types and thence to their location in the Legion Archives. Thus, for example, the direct quotes used to indicate a Legion position or policy, if obviously derived from correspondence, can be found in the relevant Legion program subject files by date of utterance. Other quotes, if said to have occurred during a National Convention, National Executive Committee meeting or other gathering, can be found in the verbatim records of such meeting, or in the official printed proceedings. The remarks of more recent officials, particularly those of Past National Commanders, may be found in oral history transcripts. Statistical information, as well as being included often in the subject files, can also be found in the extensive commission, committee, sub-committee or special group report file for which full cross-referencing is underway.

APPENDIX

JOINT NATIONAL EXECUTIVE COMMITTEE OF THIRTY-FOUR

Henry D. Lindsley, Tex., Chairman
Bennett C. Clark, Mo., Vice-Chairman
Eric Fisher Wood, Pa., Secretary
Gaspar G. Bacon, N.Y., Treasurer
William S. Beam, N.C.
Charles H. Brent, N.Y.
William H. Brown, Conn.
G. Edward Buxton, Jr., R.I.
Richard Derby, N.Y.
Franklin D'Olier, Pa.
L. H. Evridge, Tex.
Milton J. Foreman, Ill.
Ruby D. Garrett, Mo.
Fred J. A. Griggith, Okla.
Roy C. Haines, Me.
John F. J. Herbert, Mass.
Roy Hoffman, Okla.
Fred B. Humphrey, N.M.
John W. Inzer, Ala.
Stuart S. Janney, Md.
Luke Lea, Tenn.
Henry Leonard, D.C.
Thomas W. Miller, Del.
Ogden L. Mills, Jr., N.Y.
Edward Myers, Pa.
Richard C. Patterson, N.Y.
William G. Price, Jr., Pa.
S. A. Ritchie, N.Y.
Theodore Roosevelt, Jr., N.Y.
Dale Shaw, Iowa
Albert A. Sprague, Ill.
Daniel G. Stivers, Mont.
John J. Sullivan, Wash.
Hubert J. Turney, Ohio
George A. White, Ore.
George H. Wood, Ohio

NATIONAL COMMANDERS

Franklin D'Olier, Pa., 1919–20
Frederick W. Galbraith, Jr., Ohio, 1920–21
John G. Emery, Mich., 6-14-21–11-2-21
Hanford MacNider, Iowa, 1921–22
Alvin M. Owsley, Tex., 1922–23
John R. Quinn, Cal., 1923–24
James A. Drain, Wash., 1924–25
John R. McQuigg, Ohio, 1925–26
Howard P. Savage, Ill., 1926–27
Edward E. Spafford, N.Y., 1927–28
Paul V. McNutt, Ind., 1928–29
O. L. Bodenhamer, Ark., 1929–30
Ralph T. O'Neil, Kans., 1930–31
Henry L. Stevens, Jr., N.C., 1931–32
Louis A. Johnson, W.Va., 1932–33
Edward A. Hayes, Ill., 1933–34
Frank N. Belgrano, Cal., 1934–35
Ray Murphy, Iowa, 1935–36
Harry W. Colmery, Kans., 1936–37
Daniel J. Doherty, Mass., 1937–38
Stephen F. Chadwick, Wash., 1938–39
Raymond J. Kelly, Mich., 1939–40
Milo J. Warner, Ohio, 1940–41
Lynn U. Stambaugh, N.D., 1941–42
Roane Waring, Tenn., 1942–43
Warren H. Atherton, Cal., 1943–44
Edward N. Scheiberling, N.Y., 1944–45
John Stelle, Ill., 1945–46
Paul H. Griffith, Pa., 1946–47
James F. O'Neil, N.H., 1947–48
S. Perry Brown, Tex., 1948–49
George N. Craig, Ind., 1949–50
Erle Cocke, Jr., Ga., 1950–51
Donald R. Wilson, W.Va., 1951–52
Lewis K. Gough, Cal., 1952–53
Arthur J. Connell, Conn., 1953–54
Seaborn P. Collins, N.M., 1954–55
J. Addington Wagner, Mich., 1955–56
W. C. (Dan) Daniel, Va., 1956–57
John S. Gleason, Jr., Ill., 1957–58
Preston J. Moore, Okla., 1958–59
Martin B. McKneally, N.Y., 1959–60
William R. Burke, Cal., 1960–61
Charles L. Bacon, Mo., 1961–62
James E. Powers, Ga., 1962–63
Daniel F. Foley, Minn., 1963–64
Donald E. Johnson, Iowa, 1964–65
L. Eldon James, Va., 1965–66
John E. Davis, N.D., 1966–67
William E. Galbraith, Neb., 1967–68
William C. Doyle, N.J., 1968–69
J. Milton Patrick, Okla., 1969–70
Alfred P. Chamie, Cal., 1970–71
John H. Geiger, Ill., 1971–72
Joe L. Matthews, Tex., 1972–73
Robert E. L. Eaton, Md., 1973–74
James M. Wagonseller, Ohio, 1974–75
Harry G. Wiles, Kans., 1975–76
William J. Rogers, Me., 1976–77
Robert Charles Smith, La., 1977–78
John M. Carey, Mich., 1978–79
Frank I. Hamilton, Ind., 1979–80
Michael J. Kogutek, N.Y., 1980–81
Jack W. Flynt, Tex., 1981–82
Albert Keller, Jr., Ill., 1982–83
Keith A. Kreul, Wis., 1983–84
Clarence M. Bacon, Md., 1984–85
Dale L. Renaud, Iowa, 1985–86
James P. Dean, Miss., 1986–87
John P. Comer, Mass., 1987–88
H. F. "Sparky" Gierke, N.D., 1988–89
Miles S. Epling, W.Va., 1989–90

PAST NATIONAL COMMANDERS (Honorary Title, National Convention Bestowed)

Five men who presided as temporary chairmen or chairmen at the Paris and Saint Louis caucuses in 1919 were voted the title of Past National Commander:

Henry D. Lindsley (Tex.) 1919
Milton J. Foreman (Ill.) 1921
Bennett Champ Clark (Mo.) 1926
Theodore Roosevelt, Jr. (N.Y.) 1949
Eric Fisher Wood (Pa.) 1955

Subsequently, four others have been so honored:

Thomas W. Miller (Nev.) 1968
Maurice Stember (N.Y.) 1975
Hamilton Fish (N.Y.) 1979
E. Roy Stone, Jr. (S.C.) 1987

AMERICAN LEGION AUXILIARY NATIONAL PRESIDENTS

Mrs. Lowell F. Hobart, Sr., Ohio, 1921–22
Dr. Kate Waller Barrett, Va., 1922–23
Mrs. Franklin Lee Bishop, Mass., 1923–24
Mrs. O. D. Oliphant, N.J., 1924–25
Mrs. Eliza London Shepard, Cal., 1925–26
Mrs. John William Macauley, Wis., 1926–27
Mrs. Robert Walbridge, N.H., 1927–28
Mrs. Boyce Ficklen, Ga., 1928–29
Mrs. Donald Macrae, Iowa, 1929–30
Mrs. Robert Lincoln Hoyal, Ariz., 1930–31
Mrs. Frederick C. Williams, N.Y., 1931–32
Mrs. S. Alford Blackburn, Ky., 1932–33
Mrs. William H. Biester, Jr., Pa., 1933–34
Mrs. Albin C. Carlson, Minn., 1934–35
Mrs. Melville Mucklestone, Ill., 1935–36
Mrs. Oscar W. Hahn, Neb., 1936–37
Mrs. Malcolm Douglas, Wash., 1937–38
Mrs. James Morris, N.D., 1938–39
Mrs. William H. Corwith, N.Y., 1939–40
Mrs. Louis J. Lemstra, Ind., 1940–41
Mrs. Mark W. Murrill, Mass., 1941–42
Mrs. Alfred J. Mathebat, Cal., 1942–43
Mrs. Lawrence H. Smith, Wis., 1943–44
Mrs. Charles B. Gilbert, Conn., 1944–45
Mrs. Walter G. Craven, N.C., 1945–46
Mrs. Norton H. Pearl, Mich., 1946–47
Mrs. Lee W. Hutton, Minn., 1947–48
Mrs. Hubert A. Goode, Ore., 1948–49
Mrs. Norman L. Sheehe, Ill., 1949–50
Mrs. Willis C. Reed, Okla., 1950–51
Mrs. E. A. Campbell, La., 1951–52
Mrs. Rae Ashton, Utah, 1952–53
Mrs. Harold S. Burdett, N.Y., 1953–54

Mrs. Percy A Lainson, Iowa, 1954–55
Mrs. Bowden D. Ward, W.Va., 1955–56
Mrs. Carl W. Zeller, Ohio, 1956–57
Mrs. J. Pat Kelly, Ga., 1957–58
Mrs. Charles W. Gunn, Ore., 1958–59
Mrs. Alexander H. Gray, Tenn., 1959–60
Mrs. Henry Ahnemiller, Wash., 1960–61
Mrs. J. Howard McKay, Pa., 1961–62
Mrs. O. L. Koger, Kans., 1962–63
Mrs. Luther D. Johnson, Neb., 1963–64
Mrs. Walter W. Andrews, Ala., 1964–65
Mrs. Walter H. Glynn, Iowa, 1965–66
Mrs. A. J. Ryan, Sr., Fla., 1966–67
Mrs. Vernon H. Randall, Md., 1967–68
Mrs. Arthur B. Hanell, Cal., 1968–69
Mrs. H. Milton Davidson, N.M., 1969–70
Mrs. Charles C. Shaw, Ill., 1970–71
Mrs. Robert L. Parker, Okla., 1971–72
Mrs. T. G. Chilton, Ariz., 1972–73
Mrs. B. M. Jarrett, N.C., 1973–74
Mrs. Maurice Kubby, Tex., 1974–75
Mrs. Alan M. Schanel, R.I., 1975–76
Mrs. Paul Brown, Id., 1976–77
Mrs. Alvin Moltzen, N.D., 1977–78
Mrs. Earl B. Bigalow, Ore., 1978–79
Mrs. Bernard F. Kennedy, N.J., 1979–80
Mrs. Lyle Seymour, Kans., 1980–81
Mrs. John J. Roethel, Mich., 1981–82
Mrs. Walter Stolte, Mo., 1982–83
Mrs. Thomas J. Gear, Va., 1983–84
Mrs. Wayne Gardner, Fla., 1984–85
Mrs. Robert Melgard, Cal., 1985–86
Mrs. James E. Starr, Minn., 1986–87
Mrs. H. B. Behrend, Wis., 1987–88
Mrs. Ted Galka, Ind., 1988–89
Mrs. William M. Calder, Utah, 1989–90

NATIONAL VICE-COMMANDERS

Allan A. Tukey, Neb., 1919–20
Joyce S. Lewis, Minn., 1919–20
Alden B. Chambers, Mass., 1919–20
Wm. B. Follett, Ore., 1919–20
James O'Brien, Cal., 1919–20

John G. Emery, Mich., 1920–21
Thomas Goldingay, N.J., 1920–21
Claudius G. Pendill, Wis., 1920–21
J. G. Scrugham, Nev., 1920–21
E. Jackson Winslett, Ala., 1920–21

George L. Berry, Tenn., 1921–22
Raymond O. Brackett, Mass., 1921–22
H. Nelson Jackson, Vt., 1921–22
Charles H. Kendrick, Cal., 1921–22
John A. McCormack, Colo., 1921–22

Edward J. Barrett, Wis., 1922–23
Watson B. Miller, D.C., 1922–23
Erle E. Cocke, Sr., Ga., 1922–23
Robert O. Blood, N.H., 1922–23
C. P. Plummer, Wyo., 1922–23

Dr. Ira Thurman Mann, N.C., 1923–24
F. Ryan Duffy, Wis., 1923–24
Celora M. Stoddard, Ariz., 1923–24
Lester F. Albert, Id., 1923–24
William B. Healy, Pa., 1923–24

Frank McFarland, Kans., 1924–25
Eugene P. Armstrong, Conn., 1924–25
A. L. Perry, Panama, C.Z., 1924–25
Wm. Stern, N.D., 1924–25
Peyton H. Hoge, Jr., Ky., 1924–25

Joseph Y. Cheney, Fla., 1925–26
Hughes B. Davis, Okla., 1925–26
Vincent A. Carroll, Pa., 1925–26
Raymond B. Littlefield, R.I., 1925–26
Judge James A. Howell, Utah, 1925–26

John G. Sims, Tenn., 1926–27
C. Thomas Busha, Jr., Mont., 1926–27

Dr. John G. Towne, Me., 1926–27
John E. Curtiss, Neb., 1926–27
Stafford King, Minn., 1926–27

John T. Raftis, Wash., 1927–28
Ralph T. O'Neil, Kans., 1927–28
Paul R. Younts, N.C., 1927–28
Dan Spurlock, La., 1927–28
J. M. Henry, Minn., 1927–28

Lawrence E. McGann, Jr., Ill., 1928–29
George W. Malone, Nev., 1928–29
E. L. White, Conn., 1928–29
Miller C. Foster, S.C., 1928–29
Walton D. Hood, Tex., 1928–29

Milt D. Campbell, Ohio, 1929–30
John J. Dugan, Del., 1929–30
Frank Schoble, Jr., Pa., 1929–30
Willis M. Brewer, Mich., 1929–30
Morton M. David, Colo., 1929–30

Dr. Neal D. Williams, Mo., 1930–31
Dr. James A. Duff, W.Va., 1930–31
Harry B. Henderson, Jr., Wyo., 1930–31
Bert S. Hyland, Vt., 1930–31
Roland B. Howell, La., 1930–31

Richard F. Paul, Mass., 1931–32
Harold L. Plummer, Wis., 1931–32
Forrest G. Cooper, Miss., 1931–32
Roy L. Cook, N.M., 1931–32
Frank N. Brooks, Wash., 1931–32

Russell Meadows, Ariz., 1932–33
Robert D. Flory, Neb., 1932–33
Wm. E. Easterwood, Jr., Tex., 1932–33
John J. Maloney, Me., 1932–33
Chas. A. Mills, Fla., 1932–33

Charles R. Mabey, Utah, 1933–34
R. L. Gordon, Ark., 1933–34
Miguel Munoz, P.R., 1933–34
Edward Carruth, Kans., 1933–34
Charles L. Woolley, R.I., 1933–34

Daniel J. Doherty, Mass., 1934–35
Harold J. Warner, Ore., 1934–35
John K. Kennelly, N.D., 1934–35
Milo J. Warner, Ohio, 1934–35
Quimby Melton, Ga., 1934–35

Raymond F. Gates, Conn., 1935–36
Dr. W. E. Whitlock, Fla., 1935–36
Oscar W. Worthwine, Id., 1935–36
Dr. F. Whitney Godwin, Va., 1935–36
Louis R. Probst, Wyo., 1935–36

Salvatore A. Capodice, Cal., 1936–37
Leo A. Temmey, S.D., 1936–37
Leonard Sisk, Tenn., 1936–37
J. Fred Johnson, Jr., Ala., 1936–37
Jack Crowley, D.C., 1936–37

Drury M. Phillips, Tex., 1937–38
Phil M. Conley, W.Va., 1937–38
Harry M. Johnson, Mont., 1937–38
James F. Daniel, Jr., S.C., 1937–38
James R. Mahaffy, Hawaii, 1937–38

Edward J. Quinn, Me., 1938–39
Charles W. Crush, Va., 1938–39
Earl T. Ross, Nev., 1938–39
James T. Crawley, Miss., 1938–39
Henry C. Oakey, Wis., 1938–39

Leo E. Ray, N.H., 1939–40
Charles Q. Kelley, D.C., 1939–40
Matthew J. Murphy, Ill., 1939–40
James B. Fitzgerald, Md., 1939–40
H. Elwyn Davis, Colo., 1939–40

Erwin A. Froyd, Wyo., 1940–41
James L. McCrory, Neb., 1940–41
Harold P. Redden, Mass., 1940–41
Edward R. Stirling, Pa., 1940–41
Alcee S. Legendre, La., 1940–41

W. C. "Tom" Sawyer, Ariz., 1941–42
William DeLacey Allen, Ga., 1941–42
Charles W. Booth, W.Va., 1941–42
V. M. Armstrong, Ind., 1941–42
John F. Sullivan, Vt., 1941–42

John T. Batten, Ala., 1942–43
Fred G. Fraser, D.C., 1942–43
Arthur J. Connell, Conn., 1942–43
Herman H. Lark, Mo., 1942–43
Jefferson Davis Atwood, N.M., 1942–43

Martin V. Coffey, Ohio, 1943–44
E. A. Littlefield, Utah, 1943–44
Roy L. McMillan, N.C., 1943–44

Edward A. Mulrooney, Del., 1943–44
Hector G. Staples, Me., 1943–44

Bascom F. Jones, Tenn., 1944–45
Frank E. McCaffrey, R.I., 1944–45
Dan McDade, Ore., 1944–45
Ray S. Pierson, Kans., 1944–45
William P. Shadoan, Ky., 1944–45

R. Graham Huntington, N.J., 1945–46
Fred LaBoon, Kans., 1945–46
Sam L. Latimer, Jr., S.C., 1945–46
H. Dudley Swim, Id., 1945–46
Jeremiah Twomey, Mass., 1945–46

Richard C. Cadwallader, La., 1946–47
Joseph W. Brown, N.H., 1946–47
Edward J. Sharkey, Cal., 1946–47
Ernest H. Dervishian, Va., 1946–47
Martin B. Buckner, Mich., 1946–47

Albert A. Cree, Vt., 1947–48
Myron R. Renick, W.Va., 1947–48
Joe W. White, Ga., 1947–48
Richard B. Ott, Wash., 1947–48
L. W. Barns, S.D., 1947–48

James Lane, Ala., 1948–49
Leonard W. Moody, Ark., 1948–49
James Annin, Mont., 1948–49
Edward J. Kelly, Conn., 1948–49
Walter W. Alessandroni, Pa., 1948–49

Frank E. Lowe, Me., 1949–50
Dr. D. R. Perry, N.C., 1949–50
Dave H. Fleischer, Mo., 1949–50
J. E. Martie, Nev., 1949–50
Milton G. Boock, Minn., 1949–50

Joe H. Adams, Fla., 1950–51
Herbert J. Jacobi, D.C., 1950–51
Felix Pogliano, Colo., 1950–51
Lewis K. Gough, Cal., 1950–51
Frederick C. Bramlage, Kans., 1950–51

Adolph F. Bremer, Minn., 1951–52
Frank R. Kelley, Mass., 1951–52
Thomas E. Paradine, N.Y., 1951–52
Oscar B. Rohlff, Wyo., 1951–52
Audley H. Ward, S.C., 1951–52

William Ralph Bourdon, Ariz., 1952–53
Lyon Wright Brandon, Miss., 1952–53
Wilbur C. Daniel, Va., 1952–53
Harry V. Groome, N.J., 1952–53
J. Addington Wagner, Mich., 1952–53

John A. High, N.H., 1953–54
Dr. Deward H. Reed, N.M., 1953–54
Truman C. Wold, N.D., 1953–54
Herbert M. Walker, Pa., 1953–54
Thomas W. Bird, N.C., 1953–54

Leonard L. Jackson, La., 1954–55
Patrick H. Mangan, Jr., Vt., 1954–55
Howard C. Kingdom, Ohio, 1954–55
Dr. Carl J. Rees, Del., 1954–55
Robert L. Shelby, Utah, 1954–55

Guy O. Stone, Ga., 1955–56
John H. Van Horn, Alaska, 1955–56
L. Everett Page, Tex., 1955–56
James V. Day, Me., 1955–56
Gilman H. Stordock, Wis., 1955–56
William J. Holliman, Va., 1955–56

J. Edward Walter, Md., 1956–57
Gaylor M. Brown, Iowa, 1956–57
Carl R. Moser, Ore., 1956–57
John F. Stay, Pa., 1956–57
George T. Lewis, Jr., Tenn., 1956–57

William A. Cottrell, Hi., 1957–58
Ramon R. Guas, P.R., 1957–58
Harry W. Miller, W.Va., 1957–58
Lee A. Lemos, R.I., 1957–58
Isadore E. Levine, Ind., 1957–58

C. D. DeLoach, Va., 1958–59
John W. Collins, Pa., 1958–59
James B. Kerrigan, Mo., 1958–59
Robert Charles Smith, La., 1958–59
James C. Bangs, Id., 1958–59

Nate V. Keller, Minn., 1959–60
Willard W. Brandt, N.D., 1959–60
A. Layman Harman, S.C., 1959–60
Charles C. McGonegal, Cal., 1959–60
Corydon T. Hill, Cal., 5–5–60—10–20–60

William A. Brennan, Jr., Ind., 1959–60
I. Frank Gianotti, Minn., 9–14–60—10–20–60

George K. Walker, Mass., 1960–61
James M. Wagonseller, Ohio, 1960–61
Vincent J. Maxheim, Iowa, 1960–61
Dr. Harry H. Kretzler, Wash., 1960–61
R. C. Godwin, N.C., 1960–61

Walter W. Barnard, Mont., 1961–62
Edward T. Hoak, Pa., 1961–62
Wilson H. Morrison, Mich., 1961–62
J. Milton Patrick, Okla., 1961–62
Edward Wysocki, N.J., 1961–62

Claude A. Hamilton, S.D., 1962–63
Paschal C. Reese, Fla., 1962–63
Harold D. Beaton, D.C., 1962–63
James W. Doon, N.H., 1962–63
Victor F. Whittlesea, Nev., 1962–63

Dr. Garland D. Murphy, Jr., Ark., 1963–64
Earl D. Franklin, Jr., Colo., 1963–64
Harry Wright, N.M., 1963–64
Emilio S. Iglesias, Vt., 1963–64
George Emory Sipple, Wis., 1963–64

Edward H. Lynch, Jr., Conn., 1964–65
Joseph Paul, Mich., 1964–65
Herbert D. Black, S.C., 1964–65
Ward W. Husted, Wyo., 1964–65
David Aronberg, Ky., 1964–65

A. R. Choppin, La., 1965–66
William J. Rogers, Me., 1965–66
William E. Galbraith, Neb., 1965–66
Soleng Tom, Ariz., 1965–66
Robert O. Phillips, R.I., 1965–66

Robert M. Fritz, Ind., 1966–67
Frank L. Orfanello, Mass., 1966–67
James A. Tadlock, N.M., 1966–67
Harry V. Klein, Pa., 1966–67
Lewis W. Emerich, Tex., 1966–67

Coleman Nolen, Okla., 1967–68
Louis R. J. Malo, R.I., 1967–68
Roscoe D. Curtiss, Tenn., 1967–68
Edwin L. Peterson, Ph.D., Utah, 1967–68
Marvin W. Roth, Wis., 1967–68

C. Russel Huber, Alaska, 1968–69
John A. Jones, W.Va., 1968–69
Howard E. Lohman, Minn., 1968–69
Lewis E. McCray, Ala., 1968–69
Maurice R. Parisien, Me., 1968–69

Kent T. Lundgren, Mich., 1969–70
Roland D. Marble, Miss., 1969–70
Raymond F. Mudge, N.H., 1969–70
Earl R. Norgard, Ore., 1969–70
Gilberto M. Font, P.R., 1969–70

Claude Carpenter, Ark., 1970–71
Max Hanson, Id., 1970–71
Robert E. L. Eaton, Md., 1970–71
Gabriel T. Olga, Mass., 1970–71
John E. Gilbert, Pa., 1970–71

Harold W. Fann, Ky., 1971–72
Arthur M. MacCarthy, Fla., 1971–72
Roy Sweet, Vt., 1971–72
Harry G. Wiles, Kans., 1971–72
Wallace C. S. Young, Hi., 1971–72

Tim T. Craig, N.C., 1972–73
Sam Gray, Cal., 1972–73
Donald L. Gruenbaum, Ohio, 1972–73
Albert J. Moeller, N.J., 1972–73
Raymond J. Novak, S.D., 1972–73

Frank C. Brooks, Wash., 1973–74
N. E. Brown, S.C., 1973–74
John N. Roberto, Conn., 1973–74
Gilbert E. Sheeks, Ind., 1973–74
Merrick W. Swords, Jr., La., 1973–74

Boyd H. Clemens, N.D., 1974–75
Jack W. Flynt, Tex., 1974–75
Jay E. Harville, Tenn., 1974–75
Donald H. Jeffery, Pa., 1974–75
William A. Lindsay, Mont., 1974–75

John W. Adams, Jr., Ky., 1975–76
Fred W. Anderson, Jr., Nev., 1975–76
Leo F. Malloy, Mass., 1975–76
T. W. "Tom" Miller, Ark., 1975–76
James F. Walker, Minn., 1975–76

Lloyd J. Berken, Wis., 1976–77
Thomas B. Coll, D.C., 1976–77
Robert B. Grauberger, Colo., 1976–77
Frank A. Kelly, Ga., 1976–77
Wilbur Walker, Va., 1976–77

Eugene V. Lindquist, Minn., 1977–78
Roger A. Munson, Ohio, 1977–78
John J. O'Connell, R.I., 1977–78
Chester Phillips, W.Va., 1977–78
Irving B. Selmer, Wyo., 1977–78

L. Max Connolly, Ariz., 1978–79
Alvin F. Grauerholz, Kans., 1978–79
Joseph F. Ward, N.J., 1978–79
John H. Wienand, Ala., 1978–79
Nathan M. Wolfe, S.C., 1978–79

G. Y. Fails, N.M., 1979–80
Keith A. Kreul, Wis., 1979–80
Bob Legan, Ariz., 1979–80
Max E. Robinson, N.C., 1979–80
Laurence R. Spaulding, N.H., 1979–80

Ralph M. Godwin, Miss., 1980–81
Keith H. Gwilliam, Utah, 1980–81
Matthew W. Jamieson, Mich., 1980–81
Robert W. Lowry, Neb., 1980–81
Almo J. Sebastianelli, D.D.S., Pa., 1980–81

Frank T. Markovich, Mo., 1981–82
Dan C. McDonough, Alaska, 1981–82
Percy C. Miller, Tenn., 1981–82
Melvin "Doc" Simon, Vt., 1981–82
David A. Wade, Md., 1981–82

R. C. Gabrielson, S.D., 1982–83
Margaret M. Malone, N.J., 1982–83
H. Melvin Napier, Ind., 1982–83
Jack C. Plato, Ore., 1982–83
Lee O. Walker, Okla., 1982–83

J. Leslie Brown, Ky., 1983–84
Roberto Gonzalez, P.R., 1983–84
Charles R. Green, Ohio, 1983–84
Robert W. Groccia, Mass., 1983–84
John N. Lockhart, Hawaii, 1983–84

Ronald D. Birk, Kans., 1984–85
Harold W. Collett, Id., 1984–85
Stewart R. Kunde, Minn., 1984–85
Stephen J. Mikosky, Pa., 1984–85
Robert S. Turner, Ga., 1984–85

Bernard L. Black, S.C., 1985–86
Norman Conn, Cal., 1985–86
Vito M. DeFilipp, Me., 1985–86
Miles S. Epling, W.Va., 1985–86
H. F. "Sparky" Gierke, N.D., 1985–86

William M. Detweiler, La., 1986–87
Doris R. Gross, Wash., 1986–87
Donald E. Neil, Del., 1986–87
Allen L. Titus, Ind., 1986–87
Ervin F. Van Dyke, Wis., 1986–87

Neale V. Cabral, Conn., 1987–88
Joe Frank, Jr., Mo., 1987–88
W. P. "Bill" Petersen, Mont., 1987–88
Paul B. Phifer, Jr., Va., 1987–88
Leon Reed, Ark., 1987–88

Thomas L. Gabel, Ohio, 1988–89
Harvey Holcomb, Tex., 1988–89
Archie Pozzi, Jr., Nev., 1988–89
Ray G. Smith, Sr., N.C., 1988–89
John P. Tipping, N.Y., 1988–89

Vincent E. Blank, Iowa, 1989–90
Joseph E. Caouette, N.H., 1989–90
Andrew J. Cooper, Ala., 1989–90
Gerald Goetzinger, S.D., 1989–90
Vinton R. Guy, Colo., 1989–90

NATIONAL ADJUTANTS

Lemuel Bolles, Wash., 11-13-19–2-1-24
Russell G. Creviston, Ind., 2-1-24–7-31-25
James F. Barton, Iowa, 8-1-25–9-15-32
Frank Edward Samuel, Kans., 11-14-32–7-25-43

Donald G. Glascoff, Mich., 7-27-43–9-23-43 (acting); 9-23-43–1-31-48
Henry H. Dudley, Neb., 2-1-48–5-5-48 (acting); 5-5-48–7-1-56
Emil A. Blackmore, Wyo., 7-1-56–4-21-67
Ernest N. Schmit, N.D., 5-4-67–8-31-67
William F. Hauck, Ind., 8-31-67–10-18-67 (acting); 10-18-67–1-25-78
Frank C. Momsen, Minn., 1-25-78–6-30-81
Robert W. Spanogle, Mich., 6-30-81–

ASSISTANT NATIONAL ADJUTANTS

(Indianapolis Office)

Russell G. Creviston, Ind., 1919–2-1-24
(No one appointed) 2-1-24–4-4-25
James F. Barton, Iowa, 4-4-25–8-1-25
(No one appointed) 8-1-25–1-15-26
Frank E. Samuel, Kans., 1-15-26–11-14-32
Harold L. Plummer, Wis., 10-1-32–2-15-40
Donald G. Glascoff, Mich., 4-22-40–7-27-43
Henry H. Dudley, Neb., 10-1-43–2-1-48
Robert R. Poston, Tex., 2-1-48–5-1-48 (acting); 5-1-48–2-14-49
Joe E. Rabinovich, N.D., 5-1-48–11-7-49
William E. Sayer, Ind., 10-24-49–12-31-52
Emil A. Blackmore, Wyo., 1-5-53–7-1-56
Robert E. Lyngh, Colo., 7-1-56–11-8-67

ASSISTANT NATIONAL ADJUTANTS

(Washington Office)

Elbert H. Burns, Ill., 1944–45
Leonce R. Legendre, La. 1946–51
John M. (Jack) Oakey, Colo., 1951–52

ADMINISTRATIVE ASSISTANT TO THE NATIONAL COMMANDER

(Washington Office)

William F. Hauck, Ind., 1951–52

NATIONAL JUDGE ADVOCATES

Robert A. Adams, Ind., 1919–27
Scott W. Lucas, Ind., 1927–31
Robert A. Adams, Ind., 6-24-31–9-24-31
Remster A. Bingham, Ind., 9-24-31–1934
James A. Drain, Wash., 1934–35
Ralph B. Gregg, Ind., 1935–60
Bertram G. Davis, N.Y., 1960–83
Philip B. Onderdonk, Jr., Md., 1983–

NATIONAL CHAPLAINS

The Very Reverend Charles H. Brent, N.Y., 1919 National Convention. Granted title of Past National Chaplain by April 30–May 1, 1964, National Executive Committee and the 46th National Convention, September 22–24, 1964, Dallas, Texas.

Thomas H. Wiles, Colo., 1919
Rev. Francis A. Kelly, N.Y., 1919–20
Rev. John W. Inzer, Tenn., 1920–21
Rev. Earl A. Blackman, Kans., 1921–22
Rev. Wm. P. O'Connor, Ohio, 1922–23
Rev. Ezra Clemens, Minn., 1923–24
Rev. Joseph M. Lonergan, Ill., 1924–25
Rev. Wm. E. Patrick, Cal., 1925–26
Rev. Joseph L. N. Wolfe, Pa., 1926–27
Rev. Gill Robb Wilson, N.J., 1927–28
Rabbi Lee J. Levinger, Del., 1928–29
Rev. George F. Kettell, D.D., N.Y., 1929–30
Rev. Jos. N. Barnett, Wis., 1930–31
Rev. Harris A. Darche, Ill., 1931–32
Rev. Irwin Q. Wood, Id., 1932–33
Rev. Robert J. White, Mass., 1933–34
Rev. Dr. Park W. Huntington, Sr., Del., 1934–35
Rt. Rev. Msgr. Thomas D. Kennedy, Mo., 1935–36
Rev. Bryan H. Keathley, D.D., Tex., 1936–37
Rev. Fr. Frank J. Lawler, Ill., 1937–38
Rev. Jerome L. Fritsche, Neb., 1938–39
Msgr. Patrick N. McDermott, Iowa, 1939–40
Rev. Brigadier Wm. G. Gilks, Tex., 1940–41
Rev. Frederick J. Halloran, N.J., 1941–42
Dr. Paul Deforest Mortimore, Wash., 1942–43
Rev. John F. McManus, Kans., 1943–44
Rev. DeWitt C. Mallory, Fla., 1944–45
Rt. Rev. Msgr. Edward J. Smith, Iowa, 1945–46
Rev. Arthur L. Rustad, Minn., 1946–47
Rev. Fr. Frank L. Harrington, Mont., 1947–48
Rev. Thomas Grice, Cal., 1948–49
Rev. Fr. Edward J. Carney, O.S.A., Mass., 1949–50
Rabbi David Lefkowitz, La., 1950–51
Rev. Olaf G. Birkeland, Wis., 1951–52
Rev. Fr. John E. Duffy, Ohio, 1952–53
Dr. Tom B. Clark, Okla., 1953–54
Rev. Albert J. Hoffman, Iowa, 1954–55
Rev. Joseph MacCarroll, N.J., 1955–56
Rev. Bernard W. Gerdon, Ind., 1956–57
Rev. Dr. Feltham S. James, S.C., 1957–58
Rt. Rev. Msgr. John J. Twiss, Mass., 1958–59
Rabbi Robert I. Kahn, D.H.L., Tex., 1959–60
Rev. Wm. H. Moss, Tenn., 1960–61
Rev. Fr. Robert G. Keating, Conn., 1961–62
Rabbi Albert M. Shulman, Ind., 1962–63
Rev. Fr. John J. Howard, Va., 1963–64
Rev. Fr. Morris N. Dummet, La., 1964–65
Rev. Alfred C. Thompson, N.Y., 1965–66
Rev. Fr. Anthony J. O'Driscoll, O.F.M., N.J., 1966–67
Rev. Fr. Edward P. Nolan, Pa., 1967–68
Rev. Carl J. Olander, Miss., 1968–69
Rev. Fr. William D. Curtis, Minn., 1969–70

Rev. Milton B. Faust, N.C., 1970–71
Rev. Fr. Paul J. Schwaab, Neb., 1971–72
Rev. Dr. Lawrence P. Fitzpatrick, Iowa, 1972–73
Rev. Jerome D. Fortenberry, Mo., 1973–74
Rev. Harvey T. Goodling, Ore., 1974–75
Rev. Claude E. Smithmier, Ga., 1975–76
Rev. Fr. James C. Tuxbury, N.D., 1976–77
Rev. Fr. Walter D. Power, Md., 1977–78
Rev. R. Drew Wolcott, Mexico, 1978–79
Rev. Karl E. Kniseley, D.D., Cal., 1979–80
Rev. George S. Macres, Minn., 1980–81
Rev. George R. M. Rumney, Va., 1981–82
Rev. Fr. John D. Kempf, Ohio, 1982–83
Rev. James C. McKee, Utah, 1983–84
Rev. Charles G. Rice, Jr., N.Y., 1984–85
Gordon L. Patterson, Th.D., Neb., 1985–86
Rev. Fr. Arthur J. Jakobiak, N.M., 1986–87
Rev. Jerry Salveson, Minn., 1987–88
Rev. F. Robert Davidson, Mich., 1988–89
Lynn S. Kearsley, Id., 1989–90

NATIONAL TREASURERS

Gaspar G. Bacon, Mass., 11-13-19–12-20-19
Robert H. Tyndall, Ind., 12-20-19–10-18-27
Bowman Elder, Ind., 10-18-27–11-20-33
Neal Grider, Ind., 11-20-33–11-1-34
James A. Drain, Wash., 1934–35
John R. Ruddick, Ind., 1935–7-13-45
Neal Grider, Ind., 7-13-45–1958
William Francis Polen, Ind., 1958–1978
Webber LaGrange, Ind., 1978–

NATIONAL HISTORIANS

Eben Putnam, Mass., 1920–33
Thomas M. Owen, Jr., Ala., 1933–48
Monte C. Sandlin, Ala., 1948–53
Robert T. Fairey, S.C., 1953–57
Mrs. Emily Herbert, N.J., 1957–60
Glenn B. Hoover, Iowa, 1960–61
Earl D. Young, Colo., 1961–62
H. Armand deMasi, Italy, 1962–64
Harold A. Shindler, Ind., 1964–69
John A. May, S.C., 1969–70
Howard W. Swinney, Ky., 1970–71
G. Greer McCallister, Ohio, 1971–72
Loretta O. Phillips, Cal., 1972–73
R. Robert Filter, Wis., 1973–74
Nolie C. Deas, Sr., Fla., 1974–75
Dorothy Grimes Long, Colo., 1975–76
Alton H. Carpenter, N.Y., 1976–77
Arnold J. Stockstad, N.D., 1977–78
Harry H. Kretzler, Sr., M.D., Wash., 1978–79
Phillip E. Haddad, Okla., 1979–80
Neal S. Sundeen, Ariz., 1980–81
Bernard J. Chisholm, Minn., 1981–82
James W. Conway, Mass., 1982–83
Herberta T. Stark, N.H., 1983–84
Roy R. Mahoney, Fla., 1984–85
Ethel M. Matushka, Wis., 1985–86
J. Ruffin Apperson, Va., 1986–87
Edward F. Brennan, Ill., 1987–88
Richard A. Stevens, Sr., La., 1988–89
C. Carl Pilgrim, S.C., 1989–90

NATIONAL SERGEANTS-AT-ARMS

Lewis P. Fields, Tex., 1927–28*
No record, 1928–29
William A. Carey, Mass., 1929–30
Don Pierce, Kans., 1930–31
William D. Browne, Ore., 1931–32
Henry Rhode, Ill., 1932–33
No record, 1933–34
Rowan F. Howard, Tex., 1934–35
Ed. I. Lindsay, Iowa, 1935–36
Frank H. McFarland, Kans., 1936–37
Richard A. Morrissey, Mass., 1937–38
Andy Viland, Wash., 1938–39
John G. Dunn, Mich., 1939–40
Val W. Ove, Wis., 1940–41
William D. Browne, Ore., 1941–42
Paul B. Dague, Pa., 1942–43
John E. "Jack" Short, Cal., 1943–44
Edward F. O'Neill, N.Y., 1944–45
George A. Dustin, Ill., 1945–46
Fred G. Fraser, D.C., 1946–47
Edward F. Humer, Fla., 1947–48
Richard C. Gusman, Tex., 1948–49
John W. Webster, Ind., 1949–50
Thomas L. "Doc" Jennings, Ga., 1950–51
Harry E. Engelund, Cal., 1952–56
C. Howard Larsen, N.Y., 1956–60
Harry E. Engelund, Cal., 1960–61
Kenneth Cruse, Mo., 1961–62
C. Howard Larsen, N.Y., 1962–63
Frank C. Momsen, Minn., 1963–64
C. Howard Larsen, N.Y., 1964–77
Norman Conn, Cal., 1977–78
C. Howard Larsen, N.Y., 1977–78 (Sergeant-at-Arms Emeritus)
John J. Harris, N.Y., 1978–79
C. Howard Larsen, N.Y., 1978–79 (Sergeant-at-Arms Emeritus)
Charles J. Brynak, Ohio, 1979–80
C. Howard Larsen, N.Y., 1979–80 (Sergeant-at-Arms Emeritus)
R. M. "Sonny" Singletary, Jr., S.C., 1980–81
C. Howard Larsen, N.Y., 1980–81 (Sergeant-at-Arms Emeritus)
Herbert W. Odell, Tex., 1981–82
Gary L. Walling, Ill., 1982–83
Kenneth Gassman, Wis., 1983–84
Charles A. St. Clair, Md., 1984–85
Peter G. Hass, Iowa, 1985–86
Hubert V. Culver, Miss., 1986–87
Timothy A. Ryan, Mass., 1987–88
Paul R. Evenson, S.D., 1988–89
William E. Burkett, W.Va., 1989–90

FEDÉRATION INTERALLIÉE DES ANCIENS COMBATTANTS

Legion Officers

PRESIDENT

Thomas W. Miller, Del., 1925
Edward L. White, Conn., 1932

U.S.A. VICE-PRESIDENTS

Cabot Ward, France, 1920–22
H. Nelson Jackson, Vt., 1922–24
Roy Hoffman, Okla., 1924–25
Lemuel Bolles, Wash., 1925–26
Henry D. Lindsley, Tex., 1926–27
L. R. Gignilliat, Ind., 1927–28
E. Arthur Ball, Ind., 1928–29
Julius I. Peyser, D.C., 1930
Lamar Jeffers, Ala., 1930–31
Frank D. Rash, Ky., 1931–32

* Have no record prior to 1927–28

Charles Hann, Jr., N.Y., 1932–33
Louis A. Johnson, W.Va., 1933–34
Robert J. White, Mass., 1934–37
Nathaniel Spear, Jr., Pa., 1937–38
F. Whitney Godwin, Va., 1938–39

DIRECTORS OF WASHINGTON NATIONAL HEADQUARTERS OFFICE

Paul H. Griffith, Pa., 1935–44
Elbert H. Burns, Ill., 1944–46
Leonce R. Legendre, La., 1946–51
William F. Hauck, Ind., 1952–66

EXECUTIVE DIRECTORS OF WASHINGTON NATIONAL HEADQUARTERS OFFICE

William F. Hauck, Ind., 1967–78
G. Michael Schlee, Md., 1978–79
Robert W. Spanogle, Mich., 1979–81
Mylio S. Kraja, Ohio, 1981–

DIVISION DIRECTORS AT NATIONAL HEADQUARTERS, WASHINGTON, D.C.

Economic

Elbert H. Burns, Ill., 1947–49
Ralph H. Lavers, Mass., 1949–54
Clarence W. Bird, Vt., 1954–66
Austin E. Kerby, Md., 1966–80
James G. Bourie, D.C., 1980–85
Dennis K. Rhoades, Va., 1985–88
James B. Hubbard, Mich., 1989–

FOREIGN RELATIONS (became NATIONAL SECURITY-FOREIGN RELATIONS)

For many years under direction of Director of Washington Office

RESEARCH AND FOREIGN RELATIONS

Warren H. MacDonald, Md., 1968–69

LEGISLATIVE

Thomas W. Miller, Del., 1919–20
John Thomas Taylor, Pa., 1935–41
Francis M. Sullivan, Conn., 1941–45
John Thomas Taylor, Pa., 1945–49
Miles D. Kennedy, N.Y., 1949–62
Clarence H. Olson, Mont., 1962–64

Herold E. Stringer, Ak., 1965–74
Mylio S. Kraja, Ohio, 1975–81
E. Philip Riggin, Md., 1981–

NATIONAL SECURITY (became NATIONAL SECURITY–FOREIGN RELATIONS)

Milton D. Campbell, Ohio, 1942–48
Martin B. Buckner, Mich., 1948–52
James R. Wilson, Jr., Pa., 1952–69

NATIONAL SECURITY–FOREIGN RELATIONS

James R. Wilson, Jr., Pa., 1969–77
G. Michael Schlee, Md., 1977–

REHABILITATION (became VETERANS AFFAIRS AND REHABILITATION)

Watson B. Miller, Md., 1923–41
T. O. Kraabel, N.D., 1941–58
John J. Corcoran, N.Y., 1958–67
Edward H. Golembieski, Pa., 1967–77
Robert E. Lyngh, Colo., 1977–87
John F. Sommer, Jr., Ohio, 1987–

EXECUTIVE DIRECTORS OF INDIANAPOLIS OFFICE

James A. Whitfield, Mo., 1967–78
William D. Jackson, Ind., 1978–

DIRECTORS OF DIVISIONS AND SECTIONS AT NATIONAL HEADQUARTERS, INDIANAPOLIS, INDIANA

AMERICANISM

Alvin M. Owsley, Tex., 1921–22
Garland W. Powell, Md., 1923–24
Frank C. Cross, Md., 1925–27
Dan Sowers, W.Va., 1927–30
Russell Cook, Ind., 1930–34
Homer L. Chaillaux, Cal., 1934–45
Elmer W. Sherwood, Ind., 1945–46
Waldo Curtis "Tom" Sawyer, Ariz., 1947–50
Allen B. Willand, N.Y., 1950–53
Lee R. Pennington, D.C., 1953–56
C. A. "Bud" Tesch, W.Va., 1956–63
Maurice T. "Spider" Webb, Ga., 1963–70
A. R. Tyner, Jr., Okla., 1970–71

AMERICANISM AND CHILDREN & YOUTH

Fred T. Kuszmaul, Ind., 1971–77
Raymond C. Patterson, Iowa, 1977–83
K. Michael Ayers, Ind., 1983–

WORLD WAR II LIAISON COMMITTEE (became EXPANSION AND STABILIZATION COMMITTEE)

J. Ernest Isherwood, Pa., 1943–44
Vilas H. Whaley, Wis., 1944–45

EXPANSION AND STABILIZATION COMMITTEE (became MEMBERSHIP AND POST ACTIVITIES COMMITTEE)

Vilas H. Whaley, Wis., 1945–46

MEMBERSHIP AND POST ACTIVITIES COMMITTEE (formerly WORLD WAR II LIAISON COMMITTEE AND EXPANSION AND STABILIZATION COMMITTEE)

J. Fred Johnson, Jr., Ala., 1946–47

AMERICAN LEGION LIFE INSURANCE

Paul L. Weber, Neb., 1965–75
Eugene L. Fattig, Ind., 1975–85

CHILD WELFARE (became CHILDREN & YOUTH)

John W. Gorby, Ill., 1925–26
Emma C. Puschner, Mo., 1927–50
Randel Shake, Ind., 1950–70

CHILDREN & YOUTH (became AMERICANISM AND CHILDREN & YOUTH)

Randel Shake, Ind., 1970–71

COMPUTER CENTER

Russell K. Hulse, 1963–64
A. E. (Gene) Floyd, 1964–67
Ed Schultz, 1967–68
Herman A. Koehl, 1969–73
Donald C. Mote, 1973–90
Gary Garver 1990–

NATIONAL CONVENTION

Vic MacKenzie, Ore., 1931–42
Joseph L. Lumpkin, Tenn., 1945–47
Edward McGrail, W.Va., 1947–49
Edward W. Bolt, Cal., 1949–51
Edith Shutters, 1951–58
William H. Miller, Ore., 1958–84
Robert P. Radke, Ohio, 1984–

MANAGING DIRECTOR

Hubert R. Dagley, II, Ind., 1989–

MEMBERSHIP (became MEMBERSHIP AND POST ACTIVITIES)

Charles M. "Chuck" Wilson, Ill., 1949–57
George W. Rulon, N.D., 1957–61
C. W. "Pat" Geile, Ind., 1961–66

MEMBERSHIP AND POST ACTIVITIES (became MEMBERSHIP MARKETING, SERVICES, AND PROCESSING)

J. Lloyd Wignall, Utah, 1966–76
Robert W. Spanogle, Mich., 1976–78
Thomas J. Haynes, Colo., 1978–79
James L. Adcox, N.C., 1980–85
James M. Lindsey, Mich., 1985–86

MEMBERSHIP MARKETING

James M. Lindsey, Mich., 1986–89
James E. Roodvoets, Mich., 1990–

MEMBERSHIP SERVICES

Jeffry L. Wonder, Ind., 1986–

MEMBERSHIP PROCESSING

Mary Ellen Van Treese, Ind., 1986–

LIBRARIANS

Verna B. Grimm, Wash., 1925–57
Thomas V. Hull, Ind., 1957–87
Joseph J. Hovish, N.Y., 1987–

EMIL A. BLACKMORE MUSEUM (at National Headquarters)

CURATORS

Thomas V. Hull, Ind., 1967–87
Joseph J. Hovish, N.Y., 1987–

PRINTING AND COMMUNICATIONS

Warren E. Baker, Neb., 1968–83
Lori L. Bede, Ind., 1983–

PUBLICATIONS (THE AMERICAN LEGION PUBLISHING CORP.–LATER became THE AMERICAN LEGION MAGAZINE)

George A. White, Ore.-Editor & General Manager-1919–1920
C. R. Baines-General Manager-1920–1921
H. D. Cushing-General Manager-1921–1924
Robert F. Smith, Cal.-General Manager-1924–1932
James F. Barton, Iowa-General Manager-1932–1937
James F. Barton, Iowa-Director of Publications-1937–1950
James F. O'Neil, N.H.-Director of Publications-1950–1955
James F. O'Neil, N.H.-Publisher-1955–1978
Bertram G. Davis, N.Y.-Publisher-1978–1981
Dean B. Nelson, Iowa-Publisher-1981–1983
James N. Sites, D.C.-Publisher/Editor-In-Chief-1983–1985
Daniel S. Wheeler, Va.-Publisher/Editor-In-Chief-1985–

PUBLICITY (became PUBLIC RELATIONS)

Thomas J. Ross-1919
Marquis James-1920–1922
Humphrey Sullivan-1922
Frederick C. Painton-1923–1928
Fred C. Condict-1928–1934
Harold K. Philips-1934–1937
Edward McGrail-1937–1945 (with military leave from 1942–1945)

PUBLIC RELATIONS (formerly PUBLICITY)

Raymond H. Fields, Okla., 1945–49
Edward F. McGinnis, Ill., 1949–54
George J. Kelly, Va., 1954–56
James V. Day, Me., 1956–61
Charles J. Arnold, Ind., 1961–63
James C. Watkins, D.C., 1963–78
Fredrick Woodworth, D.C., 1978–79
Frederick A. Woodress, Ky., 1979–82
Michael E. Alexander, Ind., 1982
Hubert R. Dagley, II, Ind., 1983–88
Lew Wood, Ind., 1989–

PURCHASING

Warren E. Baker, Neb., 1968–83
Bill D. Kroeker, Kans., 1983–

EMBLEM SALES

E. O. Marquette, Ind., 1924–41
Carlos A. Morris, Ind., 1942–57
James S. Whitfield, Mo., 1957–67
Hollis C. Hull, Ore., 1967–68
Jack L. Spore, Wis., 1968–69
Alfred L. Lankenau, N.Y., 1969–

FIELD SERVICE

Bert L. Halligan, Iowa, 1936–42
Henry H. Dudley, N.Y., 1942–43
John M. (Jack) Oakey, Colo., 1943–54
Nicholas Lynch, Jr., N.Y., 1954–61

FINANCE

Glenn D. Crawford, Ind., 1920–60
Robert R. Fleming, Ind., 1960–69
James E. Smith, Ind., 1969–76
Paul M. Allen, Minn., 1976–

HUMAN RESOURCES (PERSONNEL)

William J. Caldwell, Ind., 1978–89
Roger S. King, Ind., 1989–

INTERNAL AFFAIRS

Charles W. "Pat" Geile, Ind., 1966–76
J. Lloyd Wignall, Utah, 1976–77
Robert W. Spanogle, Mich., 1977–79
Thomas J. Haynes, Colo., 1979–83
Raymond C. Patterson, Iowa, 1983–

NATIONAL EXECUTIVE COMMITTEEMEN

Alabama

Crampton F. Harris 1919–20
E. Jackson Winslett 1920–21
Frank M. Dixon 1921–22
Walter E. Bare 1922–25
Mathew H. Murphy 1925–26
M. E. Frohlich 1926–28
Headley E. Jordan 1928–30
E. R. Wren 1930–32
Rufus H. Bethea 1932–34
Catesby R. Jones 1934–36
Dr. Francis Marion Inge 1936–44
George L. Cleere 1944–50
Hugh W. Overton 1950–74
Joe S. Foster 1974–78
Lewis E. McCray 1978–82
Andrew J. Cooper 1982–88
Floyd E. Fann 1988–

Alaska

George A. Getchell 1919–May 1920
Walter B King May–Oct. 1920
Harold F. Dawes 1920–21
Homer G. Nordling 1921–22
N. R. Walker 1922–23
John A. Talbot 1923–25
Dayton W. Stoddard 1925–26
Nicholas Nussbaumer 1926–28
Howard J. Thompson 1928–30
David Adler 1930–32
Ralph R. Reeser 1932–34
John A. Talbot 1934–36
Anthony E. Karnes 1936–38
Clyde R. Ellis 1938–39
Roland H. Stock 1939–48
Walter B. King 1948–50
Perry S. McLain 1950–52
John H. Van Horn 1952–54
Perry S. McLain 1954–56
Herald E. Stringer 1956–64
George Petrovich 1964–76
Robert G. Blair 1976–87
William M. Bishop 1987–

Arizona

Clifford C. Faires 3-11-20–9-29-20
Andrew P. Martin 1920–21
Bert H. Clingan 1921–22
Duane Bird 1922–23
John P. Greeway 1923–24
George V. Hays 1924–26
A. J. Dougherty 1926–2-15-28
W. V. DeCamp 2-15-28–8-23-28
W. Paul Geary 1928–12-5-29
John H. Moeur 12-31-29–1934
Irving A. Jennings 1934–2-3-40
W. C. "Tom" Sawyer 2-3-40–8-24-40
William R. Bourdon 1940–42
Al N. Zellmer 1942–46
William R. Bourdon 1946–48
John R. Stille 1948–56
Calvin R. Sanders 1956–60
Soleng Tom 1960–64
Ralph A. Watkins, Jr. 1964–66
Robert E. Cockrill 1966–76
Ronald C. Murphy, Jr. 1976–80
Louis M. Pellon 1980–84
Dr. Charles L. Vawter, Jr. 1984–88
Julian F. Santos 1988–

Arkansas

Thomas A. Jackson 2-24-20–3-26-20
Frank B. Nelson 3-26-20–8-27-20
Joseph F. W. Morrison 1920–21
Dr. L. J. Kosminsky 1921–23
J. Robert Reichardt 1923–25
Frank D. Clancy, Jr. 1925–27
O. L. Bodenhamer 1927–30
Frank D. Clancy, Jr. 1930–31
Robert L. Gordon 1931–33
Oran J. Vaughan 1933–35
Charles Q. Kelley 1935–37
James H. Graves 1937–39
Sam Rorex 1939–46
Jordan B. Lambert 1946–47
Guy Hendrix Lackey, Sr. 1947–49
Harry G. Miller 1949–51
Leonard W. Moody 1951–53
Sam Rorex 1953–55
Dr. Garland D. Murphy, Jr. 1955–59
Abe J. Davidson 1959–61
Marshall Blackard 1961–63
Claude B. Carpenter, Jr. 1963–65
Ulys A. Lovell 1965–67
Lawrence E. Fisher 1966–69
J. W. Steinsiek 1969–71
Lawrence E. Fisher 1971–77
Bob Legan 1977–79
Lawrence E. Fisher 1979–89
Claude B. Carpenter, Jr. 1989–

California

Walter K. Tuller 1919–20
Charles H. Kendrick 1920–21
Buron R. Fitts 1921–22
John R. Quinn 1922–23
Seth Millington, Jr. 1923–24
George J. Hatfield 1924–26
Nathan F. Coombs 1926–28
Philip Dodson 1928–30
Frank N. Belgrano, Jr. 1930–32
Bertrand W. Gearhart 1932–34
Homer L. Chaillaux 1934–1-22-35
Clifton A. Hix 1-22-35–1936
Warren H. Atherton 1936–38
Joseph S. Long 1938–40
Thomas J. Riordan 1940–42
Leon V. McCardle 1942–44
Leon E. Happell 1944–46
William P. Haughton 1946–48
Edward W. Bolt 1948–49
Harry L. Foster 1949–52
Jack F. Ahern 1952–54
William R. Burke 1954–56
Malcolm M. Champlin 1956–58
Alfred P. Chamie 1958–60
John J. Flynn 1960–62
Roscoe T. Morse 1962–64
A. Lee Order 1964–66
William K. Kreitz 1966–68
Leo W. Crawford 1968–70
James A. Gilbert 1970–72
Bradley J. Stephens 1972–74
Cecil L. Bandy 1974–76
Bernard L. Weddel 1976–78
Donald W. Foote 1978–80
Leo P. Burke 1980–82
Robert L. Schwartz 1982–84
Don A. Drumheller 1984–86
Lloyd Higginson 1986–88
Bruce Thiesen 1988–

Canada

Howard Bird 1923–24
William H. Wardwell 1924–26
Christian A. Thomson 1926–28
Carl B. Cooper 1928–30
Harry J. Bohme 1930–31
W. N. Millar 1931–32
Albert C. Doyle 1932–34
Clarence M. Simpson 1934–36
Paul B. Hinder 1936–40
Clarence M. Simpson 1940–52
John B. Finucane 1952–62
Francis S. Kaszas 1962–64
Forrest Monner 1964–66
Cooper L. Williams 1966–68
Robert I. Hendershott 1968–76
Dr. Robert J. Hitesman 1976–78
J. Archie Corriveau 1979–86
Mrs. H. Rena Chaplin 1986–

Colorado

Erskine Reed Myer, Jr. 2-15-20–9-1-20
Harry A. Sullivan 1920–22
Wilkie Ham 1922–25
Orla A. Garris 1925–27
Raymond M. Sandhouse 1927–29
Earl E. Ewing 1929–31
Kenaz Huffman 1931–33
Howard E. Reed 1933–35
Wilbur M. Alter 1935–37
H. Elwyn Davis 1937–39
James P. Logan 1939–41
John R. Decker 1941–43
Ben C. Hilliard, Jr. 1943–45
Trevor P. Thomas 1945–7-30-47
Albert F. Cruse 7-30-47–9-1-47
Ben C. Hilliard, Jr. 9-1-47–10-16-47
John C. Vivian 1947–4-26-48
Albert F. Cruse 4-26-48–6-5-49
Leo J. Crowley 1949–51
Albert F. Cruse 1951–53
William R. Egan 1953–61
Robert B. Grauberger 1961–73
Paul B. Rodden 1973–79
Harold M. Burdick 1979–81
Charles Pat Smith 1981–89
James McNeal 1989–

Connecticut

Justus J. Fennell 1919–21
Thomas J. Bannigan 1921–22
Justus J. Fennell 1922–23
E. L. Barlow 1923–25
Eugene P. Armstrong 1925–27
Harry C. Jackson 1927–31
Kenneth F. Cramer 1931–33
Anson T. McCook 1933–34
Edward L. Newmarker 1934–35
Sydney A. R. Finer 1935–37
William J. Miller 1937–38
Arthur L. Baldwin 1938–39
J. Fred Collins 1939–41
Raymond F. Gates 1941–45
Herbert L. Emanuelson 1945–47
Arthur J. Connell 1947–53
Joseph G. Leonard 1953–79
Henry S. Bialoglowy 1979–85
Lionel F. Dugas 1985–87
Richard W. Anderson 1987–

Delaware

Thomas W. Miller 3-25-20–1928
J. Alexander Crothers 1928–29
Earl Sylvester 1929–30
John J. Dugan 1930–34
Herman H. Hanson 1934–36
Howard T. Ennis 1936–38
Edward A. Mulrooney 1938–40
George D. Hill 1940–42
John R. Fader 1942–44
William E. Matthews, Jr., 1944–46
Samuel Green 1946–48
George Ehinger 1948–50
Samuel S. Fried 1950–52
Dr. Carl J. Rees 1952–54
William J. B. Regan 1954–56
Charles A. Burrous, Jr. 1956–57
Harry S. Zerby 1-8-58–6-22-58
Garland D. Bloodsworth 1958–60
Morris Wasserman 1960–62
Dr. Park W. Huntington 1962–64
Charles E. Jackson 1964–66
Frank A. Lucia 1966–68
James E. Heal 1968–70
Thomas W. Mulrooney 1970–72
Raymond H. Trabbold 1972–74
William Melville 1974–76
Donald E. Neil 1976–78
Carlton L. Smith 1978–80
John E. Byrne 1980–82
Edward M. Knight 1982–84
John K. Simons 1984–86
Robert J. Lauer 1986–88
Donavon L. Orth 1988–

District of Columbia

E. Lester Jones 3-24-20–9-27-20
James A. Drain 1920–22
John Lewis Smith, Sr. 1922–23
Watson B. Miller 1923–24
Paul J. McGahan 1924–30
John Lewis Smith, Sr. 1930–36
Joseph J. Malloy 1936–48
Owen C. Holleran 1948–50
James D. Hill 1950–52
Lee R. Pennington 1952–53
David E. Kisliuk 1953–54
William J. Holliman 1954–2-24-56
Robert A. Bunch 2-24-56–7-21-56
James D. Hill 1956–58
John J. Finn 1958–60
Harold D. Beaton 1960–62
Frederick H. Livingstone 1962–64
Allyn C. Donaldson 1964–66
John J. Finn 1966–68
Stewart W. Parker 1968–70
Hy Wayne 1970–72
Albert Matthews 1972–74
Marshall C. Gardner 1974–76
James K. Scarborough 1976–78
Thomas C. Kouyeas 1978–80
A. Leo Anderson 1980–82
Joseph G. Kelly 1982–84
Richard Billig 1984–86
Robert L. Walters 1986–88
Richard R. Giasson 1988–

Florida

Dr. Davis Forster 3-3-20–1922
Joseph Y. Cheney 1922–25
H. Neil Kirkman 1925–29
Charles A. Mills 1929–33
J. A. Franklin 1933–5-21-34
Herbert R. Dyer 5-21-34–10-26-34
Joseph S. Clark 1934–44
Sam S. McCahill 1944–46
E. Meade Wilson 1946–66
Arthur M. MacCarthy 1966–70
John J. Adams 1970–74
Johnson E. Davis 1974–80
Billy Anderson 1980–82
A. L. (Tony) Ulchar 1982–86
George L. Derrick 1986–

France

Francis E. Drake 1920–21
R. Emmet Condon 1921–23
S. Prentiss Bailey 1923–36
James L. McCann 1936–52
Sedley C. Peck 1952–60
Dana W. Lyman 1960–62
Sedley C. Peck 1962–66
Walter E. Lindquist 1966–68
James E. Zulick 1968–74
Helmut Spangenthal 1974–82
William S. Lombardo 1982–88
Merwyn M. Beavers 1988–

Georgia

Eugnen Oberdorfer, Jr., 2-24-20–8-21-20
Sam A. Cann 1920–22
Asa W. Candler 1922–25
Terrell W. Hill 1925–27
Manton S. Eddy 1927–7-5-30
Charles P. Graddick 7-5-30–11-10-30
Edgar B. Dunlap 11-10-30–1933
Quimby O. Melton 1933–34
James D. Gould, Jr. 1934–35
Quimby O. Melton 1935–37
Edward F. O'Connor, Jr. 1937–39
J. Pat Kelly 1939–41
Hoyt C. Brown 1941–43
Jackson P. Dick 1943–47
Guy O. Stone 1947–54
James E. Powers 1954–62
J. S. "Jack" Langford 1962–63
W. D. Harrell 1963–89
Horance E. Borders 1989–

Hawaii

Leonard Withington 3-3-20–10-30-21
John R. Galt 1921–22
Walter F. Dillingham 1922–23
Adna G. Clarke 1923–27
James R. Mahaffy 1927–33
Adna G. Clarke 1933–35
Harold C. Hill 1935–37
Robert E. Kries 1937–39
Harry F. Cooper 1939–41
James Tice Phillips 1941–42
James R. Mahaffy 1942–43
Kennett W. Dawson 1943–44
P. L. Murphy 1944–45
Orvel T. Shonk, Sr. 1945–49
Earl L. Holman 1949–51
Orvel T. Shonk, Sr. 1951–53
Philip M. Corboy 1953–57
Wallace C. S. Young 1957–71
Jessie J. Cotter 1971–72
Wallace C. S. Young 1972–75
Bernard J. Peron 1975–77
Libert J. Pakele, Jr. 1977–83
Kenneth McAtee 1983–85
Robert J. Conrad 1985–

Idaho

George E. Edgington 2-24-20–7-19-20
Oscar W. Worthwine 1920–21
E. W. Sinclair 1921–23
Charles A. Robins 1923–24
James Harris 1924–25
Samuel E. Vance, Jr. 1925–28
Frank Estabrook 1928–30
David L. Bush 1930–32
Harry Benoit 1932–38
O. C. Wilson 1938–40
Alfred W. Shepherd 1940–42
Gardner B. Parsons 1942–44
James C. Bangs 1944–46
William T. Marineau 1946–48
Bert Weston 1948–50
Elbert S. Rawls 1950–52
Sidney E. Smith 1952–54
Harry R. Harn 1954–56
Andrew F. James 1956–58
John Hawley Atkinson 1958–60
Peter B. Wilson 1960–62
Douglas D. Kramer 1962–64
Bernard F. Gratton 1964–66
Bob W. Knudsen 1966–68
Max Hanson 1968–70
Melvin J. Alsager 1970–72
Dan McClintock 1972–74
E. B. "Jim" Newsome 1974–76
Elton Ashton 1976–82
Georg Serr 1982–84
Conrad Chisholm 1984–86
Lyle Hupfer 1986–88
Marion P. Johnson 1988–

Illinois

Milton J. Foreman 2-23-20–1922
Horatio B. Hackett 1922–23
Charles W. Schick 1923–12-2-23
S. L. Nelson 12-2-23–1925
Howard P. Savage 1925–27
Ferre C. Watkins 1927–29
David L. Shillinglaw 1929–31
Edward A. Hayes 1931–33
James P. Ringley 1933–34
Charles C. Kapschull 1934–35
Paul G. Armstrong 1935–39
Karl B. Nash 1939–41
William F. Waugh 1941–43
John H. Stelle 1943–45
James P. Ringley 1945–47
Leonard W. Esper 1947–49
John S. Gleason, Jr., 1949–51
Douglass D. Getchell 1951–53
Perce F. Brautigam 1953–55
S. William Ash 1955–57
Michael J. Healy 1957–59
Omar J. McMackin 1959–61
Charles C. Shaw 1961–63
John H. Geiger 1963–65
Karl Yost 1965–67
Morris "Bob" Nooner 1967–69
Eric H. Smith 1969–71
Norman J. Biebel 1971–73
Richard I. Nicholas 1973–75
Albert J. Swiderski 1975–77
Russell P. Bieritz 1977–79
Edward F. Brennan 1979–81

John B. Mahoney 1981–83
Charles Kinkade 1983–85
Firman E. Henricks 1985–87
James V. Kissner 1987–89
Paul E. Briese 1989–

Indiana

Dr. T. Victor Keene 2-23-20–1921
Oswald Ryan 1921–22
Bowman Elder 1922–27
Paul V. McNutt 1927–28
Frank M. McHale 1928–29
Raymond S. Springer 1929–31
Dr. A. C. Arnett 1931–33
Glen R. Hillis 1933–35
Isadore E. Levine 1935–43
V. M. Armstrong 1943–45
Charles Patriot Maloney 1945–47
George N. Craig 1947–49
Harry E. Fitch 1949–51
Vincent F. Kelley 1951–53
John C. Wilson 1953–55
Lawrence H. Hinds 1955–59
Ferd S. Badt 1959–61
Arthur M. McDowell 1961–63
Dr. Fred N. Daugherty 1963–65
Robert L. Kuntz 1965–67
Charles S. Boehm 1967–69
Melvin H. Heckman 1969–77
Gilbert E. Sheeks 1977–

Iowa

Daniel F. Steck 2-23-20–1921
John H. Kelly 1921–23
Dr. R. J. Laird 1923–25
Maurice P. Cahill 1925–27
Volney Diltz 1927–29
Ray Murphy 1929–33
Wm. J. O'Connell 1933–35
Leo J. Duster 1935–39
Ray O. Garber 1939–41
Morris Y. Kinne 1941–43
Fred E. Keating 1943–45
Gaylor M. Brown 1945–49
Paul A. Tornquist 1949–53
Theodore E. Murphy 1953–55
Ward M. Loftus 1955–57
Donald E. Johnson 1957–61
John W. Moore 1961–63
Ward M. Loftus 1963–2-7-65
Robert H. Lounsberry 1965–69
Raymond C. Patterson 1969–71
Stewart H. M. Lund 1971–75
Donald H. Harmeyer 1975–79
Dale L. Renaud 1979–83
Mark J. Studer 1983–87
Leo Maynard 1987–

Italy

Edward R. Warner McCabe 1-8-27–11-14-27
Mrs. Julia Woodruff Wheelock 1927–46
Amerigo Vitelli 1946–52
H. Armand deMasi 1952–62
Sexson E. Humphreys 1962–68
H. Armand deMasi 1968–73
Frank C. Bottigliero 1973–

Kansas

William F. Kurtz 2-23-20–1920
W. W. Holloway 1920–21
R. C. Meek 1921–22
Wilder S. Metcalf 1922–23
Jay H. Bracken 1923–24
Dr. C. C. Hawke 1924–26
W. D. Reilly 1926–28
Braden Johnston 1928–30
Myron C. Miller 1930–32
Rex M. Montgomery 1932–34
Leslie E. Edmonds 1934–36
Ed. Morgenstern 1936–38
Oscar Renn 1938–40
Sam Brolund 1940–42
Everett C. Garrison 1942–44
McCulley Ashlock 1944–46

Harry W. Woods 1946–48
Walter Reed Gage 1948–50
Verner C. Smith 1950–52
Guy E. Holt 1952–54
Dale L. Duncan 1954–56
Ora D. McClellan 1956–58
Harold J. Hollis 1958–60
Keith D. Brecheisen 1960–62
Robert J. Kubat 1962–64
Virgil L. Lehr 1964–66
U. S. "Udie" Grant 1966–

Kentucky

Emmet O'Neal 9-13-20–1921
Maurice K. Gordon 1921–22
Emmet O'Neal 1922–25
Frank D. Rash 1925–4-19-46
William P. Shadoan 4-28-46–1947
G. Lee McClain 1947–49
John F. Hagner 1949–51
Garland G. Bryant 1951–53
Charles M. Blackburn 1953–57
Darrell B. Hancock 1957-61
Robert W. Anderson 1961–63
Kenneth Fern 1963–67
Harry A. Greene 1967–77
J. Leslie Brown, Jr. 1977–83
Norbert H. Gadladge 1983–85
Joseph K. Goodness 1985–89
Silas M. Noel 1989–

Louisiana

Bret W. Eddy 2-23-20–1920
T. Semmes Walmsley 1920–21
Oswald W. McNeese 1921–22
Clarence J. Bourg 1922–23
Gus Blancand 1923–25
Joseph L. McHugh 1925–27
Dan W. Spurloch 1927–29
Charles E. McKenzie 1929–31
Sam H. Jones 1931–35
T. Ray Mobley 1935–37
Ernest L. Hawkins 1937–39
Joseph A. Partridge 1939–43
J. Perry Cole 1943–45
Joseph Emmett Snee 1945–49
Leonard L. Jackson 1949–51
Claude B. Duval 1951–53
Dr. Arthur R. Choppin 1953–57
Albert V. LaBiche 1957–63
Henry B. Clay 1963–67
M. C. Gehr 1967–69
Robert Charles Smith 1969–77
J. B. Broussard 1977–81
Carroll B. Fields 1981–87
Paul M. Severson 1987–

Maine

Albert Greenlaw 1919–28
Edward S. Anthoine 1928–30
Dr. John G. Towne 1930–32
Albert Beliveau 1932–34
Basil H. Stinson 1934–36
John J. Maloney, Sr., 1936–38
Raymond E. Rendall 1938–40
Edward J. Quinn 1940–44
Llewellyn C. Fortier 1944–46
Paul J. Jullien 1946–48
Hector G. Staples 1948–50
Fred A. Clough, Jr. 1950–52
Peter A. Thaanum, Jr. 1952–54
James V. Day 1954–55
Ralph M. Merrow 1955–58
Anthony J. Rumo 1958–60
William J. Rogers 1960–65
Maurice R. Parisien 1965–68
Merlon R. Kingsley 1968–70
Reginald J. Dennis 1970–72
James A. McMahon 1972–76
Clifford L. Quinney 1976–78
Vito M. DeFilipp 1978–80
Robert C. MacFarland 1980–82
Anthony G. Jordan 1982–

Maryland

Henry S. Barrett 1919–20
David John Markey 1920–22
H. Findley French 1922–23
E. Brooks Lee 1923–24
John Carmichael 1924–25
J. Moses Edlavitch 1925–28
Asa Needham 1928–32
Caesar L. Aiello 1932–33
Alex T. Grier 1933–34
John W. Jennings 1934–38
J. Bryan Hobbs 1938–42
Godfrey Child 1942–48
Harry S. Allen 1948–52
Frank T. Powers 1952–54
J. Edward Walter 1954–56
David L. Brigham 1956–64
John A. Matthews 1964–65
H. Laird Roeder 1965–66
Robert E. L. Eaton 1966–70
Jack E. Dyke 1970–76
David A. Wade 1976–78
Clarence M. Bacon 1978–80
F. Douglas Johnson 1980–82
Calvin E. Patton 1982–84
Robert W. Neal 1984–86
Talmage C. Carawan 1986–88
Earl C. Nuttall 1988–

Massachusetts

John F. J. Herbert 2-5-20–1920
James T. Duane 1920–21
Charles H. Cole 1921–22
William H. Dole 1922–23
Clarence R. Edwards 1923–24
Leo M. Harlow 1924–25
Francis J. Good 1925–26
William McGinnis 1926–27
John W. Reth 1927–28
Dr. William H. Griffin 1928–29
John J. O'Connell 1929–30
Richard F. Paul 1930–31
Stephen C. Garrity 1931–32
James P. Rose 1932–33
Stephen C. Garrity 1933–12-26-43
Harold P. Redden 3-1-44–1947
Tracy A. Dibble 1947–51
Frederick L. Mellin 1951–55
Charles N. Collatos 1955–59
Gabriel T. Olga 1959–69
Leo F. Malloy 1969–75
Robert W. Groccia 1975–81
John P. Comer 1981–87
John J. Mulkern 1987–

Mexico

Leigh H. Rovzar 1920–23
P. B. Holsinger 1923–4-12-26
R. H. Hudgens 4-12-26–11-18-27
Will S. Link 11-8-27–1928
Donald Lee McCuen 1928–30
Walter S. Sollenberger 1930–37
John Welsh 1937–38
Harry W. Berdie 1938–40
Walter S. Sollenberger 1940–46
Robert E. Feike 1946–48
Roscoe B. Gaither 1948–52
Andres J. du Bouchet, Jr. 1952–57
William J. Seibert 1957–60
Norbert W. Schmelkes 1960–64
Harry Wright 1964–70
Fred W. Soto 1970–72
Gordon A. Ballantyne 1972–80
Veit Gentry, Jr. 1980–82
Harry Wright 1982–88
Thomas L. Hogan 1988–

Michigan

Fred M. Alger, Sr. 1919–20
Alton T. Roberts 1920–21
Paul A. Martin 1921–23
Dr. Robert B. Harkness 1923–24
Dr. C. V. Spawr 1924–25
John F. Roehl 1925–26
J. Joseph Herbert 1926–27
Harold G. Edwards 1927–28
Willis M. Brewer 1928–30
Ray Charles Conlon 1930–31

Raymond J. Kelly 1931–33
Leslie P. Kefgen 1933–35
John W. Gilmore 1935–37
Don L. Beardslee 1937–38
David V. Addy 1938–41
Carl H. Smith 1941–43
W. Bea Waldrip 1943–45
Herman F. Luhrs 1945–47
Lawrence C. Knox 1947–49
Guy M. Cox 1949–51
Earl F. Ganschow 1951–53
Arthur H. Clarke 1953–55
Robert G. Mathieson 1955–57
R. Gerald Barr 1957–59
Thomas Roumell 1959–61
Donald J. Smith 1961–63
William J. Clarahan 1963–65
John M. Carey 1965–67
Marshall M. Taylor 1967–69
Duane T. Brigstock 1969–71
Edwin J. Schuitema 1971–73
Miles S. Ansbaugh 1973–75
Giles A. Reeve 1975–77
George D. Johnson 1977–79
Eugene W. Heugel 1979–81
Donald C. Huntley 1981–83
Vernon L. Henrichs 1983–85
Glenn H. Ainslie 1985–87
Andrew A. Templeton 1987–89
Roy B. Cicotte 1989–

Minnesota

Arch H. Vernon 1919–20
Dr. A. A. Van Dyke 1920–21
R. A. Rossberg 1921–22
Z. L. Begin 1922–23
Frederic D. McCarthy 1923–25
John M. Henry 1925–27
Rufus R. Rand, Jr. 1927–29
Dr. J. J. Morrow 1929–31
Earl V. Cliff 1931–33
Gerald V. Barron 1933–35
William R. Mitchell 1935–37
Lloyd B. Kolliner 1937–39
Michael F. Murray 1939–43
Roy T. Anderson 1943–53
Carl L. Lundgren 1953–57
Daniel F. Foley 1957–63
Eugene V. Lindquist 1963–73
Glenn H. Dornfeld 1973–74
Milo Blanich 1974–75
Donald R. Schroedl 1975–

Mississippi

Alexander Fitzhugh 8-18-20–1921
Dr. Ira L. Parsons 1921–22
Winfred C. Adams 1922–23
Kenneth G. Price 1923–24
Curtis T. Green 1924–26
Leon F. Hendrick 1926–27
Ben F. Hilbun 1927–28
Ernest Waldauer 1928–30
Wm. A. Schmitt 1930–32
Forrest G. Cooper 1932–36
James T. Crawley 1936–38
Adrian H. Boyd 1938–46
Fred W. Young 1946–48
H. Kirk Grantham 1948–50
Robert D. Morrow 1950–1-16-55
Ralph M. Godwin 1-31-55–7-13-55
Rollins S. (Polly) Armstrong 1955–56
Ralph M. Godwin 1956–80
Fred M. Ingellis 1980–

Missouri

Albert Linxwiler 1919–20
Jerome F. Duggan 1920–21
J. Pearce Kane 1921–22
Bennett C. Clark 1922–23
Herbert R. Booth 1923–24
Carl G. Schrader 1924–25
Harry W. Castlen 1925–26
Dr. Neal D. Williams 1926–30
Herman H. Lark 1930–32
George Fiske 1932–34
Hal S. Beardsley 1934–36
Al J. Haemerle 1936–38
Charles L. Brown 1938–42
William B. Stone 1942–50
Truman Ingle 1950–54
James B. Kerrigan 1954–56
Elmer W. Kuhlman 1956–58
William J. Kenney 1958–60
William H. Cain 1960–3-21-62
Buel A. Baclesse 3-21-62–7-29-62

Roy L. Carver 1962–64
James F. Kerr 1964–66
Frank H. Strong 1966–70
Jerome P. Dobel 1970–74
Cleo T. Martin 1974–78
Erman W. Taylor 1978–82
William F. Liddle 1982–86
Jerome N. Roach 1986–

Montana

Robert K. West 1919–20
Charles E. Pew 1920–21
Wm. G. Ferguson 1921–22
C. Thomas Busha, Jr. 1922–23
Loy J. Molumby 1923–25
N. J. Gilliland 1925–26
Charles L. Sheridan 1926–27
Harry M. Johnson 1927–28
Herbert Kibler 1928–29
Dan B. Noble 1929–31
James A. Livingston 1931–32
Arthur F. Lamey 1932–35
Hugh N. Marron 1935–37
Clarence H. Olson 1937–12-12-40
Ory J. Armstrong 12-12-40–1941
William H. Reif 1941–43
Frank E. Flaherty 1943–45
George M. Gosman 1945–47
Edwin O. Orleman 1947–49
John B. C. Knight 1949–51
Victor O. Overcash 1951–53
Walter W. Barnard 1953–55
Grover C. Schmidt, Jr. 1955–57
W. Charles Wallace 1957–59
John S. Wulf, Jr. 1959–61
Russell W. Lindborg 1961–63
Neil Shepherd 1963–65
William A. Lindsay 1965–69
P. W. Kelley 1969–71
Franklin D. Pehrson 1971–73
Earle M. Angell 1973–77
Theodore P. Crawford 1977–79
Robert R. Williams 1979–81
Pete T. Tuss 1981–83
David Shannon 1983–85
W. P. (Bill) Petersen 1985–87
C. Hal Manson 1987–89
Donald Buffington 1989–

Nebraska

Edward Patrick McDermott 1920–21
Earl M. Cline 1921–23
Frank Warner 1923–24
Samuel W. Reynolds 1924–1-22-35
Golden P. Kratz 1-30-35–4-14-36
Fred B. Winter 4-14-36–1938
Clinton Brome 1938–4-24-46
John E. Curtiss 4-24-46–5-22-60
Lyman Stuckey 7-27-60–8-28-60
Stanley M. Huffman 1960–62
Edward T. Foster 1962–64
William E. Galbraith 1964–65
Robert W. Lowry 1965–66
Jerome N. Henn 1966–76
Robert W. Lowry 1976–80
Lewis L. Adams 1980–84
Wayne Davis 1984–88
Roger L. Wild 1988–

Nevada

J. G. Scrugham 2-27-20–1922
George W. Malone 1922–23
Thomas J. D. Salter 1923–24
Earl T. Ross 1924–26
Joseph G. Allard 1926–28
E. H. Hursh 1928–30
George W. Malone 1930–32
A. C. Grant 1932–34
Ioannis A. Lougaris 1934–38
Dr. J. Dayton Smith 1938–40
Ioannis A. Lougaris 1940–46
Thomas W. Miller 1946–73
Charles F. Langel 1973–

New Hampshire

Orville E. Cain 1919–20
Reginald C. Stevenson 1920–21
Dr. Robert O. Blood 1921–22
Orville E. Cain 1922–29

Maurice F. Devine 1929–41
James J. Doyle 1941–45
William J. Johnson 1945–47
James W. Doon 1947–55
Eli A. Marcoux 1955–57
Floyd J. Daley 1957–61
Raymond F. Mudge 1961–69
Laurence R. Spalding 1969–79
M. Ray Olmstead 1979–87
Joseph E. Caouette 1987–89
George V. West 1989–

New Jersey

Philip J. Ehrhardt 1919–20
Leonidas Coyle 1920–21
Joseph D. Sears 1921–22
Harry C. Kramer 1922–23
A. Eugene Pattison 1923–26
Philip Forman 1926–27
John Grimshaw, Jr. 1927–29
Herbert H. Blizzard 1929–31
Theodore R. Crichton 1931–33
Frank A. Mathews, Jr. 1933–35
William G. McKinley 1935–67
Edmund G. Lyons 1967–73
Franklin R. Sickle 1973–79
Warren R. Davies 1979–85
James H. Hall 1985–89
Albert M. Robotti 1989–

New Mexico

Bronson M. Cutting 1919–20
Herman G. Baca 1920–21
John W. Chapman 1921–22
Joseph C. Wallach 1922–25
E. P. de Bujac 1925–27
Aud E. Lusk 1927–29
Jesus M. Baca 1929–31
Roy L. Cook 1931–33
Herman G. Baca 1933–34
Ollie A. Davis 1934–35
Edward L. Safford 1935–37
H. C. Neuffer 1937–40
Edwin G. Hobbs 1940–41
Charles Morgan 1941–43
Edward C. Smith 1943–47
Joseph H. Kirkpatrick 1947–49
Reed Mulkey 1949–57
James A. Tadlock 1957–10-21-57
Dr. Deward H. Reed 10-31-57–7-10-64
W. Peter McAtee 1964–67
G. Y. Fails 1967–73
Merrill L. Norton 1973–75
Robert W. Durand 1975–

New York

William J. Donovan 2-24-20–1920
W. R. Pooley 1920–21
Ralph K. Robertson 1921–23
Donald C. Strachan 1923–25
Albert L. Ward 1925–27
William M. Leffingwell 1927–33
Edward J. Neary 1933–35
Robert E. Minnich 1935–39
Jeremiah F. Cross 1939–44
William N. Lewis 1944–45
Leo V. Lanning 1945–57
Louis E. Drago 1957–11-27-70
Richard Pedro 1-26-71–7-17-71
Aldo R. Benedetto 7-17-71–1976
Arnold E. Swanson 1976–77
Richard M. Pedro 1977–84
John J. Harris 1984–85
William P. McLaughlin 1985–87
Donald E. Klein 1987–89
Vance E. Ketcham 1989–

North Carolina

David J. Whichard, Jr. 2-23-20–1920
Wade H. Phillips 1920–21
Dan S. Hollenga 1921–22
Cale K. Burgess 1922–23
Alice S. Gray 1923–24
Thomas W. Bird 1924–26
George K. Freeman 1926–29
E. Jack Edwards 1929–30
Wm. T. Joyner 1930–10-20-33
J. Erle McMichael 10-20-33–1934

Louis G. Ratcliffe 1934–40
Wm. Bryan Booe 1940–6-15-46
Claude S. Ramsey, Sr. 6-15-46–2-24-47
Robin S. Kirby 1947–54
R. C. Godwin 1954–56
W. Austin Gresham 1956–58
Tim T. Craig 1958–62
William Dudley Robbins 1962–66
Leroy S. Lakey 1966–72
Robert A. Tart 1972–

North Dakota

James M. Hanley 1919–20
C. L. Dawson 1920–21
M. H. Sprague 1921–22
Philip R. Bangs 1922–23
Fred A. Kraemer 1923–24
Francis Blaine Streeter 1924–25
William Stern 1925–1-1-64
Patrick T. Milloy 1964–72
Earnest N. Schmit 1972–80
Q. R. Schulte 1980–84
Robert E. Hennessey 1984–88
Howard V. Erickson 1988–

Ohio

F. W. Galbraith, Jr. 3-12-20–1920
John R. McQuigg 1920–24
Lucian Kahn 1924–26
Milo J. Warner 1926–29
George E. Denny 1929–32
Paul M. Herbert 1932–34
Thomas W. McCaw 1934–36
William S. Konold 1936–38
James R. Favret 1938–40
Eli A. Jensen 1940–42
James V. Suhr 1942–44
Martin V. Coffey 1944–48
Don W. Schoeppe 1948–50
Aaron J. Halloran 1950–52
Rossiter S. Williams 1952–54
Clarence W. Whitemyer 1954–56
James M. Wagonseller 1956–58
Edward J. Sklenicka 1958–60
Merle F. Brady 1960–64
Alec J. Blair 1964–66
Joseph S. Deutschle, Sr. 1966–68
Donald L. Gruenbaum 1968–72
Roger A. Munson 1972–76
Arthur H. Euler 1976–78
Charles R. Green 1978–82
W. Dean Scholl 1982–84
Thomas L. Gabel 1984–86
Dominic V. Belloni 1986–

Oklahoma

Roy V. Hoffman 2-23-20–1921
Robert B. Keenan, Sr. 1921–22
William S. Key 1922–23
Wm. L. Eagleton, Jr. 1923–25
Gilbert S. Fraser 1925–27
Edward L. Allison 1927–29
Raymond H. Fields 1929–35
Wm. G. Stigler 1935–37
Jack A. Porter 1937–39
Hugh Askew 1939–41
Dr. Ambrus B. Rivers 1941–49
Dr. Charles W. Hoshall 1949–51
Ike E. Crawford 1951–55
Preston J. Moore 1955–58
H. Coleman Nolen 1958–61
Gene Hassman 1961–67
W. H. (Bill) Redman 1967–69
Eldridge Colston 1969–71
W. H. (Bill) Redman 1971–73
Tom C. Smith 1973–

Oregon

Dow V. Walker 2-25-20–1920
George A. White 1920–22
Charles W. Erskine 1922–23
Dr. E. B. Stewart 1923–25
Charles J. Johnson 1925–27
Vic MacKenzie 1927–29
Ben S. Fisher 1929–30
Vic MacKenzie 1930–31
Sidney S. George 1931–37
George L. Koehn 1937–39

Willard J. Chamberlin 1939–41
E. L. Knight 1941–43
Oral E. Palmateer 1943–45
Hugh A. Bowman 1945–47
Alfred P. Kelly 1947–49
David Blakeman 1949–51
B. E. "Kelly" Owens 1951–53
Hollis C. Hull 1953–56
Karl L. Wagner 1956–65
William Stevens 1965–67
W. E. Wilkins 1967–69
Don Eva 1969–73
John W. Buether 1973–77
T. Les Galloway 1977–

Panama Canal

Fred DeVeber Sill 1920–26
Theodore M. Drake 1926–28
Fred DeVeber Sill 1928–32
Osborne E. McKay 1932–34
Theodore M. Drake 1934–36
Osborne E. McKay 1936–38
Fred DeVeber Sill 1938–40
Osborne E. McKay 1940–44
Thomas F. Sullivan 1944–46
LeRoy Schick 1946–50
Nelson W. Magner 1950–56
Claude E. Campbell 1956–60
Raymond G. Bush 1960–62
George A. Black, Jr. 1962–64
Raymond G. Bush 1964–66
Romeo J. Routhier 1966–68
Arnold A. Hannberg 1968–72
George Vieto 1972–76
James T. Wiggins 1976–78
Romeo J. Routhier 1978–81
Robert McGuinness 1981–82
Romeo J. Routhier 1982–83
Ricardo R. Machado 1983–86
Romeo J. Routhier 1986–88
Dan McDonald 1988–

Pennsylvania

Albert J. Logan 2-24-20–1920
David J. Davis 1920–21
Joseph H. Thompson 1921–22
Wm. B. Healey 1922–23
J. Leo Collins 1923–27
Lucius McK. Crumrine 1927–30
Charles A. Gebert 1930–32
Vincent A. Carroll 1932–37
J. Guy Griffith 1937–42
Harry K. Stinger 1942–52
William L. Windsor III 1952–54
Walter E. Alessandroni 1954–66
Daniel A. Drew 1966–72
E. Thomas Cammarota 1972–74
Dr. Almo J. Sebastianelli 1974–80
Stephen J. Mikosky 1980–84
Dominic D. DiFrancesco 1984–86
Joseph V. Adams 1986–

Philippines

Whipple S. Hall 1920–23
No record, 1923–24
Harry J. Morgan 1924–25
Harry D. Cranston 1925–27
Harrison S. Kerrick 1927–33
Forrest E. Williford 1933–34
Harrison S. Kerrick 1934–36
Frank Parker 1936–46
Benjamin F. Ohnick 1946–48
Marc A. Stice 1948–51
Gailey B. Underwood 1951–52
Andrew R. McKelvie 1952–54
Jose J. DeGuzman 1954–56
Bernard L. Anderson 1956–58
Robert O. Phillips 1958–60
Jose J. DeGuzman 1960–62
Robert O. Phillips 1962–63
Jose J. DeGuzman 1963–64
Robert O. Phillips 1964–65
Charles A. Park 1965–66
Robert O. Phillips 1966–68
Edward T. Berling 1968–70
Simeon C. Medalla 1970–72
Robert O. Phillips 1972–73
Manuel A. Vargas 1973–76
Carlos D. Arguelles 1976–78
Ernesto P. Golez 1978–84
Eligio Tionamba 1984–86
Ernesto P. Golez 1986–

Puerto Rico

Harry F. Besosa 1922–23
Athos W. Besosa 1923–26
Harry F. Besosa 1926–27
Manuel Font 1927–28
Noah Shepard 1928–29
Dr. Juan Lastra Charriez 1929–35
Harry L. Hall 1935–37
Manuel Font 1937–39
Dr. J. H. Font 1939–41
Ignasio Saavedra 1941–43
Jose Cantellops 1943–47
Charles H. Julia 1947–3-14-49
Vincente Reyes Fitspatrick 1949–53
Ramon Rafael Guas 1953–4-12-55
Alejo Rivera Morales 4-12-55–7-17-55
Ramon Rafael Guas 1955–57
Osvaldo Rivera 1957–59
Gilbert M. Font 1959–67
Juan H. Cintron 1967–68
Dr. Raul Barreras 1968–71
William Feliciano 1971–73
Roberto Gonzalez Vazquez 1973–83
Luis A. Andujar 1983–87
Juan H. Cintron 1987–

Rhode Island

G. Edward Buxton, Jr. 1919-20
William P. Sheffield, Jr. 1920–21
L. H. Callan 1921–22
Thomas J. H. Peirce 1922–23
Bertram W. Wall 1923–29
Raymond B. Littlefield 1929–31
Charles L. Woolley 1931–33
Bertram W. Wall 1933–35
Ralph S. Mohr 1935–37
William Beehler 1937–39
Frank E. McCaffrey 1939–43
Edward H. Ziegler 1943–45
Chester A. Follett 1945–47
George Andrews 1947–49
Arthur E. Marley 1949–51
Lee A. Lemos 1951–53
John A. Ryer 1953–69
John J. O'Connell 1969–71
Louis R. J. Malo 1971–73
Edward Denis 1973–75
John A. Adamowicz 1975–77
Kenneth O. Todd 1977–79
Matthew B. Ryan 1979–81
John E. Demers, Sr. 1981–83
Raymond S. Sanchas 1983–85
N. Pio Stizza 1985–87
Robert Miles, Jr. 1987–89
Walter R. Perry, Sr. 1989–

South Carolina

J. Monroe Johnson 1919–22
Thomas B. Spratt 1922–23
J. Monroe Johnson 1923–35
Miller C. Foster 1935–1-24-36
George D. Levy 1-24-36–1941
Sam L. Latimer, Jr. 1941–45
James F. Daniel, Jr. 1945–51
W. J. McLeod, Jr. 1951–52
Dr. Roland Hoyt Fulmer 1952–53
E. Roy Stone, Jr. 1953–

South Dakota

M. L. Shade 2-25-20–1920
Fred B. Ray 1920–22
J. H. Williams 1922–23
Dr. G. G. Cottam 1923–27
Walter H. Burke 1927–29
Frank G. McCormick 1929–30
Dr. Carle B. Lenker 1930–37
R. A. Schenkenberger 1937–41
Turner M. Rudesill 1941–4-10-44
Claude A. Hamilton 4-10-44–6-18-44
Carroll H. Lockhart 1944–49
Claude A. Hamilton 1949–57
Earl E. Hoelscher 1957–63
Glenn R. Green 1963–77
Wayne W. Slade 1977–81
Donald Clarke 1981–

Tennessee

Harry S. Berry 1919–21
Phil B. Whitaker 1921–22
L. Jere Cooper 1922–23
Dr. Samuel T. Parker 1923–24
John G. Sims, Sr. 1924–26
Oscar L. Farris 1926–28
Roane Waring 1928–30
Adam B. Bowman 1930–32
Prentice Cooper 1932–34
Roane Waring 1934–42
Bascom F. Jones 1942–44
Dr. Nat H. Copenhaver 1944–46
David N. Harsh 1946–48
Halbert Harvill 1948–50
George A. Caldwell 1950–52
Bert B. Barnes, Jr. 1952–54
Rev. William Henry Moss 1954–56
John J. Duncan 1956–58
George T. Lewis, Jr. 1958–60
Walton D. Griffin 1960–62
William S. Todd 1962–64
Whit LaFon 1964–66
Roscoe D. Curtiss 1966–67
Benton Crump 1967–68
Robert M. Summitt 1968–70
Robert J. Foster 1970–72
Jay E. Harville 1972–74
Sam Friedman 1974–76
Joe F. Hudgens 1976–78
Percy C. Miller 1978–80
Charles G. Norton 1980–82
William B. Cain 1982–84
John J. Maddux, Jr. 1984–86
James T. Waters 1986–88
Carl E. Levi 1988–

Texas

Claude V. Birkhead 2-24-20–1920
John S. Hoover 1920–21
R. G. Storey 1921–22
Charles C. Ingram 1922–23
Jay A. Rossiter 1923–24
Ben J. Dean 1924–26
Wayne B. Davis 1926–28
Yorick D. Mathes 1928–30
Ernest C. Cox 1930–32
Scott Reed 1932–34
George E. Broome 1934–36
Dr. Wm. F. Murphy 1936–38
Dr. William J. Danforth 1938–46
James M. Caviness 1946–48
H. Miller Ainsworth 1948–50
H. J. Bernard 1950–54
Albert D. Brown, Jr. 1954–58
Joseph L. Matthews 1958–62
J. Walter Janko 1962–68
Jack W. Flynt 1968–72
Clayton Mann 1972–76
Robert P. Walsh 1976–80
C. Lynn Steward 1980–84
Harvey Holcomb 1984–88
John D. Morris 1988–

Utah

Baldwin Robertson 2-19-20–1920
Murray W. McCarty 1920–22
John E. Booth 1922–23
Dr. B. W. Black 1923–25
John E. Booth 1925–27
Ray L. Olson 1927–29
E. A. Littlefield 1929–31
Joseph E. Nelson 1931–33
Darrell T. Lane 1933–35
Harry T. Reynolds, Jr. 1935–37
Norman L. Sims 1937–39
Otto A. Wiesley 1939–7-10-40
Spencer A. Eccles 7-10-40–1941
William J. Higbee 1941–43
Allison Bills 1943–45
J. Harry Hickman 1945–47
Francis J. Springer 1947–49
Robert L. Shelby 1949–51
Ferris R. Thomassen 1951–53
Victor J. Bott 1953–5
William Sutter 1955–57
Doran T. Duesler 1957–58
P. Clark Cheney 1958–63
William E. Christoffersen 1963–73
Quinn Plowman 1973–75
William E. Christoffersen 1975–

Vermont

Dr. H. Nelson Jackson 1919–20
Redfield Proctor 1920–21
Max C. Fisher 1921–22
John F. Sullivan 1922–23
Jack Crowley 1923–28
Dr. H. Nelson Jackson 1928–36
Bert S. Hyland 1936–37
Dr. H. Nelson Jackson 1937–1-14-55
Clarence S. Campbell 1-22-55–1957
Harry O. Pearson 1957–59
J. Raymond McGinn 1959–61
Edward H. Giles 1961–63
Simon J. Godfrey 1963–65
Ray Greenwood 1965–67
Albert B. Grazini 1967–69
Roy Sweet 1969–71
Francis J. Moriarity, Sr. 1971–73
Leo E. Wright 1973–75
H. Carlyle Lawson 1975–77
Melvin "Doc" Simon 1977–79
Donald A. Sisco 1979–81
Robert H. Vincelette 1981–83
John Morrissey 1983–85
Charles A. LeBeau 1985–87
Milton Willis, Jr. 1987–89
James G. Brouillette 1989–

Virginia

John J. Wicker, Jr. 2-23-20–1921
Robert T. Barton, Jr. 1921–22
Dr. J. F. Lynch 1922–23
Edward E. Goodwyn 1923–25
John J. Wicker, Jr. 1925–27
Henry M. Taylor 1927–29
Nelson C. Overton 1929–31
Roby C. Thompson 1931–33
Dr. F. Whitney Godwin 1933–35
Robert B. Crawford 1935–37
Wilmer L. O'Flaherty 1937–39
Gates R. Richardson 1939–41
Randolph H. Perry 1941–43
W. Catesby Jones 1943–7-9-44
Chapman K. Hunter 1944–45
Fred C. Buck 1945–47
Ferdinand Clinton Knight 1947–4-26-49
Fred W. Higgason 5-25-49–8-6-49
Lemuel W. Houston 1949–51
W. Marshall Geoghegan 1951–3-13-52
Dr. G. Hunter Wolfe 3-15-52–1953
Lemuel W. Houston 1953–57
L. Eldon James 1957–65
Dr. Thomas H. S. Ely 1965–67
Sam T. A. Crawford 1967–69
Thomas J. Gear 1969–81
Emmett B. Burley 1981–89
Edwin J. Dentz 1989–

Washington

Louis H. Seagrave 2-27-20–1920
Paul Edwards 1920–21
Charles S. Albert 1921–22
Dewitt M. Evans 1922–23
L. B. Donley 1923–25
Edward H. Faubert 1925–27
Stephen F. Chadwick 1927–29
Zola O. Brooks 1929–31
Harold B. King 1931–33
John J. O'Brien 1933–35
Frank N. Bruhn 1935–37
William J. Conniff 1937–39
E. C. Knoebel 1939–41
George E. Flood 1941–43
Charles A. Gonser 1943–45
Dr. Theodore J. Rasmussen 1945–47
Jack M. Baldwin 1947–49
N. P. Peterson 1949–51
John F. Shrader 1951–1-19-53
N. P. Peterson 2-1-53–8-15-53
Frank O. Sether 1953–55
Loris A. Winn 1955–57
Ralph E. Goodrich 1957–59
Langford W. Armstrong 1959–61
W. A. "Wally" Carpenter 1961–63
Russell I. Grob 1963–65
Aiden F. Russell 1965–67
Gordon Blechschmidt 1967–69
D. O. Engel 1969–71
Dr. John M. Woods 1971–73
Joseph Feldman 1973–75
Arthur J. Waldron 1975–77
Donald E. Snow 1977–79
Arthur E. Rupert 1979–81

Frank V. Buzzell 1981–83
Willard H. Dunn 1983–85
Clint Stebing 1985–89
Samuel B. White 1989–

West Virginia

Louis Johnson 2-24-20–1922
Andrew E. Edmiston, Jr., 1922–23
Spiller Hicks 1923–25
James H. McGinnis 1925–27
Robert B. McDougle 1927–34
Robert E. O'Connor 1934–9-5-35
Hubert S. Ellis 9-5-35–5-7-36
Edmund L. Jones 5-7-36–1939
W. Elliott Nefflen 1939–4-14-46
Stanley C. Morris 4-16-46–1947
Dr. P. E. Kercheval 1947–57
Leonal O. Bickel 1957–73
Charles E. Forsythe 1973–75
J. H. "Tim" Ashcraft 1975–79
Robert E. Vass, Sr. 1979–81
Jack T. Gribben 1981–

Wisconsin

Harold S. Crosby 2-23-20–1921
Edward J. Barrett 1921–22
F. Ryan Duffy 1922–10-15-23
James H. McGillan 10-15-23–1924
Vilas H. Whaley 1924–26
Harold L. Plummer 1926–28
Frank J. Schneller 1928–29
Delbert J. Kenny 1929–30
Marshall C. Graff 1930–32
Dr. C. A. Dawson 1932–34
John J. Burkhard 1934–36
George R. Howitt 1936–38
Lawrence H. Smith 1938–40
Frank L. Greenya 1940–42
Harvey V. Higley 1942–44
James R. Durfee 1944–46
William F. Trinke 1946–1-18-48
William R. Kenney 1-18-48–1950
Charles L. Larson 1950–52
Kenneth L. Greenquist 1952–54
Gordon W. Roseleip 1954–56
George Emory Sipple 1956–58
William J. Haese 1958–60
Lloyd J. Berken 1960–62
Gilman H. Stordock 1962–64
James E. Mulder 1964–66
Frank R. Schneider 1966–68
Martin T. Jansen 1968–70
L. H. "Rennie" Baker 1970–72
Vernon K. Grosenick 1972–74
Keith A. Kreul 1974–76
Bud A. Mautz 1976–78
Henry F. Renard 1978–80
Ervin Van Dyke 1980–84
Ted N. Mallow 1984–86
Jerry A. Kautzer 1986–88
James E. Chapin 1988–

Wyoming

Harry Fisher 2-24-20–1920
Valentin Colonna 1921
Charles S. Hill 1921–10-20-22
Chiles P. Plummer 10-20-22–11-29-22
Will G. Metz 11-29-22–1923
W. J. Wehrli 1923–24
Marshall S. Reynolds 1924–26
Dr. Albert B. Tonkin 1926–27
Harry B. Henderson, Jr. 1927–30
Dr. W. W. Yates 1930–32
Louis R. Probst 1932–34
George A. Heilman 1934–36
Chiles P. Plummer 1936–40
George A. Johns 1940–42
Charles J. Hughes 1942–44
T. T. Tynan 1944–46
Oscar B. Rohlff 1946–48
Ward W. Husted 1948–50
Valdemar S. Christensen 1950–52
Lyle E. Poole 1952–7-10-54
Olin F. Jacquet 7-10-54–1954
Ernest J. Goppert, Sr. 1954–56
Floyd W. Bartling 1956–60
Charles B. Metz 1960–68
J. R. "Kirk" Coulter 1968–70
Norman J. Guster 1970–74
James T. Anderson 1974–76
John A. Mokler 1976–82
Frank M. Shaffer 1982–86
David E. Nauman 1986–89
E. Lawson Schwope 1989–

CHAIRMEN OF NATIONAL COMMISSIONS AND COMMITTEES

Americanism

Arthur Woods, N.Y., 1919–20
Henry J. Ryan, Mass., 1920–21
Leonard Withington, Hi., 1921–22
No Chairman shown on National Records 1922–23
John R. Quinn, Cal., 1923–24
E. K. Bixby, Okla., 1924–26
Arthur W. Proctor, N.Y., 1926–27
Frank L. Pinola, Pa., 1927–29
Dan Spurlock, La., 1929–31
Edward J. Neary, N.Y., 1931–32
Hugh T. Williams, Va., 1932–33
Paul H. Griffith, Pa., 1933–34
Ray Murphy, Iowa, 1934–35
Stephen F. Chadwick, Wash., 1935–38
Jeremiah F. Cross, N.Y., 1938–39
Leslie P. Kefgen, Mich., 1939–40
James O'Neil, N.H., 1940–43
Robert J. Webb, Neb., 1943–46
James F. Green, Neb., 1946–50
A. Luke Crispe, Vt., 1950–51
James F. Daniel, Jr., S.C., 1952–53
J. Addington Wagner, Mich., 1953–54
James F. Daniel, Jr., S.C., 1954–11-30-60
Martin B. McKneally, N.Y., 1960–61
Charles F. Hamilton, Mo., 1961–62
Daniel J. O'Connor, N.Y., 1962–83; Chairman Emeritus 1984–
Dale L. Renaud, Iowa, 1983–85
Robert S. Turner, Ga., 1985–88
Gary W. Sammons, Mich., 1988–

Americanism Council

Rabbi Albert M. Shulman, Ind., 1963–64
Rev. John J. Howard, Va., 1964–65
Rev. Fr. Vincent S. Sikora, Va., 1965–66
Albert H. Woessner, N.Y., 1966–81
Ralph J. DeGilio, N.Y., 1981–84
Miles S. Epling, W.Va., 1984–85
Warren R. Davies, N.J., 1985–86
John J. Maddux, Tenn., 1986–

Education

Dr. Jack W. Mears, N.M., 1976–77
Leonal O. Bickel, W.Va., 1977–79
Rev. Alfred C. Thompson, N.Y., 1979–82
Dr. W. Firman Haynie, Tex., 1982–

Un-American Activities (became Counter-Subversive Activities)

Walter E. Alessandroni, Pa., 1950–51
Paul R. Selecky, Pa., 1951–52
Dr. J. E. Martie, Nev., 1952–53

Counter-Subversive Activities (formerly Un-American Activities)

Dr. J. E. Martie, Nev., 1953–76
Alvin F. Grauerholz, Kans., 1976–78
Leo F. Malloy, Mass., 1978–83
F. Rodney Loper, Pa., 1983–

American Legion Magazine (formerly Publications)

James E. Powers, Ga., 1970–72
Benjamin B. Truskoski, Conn., 1972–77
Milford A. Forrester, S.C., 1977–

Publications (became American Legion Magazine)

Milo J. Warner, Ohio, 1940–41
Lynn U. Stambaugh, N.D., 1941–42
Roane Waring, Tenn., 1942–43
Warren H. Atherton, Cal., 1943–44
Claude S. Ramsey, N.C., 1944–45
Roland Cocreham, La., 1945–47
Vilas H. Whaley, Wis., 1947–48
James F. O'Neil, N.H., 1948–50
John Stelle, Ill., 1950–57
Donald R. Wilson, W.Va., 1957–61
Edward McSweeney, N.Y., 1961–63
Charles R. Logan, Iowa, 1963–65
James E. Powers, Ga., 1965–70

Child Welfare (became Children & Youth)

George A. Withers, Kans., 1922–24 (Orphans' Home)
Mark T. McKee, Mich., 1924–27
Sherman W. Child, Minn., 1927–30
Edwin E. Hollenback, Pa., 1930–32
Milton D. Campbell, Ohio, 1932–34
Wilbur M. Alter, Colo., 1934–35
Roland B. Howell, La., 1935–37
Glen R. Hillis, Ind., 1937–39
Ed Morgenstern, Kans., 1939–40
Lawrence H. Smith, Wis., 1940–41
L. A. Williams, Wash., 1941–42
Harry C. Kehm, S.D., 1942–45
David V. Addy, Mich., 1945–47
Ralph Heatherington, W.Va., 1947–48
David V. Addy, Mich., 1948–49
A. H. Wittmann, Pa., 1949–50
David V. Addy, Mich., 1950–51
A. H. Wittmann, Pa., 1951–52
Samuel S. Fried, Del., 1952–3-21-53
David V. Addy, Mich., 3-21-53–1953
George Ehinger, Del., 1953–56
David V. Addy, Mich., 1956–57
Maurice T. Webb, Ga., 1957–58
Arthur W. Wilkie, Ind., 1958–59
Percy A. Lemoine, La., 1959–62
Garland D. Murphy, Jr., Ark., 1962–63
David V. Addy, Mich., 1963–64
Morris "Bob" Nooner, Jr., Ill., 1964–67
Earl D. Franklin, Colo., 1967–70

Children & Youth (formerly Child Welfare)

Earl D. Franklin, Colo., 1970–80
Eugene V. Lindquist, Minn., 1980–

Convention

COMMITTEE

Samuel Reynolds, Neb., 1924–25
M. S. Eddy, Ga., (France Convention Investigating Committee) 1928–29
Vincent A. Carroll, Pa., 1934–35
James P. Ringley, Ill., 1935–40
Leo J. Duster, Iowa, 1940–1-31-43
David N. Harsh, Tenn., 1943–46

COMMISSION

Vincent A. Carroll, Pa., 1946–51
Frank E. Brigham, Fla., 1951–8-4-52
Joe H. Adams, Fla., 8-7-52–1953
Harry L. Foster, Cal., 1953–54
Joe H. Adams, Fla., 1954–55
Harry L. Foster, Cal., 1955–56
Joe H. Adams, Fla., 1956–6-25-59
Harry L. Foster, Cal., 6-25-59–1959
James V. Demarest, N.Y., 1959–60
Harry L. Foster, Cal., 1960–61
James V. Demarest, N.Y., 1961–73; Chairman Emeritus 1973–76
Lawrence E. Hoffman, Fla., 1973–79
Eric H. Smith, Ill., 1979–81
Richard H. Klinge, Wash., 1981–83
Wendell G. Williams, Wis., 1983–87
James J. Charleston, Ill., 1987–

National Contests Supervisory

Dr. C. C. Hawke, Kans., 1933–34
Matty B. Bain, Pa., 1934–35
Arch M. Cantrall, W.Va., 1935–36
Matty B. Bain, Pa., 1936–42
John M. Henry, Minn., 1942–46
Arch M. Cantrall, W.Va., 1946–48
Stephen A. Manning, Mass., 1948–49
J. Earl McCurdy, Ind., 1949–50
A. L. Starshak, Ill., 1950–51
Norton R. Ganger, Fla., 1951–57
Louis R. Shealy, Ala., 1957–59
Richard H. Viancour, D.C., 1959–61
Archie Pozzi, Jr., Nev., 1961–63
Harold J. Dillon, Minn., 1963–65
Donald P. Birkett, Iowa, 1965–67
Arthur W. Mazowiecki, N.J., 1968–69
Deming Smith, S.D., 1969–76
John R. Mooradian, Me., 1976–77
Bruce L. Plumb, Ore., 1977–80
Leon M. Jackson, La., 1980–82
Robert G. Hensel, Minn., 1982–83
Archie Pozzi, Nev., 1983–84

Distinguished Guests

Alton T. Roberts, Mich., 1924–26
Milton J. Foreman, Ill., 1926–35
Jesse W. Barrett, Mo., 1935–36
Lyle O. Armel, Kans., 1936–37
Dr. William P. Ryan, Mass., 1937–38
Frank N. Brooks, Wash., 1938–39
Michael Kelleher, Mass., 1939–40
Karl K. Kitchen, Ohio, 1940–41
Robert Condon, N.Y., 1941–42
W. Percy McDonald, Tenn., 1942–43
Charles Rochester, N.Y., 1943–45
A. L. Starshak, Ill., 1945–71
William J. Rogers, D.C., 1971–75
Maurice E. Druhl, Ore., 1975–81
Thomas P. Joyce, Ill., 1981–82
Maurice E. Druhl, Ore., 1982–87
Allen L. Titus, Ind., 1987–

Economic Commission

Lawrence J. Fenlon, Ill., 1947–53
Wilbur C. Daniel, Va., 1953–54
Norman A. Johnson, Miss., 1954–55
Adolph F. Bremer, Minn., 1955–56
Stanley M. Huffman, Neb., 1956–58
Everett Richaud, La., 1958–59
Robert H. Hazen, Ore., 1959–60
George T. Lewis, Jr., Tenn., 1960–61
Almo J. Sebastianelli, Pa., 1961–63
John J. Flynn, Cal. 1963–67
Clarence S. (Larry) Campbell, Vt., 1967–74; Chairman Emeritus, 1974–82
Albert Keller, Jr., Ill., 1974–80
Frank A. Kelly, Ga., 1980–85
Bruce Thiesen, Cal., 1985–88
Joe Frank, Jr., Mo., 1988–

Employment (formerly Veterans Employment)

Frank O. Sether, Wash., 1956–57
J. Edward Walter, Md., 1957–60
Elmore R. Torn, Tex., 1960–62
Wm. J. Chisholm, Colo., 1962–68
David B. Dowd, Id., 1968–69
Walter M. Rapp, Okla., 1969–74
Merrick W. Swords, Jr., La., 1974–78
James A. McMahon, Me., 1978–

Veterans Employment (became Employment)

J. Bryan Hobbs, Md., 1935–36
Forrest G. Cooper, Miss. 1936–37
Jack Crowley, Vt. 1937–41
Lawrence J. Fenlon, Ill. 1941–47
Spence S. Boise, N.D. 1947–51
John L. Connors, Conn. 1951–53
Joseph S. McCracken, Pa. 1953–56

Earlier Employment Commission and Committees

War Risk and Compensation

Henry D. Lindsley, Tex., 1920–21

Unemployment Committee

Roy Hoffman, Okla., 1921–22
Maurice K. Gordon, Ky., 1922–23

National Employment Commission

Howard P. Savage, Ill., 1930–31
Henry L. Stevens, Jr., N.C., 1931–32

Economic Commission—Housing

Richard C. Cadwallader, La., 1946–47
Spence S. Boise, N.D., 1947–48
Bertram E. Giesecke, Tex., 1948–50
J. Neeley Peacock, Ga., 1950–51
Thomas W. Moses, W.Va., 1951–56
Sylvan King, D.C., 1956–61
Hugh Askew, Okla., 1961–62
Dr. Tom B. Clark, Okla., 1962–67

Economic Commission—Veterans Preference

Lyon W. Brandon, Miss., 1943–44
Clarence W. Lambert, R.I., 1944–46
Herbert J. Jacobi, D.C., 1946–47
Raymond R. McEvoy, Mass., 1947–69
A. B. Fennell, S.C., 1969–81
Gary W. Sammons, Mich., 1981–82
Henry J. Field, S.C., 1982–

Finance

deLancey Kountze, N.Y., 1919–20
Milton J. Foreman, Ill., 1920–22
Wilder S. Metcalf, Kans., 1922–11-1-34

Samuel W. Reynolds, Neb., 11-1-34–1935
John Lewis Smith, Sr., D.C., 1935–36
Samuel W. Reynolds, Neb., 1936–49
William J. Dwyer, N.Y., 1949–55
Harold P. Redden, Mass., 1955–68
Churchill T. Williams, Iowa, 1968–83
Walton D. Griffin, Tenn., 1983–86
George W. Boucek, Ill., 1986–

American Legion Life Insurance and Trust (formerly Group Insurance Committee)

William S. Todd, Tenn., 1964–69
Albert V. Labiche, La., 1969–77
Harold E. Heinly, Cal., 1977–83
Jerome P. Dobel, Jr., Mo., 1983–

Group Insurance (became American Legion Life Insurance and Trust Committee)

Jerome F. Duggan, Mo., 1958–63
Levi M. Hall, Minn., 1963–64

Emblem

Richard F. Paul, Mass., 1932–33
Edgar W. Carruth, Kans., 1933–36
Roy L. Cook, N.M., 1936–45
Jerome F. Duggan, Mo., 1945–46
Julius Levy, Pa., 1946–71
Clayton C. Schlick, Iowa, 1971–83
Frank Johnston, Ill., 1983–

Foreign Relations

Franklin D'Olier, Pa., 1921–22
Herbert R. Booth, Mo., 1923–24 (Permanent Peace Committee)
H. Nelson Jackson, Vt., 1924–25
Thomas A. Lee, Kans., 1924–25 (World Peace Committee)
H. Nelson Jackson, Vt., 1925–26
Henry D. Lindsley, N.Y., 1926–28 (World Peace & Foreign Relations)
Lemuel Bolles, N.Y., 1928–31 (World Peace & Foreign Relations)
Darrell T. Lane, Utah, 1931–32 (World Peace & Foreign Relations)
H. Nelson Jackson, Vt., 1932–34 (World Peace & Foreign Relations)
Robert J. White, Mass., 1934–37 (World Peace & Foreign Relations)
Darrell T. Lane, Utah, 1937–39 (World Peace & Foreign Relations)
Wilbur M. Alter, Colo., 1939–40
Harry A. Sullivan, Colo., 1940–46
Anson T. McCook, Conn., 1946–48
Leon Happell, Cal., 1948–49
William Verity, Ohio, 1949–50
Donald R. Wilson, W.Va., 1950–51
Rogers Kelley, Tex., 1951–57
Addison P. Drummond, Fla., 1957–59
Emilio S. Iglesias, Vt., 1959–63
Thomas E. Whelan, N.D., 1963–72
Dr. Robert P. Foster, Mo., 1973–78
Joseph H. Ellinwood, Mass., 1978–79
Dr. Robert P. Foster, Mo., 1979–83
Melvin "Doc" Simon, Vt., 1983–87
William M. Detweiler, La., 1987–

Foreign Relations Council

Norbert W. Schmelkes, Mexico 1965–69
Marvin W. Roth, Wis., 1969–70
Martin T. Jansen, Wis., 1970–80
Earnest N. Schmit, N.D., 1980–81
Rev. Alfred C. Thompson, N.Y., 1981–82
John F. Stay, Pa., 1982–87
Wilson R. Timmons, Fla., 1987–88
Q. R. "Kink" Schulte, N.D., 1988–

Prisoners of War Committee

William R. Burke, Cal., 1970–74

Internal Organization (became Internal Affairs)

Ben C. Hilliard, Jr., Colo., 1947–48

Internal Affairs (formerly Internal Organization)

Eli Dahlin, Kans., 1948–49
William J. Lowry, Conn., 1949–51
Ralph A. Johnson, Va., 1951–53
Charles L. Larson, Wis., 1953–54
George T. Lewis, Jr., Tenn., 1954–Sept., 1956
Addison P. Drummond, Fla., Sept., 1956–1957
Herbert J. Jacobi, D.C., 1957–61
George T. Lewis, Jr., Tenn., 1961–62
Herbert J. Jacobi, D.C., 1962–66
Donald J. Smith, Mich., Chairman Emeritus 1974–
John M. "Jack" Carey, Mich., 1974–76
James P. Dean, Miss., 1976–84
Herman G. Harrington, N.Y., 1984–

Constitution & By-Laws (formerly Constitutional Amendment & By-Laws)

Judge J. A. Howell, Utah, 1925–26
Committee inactive in years 1926–37
Harry J. Benoit, Id., 1937–44
E. E. Thompson, Mo., 1944–47
Samuel M. Birnbaum, N.Y., 1947–52
James F. Green, Neb., 1952–54
Halsey W. Stickel, N.J., 1954–65
Judge Alfonse F. Wells, 1965–73
Francis L. Giordano, N.Y., 1973–79
William W. Greeman, Ind., 1979–83
Francis L. Giordano, N.Y., 1983–

Constitutional Amendments (became Constitution & By-Laws)

Judge J. A. Howell, Utah, 1925–26

By-Laws (became Constitution & By-Laws)

C. L. Dawson, N.D., 1920–21
Paul A. Martin, Mich., 1921–22

Graves Registration (became Graves Registration and Memorials)

Eben E. Putnam, Mass., 1922–23
Thomas W. Robertson, La., 1931–32
Mancel B. Talcott, Ill., 1932–46

Graves Registration and Memorials (formerly Graves Registration—became National Cemetery Committee)

Mancel B. Talcott, Ill., 1946–58
Gordon Ward Thomas, Ill., 1958–60
Lynn Shaw Pang, Cal., 1960–61
Herbert D. Black, S.C., 1961–63
Carl L. Lundgren, Minn., 1963–64
Joseph H. Hackett, R.I., 1964–66
Francis J. Maguire, R.I., 1967–68

National Cemetery (formerly Graves Registration and Memorials)

Francis J. Maguire, R.I., 1968–69
Carl L. Lundgren, Minn., 1969–78
Robert W. Garlinger, N.Y., 1978–79
George E. Evans, Minn., 1979–80
Bob Legan, Ark., 1980–

Overseas Graves Decoration Trust (formerly Trustees Overseas Graves Endowment Fund) (1924 to the present)

Always chaired by the sitting National Commander

Membership & Post Activities

J. Fred Johnson, Jr., Ala., 1946–47
Irvin R. Snyder, Cal., 1947–49
J. Victor Giasson, Nev. 1949–50
Francis R. Heher, Nev., 1950–51
James E. Powers, Ga., 1951–54
Truman C. Wold, N.D., 1954–55
Howard C. Kingdom, Ohio, 1955–56
Churchill T. Williams, Iowa, 1956–57
Leslie K. Gridley, Ill., 1957–58
Robert E. Gates, Ind., 1958–60
William A. Brennan, Jr., Ind., 1960–62
Eugene W. Hiatt, Kans., 1962–64
Earl D. Franklin, Jr., Colo., 1964–67
William F. Gormley III, Pa., 1967–76
Steve Carver, N.C., 1976–78
J. Ray Edmundson, Va., 1978–79
Gary W. Sammons, Mich., 1979–81
Edward T. Pendarvis., S.C., 1981–82
Douglas W. Henley, Md., 1982–86
Miles S. Eipling, W.Va., 1986–87
Dominic D. DiFrancisco, Pa., 1987–88
Douglas W. Henley, Md., 1988–89
William O. Moore, Ky., 1989–

Resolutions Assignment

Paul R. Younts, N.C., 1931–32
Edward L. Blake, W.Va., 1932–33
Paul R. Younts, N.C., 1933–35
Dr. W. T. Dunning, Tex., 1935–36
Edward N. Scheiberling, N.Y., 1936–37
Dr. W. T. Dunning, Tex., 1937–38
R. O. Garber, Iowa, 1938–39
Forrest G. Cooper, Miss., 1939–41
Edward L. Blake, W.Va., 1941–43
William R. McCauley, Ill., 1943–44
Edward L. Blake, W.Va., 1944–45
Thomas J. D. Salter, Nev., 1945–50
Charles W. Griffith, S.C., 1950–70
Melvin T. Dixon, Fla., 1970–72
Alex M. Geiger, S.C., 1972–

Resolutions Subcommittee of the National Executive Committee

William G. McKinley, N.J., 1947–48
E. Meade Wilson, Fla., 1948–56
E. Roy Stone, Jr., S.C., 1957–

Trophies & Awards (became Trophies, Awards & Ceremonials)

Robert B. McDougle, W.Va., 1929–30
Wm. M. Leffingwell, N.Y., 1930–31
J. M. Henry, Minn., 1931–32
Matty B. Bain, Pa., 1932–34
John M. Henry, Minn., 1934–35
Raymond B. Townsley, Ind., 1935–36
John J. Burkhard, Wis., 1936–37
John E. Cash, N.J., 1937–41
Spencer S. Eccles, Utah, 1941–42

Trophies, Awards & Ceremonials (formerly Trophies & Awards)

Spencer S. Eccles, Utah, 1942–44
Howard F. King, Mont., 1944–48
Clyde E. Rankin, Pa., 1948–51
Joseph S. McCracken, Pa., 1951–53
Donald E. Johnson, Iowa, 1953–55
Kent T. Lundgren, Mich., 1955–56
Robert H. Lounsberry, Iowa, 1956–61
Thomas Roumell, Mich., 1961–62
Reed Beard, Ind., 1962–66
John C. Mann, Pa., 1966–71
Albert R. Walavich, Ill., 1971–74
Daniel A. Drew, Pa., 1974–79
Stephen J. Mikosky, Pa., 1979–80
Earl D. Franklin, Jr., Colo., 1980–

Legislative

Gilbert Bettman, Ohio, 1920–21
Daniel Steck, Iowa, 1921–22
Wayne Davis, Tex., 1922–23
Aaron Sapior, Ill., 1923–24
O. L. Bodenhamer, Ark., 1924–25
Hugh K. Martin, Ohio, 1925–26
Scott W. Lucas, Ill., 1926–27
Donald C. Strachan, N.Y., 1927–28
John H. Sherburne, Mass., 1928–29
Ferre C. Watkins, Ill., 1929–30
Harry W. Colmery, Kans., 1930–32
Ray Murphy, Iowa, 1932–33
Raymond J. Kelly, Mich., 1933–34
Vilas H. Whaley, Wis., 1934–35
Robert W. Colflesh, Iowa, 1935–37
Frank L. Pinola, Pa., 1937–39
Irving A. Jennings, Ariz., 1939–41
Maurice F. Devine, N.H., 1941–45
Wm. H. Doyle, Mass., 1945–47
Robert W. Colflesh, Iowa, 1947–48
Ernest S. Goens, Tex., 1948–49
Elmer W. Sherwood, Ind., 1949–50
Jerome F. Duggan, Mo., 1950–55
Herman F. Luhrs, Mich., 1955–56
Jerome F. Duggan, Mo., 1956–62
Clarence C. Horton, Ala., 1962–74; Chairman Emeritus 1974–80
Frank I. Hamilton, Ind., 1974–77
Albert C. Brown, Jr., Tex., 1977–80
Keith A. Kreul, Wis., 1980–81
Clarence M. Bacon, Md., 1981–82
Gary W. Sammons, Mich., 1982–88
Dominic D. DiFrancisco, Pa., 1988–89
Charles Pesso, N.Y., 1989–

Legislative Council

Wilbur Walker, Va., 1975–76
Clarence M. Bacon, Md., 1976–78
Wilbur Walker, Va., 1978–

National Defense (became National Security)

Roy Hoffman, Okla., 1926–28
Albert L. Cox, N.C., 1928–29
C. B. Robbins, Iowa, 1929–31
Albert L. Cox, N.C., 1931–32
Milton A. Reckord, Md., 1932–33
Amos A. Fries, D.C., 1933–34
Thomas H. Healy, D.C., 1934–35
Edward J. Neary, N.Y., 1935–36
J. O'Connor Roberts, D.C., 1936–38
Warren H. Atherton, Cal., 1938–43
Michael J. Kelleher, Mass., 1943–44
S. Perry Brown, Tex., 1944–47

National Security (formerly National Defense)

S. Perry Brown, Tex., 1947–48
Erle Cocke, Jr., Ga., 1948–50
Bruce P. Henderson, Ohio, 1950–52
Thomas E. Paradine, N.Y., 1952–53
Seaborn P. Collins N.M., 1953–54
Bruce P. Henderson, Ohio, 1954–55
Will F. Nicholson, Colo., 1955–57
Robert H. Bush, Iowa, 1957–59
Addison P. Drummond, Fla., 1959–61
Robert H. Bush, Iowa, 1961–62
William C. Doyle, N.J., 1962–66
Emmett G. Lenihan, Wash., 1966–77; Chairman Emeritus, 1977–81
Francis P. Kane, Ill., 1977–79
Milton A. Pilcher, N.C., 1979–80
Roger A. Munson, Ohio, 1980–

National Security Council

Granville S. Ridley, Tenn., 1962–77
Wilbur Walker, Va., 1977–78
Roger A. Munson, Ohio, 1978–80
Clarence M. Bacon, Md., 1980–81
David E. Munter, Ill., 1981–86
David L. Gurney, Fla., 1986–88
Wilson R. Timmons, Fla., 1988–

Aeronautics (became Aeronautics & Space)

Reed G. Landis, Ill., 1922–26
Gill Robert Wilson, N.J., 1926–27
Rufus R. Rand, Jr., Minn., 1927–28
No Aeronautics Committee 1929–32
Edward V. Rickenbacker, N.Y., 1932–33
John Dwight Sullivan, N.Y., 1933–34
Howard C. Knotts, Ill., 1934–35
Dudley M. Steele, Cal., 1935–36
W. W. Arrasmith, Neb., 1936–38
David S. Ingalls, Ohio, 1938–39
John Dwight Sullivan, N.Y., 1939–40
Norman M. (Pat) Lyon, Cal., 1940–43
Carlyle E. Godske, Wis., 1943–44
John Dwight Sullivan, N.Y., 1944–46
Edward V. Rickenbacker, N.Y., 1946–47
Roy B. Gardner, Ohio, 1947–50
Roscoe Turner, Ind., 1950–53
William C. Doyle, N.J., 1953–54
Jack K. Evans, D.C., 1954–55
Roscoe Turner, Ind., 1955–58

Aeronautics & Space (formerly Aeronautics)

Dr. William J. Danforth, Tex., 1958–61
Roscoe Turner, Ind., 1961–70
Joseph L. Hodges, Va., 1970–73

Aerospace (formerly Aeronautics & Space)

Joseph L. Hodges, Va., 1970–75
Noah L. Smalley, Fla., 1975–79
H. Vincent Strout, Mass., 1979–82
James E. Starr, Minn., 1982–

Civil Defense (became Defense Civil Preparedness)

G. Lee McClain, Ky., 1941–46
Niel R. Allen, Ore., 1946–57
Ray A. Pierce, Tex., 1957–58
William L. Weiss, Mo., 1958–59
David Aronberg, Ky., 1959–10-6-64
Ray C. Stiles, Iowa, 10-6-64
Dr. Stacey A. Garner, Tenn., 1964–74

Defense Civil Preparedness (formerly Civil Defense)

Dr. Stacey A. Garner, Tenn., 1974–77
Hugh B. Mott, Tenn., 1977–78
Donald M. Miller, Minn., 1978–82
Frank D. Riccardi, N.J., 1982–84
Frank J. D'Amico, N.Y., 1984–

Law and Order

Charles F. Ely, Mass., 1933–34
Charles R. Mabey, Utah, 1934–35
George R. Howitt, Wis., 1935–36
Richard Hartshorne, N.J., 1936–48
John Gurley, N.M., 1948–49
George Mingle, Ohio, 1949–52
William S. Todd, Tenn., 1952–53
George Mingle, Ohio, 1953–57
Paul S. Kinsey, Ohio, 1957–58
Elmer W. Kuhlmann, Mo., 1958–59
Paul S. Kinsey, Ohio, 1959–62
Elmer W. Kuhlmann, Mo., 1962–66
Paul S. Kinsey, Ohio, 1966–75
W. Dudley Robbins, N.C., 1975–

Merchant Marine

S. Perry Brown, Tex., 1941–43
Ray O. Garber, Iowa, 1943–48
Albert B. Stapp, Ala., 1948–49
Jimmy Phillips, Tex., 1949–50
Henry C. Parke, N.Y., 1950–68
James M. Wagonseller, Ohio, 1968–72
Al Olenberger, N.D., 1972–74
William D. Horan, N.Y., 1974–87
John W. Sumrall, Miss., 1987–88
Charles F. Moreland, Fla., 1988–

Military Affairs

Wade H. Hayes, N.Y., 1920–21
D. John Markey, Md., 1921–22
Wm. P. Screws, Ala., 1922–23
Milton J. Foreman, Ill., 1923–24
George E. Leach, Minn., 1924–25
Milton A. Reckord, Md., 1925–26
John R. McQuigg, Ohio, 1926–27
Edward L. Logan, Mass., 1927–28
J. Arthur Lynch, Ga., 1928–29
No committee 1929–44
Ed. J. Zoble, Wyo., 1944–45
A. D. Welsh, Mo., 1945–47
Omar J. McMackin, Ill., 1947–49
A. D. Welsh, Mo., 1949–54
William S. Todd, Tenn., 1954
William C. Doyle, N.J., 1954–62

Edwin R. Bentley, Fla., 1962–65
Monroe R. Bethman, Pa., 1966–67
Harrison R. Thyng, N.H., 1967–68
Francis P. Kane, Ill., 1968–77
Donald D. Hildebrand, Tenn., 1977–85
Henry G. Jacoby, Neb., 1985–86
Norbert G. Harmeyer, Iowa, 1986–

Naval Affairs

Edward E. Spafford, N.Y., 1920–25
Thomas Goldingay, N.J., 1925–26
Edwin Denby, Mich., 1926–27
Charles W. Schick, Ill., 1927–29
No committee appointed 1930–40
Sam Long, Tex., 1941–42
Arthur F. Duffy, N.Y., 1942–47
Paul Dever, Mass., 1947–48
Arthur F. Duffy, N.Y., 1948–54
Emmett G. Lenihan, Wash., 1954–66
L. E. Page, Tex., 1966–67
Monroe R. Bethman, Pa., 1967–68
John J. Wrenn, Mass., 1968–

Amateur Radio Network

Verlin E. Birdsell, Cal., 1957–58
Collins R. Buchner, Cal., 1958–59
Verlin E. Birdsell, Cal., 1959–60
Collins R. Buchner, Cal., 1960–68

Special Subcommittee on Uniform Code of Military Justice and Court of Military Appeals

Louis Maniatus, D.C., 1959–60
John J. Finn, D.C., 1960–66
Carl C. Matheny, Mich., 1966–68

National Security Training Committee (formerly Universal Military Training Committee)

Granville S. Ridley, Tenn., 1949–62

Universal Military Training Committee (became National Security Training Committee)

Warren H. Atherton, Cal., 1947–48
Granville S. Ridley, Tenn., 1948–49

Public Relations

PUBLICITY COMMITTEE

E. H. Risdon, Cal., 1926–29
Karl W. Detzer, N.Y., 1929–30
C. W. Motter, Neb., 1930–32
Jack R. C. Cann, Mich., 1932–34
Lawrence W. Hager, Ky., 1934–35
C. W. Motter, Neb., 1935–36

PUBLICATION & PUBLICITY COMMITTEE

Darrell T. Lane, Utah, 1936–37

PUBLISHING & PUBLICITY COMMISSION

Harry T. Colmery, Kans., 1936–37
Daniel J. Doherty, Mass., 1937–38
Stephen F. Chadwick, Wash., 1938–39
Raymond J. Kelly, Mich., 1939–40

PUBLICITY COMMISSION

Glenn H. Campbell, Ohio, 1944–45

PUBLIC RELATIONS COMMISSION

Glenn H. Campbell, Ohio, 1945–47
George A. Bideaux, Ariz., 1947–48
Frank J. Becker, N.Y., 1948–49
Herman Luhrs, Mich., 1949–53
Thomas E. Paradine, N.Y., 1953–54
W. C. Daniel, Va., 1954–55
James V. Demarest, N.Y., 1955–56
William R. Burke, Cal., 1956–58
James V. Demarest, N.Y., 1958–59
C. D. DeLoach, D.C., 1959–78
William M. Detweiler, La., 1978–86
Douglas W. Henly, Md., 1986–88
Thomas C. Kouyeas, D.C., 1988–

Hospitalization (became Hospitalization And Vocational Training)

Abel Davis, Ill., 1919–20

Hospitalization And Vocational Training (became Rehabilitation)

Abel Davis, Ill., 1920–21

Rehabilitation (became Veterans Affairs And Rehabilitation) Committee

Albert A. Sprague, Ill., 1921–22
Joe Sparks, S.C., 1922–23
Watson B. Miller, D.C., 1923–35
Daniel J. Doherty, Mass., 1935–36
Earl V. Cliff, Minn., 1936–37
Walter J. Krisp, Pa., 1937–38
William F. Smith, Pa., 1938–39
Earl V. Cliff, Minn., 1939–40
John H. Walsh, Mass., 1940–43
Robert W. Sisson, Ark., 1943–44
Robert M. McCurdy, Cal., 1944–47
W. Rex McCrosson, N.J., 1947–48
John H. Walsh, Mass., 1948–49
Robert M. McCurdy, Cal., 1949–51
Earl V. Cliff, Minn., 1951–52
Robert M. McCurdy, Cal., 1952–67
William F. Lenker, S.D., 1967–69

Veterans Affairs And Rehabilitation (formerly Rehabilitation)

William F. Lenker, S.D., 1970–89; Chairman Emeritus, 1989–
Chester F. Stellar, Ohio, 1989–

American Legion Child Welfare Foundation

(Presidents)

Garland D. Murphy, Jr., M.D., Ark., 1954–59
John E. Curtis, Neb., 1959–60
George Ehringer, Del., 1960–63
L. Eldon James, Va., 1963–65
Garland D. Murphy, Jr., M.D., Ark., 1965–66
George Ehringer, Del., 1966–70
William E. Christofferson, Utah, 1970–73
L. Eldon James, Va., 1973–79
Walton D. Griffin, Tenn., 1979–85
U. S. (Udie) Grant, Kans., 1986–

American Legion Endowment Fund Corporation

(Presidents)

James A. Drain, Wash., 1929–36
Howard P. Savage, Ill., 1936–38
Edward M. Stayton, Mo., 1938–41
Harry W. Colmery, Kans., 1941–79
S. Perry Brown, Tex., 1979–81
Robert Charles Smith, La., 1981–

Fiftieth Anniversary

Albert V. LaBiche, La., 1966–69

National Committee On The Bicentennial Of The United States Constitution

Robert S. Turner, Ga., 1985–88

The Spirit Of '76 Committee

John A. Jones, W.Va. 1970–72
Milton M. Carpenter, Mo., 1972–76

Task Force For The Future

James F. Green, Neb., 1967–68
William Eugene Galbraith, Neb., 1968–69

Joint Rehabilitation—Economic Subcommittee On Problems Of The Aged And Aging

James W. Doon, N.H., 1961–62
Milton S. Applebaum, Ill., 1962–75
Glenn R. Nielson, Minn., 1975–80

Policy Coordination And Action Group

John P. Comer, Mass., 1987–88
H. F. "Sparky" Gierke, N.D., 1988–89
Miles S. Epling, W.Va., 1989–90

Select Committee On Special Problems Of The Veterans Affairs And Rehabilitation Program

William F. Lenker, S.D., 1977–82

Veterans' Planning And Coordinating Committee

Al Keller, Jr., Ill., 1982–83 (National Commander)
Keith Kreul, Wis., 1983–84 (National Commander)
Clarence M. Bacon, Md., 1984–85 (National Commander)
James P. Dean, Miss., 1985–86 (National Commander)
John P. Comer, Mass., 1987–88 (National Commander)
H. F. "Sparky" Gierke, N.D., 1988–89 (National Commander)
Miles S. Epling, W.Va., 1989– (National Commander)

Policy Coordination And Action Group

John P. Comer, Mass., 1987–88 (National Commander)
H. F. "Sparky" Gierke, N.D., 1988–89 (National Commander)
Miles S. Epling, W.Va., 1989– (National Commander)

SONS OF THE AMERICAN LEGION NATIONAL COMMANDERS

Michael Seaton, Cal., 1968
Robert McBride, Ind., 1969
J. R. Stillwell, Ill., 1970 and 1971
John Smolinsky, Mass., 1972
Robert Faust, Ca., 1973
James Hartman, Ill., 1974
Gregory D. Reis, Ill., 1975
Grant M. Jamieson, Mich., 1976
Charles E. Gannon, Md., 1977
John M. Sherrard, Cal., 1978
Richard J. Kepler, Ariz., 1979
Ernest Wilson, Jr., N.J., 1980
Donald L. Willson, Pa., 1981
David P. Stephens, Ind., 1982
Christopher R. Cerullo, N.Y., 1983
Fred L. Hartline, Ohio, 1984
Woodrow Mudge, Colo., 1985
Royce Doucet, La., 1986
Douglas Bible, Minn., 1987
Richard L. League, Md., 1988
David R. Faust, Wis., 1989
Charles R. Belles, Va., 1990

INDEX